SOURCES FOR *CULTURES OF THE WEST*

SOURCES FOR *CULTURES OF THE WEST*

VOLUME 2: SINCE 1350

EDITED BY

Clifford R. Backman
BOSTON UNIVERSITY

OXFORD
UNIVERSITY PRESS

OXFORD
UNIVERSITY PRESS

Oxford University Press is a department of the University of Oxford. It furthers the University's objective of excellence in research, scholarship, and education by publishing worldwide. Oxford is a registered trade mark of Oxford University Press in the UK and in certain other countries.

Published in the United States of America by Oxford University Press
198 Madison Avenue, New York, NY 10016, United States of America.

For titles covered by Section 112 of the US Higher Education Opportunity Act, please visit www.oup.com/us/he for the latest information about pricing and alternate formats.

CIP data is on file at the Library of Congress

ISBN 9780197670842

CONTENTS

NEW TO THIS EDITION

The Fourth Edition of *Sources for Cultures of the West* includes fifteen new sources:

4.6 Lysias, "Against Eratosthenes," CA. 400 BCE
6.5 Sulpicia Severa, Six Poems
8.7 *The Corpus of Roman Law*
12.10 Benvenuto Cellini, *Autobiography*, 1558–1563
15.6 Daniel Defoe/Captain Charles Johnson, "The Life of Anne Bonny," 1724
15.7 The Absolutist Regimes
16.6 Germaine de Staël, *Memoirs*
17.2 Olympe de Gouges, *Declaration of the Rights of Woman and of the Female Citizen*, 1791
22.10 Pope Pius IX, *The Syllabus of Errors*, 1864
23.7 Francis Galton, "Africa for the Chinese," 1873
26.6 Victims of the Shoah
27.1 Simone Weil, "The Love of Religious Practices," 1950
27.8 Decolonization around the World
28.13 Hélène Cixous, "The Laugh of the Medusa," 1975
29.11 Vladimir Putin, "On the Historical Unity of Russians and Ukrainians," 2021

HOW TO READ A PRIMARY SOURCE

Sources for Cultures of the West is composed of two hundred primary sources. A primary source is any text, image, or other source of information that gives us a firsthand account of the past by someone who witnessed or participated in the historical events in question. Although such sources can provide significant and fascinating insight into the past, they must also be read carefully to limit modern assumptions about historical modes of thought. Here are a few elements to keep in mind when approaching a primary source.

AUTHORSHIP

Who produced this source of information? A male or a female? A member of the elite or of the lower class? An outsider looking *in* at an event or an insider looking *out*? What profession or lifestyle does the author pursue, which might influence how they are recording their information?

GENRE

What type of source are you examining? Different genres—categories of material—have different goals and stylistic elements. For example, on the one hand, a personal letter meant exclusively for the eyes of a distant cousin might include unveiled opinions and relatively trivial pieces of information, like the writer's vacation plans. On the other hand, a political speech intended to convince a nation of a leader's point of view might subdue personal opinions beneath artful rhetoric and focus on large issues like national welfare or war. Identifying genre can be useful for deducing how the source may have been received by an audience.

AUDIENCE

Who is reading, listening to, or observing the source? Is it a public or private audience? National or international? Religious or nonreligious? The source may be geared toward the expectations of a particular group; it may be recorded in a language that is specific to a particular group. Identifying audience can help us understand why the author chose a certain tone or why they included certain types of information.

HISTORICAL CONTEXT

When and why was this source produced? On what date? For what purposes? What historical moment does the source address? It is paramount that we approach primary sources in context to avoid anachronism (attributing an idea or habit to a past era where it does not belong) and faulty judgment. For example, when considering a medieval history, we must account for the fact that in the Middle Ages, the widespread understanding was that God created the world and could still interfere in the activity of mankind—such as sending a terrible storm when a community had sinned. Knowing the context (Christian, medieval, views of the world) helps us to avoid importing modern assumptions—like the fact that storms are caused by atmospheric pressure—into historical texts. In this way, we can read the source more faithfully, carefully, and generously.

BIAS AND FRAMING

Is there an overt argument being made by the source? Did the author have a particular agenda? Did any political or social motives underlie the reasons for writing the document? Does the document exhibit any qualities that offer clues about the author's intentions?

STYLISTIC ELEMENTS

Stylistic features such as tone, vocabulary, word choice, and the manner in which the material is organized and presented should also be considered when examining a source. They can provide insight into the writer's perspective and offer additional context for considering a source in its entirety.

Clifford Backman
Boston University

SOURCES FOR *CULTURES OF THE WEST*

CHAPTER 12

RENAISSANCES AND REFORMATIONS

12.1 FRANCESCO PETRARCA, "LETTER TO POSTERITY"

This letter, which Francesco Petrarca (1304–1374) never finished, represents something of an autobiographical obituary. In it, he offers a summary of his life and achievements, which, interestingly, does not include his vernacular love poetry. He wanted above all to be remembered as a scholar, a lover of classical antiquity, and a Latin poet—especially as the author of the (paralyzingly dull) epic poem *Africa*, about the Roman general Scipio Africanus. Petrarca carries his life story as far forward as 1341; he left no notes about what he intended to include in the presumed second half of the letter.

It is possible that you may have heard of me, but I doubt it; a name as obscure and insignificant as mine cannot have travelled far in either time or space. But if you have heard of me, it may interest you to know the kind of man I was, or the results of my long labors—especially those you may have heard of, or, at any rate, those whose titles may have reached you.

To begin with myself, then, I should warn you that the things men say about me will differ considerably, since men are usually more influenced by whim than by truth whenever they are passing judgment on another; there is no limit to either praise or blame. The truth is that I was one of you, a poor mortal, of no exalted origin but neither of terribly lowly birth. I simply belonged, as Augustus Caesar once said of himself, to an ancient family. In disposition, I was not naturally perverse, nor was I wanting in modesty except as the contagion of custom may have corrupted me. My youth was gone before I realized it, and young manhood carried me away. Maturity eventually brought me to my senses and taught me, through experience, the truth I had long before read in books—namely, that youth and pleasure are vain. . . . In my prime I was blessed with an agile and active, though not particularly strong, body, and although I cannot boast of having been terribly handsome, I was good-looking enough in those days. I had a clear complexion, somewhere between light and dark, and I had lively eyes. For many years I enjoyed keen vision, but it deserted me all of a sudden around my

Translation by Clifford Backman.

sixtieth birthday and forced me, reluctantly, to wear glasses. I had always been perfectly healthy, but old age brought its usual array of complaints.

My parents were good people, Florentines both, and not very well off. I may as well admit it: they were in fact on the verge of poverty. They had been expelled from their native city, which is why I was born in exile at Arezzo, in 1304. . . . I have always been contemptuous of wealth; but it is not that I would not have liked to be rich—I simply hate the work and worry that seem always to accompany wealth. I never cared to give great banquets and have led a much happier life with a plain diet and ordinary foods. . . . On the other hand, the pleasure of dining with friends is great, and nothing gives me more delight than the unexpected arrival of a friend. Nothing irks me more than ostentation, for not only is it bad in itself, being opposed to humility, but it is distracting and annoying.

In my younger years I struggled constantly with an all-consuming but pure love affair, my only one, and I would have struggled with it even longer had not my love's premature death (bitter, but in the end, salutary for me) extinguished the last flames. I wish I could say that I have been free of the lusts of the flesh, but I would be lying if I did. I can at least say this, though: even while I was occasionally swept away by the ardor of my youth and temperament, I always detested such sins from the very depths of my soul. . . .

I have taken pride in others, though never in myself, and even as insignificant as I have been, I have also thought myself even more so. In anger I have often injured myself but never another. I have always had the greatest desire for honorable friendships, and have cherished them faithfully. I can make the following boast without fear, for I know I am speaking sincerely: while I am prone to taking offense, I am quick to forget—and I never fail to remember acts of generosity. I have had the good fortune to associate with kings and princes, and to enjoy the friendship of nobles, to such a point as to excite envy. But it is the cruel fate of aging that eventually we weep for friends who have passed away. Some of the greatest kings of this age have courted and cherished my friendship. They may know why. I certainly do not. With some of them I was on such terms that they seemed, in some way, to be my guests, rather than I theirs. Their eminence in no way discomforted me; in fact, it brought me many advantages. I kept well away from many others of whom I was quite fond, for my innate longing for freedom was so strong that I carefully avoided those whose eminence seemed to threaten the liberty I loved so much.

I had more of a well-balanced mind than a keen one, one suited to many kinds of good and wholesome study but especially inclined to moral philosophy and poetry. Over time I paid less and less attention to the latter and found delight in sacred literature, discovering in it a hidden sweetness that I had earlier failed to appreciate. I came to regard works of poetry as mere amenities. I found many subjects interesting, yet focused especially on the study of antiquity, for I have always disliked our own age so much that, were it not for the love of those dearest to me, I would have preferred to live in any other period than our own. To forget the world in which we live, I have always striven to place my mind in other ages—and thus I came to love history. The conflicting opinions of people about the past have never offended me. When in doubt, I have made it a point to accept what seems to me the most probable explanation, or simply to yield to the authority of the historian I was reading. . . .

Along the breezy banks of the Rhône river I spent my boyhood, under the care of my parents, and then I spent my adolescence under the guidance of my own vanities. There were some long intervals spent abroad, though. I spent four years in the little town of Carpentras, which lies a little to the east of Avignon. In these two places I learned all that I could, considering my age, of grammar, logic, and rhetoric; or rather, I learned as much as is usually taught in school—and you, dear reader, will know how little that is. I then moved on to Montpellier for four years, to study law, and then to Bologna for three years more. . . . I was twenty-two when I finally returned home. Since habit has nearly the force of nature to it, I call Avignon—my place of exile—home. I was already beginning to make a name for myself there, and my friendship was sought by a number of prominent people. Why? I do not really know. I confess that it is now a source of surprise to me, although it seemed a natural enough thing then, when I was at the age when we are used to thinking ourselves deserving of the highest respect. I was courted first and foremost by the eminent and noble Colonna family, which then adorned the Roman Curia with their presence. . . . I spent many years in the house of Cardinal Giovanni Colonna, the brother of Giacomo, living not like a servant to Giovanni's lord but as if he were my father, or even better, my loving brother. It felt like living in my very own home. In time, though, youthful curiosity drove me to visit France and Germany. I invented a number of reasons to justify the journey to my elders, but the real impulse was simply my burning desire to see new sights. I went first to Paris, since I wanted to learn what was true in what I had heard about the city, and what was nonsense. Returning from this journey I went straightaway to Rome, which I had wanted to see ever since I was a child. There I soon came to revere Stefano Colonna, the great family's noble patriarch, an ancient hero who welcomed me in every possible way, as though I were his own son. The love and good will with which this marvelous man treated me lasted until the end of his life, and it lives on in my heart, where it will never fade until I myself cease to be.

Upon returning, I instantly felt the revulsion I have always had for city life, especially for the disgusting city of Avignon, which I truly abhorred. Seeking some means of escape, I was lucky enough to discover, about fifteen miles away, a delightful valley, narrow and secluded, called Vaucluse, where the Sorgue river (that prince of streams!) has its source. The charm of the site captivated me, and so I moved there together with all my books. If I were to tell you all that I did during my many years there, it would be a long story indeed. Almost every bit of writing I produced [in those years] was either done or begun there, or was at least conceived there; and those writings have been so numerous that even today they keep me busy and weary. My mind is like my body—more agile than strong; and while it was quite easy for me to think up new projects, I dropped many when they proved too difficult to carry out.

Inspired by the beauty of my surroundings, I undertook to write a pastoral or bucolic song: my *Bucolicum Carmen*. I also wrote *The Life of Solitude* (*De vita solitaria*), in two books, which I dedicated to the great man who is now Cardinal-Bishop Philip of Sabina, although at that time he was still the humble bishop of Cavaillon. He is the only one of my old friends who is still alive, and he has always loved me and treated me not as a bishop (as Ambrose did to Augustine) but as a brother. One Friday during Holy Week as I was hiking through those mountains I developed a powerful urge to write an epic poem, one based on Scipio Africanus the Great, who had been a favorite of mine since childhood. I began the project in a rush of enthusiasm, but because of a number of distractions I was forced to put it aside. The poem was called *Africa*, after its hero, and by some fate—my own or the poem's?—it did not fail to rouse the interest of many readers even before I published it. . . .

[In a long passage, omitted here, he describes how he was summoned to Rome by the members of the Senate, to receive the laurel crown—the highest honor for a poet in Roman tradition.]

I was very much pre-occupied with the honor I had just received, worried and fretful that I was unworthy of it, and as a result, when I was hiking through the hills again one day, I happened to cross the river Enza, in the area of Reggio Selvapiana and all of a sudden the beauty of the spot inspired me to finish writing my incomplete *Africa*. My enthusiasm for the project revived as from the dead and I wrote a number of lines that very day. More lines followed every day until I made it all the way to Parma, where I found a quiet, secluded house—which I later bought, and still own—and devoted myself to the poem with such energy that I completed it in no time at all, a fact that still amazes me to this day.

I was thirty-four years old. I returned to my home at the source of the Sorgue, to my beloved trans-Alpine solitude, after that long stay in Parma and Verona, where everyone I met, I am thankful to say, welcomed me with much greater honor that I deserved. Not long afterward, however, my reputation attracted the attention of Giacomo the Younger, of Carrara, an extraordinary man whose equal I doubt could be found even among the rulers of the age. He sent a constant stream of messengers and letters to me for years, no matter if I was in Italy or on the other side of the Alps, begging me to accept his friendship until at last, expecting little good to come of it, I decided to visit him and see what this persistence on the part of so eminent a man, a stranger to me, was all about. So I made my way to Parma, where I was received by him, who is now so dear to my memory, not as a mere mortal might be received but as the saints are received in Heaven—with so much joy and astonishing affection and respect that I cannot put it into words. Therefore, let me be silent. Among the many honors he gave me, he made me a canon of the cathedral of Padua (after he learned that I had been a cleric from boyhood) in order to strengthen my connection to him and his city. To put it bluntly, if he had not died so soon he would have put an end to all my wanderings. But alas, nothing mortal lasts forever, and everything that is sweet eventually turns bitter. Giacomo had scarcely given two years to me, to his city, and to the entire world when God, Who had given him to us, took him away. It is not out of blind love for him that I believe neither I, the city, nor the world were worthy of him. Giacomo's son and successor, a man of genuine sensibility and distinction, was likewise very friendly and respectful to me, but I could not remain with him after the death of one to whom I was so intimately connected. We were even of the same age. I returned to France, not because I was wanting to see again the old familiar place but because I wanted to get free of my misery, like a sick man wants, by a change of scene.

STUDY QUESTIONS

1. How does Petrarca come to love the past? What are the reasons he gives for his desire to "place my mind in other ages"?
2. What role do important men like Stefano Colonna and Giaccomo the Younger of Carrara play in Petrarca's life? What does this say about the role of friendship in his scholarly career?

12.2 FROM ARIOSTO, *ORLANDO FURIOSO* (*MAD ORLANDO*), 1516

Ludovico Ariosto (1474–1533) reprises the familiar characters from the "Song of Roland" (Document 10.6) in his epic romance, *Orlando Furioso,* itself a continuation of another poem (*Orlando Innamorato*). Occurring in a dreamy Renaissance version of the medieval world—including trips to Japan and the moon!—the plot centers on Orlando (a new Roland), who embodies the conflict between Muslims and Charlemagne's army by helplessly loving a pagan princess, Angelica. When Orlando discovers that Angelica has fallen in love with a Saracen named Medoro, he tips headfirst into a mania that leaves a trail of destruction across Europe. He can be saved only by his friends who bring him a flask with his "wits" inside—when he breathes it, he simultaneously falls out of love and regains his sanity.

Rudolf Gottfried, *Ariosto's Orlando Furioso.* Bloomington: Indiana University Press, 1964, pp. 184–6, 190–1, 343–7.

The day, the night to him were both alike;
Abroad upon the cold bare earth he lies;
No sleep, no food he takes, nor none would seek;
All sustenance he to himself denies.
Thus he began and ended half the week,
And he himself doth marvel whence his eyes
Are fed so long with such a spring of water,
And to himself thus reasons on the matter:

"No, no, these be no tears that now I shed;
These be no tears, nor can tears run so rife;
But fire of frenzy draw'th up to my head
My vital humor that should keep my life;
This stream will never cease till I be dead.
Then welcome, death, and end my fatal strife;
No comfort in this life my woe can minish
But thou, who canst both life and sorrow finish.

"These are not sighs, for sighs some respite have;
My gripes, my pangs no respite do permit;
The blindfold boy made me a seeing slave
When from her eyes my heart he first did hit.
Now all inflamed, I burn, I rage and rave
And in the midst of flame consume no whit:
Love sitting in my heart, a master cruel,
Blows with his wings, feeds with his will the fuel.

"I am not I, the man that erst I was;
Orlando, he is burièd and dead;
His most ungrateful love (ah, foolish lass)
Hath killed Orlando and cut off his head;
I am his ghost that up and down must pass
In this tormenting hell forever led,
To be a fearful sample and a just
To all such fools as put in love their trust."

Straightways he draweth forth his fatal blade
And hews the stones; to heave'n the shivers flee;
Accursèd was that fountain, cave, and shade,
The arbor and the flowers and every tree;
Orlando of all places havoc made
Where he those names together joined may see;
Yea, to the spring he did perpetual hurt
By filling it with leaves, boughs, stones, and dirt.

And having done this foolish, frantic feat,
He lays him down all weary on the ground,
Distempered in his body with much heat,
In mind with pains that no tongue can expound;
Three days he doth not sleep nor drink nor eat,
But lay with open eyes as in a sound;
The fourth, with rage and not with reason wakèd,
He rents his clothes and runs about stark naked.

His helmet here he flings, his pouldrons there;
He casts away his curats and his shield;
His sword he throws away, he cares not where;
He scatters all his armor in the field;
No rag about his body he doth bear
As might from cold or might from shame him
  shield;
And save he left behind this fatal blade,
No doubt he had therewith great havoc made.

But his surpassing force did so exceed
All common men that neither sword nor bill
Nor any other weapon he did need;
Mere strength sufficed him to do what he will.
He roots up trees as one would root a weed;
And e'en as birders laying nets with skill
Pare slender thorns away with easy strokes,
So he did play with ashes, elms, and oaks.

. . .

Away they fled, but he pursued so fast
That some he caught, and some surprised with
  fear
Stood still, as oft it happens, all aghast,
Not knowing how to hide themselves nor where;
Some other ploughmen, seeing what had passed,
Thought it but little wit to tarry there,
But climbed, for fear, their houses and their
  churches,
Not trusting strength of elms, of beech and
  birches.

Among the rest he takes one by his heel
And with his head knocks out another's brain,
Which causèd both of them such pain to feel

As till Doomsday they never shall complain;
Another with his fist he made to reel
Till pain itself made him past sense of pain;
And when the men fled all away afeard,
Then with like rage he set upon their herd.

. . .

And finding no man there, nor small nor great,
For all were fled away from thence for awe,
As famine forced him, he sought out some
 meat;
And were it fine or coarse, the first he saw
In greedy sort he doth devour and eat,
Not caring if it roasted were or raw;
And when thus homely he had ta'en repast,
About the country bedlamlike he passed.

Then kneeling down as if he asked some boon
Of God or some great saint, that pot he brought
Which he had carried from beyond the moon,
The jar in which Orlando's wit was caught,
And closed it to his nostrils; and eftsoon
He drawing breath, this miracle was wrought:
The jar was void and emptied every whit,
And he restored unto his perfect wit.

As one that in some dream or fearful vision
Hath dreamt of monstrous beasts and ugly fiends
Is troubled, when he wakes, with superstition
And feareth what such ugly sight intends
And lying wake thinks of that apparition
And long time after in that fancy spends:
So now Orlando lay, not little musing
At this his present state and uncouth using.

He holds his peace, but lifting up his eyes
He sees his ancient friends King Brandimart
And Oliver and him that made him wise,
All whom he knew and lovèd from his heart;
He thinks, but cannot with himself devise
How he should come to play so mad a part;
He wonders he is nak'd and that he feels
Such store of cords about his hands and heels.

At last he said, as erst Sileno said
To those that took him napping in the cave,
"Release me!" with countenance so staid
And with a sheer so sober and so grave
That they unloosèd him as he them prayed
And suffered him his liberty to have
And clothèd him and comforted his sadness
That he conceivèd of his former madness.

Thus being to his former wits restored,
He was likewise delivered clean from love;
The lady whom he erst so much adored
And did esteem all earthly joys above
Now he despised, yea rather quite
 abhorred;
Now only he applies his wits to prove
That fame and former glory to recover
Which he had not lost the while he was
 a lover.

STUDY QUESTIONS

1. In what specific respects does Orlando's passion appear as madness?
2. Is Orlando still the ideal type of a Christian knight, even before he is released from his enchantment?

12.3 MACHIAVELLI, *DISCOURSES ON LIVY*, CA. 1517

The humanist and statesman Niccolò Machiavelli (1469–1527) is best known for his Italian treatise *The Prince* on Renaissance city-state rulers—but his *Discourses on Livy* better clarify his republican ideals. In this response to Roman historian Livy, Machiavelli traces the origins of "good" republics. He comments on the maintenance of liberties, the role of religion, and the danger of societal fragmentation through conspiracy.

CHAPTER 5

WHETHER THE GUARDIANSHIP OF LIBERTY MAY BE MORE SECURELY LODGED IN THE PEOPLE OR IN THE UPPER CLASSES; AND WHO HAS MORE REASON TO CREATE AN UPRISING, HE WHO WISHES TO ACQUIRE OR HE WHO WISHES TO MAINTAIN

Among the most necessary things established by those who have founded a republic in a prudent fashion is a safeguard for liberty, and according to whether it is well established or not, that free way of life is more or less enduring. Because in every republic there are men of prominence and men of the people, some doubt has arisen over whose hands into which this guardianship would best be placed. Among the Spartans and, in our own times, among the Venetians, it was placed in the hands of the nobles, but among the Romans it was placed in the hands of the plebeians.

For this reason, it is necessary to examine which of these republics made the best choice. If we were to explore the reasons, something could be said for both sides, but if we examine the results, we would choose the side of the nobles, since the liberty of Sparta and Venice endured longer than that of Rome. Turning to the causes, let me say, while first taking the side of the Romans, that the guardianship must be given to those who have less of an appetite to usurp it. No doubt, if we consider the goal of the nobles and that of the common people, we shall see in the former a strong desire to dominate and in the latter only the desire not to be dominated, and, as a consequence, a stronger will to live in liberty, since they have less hope of usurping it than men of prominence; just so, since the common people are set up as guardians of this liberty, it is reasonable to think that they will take better care of it, and, being incapable of appropriating it for themselves, they will not permit others to do so. On the other hand, those who defend the organization of Sparta and Venice declare that those who place the guardianship in the hands of the powerful accomplish two good things: first they better satisfy their ambition, and since they have a larger part to play in the republic with this club in their hands, they have more reason to be content; second they remove a kind of authority from the restless minds of the plebeians that is the cause of countless conflicts and disagreements in any republic and is likely to drive the nobility to despair, which, in the passing of time, will produce harmful consequences.

Discourses on Livy. Translated by Julia Conway Bondanella and Peter Bondanella. Oxford: Oxford University Press, 2010, 1666w from pp. 31–2, 53–6, 256–8, 275. By permission of Oxford University Press. License granted through PLS Clear.

As an example, they offer Rome itself, where, once the tribunes of the people had this authority in their hands, they did not consider it sufficient to have one plebeian consul and wanted two of them. After this, they wanted the censorship, the praetorship, and all the other positions of power in the city; nor did this suffice, for led by this same consuming desire, they then began in time to idolize those men they saw capable of beating down the nobility; and from this arose the power of Marius and the ruin of Rome. Truly, anyone who properly considers one side or the other could remain in doubt about which of the two should be chosen as the guardian of such liberty, not knowing which human disposition is more harmful in a republic: either that which wishes to preserve honour already acquired, or that which wishes to acquire honour yet to be possessed.

. . .

CHAPTER 12

HOW IMPORTANT IT IS TO TAKE ACCOUNT OF RELIGION, AND HOW ITALY, LACKING IN RELIGION THANKS TO THE ROMAN CHURCH, HAS BEEN RUINED

Those princes or republics that wish to maintain their integrity must, above all else, maintain the integrity of their religious ceremonies, and must always hold them in veneration, because there can be no greater indication of the ruin of a state than to see a disregard for its divine worship. This is easy to understand if one knows how the religion in the place where a man is born has been founded, because the life of every religion has its foundations in one of its principal institutions. The existence of the pagan religion was founded upon the responses of the oracles and the sect of diviners and soothsayers; all the other ceremonies, sacrifices, and rites depended upon them, because they simply believed that the god who could predict your future good or evil could also grant it to you.

. . .

Since many are of the opinion that the well-being of the Italian cities arises from the Roman church, I want to discuss the arguments that occur to me against this opinion, and I shall cite as evidence two very powerful ones which, in my view, cannot be refuted. The first is that because of the evil examples set by this court, this land has lost all piety and religion; this brings with it countless disadvantages and countless disorders, because just as we take for granted every good thing where religion exists, so, where it is lacking, we take for granted the contrary. We Italians have, therefore, this initial debt to the church and to the priests, that we have become irreligious and wicked, but we have an even greater debt to them, which is the second cause of our ruin: that is, the church has kept and still keeps this land divided, and truly, no land is ever united or happy unless it comes completely under the obedience of a single republic or a single prince, as has occurred in France and Spain. The reason why Italy is not in the same condition and why it, too, does not have either a single republic or a single prince to govern it lies solely with the church, because although the church has its place of residence in Italy and has held temporal power there, it has not been so powerful nor has it possessed enough skill to be able to occupy the remaining parts of Italy and make itself ruler of this country, and, on the other hand, it has not been so weak that, for fear of losing control over its temporal affairs, it has been unable to bring in someone powerful to defend it against anyone in Italy who had become too powerful: this is seen to have happened in ancient times through a number of examples, as when with Charlemagne's assistance, the Lombards, already kings of almost all of Italy, were driven out, and when in our own times the church took power away from the Venetians with the aid of France and then chased out the French with the aid of the Swiss. Since it has not, therefore, been powerful enough to take possession of all of Italy, nor has it permitted anyone else to do so, the church has been the reason why Italy has been unable to unite under a single leader and has remained under a number of princes and lords, who have produced so much disunity and weakness that it has come to be easy prey not only to powerful barbarians but to anyone who might attack it. For this we Italians are indebted to the church and to no one else. Anyone who might wish to see this truth more clearly through actual experience needs to possess sufficient power to send the Roman court, with all the authority it possesses in Italy, to live in the lands of the Swiss, who are today the only people who live, with respect to religion and military institutions, as the ancients did, and he would observe that in a brief time the wicked customs of that court would create more disorder in that land than any other event that could at any time take place there.

. . .

CHAPTER 6

ON CONSPIRACIES

I did not think I should omit an analysis of conspiracies, since they represent a grave danger for princes and for private citizens. It is evident that many more princes have lost their lives and their states through conspiracies than through open warfare, because being able to wage open war against a prince is within the reach of very few, while the possibility of conspiring against him is open to everyone. . . . Truly golden is that maxim of Tacitus, which declares that men must honour past affairs and endure present ones, and that they should desire good princes, but regardless of what they are like, should tolerate them. And truly, anyone who does otherwise most often ruins himself and his native land.

. . .

Injuries must either be against property, lifeblood, or honour. To threaten someone's lifeblood is more dangerous than to execute him; or rather, making threats is extremely dangerous, while ordering executions involves no danger whatsoever, because a dead man cannot think about a vendetta, while those who remain alive most often leave the thinking to the dead. But anyone who is threatened and forced by necessity either to act or to suffer will become a very dangerous man to the prince, as we shall discuss in detail in the proper place. Besides this kind of necessity, injuries to property and honour are the two things that offend men more than any other kind of attack, and the prince must protect himself against them, because he can never strip a man of so much that he will not have a knife left with which to take his revenge; nor can he ever dishonour a man so much that he does not retain a heart and mind stubbornly intent on revenge.

. . .

Princes, therefore, have no greater enemy than a conspiracy, because if a conspiracy is organized against them, it either kills them or disgraces them; if it succeeds, they die, and if it is discovered and they kill the conspirators, people always believe that the conspiracy was an invention of the prince to give vent to his avarice and cruelty against their lives and property of those whom he has killed.

STUDY QUESTIONS

1. Does Machiavelli employ examples from the pre-Christian and his contemporary world equally?
2. Why does he see the church as an "impediment" to the political ambitions of Italians?

12.4 ERASMUS, "LETTER TO A FRIEND," "JULIUS EXCLUDED FROM HEAVEN," AND *INTRODUCTION TO THE GOSPELS*, FIRST PUBLISHED 1522

Desiderius Erasmus (ca. 1466–1536) was a Catholic priest who has also been called the Prince of the Humanists for his application of humanist principles to the religious disruption of the Reformation—he created new editions of the New Testament and wrote a handful of satires and other texts on Christian life. Although Erasmus was appalled by the abuses of the Catholic Church, he chose to try to address them while remaining a staunch Catholic. In 1512, Erasmus began work on a fresh Greek edition of the New Testament (with the Latin in parallel columns) that would share a beautified, holistic, and purified Word of God with Catholics in a time of religious turmoil. Interestingly, this would be the version used by Luther to make his own German translation (Document 12.6).

LETTER TO A FRIEND ON PRESENT CONDITIONS

It is no part of my nature, most learned Wolfgang, to be excessively fond of life; whether it is, that I have, to my own mind, lived nearly long enough, having entered my fifty-first year, or that I see nothing in this life so splendid or delightful, that it should be desired by one who is convinced by the Christian faith, that a happier life awaits those who in this world earnestly attach themselves to piety. But at the present moment I could almost wish to be young again, for no other reason but this, that I anticipate the near approach of a golden age; so clearly do we see the minds of princes, as if changed by inspiration, devoting all their energies to the pursuit of peace. The chief movers in this matter are Pope Leo, and Francis, King of France.

There is nothing this king does not do or does not suffer, in his desire to avert war and consolidate peace; submitting, of his own accord, to conditions which might be deemed unfair, if he preferred to have regard to his own greatness and dignity, rather than to the general advantage of the world; and exhibiting in this, as in everything else, a magnanimous and truly royal character. Therefore, when I see that the highest sovereigns of Europe, Francis of France, Charles the Catholic King, Henry of England and the Emperor Maximillian have set all their warlike preparations aside, and established peace upon solid, and as I trust adamantine foundations, I am led to a confident hope, that not only morality and Christian piety, but also a genuine and purer literature may come to renewed life or greater splendor; especially as this object is pursued with equal zeal in various regions of the world,—at Rome by Pope Leo, in Spain by the Cardinal of Toledo, in England by Henry, eighth of the name, himself not unskilled in Letters, and among ourselves by our young

From W. K. Fergison, ed., *Erasmi Opuscula*. Translated by M. P. Gilmore. The Hague: Martinus Nijhoff, 1933, pp. 65–8; From "De Libero Arbitrio" (1524). In *Desiderii Erasmi Roterodami Opera Omnia*. Edited by J. Clericus, translated by Brice M. Clagett. Lugduni Batavorum: Petri Vander Aa, 1703–1706, IX, 1240, 1244, 1248; From "De Libero Arbitrio" (1524). In *Desiderii Erasmi Roterodami Opera Omnia*. Edited by J. Clericus, translated by Brice M. Clagett. Lugduni Batavorum: Petri Vander Aa, 1703–1706, IX, 1215, 1219–20.

king Charles. In France King Francis, who seems as it were born for this object, invites and entices from all countries men that excel in merit or in learning. Among the Germans the same object is pursued by many of their excellent princes and bishops, and especially by Maximillian Caesar, whose old age, weary of so many wars, has determined to seek rest in the employments of peace, a resolution more becoming to his own years, while it is fortunate for the Christian world. To the piety of these princes it is due, that we see everywhere, as if upon a given signal, men of genius are arising and conspiring together to restore the best literature.

Polite letters, which were almost extinct, are now cultivated and embraced by Scots, by Danes and by Irishmen. Medicine has a host of champions; at Rome Nicolas of Leonice; at Venice Ambrosius Leo of Nola, in France William Cop, and John Ruelle, and in England Thomas Linacre. The Imperial Law is restored at Paris by William Budé, in Germany by Udalris Zasy; and Mathematics at Basel by Henry of Glaris. In the theological sphere there was no little to be done, because this science has been hitherto mainly professed by those who are most pertinacious in the abhorrence of the better literature, and are the more successful in defending their own ignorance as they do it under pretext of piety, the unlearned vulgar being induced to believe, that violence is offered to Religion, if any one begins an assault upon their barbarism. For in the presence of an ignorant mob they are always ready to scream and excite their followers to stone-throwing, if they see any risk of not being thought omniscient. But even here I am confident of success, if the knowledge of the three languages continues to be received in schools, as it has now begun. For the most learned and least churlish men of the profession do in some measure assist and favour the new system; and in this matter we are especially indebted to the vigorous exertions of James Lefèvrew of Étaples, whom you resemble not only in name, but in a number of accomplishments.

The humblest part of the work has naturally fallen to my lot. Whether my contribution has been worth anything, I cannot say; at any rate those who object to the world regaining its senses, are as angry with me, as if my small industry had had some influence, although the work was not undertaken by me with any confidence that I could myself teach anything magnificent; but I wanted to construct a road for other persons of higher aims, so that they might be less impeded by pools and stumbling-blocks in carrying home those fair and glorious treasures.

* * * * *

JULIUS II EXCLUDED FROM HEAVEN: JULIUS, HIS TUTELARY SPIRIT, AND SAINT PETER

JULIUS: What's the trouble here? Won't the doors open? The lock must have been changed or at least tampered with.

SPIRIT: Perhaps you haven't brought the right key, for this door will never be opened by the same key as you use for your money-box. So why haven't you brought both keys here, for this one that you have is the key of power not of knowledge?

JULIUS: This is the only one I ever had and I see no need of another as long as I have this.

SPIRIT: Nor indeed do I except that in the meantime we are shut out.

JULIUS: I am getting very angry. I will beat down these gates. Hey, someone in there, open this door at once! What is the matter? Will no one come? Why does the porter dally like this? No doubt he's snoring and probably drunk.

SPIRIT: (As always, he judges everyone else by himself!)

SAINT PETER: It's a good thing we have adamantine doors here; otherwise this man would have broken in. He must be some giant or satrap, a conqueror of cities. But, O immortal God, what stench! I will not open the door at once, but by looking out this little barred window find out what kind of a monster this may be. Who are you and what do you want?

JULIUS: Open as quickly as you can. If you had done your duty, you ought to have come out and meet me with all the pomp due an emperor.

SAINT PETER: Spoken imperiously enough. But first explain to me who you are.

JULIUS: As if you could not see for yourself!

SAINT PETER: See? Indeed I see a strange and hitherto unknown, not to say monstrous, spectacle.

JULIUS: Unless you are wholly blind, you must recognize this key even if you don't know the golden oak. And you see the triple crown and the pallium gleaming with gems and with gold.

SAINT PETER: Indeed I see a key silvered all over although it is only one and very different from those keys which Christ as the true pastor of the Church once gave over to me. And how should I recognize this proud crown? No barbarian tyrant ever wore such a one still less anyone who demanded to be admitted here. Nor does this pallium in the least move me who have always scorned and despised gold and gems as rubbish. But what is this? I see everywhere on key and crown and pallium the signs of that most wicked rogue and impostor Simon [Magus] who shares my name but not my way of life, and whom I long ago turned out of the temple of Christ.

JULIUS: If you are wise you will put aside this joking, for, in case you don't know, I am Julius the Ligurian and you will surely recognize the two letters P. M. if you learned to read at all.

SAINT PETER: I believe they stand for "Pestis Maxima" [Supreme Plague].

SPIRIT: Ha ha ha! How this soothsayer has hit the nail on the head!

JULIUS: No, "Pontifex Maximus" [Supreme Pontiff].

SAINT PETER: If you were three times "Maximus" and more even than Mercury Trismegistus, you would not come in here unless you were also "optimus," that is holy [*sanctus*].

JULIUS: If in fact it matters at all to be called "sanctus," you who are delaying the opening the doors for me have passed the bounds of imprudence since you during so many centuries have been called only "sanctus," while no one has ever called me anything but "sanctissimus." And there are six thousand bulls . . . in which I am not only named "most sacred lord" but am described by the very name of holiness itself, not *sanctus*, so that I did whatever I pleased.

SPIRIT: Even indulging in drunkenness.

JULIUS: They said that that made the sanctity of the most sacred lord Julius.

SAINT PETER: Then ask admission of those flatterers who made you most sacred and let them give you happiness who gave you sanctity. Although you think this is a question of no concern, will you be called "sanctus" whether you are or not?

JULIUS: I am exasperated. If I were only permitted to live, I should envy you neither that sanctity nor that felicity.

SAINT PETER: O what a revelation of a "most sacred mind"! Although I have now for some time been inspecting you from all sides, I notice in you many signs of impiety and none of holiness: And what does this strange crowd so very unpontifical want for itself? You bring some twenty thousand with you nor do I see anyone in such a great mob who has the countenance of a Christian. I see the loathsome dregs of men, smelling of nothing but brothels, drink-shops and gunpowder: It seems to me that hired robbers or rather infernal skeletons have rushed hither from hell to make war on heaven. Also the more I contemplate you yourself, the less do I see any vestige of an apostle. In the first place what kind of monster are you who, although you wear outside the garments of a priest, underneath bristle and clink with a covering of bloody armor? In addition to this how savage are your eyes, how stubborn your mouth, how threatening your brow and how haughty and arrogant your glance! It is shameful to have to say and at the same time disgusting to see that no part of your body is not defiled by the signs of your unrestrained and abominable lust: Not to speak of the fact that you always belch and smell of inebriation and drunkenness and indeed seem to me to have just vomited. This is so truly the condition of your whole body that you seem withered, wasted, and broken not so much by age and disease as by drunkenness.

SPIRIT: How graphically he has depicted him in all his colors.

SAINT PETER: Although I see that you have long been threatening me with your look, yet I cannot keep back what I feel. I suspect that you are that most pestilential heathen Julius returned from hell to make sport of me.

* * * * *

PARACLESIS: INTRODUCTION TO THE GOSPELS

I strongly dissent from those who are unwilling to have the Scriptures translated into the vernacular and read by the ignorant, as if Christ taught so complicated a doctrine that it can hardly be understood even by a handful of theologians or as if the arcanum of the Christian religion consisted in its not being known. It is perhaps reasonable to conceal the mysteries of kings but Christ seeks to divulge his mysteries as much as possible. I should like to have even the most humble women read the Evangel and the Epistles of St. Paul. And these ought also to be translated into all languages so that they might be read and known not only by Scots and Irishmen but also by Turks and Saracens. The first step is certainly to know the Scriptures in whatever manner. Although many will mock at them some will be captivated. Would that the ploughboy recited something from them at his ploughshare, that the weaver sang from them at his shuttle and that the traveler whiled away the tedium of his journey with their tales, indeed would that the converse of Christian men were drawn from them, for we are on the whole what our daily discourse reveals us to be. Let each attain what he can and express what he can. Let him who is behind not envy him who is ahead and let the leader encourage the follower without making him despair. Why should we restrict to a few a profession which is common to all? For since baptism in which the first profession of the philosophy of Christ is made is equally common to all Christians, since they share alike the other sacraments and finally the supreme reward of immortality, it is not fitting that the possession of dogma be relegated to those few whom we call theologians or monks. Although these latter constitute only a minute proportion of the Christian people nevertheless I could wish that they confirm more closely to what they head. For I fear lest there be found among the theologians those who are far from deserving this title, who discourse of earthly not of divine things and among the monks who profess poverty and contempt for the world you may find instead even more of the world. To me he is truly a theologian who teaches not with syllogisms and contorted arguments but with compassion in his eyes and his whole countenance, who teaches indeed by the example of his own life that riches are to be despised, that the Christian man must not put his faith in the defenses of this world but depend entirely on heaven, that he is not to return an injury for an injury, that he is to pray well for those who pray badly and do his best for those who deserve ill, that all good men ought to love and cherish each other as members of the same body and evil men tolerated if they cannot be corrected. Those who lose their goods, who are deposited of their possessions, who mourn—these are not to be pitied for they are the blessed and death is even to be desired by the pious for it is the passage to immortality. If anyone inspired by the spirit of Christ preaches things of this kind, if he inculcates, urges, invites, encourages, then he is a true theologian even if he should be a ditch digger or a weaver.

. . . For that which is especially according to nature easily comes into the minds of all. And what else is the philosophy of Christ which he himself calls a rebirth (*renascentia*) but a restoration of a nature which was originally created good?

* * * * *

ERASMUS ATTACKS LUTHER (1524)

What shall I say of the prodigal son? How could he have wasted his share of the inheritance had it not been his to do with as he pleased? But what he had, he held of his father; and we, too, remember that all our natural qualities are so many gifts of God. Besides, he enjoyed his share even when it was in his father's possession, and then it was in safer hands. What does it mean, then—his departure from his father after suddenly having demanded his share? Quite simply, to give oneself credit for one's natural qualities, and to use them, not in obeying the commandments of God, but in satisfying carnal lusts. And what means the hunger of the prodigal son? It is the sickness by which God directs the mind of the sinner towards self-knowledge, self-hatred, and regret for having left his Father. What is the meaning of the son's inner questioning, when he envisions confession and return? It is the human will adapting itself to the motivating grace that is also called, as we have said, "prevenient" grace. What about this Father who goes before his son on the way? It is the grace of God, which allows our will do to the good when we have determined to do it.

Besides, I ask, what merit could a man claim for himself who is indebted to Him from whom he received natural intelligence and free will for all he can do with these faculties? And yet God considers it meritorious in us not to turn our soul from His grace, and to enlist our talents in His service. That is enough to show that we make no mistake in attributing something to man, although we refer all his works to God as to their author: it is from Him, in fact, that man derives the power of making his strivings one with the operations of divine grace. . . . [The divine wisdom assists man] as guide and advisor, just as an architect directs his workman, draws his plans for him, explains the reason for them, corrects his faulty beginnings, and bolsters him if he loses courage: the work is attributed to the architect, without whose aid nothing would have been created, but no one pretends that the worker and pupil were worthless. What the architect is to his pupil, grace is to our will. That is why Paul writes to the Romans (8.26): "Even so His Spirit cometh to aid our weakness." Now no one calls a person who does nothing weak; that term, rather, is applied to him who lacks strength sufficient to accomplish what he undertakes; in the same sense, you do not say that some one helps you when he does everything. Now Scripture continually speaks of aid, support, succor, shelter. In order for there to be aid, the person aided has to do something. You would not say that the potter helps the clay to become a pot, or that the carpenter aids the axe in making a stool.

That is why, when our opponents declare that man can do nothing without the grace of God, therefore there are no good works by men, we confront them with this proof, which I believe more probable, that men can do everything with the aid of grace, therefore all human works can be good. As many passages as there are in Holy Scripture which mention succor, there are an equal number to establish free will, and they are countless; and I shall carry the day without any possible disagreement if the matter is judged by the number of proofs. . . .

In my opinion, similarly, free will could be preserved while completely avoiding this flagrant confidence in our own merits and the other dangers seen by Luther, without even considering those which we have cited above, and while retaining the main advantages of Lutheran teaching. This is what the doctrine means to me which attributes to grace all the first inspiration which enflames the soul, but which leaves to the human will, when it is not devoid of divine grace, a certain place in the unfolding of the drama. Now since this drama has three parts, the beginning, the development, and the fulfillment, we give the two extremities to grace and let free will enter only into the development. Thus two causes collaborate in the same given action, divine grace and the human will; but grace is the principal cause, the will a secondary one which could do nothing without the first, while grace is sufficient in itself—thus fire burns by its natural virtue, although God is the essential cause which sustains its action, without which the fire would lose all its power, if God happened to withdraw his support. . . .

But why, we are asked, leave a place for free will? In order to have something with which justly to accuse the impious who by their own decision stand outside divine grace; to acquit God of false charges of cruelty or injustice; to drive despair or arrogance far from us; to inspire us to effort. These are the reasons which have led almost all writers to admit free will; but it would remain ineffective without the perpetual aid of the grace of God, which justly prevents us from pride. But still it will be said: what good, then, is free will, if it can do nothing by itself? I shall only reply, "And what would be the use of man himself and all his faculties, if God acted on him as the potter on the clay, or even as He might act on a pebble?"

* * * * *

I take so little pleasure in dogmatizing that I should rather rank myself with the sceptics, whenever I am justified in so doing by the inviolable authority of Holy Scripture and by the decisions of the Church, to which I always submit my judgment quite willingly, whether or not I understand the reasons for what she decrees. And this temper of mind appears to me preferable to that of certain others, who, narrowly attached to their own views, never let any one deviate from them in anything, and who violently twist all the texts of Scripture in support of the position they have embraced once and for all. . . .

Here it will be objected: "Why the need of interpretation, when Scripture itself is perfectly clear?" But if it is as clear as all that, why, over the centuries, have such eminent men been blind on so important a point, as our opponents contend? If Scripture is without obscurity, why was there need for prophecies in apostolic times? That, I shall be told, was a gift of the Holy Spirit. But I should like to know whether, just as the gift of healing and the gift of tongues have ceased, this divine gift has not ceased also. And if it has not ceased, we must seek to learn to whom it could have passed. If it has passed to merely anyone at all, then every interpretation will be uncertain; if it has been received by no one, since today so many obscurities still torment the learned, no interpretation will be more certain. If I maintain that it resides in the successors of the apostles, it will be objected that over the centuries many men have succeeded the apostles who nevertheless had none of the apostolic spirit. And yet, everything else being equal, it will be sought in them, for it is more probably that God has infused His Spirit in those to whom He has given holy orders; just as we believe that grace is more clearly given to the baptized than to the unbaptized.

But, as we must, we shall admit no less than the possibility that the Spirit may actually reveal to some humble and illiterate person truths withheld from a host of learned men, as when Christ thanked His Father for the things He made known to the simple, to those whom the world thought mad—things he had hidden from the wise and the judicious, from the knowledge of scribes, Pharissees, and philosophers. And perhaps Dominic, perhaps Francis [the thirteenth century saints], were the kind of madmen who are allowed to follow their inspirations. But if Paul, in the day when this gift of the Spirit was in its full vigor, already warns men to check on whether these inspirations really come from God, what must we do in our worldly age? By what standard shall we judge opinions? By learning? But there are none but master scholars in both parties. By conduct? On both sides, likewise, there are only sinners. But we find the chorus of saints all on the same side, defending free will. I am told, it is true, "They were nothing but men." But I only meant to compare men with one another, never with God. I am asked, what does the majority prove, with regard to spiritual insight? I answer, what does the minority prove? I am asked, how can a bishop's mitre be of use in understanding Holy Scripture? I answer, what good is a mantle or cowl? Again, how can philosophical studies make it easier to understand Holy Writ? And I reply, what use is ignorance? And again, how is the comprehension of texts connected with the meeting of a council, where it might be that no member had received the Spirit of God? I answer, what then is the value of private pseudo-councils of a few individuals, where there is only too clearly no possessor of the Spirit?

Do we remember this plea of Paul's, "Don't ask for proof that Christ lives in me"? Then the apostles were only believed to the extent to which their miracles confirmed their teaching. These days, on the contrary, anyone at all demands credence just because he declares he is filled with the spirit of the Gospel. Because the apostles drove out serpents, cured the sick, brought the dead to life, and gave the gift of tongues by the laying on of hands, men decided to believe, and not without difficulty, the paradoxes they taught. And today, when we see new teachers declaring things that common sense cannot even class as paradoxes, we have not yet seen one of them capable of curing a lame horse. And would to Heaven that, if they cannot work miracles, some of them would at least show the purity and simplicity of apostolic life, which to us, poor late-comers, would be miraculous enough!

I am not speaking specifically of Luther, whom I have never met and whose works give me a confused impression, but of certain others whom I have known more closely. It is they who in biblical controversies reject the interpretation of the Fathers which we suggest to them, they who cry unrestrainedly, "The Fathers were only men!" If they are asked what criterion can be used to establish the true interpretation of Scripture, since there are only men on both sides, they rely on the revelations of the Spirit. But if they are asked why the Spirit should favor them rather than those whose miracles have shone forth throughout the world, they answer if the Gospel had disappeared from the earth thirteen centuries ago. If you insist that their life be worthy of the Spirit, they retort that they are justified by faith, not by works. If you require miracles, they tell you that the time for them has long passed, and that there is no longer any need for them, now that the Scriptures are fully clarified. And then if you doubt that Scripture is clear precisely on the point where so many great minds have erred, you fall back into the same vicious circle.

Besides if we admit that he who possesses the Spirit is sure of understanding the Scriptures, how shall I be certain of what he has seen only partially? What shall I do when several learned men bring me different interpretations, each one swearing all the time that he has the Spirit? Especially, if we add that the Spirit does not reveal all truth to them fully, even he who has the Spirit can go wrong, and err on some point.

These are my objections to those who so easily reject the traditional interpretation of the Holy Books, and who propose their own as if it had plummeted from Heaven. Finally, assuming that the Spirit of Christ could have left His people in error on some secondary point without immediate repercussions on human salvation, how can we admit that for thirteen hundred years He abandoned His Church to error, and that in all the host of holy people not one could reveal to the Church that truth which, our recent arrivals pretend, constitutes the heart of all the Gospel teaching?

But to finish this matter: whatever others may arrogate to themselves is their own affair; as for me, I claim for myself neither wisdom nor sanctity, and I take no pride in my intellect, but I shall simply and carefully set forth the views which capture my allegiance. If any one wishes to teach me, I shall not meet the truth with a closed mind.

STUDY QUESTIONS

1. What lessons, particularly concerning warfare, does Erasmus hope that the kings of Europe will draw from reading his edition of the Gospels?
2. Did the behavior of the "Warrior Pope" Julius II warrant his being "excluded" from Heaven?
3. How did Erasmus reconcile the reading of Scripture and its interpretation in the correct, Christian spirit? Can every Christian interpret what he or she reads correctly?

12.5 MARTIN LUTHER, *ON THE FREEDOM OF A CHRISTIAN*, DEDICATORY LETTER TO POPE LEO X, 1520

Martin Luther (1483–1546) wrote his great work, *On the Freedom of a Christian*, in late 1520, after his contentious meetings (described briefly here) by the papal nuncios Cardinal Cajetan, Johann Eck, Andreas von Miltitz. It is the text in which he most fully worked out his doctrine that

Translation by Clifford Backman.

salvation is the free gift offered to us by a loving God in Christ, a gift that we need not earn or deserve but simply need to be willing to accept. To this notion of *sola fide* ("by our faith alone" we are saved) he adds that of *sola Scriptura* ("by the Scriptures alone" are we authoritatively taught), emphasizing that every Christian has the right to interpret the Scriptures for himself. His dedicatory letter to Leo X follows.

For the last three years I have been waging war against the monstrous evils of our time, and more than once I have been compelled to turn my mind to you, most blessed father Leo, since everyone thinks that you are the sole cause of my struggle and that therefore I must always have you on my mind. While it is true that the pointless wrath directed at me by the evil flatterers who surround you has led me to appeal to you to call a Church Council. . . . I have never been so estranged from Your Blessedness that I have not sought, in constant and tearful prayers to the Lord, for every good thing for you. I confess that I have begun to despise, and hope to silence, those people who are trying to terrify me by invoking the majesty of your name and office. The reason I am writing to you now, blessed Leo, is that those same people are accusing me of directing my energies at you personally out of a desire to offend you.

To speak plain truth: I cannot think of anything I have said about you that was not honorable and good. . . . I am not so foolish as to attack someone whom everyone praises; and indeed, it has been my aim, and always will be, to avoid all personal attacks—even on those individuals whose personal reputations are disgraceful. I take no delight in anyone's faults since I am only too aware of the beam in my own eye. I can never be the first to cast a stone at any sinner. And while it is true that I have sharply criticized impious doctrines and have never hesitated to condemn my adversaries, I have attacked only their impiety, not their personal morals. I make no apology for this. . . .

For these reasons, dear Leo, I beg you to receive this letter in my defense and to believe that I have never thought anything wicked towards your person. I desire that every eternal blessing may befall you, and please know that I have no dispute with anyone alive regarding personal morals. My only concern is the Word of Truth. On anything else I will yield to anyone, but I cannot and will not forsake or deny the Word. If anyone thinks otherwise of me or interprets my words in any other sense, he is mistaken and does not understand me.

Neither you nor anyone can deny, however, that Your See—the Roman Curia—is more corrupt than any kingdom of Babylon or city of Sodom, lost, desperate, and hopelessly impious. Against it I have railed, and I am outraged that the people of Christ are being cheated in your name and that of the Church of Rome. I have condemned it and will keep doing so as long as a faithful spirit lives in me. . . . For many years now, as you well know, nothing has flowed from Rome into the world except the wastage of goods, bodies, and souls, the foulest of all foul things. It is as clear as day to everyone alive that the Church of Rome, once the most holy of all churches, has become the most lawless den of thieves, the most shameless of brothels, and the very realm of sin, death, and hell. If Antichrist himself were to appear on earth, he could not conjure any way to add to its wickedness.

You, dear Leo, are a lamb in the midst of wolves. Like Daniel, you are surrounded by lions; like Ezekiel, you dwell among scorpions. . . . I grieve that you, who deserve to have lived in a better age, were made Pontiff in this one, for the Curia is not worthy of you or anyone like you. It deserves a Satan—and Satan is indeed more the ruler in that wicked Babylon than you are. . . . There is nothing under the vast heavens more corrupt, diseased, and loathsome than the Curia. It surpasses even the wickedness of the Turks. Once the gateway to Heaven, it is now the opened mouth of Hell. . . .

As I was moving ahead with my studies of the Holy Scriptures, Satan opened his eyes and goaded his servant Johann Eck (that notorious enemy of Christ!), in his limitless lust for fame, to pull me into open debate, where he tripped me up on a single comment that I made in passing in regard to the primacy of the Church. In his proud insolence, foaming at the mouth and gnashing his teeth, he boasted that he would risk anything for the glory of God and the honor of the Holy See. . . . but in truth he sought to promote not the primacy of St. Peter but his own prominence among the theologians of our time. . . .

Most excellent Leo, I pray you will allow me to plead my own cause and point blame at your true enemies. I believe you have heard by now how Cardinal Cajetan acted towards me—Cajetan, that rash, miserable, and traitorous legate of yours! When, out of reverence for you, I had placed myself and all my works in his hands, he could have made peace with me by one simple word, for I had vowed to remain silent and make an end of my case if he agreed simply to order my adversaries to do the same. But he was too proud to agree to this and instead defended my adversaries. He gave them free license to speak against me, and ordered me to recant (even though this was absolutely not part of his commission). This is how our dispute turned worse just when it was in the best position to be resolved. His tyranny vexed me and continues to do so, which is why everything that has occurred since then is entirely his fault, not mine. I had begged with all my might to be allowed to remain silent and let our conflict end. What more could I have done?

Next came Karl von Miltitz, another nuncio of yours, who exerted himself in every way imaginable, trying to resolve the conflict that proud Cajetan had so boldly made even worse. But even though he was aided by the illustrious Prince-Elector Friedrich, he could accomplish nothing more than arrange a single face-to-face meeting with me. At this meeting I again yielded to your great name and offered to keep silent and to accept as my judge either the archbishop of Trier or the bishop of Naumburg. Miltitz agreed, and the matter was settled. But even as we were coming to terms, Eck (your main enemy, Leo!) rushed in, carrying his *Leipzig Disputation*—the text he had used in his debate with Andreas Karlstadt—and, taking aim against me in an unexpected way, raised a new issue in regard to papal supremacy. Our plans for peace were crushed. Miltitz stood frozen while Eck argued with me and chose different judges [than those I had agreed to]. But nothing came of all this, for Eck's lies, pretenses, and trickery had brought matters to so confused, messy, and painful a state that no matter in which direction we proceeded, a greater conflagration was sure to arise. Eck's goal, after all, was not to seek truth but his own renown. In this case too, I did nothing except what was fitting.

I must confess that on this particular occasion no small amount of the corruption in the Roman Curia came to light—but the offense was Eck's. His ambition and lust for fame revealed Rome's disgrace to the whole world. . . . Eck is your true enemy, Leo, and the enemy of your Curia. He is living proof that there is worse enemy than a flatterer, for what has been the result of his flattery but evil? Evil to the Church that is greater than any king could wreak upon it, for today the very name *Roman Curia* stinks in the nostrils of the world. . . .

Thus, I turn to you, blessed Father, and humbly beg you to stretch out your hand and silence, if possible, those flatterers who, despite their protestations, are the enemies of peace. No one should ever try to persuade you, Holy Father, that I am willing to recant—in so doing he will only make difficult matters worse. I reject all rules for how to interpret the Word of God for the simple reason that the Word, which teaches liberty in all matters, cannot be bound by rules. With the exception of these two statements, there is nothing I am not eagerly willing to do or to suffer in order to end this contention. I detest conflict, and I will challenge no one who does not challenge me. But if I am challenged, I refuse to remain silent in defense of my Lord Christ. You, blessed Leo, can put an end to all of this misery with a single word, a simple command to impose silence and peace on both sides. How I long to hear you give that command!

Beware of listening to the Sirens, dear Leo. They make you out to be more than a mere man, but partly a God who can order whatever you want in this world. It will not happen like that, not ever. You are the servant of servants, and are now in perhaps the most lamentable and dangerous position ever. Do not listen to the flatterers who say that you are the Lord of the world, that no one can be considered a Christian without your say-so, and that you have power over Heaven, Hell, and Purgatory. Such men are your enemies and a seeking to destroy your soul, as Isaiah says, "Those who led this people led them astray." They are wrong, those men who place you above Councils and the universal Church, and who claim that you alone have the right to interpret Scripture. Such men are filling the Church with their own impieties, and are doing so in your name! Satan has grown strong through such men, up to the time of your pontificate. . . .

It may seem presumptuous of me to deign to teach you; indeed, all men ought to be taught by you (especially those diseased souls who proclaim you the chief of all judges), but I am simply following in the tradition of St. Bernard [of Clairvaux], who addressed his book *Considerations* to Pope Eugenius [III]—a book, indeed, that every pope should know by heart. It is not from a desire to teach you [that I send you this book] but from that sense of duty and love that teaches us to care for our neighbors' well-being, casting aside all notions of worthiness and unworthiness, and concerned only for the dangers that threaten. I am aware how turbulently the storm-waves in Rome are tossing you about, threatening to subsume you in the infinite depths of the angry sea. So miserable is the condition in which you are now living that any help at all, even from the lowest of those who love you, is not out of place. I set aside the majesty of your office and simply offer my loving care to your person. I will not flatter one in so perilous a situation as you are in now, and if this fact alone does not convince you that I am your friend and loyal subject, I will leave it to the Lord to see and to judge.

Lest I approach you empty-handed, dear Father, I bring you this treatise, published under your name, as a token of peace and good hope; it will show you the ways in which I would prefer to occupy myself, if only your wicked flatterers would leave me be. It is a small book in size, but one whose message, I believe, encapsulates all of Christian life, if you understand it right. Being poor, I have no other gift to offer; but you need no riches, only the gifts of the spirit. I commend myself to you, dear Blessed Father, and may the Lord Jesus preserve you forever. Amen.

Wittenberg; 6th September, 1520.

STUDY QUESTIONS

1. How does Luther outline the doctrine that salvation is the free gift offered to us by a loving God in Christ?
2. How does Luther argue that salvation is a gift that we need not earn or deserve but simply be willing to accept?

12.6 MARTIN LUTHER, "PREFACE TO THE NEW TESTAMENT," FIRST PUBLISHED 1522

Martin Luther (1483–1546), known for his unplanned split from the Catholic Church, was a theologian and monk. Among other major points, Luther condemned the Catholic notion that priests enjoyed special spiritual status over other Christians that enabled them to intercede

From Preserved Smith, *Luther's Correspondence*. Philadelphia: Lutheran Publishing Co., 1913, I, pp. 91–3; (A) From Luther, *The Bondage of Will* (1525). Translated by Henry Cole. Grand Rapids, Mich.: W. B. Eerdmans Publishing Co., 1931, pp. 74, 231, 384–5, 391. Original in WA, XVIII, 551 ff.; From Luther, *To the Christian Nobility of the German Nation* (1520). In *Luther's Primary Works*. Edited by Henry Wace and C. A. Buchheim. London: Hodder and Stoughton, 1896, pp. 162–75, passim.

for ordinary sinners; he rejected the use of *indulgences* to purchase forgiveness for sins; and he claimed that only God's grace, and not something a Christian could "earn," would bring him salvation. He translated the Bible into German to make it accessible to his literate compatriots. For these actions, he was excommunicated and threatened with death, and he ultimately became the unwitting founder of the first Protestant sect, Lutheranism. In this introduction to his German translation, Luther guides his readers through Jesus's teachings so that they may come to experience them on their own.

D. PREFACE TO LUTHER'S COLLECTED WORKS, 1545

[While working on the Psalms] I was absorbed by a passionate desire to understand Paul in his Epistle to the Romans. Nothing stood in my way but that one expression, "The justice of God is revealed in the Gospel" (Romans 1:17). For I hated these words, "the justice of God," because I had been taught to understand them in the scholastic sense as the formal or active justice whereby God, who is righteous, punishes unrighteous sinners. I was in the frame of mind of feeling that although I was living a blameless life as a monk, I was still a sinner with a troubled conscience before God, and I had no confidence that I could appease Him by my efforts. I did not love—nay, I hated the righteous God who punishes sinners, and I murmured with unbridled resentment, if not with unspoken blasphemy, against Him, saying, "As if it were not enough for miserable sinners who are eternally lost through original sin to be afflicted with every kind of calamity through the law of the Ten Commandments, without God's adding woe to woe through the Gospel and even threatening us with His justice and wrath in the Gospel." Thus I raged, my conscience wild and disturbed. Still I kept hammering away at those words of Paul, wishing passionately to know what he meant.

After I had pondered the problem for days and nights, God took pity on me and I saw the inner connection between the two phrases, "The justice of God is revealed in the Gospel" and "The just shall live by faith." Then I began to understand that this "justice of God" is the righteousness by which the just man lives through the free gift of God, that is to say "by faith"; and that the justice "revealed in the Gospel" is the passive justice of God by which He takes pity on us and justifies us by our faith, as it is written, "The just shall live by faith." Thereupon I felt as if I had been born again and had entered Paradise through wide-open gates. Immediately the whole of Scripture took on a new meaning for me. I raced through the Scriptures, so far as my memory went, and found analogies in other expressions: "the work of God," i.e., what God works in us; "the strength of God," by which He gives us strength; "the wisdom of God," by which He makes us wise; "the power of God," "the blessing of God," "the glory of God."

Whereas the expression "justice of God" had filled me with hate before, I now exalted it as the sweetest of phrases with all the more love. And so this verse of Paul's became in truth the gate to Paradise for me.

* * * * *

G. LETTER TO STAUPITZ, MAY 30, 1518

I remember, reverend Father, among those happy and wholesome stories of yours, by which the Lord used wonderfully to console me, that you often mentioned the word *poenitentia*, whereupon, distressed by our consciences and by those torturers who with endless and intolerable precept taught nothing but what they called a method of confession, we received you as a messenger from Heaven, for penitence is not genuine save when it begins from the love of justice and of God, and this which they consider the end and consummation of repentance is rather its commencement.

Your words on this subject pierced me like the sharp arrows of the mighty, so that I began to see what the Scriptures had to say about penitence, and behold the happy result: the texts all supported and favored your doctrine, in so much that, while there had formerly been no word in almost all the Bible more bitter to me than *poenitentia* (although I zealously simulated it before God and tried to express an assumed and forced love), now no word sounds sweeter or more pleasant to me than that. For thus do the commands of God become sweet when we understand that they are not to be read in books only, but in the wounds of the sweetest Saviour.

After this it happened by the favor of the learned men who taught me Hebrew and Greek that I learned [from Erasmus' edition of the New Testament in Greek, note on Matthew 3:2] that the Greek word is *metanoia* from *meta* and *noun*, i.e., from "afterwards" and "mind," so that penitence or *metanoia* is "coming to one's right mind, afterwards," that is, comprehension of your own evil, after you had accepted loss and found out your error. This is impossible without a change in your affections. All this agrees so well with Paul's theology, that, in my opinion, at least, nothing is more characteristically Pauline.

Then I progressed and saw that *metanoia* meant not only "afterwards" and "mind," but also "change" and "mind," so that *metanoia* means change of mind and affection. . . .

Sticking fast to this conclusion, I dared to think that they were wrong who attributed so much to works of repentance that they have left us nothing of it but formal penances and elaborate confession. They were seduced by the Latin, for *poenitentiam agere* means rather a work than a change of affection and in no wise agrees with the Greek.

When I was glowing with this thought, behold indulgences and remissions of sins began to be trumpeted abroad with tremendous clangor, but their trumpets animated no one to real struggle. In short, the doctrine of true repentance was neglected, and only the cheapest part of it, that called penance, was magnified. . . . As I was not able to oppose the fury of these preachers, I determined modestly to take issue with them and to call their theories in doubt, relying as I did on the opinion of all the doctors and of the whole Church, who all say that it is better to perform the penance than to buy it, that is an indulgence. . . . This is the reason why I, reverend Father, who always love retirement, have unhappily been forced into the public view.

* * * * *

B. LUTHER REPLIES TO ERASMUS (1525)

You [Erasmus] alone in pre-eminent distinction from all others, have entered upon the thing itself; that is, the grand turning point of the cause; and have not wearied me with those irrelevant points about popery, purgatory, indulgences, and other like baubles, rather than causes, with which all have hitherto tried to hunt me down,—though in vain! You, and you alone, saw what was the grand hinge upon which the whole turned, and therefore you attacked the vital part at once; for which, from my heart, I thank you. . . .

The human will is, as it were, a beast between [God and Satan]. If God sit thereon, it wills and goes where God will; as the Psalm saith, "I am become as it were a beast before thee, and I am continually with thee." (Ps. 73:22–23.) If Satan sit thereon, it wills and goes as Satan will. Nor is it in the power of its own will to choose, to which rider it will run, nor which it will seek; but the riders themselves contend, which shall have and hold it. . . .

God is that Being, for whose will no cause or reason is to be assigned, as a rule or standard by which it acts; seeing that, nothing is superior or equal to it, but it is itself the rule of all things. For if it acted by any rule or standard, or from any cause or reason, it would be no longer the will of God. Wherefore, what God wills is not therefore right, because He ought or ever was bound so to will; but on the contrary, what takes place is therefore right, because He so wills. A cause and reason are assigned for the will of the creature, but not for the will of the Creator; unless you set up, over Him, another Creator. . . .

As to myself, I openly confess, that I should not wish "free-will" to be granted me, even if it could be so, nor anything else to be left in my own hands, whereby I might endeavor something towards my own salvation. And that, not merely because in so many opposing dangers, and so many assaulting devils, I could not stand and hold it fast (in which state no man could be saved, seeing that one devil is stronger than all men); but because, even though there were no dangers, no conflicts, no devils, I should be compelled to labour under a continual uncertainty, and to beat the air only. Nor would my conscience, even if I should live and work to all eternity, ever come to a settled certainty, how much it ought to do in order to satisfy God. For whatever work should be done, there would still remain a scrupling, whether or not it pleased God, or whether He required any thing more; as I proved in the experience of all those who believe in words, and as I myself learned to my bitter cost, through so many years of my own experience.

But now, since God has put my salvation out of the way of *my* will, and has taken it under *His own*, and has promised to save me, not according to my working or manner of life, but according to His own grace and mercy, I rest fully assured and persuaded that He is faithful, and will not lie, and moreover great and powerful, so that no devils, no adversaries can destroy Him or pluck me out of His hand. "No one (saith He) shall pluck them out of My hand, because My Father which gave them Me is greater than all" (John, 10:27–8). Hence it is certain, that in this way, if all are not saved, yet some, yea, many shall be saved; whereas by the power of "free-will" no one whatever could be saved, but all must perish together. And moreover, we are certain and persuaded, that in this way, we please God, not from the merit of our own works, but from the favour of His mercy promised unto us; and that, if we work less, or work badly, He does not impute it unto us, but, as a Father, pardons us and makes us better.

* * * * *

A. LUTHER CHALLENGES THE AUTHORITY OF THE ROMAN CHURCH (1520–1521)

The Romanists have, with great adroitness, drawn three walls round themselves, with which they have hitherto protected themselves, so that no one could reform them, whereby all Christendom has fallen terribly.

Firstly, if pressed by the temporal power, they have affirmed and maintained that the temporal power has no jurisdiction over them, but, on the contrary, that the spiritual power is above the temporal.

Secondly, if it were proposed to admonish them with the Scriptures, they objected that no one may interpret the Scriptures but the Pope.

Thirdly, if they are threatened with a council, they pretend that no one may call a council but the Pope.

Thus they have secretly stolen our three rods, so that they may be unpunished, and intrenched themselves behind these three walls, to act with all the wickedness and malice, which we now witness. . . .

Let us, in the first place, attack the first wall: [that the temporal power has no jurisdiction over the spiritual].

It has been devised that the Pope, bishops, priests, and monks are called the *spiritual estate*; princes, lords, artificers, and peasants are the *temporal estate*. This is an artful lie and hypocritical device, but let no one be made afraid by it, and that for this reason: that all Christians are truly of the spiritual estate, and there is no difference among them, save of office alone. As St. Paul says (I Cor. 12), we are all one body, though each member does its own work, to serve the others. This is because we have one baptism, one Gospel, one faith, and are all Christians alike; for baptism, Gospel, and faith, these alone make spiritual and Christian people.

As for the unction by a Pope or a bishop, tonsure, ordination, consecration, and clothes differing from those of laymen—all this may make a hypocrite or an anointed puppet, but never a Christian or a spiritual man. Thus we are all consecrated as priests by baptism. . . .

Therefore a priest should be nothing in Christendom but a functionary; as long as he holds his office, he has precedence of others; if he is deprived of it, he is a peasant or a citizen like the rest. Therefore, a priest is verily no longer a priest after deposition. But now they have invented *characteres indelibiles*, and pretend that a priest after deprivation still differs from a simple layman. They even imagine that a priest can never be anything but a priest—that is, that he can never become a layman. All this is nothing but mere talk and ordinance of human invention.

It follows, then, that between laymen and priests, princes and bishops, or, as they call it, between spiritual and temporal persons, the only real difference is one of office and function, and not of estate. . . .

Now see what a Christian doctrine is this: that the temporal authority is not above the clergy, and may not punish it. This is as if one were to say the hand may not help, though the eye is in grievous suffering. It is not unnatural, not to say unchristian, that one member may not help another, or guard it against harm? Nay, the nobler the member, the more the rest are bound to help it. Therefore I say, Forasmuch as the temporal power has been ordained by God for the punishment of the bad and the protection of the good, therefore we must let it do its duty throughout the whole Christian body, without respect of persons, whether it strike Popes, bishops, priests, monks, nuns, or whoever it may be. . . .

The second wall is even more tottering and weak: that they alone pretend to be considered masters of the Scriptures; although they learn nothing of them all their life. They assume authority, and juggle before us with impudent words, saying that the Pope cannot err in matters of faith, whether he be evil or good, albeit they cannot prove it by a single letter. That is why the canon law contains so many heretical and unchristian, nay unnatural laws; but of these we need not speak now. For whereas they imagine the Holy Ghost never leaves them, however unlearned and wicked they may be, they grow bold enough to decree whatever they like. But were this true, where were the need and use of the Holy Scriptures? Let us burn them, and content ourselves with the unlearned gentlemen at Rome, in whom the Holy Ghost dwells, who, however, can dwell in pious souls only. If I had not read it, I could never have believed that the devil should have put forth such follies at Rome and find a following. . . .

Therefore, it is a wickedly devised fable—and they cannot quote a single letter to confirm it—that it is for the Pope alone to interpret the Scriptures or to confirm the interpretation of them. They have assumed the authority of their own selves. And though they say that this authority was given to St. Peter when the keys were given to him, it is plain enough that the keys were not given to St. Peter alone, but to the whole community. Besides, the keys were not ordained for doctrine or authority, but for sin, to bind of loose; and what they claim besides this from the keys is mere invention. . . .

Only consider the matter. They must needs acknowledge that there are pious Christians among us that have the true faith, spirit, understanding, word, and mind of Christ; why then should we reject their word and understanding and follow a pope who has neither understanding nor spirit? Surely this were to deny our whole faith and the Christian Church. Moreover, if the article of our faith is right, "I believe in the holy Christian Church," the Pope cannot alone be right; else we must say, "I believe in the Pope of Rome," and reduce the Christian Church to one man, which is a devilish and damnable heresy. Besides that, we are all priests, as I have said, and have all one faith, one Gospel, one Sacrament; how then should we not have the power of discerning and judging what is right or wrong in matters of faith? . . . Balaam's ass was wiser than the prophet. If God spoke by an ass against a prophet, why should He not speak by a pious man against the Pope?

The third wall falls of itself, as soon as the first two have fallen. . . .

When need requires, and the pope is a cause of offence to Christendom, in these cases whoever can best do so, as a faithful member of the whole body, must do what he can to produce a true free council. This no one can do so well as the temporal authorities, especially since they are fellow-Christians, fellow-priests, sharing one spirit and one power in all things, and since they should exercise the office that they have received from God without hinderance, whenever it is necessary and useful that is should be exercised. . . .

As for their boasts of their authority, that no one must oppose it, this is idle talk. No one in Christendom has any authority to do harm, or to forbid others to prevent harm being done. There is no authority in the Church but for reformation. Therefore if the Pope wished to use his power to prevent the reformation of the Church, we must not respect him or his power; and if he should begin to excommunicate and fulminate, we must despise this as the doings of a madman, and, trusting in God excommunicate and repel him as best we may. . . .

And now I hope the false, lying spectre will be laid with which the Romanists have long terrified and stupefied our consciences. And it will be seen that, like all the rest of us, they are subject to the temporal sword; that they have no authority to interpret the Scriptures by force without skill; and that they have no power to prevent a council, or to pledge it in accordance with their pleasure, or to bind it beforehand, and deprive it of its freedom; and that if they do this, they are verily of the fellowship of antichrist and the devil, and have nothing of Christ but the name.

STUDY QUESTIONS

1. How did Luther find release from his torments by reading, closely, the book of Romans?
2. How did Luther recall developing his ideas concerning the doctrine of salvation by faith?
3. Is Luther's tone in writing excessively violent? Could his words be used to endorse actual violence?

12.7 FRANCESCO GUICCIARDINI, FLORENCE UNDER LORENZO DE' MEDICI

Francesco Guicciardini (1483–1540) was a wealthy lawyer with good political connections. Like many such figures in the Renaissance, he also had cultural and intellectual ambitions. In his later years he wrote a brilliant *History of Italy* that was one of the first works of history to combine the use of extensive archival records and a critical attitude toward political motivations and intentions. His *History of Florence*, however, is the work of a young man trying to feel his way in an unfamiliar discipline. Its most incisive passage is translated below and provides a closely observed portrait of Lorenzo de' Medici (1449–92), who ruled Florence from 1469 until his death. (Guicciardini, of course, did not know Lorenzo personally, being only nine years old when the ruler died.)

Lorenzo de' Medici was only forty-three years old when he died, after having ruled Florence for twenty-three years. He was only twenty when his father Piero died in 1469 and was still being advised by Messer Tommasso Soderini and some other elder politicians, but it took only a short time for him to come into his full strength and stature, such that he was able to govern the city just as he saw fit. . . .

Until he died in 1492 Lorenzo controlled and ran Florence as completely as if he were a Greek *tyrannos.* His renown was as widespread before his death as it has become after it. His greatness was so remarkable, and indeed without parallel in all of Florence's history, in fact, that I think it is not a mistake—and in fact may prove quite useful—if I describe his manner and character in some detail. I do not speak from my own experience, for I was still a mere boy when he died, but my information comes from reliable and trustworthy sources. Unless I have been lied to, what I am about to say is completely true.

Translation by Clifford Backman.

Lorenzo had many extraordinary virtues and a fair share of vices; some of the latter came to him naturally, while some others arose from necessity. His authority in the city was so complete that it is fair to say that Florence was not free in his time, but it enjoyed as many blessings and as much happiness as there could be in any other city that we call "free" but which is in fact under a *tyrannos*. Although not everything he did was admirable, most of his actions were so tremendous and noble that the more one studies them the more impressive they appear. Glory in arms and feats of military achievement do not figure among his successes, as they do among the great figures of antiquity, but that was more the circumstance of the times in which he lived than of his own failure. You will not read here of any brave defense of the city, a celebrated capture of a fortress, a brilliant strategy on the field of battle, or a glorious upset over enemies; Lorenzo's claim to fame includes no such military splendor. What one does find in his record is every possible sign of the virtues of civic life—no one, not even his enemies and rivals, would deny his brilliance in that regard. Who could? The simple fact that he ruled Florence for twenty-three years, always increasing its power and glory, proves the point. Bear in mind that Florence is an opinionated place, full of calculating and ambitious people, and since the city is small and cannot provide for everyone, to benefit some means to skip over others. Finally, the roster of great Italian and foreign princes who counted themselves as his friend attests to his reputation. . . .

He was generally of sound judgment and wise, but his intellect transcended politics. He committed a number of ill-considered actions, such as his war against Volterra in 1473, when he conspired to get the people of that town to rebel against him so that he could have an excuse to seize their alum mines; in so doing he ignited a fire that could have engulfed all of Italy, although things turned out well in the end. And he could have avoided the civil war of 1478 if he had handled relations with the pope [Sixtus IV, r. 1471–1484] and the king [Ferrante of Naples, r. 1458–1494] more skillfully, instead of playing the role of the aggrieved innocent for all it was worth and thereby causing the war and nearly costing himself and the city their lives. His subsequent trip to Naples, also, was too rash and hurried a decision, one that placed him directly in the hands of his enemy, an untrustworthy and traitorous king. The desperate need for peace partially excuses him, but many still live who think he could have achieved it much more safely and no less effectively had he negotiated from Florence.

He dreamed of glory and renown, and indeed he desired these more than anyone else of his time. His desire for them influenced his actions even in the most minor matters—for which he may justly be criticized. Whether he was penning verses, playing a game, or doing any little thing at all, he became enraged if someone else matched or bettered him. Even in matters of real importance his lust for glory influenced him excessively. He conspired and struggled against every prince in Italy, to the great displeasure of Duke Ludovico [Sforza of Milan, r. 1489–1500]. On the whole, his ambitions were admirable and in the end they did bring him fame and renown, both within Italy and elsewhere. He worked diligently to make Florence pre-eminent in all the arts. He founded the University of Pisa as a center for the humanities. When his advisors argued that the university would never have as many students as the universities in Padua or Pavia, he replied that he would be satisfied to have more professors than they, and indeed all the most famous and brilliant scholars in Italy taught there for a time. Lorenzo spared no expense or effort to hire them, and consequently they received extraordinarily high salaries. The humanities flourished in Florence under the tutelage of Messer Agnolo Poliziano; the study of Greek advanced under Messer Demetrios [Chalcondylas] and [Konstantinos] Lascaris; philosophy and art were the domain of Marsilio Ficino, Giorgio Benigno, Count [Giovanni] Pico della Mirandola, and other notable men. He was equally generous to the fields of vernacular poetry, music, architecture, painting, sculpture, and all other arts and disciplines. The city overflowed with superior talent, and all because Lorenzo, a universal man, was such an excellent judge of skilled men—all of whom competed with one another for his favor. In his infinite generosity, he lavished them with salaries and everything they needed for their work. For example, when he decided to establish a Greek library, he sent the learned Lascaris back to Greece to search for books of antiquity.

He employed the same liberality with princes everywhere in order to further his reputation; no expense, however great, was too much to pay if it helped him to keep the friendship of powerful people. Consequently, in places like Lyons, Milan, and Bruges, where he had business interests, his habit of spreading money everywhere made his expenses rise and his profits fall; the real fault, though, lay with some of his underlings, who did not have his talent. . . .

Lorenzo had a haughty personality. He disliked it when anyone contradicted him, and he spoke in few words, even in matters of importance, because he expected people to understand him intuitively. In casual conversation, though, he could be quite pleasant if somewhat facetious. His private home life was simple, not luxurious at all except for the banquets he threw, in which he lavished hospitality on his noble guests who visited Florence. He was lusty in his carnal appetites, and engaged in love affairs with real abandon. Some of these relationships lasted for years. So persistent was he in his conquests that many people think his extreme carnality weakened his body and brought on his early death. . . .

Many people thought him cruel and vindictive by nature, citing especially the case of the Pazzi Rebellion [of 1478], in which, after the shedding of so much blood he threw many innocents into prison and forbade the girls [of the Pazzi family] ever to marry, but one must remember how bitterly he resented the family's attempt to overthrow him, and so such harshness can hardly be surprising. Besides, he did eventually allow the Pazzi girls to marry, and freed the Pazzi boys on condition they left Florence forever. In other instances too we can see that he was not truly cruel or bloodthirsty, but simply had the flaw of excessive suspicion of others. This troublesome suspiciousness arose not from his intrinsic nature but from the fact that he had a city-state to keep under control and had to do it by means of magistrates and laws in order to maintain the appearance that Florence was a free republic. . . .

His constant distrust of others forced him not to allow powerful families to form marriage alliances. He aimed always at pairing people off in a way that did not pose any threat to his power. Sometimes he did this by forcing some young man of standing to marry a woman who was not really acceptable. In fact, the truth is that soon enough hardly any marriages took place among the important classes without his direct permission. The same suspiciousness inspired him to appoint permanent chancellors at the courts in Rome, Naples, and Milan, in order to keep an eye on the ambassadors he sent to those places. These well-paid chancellors were present to lend assistance to the various ambassadors but their real purpose was to keep Lorenzo informed of their actions.

It is true that he kept himself constantly surrounded by a large number of armed guards, who were well rewarded for their service (in fact, he even bestowed a number of hospitals and holy shrines upon some of them). He did this not out of intrinsic distrust of people, however; the truth is that the Pazzi conspiracy was to blame. Even so, it was hardly the sort of thing proper to a republic and to a private citizen; it smacked more of a tyrant ruling his subjects. In the end, one has to conclude that although Florence under Lorenzo was not a free city, it was a city that could hardly have wished for a better and more pleasing tyrant. His good qualities and virtues produced an infinity of blessings, and while the nature of his tyranny occasioned some ill-doings, these were relatively minor and never worse than they needed to be.

STUDY QUESTIONS

1. According to Guicciardini, what were the virtues of Lorenzo de' Medici? Were his virtues confined to politics? What picture of court patronage and the arts emerges from Guicciardini's portrait of Lorenzo?
2. Based on this description, would you say that Guicciardini preferred strong leaders like Lorenzo over popularly elected governments? Why?

12.8 BENVENUTO CELLINI, *MY LIFE*, 1558–1563

Benvenuto Cellini (1500–1571) was an Italian goldsmith and sculptor—and part-time soldier—who inhabited the thrilling art world dominated by masters like Michelangelo and Da Vinci. A member of the Mannerist school, Cellini was patronized by dukes, popes, and the French king; his "artistic temperament" meant that he was often in trouble with his fellow artists—he was accused of four homicides over the course of his life. This selection from his autobiography illustrates the way in which his artistic excellence framed his every experience and relationship, both personal and professional.

15. Continuing to work with Master Pagolo Arsago, I earned a great deal of money, always sending the largest part of it to my good father. By the end of two years, following my father's entreaties, I returned to Florence, and once again I went to work with Francesco Salinbene, with whom I earned a good deal and worked very hard at learning. I started going around with Francesco di Filippo again, given that I was intent upon the pursuit of some pleasure, thanks to practicing that damned music, and I always saved certain hours of the day or night which I gave over to my studies. In that period I created a silver "heart-key," which is what these objects were called at that time. This was a belt three fingers in width that new bridges were in the custom of wearing, and it was made in low relief with some little figures in the round among the others. I made it for a man who was called Raffaello Lapaccini. Although I was very poorly paid, I gained so much honour from it that it was worth much more than the recompense I justly earned. During this period I had worked with many different people in Florence, where I had made the acquaintance of some very worthy men among the goldsmiths, such as that Marcone who was my first master, as well as others who had very good reputations but who did me down in my work and blatantly robbed me whenever they could. Once I saw this, I kept away from them and considered them wicked men and thieves.

. . .

16. One day it happened that as I was leaning against the shop of one of these goldsmiths he called out to me, partly reproaching and partly threatening me; to his remarks I responded that if they had done their duty towards me, I would have said of them what one says about honest and worthy men. But, since they had done the contrary they should complain about themselves and not about me. While I was standing there talking, one of them, their cousin, who was called Gherardo Guasconti, perhaps compelled by all of them together, waited until a pack-animal with a load passed by. This was a load of bricks. When the load was near me, this Gherardo pushed it against me so forcefully that he hurt me very badly. I immediately turned on him, and when I saw that he was laughing I gave him such a hard blow with my fist on his temple that he fell down unconscious, like a dead man; then I turned to his cousins and announced: "This is how to treat thieving cowards like you!" And because they were about to make some move, since there were several of them, incensed, I put my hand on a small knife that I had

and said: "Whichever one of you leaves his shop, the other will go fetch his confessor, because there'll be no use for a doctor." These words so terrified them that no one went to the assistance of his cousin. Immediately after I had left, their fathers and children ran to the Eight and claimed that I had assaulted them with a weapon in their own shops, something which was unheard of in Florence. The Eight had me summoned before them, whereupon I appeared; they gave me a severe reprimand and scolding, since they saw me dressed in a cloak, while the Guascontis wore the mantle and hood of well-bred people, but they did so also because while my adversaries had gone to speak with all these magistrates at their homes in private, I, lacking experience, had not spoken to any of them, since I relied upon being entirely in the right.

. . .

I felt as if I had been totally discredited, and it was not long before I sent for my cousin, who was called Master Annibale the surgeon, the father of Messer Librodoro Librodori, wanting him to serve as my guarantee. Annibale refused to come: for this reason, I became very indignant and, puffing myself up like an asp, decided to do something desperate. In all of this it is obvious how much the stars not so much influence us as force us into certain courses of action. Knowing how much this Annibale owed my family, my anger became so great that it turned toward a harmful course of action—being also somewhat hot-blooded by nature—and I stood waiting until the members of the Eight had gone out to dinner, then, while I remained there alone, seeing that the guards of the Eight were no longer keeping an eye on me, and inflamed with anger, I left the Palazzo, ran to my workshop, where I seized a large dagger, and bounded into the home of my adversaries, which served as both home and workplace. I found them at table, and that young Gherardo, who had been the main cause of my interrogation, threw himself upon me: I responded by stabbing him in the chest, piercing his tunic and vest through to the shirt without touching his flesh or doing him even the slightest harm. I thought, by the way in which my hand entered his garments and by the sound his clothes made, that I had hurt him very seriously, and when he fell terrified onto the floor, I shouted: "You traitor, today is the day I kill you all." Believing that the Day of Judgment had arrived, his father, mother, and sisters threw themselves down on their knees, and at the top of their lungs they called out for mercy; once I saw that they had no defence against me and that Gherardo was stretched out on the floor like a dead man, I thought it too cowardly an act to attack them, but still furious, I ran down the stairs, and when I reached the street I came upon the rest of the clan, more than twelve of them: one of them held an iron shovel, another a huge iron pipe, while others carried hammers, anvils, and cudgels. I attacked them, like an enraged bull, throwing four or five to the ground, and I fell along with them, always striking out with my dagger, now at one, now at another. Those who had remained standing hastened as best they could to deal me some blows with both hands, with their hammers, cudgels, and anvils, and because God in His mercy sometimes intervenes in such matters, He kept us from doing each other any harm whatsoever. All I left there was my hat, captured by my adversaries although previously they had fled from it, which each one struck with his weapon; then they looked around them for their dead and wounded, but nobody had been harmed.

. . .

38. Skipping over a few things, I shall describe how Pope Clement, in order to save the papal tiaras, with all of the numerous large jewels belonging to the Apostolic Chamber, had me summoned, and he shut himself up alone in a room with me and Cavalierino. This Cavalierino had once worked in the stable of Filippo Strozzi: he was a Frenchman, a person of very humble origins, and since he was a very faithful servant, Pope Clement had made him an extremely rich man and trusted him as he did himself. This, with the Pope, Cavalierino, and me locked inside this room, they placed me before the tiaras with that large number of jewels belonging to the Apostolic Chamber, and I was given the commission of extracting them all from the gold in which they were set. And I did so: then I wrapped each of them up in small pieces of paper and sewed them up in the linings of some garments worn by the Pope and this Cavalierino. Then they gave me all the gold, which was around two hundred pounds, and

they told me to melt it down in as much secrecy as I could. I went to the Angel where my own room was located, and where I could lock the door so that no one would disturb me, and once I had built a small brick blast-furnace in the bottom of which I set a fairly large ash-tray shaped like a dish, I tossed the gold on the charcoal, which little by little dripped down into the dish. While this furnace was in operation, I constantly studied on how I could do our enemies harm, and since we had the enemy's trenches beneath us less than stone's throw away, I did them a great deal of damage in those trenches using some bits of old scrap, of which there were several piles, formerly used in the Castello as ammunition. Taking a saker and a falconet, both of which were broken a bit at the muzzle, I filled them with this scrap metal, and then as I opened fire with these weapons my shots flew down like mad, causing many unexpected injuries in the trenches. And so, keeping these weapons constantly loaded while I melted down that gold, a short time before the hour of vespers I saw a man mounted on a mule riding on the edge of the trench. This mule was moving along very swiftly, and the man was speaking to the men in the trenches. I stood ready to fire my artillery before he arrived in front of me. So, with good judgment, I commenced firing and hit him, knocking him directly in the face with one of those scraps of metal, while the rest hit the mule which fell down dead; I heard a tremendous uproar from the trench, and I fired another piece, not without doing them great damage. This man was the Prince of Orange, who was carried along the trenches to a certain inn nearby, where all the noblemen in the army quickly gathered. When Pope Clement learned what I had done, he immediately sent for me and asked about the affair, and I explained everything to him and, moreover, I told him that he must have been a man of very great importance, since all the leaders of the army, as far as one could determine, immediately gathered at the inn to which they had carried him.

. . .

After I returned to Cornaro's home, a few days later Cardinal Farnese was elected Pope, and after immediately settling matters of the greatest importance, the Pope next asked me, saying that he did not want anyone else to make his coins. Hearing these words, a certain gentleman named Messer Latino Iuvinale, who was on intimate terms with the Pope, stated that I was a fugitive from a homicide I had committed on the person of a Milanese named Pompeo, and he put all my motives in the most favourable light. At those words, the Pope said: "I didn't know about the death of Pompeo, but I knew of Benvenuto's motives perfectly well, so write him out an order of safe conduct immediately, with which he will be completely secure." There was present a great friend of that Pompeo and close confidant of the Pope named Messer Ambruogio, a Milanese, and he said: "During the first days of your papacy, it would not be good to grant pardons of this sort." Turning toward him, the Pope said: "You don't understand the matter as well as I do. You should know that men like Benvenuto, unique in their profession, need not be subject to the law: especially not Benvenuto, since I know what good reasons he had." And after my safe-conduct was made out, I immediately began to serve the new Pope and was treated with the greatest favour.

STUDY QUESTIONS

1. How does Benvenuto use violence to reinforce his sense of honor?
2. Are the endorsements of Cellini offered by the popes surprising?

12.9 VASARI, *LIVES OF ARTISTS*, FIRST PUBLISHED IN 1550, REVISED AND ADDED TO UNTIL 1568

An architect and fresco painter in his own right—and even an apprentice to Michelangelo in his youth—Giorgio Vasari (1511–1574) is most fondly remembered for his personal accounts of roughly two hundred celebrated artists of Renaissance Italy. Using art historical analysis, Vasari talks capably about the production and technical elements of paintings, ambitious architectural projects, metalworking, and sculpture. Charming anecdotes about the greats—Giotto, Michelangelo, Botticelli, etc.—bring to life the world inhabited by these incredibly talented individuals. *The Life of Donatello* (1386–1466) provides glimpses into the artistic temperament exemplified by Cellini (Document 12.8), and the preface to Part III provides an overview of artistic development throughout the Renaissance.

THE LIFE OF DONATELLO, FLORENTINE SCULPTOR [1386–1466]

Donato, who was called Donatello by his relatives and thus signed some of his works this way, was born in Florence in the year 1303. And devoting himself to the art of design, he became not only an unusually fine sculptor and a marvellous statue-maker, but also grew experienced in stucco, quite skilled in perspective, and highly esteemed in architecture. His works possessed so much grace and excellence and such a fine sense of design that they were considered to be more like the distinguished works of the ancient Greeks and Romans than those of any other artist who has ever existed, and he is therefore quite rightly recognized as the first artisan who properly used the device of scenes in bas-relief. He worked out these scenes with such careful thought, true facility, and expert skill that it was obvious he possessed a true understanding of them and executed them with extraordinary beauty. Thus, no other artisan surpassed him in this field, and even in our own times, there is no one who is his equal.

Donatello was raised from childhood in the home of Ruberto Martelli, and with his fine qualities and the diligence with which he refined his skill, he not only earned Martelli's affection but that of this entire noble family. In his youth, he worked upon so many things that they were not very highly regarded because there were so many of them. But the thing which earned him a name and brought him recognition was an Annunciation in blue-grey stone which was placed in the church of Santa Croce in Florence at the altar in the chapel of the Cavalcanti family, for which he made a decoration in the grotesque style. Its base was varied and twisted, completed by a quarter-circle to which were added six putti carrying several garlands who seem to be steadying themselves by embracing each other as if they were afraid of the height. But Donatello demonstrated above all his great ingenuity and artistry in the figure of the Virgin, who, frightened by the sudden appearance of the angel, timidly but gently moves Her body in a very chaste bow, turning towards the angel greeting Her with the most beautiful grace, so that Her face reflects the humility and gratitude one owes to the giver of an unexpected gift, and even more so when the gift is so great. Besides this, Donatello proved his ability to carve masterful folds and turns in the robes

---

Giorgio Vasari, *Lives of the Artists*. Translated by Julia Conway Bondanella and Peter Bondanella. Oxford: Oxford University Press, 2009, 2731w from pp. 147–9, 153–4, 159–60, 277–9, 281–3.

of this Madonna and the angel, and in suggesting the nude forms of his figures, he showed just how he was attempting to rediscover the beauty of the ancients which had already remained hidden for so many years. And he exhibited so much facility and skill in this work that no one could really expect more from him in design and judgement, or from the way he carved and executed the work.

In the same church below the choir screen beside the scenes frescoed by Taddeo Gaddi, Donatello took extraordinary pains in carving a wooden crucifix which, upon completing it and believing that he had produced a very rare object, he showed to Filippo di Ser Brunellesco, his very dear friend, in order to have his opinion of it. Filippo, who expected to see something much better from Donatello's description of it, smiled a bit when he saw it. When Donatello saw this, he begged Filippo for the sake of their friendship to give him his honest opinion of it, and so, Filippo, who was very candid, replied that it seemed to him as if Donatello had placed a peasant upon the cross and not a body like that of Jesus Christ, which was most delicate and represented, in all its parts, the most perfect human being born. Hearing himself criticized—and even more sharply than he had imagined—rather than receiving the praise he had hoped for, Donatello answered: "If it were as simple to create something as to criticize, my Christ would look like Christ to you and not like a peasant; take some wood and try to make one yourself." Without saying another word, Filippo returned home, and without anyone knowing, he set his hand to making a crucifix, seeking to surpass Donatello in order to vindicate his own judgement, and after many months he brought it to the highest degree of perfection. And once this was finished, he invited Donatello one morning to have lunch with him, and Donatello accepted the invitation. And so, they went together towards Filippo's home, and when they reached the Old Market, Filippo bought a few things and gave them to Donatello, saying: "Go on home with these things and wait for me there, and I'll be along shortly." Donatello therefore entered the house and, on the ground-floor, saw Filippo's crucifix in a perfect light, and stopping to examine it, he found it so perfectly finished that, realizing Filippo had outdone him, and completely stupefied, as if he had lost his wits, he relaxing his grip on his apron; whereupon, the eggs, the cheese, and everything else fell out, breaking into pieces and spilling all over, and as he stood there stunned and amazed, Filippo caught up with him, and said with a laugh: "What's your plan, Donatello? How can we have lunch if you have spilled everything?" Donatello replied: "Personally, I've had enough for this morning, but if you want your share, take it. But no more, thank you: it's for you to make Christs and for me to make peasants."

...

It was said that a Genoese merchant had Donatello execute a very handsome life-size bronze head which was thin and light so that it could be carried over a long distance, and it was through Cosimo that Donatello received the commission for such a work. When it was finished and the merchant wanted to pay Donatello, he thought that the sculptor was asking too high a price. So the deal was referred to Cosimo, who had the bust carried to a courtyard above his palace and had it placed between the battlements overlooking the street so that it could be better seen. Wishing to settle the matter, Cosimo, who found the merchant far from the price asked by Donatello, turned to the merchant and declared that Donatello's price was too low. At this, the merchant, who thought it too high, declared that Donatello had worked upon it for only a month or a little more, and that this added up to more than half a florin per day. Donatello then turned angrily away, thinking himself too greatly offended, and told the merchant that in one hundredth of an hour he could spoil the labour and value of an entire year, and he gave the bust a shove, immediately breaking it upon the street below into many pieces and telling the merchant he proved himself more accustomed to bargaining for beans than for statues. The merchant regretted what he had done and wanted to give Donatello more than double his price if he would only recast the bust, but neither the merchant's promises nor Cosimo's entreaties could ever convince Donatello to redo it.

...

It is said that when Cosimo was about to die, he commended Donatello to the care of his son Piero who, as a most conscientious executor of his father's will, gave Donatello a farm in Cafaggiulo with enough income for him to live comfortably. Donatello was delighted by this, for he felt that with this more than secure income he would not risk dying from hunger. But he had only held it for a year when he returned to Piero and gave it back to him by means of a written contract, declaring that he did not wish to lose his peace of mind having to dwell upon domestic concerns or the troubles of his peasant tenant, who was underfoot every third day—first, because the wind blew the roof off his doves' hitch; next, because the Commune seized his livestock for taxes; and then, because the storm deprived him of wine and fruit. He was so fed up and disgusted with all these things that he preferred to die from hunger rather than to think about them.

Piero laughed at Donatello's simple ways, but in order to free Donatello from this worry he accepted the farm at Donatello's insistence, and he assigned him from his own bank an allowance of the same amount or more but in cash, which was paid to Donatello every week in appropriate installments. This made Donatello exceedingly content.

PREFACE TO PART THREE

Those excellent masters we have described up to this point in the Second part of these *Lives* truly made great advances in the arts of architecture, painting, and sculpture, adding to the accomplishments of the early artists rule, order, proportion, design, and style, and if they were not perfect in every way, they drew so near to the truth that artists in the third group, whom we shall now discuss, were able, through that illumination, to rise up and reach complete perfection, the proof of which we have in the finest and most celebrated modern works. But to clarify the quality of the improvements that these artists made, it will not be out of place to explain briefly the five qualities I mentioned above and to discuss succinctly the origins of that true goodness which has surpassed that of the ancient world and rendered the modern age so glorious.

. . . Design is the imitation of the most beautiful things in Nature in all forms, both in sculpture and in painting, and this quality depends upon having the hand and the skill to transfer with great accuracy and precision everything the eye sees to a plan or drawing or to a sheet of paper, a panel, or another flat surface, and the same is true for relief in sculpture. And then the most beautiful style comes from constantly copying the most beautiful things, combining the most beautiful hands, heads, bodies, or legs together to create from all these beautiful qualities the most perfect figure possible, and using it as a model for all the figures in each one's works; and on account of this, it is said to be beautiful style.

Neither Giotto nor those artisans did this, even though they had discovered the principles underlying all such difficulties and had resolved them superficially, as in the case of drawing, which became more lifelike than it had been before and more true to Nature, and in the blending of colours and the composition of the figures in scenes, and in many other things, about which enough has already been said. And although the artists of the second period made extraordinary efforts in these crafts in all the areas mentioned above, they were not, however, sufficient to achieve complete perfection. They still lacked, within the boundaries of the rules, a freedom which—not being part of the rules—was nevertheless ordained by the rules and which could coexist with order without causing confusion or spoiling it; and this freedom required copious invention in every particular and a certain beauty even in the smallest details which could demonstrate all of this order with more decoration. In proportion, they lacked good judgement which, without measuring the figures, would bestow upon them, no matter what their dimensions a grace that goes beyond proportion. In design they did not reach the ultimate goal, for even when they made a rounded arm or a straight leg, they had not fully examined how to depict the muscles with that soft and graceful facility which is partially seen and partially concealed in the flesh of living things, and their figures were crude and clumsy, offensive to the eye and harsh in style. Moreover, they lacked a lightness in touch in making all their figures slender and graceful, especially those of women and children, whose bodies should be as natural as those of men and yet possess a volume of softness which are produced by design and good judgement rather than by the awkward example of real bodies. They also lacked an abundance of beautiful costumes, variety in imaginative details, charm in their colours, diversity in their buildings, and distance and variety in their landscapes.

. . .

The artisans who followed them succeeded after seeing the excavation of some of the most famous antiquities mentioned by Pliny: the Laocoon, the Hercules, the great torso of Belvedere, the Venus, the Cleopatra, the Apollo, and countless others, which exhibit in their softness and harshness the expressions of real flesh copied from the most beautiful details of living models and endowed with certain movements which do not distort them but lend them motion and the utmost grace. And these statues caused the disappearance of a certain dry, crude, and clear-cut style which bequeathed to this craft.

. . .

But what matters most is that the artisans of today have made their craft so perfect and so easy for anyone who possesses a proper sense of design, invention, and colouring that whereas previously our older masters could produce one panel in six years, the masters of today can produce six of them in a year. And I bear witness to this both from personal observation and from practice, and these works are obviously much more finished and perfected than those of the other reputable masters who worked before them.

But the man who wins the palm among artists both living and dead, who transcends and surpasses them all, is the divine Michelangelo Buonarroti, who reigns supreme not merely in one of these arts but in all three at once. This man surpasses and triumphs over not only all those artists who have almost surpassed Nature but even those most celebrated ancient artists themselves, who beyond all doubt surpassed Nature: and alone he has triumphed over ancient artists, modern artists, and even Nature herself, without ever imagining anything so strange or so difficult that he could not surpass it by far with the power of his most divine genius through his diligence, sense of design, artistry, judgement, and grace. And not only in painting and colouring, categories which include all the shapes and bodies, straight and curved, tangible and intangible, visible and invisible, but also in bodies completely in the round; and through the point of his chisel and his untiring labour, this beautiful and fruitful plant has already spread so many honourable branches that they have not only filled the entire world in such an unaccustomed fashion with the most luscious fruits possible, but they have also brought these three most noble arts to their final stage of development with such wondrous perfection that one might well and safely declare that his statues are, in every respect, much more beautiful than those of the ancients. When the heads, hands, arms, and feet they created are compared to those he fashioned, it is obvious his works contain a more solid foundation, a more complete grace, and a much more absolute perfection, executed at a certain level of difficulty rendered so easily in his style that it would never be possible to see anything better. The same things can be said of his paintings. If it were possible to place any of them beside the most famous Greek or Roman paintings, they would be held in even greater esteem and more highly honoured than his sculptures, which appear superior to all those of the ancients.

But if we have admired those most celebrated artists who, inspired by excessive rewards and great happiness, have given life to their works, how much more should we admire and praise to the skies those even rarer geniuses who, living not only without rewards but in a miserable state of poverty, produced such precious fruits? It may be believed and therefore affirmed that, if just remuneration existed in our century, even greater and better works than the ancients ever executed would, without a doubt, he created. But being forced to struggle more with Hunger than with Fame, impoverished geniuses are buried and unable to earn a reputation (which is a shame and a disgrace for those who might be able to help them but take no care to do so).

STUDY QUESTIONS

1. Did Donatello gain more from his relationship to his patrons Cosimo and Piero de Medici than they received from him?
2. Does Vasari claim that artists in his day can surpass the achievements of the Greeks and Romans?

12.10 BENVENUTO CELLINI, *AUTOBIOGRAPHY*, 1558–1563

Benvenuto Cellini (1500–1571) was a Florentine sculptor and goldsmith whose *Autobiography* is one of the great literary treasures of the Renaissance. As the following passage makes clear, he found himself in one sort of trouble after another throughout his life, and somehow always felt that his excellence as an artist gave him right to do whatever he wanted.

Now we turn to Pietro Torrigiani, who said to me one day while holding a drawing of me in his hand, "[Michelangelo] Buonarroti and I, when we were kids, used to go to the church of the Carmine in order to study Masaccio's chapel and Buonarroti would always make fun of everyone who was there to make sketches. One day he was really bothering me; I got much more annoyed than usual, clenched my fist, and gave him such a punch in the nose that I could feel the bone and cartilage in his nose shatter like a wafer. He'll carry the mark of that punch for the rest of his life!"

These words made me feel nothing but hatred for him, for I was then in the habit of examining the works of the divine Michelangelo almost every day, and the result of this hatred was that I no longer had any desire to travel to England with him [as we had previously planned]. I could hardly bear the sight of him, in fact.

The whole time I was in Florence I set myself to studying Michelangelo's beautiful style, a style from which I have never since strayed. At this time I also met and became close friends with a fine young man about my age—another goldsmith. His name was Francesco and he was the son of that superb painter Filippo di Fra Filippo. We worked together, which created so strong a bond of friendship between us that we were hardly ever apart, day or night. His home held many beautiful sketches drawn by his talented father and gathered together in several volumes, mostly depicting the great antiquities of Rome. When I saw these studies I fell completely in love with them. Francesco and I worked together for about two years. It was at this time that I created a bas-relief in silver, about the size of a toddler's hand. This piece was ultimately used as a man's belt buckle, for in those days large buckles were in fashion. The piece was carved in the ancient style with foliage, cherubs, and some lovely masks. I finished it in Francesco Salimbene's workshop. When several members of the goldsmith's guild saw it, they praised me as the most talented youngster then at work in the craft. Another fellow—a woodcarver of my age named Giambattista Tasso—began to say that if ever I wanted to go to Rome he would gladly come with me. One day we were discussing this idea, just after our mid-day meal. At the time I had just been arguing with my father (the usual reason: my music-playing), and so I said to Tasso, "You're the type who always talks of doing things but never does them." To which he replied, "Listen, I'm angry too—at my mother. If I had enough money to get to Rome, I wouldn't even take the time to go around to lock up that wretched little shop of mine." That's when I offered that if lack of money was the only thing keeping him in Florence, I had enough of it set aside to get both of us to Rome. We were walking as we were talking,

Translation by Clifford Backman.

and found ourselves unexpectedly at the San Pietro Gattolini Gate. "Tasso, my friend," I said, "this is God's handiwork, our arriving at this gate! Neither of us was planning it, but now that we're here it seems to me that we're half on our way!" He agreed, so we continued on, saying, "Oh, what will our parents say this evening!" We promised each other that we wouldn't give them another thought until we reached Rome, and so it was that with our aprons tied behind our backs and with scarcely another word between us, we soon reached Siena.

When we arrived there Tasso complained that his feet hurt and he could go no further and didn't even want to. He asked to borrow enough money for a ride back home. I answered, "You should have thought about this before leaving Florence! If I loaned you the money, I wouldn't have enough to continue on by myself. You say that you can't go on because your feet hurt. Well then, let's find a horse that is making a return trip to Rome! That way you won't have an excuse for not coming with me." So we hired a horse, and since Tasso made no reply, I turned the horse onto the road towards Rome. Seeing that I was determined, Tasso limped along after me as best he could, never letting up with his complaints. He was slow and fell some distance behind. By the time we reached the gate that led towards Rome I felt sorry for him and halted, and then I lifted him into the saddle. "What on earth would our friends say if they heard us declare that we were leaving for Rome but couldn't make it past Siena!" Then the good Tasso declared that what I had said was true, and since he was fundamentally a happy person he began to laugh and sing. In this way, laughing and singing together, we made our way to Rome. This happened when I was exactly nineteen years old, the same age as the century we now live in.

Once arrived in Rome, I immediately found work in the shop of a master smith called Firenzuola. His name was Giovanni and he came from the village in Lombardy called Firenzuola. He was a talented goldsmith who worked mainly on trays, dishes, and other large items. He was deeply impressed when I showed him a model of the belt buckle I had made at Salimbene's shop in Florence, and turning to his apprentice (a Florentine lad named Giannetto Giannotti who had been with him for several years) he said, "Here is a Florentine who knows a thing or two! You, on the other hand, are a Florentine know-nothing!"

I recognized Giannetto, since before setting out for Rome he used to go drawing with me and we had been good friends. I wanted to speak to him, but his master's words had so offended him that he pretended not to know me and said we had never met. This hurt me, so I said, "Giannetto! We were friends, good friends! We spent time together in this place and that place, and used to sketch together, and ate and drank and slept in your home in the country. Still, it doesn't matter if you vouch for me or not to this honest master of yours, because I intend to let the work of my hands show him the kind of man I am. I don't need your help!"

. . .

It happened one day that I was leaning against the wall of one of the Roman goldsmith's shops, and he began to yell at me in a reproachful, threatening manner. I retorted that if everyone working there had treated me honorably I would have nothing to say except how worthy and honest they were; but since they had done just the opposite, they should direct their criticism at themselves instead of at me. So I just stood there and chatted. Then one of them—a cousin, named Gherardo Guasconti, goaded by the others—bided his time until a packhorse carrying a load of bricks happened by. Gherardo then shoved the beast into me with great force. The pain was terrible. I spun around to face him—he was laughing—and drove my fist into his temple so hard that he fell unconscious to the ground, looking for all the world like a dead man. Then, turning to his cousins, I shouted, "That's how I deal with thieving good-for-nothings like you!"

Now there was a bunch of them and they were angry and ready to spring into action, so I drew my knife and said, "If anyone leaves this shop, it had better be to find a confessor, for he'll have no need of a doctor!" My words scared them so that no one moved to help his cousin. The second I left the shop all the men and boys ran to the magistrates and said I had attacked them with a weapon in their shop—something that was unheard of in Florence. The magistrates had me summoned and

I subsequently appeared before them. They gave me a harsh reprimand and scolding, for unlike the Guascontis (who had dressed in fancy mantles and hoods) I wore only a simple cloak. Moreover, the Guascontis had already pleaded their case, in private, at the magistrates' own homes, whereas I had naively trusted in the fairness of the system and had not tried to win the magistrates over beforetimes. I testified that I had indeed given Gherardo a slap in anger but only on account of the enormous and offensive injury he had done to me, and consequently I had done nothing to merit so strong a chastisement. No sooner had I spoken the word slap when one of the magistrates, Prinzivalle della Stufa, shouted, "You punched him; you didn't slap him!" Then the bell rang and we were all dismissed. While we were out, Prinzivalle spoke in my defense to his colleagues, saying, "My lords, consider how naïve this poor fellow is. He says he gave only a slap, thinking it less serious than a punch. But the penalty for a slap in the Mercato Nuovo is twenty-five scudi, whereas that for a punch is nothing, or practically so. Undoubtedly he is a very talented artist and does his best to support his family by his work. I wish to God our city had more, not fewer, young men like him!"

Some of the other magistrates were followers of Savonarola (I could tell by the cut of their cowls), and because were part of that gang and had been persuaded by all the pleadings and lies put forth by my enemies, they were only too happy to toss me into a prison cell and mete out the harshest of punishments. Fortunately, though, good Prinzivalle was there to make everything all right, and so I was hit only with a small fine of four bushels of flour that I was to donate to the Convento della Murata. After he summoned me back inside, Prinzivalle was quick to tell me not to say another word lest I risk the other magistrates' displeasure, and to obey the terms of my sentence right down to the letter. And so the full panel of magistrates gave me a proper scolding and ordered me to see the chancellor. "It was still only a slap, not a punch," I muttered under my breath—which made all eight of them laugh.

The chancellor formalized the orders on behalf of the magistracy and officially sentenced me alone to pay the four bushels of flour. I felt I had been treated unfairly. Not long afterwards I asked my cousin M. Annibale the surgeon (and father of the honorable Librodoro Librodori) to serve as my guarantor. When Annibale refused to appear in court I became indignant, puffed myself up like an asp, and decided to take a desperate measure. How clear it is, in relating all of this, how the stars not only influence us but actually drive us into certain courses of action! My anger was great, for I knew well how much this Annibale owed to my family, and being hot-blooded by nature I made a rash choice: once the magistrates had withdrawn to their dinner and I was alone (the guards had stopped paying any attention to me), I left the courthouse in a rage, ran to my workshop, grabbed a large dagger, and raced to where my enemies lived and worked. I came upon them as they were at table. Young Gherardo, the cause of all my troubles, hurled himself at me. I reacted by thrusting my dagger at his chest; it pierced his tunic and vest, and even went through his shirt, although it never touched his flesh or did him the slightest harm. But to judge from the sound his clothes made and the feeling in my hand, I was certain I had wounded him badly. When he fell to the floor, looking terrified, I shouted, "Traitors! Today I will kill you all!"

Thinking the Last Judgment had arrived, Gherardo's father, mother, and sisters all fell to their knees and cried out for mercy at the top of their lungs. Seeing that they were defenseless and Gherardo was stretched out on the floor like a dead man, I thought attacking them would be a cowardly thing to do, so instead I ran down the stairs, still in a rage, and when I got to the street I found the rest of their clan—all twelve or more of them. One held an iron shovel, another a large iron pipe. Still others were lugging hammers, anvils, and cudgels. I attacked them all like a furious bull, throwing four or five of them to the ground. I rushed at them thrusting my dagger at this one and that one. Those still on their feet did their best to strike me with their hammers, cudgels, and anvils, but since God in His mercy often intervenes in our actions, He saw to it that none of us harmed each other in any way. The only thing I left at the scene was my hat, which my enemies (who had previously run away at the sight of it) kept as a prize and which they took turns striking with their weapons. When they finally stopped and looked around to tend to their dead and wounded, they found that no one had been harmed at all.

STUDY QUESTIONS

1. What picture of Florentine and Roman artistic circles emerges from Cellini's description? Does this picture differ from the way artists are usually depicted?
2. How do networks play a role in Cellini's professional life?

CHAPTER 13

WORLDS OLD AND NEW

13.1 BARTOLOMÉ DE LAS CASAS, *A SHORT ACCOUNT OF THE DESTRUCTION OF THE INDIES*, WRITTEN 1542; PUBLISHED 1552

A Dominican friar, Bartolomé de Las Casas (ca. 1484–1566) wrote his *Short Account* to open the eyes of King Philip II of Spain to the atrocities committed upon the native peoples in newly discovered Latin America. For this early devotion to the protection of what would be called "human rights," de Las Casas was appointed "Protector of the Indians." The text itself can be difficult to read—the crimes against the Indigenous populations are recounted with a matter-of-fact tone that seems at odds with the level of horrific detail provided. De Las Casas argues that this inhumane activity must cease for two reasons: first, because "Indian" souls cannot be saved through conversion if the people continue to be murdered first, and second, because Spain will suffer God's wrath as a result of these sins.

PREFACE

The Americas were discovered in 1492, and the first Christian settlements established by the Spanish the following year. It is accordingly forty-nine years from now since Spaniards began arriving in numbers in this part of the world. They first settled the large and fertile island of Hispaniola, which boasts six hundred leagues of coastline and is surrounded by a great many other large islands, all of them, as I saw for myself, with as high a native population as anywhere on earth. Of the coast of the mainland which, at its nearest point, is a little over two hundred and fifty leagues from Hispaniola, more than ten thousand leagues had been explored by 1541, and more are being discovered every day. This coastline, too, swarming with people and it would seem, if we are to judge by those areas so far explored, that the Almighty selected this part of the world as home to the greater part of the human race.

God made all the peoples of this area, many and varied as they are, as open and as innocent as can be imagined. The simplest people in the world—unassuming, long-suffering, unassertive, and submissive—they are without malice or guile, and are utterly faithful and obedient both to their own native lords and to the Spaniards in whose service they now find themselves. Never quarrelsome or belligerent or boisterous, they harbour no grudges and do not seek to settle old scores; indeed, the notions of revenge, rancor, and hatred are quite foreign to them. At the same time, they are among the least robust of human beings: their delicate constitutions make them unable to withstand hard work or suffering and render them liable to succumb to almost any illness, no matter how mild. Even the common people are no tougher than princes or than other Europeans born with a silver spoon in their mouths and who spend their lives shielded from the rigours of the outside world. They are also among the poorest people on the face of the earth; they own next to nothing and have no urge to acquire material possessions. As a result they are neither ambitious nor greedy, and are totally uninterested in worldly power. Their diet is every bit as poor and as monotonous, in quantity and in kind, as that enjoyed by the Desert Fathers. Most of them go naked, save for a loincloth to cover their modesty; at best they may wrap themselves in a piece of cotton material a yard or two square. Most sleep on matting, although a few possess a kind of hanging net, known in the language of Hispaniola as a hammock. They are innocent and pure in mind and have a lively intelligence, all of which makes them particularly receptive to learning and understanding the truths of our Catholic faith and to being instructed in virtue; indeed, God has invested them with fewer impediments in this regard than any other people on earth. Once they begin to learn of the Christian faith they become so keen to know more, to receive the Sacraments, and to worship God, that the missionaries who instruct them do truly regard them men of exceptional patience and forbearance; and over the years I have time and again met Spanish laymen who have been so struck by the natural goodness that shines through these people that they frequently can be heard to exclaim: "These would be the most blessed people on earth if only they were given the chance to convert to Christianity."

It was upon these gentle lambs, imbued by the Creator with all the qualities we have mentioned, that from the very first day they clapped eyes on them the Spanish fell like ravening wolves upon the fold, or like tigers and savage lions who have not eaten meat for days. The pattern established at the outset has remained unchanged to this day, and the Spaniards still do nothing save tear the natives to shreds, murder them and inflict upon them untold misery, suffering and distress, tormenting, harrying and persecuting them mercilessly. We shall in due course describe some of the many ingenious methods of torture they have invented and refined for this purpose, but one can get some idea of the effectiveness of their methods from the figures alone. When the Spanish first journeyed there, the indigenous population of the island of Hispaniola stood at some three million; today only two hundred survive.

. . .

One God-fearing individual was moved to mount an expedition to seek out those who had escaped the Spanish trawl and were still living in the Bahamas and to save their souls by converting them to Christianity, but, by the end of a search lasting three whole years, they had found only the eleven survivors I saw with my own eyes. A further thirty or so islands in the region of Puerto Rico are also now uninhabited and left to go to rack and ruin as a direct result of the same practices. All these islands, which together must run over two thousand leagues, are now abandoned and desolate.

On the mainland, we know for sure that our fellow-countrymen have, through their cruelty and wickedness, depopulated and laid waste an area which once boasted more than ten kingdoms, each of them larger in area than the whole of the Iberian Peninsula. The whole region, once teeming with human beings, is now deserted over a distance of more than two thousand leagues: a distance, that is, greater than the journey from Seville to Jerusalem and back again.

At a conservative estimate, the despotic and diabolical behaviour of the Christians has, over the last forty years, led to the unjust and totally unwarranted deaths of more than twelve million souls, women and children among them, and there are grounds for believing my own estimate of more than fifteen million to be nearer the mark.

. . .

[The *conquistadores*] spared no one, erecting especially wide gibbets on which they could string their victims up with their feet just off the ground and then burn them alive thirteen at a time, in honour of our Saviour and the twelve Apostles, or tie dry straw to their bodies and set fire to it. Some they chose to keep alive and simply cut their wrists, leaving their hands dangling, saying to them: "Take this letter"—meaning that their sorry condition would act as a warning to those hiding in the hills. The way they normally dealt with the native leaders and nobles was to tie them to a kind of griddle consisting of sticks resting on pitchforks driven into the ground and then grill them over a slow fire, with the result that they howled in agony and despair as they died a lingering death.

It once happened that I myself witnessed their grilling of four or five local leaders in this fashion (and I believe they had set up two or three pairs of grills alongside so that they might process other victims at the same time) when the poor creatures' howls came between the Spanish commander and his sleep. He gave orders that the prisoners were to be throttled, but the man in charge of the execution detail, who was more bloodthirsty than the average common hangman (I know his identity and even met some relatives of his in Seville), was loath to cut short his private entertainment by throttling them so he personally went round ramming wooden bungs into their mouths to stop them making such a racket and deliberately stoked the fire so that they would take just as long to die as he himself chose. I saw all these things for myself and many others besides. And, since all those who could do so took to the hills and mountains in order to escape the clutches of these merciless and inhuman butchers, these mortal enemies of human kind trained hunting dogs to track them down—wild dogs who would savage a native to death as soon as look at him, tearing him to shreds and devouring his flesh as though he were a pig. These dogs wrought havoc among the natives and were responsible for much carnage. And when, as happened on the odd occasion, the locals did kill a European, as, given the enormity of the crimes committed against them, they were in all justice fully entitled to, the Spanish came to an unofficial agreement among themselves that for every European killed one hundred natives would be executed.

. . .

CONCLUSION

I, Bartolomé de Las Casas, or Casaus, a brother in the Dominican Order, was, by the grace of God, persuaded by a number of people here at the Spanish court, out of their concern for the Christian faith and their compassion towards the afflictions and calamities that befall their fellow-men, to write the work you have before you in order to help ensure that the teeming millions in the New World, for whose sins Christ gave His life, do not continue to die in ignorance, but rather are brought to knowledge of God and thereby saved. My deep love of Castile has also been a spur, for I do not wish to see my country destroyed as a divine punishment for sins against the honour of God and the True Faith. It has always been my intention to pen this account, although it has been long delayed by my being taken up with so many other tasks. I completed it in Valencia on the eighth day of December 1542, at a time when the violence, the oppression, the despotism, the killing, the plunder, the depopulation, the outrages, the agonies and the calamities we have described were at their height throughout the New World wherever Christians have set foot. It may be that some areas are worse than others: Mexico City and the surrounding territories are a little better than most, for there, at least, outrages cannot be committed so publicly, as there is justice of a sort, despite the crippling taxation unjustly imposed on the people. Yet I do see hope for the future, for, as the Emperor and King of Spain, Charles V (whose person and whose Empire may God preserve), learns of the crimes committed against his will and against that of God by his servants in the New World and of their treachery towards the people of the continent (for, until now, there has been an effective conspiracy of silence about what has really been happening), he will, as one wedded to the concept of justice and avid to see it prevail, put a stop to the wickedness and undertake a total reform of the administration of this New World that God has bestowed upon him and will do so for the greater glory of the Holy Catholic Church and for the salvation of his own royal soul. Amen.

STUDY QUESTIONS

1. In what terms does de Las Casas argue for the humanity of the Native Americans?
2. Is his principal interest in their souls, which can be converted if they are reached in time and by the right agents?

13.2 NICOLAUS COPERNICUS, DEDICATION OF *THE REVOLUTIONS OF THE HEAVENLY BODIES* TO POPE PAUL III, 1543

Nicolaus Copernicus's (1473–1543) heliocentric theory upset centuries of Western scientific tradition—a tradition that appeared to have the authority of the Bible behind it, since the Scriptures refer repeatedly to the sun's rising and setting. He knew that his theory would confront resistance, which is why he delayed the publication of his work for so long. In this preface he explains his work to the pope.

I can easily conceive, most Holy Father, that as soon as some people learn that in this book which I have written concerning the revolutions of the heavenly bodies, I ascribe certain motions to the Earth, they will cry out at once that I and my theory should be rejected. For I am not so much in love with my conclusions as not to weigh what others will think about them, and although I know that the meditations of a philosopher are far removed from the judgment of the laity, because his endeavor is to seek out the truth in all things, so far as this is permitted by God to the human reason, I still believe that one must avoid theories altogether foreign to orthodoxy. Accordingly, when I considered in my own mind how absurd a performance it must seem to those who know that the judgment of many centuries has approved the view that the Earth remains fixed as center in the midst of the heavens, if I should, on the contrary, assert that the Earth moves; I was for a long time at a loss to know whether I should publish the commentaries which I have written in proof of its motion, or whether it were not better to follow the example of the Pythagoreans and of some others, who were accustomed to transmit the secrets of Philosophy not in writing but orally, and only to their relatives and friends, as the letter from Lysis to Hipparchus bears witness. They did this, it seems to me, not as some think, because of a certain selfish reluctance to give their views to the world, but in order that the noblest truths, worked out by the careful study of great men, should not be despised by those who are vexed at the idea of taking great pains with any forms of literature except such as would be profitable, or by those who, if they are driven to the study of Philosophy for its own sake by the admonitions and the example of others, nevertheless, on account of their stupidity, hold a place among philosophers similar to that of drones among bees. Therefore, when I considered this carefully, the contempt which I had to fear because of the novelty and apparent absurdity of my view, nearly induced me to abandon utterly the work I had begun.

My friends, however, in spite of long delay and even resistance on my part, withheld me from this decision. First among these was Nicolaus Schonberg, Cardinal of Capua, distinguished in all branches of learning. Next to him comes my very dear friend, Tidemann Giese, Bishop of Culm, a most earnest student, as he is, of sacred and, indeed, of all good learning. The latter has often urged me, at times even spurring me on with reproaches, to publish and at last bring to the light the book which had lain in my study not nine years merely, but already going on four times nine. Not a few other very eminent and scholarly men made the same request, urging that I should no longer through fear refuse to give out my work for the common benefit of students of Mathematics. They said I should find that the more absurd most men now thought this theory of mine concerning the motion of the Earth, the more admiration and gratitude it would command after they saw in the publication of my commentaries the mist of absurdity cleared away by most transparent proofs. So, influenced by these advisors and this hope, I have at length allowed my friends to publish the work, as they had long besought me to do.

But perhaps Your Holiness will not so much wonder that I have ventured to publish these studies of mine, after having taken such pains in elaborating them that I have not hesitated to commit to writing my views of the motion of the Earth, as you will be curious to hear how it occurred to me to venture, contrary to the accepted view of mathematicians, and well-nigh contrary to common sense, to form a conception of any terrestrial motion whatsoever. Therefore, I would not have it unknown to Your Holiness that the only thing which induced me to look for another way of reckoning the movements of the heavenly bodies was that I knew that mathematicians by no means agree in their investigations thereof. For, in the first place, they are so much in doubt concerning the motion of the sun and the moon, that they cannot even demonstrate and prove by observation the constant length of a complete year; and in the second place, in determining the motions both of these and of the five other planets, they fail to employ consistently one set of first principles and hypotheses, but use methods of proof based only upon the apparent revolutions and motions. For some employ concentric circles only; others, eccentric circles and epicycles; and even by these means they do not completely attain the desired end. For, although those who have depended upon concentric circles have shown that certain diverse motions can be deduced from these, yet they have not succeeded thereby in laying down any sure principle, corresponding indisputably to the phenomena. These, on the other hand, who have devised systems of eccentric circles, although they seem in great part to have solved the apparent movements by calculations which by these eccentrics are made to fit, have nevertheless introduced many things which seem to contradict the first principles of the uniformity of motion. Nor have they been able to discover or calculate from these the main point, which is the shape of the world and the fixed symmetry of its parts; but their procedure has been as if someone were to collect hands, feet, a head, and other members from various places, all very fine in themselves, but not proportionate to one body, and no single one corresponding in its turn to the others, so that a monster rather than a man would be formed from them. Thus, in their process of demonstration which they term a "method," they are found to have omitted something essential or to have included something foreign and not pertaining to the matter in hand. This certainly would never have happened to them if they had followed fixed principles; for if the hypotheses they assumed were not false, all that resulted therefrom would be verified indubitably. Those things which I am saying now may be obscure, yet they will be made clearer in their proper place.

Therefore, having turned over in my mind for a long time this uncertainty of the traditional mathematical methods of calculating the motions of the celestial bodies, I began to grow disgusted that no more consistent scheme of the movements of the mechanism of the universe, set up for our benefit by that best and most law-abiding Architect of all things, was agreed upon by philosophers who otherwise investigate so carefully the most minute details of this world. Wherefore I undertook the task of rereading the books of all the philosophers I could get access to, to see whether anyone ever was of the opinion that the motions of the celestial bodies were other than those postulated by the men who taught mathematics in the schools, and I found first, indeed, in Cicero, that Niceta perceived that the Earth moved; and afterward in Plutarch I found that some others were of this opinion, whose words I have seen fit to quote here, that they may be accessible to all:—

"Some maintain that the Earth is stationary, but Philolaus the Pythagorean says that it revolves in a circle about the fire of the ecliptic, like the sun and moon. Heraklides of Pontus and Ekphantus the Pythagorean make the Earth move, not changing its position, however, confined in its falling and rising around its own center in the manner of a wheel."

Taking this as a starting point, I began to consider the mobility of the Earth; and although the idea seemed absurd, yet because I knew that the liberty had been granted to others before me to postulate all sorts of little circles for explaining the phenomena of the stars, I thought I also might easily be permitted to try whether by postulating some motion of the Earth, more reliable conclusions could be reached regarding the revolution of the heavenly bodies, than those of my predecessors.

And so, after postulating movements, which, farther on in the book, I ascribe to the Earth, I have found by many and long observations that if the movements of the other planets are assumed for the circular motion of the Earth and are substituted for the revolution of each star, not only do their phenomena follow logically therefrom, but the relative positions and magnitudes both of the stars and all their orbits, and of the heavens themselves, become so closely related that in none of its parts can anything be changed without causing confusion in the other parts and in the whole universe. Therefore, in the course of the work I have followed this plan: I describe in the first book all the positions of the orbits together with the movements which I ascribe to the Earth, in order that this book might contain, as it were, the general scheme of the universe. Thereafter in the remaining books, I set forth the motions of the other stars and of all their orbits together with the movement of the Earth, in order that one may see from this to what extent the movements and appearances of the other stars and their orbits can be saved, if they are transferred to the movement of the Earth. Nor do I doubt that ingenious and learned mathematicians will sustain me, if they are willing to recognize and weigh, not superficially but with that thoroughness which Philosophy demands above all things, those matters which have been adduced by me in this work to demonstrate these theories. In order, however, that both the learned and the unlearned equally may see that I do not avoid anyone's judgment, I have preferred to dedicate these investigations of mine to Your Holiness rather than to any other, because, even in this remote corner of the world where I live, you are considered to be the most eminent man in dignity of rank and in love of all learning and even of mathematics, so that by your authority and judgment you can easily suppress the bites of slanderers, albeit the proverb has it that there is no remedy for the bite of a sycophant. If perchance there shall be idle talkers, who, though they are ignorant of all mathematical sciences, nevertheless assume the right to pass judgment on these things, and if they should dare to criticize and attack this theory of mine because of some passage of Scripture which they have falsely distorted for their own purpose, I care not at all; I will even despise their judgment as foolish. For it is not unknown that Lactantius, otherwise a famous writer but a poor mathematician, speaks most childishly of the shape of the Earth when he makes fun of those who said that the Earth has the form of a sphere. It should not seem strange then to zealous students, if some such people shall ridicule us also. Mathematics are written for mathematicians, to whom, if my opinion does not deceive me, our labors will seem to contribute something to the ecclesiastical state whose chief office Your Holiness now occupies; for when not so very long ago, under Leo X, in the Lateran Council the question of revising the ecclesiastical calendar was discussed, it then remained unsettled, simply because the length of the years and months, and the motions of the sun and moon were held to have been not yet sufficiently determined. Since that time, I have given my attention to observing these more accurately, urged on by a very distinguished man, Paul, bishop of Fossombrone, who at that time had charge of the matter. But what I may have accomplished herein I leave to the judgment of Your Holiness in particular, and to that of all other learned mathematicians; and lest I seem to Your Holiness to promise more regarding the usefulness of the work than I can perform, I now pass to the work itself.

STUDY QUESTIONS

1. What argument does Copernicus offer to the pope in defense of his new theory?
2. How does Copernicus use reason to support his heliocentric theory?

13.3 GALILEO GALILEI, LETTER TO DON BENEDETTO CASTELLI, DECEMBER 21, 1613

An Italian astronomer, physicist, and mathematician, Galileo Galilei (1564–1642) made many significant contributions to science—such as improvements to the telescope and work with sunspots—but is remembered primarily for his support of a heliocentric model of the solar system. His conviction led him into conflict with the Catholic Church; he was accused of heresy and finished his days under house arrest. Aside from his astronomical texts, Galileo also corresponded with leading figures of his day. This letter, to the Benedictine mathematician Benedetto Castelli, addresses one of the main articles of the problem with Galileo's heliocentrism: how to reconcile observable scientific fact with the words of the Bible, held to be literal and inviolable in seventeenth-century Italy.

Very Reverend Father and most worthy Signore,

I received a visit yesterday from Signor Niccolò Arrighetti, who brought me news of your Reverence. I was delighted to hear what I never doubted, namely the high opinion in which you are held by the whole university, both the governors and the teachers and students of all nations. . . . But what set the seal on my pleasure was hearing his account of the arguments which you were able to put forward, thanks to the great kindness of their Serene Highnesses, first at their dinner table and later in Madame's drawing-room, in the presence of the Grand Duke and the Archduchess and the distinguished and excellent gentleman Don Antonio and Don Paolo Giordano and other excellent philosophers. What greater favour could you wish for than that their Highnesses should be pleased to hold conversation with you, to put their doubts to you, to hear you

Galileo Galilei, *Selected Writings.* Translated by William R. Shea and Mark Davie. Oxford: Oxford University Press, 2013, pp. 55–61. By permission of Oxford University Press.

resolve them and finally to be satisfied with your Reverence's replies?

The points which you made, as Signor Arrighetti reported them to me, have prompted me to think afresh about some general principles concerning the citing of Holy Scripture in disputes on matters of natural science, and in particular on the passage in Joshua which was put forward by the Dowager Grand Duchess, and to which the Archduchess offered some rejoinders, as evidence against the motion of the Earth and the fixed position of the Sun.

As regards the first general question raised by Madame, it seems to me that both she and you were entirely prudent when she asserted and you agreed that the Holy Scripture can never lie or be in error, but that its decrees are absolutely and inviolably true. I would simply have added that, although Scripture cannot err, nonetheless some of its interpreters and expositors can, and in various ways. One error in particular, which is especially serious and frequent, is to insist always on the literal meaning of the words, for this can lead not only to many contradictions but also to grave heresies and blasphemies; for it would mean attributing to God feet and hands and eyes, not to mention physical human affectations such as anger, repentance, hatred, and sometimes even forgetfulness of past events and ignorance of the future. So, since Scripture contains many statements which, if taken at their face value, appear to be at variance with the truth, but which are couched in these terms so as to be comprehensible to the ignorant, it is up to wise expositors to explain their true meaning to those few who deserve to be set apart from the common herd, and to point out the particular reasons why they have been expressed as they have.

Given, then, that Scripture in many places not only admits but necessarily requires an interpretation which differs from the apparent meaning of the words, it seems to me that it should be brought into scientific disputes only as a last resort. For while Holy Scripture and nature proceed alike from the divine Word—Scripture as dictated by the Holy Spirit, and nature as the faithful executor of God's commands—it is agreed that Scripture, in order to be understood by the multitude, says many things which are apparently and in the literal sense of the words at variance with absolute truth. But nature never transgresses the laws to which it is subject, but is inexorable and unchanging, quite indifferent to whether its hidden reasons and ways of working are accessible to human understanding or not. Hence, any effect in nature which the experience of our senses places before our eyes, or to which we are led by necessary demonstrations, should on no account be called into question because of a passage of Scripture whose words appear to suggest something different, because not every statement of Scripture is bound by such strict rules as every effect of nature.

. . .

I believe that the purpose of the authority of Holy Scripture is solely to persuade men of those articles and propositions which are necessary to their salvation and which, being beyond the scope of human reasoning, could not be made credible to us by science or by any other means, but only through the mouth of the Holy Spirit himself. I do not consider it necessary to believe that the same God who has endowed us with sense, and with the power of reasoning and intellect, should have chosen to set these aside and to convey to us by some other means those facts which we are capable of finding out by exercising these faculties. This is especially the case with those sciences of which only a tiny part is to be found in scattered references in Scripture, which as astronomy, of which Scripture contains so little that it does not even mention the planets. For if the sacred writers had intended to persuade the people of the order and motions of the heavenly bodies, they would not have said so little about them—almost nothing compared to the infinite, profound, and wonderful truths which this science contains.

So you can see, Father, if I am not mistaken, how flawed is the procedure of those who, in debating the questions of natural science which are not directly matters of faith, give priority to verses of Scripture—often verses which they have misunderstood.

. . .

To confirm this, I come now to the particular case of Joshua, about which you presented three statements to their Highnesses; and specifically, to the third of these, which you rightly attributed to me, but to which I now want to add some further considerations, which I do not believe I have yet explained to you.

So let me first concede to my adversary that the words of the sacred text should be taken in exactly their literal sense, namely that God made the Sun stand still in response to Joshua's prayers, so that the day was prolonged and Joshua was able to complete his victory. But let me claim the same concession for myself, lest my adversary should tie me down while remaining free himself to change or modify the meanings of words; and I will show that this passage of Scripture clearly demonstrates the impossibility of the Aristotelian and Ptolemaic world system, and on the contrary fits perfectly well with the system of Copernicus.

I ask first, does my adversary know in what ways the Sun moves? If he does, he must perforce reply that it has two motions, an annual motion from west to east, and a daily one in the opposite direction, from east to west.

My second question then is, do these two different and almost contrary motions both belong to the Sun, and are they both proper to it? To this the answer must be no: only the annual motion is specific and proper to the Sun, while the other belongs to the highest heaven or Primum Mobile, which draws the Sun, the other planets, and the sphere of the fixed stars along with it, making them complete a revolution around the Earth every twenty-four hours, with a motion which is, as I have said, contrary to their own natural and proper motion.

So to the third question: which of these two motions of the Sun produces day and night, the Sun's own real motion or that of the Primum Mobile? The answer has to be that day and night are the result of the motion of the Primum Mobile, and that the Sun's own motion produces not day and night but the changing seasons, and the year itself.

Hence it is clear that, if the length of the day depends not on the motion of the Sun but on that of the Primum Mobile, in order to prolong the day it is the Primum Mobile which must be made to stop, not the Sun. Indeed, anyone who understands these first elements of astronomy will realize that if God had stopped the motion of the Sun, the effect would have been to shorten the day, not to lengthen it. The motion of the Sun being in the opposite direction to the daily revolution of the heavens, the more the Sun moved towards the east, the more its progress towards the west would be held back; and if the Sun's motion were diminished or stopped altogether, it would reach the point where it sets all the more quickly. This effect can be clearly seen in the case of the Moon, whose daily revolution is slower than the Sun's by the same amount as its own proper motion is faster than the Sun's. So it is simply impossible, according to the system of Ptolemy and Aristotle, to prolong the day by stopping the motion of the Sun, as Scripture says happened. It follows therefore that either the motions of the heavens are not as Ptolemy says, or we must change the sense of the words of Scripture and say that, when Scripture says that God stopped the Sun, what it meant was that God stopped the Primum Mobile.

. . .

However, since we have agreed that we should not change the meaning of the words of Scripture, we must have recourse to another arrangement of the world to see whether it agreed with the plain meaning of the words, as indeed we shall see that it does.

I have discovered and rigorously demonstrated that the globe of the Sun turns on its own axis, making a complete revolution in all the space of roughly one lunar month, in the same direction as all the other revolutions of the heavens. Moreover, it is very probable and reasonable to suppose that the Sun, as the instrument and the highest minister of nature—the heart of the world, so to speak—imparts not only light (as it clearly does) but also motion to the planets which revolve around it. So if we follow Copernicus in attributing first of all a daily rotation to the Earth, it is clear that, to bring the whole system to a stop solely in order to prolong the extent and time of daylight without disrupting all the other relations between the planets, it was enough that the Sun should stand still, just as the words of Holy Writ say. This, then, is how the length of the day on Earth can be extended by making the Sun stand still, without introducing any confusion among the parts of the world and without altering the words of Scripture.

I have written much more than my indisposition allows, so I close by offering myself as your servant, kissing your hand and praying our Lord that you may have a joyful festive season and every happiness.

In Florence, 21 December 1613, your Reverence's devoted servant, Galileo Galilei.

STUDY QUESTIONS

1. How does Galileo, with specific reference to the story of Joshua making the sun stand still, illustrate the danger of reading Scripture in *literal* terms?
2. How does he contrast the various purposes of Scripture and science in this respect?

13.4 JOHN DONNE, SERMON, DECEMBER 12, 1626; "TO HIS MISTRESS GOING TO BED," 1633

John Donne (1572–1631) was a Catholic-turned-Anglican priest, poet, and satirist. Donne spanned the literary scale, writing hundreds of texts ranging from erotic love poems to sermonic meditations on God. After love pushed him into an economically ruinous marriage (that ultimately yielded twelve children), Donne endured fourteen years of destitution and depression—during which time he wrote some of his most poignant poetry. The sermon included here explores the lofty topics of true knowledge and change, whereas the almost bawdy poem revels in the exploration of his lover's body.

FROM A SERMON PREACHED 12 DECEMBER 1626

[THE STATE OF KNOWLEDGE]

How imperfect is all our knowledge? What one thing do we know perfectly? Whether we considered arts, or sciences, the servant knows but according to the proportion of his master's knowledge in that art, and the scholar knows but according to the proportion of his master's knowledge in that science; Young men mend not their sight by using old men's spectacles; and yet we look upon nature, but with Aristotle's spectacles, upon the body of man, but with Galen's, and upon the frame of the world, but with Ptolemy's spectacles. Almost all knowledge is rather like a child that is embalmed to make a mummy, than that is nursed to make a man; rather conserved in the stature of the first age, than grown to be greater; And if there be any addition to knowledge, it is rather new knowledge, than a greater knowledge; rather a singularity in a desire of proposing something that was not known at all before, than an improving, an advancing, a multiplying of former inceptions; and by that means, no knowledge comes to be perfect. One philosopher thinks he is dived to the bottom, when he says, he knows nothing but this, That he knows nothing; and yet another thinks, that he hath expressed more knowledge than he, in saying, That he knows not so much as that, That he knows nothing. St. Paul found that to be all knowledge, To know Christ; And Mahomet thinks himself wise therefore, because he knows not, acknowledges not Christ, as

---

John Donne, *The Major Works, Including Songs and Sonnets and Sermons*. Edited by John Carey. New York: Oxford University Press, 2008, pp. 12–13, 372–4.

St. Paul does. Though a man knew not, that every sin casts another shovel of brimstone upon him in Hell, yet if he knew that every riotous feast cuts off a year, and every wanton night even years of his seventy in this world, it were some degree towards perfection in knowledge. He that purchases a manor, will think to have an exact survey of the land: But who thinks of taking so exact a survey of his conscience, how that money was got, that purchased that manor? We call that a man's means, which he hath; But that is truly his means, what way he came by it. And yet how few are there, (when a state comes to any great proportion) that know that; that know what they have, what they are worth?

. . .

[MUTABILITY]

I need not call in new philosophy, that denies a settledness, an acquiescence in the very body of the earth, but makes the earth to move in that place, where we thought the sun had moved; I need not that help, that the earth itself is in motion, to prove this, That nothing upon earth is permanent; The assertion will stand of itself, till some man assign me some instance, something that a man may rely upon, and find permanent. Consider the greatest bodies upon earth, The monarchies; Objects, which one would think, destiny might stand and stare at, but not shake; Consider the smallest bodies upon earth, the hairs of our head, objects, which one would think, destiny would not observe, or could not discern; And yet destiny, (to speak to a natural man) and God, (to speak to a Christian) is no more troubled to make a monarchy ruinous, than to make a hair gray. Nay, nothing needs to be done to either, by God, or destiny; a monarchy will ruin, as a hair will grow gray, of itself. In the elements themselves, of which all sub-elementary things are composed, there is no acquiescence, but a vicissitudinary transmutation into one another; air condensed becomes water, a more solid body, And air rarified becomes fire, a body more disputable, and in-apparent. It is so in the conditions of men too; a merchant condensed, kneaded and packed up in a great estate, becomes a Lord; And a merchant rarified, blown up by a perfidious factor, or by riotous son, evaporates into air, into nothing, and is not seen. And if there were anything permanent and durable in this world, yet we got nothing by it, because howsoever that might last in itself, yet we could not last to enjoy it; If our goods were not amongst moveables, yet we ourselves are; if they could stay with us, yet we cannot stay with them.

. . .

ELEGY: TO HIS MISTRESS GOING TO BED

Come, Madam, come, all rest my powers defy,
Until I labour, I in labour lie.
The foe oft-times, having the foe in sight,
Is tired with standing though they never fight.
Off with that girdle, like heaven's zone glistening,
But a far fairer world encompassing.
Unpin that spangled breastplate, which you wear
That th'eyes of busy fools may be stopped there:
Unlace yourself, for that harmonious chime
Tells me from you that now 'tis your bed-time.
Off with that happy busk, which I envy,
That still can be, and still can stand so nigh.
Your gown going off, such beauteous state reveals,
As when from flowery means th'hill's shadow steals.
Off with your wiry coronet and show
The hairy diadem which on you doth grow.
Off with those shoes: and then safely tread
In this love's hallowed temple, this soft bed.
In such white robes heaven's angels used to be
Received by men; thou angel bring'st with thee
A heaven like Mahomet's paradise; and though
Ill spirits walk in white, we easily know
By this these angels from an evil sprite,
They set our hairs, but these our flesh upright.
Licence my roving hands, and let them go
Behind, before, above, between, below.
O my America, my new found land,
My kingdom, safeliest when with one man manned,
My mine of precious stones, my empery,
How blessed am I in the discovering thee.
To enter in these bonds is to be free,
Then where my hand is set my seal shall be.
Full nakedness, all joys are due to thee.
As souls unbodied, bodies unclothed must be,

To taste whole joys. Gems which you women use
Are like Atalanta's balls, cast in men's views,
That when a fool's eye lighteth on a gem
His earthly soul may covet theirs, not them.
Like pictures, or like books' gay coverings made
For laymen, are all women thus arrayed;
Themselves are mystic books, which only we
Whom their imputed grace will dignify
Must see revealed. Then since I may know,
As liberally as to a midwife show
Thyself; cast all, yea, this white linen hence,
Here is no penance, much less innocence.
To teach thee, I am naked first: why then
What needest thou have more covering than a man?

STUDY QUESTIONS

1. Does Donne seem to believe that perfect knowledge of anything can exist?
2. What do his references to "Mahomet" and "America" reveal about his time and place?

13.5 RENÉ DESCARTES, A *DISCOURSE ON METHOD*, 1637

René Descartes (1596–1650) has been called the Father of Modern Philosophy because of his work in philosophy, metaphysics, theology, and mathematics. Perhaps best known for the groundbreaking maxim "I think, therefore I am," Descartes lays out a method for creating solid foundations on which he can build theoretical arguments—an epistemology known as Cartesianism. The *Discourse* moves from autobiography to philosophical tract and recounts how Descartes came to the thoughts and processes that redefined philosophy.

PART ONE

Good sense is, of all things among men, the most equally distributed; for every one thinks himself so abundantly provided with it, that those even who are the most difficult to satisfy in everything else, do not usually desire a larger measure of this quality than they already possess. And in this it is not likely that all are mistaken the conviction is rather to be held as testifying that the power of judging aright and of distinguishing truth from error, which is properly what is called good sense or reason, is by nature equal in all men; and that the diversity of our opinions, consequently, does not arise from some being endowed with a larger share of reason than others, but solely from this, that we conduct our thoughts along different ways, and do not fix our attention on the same objects. For to be possessed of a vigorous mind is not enough; the prime requisite is rightly to

René Descartes, *A Discourse on the Method of Rightly Conducting the Reason, and Seeking Truth in the Sciences.* Translated by John Veitch and available via Project Gutenberg.

apply it. The greatest minds, as they are capable of the highest excellences, are open likewise to the greatest aberrations; and those who travel very slowly may yet make far greater progress, provided they keep always to the straight road, than those who, while they run, forsake it.

For myself, I have never fancied my mind to be in any respect more perfect than those of the generality; on the contrary, I have often wished that I were equal to some others in promptitude of thought, or in clearness and distinctness of imagination, or in fullness and readiness of memory. And besides these, I know of no other qualities that contribute to the perfection of the mind; for as to the reason or sense, inasmuch as it is that alone which constitutes us men, and distinguishes us from the brutes, I am disposed to believe that it is to be found complete in each individual; . . .

I will not hesitate, however, to avow my belief that it has been my singular good fortune to have very early in life fallen in with certain tracks which have conducted me to considerations and maxims, of which I have formed a method that gives me the means, as I think, of gradually augmenting my knowledge, and of raising it by little and little to the highest point which the mediocrity of my talents and the brief duration of my life will permit me to reach. For I have already reaped from it such fruits that, although I have been accustomed to think lowly enough of myself, and although when I look with the eye of a philosopher at the varied courses and pursuits of mankind at large, I find scarcely one which does not appear in vain and useless, I nevertheless derive the highest satisfaction from the progress I conceive myself to have already made in the search after truth, . . .

. . .

My present design, then, is not to teach the method which each ought to follow for the right conduct of his reason, but solely to describe the way in which I have endeavored to conduct my own. . . .

From my childhood, I have been familiar with letters; and as I was given to believe that by their help a clear and certain knowledge of all that is useful in life might be acquired, I was ardently desirous of instruction. But as soon as I had finished the entire course of study, at the close of which it is customary to be admitted into the order of the learned, I completely changed my opinion. For I found myself involved in so many doubts and errors, that I was convinced I had advanced no farther in all my attempts at learning, than the discovery at every turn of my own ignorance. And yet I was studying in one of the most celebrated schools in Europe, in which I thought there must be learned men, if such were anywhere to be found. I had been taught all that others learned there; and not contented with the sciences actually taught us, I had, in addition, read all the books that had fallen into my hands, treating of such branches as are esteemed the most curious and rare. I knew the judgment which others had formed of me; and I did not find that I was considered inferior to my fellows, although there were among them some who were already marked out to fill the places of our instructors. And, in fine, our age appeared to me as flourishing, and as fertile in powerful minds as any preceding one. I was thus led to take the liberty of judging of all other men by myself, and of concluding that there was no science in existence that was of such a nature as I had previously been given to believe.

I still continued, however, to hold in esteem the studies of the schools. I was aware that the languages taught in them are necessary to the understanding of the writings of the ancients; that the grace of fable stirs the mind; that the memorable deeds of history elevate it; and, if read with discretion, aid in forming the judgment; that the perusal of all excellent books is, as it were, to interview with the noblest men of past ages, who have written them, and even a studied interview, in which are discovered to us only their choicest thoughts; that eloquence has incomparable force and beauty; that poesy has its ravishing graces and delights; that in the mathematics there are many refined discoveries eminently suited to gratify the inquisitive, as well as further all the arts an lessen the labour of man; that numerous highly useful precepts and exhortations to virtue are contained in treatises on morals; that theology points out the path to heaven; that philosophy affords the means of discoursing with an appearance of truth on all matters, and commands the admiration of the more simple; that jurisprudence, medicine, and the other sciences, secure for their cultivators honors and riches; . . .

. . .

I was especially delighted with the mathematics, on account of the certitude and evidence of their reasonings; but I had not as yet a precise knowledge of their true use; and thinking that they but contributed to the advancement of the mechanical arts, I was astonished that foundations, so strong and solid, should have had no loftier superstructure reared on them. On the other hand, I compared the disquisitions of the ancient moralists to very towering and magnificent palaces with no better foundation than sand and mud: they laud the virtues very highly, and exhibit them as estimable far above anything on earth; but they give us no adequate criterion of virtue, and frequently that which they designate with so fine a name is but apathy, or pride, or despair, or parricide.

. . .

. . . But after I had been occupied several years in thus studying the book of the world, and in essaying to gather some experience, I at length resolved to make myself an object of study, and to employ all the powers of my mind in choosing the paths I ought to follow, an undertaking which was accompanied with greater success than it would have been had I never quitted my country or my books.

. . .

PART FOUR

. . . but as I then desired to give my attention solely to the search after truth, I thought that a procedure exactly the opposite was called for, and that I ought to reject as absolutely false all opinions in regard to which I could suppose the least ground for doubt, in order to ascertain whether after that there remained aught in my belief that was wholly indubitable. Accordingly, seeing that our senses sometimes deceive us, I was willing to suppose that there existed nothing really such as they presented to us; and because some men err in reasoning, and fall into paralogisms, even on the simplest matters of geometry, I, convinced that I was as open to error as any other, rejected as false all the reasonings I had hitherto taken for demonstrations; and finally, when I considered that the very same thoughts (presentations) which we experience when awake may also be experienced when we are asleep, while there is at that time not one of them true, I supposed that all the objects (presentations) that had ever entered into my mind when awake, had in them no more truth than the illusions of my dreams. But immediately upon this I observed that, whilst I thus wished to think that all was false, it was absolutely necessary that I, who thus thought, should be somewhat; and as I observed that this truth, I think, therefore I am (COGITO ERGO SUM), was so certain and of such evidence that no ground of doubt, however extravagant, could be alleged by the sceptics capable of shaking it, I concluded that I might, without scruple, accept it as the first principle of the philosophy of which I was in search.

In the next place, I attentively examined what I was and as I observed that I could suppose that I had no body, and that there was no world nor any place in which I might be; but that I could not therefore suppose that I was not; and that, on the contrary, from the very circumstance that I thought to doubt of the truth of other things, it most clearly and certainly followed that I was; while, on the other hand, if I had only ceased to think, although all the other objects which I had ever imagined had been in reality existent, I would have had no reason to believe that I existed; I thence concluded that I was a substance whose whole essence or nature consists only in thinking, and which, that it may exist, has need of no place, nor is dependent on any material thing; so that "I," that is to say, the mind by which I am what I am, is wholly distinct from the body, and is even more easily known than the latter, and is such, that although the latter were not, it would still continue to be all that it is.

After this I inquired in general into what is essential to the truth and certainty of a proposition; for since I had discovered one which I knew to be true, I thought that I must likewise be able to discover the ground of this certitude. And as I observed that in the words I think, therefore I am, there is nothing at all which gives me assurance of their truth beyond this, that I see very clearly that in order to think it is necessary to exist, I concluded that I might take, as a general rule, the principle, that all the things which we very clearly and distinctly conceive are true, only observing, however, that there is some difficulty in rightly determining the objects which we distinctly conceive.

In the next place, from reflecting on the circumstance that I doubted, and that consequently my being was not wholly perfect (for I clearly saw that it was a greater perfection to know than to doubt), I was led to inquire whence I had learned to think of something more perfect than myself; and I clearly recognized that I must hold this notion from some nature which in reality was more perfect. As for the thoughts of many other objects external to me, as of the sky, the earth, light, heat, and a thousand more, I was less at a loss to know whence these came; for since I remarked in them nothing which seemed to render them superior to myself, I could believe that, if these were true, they were dependencies on my own nature, in so far as it possessed a certain perfection, and, if they were false, that I held them from nothing, that is to say, that they were in me because of a certain imperfection of my nature. But this could not be the case with the idea of a nature more perfect than myself; for to receive it from nothing was a thing manifestly impossible; and, because it is not less repugnant that the more perfect should be an effect of, and dependence on the less perfect, than that something should proceed from nothing, it was equally impossible that I could hold it from myself: accordingly, it but remained that it had been placed in me by a nature which was in reality more perfect than mine, and which even possessed within itself all the perfections of which I could form any idea; that is to say, in a single word, which was God. And to this I added that, since I knew some perfections which I did not possess, I was not the only being in existence (I will here, with your permission, freely use the terms of the schools); but, on the contrary, that there was of necessity some other more perfect Being upon whom I was dependent, and from whom I had received all that I possessed; for if I had existed alone, and independently of every other being, so as to have had from myself all the perfection, however little, which I actually possessed, I should have been able, for the same reason, to have had from myself the whole remainder of perfection, of the want of which I was conscious, and thus could of myself have become infinite, eternal, immutable, omniscient, all-powerful, and, in fine, have possessed all the perfections which I could recognize in God.

STUDY QUESTIONS

1. How does Descartes account for the general perception of equal knowledge among people?
2. How does he find enlightenment through introspection, rather than through trusting conventional authorities of wisdom?

13.6 *THE JESUIT RELATIONS*, FRENCH NORTH AMERICA, 1649

The Jesuit Relations are the most important set of documents attesting the encounter between Europeans and native North Americans in the seventeenth century. These annual reports of French missionaries from the Society of Jesus document the conversions—or attempted conversions—of the various native peoples in what is today the St. Lawrence River basin and the Great Lakes

Paul Ragueneau, *Relation of 1648–49*. In *The Jesuit Relations: Natives and Missionaries in Seventeenth-Century North America*, edited by Allan Greer. New York: Bedford/St. Martin's, 2000, pp. 112–15.

region. When they arrived on the banks of the St. Lawrence in 1625, French Jesuits were entering a continent still very much under the control of First Nations peoples, who were divided by their own ethnic and linguistic differences. Even the catch-all terms "Huron" and "Iroquois" masked the existence of confederacies, composed of several distinct nations, who had joined together prior to the arrival of Europeans.

When the Jesuits made headway with one group, they usually lost initiative with the group's rivals—and sometimes found themselves in the midst of a conflict that they could barely understand or appreciate. This section of one of the *Relations* concerns the torture and murder of Jean Brébeuf, who had lived among the Hurons at various points from the 1620s through the 1640s, observing their culture and systematically attempting to convert them to Catholicism. However, when an Iroquois raiding party invaded his settlement, the depth of the Hurons' Christian commitment—and his own—would be tested.

The sixteenth day of March in the present year, 1649, marked the beginning of our misfortunes—if an event, which no doubt has been the salvation of many of God's elect, can be called a misfortune.

The Iroquois, enemies of the Hurons, arrived by night at the frontier of this country. They numbered about a thousand men, well furnished with weapons, most of them carrying firearms obtained from their allies, the Dutch. We had no knowledge of their approach, although they had started from their country in the autumn, hunting in the forests throughout the winter, and had made a difficult journey of nearly two hundred leagues over the snow in order to take us by surprise. By night, they reconnoitered the condition of the first place upon which they had designs. It was surrounded by a pine stockade fifteen or sixteen feet in height, and a deep ditch with which nature had strongly fortified this place on three sides. There remained only a small space that was weaker than the others.

It was at this weak point that the enemy made a breach at daybreak, but so secretly and promptly that he was master of the place before anyone could mount a defense. All were then sleeping deeply, and they had no time to recognize the danger. Thus this village was taken, almost without striking a blow and with only ten Iroquois killed. Part of the Hurons—men, women, and children—were massacred then and there, while the others were made captives and were reserved for cruelties more terrible than death.

. . .

The enemy did not stop there, but followed up his victory, and before sunrise he appeared in arms to attack the town of St. Louis, which was fortified with a fairly good stockade. Most of the women and the children had just gone from it upon hearing the news which had arrived regarding the approach of the Iroquois. The people of greatest courage, about eighty persons, being resolved to defend themselves well, courageously repulsed the first and the second assaults, killing about thirty of the enemy's boldest men, in addition to many wounded. But finally, the larger number prevailed, as the Iroquois used their hatchets to undermine the palisade of stakes and opened a passage for themselves through some considerable breaches.

About nine o'clock in the morning, we perceived from our house at St. Marie the fire which was consuming the cabins of that town, where the enemy, after entering victoriously, had reduced everything to desolation. They cast into the flames the old, the sick, the children who had not been able to escape, and all those who, being too severely wounded, could not have followed them into captivity. At the sight of those flames, and by the color of the smoke which issued from them, we understood sufficiently what was happening, for this town of St. Louis was no more than a league distant from us. Two Christians who escaped the fire arrived about this time and confirmed this.

In this town of St. Louis were at that time two of our fathers, Father Jean de Brébeuf and Father

Gabriel Lalemant, who had charge of a cluster of five towns. These formed but one of the eleven missions of which we have spoken above, and we call it the mission of St. Ignace.

Some Christians had begged the fathers to preserve their lives for the glory of God, which would have been as easy for them as for the more than five hundred persons who went away at the first alarm, for there was more than enough time to reach a place of safety. But their zeal could not permit such a thing, and the salvation of their flock was dearer to them than the love of their own lives. They employed the moments left to them as the most previous which they had ever had in the world, and through the heat of the battle their hearts were on fire for the salvation of souls. One was at the breach, baptizing the catechumens [native converts who had not yet been baptized], and the other was giving absolution to the neophytes [recently baptized Christians]. Both of them urged the Christians to die in the sentiments of piety with which they consoled them in their miseries. Never was their faith more alive, nor their love for their good fathers and pastors more keenly felt.

An infidel, seeing the desperate situation, spoke of taking flight, but a Christian named Etienne Annaotaha, the most esteemed in the country for his courage and his exploits against the enemy, would never allow it. "What!" he said. "Could we ever abandon these two good fathers, who have exposed their lives for us? Their love for our salvation will be the cause of their death, for there is no longer time for them to flee across the snows. Let us then die with them, and we shall go together to heaven." This man had made a general confession a few days previously, having had a presentiment of the danger awaiting him and saying that he wished that death should find him disposed for Heaven. And indeed he, as well as many other Christians, had abandoned themselves to fervor in a manner so extraordinary that we shall never be sufficiently able to bless the guidance of God over so many predestinated souls. His divine providence continues lovingly to guide them in death as in life.

STUDY QUESTIONS

1. How well do the Jesuits seem to have understood the conflicts among native peoples in this region?
2. How was Ragueneau's reporting of the battle designed to highlight the "success" of the mission, despite an apparent setback?

13.7 THOMAS HOBBES, "ON NATURAL LAW," *LEVIATHAN*, 1651

Thomas Hobbes (1588–1679) was an English political philosopher who examined the idea of a "social contract" existing between a ruler and society. Although he upheld absolutism as a political system, his liberal ideas—such as the belief in natural equality for all men and the idea that

From Thomas Hobbes, *Leviathan*. Edited by J. C. A. Gaskin. New York: Oxford University Press, 2010, pp. 82–6, 132–3, 138–9, 141–3.

rule should emerge from the needs of society—helped frame early American political thought. His massive work *Leviathan*, named for the biblical sea beast, explores and explains this theory of social contract during the English civil war that challenged traditional monarchy. This selection outlines Hobbes's views on natural law and the liberties it demands.

CHAPTER XIII: OF THE NATURAL CONDITION OF MANKIND AS CONCERNING THEIR FELICITY, AND MISERY

NATURE hath made men so equal, in the faculties of the body, and mind; as that though there be found one man sometimes manifestly stronger in body, or of quicker mind than another; yet when all are reckoned together, the difference between man, and man, is not so considerable, as that one man can thereupon claim to himself any benefit, to which another may not pretend, as well as he. For as to the strength of body, the weakest has strength enough to kill the strongest, either by secret machination, or by confederacy with others, that are in the same danger with himself.

And as to the faculties of the mind, (setting aside the arts grounded upon words, and especially that skill of proceeding upon general, and infallible rules, called science; which very few have, and but in few things; as being not a native faculty, born with us; nor attained (as prudence,) while we look after somewhat else,) I find yet a greater equality amongst men, than that of strength. For prudence, is but experience; which equal time, equally bestows on all men, in those things they equally apply themselves unto. That which may perhaps make such equality incredible, is but a vain conceit of one's own wisdom, which almost all men think they have in a greater degree, than the vulgar; that is, than all men but themselves, and a few others, whom by fame, or for concurring with themselves, they approve. For such is the nature of men, that howsoever they may acknowledge many others to be more witty, or more eloquent, or more learned; yet they will hardly believe there be many so wise as themselves; for they see their own wit at hand, and other men's at a distance. But this proveth rather that men are in that point equal, than unequal. For there is not ordinarily a greater sign of the equal distribution of any thing, than that every man is contented with his share.

From this equality of ability, ariseth equality of hope in the attaining of our ends. And therefore if any two men desire the same thing, which nevertheless they cannot both enjoy, they become enemies; and in the way to their end, (which principally their own conservation, and sometimes their delectation only,) endeavor to destroy, or subdue one another. And from hence it comes to pass, that where an invader hath no more to fear, than another man's single power; if one plant, sow, build, or possess a convenient seat, others may probably be expected to come prepared with forces united, to dispossess, and deprive him, not only of the fruit of his labour, but also of his life, or liberty. And the invader again is in the like danger of another.

And from this diffidence of one another, there is no way for any man to secure himself, so reasonable, as anticipation; that is, by force, or wiles, to master the persons of all men he can, so long, till he see no other power great enough to endanger him: and this is no more than his own conservation requireth, and is generally allowed. Also because there be some, that taking pleasure in contemplating their own power in the acts of conquest, which they pursue farther than their security requires; if others, that otherwise would be glad to be at ease within modest bounds, should not by invasion increase their power, they would not be able, long time, by standing only their defence, to subsist. And by consequence, such augmentation of dominion over men, being necessary to a man's conservation, it ought to be allowed him.

Again, men have no pleasure, (but on the contrary a great deal of grief) in keeping company, where there is no power able to over-awe them all. For every man looketh that his companion should value him, at the same rate he sets upon himself: and upon all signs of contempt, or undervaluing, naturally endeavours, as far as he dares (which amongst them that have no common power to keep them in quiet, is far enough to make them destroy each other,) to extort a greater value from his contemners, by damage; and from others, by the example.

So that in the nature of man, we find three principal causes of quarrel. First, competition; secondly, diffidence; thirdly, glory.

The first, maketh men invade for gain; the second, for safety; and the third, for reputation. The first use violence, to make themselves masters of other men's persons, wives, children, and cattle; the second, to defend them; the third, for trifles, as a word, a smile, a different opinion, and any other sign of undervalue, either direct in their persons, or by reflection in their kindred, their friends, their nation, their profession, or their name.

Hereby it is manifest, that during the time men live without a common power to keep them all in awe, they are in that condition which is called war; and such a war, as is of every man, against every man. For WAR, consisteth not in battle only, or the act of fighting; but in a tract of time, wherein the will to contend by battle is sufficiently known: and therefore the notion of *time*, is to be considered in the nature of war; as it is in the nature of weather. For as the nature of foul weather, lieth not in a shower or two of rain; but in an inclination thereto of many days together: so the nature of war consisteth not in actual fighting; but in the known disposition thereto, during all the time there is no assurance to the contrary. All other time is PEACE.

Whatsoever therefore is consequent to a time of war, where every man is enemy to every man; the same is consequent to the time, wherein men live without other security, than what their own strength, and their own invention shall furnish them withal. In such condition, there is no place for industry; because the fruit thereof is uncertain: and consequently no culture of the earth; no navigation, nor use of the commodities that may be imported by sea; no commodious building; no instruments of moving, and removing such things as require much force; no knowledge of the face of the earth; no account of time; no arts; no letters; no society; and which is worst of all, continual fear, and danger of violent death; and the life of man, solitary, poor, nasty, brutish, and short.

It may seem strange to some man, that has not well weighed these things; that nature should thus dissociate, and render men apt to invade, and destroy one another: he may therefore, not trusting to this inference, made from the passions, desire perhaps to have the same confirmed by experience. Let him therefore consider with himself, when taking a journey, he arms himself, and seeks to go well accompanied; when going to sleep, he locks his doors; when even in his house he locks his chests; and this when he knows there be laws, and public officers, armed, to revenge all injuries shall be done him; what opinion he has of his fellow-subjects, when he rides armed; of his fellow citizens, when he locks his doors; and of his children, and servants, when he locks his chests. Does he not there as much accuse mankind by his actions, as I do by my words? But neither of us accuse man's nature in it. The desires, and other passions of man, are in themselves no sin. No more are the actions, that proceed from those passions, till they know a law that forbids them: which till laws be made they cannot know: nor can any law be made, till they have agreed upon the person that shall make it.

It may peradventure be thought, there was never such a time, not condition of war as this; and I believe it was never generally so, over all the world: but there are many places, where they live so now. For the savage people in many places of America, except the government of small families, the concord whereof dependeth on natural lust, have no government at all; and live at this day in that brutish manner, as I said before. Howsoever, it may be perceived what manner of life there would be, where there were no common power to fear; by the manner of life, which men that have formerly lived under a peaceful government, use to degenerate into, in a civil war.

But though there had never been any time, wherein particular men were in a condition of war one against another; yet in all times, kings, and persons of sovereign authority, because of their independency, are in continual jealousies, and in the state and posture of gladiators; having their weapons pointing, and their eyes fixed on one another; that is, their forts, garrisons, and guns upon the frontiers of their kingdoms; and continual spies upon their neighbours; which is a posture of war. But because they uphold thereby, the industry of their subjects; there does not follow from it, that misery, which accompanies the liberty of particular men.

To this war of every man against every man, this also is consequent; that nothing can be unjust. The notions of right and wrong, justice and injustice have there no place. Where there is no common power, there is no law: where no law, no injustice. Force, and fraud, are in war the two cardinal virtues. Justice, and injustice are none of the faculties neither of the body, nor mind. If they were, they might be in a man that were alone in the world, as well as his senses, and passions. They are qualities, that relate to men in society, not in solitude. It is consequent also to the same condition, that there be no property, no dominion, no *mine* and *thine* distinct; but one that to be every man's, that he can get; and for so long, as he can keep it. And thus much for the ill condition, which man by mere nature is actually placed in; though with a possibility to come out of it, consisting partly in the passions, partly in his reason.

The passions that incline men to peace, are fear of death; desire of such things as are necessary to commodious living; and a hope by their industry to obtain them. And reason suggesteth convenient articles of peace, upon which men may be drawn to agreement. These articles, are they, which otherwise are called the Laws of Nature: whereof I shall speak more particularly, in the two following chapters.

. . .

CHAPTER XX: OF DOMINION PATERNAL, AND DESPOTICAL

A COMMONWEALTH *by acquisition*, is that, where the sovereign power is acquired by force; and it is acquired by force, when men singly, or many together by plurality of voices, for fear of death, or bonds, do authorize all the actions of that man, or assembly, that hath their lives and liberty in his power.

And this kind of dominion, or sovereignty, differeth from sovereignty by institution, only in this, that men who choose their sovereign, do it for fear of one another, and not of him whom they institute: but in this case, they subject themselves, to him they are afraid of. In both cases they do it for fear: which is to be noted by them, that hold all such covenants, as proceed from fear of death, or violence, void: which if it were true, no man, in any kind of commonwealth, could be obliged to obedience. It is true, that in a commonwealth once instituted, or acquired, promises proceeding from fear of death, or violence, are no covenants, nor obliging, when the thing promised is contrary to the laws; but the reason is not, because it was made upon fear, but because he that promiseth, hath no right in the thing promised. Also, when he may lawfully perform, and doth not, it is not the invalidity of the covenant, that absolveth him, but the sentence of the sovereign. Otherwise, whensoever a man lawfully promiseth, he unlawfully breaketh: but when the sovereign, who is the actor, acquitteth him, then he is acquitted by him than extorted the promise, as by the author of such absolution.

But the rights, and consequences of sovereignty, are the same in both. His power cannot, without his consent, be transferred to another: he cannot be punished by them: he is judge of what is necessary for peace; and judge of doctrines: he is sole legislator; and supreme judge of controversies; and of the times, and occasions of war, and peace: to him it belongeth to choose magistrates, counselors, commanders, and all other officers, and ministers; and to determine of rewards, and punishments, honour, and order. The reasons whereof, are the same which are alleged in the precedent chapter, for the same rights, and consequences of sovereignty by institution.

. . .

So that it appeareth plainly, to my understanding, both from reason, and Scripture, that the sovereign power, whether placed in one man, as in monarchy, or in one assembly of men, as in popular and artistocratical commonwealths, is as great, as possibly men can be imagined to make it. And though of so unlimited a power, men may fancy many evil consequences, yet the consequences of the want of it, which is perpetual war of every man against his neighbor, are much worse. The condition of man in this life shall never be without inconveniences; but there happeneth in no commonwealth any great inconvenience, but what proceeds from the subject's disobedience, and breach of those covenants, from which the commonwealth hath its being. And whosoever thinking sovereign power too great, will seek to make it less, must subject himself, to the power that can limit it; that is to say, to a greater.

The greatest objection is, that of the practice; when men ask, where, and when, such power has by subjects been acknowledged. But one may ask them again, when, or where has there been a kingdom long free from sedition and civil war. In those nations, those commonwealths have been long-lived, and not been destroyed but by foreign war, the subjects never did dispute of the sovereign power. But howsoever, an argument from the practice of men, that have not been sifted to the bottom, and with exact reason weighed the causes, and nature of commonwealths, and suffer daily those miseries, that proceed from the ignorance thereof, is invalid. For though in all places of the world, men should lay the foundation of their houses on the sand, it could not thence be inferred, that so it ought to be. The skill of making, and maintaining commonwealths, consisteth in certain rules, as doth arithmetic and geometry; not (as tennis-play) on practice only: which rules, neither poor men have the leisure, nor men that have had the leisure, have hitherto had the curiosity, or the method to find out.

. . .

But as men, for the attaining of peace, and conservation of themselves thereby, have made an artificial man, which we call a commonwealth; so also have they made artificial chains, called *civil laws,* which they themselves, by mutual covenants, have fastened at one end, to the lips of that man, or assembly, to whom they have given the sovereign power; and at the other end to their own ears. These bonds in their own nature but weak, may nevertheless be made to hold, by the danger, though not by the difficulty of breaking them.

In relation to these bonds only it is, that I am to speak now, of the *liberty of subjects.* For seeing there is no commonwealth in the world, wherein there be rules enough to set down, for the regulating of all the actions, and words of men; (as being a thing impossible:) it followeth necessarily, that in all kinds of actions, by the laws praetermitted [passed over], men have the liberty, of doing what their own reasons shall suggest, for the most profitable to themselves. For if we take liberty from chains and prison, it were very absurd for men to clamour as they do, for the liberty they so manifestly enjoy. Again, if we take liberty, for an exemption from laws, it is no less absurd, for men to demand as they do, that liberty, by which all other men may be masters of their lives. And yet as absurd as it is, this is it they demand; not knowing that the laws are of no power to protect them, without a sword in the hands of a man, or men, to cause those laws to be put into execution. The liberty of a subject, lieth therefore only in those things, which in regulating their actions, the sovereign hath praetermitted: such as is the liberty to buy, and sell, and otherwise contract with one another; to choose their own abode, their own diet, their own trade of life, and institute their children as they themselves think fit; and the like.

Nevertheless we are not to understand, that by such liberty, the sovereign power of life, and death, is either abolished, or limited. For it has been already shown, that nothing the sovereign representative can do to a subject, on what pretence soever, can properly be called injustice, or injury; because every subject is author of every act the sovereign doth; so that he never wanteth right to any thing, otherwise, than as he himself is the subject of God, and bound thereby to observe the laws of nature. And therefore it may, and doth often happen in commonwealths, that a subject may be put to death by the command of the sovereign power; and yet neither do the other wrong: as when Jeptha caused his daughter to be sacrificed: in which, and the like cases, he that so dieth, had liberty to do the action, for which he is nevertheless, without injury put to death. And the same holdeth also in a sovereign prince, that putteth to death an innocent subject. For though the action be against the law of nature, as being contrary to equity, (as was the killing of Uriah, by David;) yet it was not an injury to Uriah, but to God. Not to Uriah, because the right to do what he pleased, was given him by Uriah himself: and yet to God, because David was God's subject; and prohibited all iniquity by the law of nature. Which distinction, David himself, when he repented the fact, evidently confirmed, saying, *To thee only have I sinned.* In the same manner, the people of Athens, when they banished the most potent of their commonwealth for ten years, thought they committed no injustice; and yet they never questioned what crime he had done; but what hurt he would do: nay they commanded the banishment of they knew not whom; and every citizen bringing his oystershell into the market place, written with the name of him he desired should be banished, without actually accusing him, sometimes banished an Aristides, for his reputation of justice; and sometimes a scurrilous jester, as Hyperbolus, to make a jest of it. And yet a man cannot say, the sovereign people of Athens wanted right to banish them; or an Athenian the liberty to jest, or to be just.

The liberty, whereof there is so frequent, and honourable mention, in the histories, and philosophy of the ancient Greeks, and Romans, and in the writings, and discourse of those that from them have received all their learning in the politics, is not the liberty of particular men; but the liberty of the commonwealth: which is the same with that, which every man then should have, if there were no civil laws, no commonwealth at all. And the effects of it also be the same. For as amongst his neighbor; no inheritance, to transmit to the son, nor to expect from the father; no propriety of goods, or lands; no security; but a full and absolute liberty in every particular man: so in states, and commonwealths not dependent on one another, every commonwealth, (not every man) has an absolute liberty, to do what it shall judge (that is to say, what that man, or assembly that representeth it, shall judge) most conducing to their benefit. But withal, they live in the condition of a perpetual war, and upon the confines of battle, with their frontiers armed, and cannons planted against their neighbours round about. The Athenians, and Romans were free; that is, free commonwealths: not that any particular man had the liberty to resist their own representative; but that their representative had the liberty to resist, or invade other people. There is written on the turrets of the city of Lucca in great characters at this day, the word LIBERTAS; yet no man can thence infer, that a particular man has more liberty, or immunity from the service of the commonwealth there, than in Constantinople. Whether a commonwealth be monarchical, or popular, the freedom is still the same.

STUDY QUESTIONS

1. Does Hobbes see war as a natural and even necessary experience for humanity?
2. How does he contrast the "freedom" of the individual with the freedom of the commonwealth as a whole?

CHAPTER 14

THE WARS OF ALL AGAINST ALL

14.1 JOHN FOXE, *FOXE'S BOOK OF MARTYRS*, TRIAL OF ANNE ASKEW

John Foxe (1517–1587) authored this martyrology that especially focuses on the martyrdoms of sixteenth-century Protestants at the hands of Catholic inquisitors. This selection recounts the trial against Anne Askew, an Englishwoman who became actively involved in propagating Protestant beliefs—even being rejected by her husband as a result of her zeal. As in medieval inquisitions, the questions asked to Anne are aimed at clarifying where the error arises; here, she rejects the doctrine of transubstantiation and challenges the authority of "improper" priests. Her answers are logical and coherent as she unwittingly condemns herself. Anne was tortured in the Tower of London and burned at the stake in 1546 at the age of twenty-five.

To satisfy your expectation: good people (saith she) this was my first examination in the year of our Lord 1545 and in the month of March.

First Christopher Dare examined me at Sadler's Hall; being one of the quest, and asked if I did not believe that the sacrament, hanging over the altar, was the very body of Christ really. Then I demanded this question of him: wherefore Saint Stephen was stoned to death, and he said, he could not tell. Then I answered that no more would I assoil his vain question.

Secondly, he said that there was a woman, which did not testify that I should read, how God was not in temples made with hands. Then I showed him the seventh and seventeenth chapters of the Acts of Apostles, what Stephen and Paul had said therein. Whereupon he asked me how I took those sentences? I answered, "I would not throw pearls among swine, for acorns were good enough."

Thirdly, he asked me wherefore I said that I had rather read five lines in the Bible, than to hear five masses in the temple? I confessed, that I had said no less: not for the dispraise of either the epistle or the gospel, but because the one did greatly edify me, and the other nothing at all. As Saint Paul doth witness in the fourteenth chapter of his first epistle to the Corinthians, whereas he saith, "If the trumpet giveth an uncertain sound who will prepare himself to the battle?"

John Foxe, *Foxe's Book of Martyrs: Select Narratives*. Edited by John N. King. New York: Oxford University Press, 2009, pp. 22–35.

Fourthly: he laid unto my charge that I should say: "If an ill priest ministered, it was the devil and not God."

My answer was, that I never spake any such thing. But this was my saying: that whosoever he were that ministered unto me, his ill conditions could not hurt my faith, but in spirit I received nevertheless, the body and blood of Christ.

He asked me what I said concerning confession? I answered him my meaning, which was as Saint James saith, that every man ought to acknowledge his faults to other, and the one to pray for the other.

Sixthly, he asked me what I said to the King's Book? And I answered him, that I could say nothing to it, because I never saw it.

Seventhly, he asked me if I had the spirit of God in me? I answered, "If I had not, I was but a reprobate or castaway." Then he said he had sent for a priest to examine me, which was here at hand.

The priest asked me what I said to the sacrament of the altar, and required much to know therein my meaning. But I desired him again, to hold me excused concerning that matter. None other answer would I make him, because I perceived him to be a papist.

Eighthly he asked me, if I did not think that private Masses did help souls departed? I said it was great idolatry to believe more in them, than in the death which Christ died for us.

Then they had me thence unto my Lord Mayor, and he examined me, as they had before, and I answered him directly in all things I answered the quest before. Besides this my Lord Mayor laid one thing to my charge, which was never spoken of me, but of them: and that was, whether a mouse eating the host, received God or no? This question did I never ask, but indeed they asked it of me, whereunto I made them no answer but smiled.

Then the bishop's chancellor rebuked me and said, that I was much to blame for uttering the scriptures. For Saint Paul (he said) forbade women to speak, or to talk of the word of God. I answered him that I knew Paul's meaning as well as he, which is in 1 Corinthians 14, that a woman ought not to speak in the congregation by the way of teaching. And then I asked him, how many women he had seen go into the pulpit and preach? He said he never saw none. Then I said he ought to find no fault in poor women, except they had offended the law.

Then the Lord Mayor commanded me to ward, I asked him if sureties would not serve me, and he made me short answer, that he would take none. Then was I had to the Counter, and there remained eleven days, no friend admitted to speak with me. But in the meantime there was a priest sent to me, which said that he was commanded of the bishop to examine me, and to give me good counsel, which he did not. But first he asked me for what cause I was put in the Counter, and I told him, I could not tell. Then he said it was great pity that I should be there without cause, and concluded that he was very sorry for me.

Secondly, he said, it was told him, that I should deny the sacrament of the altar. And I answered again that, that I have said, I have said.

Thirdly he asked me if I were shriven, I told him, so that I might have one of these three, that is to say, Doctor Crome, Sir Guillam, or Huntington. I was contented because I knew them to be men of wisdom, "as for you or any other I will not dispraise, because I know you not." Then he said, "I would not have you think, but that I, or another that shall be brought to you, shall be as honest as they, for if we were not, you may be sure the kind would not suffer us to preach." Then I answered by the saying of Solomon: "By communing with the wise, I may learn wisdom, but by talking with a fool, I shall take scathe." Pro[verbs, ch. 1].

Fourthly he asked, "If the host should fall and a beast did eat it, whether the beast did receive God or no?" I answered, "Seeing you have taken the pains to ask the question, I desire you also to assoil it yourself: for I will not do it, because I perceive you come to tempt me." And he said, "It was against the order of schools that he which asked the question should answer it." I told him [that] I was but a woman and knew not the course of schools.

Fifthly he asked me, if I intended to receive the sacrament at Easter, or no? I answered, that else I were not Christian woman, and thereat I did rejoice, that the time was so near at hand, and then he departed thence with many fair words.

The twenty-third day of March, my cousin Brittain came into the Counter unto me, and asked me whether I might be put to bail or no? Then went he immediately unto my Lord Mayor, desiring of him to be so good unto me. That I might be bailed. My Lord answered him, and said that he would be glad to do the best that in him lay. Howbeit he could not bail me, without the consent of a spiritual officer: requiring him to go and speak with the chancellor of London. For he said, like as he could not commit me to prison without the consent of a spiritual officer, no more could he bail me without consent of the same.

. . .

On the morrow after, the Bishop of London sent for me, at one of the clock, his hour being appointed at three, and as I came before him, he said he was very sorry for my trouble, and desired to know my opinion in such matters as were laid against me.

. . .

In the mean while he commanded his archdeacon to common with me, who said unto me: "Mistress wherefore are you accused and thus troubled here before the bishop?" To whom I answered again and said: "Sir, ask I pray you my accusers, for I know not as yet." Then took he my book out of my hand, and said: "Such books as this, have brought you to the trouble you are in. Beware," (saith he), "beware, for he that made this book and was the author thereof, was an heretic I warrant you, and burnt in Smithfield." Then I asked him, if he were certain and sure, that it was true that he had spoken. And he said he knew well the book was of John Frith's making. Then I asked him if he were not ashamed for to judge of the book before he saw it within, or yet knew the truth thereof. I said also, that such unadvised and hasty judgement is a token apparent of a very slender wit. Then I opened the book and showed it to him. He said he thought it had been another, for he could find no fault therein. Then I desired him no more to be so unadvisedly rash and swift judgement, till he thoroughly knew the truth, and so he departed from me.

. . .

Then brought he forth this unsavoury similitude: that if a man had a wound, no wise surgeon would minister help unto it before he had seen it uncovered. "In like case," saith he, "can I give you no good counsel, unless I know wherewith your conscience is burdened." I answered, that my conscience was clear in all things: and for to lay a plaster unto the whole skin, it might appear much folly.

. . .

Then said my Lord unto me, that I had alleged a certain text of the scripture. I answered that I alleged none other but Saint Paul's own saying to the Athenians in the eighteenth chapter in the Apostle's acts, that God dwelleth not in temples made with hands. Then asked he me what my faith and belief was in that matter? I answered him, "I believe as the scripture doth teach me."

Then enquired he of me, "What if the scripture do say that it is the body of Christ?" "I believe," said I, "as the scripture doth teach me." Then asked he again, "What if the scripture do say that it is not the body of Christ?" My answer was still, "I believe as the scripture informeth me." And upon this argument he tarried a great while, to have driven me to make him an answer to his mind. Howbeit I would not: but concluded this with him, that I believe therein and in all other things as Christ and his holy apostles did leave them.

Then he asked me why I had so few words? And I answered, "God hath given me the gift of knowledge, but not of utterance. And Solomon saith: "That a woman of few words is a gift of God." Proverbs nineteen.

. . .

"Be it known," (saith he), "of all men, that I Anne Askew do confess this to be my faith and belief, notwithstanding my reports made afore to the contrary. I believe that they which are houseled at the hands of a priest, whether his conversation be good or not, do receive the body and blood of Christ in substance really. Also I do believe, that after the consecration, whether it be received or reserved, it is no less than the very body and blood of Christ in substance. Finally I do believe in this and in all other sacraments of holy church, in all points according to the old Catholic faith of the same. In witness whereof I the said Anne have subscribed my name."

There was somewhat more in it, which because I had not the copy, I cannot not remember. Then he read it to me and asked me if I did agree to it. And I said again, "I believe so much thereof, as the holy scripture both agree unto: wherefore I desire you, that ye will add that thereunto." Then he answered, that I should not teach him what he should write. With that, he went forth into his great chamber, and read the same bill before the audience, which inveigled and willed me to set to my hand, saying also, that I have favour showed me..

. . .

"The true copy of the confession and belief of Anne Askew, otherwise called Anne Kime, made before the Bishop of London, the twentieth day of March, in the year of our Lord God after the computation of the Church of England, 1545, and subscribed with her own hand, in the presence of the said bishop and other, whose names hereafter are recited, set forth and published at this present, to the intent the world may see what credence is now to be given unto the same woman, who in so short a time hath most damnably altered and changed her opinion and belief, and therefore rightfully in open court arraigned and condemned," *Ex. Registrum.*

"Be it known to all faithful people, that as touching the blessed sacrament of the altar, I do firmly and undoubtedly believe, that after the words of consecration be spoken by the priest, according to the common usage of this Church of England, there is present really the body and blood of our saviour Jesus Christ, whether the minister which both consecrate, be a good man, or a bad man, and that also whensoever the said sacrament is received, whether the receiver be a good man or a bad man, he doth receive it really and corporally. And moreover, I do believe, that whether the said sacrament then received of the minister, or else reserved to be put into the pix, or to be brought to any person that is impotent or sick, yet there is the very body and blood of our said saviour: so that whether the minister or the receiver be good or bad, yea whether the sacrament be received or reserved, always there is the blessed body of Christ really.

"And this thing with all other things touching the sacrament and other sacraments of the church, and all things else touching the Christian belief, which are taught and declared in the king's majesty's book lately set forth for the erudition of the Christian people, I Anne Askew, otherwise called Anne Kime, do truly and perfectly believe, and so here presently confess and knowledge. And here I do promise that henceforth I shall never say or do anything against the promises, or against any of them. In witness whereof, I the said Anne have subscribed my name unto these presents. Written the twentieth day of March, in the year of our Lord God 1545." *Ex Registrum.*

By me Anne Askew, otherwise called Anne Kime.

. . .

Here mayest thou note gentle Reader in this confession, both in the bishop and his register: a double sleight of false conveyance. For although the confession purporteth the words of the bishop's writing, whereunto she did not set her hand, yet by the title prefixed before, mayest thou see that both she was arraigned and condemned before this was registered, and also that she is falsely reported to have put to her hand, which indeed by this her own book appeareth not so to be, but after this manner and condition: "I Anne Askew do believe all manner things contained in the faith of the Catholic Church, and not otherwise." It followeth more in the story.

Then because I did add unto it the Catholic Church he flang into his chamber in a great fury. With that my cousin Brittain followed him, desiring him for God's sake to be good Lord unto me. He answered that I was a woman, and that he was nothing deceived in me. Then my cousin Brittain desired him to take me as a woman, and not to set my weak woman's wit to his lordship's great wisdom.

Then went in unto him Doctor Weston, and said, that the cause why I did write there "the Catholic Church," was that I understood not "the church" written afore. So with much ado, they persuaded my Lord to come out again, and to take my name with the names of my sureties, which were my cousin Brittain, and Master Spilman of Gray's Inn.

This being done, we thought that I should have been put to bail immediately according to the order of the law. Howbeit, he would not suffer it, but committed me from thence to prison again, until the next morrow, and then he willed me to appear in the Guildhall, and so I did. Notwithstanding, they would not put me to bail there neither, but read the bishop['s] writing unto me, as before, and so commanded me again to prison.

Then were my sureties appointed to come before them on the next morrow in Paul's Church: which did do indeed. Notwithstanding they would once again have broken off with them because they would not be bound also for another woman at their pleasure, whom they knew not nor yet what matter was laid unto her charge. Notwithstanding at the last, after much ado and reasoning to and fro, they took a bond of them recognizance for my forthcoming. And thus I was at the last delivered.

Written by me Anne Askew.

. . .

Hitherto we have entreated of this good woman. Now it remaineth that we touch somewhat as concerning her end and martyrdom. After that she, being born of such stock and kindred, that she might have lived in great wealth and prosperity, if she would rather have followed the world, than Christ, now had been so tormented, that she could neither live long in so great distress, neither yet by her adversaries be suffered to die in secret: the day of her execution being appointed, she was brought into Smithfield in a chain, because she could not go on her feet, by means of her great torments. When she was brought unto the stake, she was tied by the middle with a chain that held up her body. When all things were thus prepared to the fire, Doctor Shaxton who was then appointed to preach, began his sermon. Anne Askew hearing, and answering again unto him, where he said well, confirmed the same: where he said amiss, there said she, "He misseth, and speaketh without the book."

The sermon being finished, the martyrs standing there tied at three stakes ready to their martyrdom, began their prayers. The multitude and concourse of the people was exceeding, the place where they stood being railed about to keep out the press. Upon the bench under Saint Bartholomew's Church, sat Wriothesley Chancellor of England, the old Duke of Norfolk, the old Earl of Bedford, the Lord Mayor with diverse other more. Before the fire should be set unto them, one of the bench hearing that they had gunpowder about them, and being afraid lest the faggots by strength of the gunpowder would come flying about their ears, began to be afraid, but the Earl of Bedford declaring unto him how the gunpowder was not laid under the faggots, but only about their bodies to rid them out of their pain, which having vent, there was no danger to them of the faggots, so diminished that fear.

Then Wriothesley Lord Chancellor, sent to Anne Askew letters, offering to her the king's pardon, if she would recant. Who refusing once to look upon them, made this answer again: that she came not thither to deny her lord and master. Then were the letters likewise offered unto the other, who in like manner, following the constancy of the woman, denied not only to receive them, but also to look upon them. Whereupon the Lord Mayor commanding fire to be put unto them, cried with a loud voice, "*Fiat justitia.*"

And thus the good Anne Askew with these blessed martyrs, being troubled so many manner of ways, and having passed through so many torments, having now ended the long course of her agonies, being compassed in with flames of fire, as a blessed sacrifice unto God, she slept in the Lord, anno 1546, leaving behind her singular example of Christian constancy for all men to follow.

STUDY QUESTIONS

1. How does Anne Askew appeal to her own reading of the Bible throughout her interrogation?
2. Why were her interrogators so insistent on the point of transubstantiation, and how does this reflect the larger goals of Henry VIII's Church of England in the 1540s?

14.2 OGIER GHISELIN DE BUSBECQ, "THE COURT OF SULEIMAN THE MAGNIFICENT," 1581

Ghiselin (1522–1592) was a Flemish ambassador who represented the Austrian Habsburgs at the court of Suleiman the Magnificent (1520–1566) in Istanbul. In 1581, he published an account of his time among the Ottomans as *Itinera Constantinopolitanum et Amasianum* (*Travels in Constantinople and Asia Minor*). A polymath, a sensitive observer of court politics, and an adventurous intellectual, Ghiselin also discovered a nearly intact copy of the autobiography of the Roman emperor Augustus that had been inscribed at Ankara, and he publicized the contents of this *Monumentum Ancyranum* for scholars around the world—and up to the present day. However, in this segment of his travel narrative, he draws attention to the personal habits and behaviors of a contemporary emperor—and one who saw himself as the heir to the Romans as well as to the other monarchs who had held Constantinople/Istanbul.

The Sultan was seated on a very low ottoman, not more than a foot from the ground, which was covered with a quantity of costly rugs and cushions of exquisite workmanship; near him lay his bow and arrows. His air, as I said, was by no means gracious, and his face wore a stern, though dignified, expression. On entering we were separately conducted into the royal presence by the chamberlains, who grasped our arms. . . . After having gone through a pretense of kissing his hand, we were conducted backwards to the wall opposite his seat, care being taken that we should never turn our backs on him. The Sultan then listened to what I had to say; but the language I held was not at all to his taste, for the demands of his Majesty breathed a spirit of independence and dignity . . . and so he made no answer beyond saying in a tetchy way, "Giusel, giusel," i.e. well, well. . . .

. . .

With all this luxury great simplicity and economy are combined; every man's dress, whatever his position may be, is of the same pattern; no fringes or useless points are sewn on, as is the case with us. . . . They were quite as much surprised at our manner of dressing as we were at theirs. They use long robes reaching down to the ankles, which have a stately effect and add to the wearer's height, while our dress is so short and scanty that it leaves exposed to view more than is comely of the human shape; . . .

I was greatly struck with the silence and order that prevailed in this great crowd. There were no cries, no hum of voices, the usual accompaniments of a motley gathering, neither was there any jostling; without the slightest disturbance each man took his proper place according to his rank. The Agas, as they call their chiefs, were seated, to wit, generals, colonels (*bimbashi*), and captains (*soubashi*). Men of a lower position stood. The most interesting sight in this assembly was a body of several thousand Janissaries, who were drawn up in a long line apart from the rest; their array was so steady and motionless that, being at a little distance, it was some time before I could make up my mind as to whether they were human beings or statues; at last I received a hint to salute them, and saw all their heads bending at the same moment to return my bow.

. . .

Wayne S. Vucinich, *The Ottoman Empire: Its Record and Legacy*. Princeton: Van Nostrand, 1965, pp. 127–9. Wayne S. Vucinich, *The Ottoman Empire: Its Record and Legacy*, Krieger Publishing Company, Malabar, FL © 1979.

When the cavalry had ridden past, they were followed by a long procession of Janissaries, but few of whom carried any arms except their regular weapon, the musket. They were dressed in uniforms of almost the same shape and colour, so that you might recognize them to be the slaves, . . . There is only one thing in which they are extravagant, viz., plumes, head-dresses, etc., and veterans who formed the rear guard were specially distinguished by ornaments of this kind. The plumes which they insert in their frontlets might well be mistaken for a walking forest.

STUDY QUESTIONS

1. Why were order and discipline apparently so important at Suleiman's court?
2. Why might Ghiselin have found the Janissaries particularly impressive?

14.3 FROM CHRISTOPHER MARLOWE, *THE MASSACRE AT PARIS*, CA. 1593

Christopher Marlowe (before 1564–1593) was an Elizabethan poet and playwright, historically connected with Shakespeare's work. Until his mysterious assassination, Marlowe was England's most celebrated dramatist—a title Shakespeare then inherited. His play *Massacre at Paris* describes the horrific event known as the Saint Bartholomew's Day massacre (beginning on August 23, 1572), in which the ruling Catholic majority arranged the simultaneous assassination of the leaders of the dissenting Protestant (Huguenot) party. The surviving manuscript is most likely reconstructed from the memory of the play's actors, but nonetheless gives a glimpse into how deadly religious disagreement could become in early modern France. These scenes show the Catholic Duke of Guise's attempts to limit Huguenot survivors, attitudes toward "heretical" corpses, and concerns about inheritance of the French throne in this era of dramatic turmoil.

GUISE: My Lord of *Anjoy*, there are a hundred
Protestants.
Which we have chased into the river rene,
That swim about and so preserve their lives:
How may we do? i fear me they will live.

DUMAINE: Go place some men upon the bridge,
With bows and darts to shoot at them as
they flee,
And sink them in the river as they swim.
Guise.

Christopher Marlowe, *The Massacre at Paris*. Oxford: The Malone Society Reprints, 1928, lines 504–42, 578–633.

GUISE: Tis well advice *Dumaine*, go see that it be done.
And in the meantime my Lord, could we devise
To get those pedants from the King *Navarre*, that are tutors to him and the prince of *Condy*.

ANJOY: For that let me alone, Cousin stay you here,
And when you see me in, then follow hard. *He knocks, and enter the King of* Navarre *and Prince of* Condy, *with their schoolmasters.*
How now my Lords, how fare you?

NAVARRE: My Lord, they say that all the Protestants are massacred.

ANJOY: I, so they are, but yet what remedy: I have done what I could to stay this broil.

NAVARRE: But yet my Lord the report does run, That you were one that made this Massacre.

AN: Who I, you are deceived, I rose but now.

ENTER GUISE. HENCE.

GUISE: Murder the Hugonets, take those pedants

NA: Thou traitor *Guise*, lay off thy bloody hands.

CONDY: Come let us go tell the King. *Exeunt.*

GUISE: Come sirs, I'll whip you to death with my Dagger's point. *He kills them.*

AN: Away with them both. *Exit* Anjoy.

GUISE: And now sirs for this night let our fury stay.
Yet will we not that the Massacre shall end,
Gonzago posse you to Orleance, *Retes* to Deep,
Mountsorrell unto Roan, and spare not one that you suspect of heresy.
And now stay that bell that to the devils Mattins rings.
Now.

. . .

Enter two with the Admirals *body.* *sc. vii*

1. Now sirra, what shall we do with the Admiral?
2. Why let us burn him for a heretic.
1. O no, his body will infect the fire, and the fire the air, and so we shall be poisoned with him.
2. What shall we do then?
1. Let's throw him into the river.
2. Oh it will corrupt the water, and the water the fish, and by the fish ourselves when we eat them.
1. Then throw him into the ditch.
2. No, no, to decide all doubts, be ruled by me, let's hang him here upon this tree.
1. Agreed. *They hang him.*

Enter the Duke of Guise, and Queen Mother, *and* the Cardinal.

GUISE: Now Madame, how like you our lusty Admiral?

[B 5] *Queen.*

QUEEN: Believe me *Guise* he becomes the place so well, As I could long before this have wished him there.
But come let's walk aside, the air is not very sweet.

GUISE: No by my faith Madam.
Sire, take him away and throw him in some ditch.
carry away the dead body.
And now Madam as I understand,
There are a hundred Hugonets and more,
Which in the woods do horde their synagogue:
And daily meet about this time of day,
And thither will I to put them to the sword.

QU: Do so sweet *Guise*, let us delay no time,
For if these stragglers gather head again,
And disperse themselves throughout the Realm of France,
It will be hard for us to work their deaths.
Be gone, delay no time sweet *Guise*.

GUISE: Madam I go as whirl-winds rage before a storm. *Exit* Guise.

QU: My Lord of Loraine have you marked of late,
How *Charles* our son begins for to lament: For the late nights work which my Lord of *Guise*
Did make in Paris amongst the Hugonites?

CARD: Madam, I have heard him solemnly vow, With the rebellious King of *Navarre*, For to revenge their deaths upon us all.

QU: I, but my Lord let me alone for that, For *Katherine* must have her will in France: As I do live, for surely he die.
And
The Massacre
And *Henry* then shall wear the diadem.
And if he grudge or cross his Mothers will,
I'll disinherit him and all the rest:
For I'll rule France, but they shall wear the crown:
And if they storm, I then may pull them down.
Come my Lord lets us go. *Exeunt.*

STUDY QUESTIONS

1. What seems to be motivating Guise, Anjou, and the Queen Mother Catherine in their deliberations about the impending massacre?
2. How might this play have appealed to Elizabethan English audiences, who had not experienced the French Wars of Religion in the 1570s and 1580s?

14.4 JOHANNES JUNIUS, LETTER TO HIS DAUGHTER AND TRIAL TRANSCRIPT, 1628

Johannes Junius (1573–1628), the mayor of Bamberg, Germany, was accused of witchcraft during the craze of 1628. Before his tragic execution, Junius wrote a moving letter to his daughter Veronica so that she would understand the charges brought against him and the torture he endured. Amid prayers to keep him in God's care, Junius describes false witnesses brought against him, his sufferings, and the lies that he finally "confessed" to no avail. The transcript of his trial has survived as well and permits a glimpse into the terrifying machinery of the witch-hunts.

A hundred thousand Good Nights, my darling Veronica, my daughter. Innocent have I been imprisoned, innocent have I been tortured, and innocent must I die—for whoever comes into this place must become a witch, or else he will be tortured until he invents something (may God have mercy) and confesses to it. I will tell you everything that has happened to me. The first time I was brought before the court Doctor Braun, Doctor Kötzendorffer, and two other doctors whom I did not know were there [SEVERAL WORDS MISSING] Then Doctor Braun asked me from the gallery, "How did you end up here, brother?" "Bad luck," I answered. "Listen!" he said, "You are a witch! Will you confess it freely? If not, they will put witnesses and the executioner in front of you." I said, "I've been betrayed! My conscience is clean. Even if they bring a thousand witnesses, I'm not worried. I'll gladly listen to their witnesses." Then the Chancellor's son was brought forth. I asked him, "Herr Doctor, what do you know about me? I have never seen you before in all my life, whether for good or for bad." And he gave me in answer, "Friend, I know you from the district court. I asked you for a pardon when I appeared before you in court." "Yes, but so what?" He said nothing. So I asked the Lord Commissioner to question him under oath. Doctor Braun said that "he need not do what he does not wish to do; it is enough that he has stated he saw you. Step down now, Herr Doctor!" I said, "My lords, what kind of evidence is that? If that is how this process goes, then how can you be any more sure it was me [he saw] than some other honest man?" But no one would listen to me. Then the Chancellor came up and said that he too, just like his son, had seen me [at a witch-gathering]. But he knew me only by reputation, nothing more. Then came Hopfen-Else, who said she had seen me dance on the Hauptmoor. "With whom?"

From Johannes Junius, "Letter from Prison." Bamberg, 1628. Translation by Clifford Backman.

I asked. She replied that she didn't know. I then swore on oath to the lord justices that what they had heard was all pure lies, so help me God, and that they should ask these witnesses of theirs to be truthful and honest. But they did not wish to know the truth, or else they would have said so; instead they wanted me to confess freely, or else the executioner would drag it out of me. I answered, "I have never renounced God and will never do so. May God in His grace keep me from such a thing! I would rather suffer anything, than that." And that was when—O God in Highest Heaven have pity!—in came the executioner, who tied my hands together and twisted thumbscrews on them until blood flowed out from my nails and all over; for four weeks I couldn't use my hands, as you can see by my writing. I thought about the five Holy Wounds suffered by God and said, since as far as the name and glory of God was concerned I had not renounced them, I would commend my innocence and all my agony and suffering to His Five Wounds. He would ease my pain, so that I could endure any amount of it. But then they hauled me up, hands bound behind my back, and lifted me in the hanging torture. I thought then that heaven and earth were ending. Six times they hoisted me up in this way, and then let me fall. The pain was horrible.

All of this happened while I was stark naked, since they had stripped me and left me that way. Since no one but Our Lord God could help me, I called out to Him, saying, "Forgive them. O God, for they are hurting an innocent man! They care nothing for my life and soul! They only want to seize my wealth and possessions!" Then Doctor Braun said, "You are a devil!" I answered, "I'm no devil or any such thing. I'm as innocent as any one of you! And if anyone doubts me, then no honest man in all of Bamberg is safe—not you, not me, not anyone else!"

The Doctor then cried out that he would not be challenged by a devil. "Neither will I!" I shouted. "But these false witnesses are the devil, and so is this wretched torture of yours—for it lets no one go free, and no one can endure it."

All of this occurred on Friday, 30 June, when I was forced to endure, with God's help, the torture. Throughout that entire time I was strung up and could not use my hands, but suffered pain upon pain despite my innocence. When the executioner finally led me back to my prison cell he said to me, "I beg you, sir! For God's sake, confess to something, whether it's true or not! Invent something—for you won't be able to survive the torturing they plan for you. Even if you do survive, you'll never go free. Not even if you were an earl. It will just be one torture after another, until you confess and say that you are a witch. Only then will they let you go free. That's how all these trials go, each one just like the other."

Sometime after this, Georg came and told me that the Commissioner had declared he wanted to make such an example of me that people would talk about it for a long time. They had already brought in several more torturers, just for me. Georg too pleaded with me, for God's sake, to confess to something, for even if I were entirely innocent I would never again go free. The candle-maker, the lamplighter, and a few others, too, told me the same thing. Since I was in such a sad plight, I asked to be granted a day to think things over and consult with a priest. They denied me a priest but allowed me some time to think.

So now, dear daughter, what do you think about the danger I was in, and still am in? I have to confess to being a witch even though I am not one, and must do for the first time something that I have never before considered—renounce God. I wrestled with myself day and night over this, until finally an idea came to me one night as I was praying, showing how I need not be troubled: since I was denied a priest, with whom I could take counsel, I would simply invent something and say it. How much better it would be to simply confess something by the words of my mouth even though it was not actually true. I could confess my lie later, and the fault would be on those who had forced me to do it. I could explain that I had asked to see a priest from the Dominican cloister but had been refused. And so, here follows my sworn statement—the entire thing a lie. Dearest child, what follows is the affidavit I made on account of the horrible pain, the cruel torture, I suffered and could endure no longer.

In 1624 or 1625 I had gone on city business to the town of Rottweil, and had to carry about six hundred florins with me in order to conduct some legal affairs on behalf of Doctor Braun and the city—which is why I had taken counsel with so many honest people who had helped me out. Everything that follows appears in my affidavit, but is nothing but a pure lie—a lie I told in light of the horrible, monstrous torture that compelled me, and for which I now must die. In my affidavit it says that I went into my field at Friedrichsbrunnen, and was so troubled that I had to sit down. While I was there a peasant girl approached and asked, "What's wrong, sir? Why are you so sad?" "I don't know," I replied. She drew closer to me and did several things to me that resulted in my lying with her, and no sooner was this done than she turned into a goat and said, "Behold, now you can see who you've been dealing with." Then he grabbed me by the throat and said, "You must be mine now, or else I'll kill you!" "God save me!" I cried. He disappeared suddenly, then just as suddenly he reappeared with two women and two men at his side. I was forced to renounce God, which I did, and at the same time I renounced the Lord of Heaven. After this, he baptized me—and the two women he had brought became my godmothers. Then they gave me a gold coin as a token, but it was really just a potsherd. It seemed to me that I had survived, for they then led me to stand alongside the executioner. Where was I during the dances? I confessed then and there, after giving it some thought, what I had heard from the Chancellor, his son, and Hopfen-Else, and all the elders of the court, the council-room: the Hauptmoor—just as I had heard in the reading of the initial charges against me. So that was the name of the site that I gave.

Next I was told to identify the people I had seen there. I said that I had not recognized anyone. "You devil! I'll put the executioner at your throat! Tell us! Wasn't the Chancellor there?" I said he was. "Who else?" I said I hadn't recognized anyone else. So he said, "Take one street after another; start at the market then go up one street and down the next." I had to name a few people at least. Then came the long street—I had to name at least one person there. Next the Zinkenwörth—one person more. Then over the upper bridge to both sides of the Bergtor. I knew nobody. Did I recognize anyone from the castle, anyone at all? I should speak without fear. They carried on this way for street after street, but there was nothing more I could or would say, so they handed me over to the executioner, saying that he should strip me, cut off all my hair, and start to torture me again. "This devil knows someone in the market, sees him every day, and yet refuses to identify him!" They meant Dietmeyer—so I had to identify him too.

Then they made me tell what evils I had committed. "None," I replied, "the Devil had wanted me to do something, but I had refused, and so he beat me." "Haul the fellow up!" So I said that I was supposed to murder my own children, but I had killed a horse instead. That didn't help, though, [so I said that] I had also taken a piece of the Host and had desecrated it. Once I had said this, they left me in peace.

Dear child, you now have my entire confession and the reasons for which I must die. They are nothing but lies and imaginings, so help me God. I said all these things out of fear of the wretched torture that was threatened beyond what I had already suffered; they never stop with the torturing until one confesses something. No matter how pious a man might be, he will confess to being a witch. No one escapes, not even a lord. If God allows no remedy that would let the light of day shine through, the whole family is done for. One has to denounce other people, even if one knows nothing at all about them, as I have had to do—and God in Heaven knows that I know next to nothing about [the people I accused]. I die an innocent man, like a martyr. Dearest child, I know that you are every bit as devout as I am, but even you have told a few lies in your time, and if I may be permitted to give you some advice: take all the money and letters you have [SEVERAL WORDS MISSING] and devote half a year to a holy pilgrimage, and do everything you can, in that time period, to [SEVERAL WORDS MISSING]. I recommend doing this until it becomes clear that your resources have run out. This way, at least, there will be some honest men and women in Bamberg, both in the church and in the world of business—people who do not know evil and who have clean consciences, as I once was (as you know) before my arrest. Nevertheless, they very well may find themselves in the witch-prison; for all it takes is for a rumor about an individual to go around, no matter if he is honest or not. Herr Neudecker, the Chancellor, his son, the candle-maker, the daughter of Wolff Hoffmeister, and Hopfen-Else have all testified against me, all at the same time. Their testimony was all false, drawn out of them by force, as they all told me later when they begged my forgiveness in God's name before they were executed. Their last words to me were that they knew nothing but good of me. They had been forced to lie, just as I was. I am done for, for sure. That's how it is for many people now, and will be for many more yet to come, if God does not shine a path out of this darkness. I have nothing more to say.

Dear child, hide this letter so that no one ever sees it. Or else I will be tortured yet again, and piteously; more than that, my jailers would be beheaded—so strongly is it forbidden [to smuggle out letters]. Herr Steiner, my cousin, is familiar to you—you can trust him and [SEVERAL WORDS MISSING] him read it. He is a discreet man.

Dear child, pay this man a Reichstaler [SEVERAL WORDS MISSING].

It has taken me several days to write this, since my hands are broken. I am in a wretched state. I beg you, in the light of Judgment Day, to keep this letter safe, and to pray for me, your father, as you would for a true martyr. After my death, do as you wish but be careful not to let anyone see this letter. Please ask Anna Maria also to pray for me. You can swear it on oath that I was not a witch but a martyr, and that I died as such.

A thousand times Good Night. Your father, Johannes Junius, will never see you again. 24 July 1628.

STUDY QUESTION

1. Why does Junius fail to convince his accusers of his innocence of witchcraft?

CHAPTER 15

FROM WESTPHALIA TO PARIS: REGIMES OLD AND NEW

15.1 ANNE OF FRANCE, *LESSONS FOR MY DAUGHTER*, 1560–1600

"Madame la Grande," as she was called, was the daughter of King Louis XI of France and briefly the regent for her brother Charles VIII. Anne (1461–1522) was an able stateswoman who managed royal lands and the ducal territories of her husband and oversaw the education and raising of aristocratic offspring. In this vein, Anne wrote a handbook for her only daughter, Suzanne, guiding her through the courtly gauntlet. Like Dhuoda's handbook to her son (Document 8.6), Anne here attempts to help her daughter avoid the pitfalls of courtly life—but in this case, a woman's worst enemies are frivolity, immodesty, and a quick tongue. The Dr. Lienard referred to several times in this passage cannot be identified.

And so, my daughter, devote yourself completely to acquiring virtue. Behave so that your reputation may be worthy of perpetual memory: whatever you do, above all, be truly honest, humble, courteous, and loyal. Believe firmly that if even a small fault or lie were to be found in you, it would be a great reproach. As Doctor Lienard writes in his argument about lying, it is the worst of all the vices, foul and dishonest to God and the world. Now then, my daughter, if you would like to be numbered among worthy women and to have a good and honest reputation, be very careful to avoid it. And as Socrates says, do not be like those foolish idlers who, in their idiocy, think themselves wise and worthy when they deceive and abuse many people with their evil and venomous cunning, which is detestable to God and abominable to the world. And as the aforementioned Doctor Lienard says, no man or woman of great rank who has good judgment wants to have such a reputation. And he also says there are many dishonest and evil nobles in the world today who come from good families and have a large following, but, to speak frankly and truthfully, those who follow them are either fools or have business with them. Be assured, as the aforesaid doctor says, that if their followers flatter them to their faces, they damn them behind their backs. Finally, as Saint Ambrose says, whatever pretenses they make and however long it takes, in the end such people are neither loved by

Translation by Clifford Backman.

God nor by the world. Wise men say you should fly from them as if they were poison no matter how pleasing their greetings and no matter how charming their pastimes—in the end, associating with them is too perilous. And so, my daughter, protect yourself from them and their deceptive company.

. . .

And so, my daughter, because virtues and good works are as well praised, loved, and valued in this world as they are in the next, you should take great pains to be virtuous; to this end, make sure that your conversation is always honest and good, that you are courteous and amiable in all things, and that you are pleasant to all and loved by all. And, truly, when it comes to love, the Philosopher says honesty must be its foundation because any other "love" is only false treachery and hypocrisy—with all the authority and power that a mother can and should have over a daughter, I command you to flee from such love. It is important to control your bearing, your expressions, your words, your sentiments, your thoughts, your desires, your wishes, and your passions. As Saint Paul says, of all the temptations and subtle deceptions in the world, this is one of the worst, and from such "love" comes great evil, so dishonestly is it practiced today. As many doctors agree, there is no man of worth, however, noble he may be, who does not use treachery, nor to whom it does not seem good sport to deceive or trick women of rank from one good family or another, it doesn't matter which. And Doctor Lienard says there is no man so perfect who, in matters of love, is truthful or keeps his word, however firm or fervent—which I certainly believe. One time I heard a noblewoman of great rank tell about a knight she knew who, in such a situation, took a solemn oath of his own free will, on his honor as a gentleman, on the altar and on a missal where Mass is said everyday—and this knight did not keep his oath for more than four hours! And, as she told me, the oath was very reasonable and, with all respect to his honor and conscience, he had no excuse whatsoever for breaking it except his own lust, weak will, and sudden change of heart. Therefore, my daughter, whatever flattering speeches or great signs of love that someone may make you, trust none of them. As Doctor Lienard says, those who are wisest and think they are following the right path are often the first to be misled. . . . Although, certainly, it must be said that when those of virtuous character come together, by one means or another, love can be marvelously great and, in the end, good and honest. But when this does happen, as Doctor Lienard says at the end of his argument about true love, the enemy, who is full of venomous subtlety, uses his power to break and distance such love because of the great goods and honors that result from it. . . . Therefore, for the greatest certainty in such situations, I advise you to avoid all private meetings, no matter how pleasant they are, because, as you have seen, many an honest beginning comes to a dishonest and harmful end. And even when it seems all is for the best, you must also fear the foolish and the irresponsible opinions others often express, to the prejudice of women and at their expense. As Doctor Lienard says, in this situation and in others, the world is so vile and so corrupt that true love is hardly understood or recognized.

. . .

For this reason, my daughter, heed this example and, wherever you are, avoid making any unpleasant faces and shaking or turning your head this way and that, and do not stare, peer around you, or let your eyes wander. Also, make sure you do not laugh too much for any reason because it is very unbecoming, especially for young noblewomen, whose manners should be more solemn, gentler, and more controlled than the manners of others. Nor should you talk too much or too sharply like many foolish and conceited women who want to attract attention and, to be more admired, speak boldly and in a flighty way, responding to everyone and on all topics, which is very unbecoming in all women, whatever their state, but especially so for young virgins, rich and poor alike, who must protect their reputations. Because of their careless talk, many young women are judged to be foolish and unchaste; as one philosopher says, the way a woman minds her eyes and her tongue is an indication of her chastity. For this reason, my daughter, always use your eyes and tongue cautiously and carefully; that is, know when to speak and where your eyes belong, never be the first or the last to talk, and do not be a tale-teller, especially of anything unpleasant or prejudicial. Also, be slow and cool in all your responses because, as wise men say, on some subjects a reply cannot be avoided. Also, take care not to run or jump, and do not pinch or hit anyone. Likewise suffer no man to touch your body, no matter who he is, no holding of hands or pressing of feet. In conclusion, my daughter, remember those three aforementioned daughters who were the cause of their mother's death, and do not behave so that your bad conduct is the cause of mine.

. . .

I do not wish to say that . . . in hearing, speaking, and responding to honest questions and proposals you might not sometimes encounter the bad as well as the good. But, suppose a castle is beautiful and so well-guarded that it is never assailed—then it is not to be praised, nor is a knight who has never proven himself to be commended for his prowess. To the contrary, the thing most highly commended is that which has been in the fire yet cannot be scorched (or worse) or that which has been in the terrible depths of the sea yet cannot be drowned or that which has been in the mire of this world yet cannot be soiled in any way. Worthy of being praised, therefore, are women who in this miserable world know to live in purity of conscience and chastity; they are worthy of eternal glory because by their steadfast chastity and good virtue they redirect fools, disordered in their carnality, to the good road. As the saying goes, the habit does not make the monk, and sometimes those you think are the biggest deceivers and the most worldly are easiest to convert and are then greatly to be commended. Nevertheless, in this situation there is no certainty, and I counsel more doubt than surety. As Saint Paul says, the assaults and stings of this world are hard to endure except with the help of God, with which nothing is impossible.

STUDY QUESTIONS

1. Is it even more essential for women to channel their thoughts and words into virtuous paths than for their male counterparts?
2. How can a woman avoid scandalous talk, even if standards of behavior are applied unequally to females?

15.2 MOLIÈRE, *THE MISANTHROPE*, FIRST PERFORMED 1666

An actor who abandoned social prestige for the stage, Jean-Baptiste Poquelin (1622–1673), better known as Molière, numbers among the greatest comedy playwrights. His plays incorporated traits of *commedia dell'arte* while poking fun at the foibles of humankind—such as the hypochondriac obsessions of the main character in his popular *The Imaginary Invalid*. *The Misanthrope*, another comedy of manners, centers around the plight of Alceste, who adores the flirtatious Célimène while simultaneously condemning her for blindly obeying social niceties, such as politeness toward strangers. When he ultimately discovers that Célimène has led him on, Alceste decides that self-imposed exile from society is the only solution to his misanthropic loathing.

Molière, *The Misanthrope, Tartuffe, and Other Plays*. Translated by Maya Slater. Oxford: Oxford University Press, 2009, 1397w from pp. 209–13. By permission of Oxford University Press.

ACT I, SCENE 1

ALCESTE, PHILINTE

PHILINTE: Oh, what's the matter? What's wrong now?
ALCESTE: Leave me alone.
Go away.
PHILINTE: But why must you adopt this angry tone? . . .
ALCESTE: Oh, leave me here, I said. Go, run away and hide.
PHILINTE: Alceste, don't lose your temper. Listen, then decide.
ALCESTE: I want to lose my temper, and to make a stand.
PHILINTE: I find your angry rantings hard to understand.
Although we're still good friends, I really must insist . . .
ALCESTE: What? Me, your friend? Why don't you cross me off your list?
It's true I've always made a show of liking you;
But now I've witnessed your behaviour, we're through.
I tell you, I don't want your friendship any more—
I hate you, now I know you're rotten to the core.
PHILINTE: You seem to have decided I'm the one to blame . . .
ALCESTE: That's right. Why don't you crawl away and die of shame?
I'm telling you, there's no excuse for what you've done—
Your antics must seem scandalous to everyone.
You met a man, you treated him as your best friend,
You were all over him, you hugged him without end,
You said he mattered to you, swore by Heaven above
That what you felt for him was liking, even love.
I asked you for the fellow's name, when he had gone,
And you scarcely remembered who he was—come on!
No sooner had he turned his back on you, I swear,
You spoke of him to me, as if you didn't care.
Good grief! The way you carry on is a disgrace.
You worthless coward, must you really be so base?
If I had done what you've just done, do you know what
I'd do? I'd go and hang myself, right on the spot.
PHILINTE: Come on, it's not a hanging matter, so don't tease.
I beg leave to appeal against my sentence, please.
It's time you showed some mercy. Don't be quite so hard.
What, make me hang myself for that? What a charade!
ALCESTE: Oh, very funny! That was typical of you.
PHILINTE: But, seriously, what am I supposed to do?
ALCESTE: You should be honourable, honest, without art,
And everything you say should come straight from the heart.
PHILINTE: But when a stranger rushes up and hugs you tight,
You have to hug him back—it seems only polite;
You can't keep him at arm's length, you must play the game,
And if he swears you're his best friend, you do the same.
ALCESTE: No. Your hypocrisy disgusts me, and that's flat.
You fashionable types, you all behave like that.
I tell you, I can't stand the phoney posturing
Of men who claim they like you more than anything,
And fling their arms around you, kiss you on the cheek,
Insist that they adore you, every time they speak.
They've perfect manners, and they obey the rules,
But decent men are treated on a par with fool.
Look, I mean, what's the point of someone kissing you,
And swearing he appreciates and loves you too,
Proclaiming to the world that you're the only one,
Then rushing off to do the same to everyone?
No. If a man who has the slightest self-respect
Is faced with such hypocrisy, he must object.
For very little's added to our sense of worth
If we're the same as all the others on this earth.
If you respect a man, believing he's the best,
Don't put him on an equal footing with the rest.
Now you're no different from the other fellows, so,
Damn it, you're not the sort of man I want to know.
I can't value a friend who puts himself about,
And doesn't see why merit should be singled out.

I want to be distinguished from the rest, you see:
The friend of all humanity's no friend to me.
PHILINTE: But, in polite society, you have to do
Your bit, or people won't think very well of you.
ALCESTE: Nonsense! I say, the time has come to make a stand
Against these hypocrites. I want them to be banned.
I want us to be proper men, and when we meet,
To show our secret, inner thoughts, without deceit.
We must speak from the heart, lay bare our sentiments,
Not hide the truth with empty, formal compliments.
PHILINTE: It won't work. There are times when total frankness would
Be idiotic, totally misunderstood.
And sometimes, even if we find it an ordeal,
It's better to suppress the truth of what we feel.
Truth can be inappropriate; most people shrink
From telling everyone precisely what they think.
What if we know someone we hate, or find uncouth—
Are we supposed to tell the whole, unvarnished truth?
ALCESTE: Yes.
PHILINTE: What, you want to go to poor old Emilie,
And tell her she's too old to dress so prettily—
With all that make-up, she looks like a painted whore?
ALCESTE: That's right.
PHILINTE: Should we tell Dorilas he's a great bore?
The courtiers hate the way he shows off endlessly,
And boasts about his courage, and his pedigree.
ALCESTE: We should.
PHILINTE: You must be joking.
ALCESTE: Joking? not at all.
I tell you, we must spare nobody, great or small.
My eyes are never spared, at court or in the town:
I'm always shaving to see sights that make me frown.
It puts me in a rage, to see what I detest:
The way men treat each other makes me so depressed.
Hypocrisy is everywhere, and flattery,
And crude self-interest, and even treachery.
I've had enough. Mankind's an absolute disgrace.
I'll make a stand, alone against the human race.
PHILINTE: Your grim philosophy is too morose by half.
Your fits of black depression simply make me laugh.
It strikes me we resemble, in a curious way,
The brothers in *The School for Husbands*, Molière's play,
Who . . .
ALCESTE: Good God! Some comparison. Please, let that drop.
PHILINTE: Fine. Let's be serious. I'm asking you to stop
This madness. You won't change the world with what you do,
And since this frankness seems to have such charms for you,
I tell you, frankly, you've become so querulous,
That, nowadays, the world finds you ridiculous.
You turn your nose up, claim our modern manners shock,
But everyone around thinks you're a laughingstock.
ALCESTE: Well, good, damn it! Yes, good! I ask for nothing more.
I'm quite delighted, that's what I've been hoping for.
Since everyone I know seems hateful in my eyes,
I'd be disgusted, if they thought that I was wise.
PHILINTE: Why blame the human race? You're eaten up with hate.
ALCESTE: It overwhelms me totally—I'm desperate.
PHILINTE: You say you loathe us all, without exception, and
There's not a single human being you can stand?
Can't you imagine any situation when . . .?
ALCESTE: No. My disgust is general. I hate all men—
Hate some of them because they are in an evil crew,
And others for condoning what the villains do,
Instead of treating them with loathing and contempt,
As they deserve. They might at least make an attempt
To judge that fellow who's no better than he ought,

I mean the filthy beast who's taken me to court:
His wickedness shines out behind his bland façade,
And everybody knows his manner's a charade.
He sighs and rolls his eyes, and mouths his platitudes,
But no one's taken in, save idiots or prudes.
Confound him! He's got his flat foot in every door.
He gets on in the world by dirty tricks, what's more.
He does so well, living off his ill-gotten gains,
Ironically, he's rewarded for his pains—
He has some sort of title, which he likes to use,
But all his posturing can't alter people's views.
Call him confounded liar, no one will object;
Say he's a fraud, and nobody will contradict.
Yet, with his smirking face, he gets himself received
In the best circles, though his hosts are not deceived.
He knows all the right people, so he always wins.
He beats his rivals, though he can't conceal his sins.
Yes, curse him, every time! It cuts me to the quick
To see him get away with every dirty trick.
Sometimes, it overwhelms me. I feel mortified
By all mankind, and long to run away and hide.

STUDY QUESTIONS

1. How does Alceste skewer the phoniness and hypocrisy of "polite society"?
2. What does he believe will happen, even if the essentially fraudulent nature of this society is exposed?

15.3 CARDINAL RICHELIEU, "THE ROLE OF THE KING," *POLITICAL TESTAMENT*, CA. 1638, FIRST PUBLISHED 1688

Armand Jean du Plessis (1585–1642), the Duke of Richelieu and a Catholic bishop, became the first minister for King Louis XIII. He worked to centralize the French state at the expense of the nobility and factions; this included curtailing the political liberties of the Huguenots but supporting them in the Thirty Years' War (1618–1648) to limit Austrian and Spanish power before a strong French king. His *Political Testament*, one of many works, would have served as a guide for the young Louis XIII in case Richelieu fell victim to one of his frequent illnesses—which explains its hasty, jotted-down feel. This selection outlines the proper role of the king in Richelieu's vision of a strongly centralized France.

God is the principle of all things, the sovereign master of kings, and the only one who can make their reigns happy. If the devotion of Your Majesty were not known to all, I would begin this chapter, which is concerned with your person, by stating to you that should you not follow the wishes of your Creator and submit to His laws you could not hope to have yours observed by subjects obedient to your orders.

But it would be a superfluous gesture to exhort Your Majesty in the matter of devotion. You are so bent toward it by inclination and so confirmed in it by virtuous habit that there is no reason to fear you might turn away from it. It is because of this that in place of showing you the advantage religious principles have over others I will content myself with observing that although devotion is necessary for kings, it ought to be devoid of all over-scrupulousness. I say this, Sire, because the sensitiveness of Your Majesty's conscience has often made you fear to offend God in reaching even those decisions which you cannot abstain from making without sin.

I well know that faults of such a nature in a prince are much less dangerous for a state than those which lean in the direction of presumption and disrespect toward that which a monarch should revere. But since they are faults, it is necessary to correct them, as it is most certain that they have resulted in many inconveniences prejudicial to the interests of the state. I beseech you, in this matter, to try to fortify yourself against your scruples, reminding yourself that you can never be guilty in the eyes of God if, on occasions involving difficult discussions of matters of conscience, you follow the advice of your council, confirmed by that of several competent theologians not suspected of having an interest in the question.

The basic problem recognized, there remains nothing else of a personal nature intrinsically necessary to the successful conducting of your affairs save the preservation of your health, and I cannot go on without giving it special emphasis. Long, thorough, and persistent observation of your conduct in all sorts of circumstances emboldens me to say that nothing is more important than the proper direction of your will, which otherwise can be a most powerful enemy, as it so often is with princes who cannot be prevailed upon to do not only what is useful but what is even absolutely necessary. Your Majesty's mind so completely dominates your body that the slightest emotional upset affects your whole being. Many occurrences of this have made me so certain of the truth of my diagnosis that I am convinced I have never seen you ill in any other way.

God has seen fit to give Your Majesty the force of character necessary to act with firmness when confronted with business of the greatest importance. But as a balance to this noble quality He has often allowed you to be sensitive to matters so small that no one in advance would suspect they might trouble you and thus try to protect you from their bothersome quality. So far, time alone has provided the only remedy for these overwhelming experiences of which the inward consequence has always been a bodily indisposition. You are, in this regard, much like those whose great courage makes them disdain the blows of a sword but who cannot, because of a certain natural antipathy, stand the puncture of the scalpel. It is impossible for many men to anticipate the surprises which will come from their emotions. I do not think, however, that such is the case with Your Majesty, who has many excellent qualities most people do not have. I believe that, in all likelihood, the first ebullience of your ardent youth having passed, the stability of a greater maturity will help you protect yourself by forethought in the future from an enemy which is all the more dangerous because it is internal and domestic, and which has already caused you misfortune serious enough on two or three occasions to have brought your life in jeopardy.

Just as this is a matter of great importance for your health, so is it also for your reputation and glory, for which it should always appear that reason prevailed over your emotions. I cannot help repeating again a plea that I have made many times before to Your Majesty, begging you to apply yourself to the matters of greatest importance to your country, disdaining the little ones as beneath your thought and interest. It would be useful and inspiring for you to dwell often upon the vast prospects of the trend of events. If you preoccupy yourself with the small matters, you will not only fail to gain benefit therefrom, you will even bring misfortune upon yourself. Not only does such a preoccupation divert you from a better one.

Just as little thorns are more capable of pricking than larger ones, which are more easily seen, so it would be impossible for you to protect yourself from many unpleasant happenings inconsequential for public business and bad for your own health.

The great emotional outbursts to which you have been subject on several occasions urge me to tell you here, as I have earlier done more than once, that while there are certain public charges necessary to the furtherance of state affairs which you must perform, there are others the performance of which can do no less than destroy the good disposition of whoever plunges into them. This in turn so adversely affects those charged with carrying out decisions that they too are less able to do what is expected of them. The experience of governing that Your Majesty has acquired from a reign which thus far has lasted twenty-five years makes you well aware of the fact that the outcome of large undertakings rarely confirms directly with the orders initially given. It also teaches you that you might better have compassion for those charged with the execution of your commands when their efforts do not succeed, rather than to blame them for the poor results for which they may not be responsible. It is only God whose acts are infallible, and yet His goodness is such that, letting men act as their weakness directs, He even so overlooks the gulf between their deeds and His standards. This should teach kings to tolerate with patient reasonableness what the Creator endured assuredly because of His benevolence.

Your Majesty being by nature delicate, with a weak constitution, and a restless, impatient disposition, particularly when you are with the army where you always insist on taking the command, I believe it would be committing a crime if I did not beseech you to avoid war in the future in as far as it is possible. This plea I base upon the fact that the frivolousness and unreliability of the French can generally be overcome only by their master's presence and that Your Majesty cannot, without endangering your health, commit yourself to a program of long duration with the hope of success. You have made the valor and strength of your arms well enough known to entitle you in the future to think only of how to enjoy the peace your efforts have brought to the realm, while ever being on the alert to defend it against all those who might break their pledge and attack it again.

Although it is common enough with many men to act only when driven by some emotion, so that one may conceive of them as being like incense which smells sweet only when it is being burned, I cannot help reminding Your Majesty that such a character trait is dangerous in any kind of person, and it is particularly so in kings, who more than all others should be motivated by reason. If emotion once in a while does in fact bring good results, it is only a matter of luck, since by its very nature it misleads men so much that it blinds those who are possessed by it. If a man so deprived of sight occasionally does find the proper course, it is a marvel if he does not stray and get lost completely. And if he does not fall down he will certainly need the best of good fortune not to falter many times. Often indeed have evils befallen princes and their countries when they have been more inclined to follow their emotions than their minds, especially when guided by their whims rather than by considerations of the public interest. Because of this is it impossible for me not to beg Your Majesty to reflect frequently on this matter in order to confirm more and more in yourself your natural tendency to do the right thing.

I also plead with you to think often of how I have reminded you many times that there is no prince in a worse position than he who, not always able to do those things by himself which it is nevertheless his duty to perform, finds it even harder to let others do them for him. The capability of allowing himself to be served is not one of the least qualities a great king should have. Without this quality, opportunities are often quickly and senselessly lost when favorable action could be taken in settling matters for the advancement of the state.

The late king, your father, being in dire extremity, paid with kind words those who served him, accomplishing with caresses what his lack of funds would not permit him to encourage by other means. Your Majesty is unable to follow the late king in this practice, not being of the same make-up, having instead a natural dryness which you inherited from your mother the Queen, who herself has told you this in my presence several times. I cannot help reminding you that the public interest requires that you treat with consideration those who serve you, and at the least it is wise for you to be particularly careful not to say anything that would offend them.

Since I am going to deal later with the subject of the liberality princes should exercise I will say no more about it here, but I will dwell a bit on the bad effects which result from the remarks of those who speak too loosely about their subjects. The blows from a sword are easily healed. But it is not the same with blows of the tongue, especially if they be from the tongue of a king, whose authority renders the pain almost without remedy unless it be provided by the king himself. The higher a stone is thrown, the greater its striking force when it returns. There are many who would give no thought to being cut to pieces by the enemies of their master but who cannot suffer the slightest scratch from his hand. Just as flies do not constitute the diet of the eagle, so the lion is contemptuous of all animals with less than his strength. Likewise, a man who attacked a child would be blamed by everyone. In similar fashion, I make bold to say, a great king should never insult his subordinates since they too are relatively weak. History is full of the unfortunate episodes which have resulted from the excessively free rein great men have given to their tongues, causing the unhappiness of those they considered beneath them.

God has seen fit to so endow Your Majesty as to make it natural for you not to do evil, and such being the case, it is only reasonable that you should carefully guard what you say, so that even your words will give no offense. I am sure, in this matter, that you will not by intent speak offensively, but it is difficult for you not to act impulsively, and sudden waves of emotion occasionally overtake you when you least expect them. I would not be your loyal servant if I did not warn you that both your reputation and your interests require that you have a particular care with regard to them, because such looseness of the tongue, while it may not disturb your conscience, can do much harm to your affairs. Just as to speak well of your enemies is an heroic virtue, so also a prince cannot speak offensively about those who would lay down their lives a thousand times for him and his interests without committing a great fault against the laws of Christianity, to say nothing of those of political wisdom.

A king who has clean hands, a pure heart, and a gentle tongue is not of little virtue, and he who has the first two qualities so eminently as Your Majesty, can with great facility acquire the third. As it is part of the grandeur of kings to be so reserved in their speech that nothing comes out of their mouths which could give offense to their subordinates, so too it is prudent to say nothing derogatory about the principal governmental agencies. Indeed, they should be so spoken of as to give occasion for the belief they are held in high regard. The most important undertakings of state so frequently require that they be thwarted, that prudence itself indicates they should be pampered in lesser matters.

It is not enough for great princes to resolve never to speak evil of anyone. Good sense requires that they also close their ears to slander and false information, pursuing and even banishing authors as most dangerous plagues, often capable of poisoning the hearts of princes, as well as the minds of all those who approach them. All those who have free access to the ears of kings, without meriting it, are dangerous, and those who possess their hearts out of pure favoritism are even more so, for in order to preserve such a great treasure it is necessary to have recourse to artifice and malice, in default of the true virtues which invariably are lacking in such people.

I am compelled to say further in this matter that I have always been more apprehensive about the power of such influences over Your Majesty than of the world's greatest kings, and you have more need to guard yourself from the artifice of a valet who wants to take you by surprise than of all the factions the high nobles might form within your realm, even if they should have a common goal. When I first entered your service, I learned that those who previously had the honor of serving you were absolutely convinced you were easily persuaded to suspect them, and having such a conviction their principal care was ever to keep their agents close to you to counteract the suspected evil. The fact of the firmness of Your Majesty in supporting me obliges me to recognize either that this judgment was without foundation or else that mature reflection has erased your youthful weakness. Even so, I cannot help beseeching you to strengthen this trait in your character so that the attitude you have been pleased to take toward me will be the one naturally expected by anyone who may succeed me. In addition, I must also say to you that just as the ears of princes ought to be closed to calumny, so also should they be open to all truths useful to the state, and in like manner just as their tongues should never give utterance to words prejudicial to the reputation of others, so they should be able to speak freely and boldly when questions of public interest are at stake.

STUDY QUESTIONS

1. How does the cardinal mix flattery with sound advice?
2. Did Richelieu have an interest in warning the king against listening to gossip about his subordinates?

15.4 JEAN DOMAT, *THE CIVIL LAW AND ITS NATURAL ORDER*, 1689

Jean Domat (1625–1696) was a lawyer and legal scholar who served as royal prosecutor in the city of Clermont from 1655 to 1683, after which he retired to his study and dedicated himself to compiling his massive legal code. Apart from reordering the bulk of the Roman law tradition, Domat's work is significant for its concern to emphasize natural law as the basis for civil law—that is, the idea that law arises from, and represents, the innate moral values of a society. Although he accepted the then-popular idea of the divine right of kings to rule, Domat presents law as an organic system over which the king presides but which does not emanate from him.

It is well-known that human society forms a kind of organic body, of which each person forms a part—and this truth, as the Bible has shown and the light of reason makes clear, is the foundation upon which all the duties and obligations that govern all men's actions toward one another individually and toward the body as a whole is based. These duties, moreover, are nothing less than the prescribed functions expected of each person, whatever his position in society. In this principle we find the origin of those laws that determine the duties of those who govern and of those who are governed. . . . As the Lord commands everyone to faithfully obey the precepts of His law that pertain to everyone, so does He command every person to faithfully obey the precepts that pertain to whatever specific condition or status

Jean Domat, "Le droit public, suite des lois civiles dans leur ordre naturel." In *Oeuvres completes, nouvelle edition revue corrigée*, vol. 3, edited by Joseph Remy. Paris: Firmin-Didot, 1829, pp. 1–2, 15–21, 26–27, 35, 39, 40, 44–5. Translation by Clifford Backman.

he holds in the body politic. . . . But since, in their fundamental nature, all men are equal simply by virtue of being human, nature does not decree that any one person is subject to another. . . . Within this state of natural equality, however, individuals are differentiated by various qualities that result in their being of unequal status, and thus people must develop relationships and dependencies that determine their duties toward each other. Thus, government is made necessary.

And since government, as established by God, is necessary for the good of society, it is therefore also incumbent upon all who are subject to it to submit to it and obey it—for if not, they would be resisting God Himself, and government (which ought to be the guarantor of peace and unity and the mainstay of the public good) would become the cause of division and conflict, and thus bring about its own downfall. . . .

To obey a government entails accepting its laws as laws, not attempting any action that runs counter to them, performing whatever action they require, avoiding all that they forbid, shouldering the public responsibilities they assign—whether in terms of serving in office or in payment of taxes—and in general to accept the obligation not to disturb public order but to endorse and assist it as one's circumstances allow.

Such obedience being necessary to maintain the harmonious order that should unite the head and other members that make up the state, it remains an essential duty for all subjects to obey without question the ruler's commands, without presuming to judge which orders they will or will not obey. For if everyone had the right to determine what is or is not justice, then every person would in effect be his own master—and sedition would arise. . . .

Among the rights given to the sovereign by the law is the right to possess and display whatever accoutrements of grandeur and majesty he needs to make known the tremendous authority and dignity of the all-encompassing power he possesses, in order to impress upon the minds of his subjects a proper attitude of veneration. . . . For it is by God's grace that He invests His power in sovereigns, and He permits rulers to adorn the authority He gives them with whatever seems to them to be appropriate, as a means of assuring the people's respect. This can be best achieved by having an aura of splendor radiate from their magnificent palaces, amid other visible signs of that splendor. . . .

The primary and most absolute of all the duties owed by those to whom God has entrusted the power of government is this: to acknowledge that they hold all of their power from God Himself, that it is His place they are taking, that it is through Him that they govern, and that it is God to Whom they should turn for guidance and wisdom in the matter of governing. May these truths form the foundation of all their conduct, and guide all of their actions in the performance of their duties. . . . [duties which include]: maintaining public order throughout the state, the peaceful lives of his subjects and the peace of mind of their families, care for every matter that pertains to the common good, the selection of capable ministers who love justice and truth, the appointment of worthy men to all public offices. . . . the discreet application of either severity or mercy in cases where the strong hand of justice may perhaps be restrained. . . . the good administration of public finances, prudence in relations with foreign states—in all, everything that can make government a blessing to good people, a terror to the wicked, and a worthy exemplar to Heaven's mandate to govern.

STUDY QUESTIONS

1. What metaphor does Domat use to present natural law?
2. How would Louis XIV—who ruled France when Domat composed *Civil Laws According to the Natural Order*—have responded to Domat's view of law as an organic system over which the king presides but which does not emanate from him?

15.5 FRANÇOIS FÉNELON, *THE ADVENTURES OF TELEMACHUS*, 1699

A Catholic priest and writer, François Fénelon (1651–1715) was enlisted by the church to preach to French Protestants (Huguenots) to bring them back to orthodox belief. His bestseller work, *The Adventures of Telemachus*, adds to the story of the *Odyssey* (see Document 3.2) by describing the travels of Odysseus's son, Telemachus. Guiding Telemachus is his tutor, simply called Mentor (but later revealed as Diana, goddess of wisdom), who explains the tenets of a truly good society—one that abolished government, upheld the brotherhood of citizens, and looked back to ancient Greece as a model. Thus, Telemachus served as a fierce criticism of the rule of the Sun King, Louis XIV of France (1638–1715).

The bark now touched the dominions of Pluto, and the shades ran down in crowds to the shore, gazing, with the utmost curiosity and wonder, at the living mortal who stood distinguished among the dead in the boat; but, the moment Telemachus set his foot on the shore, they vanished like the darkness of night before the first beams of morning. Then Charon, turning towards him, with a brow less contracted into frowns than usual, said to him: "O favored of heaven, since thou art permitted to enter the realms of darkness, which to all the living, besides thyself, are interdicted, make haste to go whithersoever the Fates have called thee; proceed by this gloomy path to the palace of Pluto, whom thou wilt find sitting upon his throne, who will permit thee to enter those recesses of his dominion, the secrets of which I am not permitted to reveal."

Telemachus, immediately pressing forward with a hasty step, discovered the shades gliding about on every side, more numerous than the sands on a seashore; and he was struck with a religious dread to perceive that, in the midst of the tumult and hurry of this incredible multitude, all was silent as the grave. He sees, at length, the gloomy residence of unrelenting Pluto: his hair stands erect, his legs tremble, and his voice fails him. "Tremendous power!" said he, with faltering and interrupted speech, "the son of unhappy Ulysses now stands before thee. I come to inquire whether my father is descended into your dominions, or whether he is still a wanderer upon the earth?"

Pluto was seated upon a throne of ebony: his countenance was pale and severe, his eyes hollow and ardent, and his brow contracted and menacing. The sight of a mortal still breathing the breath of life was hateful to his eyes, as the day is hateful to those animals that leave their recesses only by night. At his side sat Proserpine, who was the only object of his attention, and seemed to soften him into some degree of complacency. She enjoyed a beauty that was perpetually renewed but there was mingled with her immortal charms something of her lord's inflexible severity.

At the foot of the throne sat the pale father of destruction, Death, incessantly whetting a scythe which he held in his hand. Around this horrid spectre hovered repining Cares and injurious Suspicions; Vengeance, distained with blood and covered with wounds; causeless Hatred; Avarice, gnawing her own flesh; Despair, the victim of her own rage; Ambition,

From François Fénelon, *The Adventures of Telemachus.* Translated by Dr. Hawkesworth. New York: Hurd and Houghton, 1872, pp. 450–8.

whose fury overturns all things like a whirlwind; Treason, thirsting for blood, and not able to enjoy the mischief she produces; Envy, shedding round her the venom that corrodes her heart, and sickening with rage at the impotence of her malice; Impiety, that opens for herself a gulf without bottom, in which she shall plunge at last without hope; Spectres, all hideous to behold; Phantoms, that represent the dead to terrify the living; frightful Dreams; and the horrid Vigils of disease and pain. By these images of woe was Pluto surrounded: such were the attendants that filled his palace. He replied to the son of Ulysses in a hollow tone, and the depths of Erebus remurmured to the sound: "If it is by fate, young mortal, that thou hast violated this sacred asylum of the dead, that fate, which has thus distinguished thee, fulfill. Of thy father I will tell thee nothing; it is enough that here thou art permitted to seek him. As upon the earth he was a king, thy search may be confined, on one side, to that part of Tartarus where wicked kings are consigned to punishment, and, on the other, to that part of Elysium, where the good receive their reward. But, from hence thou canst not enter the fields of Elysium till thou hast passed through Tartarus. Make haste thither, and linger not in my dominions."

Telemachus instantly obeyed, and passed through the dreary vacuity that surrounded him with such speed that he seemed almost to fly; such was his impatience to behold his father and to quit the presence of a tyrant equally the terror of the living and the dead. He soon perceived the gloomy tract of Tartarus at a small distance before him: from this place ascended a black cloud of pestilential smoke, which would have been fatal in the realms of life. This smoke hovered over a river of fire, the flames of which, returning upon themselves, roared in a burning vortex with a noise like that of an impetuous torrent precipitated from the highest rock, so that in this region of woe no other sound could be distinctly heard.

Telemachus, secretly animated by Minerva, entered the gulf without fear. He first saw a great number of men, who, born in a mean condition, were now punished for having sought to acquire riches by fraud, treachery, and violence. Among them he remarked many of the impious hypocrites, who, affecting a zeal for religion, played upon the credulity of others and gratified their own ambition. These wretches, who had abused virtue itself, the best gift of heaven, to dishonest purposes, were punished as the most criminal of men. Children who had murdered their parents, wives who had sold their country in violation of every tie, were punished with less severity than these. Such was the decree pronounced by the judges of the dead, because hypocrites are not content to be wicked upon the common terms; they would be vicious, with the reputation of virtue; and by an appearance of virtue, which at length is found to be false, they prevent mankind from putting confidence in the true. The gods, whose omniscience they mock and whose honor they degrade, take pleasure in the exertion of all their power to avenge the insult.

After these appeared others, to whom the world scarcely imputes guilt, but whom the divine vengeance pursues without pity—the liar, the ingrate, the parasite who lavishes adulation upon vice, and the slanderer who falsely detracts from virtue—all those who judge rashly of what they know but in part, and thus injure the reputation of the innocent.

But, among all who suffered for ingratitude, those were punished with most severity who had been ungrateful to the gods. "What!" said Minos, "is he considered as a monster who is guilty of ingratitude to his father or his friend, from whom he has received some such benefits as mortals can bestow, and shall the wretch glory in his crime who is ungrateful to the gods, the givers of life and of every blessing it includes? Does he not owe his existence rather to the authors of nature than to the parents through whom his existence was derived? The less these crimes are censured and punished upon earth, the more are they obnoxious in hell to implacable vengeance, which no force can resist and no subtlety elude."

Telemachus, seeing a man condemned by the judges, whom he found sitting, ventured to ask them what was his crime. He was immediately answered by the offender himself. "I have done," said he, "no evil; my pleasure consisted wholly in doing good. I have been just, munificent, liberal, and compassionate; of what crime, then, can I be accused?" "With respect to man," replied Minos, "thou art accused of none; but didst thou not owe less to man than to the gods? If so, what are thy pretensions to justice? Thou hast punctually fulfilled thy duty to men, who are but dust; thou hast been virtuous, but thy virtue terminated wholly in thyself, without reference to the gods who gave it: thy virtue was to be thy own felicity, and to thyself thou wast all in all. Thou hast, indeed, been thy own deity. But the gods, by whom all things have been created, and who have created all things for themselves, cannot give up their rights: thou hast forgotten them, and they will forget thee. Since thou hast desired to exist for thyself, and not for them, to thyself they will deliver thee up. Seek, then, thy consolation in thine own heart. Thou art separated forever from man, whom, for thy own sake, thou hast desired to please, and art left to thyself alone, that idol of thy heart. Learn now, at least, that piety is that virtue of which the gods are the object, and that without this no virtue can deserve the name. The false lustre of that which thou hast long dazzled the eyes of men, who are easily deceived, will deceive no more. Men distinguish that only from which they derive pain or pleasure, into virtue and vice, and are, therefore, alike ignorant both of good and evil: but here the perspicacity of divine wisdom discerns all things as they are; the judgment of men, from external appearance, is reversed; what they have admired is frequently condemned, and what they have condemned, approved."

These words, to the boaster of philosophic virtue, were like a stroke of thunder, and he was unable to sustain the shock. The self-complaisance with which he had been used to contemplate his moderation, his fortitude, his generosity, was now changed to despair. The view of his own heart, at enmity with the gods, became his punishment. He now saw, and was doomed forever to see, himself by the light of truth. He perceived that the approbation of men, which all his actions had been directed to acquire, was erroneous and vain. When he looked inward, he found every thing totally changed; he was no longer the same being, and all comfort was eradicated from his heart. His conscience, which had hitherto witnessed in his favor, now rose up against him, and reproached him even with his virtues, which, not having deity for their principle and end, were erroneous and illusive. He was overwhelmed with consternation and trouble, with shame, remorse, and despair. The Furies, indeed, forbore to torment him; he was delivered over to himself, and they were satisfied; his own heart was the avenger of the gods, whom he had despised. As he could not escape from himself, he retired to the most gloomy recesses, that he might be concealed from others: he sought for darkness, but he found it not; light still persecuted and pursued him: the light of truth, which he had not followed, now punished him for neglect. All that he had beheld with pleasure became odious in his eyes, as the source of misery that could never end. "O fool!" said he, "I have known neither the gods, men, nor myself; I have, indeed, known nothing, since I have not known the only and true good. All my steps have deviated from the path I should have trodden; all my wisdom was folly and all my virtue was pride, which sacrificed, with a blind impiety, only to that vile idol, myself!"

The next objects that Telemachus perceived, as he went on, were the kings that had abused their power. An avenging Fury held up before them a mirror which reflected their vices in all their deformity. In this they beheld their undistinguishing vanity, that was gratified by the grossest adulation; their want of feeling for mankind, whose happiness should have been the first object of their attention; their insensibility to virtue, their dread of truth, their partiality to flatterers, their dissipation, effeminacy, and indolence; their causeless suspicions; their vain parade and ostentatious splendor, an idle blaze, in which the public welfare is consumed; their ambition of false honor, procured at the expense of blood; and their inhuman luxury, which extorted a perpetual supply of superfluous delicacies from the wretched victims of grief and anguish. When they looked into this mirror, they saw themselves faithfully represented; and they found the picture more monstrous and horrid than the Chimera vanquished by Bellerophon, the Lernaean hydra slain by Hercules, and even Cerebus [Cerberus] himself, though from his three howling mouths he disgorges a stream of black venomous blood, that is sufficient to infect the whole race of mortals that breathe upon the earth.

At the same time another Fury tauntingly repeated all the praises which sycophants had lavished upon them in their lives, and held up another mirror, in which they appeared as flattery had represented them.

The contrast of these pictures, widely different, was the punishment of their vanity. It was remarkable that the most wicked were the objects of the most extravagant praise; because the most wicked are most to be feared, and because they exact, with less shame, the servile adulation of the poets and orators of their time.

Their groans perpetually ascended from this dreadful abyss, where they saw nothing but the derision and insult of which they were themselves the objects—where every thing repulsed, opposed, and confounded them. As they sported with the lives of mankind upon the earth, and pretended that the whole species were created for their use, they were, in Tartarus, delivered over to the capricious tyranny of slaves, who made them taste all the bitterness of servitude in their turn. They obeyed with unutterable anguish, and without hope that the iron hand of oppression would lie lighter upon them. Under the strokes of these slaves, now their merciless tyrants, they lay passive and impotent, like an anvil under the hammers of the Cyclops, when Vulcan urges their labor at the flaming furnaces of Mount Aetna.

Telemachus observed the countenance of these criminals to be pale and ghastly, strongly expressive of the torment they suffered at the heart. They looked inward with a self-abhorrence, now inseparable from their existence. Their crimes themselves had become their punishment, and it was not necessary that greater should be inflicted. They haunted them like hideous spectres, and continually started up before them in all their enormity. They wished for a second death, that might separate them from these ministers of vengeance, as the first had separated their spirits from the body—a death that might at once extinguish all consciousness and sensibility. They called upon the depths of hell to hide them from the persecuting beams of truth, in impenetrable darkness; but they are reserved for the cup of vengeance, which, though they drink it forever, shall be ever full. The truth, from which they fled, has overtaken them, an invincible and unrelenting enemy. The ray which once might have illuminated them, like the mild radiance of the day, now pierces them like lightning—a fierce and fatal fire, that, without injury to the external parts, infixes a burning torment at the heart. By truth, now, an avenging flame, the very soul is melted, like metal in a furnace; it dissolves all, but destroys nothing; it disunites the first elements of life, yet the sufferer can never die. He is, as it were, divided against himself, without rest and without comfort; animated by no vital principle, but the rage that kindles at his own misconduct, and the dreadful madness that results from despair.

Among these objects, at the sight of which the hair of Telemachus stood erect, he beheld many of the ancient kings of Lydia who were punished for having preferred the selfish gratification of others, which, to royalty, is a duty of indispensable obligation.

These kings mutually reproached each other with their folly. "Did I not often recommend to you," said one of them to his son, "during the last years of my life, when old age had given weight to my counsel, the reparation of the mischiefs that my negligence had produced?" "Unhappy father!" replied the son, "thou art the cause of my perdition; it was thy example that made me vain-glorious, proud, voluptuous, and cruel. While I saw thee surrounded with flattery, and relaxed into luxury and sloth, I also insensibly acquired the love of pleasure and adulation. I thought the rest of men were to kings what horses and other beasts of burden are to men—animals wholly unworthy of regard, except for the drudgery they perform and the conveniences they procure. This was my opinion, and I learnt it of thee. I followed thy example, and share thy misery." These reproaches were mingled with the most horrid execrations: mutual rage and indignation aggravated the torments of hell.

Around these wretched princes there still hovered, like owls in the twilight, causeless Jealousies and vain Alarms, Mistrust and Dread, which revenge upon kings their disregard of mankind; Avarice, insatiable of wealth; False-Honor, ever tyrannical and oppressive; and effeminate Luxury, a deceitful demon that aggravated every evil, and bestows only imaginary good.

Many kings were also severely punished, not for the mischief they had done, but for the good they had neglected to do. Every crime that is committed by the subject in consequence of laws not enforced, is the crime of the kings, for kings reign only as ministers of the law. To kings also are imputed all the disorders that arise from pomp, luxury, and every other excess which excites irregular and impetuous passions that cannot be gratified but by the violation of the common rights of mankind. But the princes who, instead of watching over their people as a shepherd watches over his flock, worried and devoured them like the wolf were punished with the most exemplary severity.

In this abyss of darkness and misery, Telemachus beheld, with yet greater astonishment, many kings who had been honored for their personal virtues upon earth, but were, notwithstanding, condemned to the pains of Tartarus for having left the administration of government to wicked and crafty men. They were punished for mischiefs which they had suffered to be perpetrated under the sanction of their authority. The greater part of them, indeed, had been by principle neither virtuous nor vicious; supinely taking the color impressed upon them from without, they did not shun the truth when it presented itself, but they had no relish for virtue, no delight in doing good.

When Telemachus left Tartarus, he felt himself relieved, as if a mountain had been removed from his breast. This relief, so sudden and so great, impressed him with a strong sense of the misery of those who are confined there without hope of deliverance. He was terrified at having seen so many kings punished with much greater severity than any other offenders. "Have kings, then," said he, "so many duties to fulfill, so many difficulties to surmount, and so many dangers to avoid? Is the knowledge that is necessary to put them upon their guard, as well against themselves as others, so difficult to be acquired? and, after all the envy, tumult, and opposition of a transitory life, are they consigned to the intolerable and eternal pains of hell? What folly, then, to wish for royalty! How happy the peaceful private station, in which the practice of virtue is comparatively easy!"

STUDY QUESTIONS

1. How are the tribunals and monarchs of Hades modeled on those of Louis XIV's France?
2. Does the document serve as a warning to kings against the powers of sycophants and the long-term consequences of poor decisions?

15.6 DANIEL DEFOE/CAPTAIN CHARLES JOHNSON, "THE LIFE OF ANNE BONNY," 1724

The popular *General History of the Pyrates*, credited in its title page to Captain Charles Johnson, has long been thought to be the pseudonymous work of the English novelist Daniel Defoe (1667–1731), the author of *Robinson Crusoe* (1719) and *Moll Flanders* (1722). Defoe, who was frequently in legal trouble for his political stances and many debts, is known to have used nearly two hundred pseudonyms in his lifetime. The question of the book's authorship continues to be debated. The *General History* consists of thirty-nine short biographies of the most notorious pirates who sailed in the Caribbean during the so-called "Golden Age" of piracy. Some of the pirates, including the one treated below, may have been wholly fictional. The text is complete.

As we have been more particular in the Lives of these two Women, than those of other Pyrates, it is incumbent on us, as a faithful Historian, to begin with their Birth. Anne Bonny was born at a Town near Cork, in the Kingdom of Ireland, her Father an Attorney at Law, but Anne was not one of his legitimate Issue, which seems to cross an old Proverb, which says, that Bastards have the best Luck. Her Father was a married Man, and his Wife having been brought to Bed, contracted an Illness in her lying in, and in order to recover her Health, she was advised to remove for Change of Air; the Place she chose, was a few Miles distance from her Dwelling, where her Husband's Mother liv'd. Here she sojourn'd some Time, her Husband staying at Home, to follow his Affairs. The Servant-Maid, whom she left to look after the House, and attend the Family, being a handsome young Woman, was courted by a young Man of the same Town, who was a Tanner; this Tanner used to take his Opportunities, when the Family was out of the Way, of coming to pursue his Courtship; and being with the Maid one Day as she was employed in the Household Business, not having the Fear of God before his Eyes, he takes his Opportunity, when her Back was turned, of whipping three Silver Spoons into his Pocket. The Maid soon miss'd the Spoons, and knowing that no Body had been in the Room, but herself and the young Man, since she saw them last, she charged him with taking them; he very stifly denied it, upon which she grew outragious, and threatned to go to a Constable, in order to carry him before a Justice of Peace. These Menaces frighten'd him out of his Wits, well knowing he could not stand Search; wherefore he endeavoured to pacify her, by desiring her to examine the Drawers and other Places, and perhaps she might find them; in this Time he slips into another Room, where the Maid usually lay, and puts the Spoons betwixt the Sheets, and then makes his Escape by a back Door, concluding she must find them, when she went to Bed, and so next Day he might pretend he did it only to frighten her, and the Thing might be laugh'd off for a Jest.

As soon as she miss'd him, she gave over her Search, concluding he had carry'd them off, and went directly to the Constable, in order to have him apprehended. The young Man was informed, that a Constable had been in Search of him, but he regarded it but little, not doubting but all would be well next Day. Three or four Days passed, and still he was told, the Constable was upon the Hunt for him, this made him lye concealed; he could not comprehend the Meaning of it, he imagined no less, than that the Maid had a Mind to convert the Spoons to her own Use, and put the Robbery upon him.

It happen'd, at this Time, that the Mistress being perfectly recovered of her late Indisposition, was returned Home, in Company with her Mother-in-Law; the first News she heard, was of the Loss of the Spoons, with the Manner how; the Maid telling her, at the same Time, that the young Man was run away. The young Fellow had Intelligence of the Mistress's Arrival, and considering with himself, that he could never appear again in his Business, unless this Matter was got over, and she being a good-natured Woman, he took a Resolution of going directly to her, and of telling her the whole Story, only with this Difference, that he did it for a Jest.

The Mistress could scarce believe it, however, she went directly to the Maid's Room, and turning down the Bed Cloaths, there, to her great Surprize, found the three Spoons; upon this she desired the young Man to go Home and mind his Business, for he should have no Trouble about it.

The Mistress could not imagine the Meaning of this, she never had found the Maid guilty of any pilfering, and therefore it could not enter her Head, that she designed to steal the Spoons her self; upon the whole, she concluded the Maid had not been in her Bed, from the Time the Spoons were miss'd, she grew immediately jealous upon it, and suspected, that the Maid supply'd her Place with her Husband, during her Absence, and this was the Reason why the Spoons were no sooner found.

She call'd to Mind several Actions of Kindness, her Husband had shewed the Maid, Things that pass'd unheeded by, when they happen'd, but now she had got the Tormentor, Jealousy, in her Head, amounted to Proofs of their Intimacy; another Circumstance which strengthen'd the whole, was, that tho' her Husband knew she was to come Home that Day, and had had no Communication with her in four Months, which was before her last lying in, yet he took an Opportunity of going out of Town that

Morning, upon some slight Pretence. All these Things put together, confirm'd her in her Jealousy.

As Women seldom forgive Injuries of this Kind, she thought of discharging her Revenge upon the Maid. In order to this, she leaves the Spoons where she found them, and orders the Maid to put clean Sheets upon the Bed, telling her, she intended to lye there herself that Night, because her Mother-in-Law was to lye in her Bed, and that she (the Maid) must lye in another Part of the House; the Maid in making the Bed, was surprized with the Sight of the Spoons, but there were very good Reasons, why it was not proper for her to tell where she found them, therefore she takes them up, puts them in her Trunk, intending to leave them in some Place, where they might be found by Chance.

The Mistress, that every Thing might look to be done without Design, lyes that Night in the Maid's Bed, little dreaming of what an Adventure it would produce. After she had been a Bed some Time, thinking on what had pass'd, for Jealousy kept her awake, she heard some Body enter the Room; at first she apprehended it to be Thieves, and was so fright'ned, she had not Courage enough to call out; but when she heard these Words, Mary, are you awake? She knew it to be her Husband's Voice; then her Fright was over, yet she made no Answer, least he should find her out, if she spoke, therefore she resolved to counterfeit Sleep, and take what followed.

The Husband came to Bed, and that Night play'd the vigorous Lover; but one Thing spoiled the Diversion on the Wife's Side, which was, the Reflection that it was not design'd for her; however, she was very passive, and bore it like a Christian. Early before Day, she stole out of Bed, leaving him asleep, and went to her Mother-in-Law, telling her what had passed, not forgetting how he had used her, as taking her for the Maid; the Husband also stole out, not thinking it convenient to be catched in that Room; in the mean Time, the Revenge of the Mistress was strongly against the Maid, and without considering that to her she owed the Diversion of the Night before, and that one good turn should deserve another; she sent for a Constable, and charged her with stealing the Spoons. The Maid's Trunk was broke open, and the Spoons found, upon which she was carry' d before a Justice of Peace, and by him committed to Gaol.

The Husband loiter'd about till twelve a-Clock at Noon, then comes Home, pretending he was just come to Town; as soon as he heard what had pass'd, in Relation to the Maid, he fell into a great Passion with his Wife; this set the Thing into a greater Flame, the Mother takes the Wife's Part against her own Son, insomuch that the Quarrel encreasing, the Mother and Wife took Horse immediately, and went back to the Mother's House, and the Husband and Wife never bedded together after.

The Maid lay a long Time in the Prison, it being near half a Year to the Assizes; but before it happened, it was discovered she was with Child; when she was arraign'd at the Bar, she was discharged for want of Evidence; the Wife's Conscience touch'd her, and as she did not believe the Maid Guilty of any Theft, except that of Love, she did not appear against her; soon after her Acquittal, she was delivered of a Girl.

But what alarm'd the Husband most, was, that it was discovered the Wife was with Child also, he taking it for granted, he had had no Intimacy with her, since her last lying in, grew jealous of her, in his Turn, and made this a Handle to justify himself, for his Usage of her, pretending now he had suspected her long, but that here was Proof; she was delivered of Twins, a Boy and a Girl.

The Mother falling ill, sent to her Son to reconcile him to his Wife, but he would not hearken to it; therefore she made a Will, leaving all she had in the Hands of certain Trustees, for the Use of the Wife and two Children lately born, and died a few Days after.

This was an ugly Turn upon him, his greatest Dependance being upon his Mother; however, his Wife was kinder to him than he deserved, for she made him a yearly Allowance out of what was left, tho' they continued to live separate. It lasted near five Years; at this Time having a great Affection for the Girl he had by his Maid, he had a Mind to take it Home, to live with him; but as all the Town knew it to be a Girl, the better to disguise the Matter from them, as well as from his Wife, he had it put into Brecches, as a Boy, pretending it was a Relation's Child he was to breed up to be his Clerk.

The Wife heard he had a little Boy at Home he was very fond of, but as she did not know any Relation of his that had such a Child, she employ'd a Friend to enquire further into it; this Person by talking with the Child, found it to be a Girl, discovered that the Servant-Maid was its Mother, and that the Husband still kept up his Correspondence with her.

Upon this Intelligence, the Wife being unwilling that her Children's Money should go towards the Maintainance of Bastards, stopped the Allowance. The Husband enraged, in a kind of Revenge, takes the Maid home, and lives with her publickly, to the great Scandal of his Neighbours; but he soon found the bad Effect of it, for by Degrees he lost his Practice, so that he saw plainly he could not live there, therefore he thought of removing, and turning what Effects he had into ready Money; he goes to Cork, and there with his Maid and Daughter embarques for Carolina.

At first he followed the Practice of the Law in that Province, but afterwards fell into Merchandize, which proved more successful to him, for he gained by it sufficient to purchase a considerable Plantation: His Maid, who passed for his Wife, happened to die, after which his Daughter, our Anne Bonny, now grown up, kept his House.

She was of a fierce and couragious Temper, wherefore, when she lay under Condemnation, several Stories were reported of her, much to her Disadvantage, as that she had kill'd an English Servant-Maid once in her Passion with a Case-Knife, while she look'd after her Father's House; but upon further Enquiry, I found this Story to be groundless. It was certain she was so robust, that once, when a young Fellow would have lain with her, against her Will, she beat him so, that he lay ill of it a considerable Time.

While she lived with her Father, she was look'd upon as one that would be a good Fortune, wherefore it was thought her Father expected a good Match for her; but she spoil'd all, for without his Consent, she marries a young Fellow, who belong'd to the Sea, and was not worth a Groat; which provoked her Father to such a Degree, that he turn'd her out of Doors, upon which the young Fellow, who married her, finding himself disappointed in his Expectation, shipped himself and Wife, for the Island of Providence, expecting Employment there.

Here she became acquainted with Rackam the Pyrate, who making Courtship to her, soon found Means of withdrawing her Affections from her Husband, so that she consented to elope from him, and go to Sea with Rackam in Men's Cloaths. She was as good as her Word, and after she had been at Sea some Time, she proved with Child, and beginning to grow big, Rackam landed her on the Island of Cuba; and recommending her there to some Friends of his, they took Care of her, till she was brought to Bed. When she was up and well again, he sent for her to bear him Company.

The King's Proclamation being out, for pardoning of Pyrates, he took the Benefit of it, and surrender'd; afterwards being sent upon the privateering Account, he return'd to his old Trade, as has been already hinted in the Story of Mary Read. In all these Expeditions, Anne Bonny bore him Company, and when any Business was to be done in their Way, no Body was more forward or couragious than she, and particularly when they were taken; she and Mary Read, with one more, were all the Persons that durst keep the Deck, as has been before hinted.

Her Father was known to a great many Gentlemen Planters of Jamaica, who had dealt with him, and among whom he had a good Reputation; and some of them, who had been in Carolina, remember'd to have seen her in his House; wherefore they were enclined to show her Favour, but the Action of leaving her Husband was an ugly Circumstance against her. The Day that Rackam was executed, by special Favour, he was admitted to see her; but all the Comfort she gave him, was, that she was sorry to see him there, but if he had fought like a Man, he need not have been hang'd like a Dog.

She was continued in Prison, to the Time of her lying in, and afterwards reprieved from Time to Time; but what is become of her since, we cannot tell; only this we know, that she was not executed.

STUDY QUESTIONS

1. What are the circumstances that led to Anne becoming a pirate?
2. How would you describe Anne's relationship with Rackham?

15.7 THE ABSOLUTIST REGIMES

Four families—the Bourbons (France), Hohenzollerns (Brandenburg-Prussia), the Habsburgs (Austria and Spain), and the Romanovs (Russia)—ruled over much of Europe during the Old Regime. A web of intermarriages connected the royal families to one another.

The Absolutist Regimes

Habsburg	Hohenzollern	Bourbon	Romanov	Bourbon
Austria	Brandenburg-Prussia	France	Russia	Spain
Leopold I	Friedrich Wilhelm	Louis XIII	Alexis	Felipe IV (*)
1658–1705	1640–1688	1610–1643	1645–1676	1621–1665
Josef I	Friedrich III	Louis XIV	Theodore II	Carlos II (*)
1705–1711	1688–1713	1643–1715	1676–1682	1665–1700
Karl VI	Friedrich Wilhelm I	Louis XV	Ivan V	Felipe V
1711–1740	1713–1740	1715–1774	1682–1689	1700–1746
Maria Theresa	Friedrich II the Great	Louis XVI	Piotr I the Great	Ferdinando VI
1740–1780	1740–1786	1774–1792	1689–1725	1746–1759
Josef II	Friedrich Wilhelm II		Katerina I	Carlos III
1780–1790	1786–1797		1725–1727	1759–1788
Leopold II	Friedrich Wilhelm III		Piotr II	Carlos IV
1790–1792	1797–1840		1727–1730	1788–1808
Francis II			Anna	
1792–1835			1730–1740	
			Ivan VI	
			1740–1741	
			Lizaveta	
			1741–1762	
			Piotr III	
			1762	
			Katerina II the Great	
			1762–1796	
			Pavel	
			1796–1801	
			Aleksandr I	
			1801–1825	

(*)= last two Habsburg kings of Spain.

CHAPTER 16

THE ENLIGHTENED

16.1 JOHN LOCKE, "OF TYRANNY," *TWO TREATISES OF GOVERNMENT*, 1689

An English Enlightenment philosopher, John Locke (1632–1704) developed ideas of empiricism, liberalism, and classical republicanism—which influenced the American Declaration of Independence (1776) and justified humankind's move toward self-rule. His work *Two Treatises of Government* was so controversial that Locke published it anonymously. Book II, from which this selection comes, is provisionally called "An Essay Concerning the True Original, Extent and End of Civil Government," giving insight into Locke's aims. As the discussion of tyranny exemplifies, Locke was fundamentally concerned with initial human equality and the rights to property and legitimate government. Consider his "ideal" ruler compared with the absolutists of his age.

Sect. 199. As usurpation is the exercise of power, which another hath a right to; so tyranny is the exercise of power beyond right, which no body can have a right to. And this is making use of the power any one has in his hands, not for the good of those who are under it, but for his own private separate advantage. When the governor, however intitled, makes not the law, but his will, the rule; and his commands and actions are not directed to the preservation of the properties of his people, but the satisfaction of his own ambition, revenge, covetousness, or any other irregular passion.

Sect. 200. If one can doubt this to be truth, or reason, because it comes from the obscure hand of a subject, I hope the authority of a king will make it pass with him. King James the first, in his speech to the parliament, 1603, tells them thus,

> I will ever prefer the weal of the public, and of the whole commonwealth, in making of good laws and constitutions, to any particular and private ends of mine; thinking ever the wealth and weal of the commonwealth to be my greatest weal and worldly felicity; a point wherein a lawful king doth directly differ from a tyrant: for I do acknowledge, that the special and greatest point of difference that is between a rightful king and an usurping tyrant, is this, that whereas the proud and ambitious tyrant doth think his kingdom and people are only ordained for satisfaction of his desires and unreasonable appetites, the righteous and just king doth by the contrary

From John Locke, "Second Treatise of Government," 1690.

> acknowledge himself to be ordained for the procuring of the wealth and property of his people.

And again, in his speech to the parliament, 1609, he hath these words:

> The king binds himself by a double oath, to the observation of the fundamental laws of his kingdom; tacitly, as by being a king, and so bound to protect as well the people, as the laws of his kingdom; and expressly, by his oath at his coronation, so as every just king, in a settled kingdom, is bound to observe that paction made to his people, by his laws, in framing his government agreeable thereunto, according to that paction which God made with Noah after the deluge. Hereafter, seed-time and harvest, and cold and heat, and summer and winter, and day and night, shall not cease while the earth remaineth. And therefore a king governing in a settled kingdom, leaves to be a king, and degenerates into a tyrant, as soon as he leaves off to rule according to his laws.

And a little after,

> Therefore all kings that are not tyrants, or perjured, will be glad to bound themselves within the limits of their laws; and they that persuade them the contrary, are vipers, and pests both against them and the commonwealth.

Thus that learned king, who well understood the notion of things, makes the difference betwixt a king and a tyrant to consist only in this, that one makes the laws the bounds of his power, and the good of the public, the end of his government; the other makes all give way to his own will and appetite.

Sect. 201. It is a mistake, to think this fault is proper only to monarchies; other forms of government are liable to it, as well as that: for wherever the power, that is put in any hands for the government of the people, and the preservation of their properties, is applied to other ends, and made use of to impoverish, harass, or subdue them to the arbitrary and irregular commands of those that have it; there it presently becomes tyranny, whether those that thus use it are one or many. Thus we read of the thirty tyrants at Athens, as well as one at Syracuse; and the intolerable dominion of the Decemviri at Rome was nothing better.

Sect. 202. Where-ever law ends, tyranny begins, if the law be transgressed to another's harm; and whosoever in authority exceeds the power given him by the law, and makes use of the force he has under his command, to compass that upon the subject, which the law allows not, ceases in that to be a magistrate; and, acting without authority, may be opposed, as any other man, who by force invades the right of another. This is acknowledged in subordinate magistrates. He that hath authority to seize my person in the street, may be opposed as a thief and a robber, if he endeavours to break into my house to execute a writ, notwithstanding that I know he has such a warrant, and such a legal authority, as will impower him to arrest me abroad. And why this should not hold in the highest, as well as in the most inferior magistrate, I would gladly be informed. Is it reasonable, that the eldest brother, because he has the greatest part of his father's estate, should thereby have a right to take away any of his younger brothers portions? or that a rich man, who possessed a whole country, should from thence have a right to seize, when he pleased, the cottage and garden of his poor neighbour? The being rightfully possessed of great power and riches, exceedingly beyond the greatest part of the sons of Adam, is so far from being an excuse, much less a reason, for rapine and oppression, which the endamaging another without authority is, that it is a great aggravation of it: for the exceeding the bounds of authority is no more a right in a great, than in a petty officer; no more justifiable in a king than a constable; but is so much the worse in him, in that he has more trust put in him, has already a much greater share than the rest of his brethren, and is supposed, from the advantages of his education, employment, and counsellors, to be more knowing in the measures of right and wrong.

Sect. 203. May the commands then of a prince be opposed? may he be resisted as often as any one shall find himself aggrieved, and but imagine he has not right done him? This will unhinge and overturn all polities, and, instead of government and order, leave nothing but anarchy and confusion.

Sect. 204. To this I answer, that force is to be opposed to nothing, but to unjust and unlawful force; whoever makes any opposition in any other case, draws on himself a just condemnation both from God and man; and so no such danger or confusion will follow, as is often suggested: for,

Sect. 205. First, As, in some countries, the person of the prince by the law is sacred; and so, whatever he commands or does, his person is still free from all question or violence, not liable to force, or any judicial censure or condemnation. But yet opposition may be made to the illegal acts of any inferior officer, or other commissioned by him; unless he will, by actually putting himself into a state of war with his people, dissolve the government, and leave them to that defence which belongs to every one in the state of nature: for of such things who can tell what the end will be? and a neighbour kingdom has shewed the world an odd example. In all other cases the sacredness of the person exempts him from all inconveniencies, whereby he is secure, whilst the government stands, from all violence and harm whatsoever; than which there cannot be a wiser constitution: for the harm he can do in his own person not being likely to happen often, nor to extend itself far; nor being able by his single strength to subvert the laws, nor oppress the body of the people, should any prince have so much weakness, and ill nature as to be willing to do it, the inconveniency of some particular mischiefs, that may happen sometimes, when a heady prince comes to the throne, are well recompensed by the peace of the public, and security of the government, in the person of the chief magistrate, thus set out of the reach of danger: it being safer for the body, that some few private men should be sometimes in danger to suffer, than that the head of the republic should be easily, and upon slight occasions, exposed.

Sect. 206. Secondly, But this privilege, belonging only to the king's person, hinders not, but they may be questioned, opposed, and resisted, who use unjust force, though they pretend a commission from him, which the law authorizes not; as is plain in the case of him that has the king's writ to arrest a man, which is a full commission from the king; and yet he that has it cannot break open a man's house to do it, nor execute this command of the king upon certain days, nor in certain places, though this commission have no such exception in it; but they are the limitations of the law, which if any one transgress, the king's commission excuses him not: for the king's authority being given him only by the law, he cannot impower any one to act against the law, or justify him, by his commission, in so doing; the commission, or command of any magistrate, where he has no authority, being as void and insignificant, as that of any private man; the difference between the one and the other, being that the magistrate has some authority so far, and to such ends, and the private man has none at all: for it is not the commission, but the authority, that gives the right of acting; and against the laws there can be no authority. But, notwithstanding such resistance, the king's person and authority are still both secured, and so no danger to governor or government.

Sect. 207. Thirdly, Supposing a government wherein the person of the chief magistrate is not thus sacred; yet this doctrine of the lawfulness of resisting all unlawful exercises of his power, will not upon every slight occasion indanger him, or imbroil the government: for where the injured party may be relieved, and his damages repaired by appeal to the law, there can be no pretence for force, which is only to be used where a man is intercepted from appealing to the law: for nothing is to be accounted hostile force, but where it leaves not the remedy of such an appeal; and it is such force alone, that puts him that uses it into a state of war, and makes it lawful to resist him. A man with a sword in his hand demands my purse in the high-way, when perhaps I have not twelve pence in my pocket: this man I may lawfully kill. To another I deliver 100 pounds to hold only whilst I alight, which he refuses to restore me, when I am got up again, but draws his sword to defend the possession of it by force, if I endeavour to retake it. The mischief this man does me is a hundred, or possibly a thousand times more than the other perhaps intended me (whom I killed before he really did me any); and yet I might lawfully kill the one, and cannot so much as hurt the other lawfully. The reason whereof is plain; because the one using force, which threatened my life, I could not have time to appeal to the law to secure it: and when it was gone, it was too late to appeal. The law could not restore life to my dead carcass: the loss was irreparable; which to prevent, the law of nature gave me a right to destroy him, who had put himself into a state of war with me, and threatened my destruction. But in the other case, my life not being in danger, I may have the benefit of appealing to the law, and have reparation for my 100 pounds that way.

Sect. 208. Fourthly, But if the unlawful acts done by the magistrate be maintained (by the power he has got), and the remedy which is due by law, be by the same power obstructed; yet the right of resisting, even in such manifest acts of tyranny, will not suddenly, or on slight occasions, disturb the government: for if it reach no farther than some private men's cases, though they have a right to defend themselves, and to recover by force what by unlawful force is taken from them; yet the right to do so will not easily engage them in a contest, wherein they are sure to perish; it being as impossible for one, or a few oppressed men to disturb the government, where the body of the people do not think themselves concerned in it, as for a raving mad-man, or heady malcontent to overturn a well settled state; the people being as little apt to follow the one, as the other.

STUDY QUESTIONS

1. How does Locke employ reason and appeal to justice to make his arguments?
2. Where would Locke have stood on the execution (regicide) of King Charles I? What does he say about a "heady prince" and a theoretically "heady malcontent"?

16.2 DANIEL DEFOE, *JOURNAL OF THE PLAGUE YEAR*, 1722

Although most famous for his novel *Robinson Crusoe*, Daniel Defoe (ca. 1660–1731) was also a prolific pamphleteer and journalist, focusing on issues such as English religious intolerance between Catholics and Anglicans and the political tumult around the 1706 unification of England, Wales, and Scotland into "Great Britain"—topics for which he was a frequent visitor to the pillory. In this work, Defoe narrativizes the Plague of London (1665) through the viewpoint of a fictional main character—although Defoe himself was a child when the pestilence hit and purportedly used his uncle's journals to flesh out the chilling subject matter.

Business led me out sometimes to the other End of the Town, even when the Sickness was chiefly there; and as the thing was new to me, as well as to every Body else, it was a most surprising thing, to see those Streets, which were usually so thronged, now grown desolate, and so few People to be seen in them, that if I had been a Stranger, and at a Loss for my Way, I might sometimes have gone the Length of a whole

From Daniel Defoe, *A Journal of the Plague Year* (revised edition). Edited by Louis Landa and David Roberts. New York: Oxford University Press, 2011, pp. 16, 49–50, 68–9, 105.

Street, I mean of the by-Streets, and see no Body to direct me, except the Watchman, set at the Doors of such Houses as were shut up; of which I shall speak presently.

One Day, being at the Part of the Town, on some special Business, Curiosity led me to observe things more than usually; and indeed I walk'd a great Way where I had no Business; I went up to *Holbourn*, and there the Street was full of People; but they walk'd in the middle of the great Street, neither on one Side or other, because, as I suppose, they would not mingle with nay Body that came out of Houses, or meet with Smells and Scents from Houses that might be infected.

. . .

But I come back to the Case of Families infected, and shut up by the Magistrates; the Misery of those Families is not to be express'd, and it was generally in such Houses that we heard the most dismal Shrieks and Out-cries of the poor People terrified, and even frightened to Death, by the Sight of the Condition of their dearest Relations, and by the Terror of being imprisoned as they were.

I remember, and while I am writing this Story, I think I hear the very Sound of it, a certain Lady had an only Daughter, a young Maiden about 19 years old, and who was possessed of a very Considerable Fortune; they were only Lodgers in the House where they were: The young Woman, her Mother, and the Maid, had been abroad on some Occasion, I do not remember what, for the House was not shut up; but about two Hours after they came home, the young Lady complain'd she was not well; in a quarter of a Hour more, she vomited, and had a violent Pain in her Head. Pray God, says her Mother in a terrible Fright, my Child has not the Distemper! The Pain in her Head increasing, her Mother ordered the Bed to be warm'd, and resolved to put her to Bed; and prepared to give her things to sweat, which was the ordinary Remedy to be taken, when the first Apprehensions of the Distemper began.

While the Bed was airing, the Mother undressed the young Woman, and just as she was laid down in the Bed, she looking upon her Body with a Candle, immediately discovered the fatal Tokens on the Inside of her Thighs. Her Mother not being able to contain herself, threw down her Candle, and shriekt out in such a frightful Manner, that it was enough to place Horror upon the stoutest Heart in the World; not was it one Skream, or one Cry, but the Fright having seiz'd her Spirits, she fainted first, then recovered, then ran all over the House, up the Stairs and down the Stairs, like one distracted, and indeed really was distracted, and continued screeching and crying out for several Hours, void of all Sense, or at least, Government of her Senses, and as I was told, never came thoroughly to herself again: As to the young Maiden, she was a dead Corpse from that Moment; for the Gangren which occasions the Spots had spread [over] her whole Body, and she died in less than two Hours: But still the Mother continued crying out, not knowing any Thing more of her Child, several Hours after she was dead. It is so long ago, that I am not certain, but I think the Mother never recover'd, but died in two or three Weeks after.

This was an extraordinary Case, and I am therefore the more particular in it, because I came so much to the Knowledge of it; but there were innumerable such like Cases; and it was seldom; that the Weekly Bill came in, but there were two or three put in *frighted*, that is, *that may well be call'd*, frighted to Death: But besides those, who were so frighted to die upon the Spot there were great Numbers frighted to other Extreams, some frighted out of their Senses, some out of their Memory and some out of their Understanding: . . .

. . .

It is true, People us'd all possible Precaution, when any one bought a Joint of Meat in the Market, they would not take it of the Butchers Hand, but take it off the Hooks themselves. On the other Hand, the Butcher would not touch the Money, but have it put into a Pot full of Vinegar which he kept for that purpose. The Buyer carry'd always small Money to make up any odd Sum, that they might take no Change. They carry'd Bottles for Scents, and Perfumes in their Hands, and all the Means that could be us'd, were us'd: But then the Poor cou'd not do even these things, and they went at all Hazards.

Innumerable dismal Stories were heard every Day on this very Account: Sometimes a Man or Woman dropt down Dead in the very Markets; for many

People that had the Plague upon them, knew nothing of it; till the inward Gangreen had affected their Vitals and they dy'd in a few Moments; this caus'd, that many died frequently in that Manner in the Streets suddainly, without any warning: Others perhaps had Time to go to the next Bulk or Stall; or to any Door, Porch, and just sit down and die, as I have said before.

...

I must say, when all that will fly are gone, those that are left and must stand it, should stand stock still where they are, and not shift from one End of the Town, or one Part of the Town to the other; for that is the Bane and Mischief of the whole, and they carry the Plague from House to House in their very Clothes.

Wherefore, were we ordered to kill all the Dogs and Cats: But because as they were domestick Animals, and are apt to run from House to House, and from Street to Street; so they are capable of carrying the Effluvia or Infectious Steams of Bodies infected, even in their Furrs or Hair; and therefore, it was that in the beginning of the Infection, an Order was published by the Lord Mayor, and by the Magistrates, according to the Advice of the Physicians; that all the Dogs and Cats should be immediately killed, and an Officer was appointed for the Execution.

It is incredible, if their Account is to be depended upon, what a prodigious Number of those Creatures were destroy'd: I think they talk'd of forty thousand Dogs, and five times as many Cats, few Houses being without a Cat, and some having several, and sometimes five or six in a House. All possible Endeavours were us'd also to destroy the Mice and Rats, especially the latter; by laying Rats-Bane, and other Poisons for them, and a prodigious multitude of them were also destroy'd.

STUDY QUESTIONS

1. How does Defoe chronicle the psychological effects of the plague on sufferers and their families?
2. Does the excerpt reveal the principle of "quarantine"? Is this more sophisticated than one might imagine?

16.3A. ROUSSEAU, "A DISCOURSE ON THE ORIGIN OF INEQUALITY," 1755

François-Marie Arouet (1694–1778), who published under the pen name Voltaire, and Jean-Jacques Rousseau (1712–1778) were two of the most influential of the Enlightenment thinkers. Both were somewhat cynical about the limits of human goodness; Voltaire, however, believed in progress only if the lower orders were firmly directed by a political and intellectual elite. For commoners—rural and urban alike—he had nothing but disdain. Voltaire was known for throwing literary punches and

From J. J. Rousseau, "A Discourse on the Origin of Inequality." In *The Social Contract*, Everyman's ed., translated by G. D. H. Cole. New York: E. P. Dutton and Co., n.d., pp. 236–8.

was imprisoned twice, beaten up by hired thugs, and spent several years in exile (in England) for his troubles. On his return he published his *Philosophical Letters on the English* (1733), which made him famous. Rousseau, apart from sharing a giant ego with Voltaire, was in every way his opposite. A commoner by birth, Rousseau came from Geneva and was almost entirely self-educated. Although he was a morally suspect misanthrope himself, in his writings he proposed that goodness is an inherent human capability. It is society that corrupts people, he believed, imposing false inequalities on them. In *On the Origin of Inequality* Rousseau discusses two types of inequality, natural (based on physical attributes) and moral (based on political or social circumstances). His main concern, however, is with the latter, what he calls civil society, which allows man to enslave man. Voltaire's letter to Rousseau, acknowledging his essay, illustrates the former's style and his flippant dismissal of Rousseau's critique of civilization, suggesting that it made him want to "walk on all fours."

If the reader thus discovers and retraces the lost and forgotten road, by which man must have passed from the state of society; if he carefully restores, along with the intermediate situations which I have just described, those which want of time has compelled me to suppress, or my imagination has failed to suggest, he cannot fail to be struck by the vast distance which separates the two states. It is in tracing this slow succession that he will find the solution of a number of problems of politics and morals, which philosophers cannot settle. He will feel that, men being different in different ages, the reason why Diogenes could not find a man was that he sought among his contemporaries a man of an earlier period. He will see that Cato died with Rome and liberty, because he did not fit the age in which he lived; the greatest of men served only to astonish a world which he would certainly have ruled, had he lived five hundred years sooner. In a word, he will explain how the soul and the passions of men insensibly change their very nature; why our wants and pleasure in the end seek new objects; and why, the original man having vanished by degrees, society offers to us an assembly of artificial men and fictitious passions, which are the work of all these new relations, and without any real foundation in nature. We are taught nothing on this subject, by reflection, that is not entirely confirmed by observation. The savage and the civilized man differ so much in the bottom of their hearts and in their inclinations, that what constitutes the supreme happiness of one would reduce the other to despair. The former breathes only peace and liberty; he desires only to live and be free from labour; even the *ataraxia* [imperturbability] of the Stoic falls far short of his profound indifference to every other object. Civilized man, on the other hand, is always moving, sweating, toiling and racking his brains to find still more laborious occupations: he goes on in drudgery to his last moment, and even seeks death to put himself in a position to live, or renounces life to acquire immortality. He pays his court to men in power, whom he hates, and to the wealthy, whom he despises; he stops at nothing to have the honour of serving them; he is not ashamed to value himself on his own meanness and their protection; and, proud of his slavery, he speaks with disdain of those, who have not the honour of sharing it. What a sight would the perplexing and envied labours of a European minister of State present to the eyes of a Caribean! [sic] How many cruel deaths would not this indolent savage prefer to the horrors of such a life, which is seldom even sweetened by the pleasure of doing good! But, for him to see into the motives of all this solicitude, the words *power* and *reputation*, would have to bear some meaning in his mind; he would have to know that there are men who set a value on the opinion of the rest of the world; who can be made happy and satisfied with themselves rather on the testimony of other people than on their own. In reality, the source of all these differences is, that the savage lives within himself, while social man lives constantly outside himself, and only knows how to live in the opinion of others, so that he seems to receive the consciousness of his own existence merely from the judgment of others concerning him. It is not to my present purpose to insist on the indifference to good and evil which arises from this disposition, in spite of our many fine works on morality, or to show how, everything being reduced to appearances, there is but art and mummery in even honour, friendship, virtue, and often vice itself, of which we all at length learn the secret of boasting; to show, in short, how, always asking others what we are, and never daring to ask ourselves, in the midst of so much philosophy, humanity and civilization, and of such sublime codes of morality, we have nothing to show for ourselves but a frivolous and deceitful appearance, honour without virtue, reason without wisdom, and pleasure without happiness. It is sufficient that I have proved that this is not by any means the original state of man, but that it is merely the spirit of society, and the inequality which society produces, that thus transform and alter our natural inclinations.

I have endeavoured to trace the origin and progress of inequality, and the institution and abuse of political societies, as far as these are capable of being deduced from the nature of man merely by the light of reason, and independently of those sacred dogmas which give sanction of divine right to sovereign authority. It follows from this survey that, as there is hardly an inequality in the state of nature, all the inequality which now prevails owes its strength and growth to the development of our faculties and the advance of the human mind, and becomes at last permanent and legitimate by the establishment of property and laws. Secondly, it follows that moral inequality, authorized by positive right alone, clashes with natural right, whenever it is not proportionate to physical inequality; a distinction which sufficiently determines what we ought to think of that species of inequality which prevails in all civilised countries; since it is plainly contrary to the law of nature, however defined, that children should command old men, fools wise men, and that the privileged few should gorge themselves with superfluities, while the starving multitude are in want of the bare necessities of life.

STUDY QUESTIONS

1. For Rousseau, what is the difference between the savage and the civilized man?
2. What, for Rousseau, is the source of inequality? Why does it "prevail in all civilized societies?"

16.3B. VOLTAIRE, LETTER TO ROUSSEAU ON THE LATTER'S "A DISCOURSE ON THE ORIGIN OF INEQUALITY," 1755

Voltaire first met the younger Jean-Jacques Rousseau in 1754. In 1755, Rousseau had written an essay entitled "The Discourse on the Origin of Inequality among Men" (but renamed by his friends "The Essay against Civilization"), which he sent to Voltaire. Voltaire replied in the following letter.

From E. B. Hall [S. G. Tallentyre, pseud.], *Voltaire in His Letters*. New York: G. P. Putnam's Sons, 1919, pp. 149–54.

I have received, sir, your new book against the human species, and I thank you for it. You will please people by your manner of telling them the truth about themselves, but you will not alter them. The horrors of that human society—from which in our feebleness and ignorance we expect so many consolations—have never been painted in more striking colours: no one has ever been so witty as you are in trying to turn us into brutes: to read your book makes one long to go on all fours. Since, however, it is now some sixty years since I gave up the practice, I feel that it is unfortunately impossible for me to resume it: I leave this natural habit to those more fit for it than are you and I. Nor can I set sail to discover the aborigines of Canada, in the first place because my ill-health ties me to the side of the greatest doctor in Europe, and I should not find the same professional assistance among the Missouris: and secondly because war is going on in that country, and the example of the civilised nations has made the barbarians almost as wicked as we are ourselves. I must confine myself to being a peaceful savage in the retreat I have chosen—close to your country, where you yourself should be.

I agree with you that science and literature have sometimes done a great deal of harm. Tasso's enemies made his life a long series of misfortunes: Galileo's enemies kept him languishing in prison, at seventy years of age, for the crime of understanding the revolution of the earth: and, what is still more shameful, obliged him to forswear his discovery. Since your friends began the Encyclopaedia, their rivals attack them as deists, atheists—even Jansenists.

If I might venture to include myself among those whose works have brought them persecution as their sole recompense, I could tell you of men set on ruining me from the day I produced my tragedy *Oedipe*: of a perfect library of absurd calumnies which have been written against me: of an ex-Jesuit priest whom I saved from utter disgrace rewarding me by defamatory libels: of a man yet more contemptible printing my *Century of Louis XIV* with *Notes* in which crass ignorance gave birth to the most abominable falsehoods: of yet another, who sold to a publisher some chapters of a *Universal History* supposed to be by me: of the publisher avaricious enough to print this shapeless mass of blunders, wrong dates, mutilated facts and names: and, finally, of men sufficiently base and craven to assign the production of their farrago to me. I could show you all society poisoned by this class of person—a class unknown to the ancients—who, not being able to find any honest occupation—be it manual labour or service—and unluckily knowing how to read and write, become the brokers of literature, live on our works, steal our manuscripts, falsify them, and sell them. I could tell of some loose sheets of a gay trifle which I wrote thirty years ago (on the same subject that Chapelain was stupid enough to treat seriously) which are in circulation now through the breach of faith and the cupidity of those who added their own grossness to my *badinage* and filled in the gaps with a dullness only equaled by their malice; and who, finally after twenty years, are selling everywhere a manuscript which, in very truth, is theirs and worthy of them only. . . .

Confess, sir, that all these things are, after all, but little personal pin-pricks, which society scarcely notices. What matter to humankind that a few drones steal the honey of a few bees? Literary men make a great fuss of their petty quarrels: the rest of the world ignores them, or laughs at them.

They are, perhaps, the least serious of all the ills attendant on human life. The thorns inseparable from literature and a modest degree of fame are flowers in comparison with the other evils which from all time have flooded the world. Neither Cicero, Varro, Lucretius, Virgil, or Horace had any part in the proscriptions of Marius, Sulla, that profligate Antony, or that fool Lepidus; while as for that cowardly tyrant, Octavius Caesar—servilely entitled Augustus—he only became an assassin when he was deprived of the society of men of letters.

Confess that Italy owed none of her troubles to Petrarch or to Boccaccio: that Marot's jests were not responsible for the massacre of St. Bartholomew: or the tragedy of the *Cid* for the wars of the Fronde. Great crimes are always committed by great ignoramuses. What makes, and will always make, this world a vale of tears is the satiable greediness and the indomitable pride of men, from Thomas Koulikan, who did not know how to read, to a customhouse officer who can just count. Letters support, refine, and comfort the soul: they are serving you, sir, at the very moment you decry them: you are like Achilles declaiming against fame, and Father Malebranche using his brilliant imagination to belittle imagination.

If anyone has a right to complain of letters, I am that person, for in all times and in all places they have led to my being persecuted: still, we must needs love them in spite of the way they are abused—as we cling to society, though the wicked spoil of its pleasantness: as we must love our country, though it treats us unjustly: and as we must love and serve the Supreme Being, despite the superstition and fanaticism which too often dishonour His service.

M. Chappus tells me your health is very unsatisfactory: you must come and recover here in your native place, enjoy its freedom, drink (with me) the milk of its cows, and browse on its grass.

I am yours most philosophically and with sincere esteem.

STUDY QUESTIONS

1. How is inequality in society the result of the society itself and not the result of a "state of nature"?
2. How does Voltaire mock the idea of a "natural" state of man?

16.4 CESARE BECCARIA, "ON TORTURE," *OF CRIMES AND PUNISHMENTS*, 1764

A politician and legal professional, Cesare Beccaria (1738–1794) was an Italian Enlightenment thinker who sought to reform the penal system and therefore improve society. In his work *Of Crimes and Punishments*, Beccaria argues against the death penalty as a transgression of the state's authority over its citizens and a fundamentally unhelpful method of punishment. The work asserts that punishment must fit the crime and that it should deter crime instead of being a source of vengeance. This portion of the work outlines Beccaria's theories on the rationales and justifications for torture.

As the great Montesquieu says, every punishment that does not derive from absolute necessity is tyrannical. This proposition can be stated more generally in the following manner: every act of authority of one man over another that does not derive from absolute necessity is tyrannical. This is the foundation, therefore, upon which the sovereign's right to punish crimes is based: the necessity to defend the depository of the public welfare from individual usurpations; and the more just the punishments, the more sacred

From Cesare Beccaria, *On Crimes and Punishments and Other Writings*. Edited by Aaron Thomas, translated by Aaron Thomas and Jeremy Parzen. Toronto: University of Toronto Press, © 2009.

and inviolable the security and the greater the liberty the sovereign preserves for his subjects. Let us consult the human heart, and in it we will find the fundamental principles of the sovereign's true right to punish crimes, for no lasting advantage can be expected from political morality, unless that morality is founded upon the indelible sentiments of mankind. Any law that deviates from these sentiments will always encounter a contrary resistance that will prevail in the end, just as any force, however small, if continuously exerted will prevail over any violent jolt transmitted to a body.

No man ever freely surrendered a portion of his own liberty for the sake of the public good; such a chimera appears only in fiction. If it were possible, we would each prefer that the pacts binding others did not bind us; every man sees himself as the centre of all the world's affairs.

. . .

The torture of a criminal while his trial is being prepared is a cruelty condoned by custom in most nations, whether to compel him to confess a crime, to contradict himself, to discover his accomplices, or for some kind of metaphysical and incomprehensible purgation of infamy, or, lastly, in order to discover other crimes of which he may be guilty but of which he is not accused.

No man can be considered *guilty* before the judge has reached a verdict, nor can society deprive him of public protection until it has been established that he has violated the pacts that granted him such protection. What right, then, other than that of force, can empower the judge to inflict punishment on a citizen while his guilt or innocence remains in doubt? This dilemma is not new: either the crime is certain or it is not; if certain; no punishment awaits him other than that which has been established by the laws, and torture is useless because the criminal's confession is useless; if it is not certain, then one must not torture an innocent man, because in the eyes of the law he is a man whose crimes have not been proven. . . .

What is the political purpose of punishment? To instill fear in others. But what justification can we possibly give for the secret and private carnage that the tyranny of custom inflicts on the guilty and the innocent? It is important that no manifest crime go unpunished, but there is no point in discovering who committed a crime that lies buried in darkness. A wrong that has already been committed, and for which there is no remedy, cannot be punished by political society except when it entices others with false hopes of impunity. If it is true that more men, whether from fear or virtue, respect the laws than break them, the risk of torturing an innocent should be considered greater, since there is a greater likelihood that any given man has respected the laws than defied them.

. . .

This shameful crucible of truth is an enduring monument to the law of ancient and savage times, when ordeals by fire, by boiling water, and the uncertain fate of armed combat were called *judgments* of God, as if the links to the eternal chain that emanates from the bosom of the First Mover had to be uncoupled and thrown into disarray at every moment for the sake of frivolous human institutions. The only difference between torture and ordeals by fire or boiling water is that the outcome of the former seems to depend upon the will of the accused, while the outcome of the latter depends upon a purely physical and extrinsic fact; but this difference is only apparent, not real. Speaking the truth in the midst of spasms and agony is as little a free action as was in an earlier era the attempt to thwart the effects of fire and boiling water without recourse to trickery. Every act of our will is always proportional to the force of the sensory impression from which it springs; and the sensory capacity of every man is limited. Therefore, the impression of pain may increase to such a degree that, filling the entire sensory capacity, it leaves the torture victim no liberty but to choose the shortest route to relieve his pain momentarily. Under these circumstances, the statements made by the accused are as inevitable as the impressions made by fire and water. And thus the innocent and sentient man will declare himself guilty if he thinks that doing so will make the pain cease.

. . .

A confession made under torture is not valid unless it is confirmed by oath after the torture has ceased, but if the accused does not confirm the crime, he is tortured anew. Some learned men and some nations allow this infamous question-begging only three times; other nations and learned men leave it to the discretion of the judge, and in this way, of two men who are equally innocent or guilty, the robust and courageous man will be acquitted and the feeble and timid man will be convicted by virtue of this strict line of reasoning: *I, the judge, was supposed to find you guilty of such-and-such a crime; you, the strong, were able to resist the pain, so I acquit you; you, the weak, succumbed, so I convict you. I feel that the confession wrung from you by torture will carry no weight at all, but I will torture you anew if you do not confirm what you have confessed.*

A strange consequence that necessarily follows from the use of torture is that the innocent individual is placed in a worse condition than the guilty; for if both are tortured, every outcome is stacked against him, because either he confesses to a crime and is convicted or he is declared innocent and has suffered to undeserved punishment. The criminal, on the other hand, is in a favourable position, for when he firmly withstands the torture he must be acquitted as innocent; he will have exchanged a greater punishment for a lesser one. Thus, the innocent cannot but lose and the guilty only stand to gain.

STUDY QUESTIONS

1. Was torture in this period an unjust—and an ineffective—interrogation technique?
2. How did the guilty "stand to gain" from withstanding torture, and is Beccaria's argument convincing?

16.5 ADAM SMITH, "OF THE PRINCIPLE OF THE COMMERCIAL OR MERCANTILE SYSTEM," *THE WEALTH OF NATIONS*, 1776

Adam Smith (1723–1790) was a Scottish Enlightenment thinker, a renowned lecturer, and a social philosopher. Interested in how humans work and think together to form functioning societies, Smith produced two major works: *The Theory of Moral Sentiments* (1759) and *An Inquiry into the Nature and Causes of the Wealth of Nations* (1776) (known by its abbreviated title, *The Wealth of Nations*). In *The Wealth of Nations*, Smith argues that society will be best served by a free-market economy that utilizes division of labor, operates via the theory of supply and demand, and is ruled by an "invisible hand"—that is, the market's self-regulating nature. In this selection, Smith describes the fundamental basis of his economic theory and the role of that mere "utensil," money.

From Adam Smith, *An Inquiry into the Nature and Causes of the Wealth of Nations*. Edited by C. J. Bullock. New York: P. F. Collier & Son, 1909, pp. 332–3, 335–8.

The quantity of every commodity which human industry can either purchase or produce, naturally regulates itself in every country according to the effectual demand, or according to the demand of those who are willing to pay the whole rent, labour and profits which must be paid in order to prepare and bring it to market. But no commodities regulate themselves more easily or more exactly according to this effectual demand than gold and silver; because, on account of the small bulk and great value of those metals, no commodities can be more easily transported from one place to another, from the places where they are cheap, to those where they are dear, from the places where they exceed, to those where they fall short of this effectual demand. If there were in England, for example, an effectual demand for an additional quantity of gold, a packet-boat could bring from Lisbon, or from wherever else it was to be had, fifty tuns of gold, which could be coined into more than five million guineas. But if there were an effectual demand for grain to the same value, to import it would require, at five guineas a tun, a million of tuns of shipping, or a thousand ships of a thousand tuns each. The navy of England would not be sufficient.

. . .

It would be too ridiculous to go about seriously to prove, that wealth does not consist in money, or in gold and silver; but in what money purchases, and is valuable only for purchasing. Money, no doubt, makes always a part of the national capital; but it has already been shown that it generally makes but a small part, and always the most unprofitable part of it.

It is not because wealth consists more essentially in money than in goods, that the merchant finds it generally more easy to buy goods with money, than to buy money with goods; but because money is the known and established instrument of commerce, for which every thing is readily given in exchange, but which is not always with equal readiness to be got in exchange for every thing. The greater part of goods besides are more perishable than money, and he may frequently sustain a much greater loss by keeping them. When his goods are upon hand too, he is more liable to such demands for money as he may not be able to answer, than when he has got their price in his coffers. Over and above all this, his profit arises more directly from selling than from buying, and he is upon all these accounts generally much more anxious to exchange his goods for money, than his money for goods. But though a particular merchant, with abundance of goods in his warehouse, may sometimes be ruined by not being able to sell them in time, a nation or country is not liable to the same accident. The whole capital of a merchant frequently consists in perishable goods destined for purchasing money. But it is but a very small part of the annual produce of the land and labour of a country which can ever be destined for purchasing gold and silver from their neighbours. The far greater part is circulated and consumed among themselves; and even of the surplus which is sent abroad, the greater part is generally destined for the purchase of other foreign goods. Though gold and silver, therefore, could not be had in exchange for the goods destined to purchase them, the nation would not be ruined. It might, indeed, suffer some loss and inconveniency, and be forced upon some of those expedients which are necessary for supplying the place of money. The annual produce of its land and labour, however, would be the same, or very nearly the same, as usual, because the same, or very nearly the same consumable capital would be employed in maintaining it. And though goods do not always draw money so readily as money draws goods, in the long-run they draw it more necessarily than even it draws them. Goods can serve many other purposes besides purchasing money, but money can serve no other purpose besides purchasing goods. Money, therefore, necessarily runs after goods, but goods do not always or necessarily run after money. . . .

Consumable commodities, it is said, are soon destroyed; whereas gold and silver are of a more durable nature, and, were it not for this continual exportation, might be accumulated for ages together, to the incredible augmentation of the real wealth of the country. Nothing, therefore, it is pretended, can be more disadvantageous to any country, than the trade which consists in the exchange of such lasting for such perishable commodities. We do not, however, reckon that trade disadvantageous which consists in the exchange of the hard-ware of England for the wines of France; and yet hard-ware is a very durable commodity, and were it not for this continual exportation, might too be accumulated for ages together, to the incredible augmentation of the pots and pans of the country. But it readily occurs that the number of such utensils is in every country necessarily limited by the use which there is for them; that it would be absurd to have more pots and pans than were necessary for cooking the victuals usually consumed there; and that if the quantity of victuals were to increase, the number of pots and pans would readily increase along with it, a part of the increased quantity of victuals being employed in purchasing them, or in maintaining an additional number of workmen whose business it was to make them. It should as readily occur that the quantity of gold and silver is in every country limited by the use which there is for those metals; that their use consists in circulating commodities as coin, and in affording a species of household furniture as plate; that the quantity of coin in every country is regulated by the value of the commodities which are to be circulated by it: increase that value, and immediately a part of it will be sent abroad to purchase where it is to be had, the additional quantity of coin requisite for circulating them: that the quantity of plate is regulated by the number of wealth of those private families who chuse to indulge themselves in that sort of magnificence: increase the number and wealth of such families, and a part of this increased wealth will most probably be employed in purchasing, wherever it is to be found, an additional quantity of plate: that to attempt to increase the wealth of any country, either by introducing or by detaining in it an unnecessary quantity of gold and silver, is absurd as it would be to attempt to increase the good cheer of private families by obliging them to keep an unnecessary number of kitchen utensils. As the expence of purchasing those unnecessary utensils would diminish instead of increasing either the quantity or goodness of the family provisions; so the expence of purchasing an unnecessary quantity of gold and silver must, in every country, as necessarily diminish the wealth which feeds, clothes, and lodges, which maintains and employs the people. Gold and silver, whether in the shape of coin or of plate, are utensils, it must be remembered, as much as the furniture of the kitchen. Increase the use for them, increase the consumable commodities which are to be circulated, managed, and prepared by means of them, and you will infallibly increase the quantity; but if you attempt by extraordinary means, to increase the quantity, you will as infallibly diminish the use and even the quantity too, which in those metals can never be greater than what the use requires. Were they ever to be accumulated beyond this quantity, their transportation is so easy, and the loss which attends their lying idle and unemployed so great, that no law could prevent their being immediately sent out of the country.

STUDY QUESTIONS

1. How does Smith contrast money as an instrument with "wealth" when applied to nations?
2. In what ways does he enhance his argument with supply-and-demand arguments?

16.6 GERMAINE DE STAËL, *MEMOIRS*

Germaine de Staël (1766–1817) was one of the great literary figures of the Enlightenment, though perhaps known more for championing the cause of reform in her salons and her political activity than for her literary output. She was born to a wealthy family—her father was the minister

Translation by Clifford Backman.

of finance to Louis XVI, her mother a prominent salon hostess—who married a Swedish nobleman who served as his country's ambassador to France. Active in the Revolution, she worked tirelessly to moderate the increasingly radical programs of the National Assembly, and when the National Convention came to power in 1792 she fled to Switzerland and spent time in Britain. She remained a champion of constitutional monarchy and opposed the radical developments in France's revolutionary regime, but returned to Paris in 1797 in order to mitigate the tensions and rivalries that were destroying the Revolution. When Napoleon Bonaparte came to power in 1799, de Staël found herself in frequent trouble with the new regime and had to go into brief exiles to avoid being arrested. In 1810 she left France and went on a long journey through eastern Europe and Russia and did not return to France until after Napoleon's fall. Her novels, essays, and travelogues have remained popular. What follows here are two chapters from her memoirs (published posthumously) in which she records her impressions of Russia and its people.

CHAPTER 13: THE COUNTRYSIDE AND THE CHARACTER OF THE PEOPLE

As I drew nearer and nearer to Moscow, nothing seemed to announce that I was approaching a capital city, only isolated wooden villages and no signs of life or movement along the roads that stretched across the immense plains. No sound, no country houses, no people. Russia is so vast that everything seemed to be swallowed up by the sheer space of it. One feels that one is passing through a countryside from which the entire population has just left. There were no birds and few cattle, at least hardly any visible from the road. The vastness of the place makes everything seem to disappear except the vastness itself—like a metaphysical concept that one can never shake once one has thought of it.

One evening before I arrived in the city I stopped in a pleasant meadow. It had been a hot day and I saw some peasant women dressed in quaint traditional clothes who were heading home from their work in the fields and singing some Ukrainian songs, the words of which were an ode to love and liberty. The tunes breathed an air of melancholy—almost of regret. I asked them if they would dance for me, and they consented. I have seen nothing more graceful than these country dances which were as refined as anything to be found in the finest arts of nature; they were remarkably sensual yet modest, and indeed I imagine that only the *bayadères* of India are their equal in that combination of languor and vitality that characterizes dancing in Russia and is suggestive of both reverie and passion (two human qualities that civilization can neither create nor subdue). The modest gaiety of these peasant women resonated with me, as indeed to one extent or another did that of most of the common folk I encountered in Russia. At the same time, I can easily imagine that they are fearsome once their passions are stirred since lacking all education they do not know how to control their own violent emotions. Being ignorant, they have no true moral values and are as much given to theft as to generosity. They take as readily as they give and are as conniving as they are gracious, depending on their mood, and they value both traits in themselves. Thus they resemble brutes in no small way in their approach to life, although I must add that only people tinged with barbarousness seem truly alive in Europe today—that is to say, people who are unaffected by Enlightenment and are therefore free. Only a people who have acquired from civilization an indifference to whatever oppresses them, provided their hearth-fires are left undisturbed, are truly free; and those nations whom civilization has taught nothing but how to explain power and rationalize servitude are doomed to be crushed. How many times I have wondered what became of those lovely peasant girls and those long-bearded peasant men, who accepted so peaceably the fate which Providence decreed for them! They must all have perished, for not a single one of them would ever have entered the service of their oppressors.

It is worth noting how much the people of Russia show a sense of public spiritedness. Their many military victories have given them a sense of invincibility, and this feeling, combined with the haughtiness of their aristocracy, the common people's sense of loyalty, the depth of their religious convictions, their hatred of foreigners (which is precisely what Peter I tried to suppress in them in his desire to bring enlightenment and civilization to them, but is nevertheless still coursing through their veins and ready to lash out)—all these things together account for their passionate energy. Many French people believe that Russia consists entirely of corrupt rulers, military yes-men, and a slave-like populace, but this is a grave misunderstanding that results merely from some old anecdotes spread by Parisian shopkeepers who have not been paid by their Russian debtors and a few clever witticisms of Diderot. Russia is a nation that it takes a long period of study to understand. I have observed it under circumstances when its many traits stood out, for the truth of a country is never more exposed than when it is in hard times and in need of courage. It cannot be over-stated that Russia is a nation of the most marked contrasts—the result, perhaps, of its mixed European and Asiatic cultural make-up. The people are so outgoing that one might think oneself their intimate friend after knowing them only a day, and yet one would be nothing of the kind even after ten years.

A Russian's silence is extraordinary and occurs only when he takes a profound interest in something. Otherwise he will talk as much as anyone, except his conversation evinces nothing but politeness and yields nothing of his true thoughts or feelings. Some people draw comparisons between the Russians and the French in this regard, although I think this entirely unjust, for the Russians are so changeable that they can speak and act so as to resemble the British, the French, or the Germans, depending on their circumstance; and yet they never cease to be essentially Russian, by which I mean they unite impulsiveness and restraint. Russians are more inclined to passionate feeling than intimate friendship, more daring that discerning, more devout than virtuous, more bold than gentlemanly, and so single-minded in pursuit of whatever they desire that nothing can stop them. More sociable than we French, their socializing nevertheless does not resemble our own, for their preference is not for the company of men and women engaged in an evening of clever conversation. When they gather, they wish to eat delicacies and watch the newest entertainments from around Europe and Asia; to hear music; to engage in play—in short, to do whatever activities will satisfy their desire for great amusement. They seek satisfactions of the heart and mind not in the company they keep but in the actions they undertake. They are, on the whole, quite an ignorant people who take little or no pleasure in serious conversation and do not care whether or not they exhibit any wit or cleverness by means of it. One looks in vain for any poetry, eloquent expression, or literature in Russia; luxury, power, and boldness are what they pursue and pride themselves on. Any other means of acquiring distinction they regard as effeminate and silly.

All of which will lead many people to say that this is no surprise since the Russians, being slaves, cannot develop any true civilized character. I need hardly say that all enlightened men and women wish to see Russia liberated from this condition, and probably no one desires it more than Tsar Alexander. Russian servitude has not resulted, though, in the same social effects that the West is familiar with as a consequence of feudalism, that is, one of conquerors imposing their wills upon the vanquished. Here the bonds connecting the elites and the common people resemble that of the free citizens and the slaves in the ancient Roman *familia* [household], rather than the lords and serfs of our tradition. In Russia there is no urban class interposed between high and low, and the nation's art and literature suffer for it since it is generally among such a middling class that knowledge advances. But it must be said that the lack of an in-between class means that the high and the low are united by close bonds of affection even though the material and social differences between them are so stark since they exist side by side without any buffer between them. The manner of social organization is a detriment to the intellectual culture of the upper class but not to the happiness of the lower since nations that do not have representative governments—that is, where monarchs still issue and execute the laws themselves—people are generally more debased by the absence of rational thinking and morality than they are in this vast Russian empire, in which a handful of simple religious teachings and social traditions suffice to keep the masses of people under the guidance of the elites. The sheer immensity of the empire prevents the authority of the powerful from oppressing the people too much. Finally, and most important of all, the spirit of religious faith and military-like discipline is so strong among the people that they are tolerant of most abuses. A wise writer once justly said that Russians resemble the plays of Shakespeare in the sense that everything about them that is not deficient is sublime, and everything that is not sublime is deficient.

Considering the tremendous crises that Russia was undergoing when I travelled through it, I could not help but admire the resolute strength and readiness to endure sacrifice that I saw everywhere; the contemplation of those virtues was nearly enough, indeed, to allow me to overlook aspects of the people that I might otherwise have condemned.

CHAPTER 15: THE JOURNEY FROM MOSCOW TO PETERSBURG

I was sad to leave Moscow and stopped for a while in a woodland not far from the city, a site where Muscovites often go on holidays in order to frolic and simply enjoy the sunshine (which lasts only a short time there). What did I see as I made my way north? Even the seemingly innumerable birch trees, which can wear you out with monotony, start to become rare as you approach Archangel, where, I am told, they are still cared for [despite the conditions] as we do with orange trees in France. The countryside from Moscow to Petersburg is dusty at first, then turns marshy. When it rains, the earth turns black and the roads all but disappear. The peasants' houses one sees, however, look comfortable and are decorated with pilasters and windows that are surrounded by wooden arabesque carvings. It was summer when I passed through this region but I could already sense the approach of winter in the cloud banks. The local fruits I ate were all bitter since they ripen so quickly. I saw a rose that stirred my memory of those in our own country, but all the other flowers I beheld appeared to have their heads lowered in submission, as though the icy hand of the north wind was preparing to pluck them.

I rode through Novgorod, a city with a long tradition of republican independence that dates back six centuries to the days of the Hanseatic League. It is common for people today to say that Europe regained its freedom in the last century, but it actually despotism that is the modern invention. In Russia, in fact, serfdom was only introduced in the sixteenth century. Until Peter I's reign imperial edicts used the formula *The boyars* [high nobility] *have advised and the Tsar decrees*. Peter introduced many excellent things in Russia, and in order to do so he had to bring low many of the traditional elites and ally himself with civil and spiritual authorities—which is precisely what Richelieu did in France, and indeed Peter was a great admirer of the cardinal. I recall learning that when he was shown the cardinal's tomb he exclaimed, "What a great man! I would gladly give up half my empire in order to learn from him how to govern the other half!" Peter was too modest in saying this, for he had the advantage of being a great general (something Richelieu was not) and both the founder of a navy and the instigator of commerce. Richelieu, in contrast, did nothing but govern despotically at home and deal craftily abroad. But as for Novgorod, Ivan Vasilievich [Ivan III, r. 1462–1505] acquired it in 1470 and put an end to its liberties. He also brought to the Kremlin in Moscow the great Veche Bell whose ringing had long signaled to the citizens that it was time to congregate in the market square to deliberate on public affairs. When Novgorod thus lost her liberty, the city saw its population, commerce, and wealth all plummet. Such, according to Russia's finest historian, is the disastrous effect of arbitrary power. Even today Novgorod emits an atmosphere of melancholy, whose vast enclosed area indicates that it was once a large and populous city although now you see only scattered homes whose inhabitants seem almost to have been placed there like figurines weeping over tombs. Moscow today, though beautiful, has much the same aspect, although the public spirit of its people will certainly bring about its recovery as it rebuilds.

STUDY QUESTIONS

1. What main impressions does Russia make on de Staël? How is Russia different from France? How are Russians different from the French?
2. For de Staël, which obstacles impede the development of "true civilized character" among the Russians? Why does she describe them as "slaves"?

CHAPTER 17

THE FRENCH REVOLUTION AND THE NAPOLEONIC EMPIRE

17.1 EDMUND BURKE, *REFLECTIONS ON THE REVOLUTION IN FRANCE*, 1790

Edmund Burke (1729–1797) was an Irish politician and writer who moved to England to become involved in politics as a supporter of constitutional monarchy. The moderate Burke opposed every form of absolutism, which led him to support the American colonies as they resisted the encroachments of King George III, but to condemn the French revolutionaries as being iconoclastic of the ancient regime instead of returning to what he considered a stable political tradition. In a widely disseminated popular pamphlet, Burke responded to the excesses of the French Revolution, from women marching on Versailles to the sweeping change—disconnected from the needs of a newly created social structure—that was demanded by revolutionaries. Consider his wary tone in discussing the events across the Channel.

Sollicitous chiefly for the peace of my own country, but by no means unconcerned for yours, I wish to communicate more largely, what was at first intended only for your private satisfaction. I shall still keep your affairs in my eye, and continue to address myself to you. Indulging myself in the freedom of epistolary intercourse, I beg leave to throw out my thoughts, and express my feelings, just as they arise in my mind, with very little attention to formal method. I set out with the proceedings of the Revolution Society; but I shall not confine myself to them. Is it possible I should? It looks to me as if I were in great crisis, not of the affairs of France alone, but of all Europe, perhaps of more than Europe. All circumstances taken together, the French revolution is the most astonishing that has hitherto happened in the world. The most wonderful things are brought about in many instances by means the most absurd and ridiculous; in the most ridiculous modes; and apparently, by the most contemptible instruments. Every thing seems out of nature in this strange chaos of levity and ferocity, and of all sorts of crimes jumbled together with all sorts of follies.

From Edmund Burke, *Reflections on the Revolution in France, 1790*, pp. 10, 37–40, 54–5, 60–1, 96–7, 169–70, 248–9.

In viewing this monstrous tragi-comic scene, the most opposite passions necessarily succeed, and sometimes mix with each other in the mind; alternate contempt and indignation; alternate laughter and tears; alternate scorn and horror.

. . .

Compute your gains: see what is got by those extravagant and presumptuous speculations which have taught your leaders to despise all their predecessors, and all their contemporaries, and even to despise themselves, until the moment in which they became truly despicable. By following those false lights, France has brought undisguised calamities at a higher price than any nation has purchased the most unequivocal blessings! France has brought poverty by crime! France has not sacrificed her virtue to her interest; but she has abandoned her interest, that she might prostitute her virtue. All nations have begun the fabric of a new government, or the reformation of an old, by establishing originally, or by enforcing with greater exactness, some rites or other of religion. All other people have laid the foundations of civil freedom in severer manners, and a system of a more austere and masculine morality. France, when she let loose the reins of regal authority, doubled the license, of a ferocious dissoluteness in manner, and of an insolent irreligion in opinion and practices; and has extended through all ranks of life, as if she were communicating some privilege, or laying open some secluded benefit, all the unhappy corruptions that usually were the disease of wealth and power. This is one of the new principles of equality in France.

France, by the perfidy of her leaders, has utterly disgraced the tone of lenient council in the cabinets of princes, and disarmed it of its most potent topics. She has sanctified the dark suspicious maxims of tyrannous distrust; and taught kings to tremble at (what will hereafter be called) the delusive plausibilities, of moral politicians. Sovereigns will consider those who advise them to place an unlimited confidence in their people, as subverters of their thrones; as traitors who aim at their destruction, by leading their easy good-nature, under specious pretences, to admit combinations of bold and faithless men into a participation of their power. This alone (if there were nothing else) is irreparable calamity to you and to mankind. Remember that your parliament of Paris told your king, that in calling the states together, he had nothing to fear but the prodigal excess of their zeal in providing for the support of the throne. It is right that these men should hide their heads. It is right that they should bear their part in the ruin which their counsel has brought on the sovereign and their country. Such sanguine declarations tend to lull authority asleep; to encourage it rashly to engage in perilous adventures of untried policy; to neglect those provisions, preparations, and precautions, which distinguish benevolence from imbecility; and without which no man can answer for the salutary effect of any abstract plan of government or of freedom. For want of these, they have seen the medicine of the state corrupted into its poison. They have seen the French rebel against a mild and lawful monarch, with more fury, outrage, and insult, than ever any people has been known to rise against the most illegal usurper, or the most sanguinary tyrant. Their resistance was made to concession; their revolt was from protection; their blow was aimed at a hand holding out graces, favours, and immunities.

This was unnatural. The rest is in order. They have found their punishment in their success. Laws overturned; tribunals subverted; industry without vigour; commerce expiring; the revenue unpaid, yet the people impoverished; a church pillaged, and a state not relieved; civil and military anarchy made the constitution of the kingdom; every thing human and divine sacrificed to the idol of public credit, and national bankruptcy the consequence; and to crown all, the paper securities of new, precarious, tottering power, the discredited paper securities of impoverished fraud, and beggared rapine, held out as currency for the support of an empire, in lieu of the two great recognized species that represent the lasting conventional credit of mankind, which disappeared and hid themselves in the earth from whence they came, when the principle of property, whose creatures and representatives they are, was systematically subverted.

Were all these dreadful things necessary? were they the inevitable results of the desperate struggle of determined patriots, compelled to wade through blood and tumult, to the quiet shore of a tranquil and prosperous liberty? No! nothing like it. The fresh ruins of France, which shock our feelings whenever we can turn our eyes, are not the devastation of civil war; they are the sad but instructive monuments of rash and ignorant counsel in time of profound peace. They are the display of inconsiderate and presumptuous, because unresisted and irresistible authority. The persons who have thus squandered away the precious treasure of their crimes, the persons who have made this prodigal and wild waste of public evils (the last stake reserved for the ultimate ransom of the state) have met in the progress with little, or rather with no opposition at all. Their whole march was more like a triumphal procession than the progress of a war. Their pioneers have gone before them, and demolished and laid every thing level at their feet. Not one drop of *their* blood have they shed in the cause of the country they have ruined. They have made no sacrifices to their projects of greater consequences than their shoe-buckles, whilst they were imprisoning their king, murdering their fellow citizens, and bathing in tears, and plunging in poverty and distress, thousands of worthy men and worthy families. Their cruelty has not even been the base result of fear. It has been the effect of their sense of perfect safety, in authorizing treasons, robberies, rapes, assassinations, slaughters, and burnings throughout their harassed land. But the cause of all was plain from the beginning.

. . .

What is that cause of liberty, and what are those exertions in its favour, to which the example of France is so singularly auspicious? Is our monarchy to be annihilated, with all the laws, all the tribunals, and all the antient corporations of the kingdom? Is every land-mark of the country to be done away in favour of a geometrical and arithmetical constitution? Is the house of lords to be voted useless? Is episcopacy to be abolished? Are the church lands to be sold to Jews and jobbers; or given to bribe new-invented municipal republics into a participation in sacrilege? Are all the taxes to be voted grievances, and the revenue reduced to a patriotic contribution, or patriotic presents? Are silver shoe-buckles to be substituted in the place of the land tax and the malt tax, for the support of the naval strength of this kingdom? Are all orders, ranks, and distinctions to be confounded, that out of universal anarchy, joined to national bankruptcy, three or four thousand democracies should be formed into eighty-three, and that they may all, by some sort of unknown attractive power, be organized into one? For this great end, is the army to be seduced from its discipline and its fidelity, first, by every kind of debauchery, and then by the terrible precedent of a donative in the increase of pay? Are the curates to be seduced from their bishops, by holding out to them the delusive hope of a dole out of the spoils of their own order? Are the citizens of London to be drawn from their allegiance, by feeding them at the expence of their fellow-subjects? Is a compulsory paper currency to be substituted in the place of the legal coin of this kingdom? Is what remains of the plundered stock of public revenue to be employed in the wild project of maintaining two armies to watch over and to fight with each other?—If these are the ends and means of the Revolution Society, I admit they are well assorted; and France may furnish them for both with precedents in point.

I see that your example is held out to shame us. I know that we are supposed a dull sluggish race, rendered passive by finding our situation tolerable; and prevented by a mediocrity of freedom from ever attaining to its full perfection. Your leaders in France began by affecting to admire, almost to adore, the British constitution; but as they advanced they came to look upon it with a sovereign contempt. The friends of your National Assembly amongst us have full as mean an opinion of what was formerly thought the glory of their country. The Revolution Society has discovered that the English nation is not free.

. . .

Government is not made in virtue of natural rights, which may and do exist in total independence of it; and exist in much greater clearness, and in a much greater degree of abstract perfection: but their abstract perfection is their practical defect. By having a right to every thing they want every thing. Government is a contrivance of human wisdom to provide human *wants*. Men have a right that these wants should be provided for by this wisdom. Among these wants is to be reckoned the want, out of civil society, of a sufficient restraint upon their passions. Society requires not only that the passions of individuals should be subjected, but that even in the mass and body as well as in the individuals, the inclinations of men should frequently be thwarted, their will controlled, and their passions brought into subjection. This can only be done *by a power of themselves;* and not, in the exercise of its function, subject to that will and to those passions which it is its office to bridle and subdue. In this sense the restraints on men, as well as their liberties, are to be reckoned among their rights. But as the liberties and the restrictions vary with times and circumstances, and admit of infinite modifications, they cannot be settled upon any abstract rule; and nothing is so foolish as to discuss them upon that principle.

The moment you abate any thing from the full rights of men, each to govern himself, and suffer any artificial positive limitation upon those rights, from that moment the whole organization of government becomes a consideration of convenience. This it is which makes the constitution of a state, and the due distribution of its powers, a matter of the most delicate and complicated skill. It requires deep knowledge of human nature and human necessities, and of the things which facilitate or obstruct the various ends which are to be pursued by the mechanism of civil institutions. The state is to have recruits to its strength, and remedies to its distempers. What is the use of discussing a man's abstract right to food or to medicine? The question is upon the method of procuring and administering them. In that deliberation I shall always advise to call in the aid of the farmer and the physician, rather than the professor of metaphysics.

The science of constructing a commonwealth, or renovating it, or reforming it, is, like every other experimental science, not to be taught *a priori.* Nor is it a short experience that can instruct us in that practical science; because the real effects of moral causes are not always immediate; but that which in the first instance is prejudicial may be excellent in its remoter operation; and its excellence may arise even from the ill effects it produces in the beginning. The reverse also happens; and very plausible schemes, with very pleasing commencements have often shameful and lamentable conclusions.

. . .

To avoid therefore the evils of inconstancy and versatility, ten thousand times worse than those of obstinacy and the blindest prejudice, we have consecrated the state, that no man should approach to look into its defects or corruptions but with due caution; that he should never dream of beginning its reformation by its subversion; that he should approach to the faults of the state as to the wounds of a father, with pious awe and trembling solicitude. By this wise prejudice we are taught to look with horror on those children of their country who are prompt rashly to hack that aged parent in pieces, and put him into the kettle of magicians, in hopes that by their poisonous weeds, and wild incantations, they may regenerate the paternal constitution, and renovate their father's life.

Society is indeed a contract. Subordinate contracts for objects of mere occasional interest may be dissolved at pleasure—but the state ought not to be considered as nothing better than a partnership agreement in a trade of pepper and coffee, callico or tobacco, or some other such low concern, to be taken up for a little temporary interest, and to be dissolved by the fancy of the parties. It is to be looked on with other reverence; because it is not a partnership in things subservient only to the gross animal existence of a temporary and perishable nature. It is a partnership in all science; a partnership in all art; a partnership in every virtue, and in all perfection. As the ends of such a partnership cannot be obtained in many generations, it becomes a partnership not only between those who are living, but between those who are living, those who are dead, and those who are to be born. Each contract of each particular state is but a clause in the great primeval contract of eternal society, linking the lower with the higher natures, connecting the visible and invisible world, according to a fixed compact sanctioned by the inviolable oath which holds all physical and all moral natures, each in the appointed place. This law is not subject to the will of those, who by an obligation above them, and infinitely superior, are bound to submit their will to that law. The municipal corporations of that universal kingdom are not morally at liberty at their pleasure, and on the speculations of a contingent improvement, wholly to separate and tear asunder the bands of the subordinate community, and to dissolve it into an unsocial, uncivil, unconnected chaos of elementary principles. It is the first and supreme necessity only, a necessity that is not chosen but chooses, a necessity paramount to deliberation, that admits no discussion, and demands no evidence, which alone can justify a resort to anarchy. This necessity is not exception to the rule; because this necessity itself is a part too of that moral and physical disposition of things to which man must be obedient by consent or force; but if that which is only submission to necessity should be made the object of choice, the law is broken, nature is disobeyed, and the rebellious are outlawed, cast forth, and exiled, from this world reason, and order, and peace, and virtue, and fruitful penitence, into the antagonist world of madness, discord, vice, confusion, and unavailing sorrow.

. . .

At once to preserve and to reform is quite another thing. When the useful parts of an old establishment are kept, and what is superadded is to be fitted to what is retained, a vigorous mind, steady persevering attention, various powers of comparison and combination, and the resources of an understanding fruitful in expedients are to be exercised; they are to be exercised in a continued conflict with the combined force of opposite vices; with the obstinacy that rejects all improvement, and the levity that is fatigued and disgusted with every thing of which it is in possession. But you may object—"A process of this kind is slow. It is not fit for an assembly, which glories in performing in a few months the work of ages. Such a mode of reforming, possibly might take up many years." Without question it might; and it ought. It is one of the excellences of a method in which time is amongst the assistants, that its operation is slow, and in some cases almost imperceptible. If circumspection and caution are a part of wisdom, when we work only upon inanimate matter, surely they become a part of duty too, when the subject of our demolition and construction is not a brick and timber, but sentient beings, by the sudden alteration to whose state, condition, and habits, multitudes may be rendered miserable. But it seems as if it were the prevalent opinion in Paris, that an unfeeling heart, and an undoubting confidence, are the sole qualifications for a perfect legislator. Far different are my ideas of that high office. The true lawgiver ought to have a heart full of sensibility. He ought to love and respect his kind, and to fear himself. It may be allowed to his temperament to catch his ultimate object with an intuitive glance; but his movements towards it ought to be deliberate. Political arrangement, as it is a work for social ends, is to be only wrought by social means. There mind must conspire with mind. Time is required to produce that union of minds which alone can produce all the good we aim at. Our patience will achieve more than our force. If I might venture to appeal to what is so much out of fashion in Paris, I mean to experience, I should tell you, that in my course I have known, and, according to my measure, have co-operated with great men; and I have never yet seen any plan which has not been mended by the observations of those who were much inferior in understanding to the person who took the lead in the business. By a slow but well-sustained progress, the effect of each step is watched; the good or ill success of the first, gives light to us in the second; and so, from light to light, we are conducted with safety through the whole series. We see, that the parts of the system do not clash. The evils latent in the most promising contrivances are provided for as they arise. One advantage is as little as possible sacrificed to another. We compensate, we reconcile, we balance. We are enabled to unite into a consistent whole the various anomalies and contending principles that are found in the minds and affairs of men. From hence arises, not an excellence in simplicity, but one far superior, an excellence in composition. Where the great interests of mankind are concerned through a long succession of generations, that succession ought to be admitted into some share in the councils which are so deeply to affect them. If justice requires this, the work itself requires the aid of more minds than one age can furnish. It is from this view of things that the best legislators have been often satisfied with the establishment of some sure, solid, and ruling principle in government; a power like that which some of the philosophers have called a plastic nature; and having fixed the principle, they have left it afterwards to its own operation.

. . .

I wish my countrymen rather to recommend to our neighbors the example of the British constitution, than to take models from them for the improvement of our own. In the former they have got an invaluable treasure. They are not, I think, without some causes of apprehension and complaint; but they do not owe to their constitution, but to their own conduct. I think our happy situation owing to our constitution; but owing to the whole of it, and not to any part singly; owing in a great measure to what we have left standing in our several reviews and reformations, as well as to what we have altered or superadded. Our people will find employment enough for a truly patriotic, free, and independent spirit, in guarding what they possess, from violation. I would not exclude alteration neither; but even when I changed, it should be to preserve. I should be led to my remedy by a great grievance. In what I did, I should follow the example of our ancestors. I would make the reparation as nearly as possible in the style of the building. A politic caution, a guarded circumspection, a moral rather than a complexional timidity were among the ruling principles of our forefathers in their most decided conduct. Not being illuminated with the light of which the gentlemen of France tell us they have got so abundant a share, they acted under a strong impression of the ignorance and fallibility of mankind. He that had made them thus fallible, rewarded them for having in their conduct attended to their nature. Let us imitate their caution, if we wish to deserve their fortune, or to retain their bequests. Let us add, if we please, but let us preserve what they have left; and, standing on the firm ground of the British constitution, let us be satisfied to admire rather than attempt to follow in their desperate flights the aëronauts of France.

I have told you candidly my sentiments. I think they are not likely to alter yours. I do not know that they ought. You are young; you cannot guide, but must follow the fortune of your country. But hereafter they may be of some use to you, in some future form which your commonwealth may take. In the present it can hardly remain; but before its final settlement it may be obliged to pass, as one of our poets says, "through great varieties of untried being," and in all its transmigrations to be purified by fire and blood.

I have little to recommend my opinions, but long observation and much impartiality. They come from one who has been no tool of power, no flatterer of greatness; and who in his last acts does not wish to belye the tenour of his life. They come from one, almost the whole of whose public exertion has been a struggle for the liberty of others; from one in whose breast no anger durable or vehement has ever been kindled, but by what he considered as tyranny; and who snatches from his share in the endeavors which are used by good men to discredit opulent oppression, the hours he has employed on your affairs; and who in so doing persuades himself he has not departed from his usual office: they come from one who desires honours, distinctions, and emoluments, but little; and who expects them not at all; who has not contempt for fame, and no fear of obloquy; who shuns contention, though he will hazard an opinion: from one who wishes to preserve consistency; but who would preserve consistency by varying his means to secure the unity of his end; and, when the equipoise of the vessel in which he sails, may be endangered by overloading it upon one side, is desirous of carrying the small weight of his reasons to that which may preserve its equipoise.

STUDY QUESTIONS

1. Does Burke consider all rash, hasty behavior essentially immoral?
2. Are conservatism's principles based only in reason, or do they sometimes make appeal to faith and loyalty?

17.2 OLYMPE DE GOUGES, *DECLARATION OF THE RIGHTS OF WOMAN AND OF THE FEMALE CITIZEN*, 1791

Olympe de Gouges (1748–1793) was a proud abolitionist, political activist, social reformer, and playwright. Born as Marie Gouze, at the age of seventeen she was married against her will to a man she abhorred and soon had a child. Her husband died shortly thereafter, leaving her to shift for herself. She changed her name to Olympe de Gouges and never married again, although she did take a series of well-to-do lovers (she once called the institution of marriage "a tomb where love and trust lie buried"). She was largely self-educated and after her move to Paris became a regular presence at prominent salons. She published a novel in 1784 and then turned to playwrighting. A speedy writer, she produced forty plays and dozens of political pamphlets (the "blogs" of the eighteenth century). She enthusiastically supported the Revolution at the start but soon became critical of its excesses and chaos, as well as its neglect of women as rightful citizens of the nation. She was executed for treason in 1793, during the Reign of Terror, falsely accused of trying to aid the restoration of the monarchy. Her *Declaration of the Rights of Woman and of the Female Citizen* remains her best-known work.

PREAMBLE

The mothers, daughters, sisters, and representatives of the nation propose to establish a National Assembly, and in consideration of the fact that ignorance, oversight, and contempt for the rights of women are the principal causes of public misery and governmental corruption they resolve to proclaim in a solemn declaration the natural, inalienable, and sacred rights of women. May this declaration remain always in the minds of all of society and forever remind everyone of their rights and duties; and may the actions of empowered women and men together be ever judged by the goals of all political institutions, and thus earn the people's respect; and may the just concerns of female citizens, based henceforth on fundamental and unchallenged principles, always aim at maintaining the Constitution and the good morals and welfare of all.

Therefore, the sex superior in beauty and courage, acting out of womanly suffering, recognizes and declares in the presence and under the guidance of the Supreme Being the following Rights of Woman and the Female Citizen:

1. Women are born free and remain equal to men in their rights. Social distinctions apply only on the basis of what serves the public good.
2. The goal of every political institution is the preservation of the natural, un-created rights of both men and women—namely liberty, prosperity, security, and above all resistance to oppression.
3. The nation itself, which is the union of its men and women, is the source of all sovereignty. No political body or individual can legitimately exercise any authority that does not derive from the nation.

Translation by Clifford Backman.

4. Liberty and justice consist of rendering to all that which belongs to them. The limits that exist on women's ability to exercise their natural rights are those imposed by the timeless tyranny imposed upon them by men, and these limits must be reformed by the laws of nature and reason.
5. The laws of nature and reason stand opposed to all actions harmful to society. Whatever is not forbidden by these wise and divine laws cannot be denied to anyone, and no person can be forced to act contrary to them.
6. Just law is the expression of the general will, and all citizens—male and female alike—must agree to its formulation either personally or through their representatives.
7. There can be no exceptions for any woman. In all cases she is to be accused, arrested, and imprisoned according to the same law and rigorous standards as any man.
8. Law must establish penalties that are strictly and clearly necessary, and no woman henceforth may be held accountable for violating any law that predates this pronouncement and applies to her specifically because she is a woman.
9. Any woman who is declared guilty [under new law] must face the full severity of that law.
10. The law may not take action against any person solely on the basis of his or her opinions, no matter how offensive they might be. Since a woman has the right to mount a scaffold she must have a right to address the Government so long as her statements do not disturb public order as established by law.
11. Free expression of ideas and opinions is one of woman's most precious rights, since only this freedom can ensure legal paternity as regards children. Every female citizen has the right to assert freely *I am the mother of this child, who belongs to you* without being forced to conceal this truth because of a barbarous prejudice; although she is answerable for any abuse of this freedom, as determined by law.
12. It is a necessary boon to society to safeguard the rights of woman and the female citizen. This guarantee serves the advantage of everyone, not just the women whom it pertains to.
13. Women contribute as much as men to the maintenance of public service and administration, and share equally in the onerous duties and responsibilities established by law, and therefore they must join equally in the performance of offices, employments, trusts, dignities, and other activities.
14. Women and men, as citizens, acting either for themselves or through their representatives, have an equal right to decide on the need for public taxation. Women share equally in producing the nation's wealth and therefore should share equally in the reckoning, administering, collecting, and timing of taxes.
15. The women of the nation, in contributing equally to the payment of taxes, have a right to demand from every public official an accounting of his or her actions in office.
16. Any society that does not guarantee the rights of its citizens and the separation of governmental powers is a society without a Constitution; and any Constitution that was created without the participation of the majority of its citizens is null and void.
17. Ownership of property is a sacred and inviolable right belonging to both sexes, whether mutually or individually. No one can be deprived of it by any claim to natural law unless it is to serve the public good as established by recognized law and all due indemnity.

Arise, women! The clarion bell of Reason rings throughout the universe! Recognize your rights! The mighty structure of the world is no longer beset by prejudice, fanaticism, superstition, and lies, and the torch of Truth has dispelled the clouds of stupidity and transgression. Society's enslaved men have marshalled their forces but needed yours too in order to break chains of their servitude—but then, once freed, these men imposed injustice upon you! O women, women! When will you stop being so blind! What have you gained from the Revolution so far but sharper scorn and bitterer contempt? During the centuries of [monarchical] decadence your only power was what you wielded over the weakness of your own men; but that world is now destroyed, so what is left for you but the complaint that men are unjust and that their claim upon your patrimony is properly legal and wise? The wise words of the Lawgiver at the marriage of Cana?[1] Are you afraid that our nation's lawgivers, in setting right this moral problem that dates to an out-of-style politics, will say, "Women, what makes you equal to us?" If so, you must answer, "Everything!" If men are going to persist in this imbecility that contradicts their own stated principles, you must have the courage to attack their pretensions of superiority with the force of Reason. Unite under the banner of philosophy; unleash the energy of your spirit; and you will soon see these proud men, your servile adorers, crawl at your feet and become willing to share with you the blessings of the Supreme Being. No matter what obstacles stand in your way, it is in your power to free us all, if only you will it.

[1] A reference to the story of Jesus attending a marriage celebration. According to John's gospel (ch. 2) when the party's host ran out of wine Jesus's mother asked her son to do something to rectify the situation. Jesus turned to her and complained, "Woman, what do you want from me?"

STUDY QUESTIONS

1. What are the principal declarations set forth by de Gouges? What are the main bases of her argument?
2. How does de Gouges view "nature"? What, for her, is the connection between law and nature?

17.3 MAXIMILIEN ROBESPIERRE, *REPORT ON THE PRINCIPLES OF PUBLIC MORALITY*, 1794

Maximilien de Robespierre (1758–1794) was a philosopher, activist, and staunch *Jacobin*. In his early life, Robespierre championed the fundamental goodness of French citizens, for whom he sought an array of political rights. However, when King Louis XVI "betrayed" France with his abuses of constitutional protection for citizens, Robespierre argued that the only solution was death; his belief that traitors were undermining the revolution made him determined to root them out. Two years later, it was his rhetoric that justified the use of mass executions during the Reign of Terror (1793–1794) as protection of the Republic. In this work, Robespierre appeals to his compatriots' sense of virtue to push on through revolution and abolishment of tyranny to arrive safely at a republican government.

But what is our goal, the point toward which we are striving? The peaceful enjoyment of freedom and equality; the rule of that Eternal Justice whose laws are not carved in marble or stone but are inscribed in the hearts of all men—even the heart of a slave, who forgets them, and that of a tyrannical ruler, who denies them. We seek an ordering of society in which all base and cruel passions are held in check, and all benevolent

Translation by Clifford Backman.

and generous passions are brought to life, by laws; in which the noblest ambition is to earn glory and serve the nation; in which social honors are based on the fundamental notion of equality; in which any given citizen is subject to the magistrate, while the magistrate is subject to the people, and the people to the cause of justice. . . . We desire a society in which morality takes the place of egotism; integrity takes that of formal codes of behavior; principles replace habits; the rule of reason substitutes for the tyranny of tradition—scorn of vice takes the place of scorn of the unfortunate, the love of honor takes over for the love of money, and good people replace "proper society." We want a society in which merit replaces intrigue, genius replaces wit, truth replaces glamour, genuine happiness displaces luxurious boredom, and human greatness displaces the pettiness of "great people." . . . In short, a society in which the miraculous virtue of a republic takes the place of the ridiculous vice of a monarchy. . . .

A democratic state is one in which the sovereign people, guided by laws of their own making, do for themselves everything that they can do effectively, and their representatives, guided by those same laws, do everything that they cannot. This is why you must seek the rules for your political conduct in the principles of democracy. But before we can lay the foundations of democracy and set them on firm ground, we must first (if we are ever to achieve the stable society ruled by constitutional laws) finish Liberty's war against Tyranny and pass safely through the storms of Revolution. . . . Therefore you ought to conduct yourself with the stormy conditions through which our revolution is passing always in mind. . . . And what is the fundamental principle of our popular democracy, the mainspring that sustains and drives it? Virtue. The type of public virtue that worked wonders in ancient Greece and Rome and is bound to produce even more astonishing feats in republican France. . . .

It follows that the first rule of your public conduct should be to dedicate yourselves to equality and virtue. . . . and you should embrace everything that inspires patriotism, purifies morals, elevates the soul, and directs the passions of the heart toward serving the public interest. . . . Insofar as our French Revolution is concerned, any personal immorality is an attack on our society, any personal corruption is counter-revolutionary. Weakness, vice, and prejudice are paving stones on the road to another monarchy. Under the heavy weight of our former customs, human frailty can succumb to false ideas and faint-hearted sentiments, and thus we are in greater danger from too much weakness that we are from an excess of zeal. . . .

But I speak these words not to justify any and all excesses. Even the most sacred of principles can be abused. Our government must be wise enough to allow for circumstances, to seize the right moments, to select the appropriate methods. Proper preparation is necessary to the correct performance of weighty deeds, just as wisdom is a precondition of virtue. From this way of thinking we deduce an important truth: a government of the people must trust those people and be suspicious of itself.

And this is all that would need to be said, if we were steering the great ship of our revolution through calm waters. But storms rage against us, and the condition of our revolution at the moment imposes a special obligation upon all. . . . Wicked men with plans in their hearts to steal from the people or who have already done so and now seek impunity, evildoers for whom the liberty of all is a personal tragedy or who have embraced the call of our revolution but treat our republic as an object on which to prey, abound. So many self-serving and greedy men who once stood at our side have now abandoned us and our cause, which they probably never shared with us at all. One could say that two opposed foes—Virtue and Vice—are competing for mastery of the natural world, and at the present hour are fighting to control the destiny of the world. At this moment, in this great epoch of human history, France is the main stage of this titanic struggle. On the outside, all the tyrants of the world have us encircled; on the inside, all their friends are conspiring against us and will keep doing so until there is no hope. Therefore, we must either smother our Republic's internal and external enemies, or perish with them. Our guiding maxim will be to deal with the people by reason, and to the enemies of the people by terror. In peaceful times, of course, virtue is the source from which the people's government derives its authority. But now, at this point in our revolution, there are two sources: virtue and terror. Virtue, without which terror would be disastrous; and terror, without which virtue is powerless—terror that is nothing more nor less than swift, severe, and unbending justice. . . .

Some will say that terror is how a despotism rules. But has our government anything in common with despotism? Yes—but only in the sense that a sword in one hand resembles a sword in another, whether one champions liberty or tyranny. When tyrants hold power because their subjects are terrified of them, then tyrants are justified—but only as tyrants. When we strike down the enemies of liberty by means of terror, we too are justified—but as founders of a republic. The government of our revolution is the despotism of liberty against tyranny.

STUDY QUESTIONS

1. What is the context for Robespierre arguing that virtue without terror is disastrous? How does he portray the position of France?
2. What does Robespierre mean when he says "the government of our revolution is the despotism of liberty against tyranny"? Can you say that events made "despotism of tyranny against liberty" to be more true?

17.4 NAPOLEON, LETTERS TO HIS BROTHER JÉRÔME, 1801–1812

Napoleon Bonaparte (1769–1821) started his political career as a Corsican officer in the French army and rose to be the self-styled "First Consul of the French Republic, and later Emperor of France"—thus reviving ancient Roman means of rule. An ambitious man, Napoleon led many successful military campaigns against Western European nations who objected to his consolidated power; British Duke Wellington defeated his army at Waterloo (Belgium) in 1815, thus ending Napoleon's imperial rule. This letter, written to his brother Jérôme Napoleon (1784–1860), the King of Westphalia, reveals a reformist side to the great conqueror: here, Napoleon advocates for enlightened rule over a grateful, liberated population.

TO JÉRÔME BONAPARTE

PARIS, *16th August* 1801.

I'm glad to hear you are getting used to the life of a sailor. There's no better career in which to win a name for yourself. Go up aloft, get to know every part of the ship; and when you come back from your voyage, I hope to hear that you are as active as any powder-monkey. Don't let anyone dictate your profession to you. Make up your mind that you are going to be a sailor. I hope you have already learnt to keep your watch, and box the compass.

. . .

From J. M. Thompson, trans. and ed., *Napoleon's Letters*. London: J. M. Dent & Sons Ltd, 1999, pp. 94, 190–1, 121–2, 194–5, 202, 218–9, 270–1.

TO MADAME MÈRE

CHÂTEAU DE STUPINIGI, *22nd April* 1805.

M. Jérôme Bonaparte has arrived at Lisbon with the woman he is living with. I have ordered the prodigal son to travel by Perpignan, Toulouse, Grenoble, and Turin, and to report himself at Milan. I have told him that if he varies this route he will be arrested. Miss Paterson, who is living with him, has taken the precaution of bringing a brother with her. I have given orders that she is to be sent back to America. If she attempts to evade these orders, and appears either at Bordeaux or in Paris, she will be escorted to Amsterdam, and put on board the first ship for America. As for the young man himself, I shall only give him one interview. If he shows himself unworthy of the name he bears, and seems inclined to persist in his liaison, I shall show him no mercy. If he shows no disposition to wipe out the dishonour with which he has stained my name by deserting the colours for a wretched woman, I shall utterly disown him, and perhaps make an example of him, to teach young officers the sanctity of military service, and the enormity of the crime they commit, if they prefer a female to the flag. Assuming that he comes to Milan, I want you to write to him. Tell him that I have been like a father to him. Tell him that it is his sacred duty to obey me, and that his only hope is to do as I command. Get his sisters to write too: for, once I have pronounced his sentence, I shall be inflexible, and his whole career will be ruined.

. . .

TO JÉRÔME NAPOLEON, KING OF WESTPHALIA

FONTAINEBLEAU, *15th November* 1807.

I enclose the constitution for your Kingdom. It embodies the conditions on which I renounce all my rights of conquest, and all the claims I have acquired over your state. You must faithfully observe it. I am concerned for the happiness of your subjects, not only as it affects your reputation, and my own, but also for its influence on the whole European situation. Don't listen to those who say that your subjects are so accustomed to slavery that they will feel no gratitude for the benefits you give them. There is more intelligence in the Kingdom of Westphalia than they would have you believe; and your throne will never be firmly established except upon the trust and affection of the common people. What German opinion impatiently demands is that men of no rank, but of marked ability, shall have an equal claim upon your favour and your employment, and that every trace of serfdom, or of a feudal hierarchy between the sovereign and the lowest class of his subjects, shall be done away with. The benefits of the Code Napoleon, public trial, and the introduction of juries, will be the leading features of your Government. And to tell you the truth, I count more upon their effects, for the extension and consolidation of your rule, than upon the most resounding victories. I want your subjects to enjoy a degree of liberty, equality, and prosperity hitherto unknown to the German people. I want this liberal regime to produce, one way or another, changes which will be of the utmost benefit to the system of the Confederation, and to the strength of your monarchy. Such a method of government will be a stronger barrier between you and Prussia than the Elbe, the fortresses, and the protection of France. What people will want to return under the arbitrary Prussian rule, once it has tasted the benefits of a wise and liberal administration? In Germany, as in France, Italy, and Spain, people long for equality and liberalism. I have been managing the affairs of Europe long enough now to know that the burden of the privileged classes was resented everywhere. Rule constitutionally. Even if the reason, and the enlightenment of the age, were not sufficient cause, it would be good policy for one in your position; and you will find that the backing of public opinion gives you a great natural advantage over the absolute kings who are your neighbours.

. . .

TO JÉRÔME NAPOLEON, KING OF WESTPHALIA

PARIS, *6th March* 1808.

I have read your letter to Beugnot. I fancy I told you that you could keep Beugnot and Siméon as long as you want them: but is it absurd to make them take an oath. No sober-minded Frenchman, who seriously considered the results of such an act, would do so. I pardon their taking the oath only because I cannot believe they did so *ex animo*. If it is an oath of fidelity to your person, that is already contained in the oath of fidelity to mine taken by every Frenchman. If it is an oath taken as a subject of Westphalia, you are asking something that would be refused by the humblest drummer-boy in my army. No such oath has been taken by the senators or State councilors employed at Naples. Frenchmen employed in the king's household have sworn fidelity to him as a French prince. And even supposing these reasons were not enough, this is not the moment, when you are surrounded by foes and foreigners, to ask of men who might be useful to you the criminal act of renouncing their fatherland. I have seldom seen anyone with so little sense of proportion as yourself. You know nothing, yet you never take advice. You decide nothing by reason, everything by impulse and passion. I have no wish to correspond with you more than is indispensable for matters involving foreign courts, for there you put yourself forward, and publish your disagreements with me to all Europe; and that I am hardly disposed to allow. As for your financial and home affairs, I repeat, as I said before, that nothing you do squares either with my opinions or my experience: if you go on as you are going you will get nowhere. All the same, I should be obliged if you would practice a little less pomp and ostentation in *demarches* whose consequences you fail to appreciate. Nothing could be more absurd than the audience you gave to the Jews. Nothing could be worse than your parody of the French *Moniteur*. I have undertaken to reform the Jews, but I have made no attempt to attract more of them into my states. Far from it. I have been careful to do nothing suggesting a good opinion of the most despicable race in the world.

P. S. My dear fellow, I'm very fond of you, but you're a mere babe. Keep Siméon and Beugnot for at least a year longer, oath or no oath. Then we shall see what we shall see!

. . .

TO JÉRÔME NAPOLEON, KING OF WESTPHALIA

BAYONNE, 16*th July* 1808

You owe the bank two millions. You allow your notes to be repudiated. It is thoroughly dishonest of you. I will not be let down like this. You must sell your diamonds and your plate. There must be an end to the mad extravagance which already makes you the laughing-stock of Europe, and will end by rousing the indignation of your subjects. Sell your furniture, sell your horses, sell your jewellery, and pay your debts. Honour is the best currency. It is bad form to leave your debts unpaid, whilst everyone can see the kind of presents you give. The luxury you indulge in bewilders and shocks your subjects. You are young and light-headed, and care nothing for the value of money—and that at a time when your people are suffering from the after-effects of war.

. . .

TO JÉRÔME NAPOLEON, KING OF WESTPHALIA

SCHÖNBRUNN, 17*th July* 1809.

I have seen an Army Order of yours which makes you the laughing-stock of Germany, Austria, and France. Have you no friend at your side to tell you a few home truths? You are a king, and the Emperor's brother: but those are no qualifications for war. In war one must begin as a soldier, continue as a soldier, and end as a soldier. No ministers, no foreign attachés, no ceremonial. War means bivouacking at the head of the army, spending days and nights on horseback, and marching with the advance guard, to get the news—otherwise one had better stay behind in the women's quarters.

You go to war like a Persian satrap. Good God! Did I teach you such methods?—I who, with an army of 200,000 men, march at the head of my skirmishers, and do not even let Champagny come with me, but leave him behind at Munich or Vienna?

What has been the result? Everyone complains of you. Kienmayer, with his 20,000 men, despises you, and your absurd pretensions: he has concealed his movements from you, and fallen upon Junot. This would never have happened if you had been with your advance guard, and had given your orders from that position. Then you would have known what he was doing, and could have pursued him, whether along his line of retreat, or by way of Bohemia. You have plenty of ambition, some intelligence, and a few good qualities: but they are spoilt by silliness, and gross conceit; and you have no knowledge of the world. Meanwhile, unless an armistice has been declared, Kienmayer will have put Junot out of action, and turned upon you.

Stop making a fool of yourself. Send the foreign attachés back to Cassel. Do without your procession of luggage-carts: cut down your dinners to one table. Go to war like any young soldier who wants to win honour and glory. Try to deserve the rank you have reached, and the esteem of France and Europe, who are watching everything you do. And, for Heaven's sake, have the sense to write and speak as becomes your rank!

. . .

TO JÉRÔME NAPOLEON

VILNA, 14*th July* 1812.

The messenger you sent from Grodno yesterday at 4 p.m. has arrived. I was looking forward to his coming with pleasurable anticipation, thinking you would have sent the major-general news of Bagration's army, of the direction taken by Poniatowski in his pursuit, and of movements in Volhynia. Imagine my astonishment on hearing that he had received nothing but a compliment about a general! I can only express my displeasure at the scanty information you send me. I know neither the number of Bagration's divisions, nor their names, nor the position he occupied, nor the particulars of your captures at Grodno, nor what you are now doing. I have five or six columns on the move to cut off Bagration's retreat. I assume that you cannot so far have neglected your duty as not to have been pursuing him since yesterday. I hope, at any rate, that Prince Poniatowski has pursued him with the whole of the 5th corps. My operations are held up for lack of information from Grodno. I have had no news since the 30th. Not a word from your Chief of Staff. Not a word from Poniatowski. It is impossible to carry on a war in this fashion. You think and talk of nothing but trifles. I am distressed to see how paltry all your interests are. If General Vandamme has been guilty of embezzlement, you were quite right to send him to the rear: but the matter is of such minor importance at the moment that I am sorry you did not send me, by your messenger, information which would have been useful to me, and particulars as to your position.

I don't know why Prince Poniatowski doesn't write to the major-general twice a day. I told him to.

P. S. You are compromising the whole success of the campaign on the right flank. It is impossible to carry on war in this fashion.

STUDY QUESTIONS

1. Was Napoleon's endorsement of a "wise and liberal administration" of Westphalia simply a practical means of fostering loyalty to his regime?
2. Was Napoleon principally frustrated with Jérome's despotic behavior or his personal failings?

17.5 JAKOB WALTER, *DIARY OF A NAPOLEONIC FOOT SOLDIER*, WRITTEN 1856, FIRST PUBLISHED 1932

Jakob Walter (1788–1864), who fought in Napoleon's Grande Armée for two stints, records the experiences of the average foot soldier. The poorly organized nature of early nineteenth-century armies meant that little more than bread was supplied by the state; even housing had to

From Walter Jakob, *The Diary of a Napoleonic Foot Soldier*, ed. Marc Raeff. New York: Penguin Publishing Co., 1993, pp. 85–7, 145–6, 149–54, 163–5, 180–3, 187–8, 230–1.

be provided by local communities. Walter's goal was to record the details of his campaigns as objectively as possible, not to lay out moral commentary on his lot as a lowly soldier. He mailed his diary to his son; it fell out of view only to be rediscovered and published some eighty years later. Consider the stripped-down nature of Walter's language and his hesitation to outwardly lament the difficulties he and his fellow foot soldiers endured. In the following passage Walter describes the political upheavals that marked France from the start of the July Monarchy, in 1830 to the revolutions of 1848.

I had spent the best days of my youth amid a society which seemed to increase in greatness and prosperity as it increased in liberty; I had conceived the idea of a balanced, regulated liberty, held in check by religion, custom and law; the attractions of this liberty had touched me; it had become the passion of my life; I felt that I could never be consoled for its loss, and that I must renounce all hope of its recovery.

I had gained too much experience of mankind to be able to content myself with empty words; I knew that, if one great revolution is able to establish liberty in a country, a number of succeeding revolutions make all regular liberty impossible for very many years. . . .

I began to pass in review the history of our last sixty years, and I smile bitterly when I thought of the illusions formed at the conclusion of each period in this long revolution.

The Constitutional Monarchy had succeeded the Ancien Régime; the Republic, the Monarchy; the Empire, the Republic; the Restoration, the Empire; and then came the Monarchy of July. After each of the successive changes it was said that the French Revolution, having accomplished what was presumptuously called its work, was finished; this had been said and it had been believed. Alas! I myself had hoped it under the Restoration, and again after the fall of the Government of the Restoration; and here is the French Revolution beginning over again, for it is still the same one. As we go on, its end seems farther off and shrouded in greater darkness. Shall we ever—as we are assured by other prophets, perhaps as delusive as their predecessors—shall we ever attain a more complete and more far-reaching social transformation than our fathers foresaw and desired, and than we ourselves are able to foresee; or are we not destined simply to end in a condition of intermittent anarchy, the well-known chronic and incurable complaint of old races? . . .

All the deputies who came to Paris [for the National Assembly in early May] with the desire to put down the excesses of the Revolution had to combat the demagogic party regarded him [Lamartine] beforehand as their only possible leader, and looked to him unhesitatingly to place himself at their head to attack and overthrow the Socialists and demagogues. They soon discovered that they were deceived, and that Lamartine did not see the part he was called upon to play in so simple a light. It must be confessed that his was a very complex and difficult position. It was forgotten at the time, but he could not himself forget, that he had contributed more than any other to the success of the Revolution of February. . . .

He was then following the tortuous road that was soon to lead him to his ruin, struggling to dominate the Mountain without overthrowing it, and to slacken the revolutionary fire without extinguishing it, so as to give the country a feeling of security strong enough for it to bless him, not strong enough to cause it to forget him. . . .

The nation saw in Ledru-Rollin the bloody image of the Terror; it beheld in him the genius of evil as in Lamartine the genius of good, and it was mistaken in both cases. . . .

Lamartine, who had seen nothing but Paris during the last two months, and who had there, so to speak, lived in the very heart of the revolutionary party, exaggerated the power of the Capital and the inactivity of the rest of France. He over-estimated both. But I am not sure that I, on my side, did not strain a point on the other side. . . . In any case, I am led to believe that it was Lamartine's tergiversations and his semi-connivance with the enemy that saved us, while it ruined him. Their effect was to amuse the leaders of the Mountain and to divide them. The Montagnards of the old school, who were retained in the Government, separated themselves from the Socialists, who were excluded from it. . . .

Lamartine saw these dangers more closely and clearly than I, and I believe today that the fear of arousing a mortal conflict influenced his conduct as much as did his ambition. . . .

It was then [at the May 15 uprising against the National Assembly on the pretext of demonstrations of sympathy for the Prussian repression of Polish riots] that I saw appear, in his turn, in the tribune a man whom I have never seen since, but the recollection of whom has always filled me with horror and disgust. He had wan, emaciated cheeks, white lips, a sickly, wicked and repulsive expression, a dirty pallor, the appearance of a mouldy corpse; he wore no visible linen; an old black frock-coat tightly covered his lean, withered limbs; he seemed to have passed his life in a sewer and to have just left it. I was told it was Blanqui.

Blanqui said one word about Poland; then, turning sharply to domestic affairs, he asked for revenge for what he called the massacres of Rouen, recalled with threats the wretchedness in which the people had been left, and complained of the wrongs done to the latter by the Assembly. After thus exciting his hearers, he returned to the subject of Poland and, like Raspail, demanded an immediate vote. . . .

A long interval passed; at last Barbès darted up and climbed, or rather leapt, into the tribune. He was one of those men in whom the demagogue, the madman and the knight errant are so closely intermingled that it is not possible to say where one ends or the other commences, and who can only make their way in a society as sick and troubled as ours. . . .

"I demand," said he, in panting, jerking tones, "that, immediately and before rising, the Assembly shall vote the departure of an army for Poland, a tax of a milliard upon the rich, the removal of the troops from Paris, and shall forbid the beating to arms; if not, the representatives to be declared traitors to the country." . . .

The whole time elapsing between the [insurrections of May] and the days of June was filled with the anxiety caused by the approach of these latter days. . . . The National Assembly was so constantly possessed by this thought that one might have said that it read the words "Civil War" written on the four walls of the House. . . .

The danger was perceived afar off as well as near at hand. The provinces grew indignant and irritated with Paris; for the first time for sixty years they ventured to entertain the idea of resisting it. . . . The ruin of commerce, universal war, the dread of Socialism made the Republic more and more hateful in the eyes of provinces. This hatred manifested itself especially beneath the secrecy of the ballot. The electors were called upon to re-elect in twenty-one departments; and in general they elected the men who in their eyes represented the Monarchy in some form or other. . . .

It was then that suddenly, for the first time, the name of Louis Napoleon came into notice. The Prince was elected at the same time in Paris and in several departments. Republicans, Legitimists and demagogues gave him their votes; for the nation at that time was like a frightened flock of sheep, which runs in all directions without following any road. . . .

I come at last to the insurrection of June, the most extensive and the most singular that has occurred in our history, and perhaps in any other. . . .

What distinguished it also, among all the events of this kind which have succeeded one another in France for sixty years, is that it did not aim at changing the form of government, but at altering the order of society. It was not, strictly speaking, a political struggle, in the sense which until then we had given to the world, but a combat of class against class, a sort of Servile War. It represented the facts of the Revolution of February in the same manner as the theories of Socialism represented its ideas; or rather it issued naturally from these ideas, as a son does from his mother. We behold in it nothing more than a blind and rude, but powerful, effort on the part of the workmen to escape from the necessities of their condition, which had been depicted to them as one of unlawful oppression, and to open up by main force a road towards that imaginary comfort with which they had been deluded. It was this mixture of greed and false theory which first gave birth to the insurrection and then made it so formidable. These poor people had been told that the wealth of the rich was in some way the produce of a theft practiced upon themselves. They had been assured that the inequality of fortunes was as opposed to morality and the welfare of society as it was to nature. Prompted by their needs and their passions, many had believed this obscure and erroneous notion of right, which, mingled with brute force, imparted to the latter an energy, a tenacity and a power which it would never have possessed unaided.

It must also be observed that this formidable insurrection was not the enterprise of a certain number of conspirators, but the revolt of one whole section of the population against another. . . .

Such were the days of June, necessary and disastrous days. They did not extinguish revolutionary ardour in France, but they put a stop, at least for a time, to what may be called the work appertaining to the Revolution of February. They delivered the nation from tyranny of the Paris workmen and restored it to possession of itself.

Socialist theories continued to penetrate into the minds of the people in the shape of envious and greedy desires, and to sow the seed of future revolutions; but the socialist party itself was beaten and powerless. The Montagnards, who did not belong to it, felt that they were irrevocably affected by the blow that had struck it. The moderate Republicans themselves did not fail to be alarmed lest this victory had led them to a slope which might precipitate them from the Republic, and they made an immediate effort to stop their descent, but in vain. Personally I detested the Mountain, and was indifferent to the Republic; but I adored Liberty, and I conceived great apprehensions for it immediately after these days. I at once looked upon the June fighting as a necessary crisis, after which, however, the temper of the nation would undergo a certain change. The love of independence was to be followed by a dread of, and perhaps a distaste for, free institutions; after such an abuse of liberty a return of this sort was inevitable. This retrograde movement began, in fact, on the 27th of June. At first very slow and invisible, as it were, to the naked eye, it grew swifter, impetuous, irresistible. Where will it stop? I do not know.

STUDY QUESTIONS

1. Is the author an advocate of socialism or a class revolt?
2. Are the reality of power politics and the remembered rhetoric of the Revolution in conflict?

CHAPTER 18

INDUSTRIALIZATION AND ITS DISCONTENTS

18.1 WILLIAM WORDSWORTH, "TINTERN ABBEY," 1798; "THE WORLD IS TOO MUCH WITH US," 1806

A renowned Romantic poet and friend of Samuel Taylor Coleridge, William Wordsworth (1770–1850) was a prolific writer who had grown up reading the great British poets. His own large work, the *Prelude* (which he worked on throughout his life), is a protoautobiography in which he examines his spiritual development through exposure to nature. In "Tintern Abbey," Wordsworth revisits this delight in sublime nature; in "The World Is Too Much with Us," he laments being enslaved by the daily woes that pull us out of sync with our natural inclinations.

"LINES WRITTEN A FEW MILES ABOVE TINTERN ABBEY, ON REVISITING THE BANKS OF THE WYE DURING A TOUR, JULY 13, 1798"

Five years have passed; five summers, with the length
Of five long winters! and again I hear
These waters, rolling from their mountain-springs
With a sweet inland murmur.—Once again
Do I behold these steep and lofty cliffs,
Which on a wild secluded scene impress
Thoughts of more deep seclusion; and connect
The landscape with the quiet of the sky.
The day is come when I again repose
Here, under this dark sycamore, and view
These plots of cottage-ground, these orchard-tufts,
Which, at this season, with their unripe fruits,
Among the woods and copses lose themselves,
Nor, with their green and simple hue, disturb
The wild green landscape. Once again I see
These hedge-rows, hardly hedge-rows, little lines
Of sportive wood run wild; these pastoral farms
Green to the very door; and wreathes of smoke
Sent up, in silence, from among the trees,
With some uncertain notice, as might seem,
Of vagrant dwellers in the houseless woods,
Or of some hermit's cave, where by his fire
The hermit sits alone.
                    Though absent long,

William Wordsworth, *The Major Works—Including the Prelude*. Edited by Stephen Gill. New York: Oxford University Press, 2008.

These forms of beauty have not been to me,
As is a landscape to a blind man's eye:
But oft, in lonely rooms, and mid the din
Of towns and cities, I have owed to them,
In hours of weariness, sensations sweet,
Felt in the blood, and felt along the heart,
And passing even into my purer mind
With tranquil restoration:—feelings too
Of unremembered pleasure; such, perhaps,
As may have had no trivial influence
On that best portion of a good man's life;
His little, nameless, unremembered acts
Of kindness and of love. Nor less, I trust,
To them I may have owed another gift,
Of aspect more sublime; that blessed mood,
In which the burthen of the mystery,
In which the heavy and the weary weight
Of all this unintelligible world
Is lightened:—that serene and blessed mood,
In which the affections gently lead us on,
Until, the breath of this corporeal frame,
And even the motion of our human blood
Almost suspended, we are laid asleep
In body, and become a living soul:
While with an eye made quiet by the power
Of harmony, and the deep power of joy,
We see into the life of things.

. . .

"THE WORLD IS TOO MUCH WITH US"

The world is too much with us; late and soon,
Getting and spending, we lay waste our powers:
Little we see in nature that is ours;
We have given our hearts away, a sordid boon!
The Sea that bares her bosom to the moon;
The Winds that will be howling at all hours
And are up-gathered now like sleeping flowers;
For this, for every thing, we are out of tune;
It moves us not—Great God! I'd rather be
A Pagan suckled in a creed outworn;
So might I, standing on this pleasant lea,
Have glimpses that would make me less forlorn;
Have sight of Proteus coming from the sea;
Or hear old Triton blow his wreathed horn.

STUDY QUESTIONS

1. What does the poet reveal about his consistent state of introspection and his reaction to the natural world?
2. In what ways is the author connected to the mood and perceptivity of the Romantic movement in the arts?

18.2 LETTER OF BETTINA VON ARNIM TO JOHANN GOETHE, 1810

This excerpt is from a letter of Bettina von Arnim (Elisabeth Brentano [1785–1859]) to Johann Wolfgang von Goethe (1749–1832), Vienna, May 28, 1810. Arnim here describes the overpowering effect on her of the composer Ludwig von Beethoven (1770–1827) and his music.

From Walter Schmitz and Sibylle von Steinsdorff, eds., *Bettine von Arnim Werke und Briefe*, 4 vols. (Frankfurt, 1992), 2.344–51. Translation by Clifford Backman.

When I first met this man, whom I so much wish to tell you about, the entire world as I had known it vanished. True, I am quite young—a girl, still,—but I make no mistake when I assert something that no one else now alive will understand or agree with, namely that [Beethoven] has raced far ahead of the rest of the civilized world. Will any of us ever catch up with him? I doubt it. I pray he lives long enough to achieve the apotheosis of the sublimely powerful mystery he carries within him—but no longer. Oh, may he achieve the Ineffable! If he does, he will bequeath us the secret to a divine baptism that will lift us ever closer to true bliss. For I will make a confession to you: I believe in divine magic that is part of the spiritual world. Beethoven, in his music, possesses and expresses it. What is more—everything he could tell you about his music in words is also pure magic. Every impulse and desire he has expresses this superior existence. In fact, he believes himself to be the founder of a new realm of spiritual life.

You will understand in your own way what I am trying to say, and know whether it is the truth. But who is there alive today who could take the place of this genius? Who could achieve what he has achieved? Human actions are like the movement of the pendulum of a clock, coming and going for him alone; he alone is free and creates as acts of a free will what is uncreated and unknown. The little busyness of the everyday world means nothing to him: the sun at dawn finds him already engaged in his sacred work, and at dusk he scarcely notices anything around him. He forgets to eat, and the storm of Inspiration sets him apart from the commonalities of every-day life.

Beethoven himself said as much to me. "From the moment I open my eyes in the morning, I begin to groan, because everything I see offends my soul. I have no choice but to hate a world that cannot understand that music is more sublime, more transcendent, than all knowledge and philosophy. It is a wine that inspires all new creativity, and I am the Bacchus who produces this ennobling wine and intoxicates men's spirits. When the people hunger once more, they realize that in their intoxication that they have procured already, like fishers of the sea, the nourishment they will need back on shore. I have no friends, and I must live alone, and yet I know God is closer to me, in my art, than He is to anyone else. I move forward with Him, seeing Him and understanding Him completely. I do not worry about my music's fate. Anyone who opens his mind and heart to it will be forever released from the miseries that are the daily burden of everyone else."

Beethoven said all these things, and more, to me at our very first meeting. A feeling of exultation poured over me, to think that so great a man revealed his innermost thoughts to one so insignificant as me. This was all the greater a surprise since I had been told he was a misanthrope who would talk to no one. No one, in fact, even bothered to introduce me to him; I sought him out on my own. Beethoven owns three residences and takes turns hiding out in each: one in the country, one in the city, and one in the citadel. It was there, in the citadel, that I first met him. I went in unannounced and found him at his piano. After I had given him my name he welcomed me with great warmth and asked if I would like to hear a new song, a poem he had just finished setting to music. Then he played *Kennst du das Land*, singing in a voice so compelling that I fell immediately under its melancholy spell.

"Beautiful, isn't it?" he asked in a passion.
"It is magnificent," I replied.

Pleased with my approval, he declared, "I'll play it again!" then continued, "Most people are moved by good art, but that doesn't mean they possess artistic souls. True artists are made of fire, and they never weep."

Then he started to play another song, composed only a few days earlier, that was also based on one of your poems—*Tröcknet nicht, Tränen der ewigen Liebe*. Afterwards he walked me home, stopping on occasion and speaking so loudly that it took some fortitude to listen to him, for he speaks so passionately and says such unsettling things that one has constantly to remind oneself that one is in public. There was a large crowd at home, and everyone was astonished to see him with me. He stayed for dinner and then sat down at the piano of his own accord, without being asked, and he played a long time, all so wonderfully. His sense of pride is an intrinsic part of his genius, and when inspired, his genius creates the Ineffable while bidding his fingers to do the Impossible.

Since then, we see each other almost every day. Sometimes he comes here, others I go there. So it is that I have all but given up the social scene, exhibitions, concerts, even attending [Mass] at St. Stephen's. Beethoven once said, "What on earth do you want to go there for? Instead, I will call for you towards evening and we'll go for a walk on the paths around Schönbrunn [Palace]."

Yesterday we walked through a beautiful garden in full flower. The greenhouses were open, and the scents were intoxicating. All of a sudden Beethoven stopped, and standing in a blaze of sunlight declared:

"Goethe's poetry moves me profoundly. Not only in what the poems say, but in their rhythms. The language itself is transcendent, as though raised on high by fairy spirits, and carries the very essence of harmony within itself, as though it were driving me to set it to music. And at that moment, that incandescent moment of inspiration, I can only let the melody flow out and escape me. I run after it. But once I think I have captured it, it flits away, bobbing and weaving, in a perfect storm of feeling, going every which way. If I grab it again, seething with passion, I become inseparable from it. Full of enthusiasm, I then trace out my variations on it. Only then, you see, do I triumph over my first inspiration and create a symphony. Yes, music is the union of the life of the mind and the life of the senses. How I wish I could talk to Goethe about this! Would he understand me? Melody is poetry made perceptible, don't you think? It translates the spiritual essence of poetry into a physical sensation. Isn't it by setting it to music that one truly understands the feelings expressed in one of Mignon's poems? And that this heightened understanding awakens still more powerful emotions? In music the spirit stretches out into the eternal universe and becomes a channel for the great perception that can arise from a few simple musical lines—a perception without which those lines would remain hidden, unknown, and unimagined. That is the harmony expressed in my symphonies, a harmony in which various expressions push forward until they fuse into a single wholeness. When that happens, one truly senses the Eternal, the Infinite, the Ineffable, that exists in the realm of the spirit. With my compositions I invariably have a sensation of accomplishment, of achieved wholeness, but at the same time I also feel an unquenchable desire to start again. Like a child I want to experience again the sensation that only a moment before had seemed completely fulfilled and finished with the last clang of cymbals, the sensation that hammered into my listeners' ears, like a chisel, all of my musical joy and conviction. Talk to Goethe about me! Tell him that if he hears my symphonies he will know that I'm right in saying that music is the sole mystical gate that leads one to the supernal world of true wisdom—a world that envelops all mankind but which most fail to grasp.

"One needs a kind of spiritual rhythm in order to grasp the essence of music. It gives a sensation or inkling of divine knowledge; what the mind extracts from it is the very essence of spiritual knowledge. Of course, everyone's mind lives on music just as our bodies live on air—but it is an altogether different thing to understand music with deep intellect. The more the spirit receives of this sort of nourishment, the more the mind matures and develops, until it achieves perfect harmony with it. But these people are the rarest of all. Even as there are multitudes who marry for love but never know what true love is (though they may believe they do), so are there multitudes who follow the Siren-call of music without ever realizing its greatest revelations. Like every art, music's foundation—its groundwork, if you will—is moral sentiment; its every sensation marks a moral progress. To submit to music's inscrutable laws, to make one's soul obey and to live according to them, is to allow its revelatory truths to emerge; this is art's unique principle—that the surrender of one's soul to artistic revelation is to unite with the Sublime! Only surrender to the divinity of its sublime authority can help us to over-master our passionate impulses and allow our imaginations to achieve their fullest expression! You must understand this: art proceeds from divine power, and all human interaction with it is religion itself. What we derive from pure art, we derive from God. Art channels divine inspiration and allows us to achieve that to which we aspire.

"We never know what enlightenment awaits us. The young seed needs fertile soil, charged with warmth, in order to sprout, develop, and express itself. Music is that warm soil in which the spirit lives, thinks, and discovers. Philosophy is a mere by-product, an echoing spark of the lightning-struck spirit. No, only music can fill the need felt by all of us to relate everything we experience to an essential truth. No individual mind can ever master what it creates, of course, but it can at least know the joy of creating. Every work of true art is self-sufficient and is greater than the artist who made it. Once created, it returns to its sacred source and remains with mankind only as a reminder of the divine power working within him. Music connects the intellect with divine harmony, and every single thought in the mind carries with it the essence of that connection, of participation by analogy in a larger truth. This explains why all musical expression comprises so intimate and critical an element of the wider community of the unified celestial harmony. Everything that is lightning-struck in inspiration causes the soul to expand and express itself in music. Mine, of course, is just such an electric nature.

"But listen to me, carrying on like this! I must stop with this un-wise wisdom, or else I might miss my rehearsal. Do write to Goethe and tell him whatever you understand of what I've been saying. I can't be held accountable for what you write, but I shall be glad to hear what he has to say on these matters."

I promised that I would write to you and describe his thoughts the best I could. He then took me to a dress-rehearsal of the entire orchestra, and I sat alone in that great, dark, empty space. A few rays of light shone through some small tears and holes in the curtains, and tiny specks floated in them as in a river. One could have thought of them as numberless souls riding on heavenly beams. But then, oh Goethe! This genius, this immense, compelling genius began to conduct. No king or emperor was ever so aware of the power at his command or exercised it like this man. Beethoven—who only a few minutes before, in the garden, tried to find the words to express the source of his inspiration. If I could understand him as well as I feel him, I would be omniscient indeed. There he stood, upright and full of purpose, his gestures and face expressing the utter perfection of his music. He noted every minor mistake, every tiny failure in interpretation. Not a single breath was drawn that he did not direct. Everything was ordered, controlled, and above all inspired by the extraordinary charisma of his genius. It would have been easy to imagine his spirit re-incarnated as the master of the whole world!

I wrote this letter yesterday evening, and this morning I read the whole thing to Beethoven. "Did I really say that?" he kept asking. "I must have been in a trance!" Then he re-read the whole thing, carefully striking out bits and re-writing them between the lines—as you can see above—because he so deeply desires that you understand him.

Do make me happy by replying promptly, so Beethoven knows how much you respect him. You and I had always intended to have a discussion about music some day, because I am so fond of it. But now, because of Beethoven, I think I couldn't possibly carry on such a conversation.

My address is: Erdberggasse, Birkenstockhaus. Your letter will find me there for the next two weeks.

Bettina

STUDY QUESTIONS

1. According to von Arnim, what is the genius of Beethoven? What qualities make it Romantic?
2. What special power does music have in von Arnim's view? What makes it superior to philosophy?

18.3 THOMAS CARLYLE, "SIGNS OF THE TIMES," 1829

A Scottish historian and writer, Thomas Carlyle (1795–1881) turned the difficulties of his life—a sickly nature, a crisis of faith in the Christian Church, and a tempestuous marriage—toward writing a harsh-toned and often argumentative series of works. Friends with Ralph Waldo Emerson, Carlyle was an important mouthpiece for a dissatisfied Victorian generation. His essay "Signs of the Times," first published in the *Edinburgh Review*, examines a nineteenth-century "mechanical age" that fundamentally altered the role of man in his "modern" society.

How often have we heard, for the last fifty years, that the country was wrecked, and fast sinking; whereas, up to this date, the country is entire and afloat! The "State in Danger" is a condition of things, which we have witnessed a hundred times; and as for the Church, it has seldom been out of "danger" since we can remember it.

All men are aware that the present is a crisis of this sort; and why it has become so. The repeal of the Test Acts, and then of the Catholic disabilities, has struck many of their admirers with an indescribable astonishment. Those things seemed fixed and immovable; deep as the foundations of the world; and lo, in a moment they have vanished, and their place knows them no more!

. . .

Were we required to characterise this age of ours by any single epithet, we should be tempted to call it, not an Heroical, Devotional, Philosophical, or Moral Age, but, above all others, the Mechanical Age. It is the Age of Machinery, in every outward and inward sense of that word; the age which, with its whole undivided might, forwards, teaches and practises the great art of adapting means to ends. Nothing is now done directly, or by hand; all is by rule and calculated contrivance. For the simplest operation, some helps and accompaniments, some cunning abbreviating process is in readiness. Our old modes of exertion are all discredited, and thrown aside. On every hand, the living artisan is driven from his workshop, to make room for a speedier, inanimate one. The shuttle drops from the fingers of the weaver, and falls into iron fingers that ply it faster. The sailor furls his sail, and lays down his oar; and bids a strong, unwearied servant, on vaporous wings, bear him through the waters. Men have crossed oceans by steam; the Birmingham Fire-king has visited the fabulous East; and the genius of the Cape, were there any Camoens now to sing it, has again been alarmed, and with far stranger thunders than Gamas. There is no end to machinery. Even the horse is stripped of his harness, and find a fleet fire-horse yoked in his stead. Nay, we have an artist that hatches chickens by steam; the very brood-hen is to be superseded! For all earthly, and for some unearthly purposes, we have machines and mechanic furtherances; for mincing our cabbages; for casting us into magnetic sleep. We remove mountains, and make seas our smooth highway; nothing can resist us. We war with rude Nature; and, by our resistless engines, come off always victorious, and loaded with spoils.

What wonderful accessions have thus been made, and are still making, to the physical power of

From G. B. Tennyson, ed., *A Carlyle Reader: Selections from the Writings of Thomas Carlyle.* Cambridge, UK: Cambridge University Press, 2001, pp. 32–3, 34–6, 37, 40–1, 46–7.

mankind; how much better fed, clothed, lodged and, in all outward respects, accommodated men now are, or might be, by a given quantity of labour, is a grateful reflection which forces itself on every one. What changes, too, this addition of power is introducing into the Social System; how wealth has more and more increased, and at the same time gathered itself more and more into masses, strangely altering the old relations, and increasing the distance between the rich and the poor, will be a question for Political Economists, and a much more complex and important one than any they have yet engaged with.

But leaving these matters for the present, let us observe how the mechanical genius of our time has diffused itself into quite other provinces. Not the external and physical alone is now managed by machinery, but the internal and spiritual also. Here too nothing follows its spontaneous course, nothing is left to be accomplished by old natural methods. Everything has its cunningly devised implements, its preëstablished apparatus; it is not done by hand, but by machinery. Thus we have machines for Education: Lancastrian machines; Hamiltonian machines; monitors, maps and emblems. Instruction, that mysterious communing of Wisdom with Ignorance, is no longer an indefinable tentative process, requiring a study of individual aptitudes, and a perpetual variation of means and methods, to attain the same end; but a secure, universal, straightforward business, to be conducted in the gross, by proper mechanism, with such intellect as comes to hand. Then, we have Religious machines, of all imaginable varieties; the Bible-Society, professing a far higher and heavenly structure, is found, on inquiry, to be altogether an earthly contrivance: supported by collection of moneys, by fomenting of vanities, by puffing, intrigue and chicane; a machine for converting the Heathen. It is the same in all other departments. Has any man, or any society of men, a truth to speak, a piece of spiritual work to do; they can nowise proceed at once and with the mere natural organs, but must first call a public meeting, appoint committees, issue prospectuses, eat a public dinner; in a word, construct or borrow machinery, wherewith to speak it and do it. Without machinery they were hopeless, helpless; a colony of Hindoo weavers squatting in the heart of Lancashire. Mark, too, how every machine must have its moving power, in some of the great currents of society; every little sect among us, Unitarians, Utilitarians, Anabaptists, Phrenologists, must have its Periodical, its monthly or quarterly Magazine;—hanging out, like its windmill, into the *popularis aura*, to grind meal for the society.

With individuals, in like manner, natural strength avails little. No individual now hopes to accomplish the poorest enterprise single-handed and without mechanical aids; he must make interest with some existing corporation, and till his field with their oxen. In these days, more emphatically than ever, "to live, signifies to unite with a party, or to make one." Philosophy, Science, Art, Literature, all depend on machinery. No Newton, by silent meditation, now discovers the system of the world from the falling of an apple; but some quite other than Newton stands in his Museum, his Scientific Institution, and behind whole batteries of retorts, digesters, and galvanic piles imperatively "interrogates Nature,"—who, however, shows no haste to answer. In defect of Raphaels, and Angelos, and Mozarts, we have Royal Academies of Painting, Sculpture, Music; whereby the languishing spirit of Art may be strengthened, as by the more generous diet of a Public Kitchen. Literature, too, has its Paternoster-row mechanism, its Trade-dinners, its Editorial conclaves, and huge subterranean, puffing bellows; so that books are not only printed, but, in a great measure, written and sold, by machinery.

. . .

These things, which we state lightly enough here, are yet of deep import, and indicate a mighty change in our whole manner of existence. For the same habit regulates not our modes of action alone, but our modes of thought and feeling. Men are grown mechanical in head and in heart, as well as in hand. They have lost faith in individual endeavor, and in natural force, of any kind. Not for internal perfection, but for external combinations and arrangements, for institutions, constitutions,—for Mechanism of one sort or other, do they hope and struggle. Their whole efforts, attachments, opinions, turn on mechanism, and are of a mechanical character.

We may trace this tendency in all the great manifestations of our time; in its intellectual aspect, the studies it most favours and its manner of conducting them; in its practical aspects, its politics, arts, religion, morals; in the whole sources, and throughout the whole currents, of its spiritual, no less than its material activity.

Nowhere, for example, is the deep, almost exclusive faith we have in Mechanism more visible than in the Politics of this time. Civil government does by its nature include much that is mechanical, and must be treated accordingly. We term it indeed, in ordinary language, the Machine of Society, and talk of it as the grand working wheel from which all private machines must derive, or to which they must adapt, their movements. Considered merely as a metaphor, all this is well enough; but here, as in so many other cases, the "foam hardens itself into a shell," and the shadow we have wantonly evoked stands terrible before us and will not depart at our bidding. Government includes much also that is not mechanical, and cannot be treated mechanically; of which latter truth, as appears to us, the political speculations and exertions of our time are taking less and less cognisance.

Nay, in the very outset, we might note the mighty interest taken in *mere political arrangements*, as itself the sign of a mechanical age. The whole discontent of Europe takes this direction. The deep, strong cry of all civilised nations,—a cry which, every one now sees, must and will be answered, is: Give us a reform of Government! A good structure of legislation, a proper check upon the executive, a wise arrangement of the judiciary, is *all* that is wanting for human happiness. The Philosopher of this age is not a Socrates, a Plato, a Hooker, or Taylor, who inculcates on men the necessity and infinite worth of moral goodness, the great truth that our happiness depends on the mind which is within us, and not on the circumstances which are without us; but a Smith, a De Lolme, a Bentham, who chiefly inculcates the reverse of this,—that our happiness depends entirely on external circumstances; nay, that the strength and dignity of the mind within us is itself the creature and consequence of these. Were the laws, the government, in good order, all were well with us; the rest would care for itself! Dissentients from this opinion, expressed or implied, are now rarely to be met with; widely and angrily as men differ in its application, the principle is admitted by all.

Equally mechanical, and of equal simplicity, are the methods proposed by both parties for completing or securing this all-sufficient perfection of arrangement. It is no longer the moral, religious, spiritual condition of the people that is our concern, but their physical, practical, economical condition, as regulated by public laws. Thus is the Body-politic more than ever worshipped and tendered; but the Soul-politic less than ever. Love of country, in any high or generous sense, in any other than an almost animal sense, or mere habit, has little importance attached to it in such reforms, or in the opposition shown them. Men are to be guided only by their self-interests. Good government is a good balancing of these; and, except a keen eye and appetite for self-interest, requires no virtue in any quarter. To both parties it is emphatically a machine: to the discontented, a "taxing-machine"; to the contented, a "machine for securing property." Its duties and its faults are not those of a father, but of an active parish-constable.

Thus it is by the mere condition of the machine, by preserving it untouched, or else by reconstructing it, and oiling it anew, that man's salvation as a social being is to be ensured and indefinitely promoted. Contrive the fabric of law aright, and without farther effort on your part, that divine spirit of Freedom, which all hearts venerate and long for, will of herself come to inhabit it; and under her healing wings every noxious influence will wither, every good and salutary one more and more expand. Nay, so devoted are we to this principle, and at the same time so curiously mechanical, that a new trade, specially grounded on it, has arisen among us, under the name of "Codification," or codemaking in the abstract; whereby any people, for a reasonable consideration, may be accommodated with a patent code;—more easily than curious individuals with patent breeches, for the people does *not* need to be measured first.

. . .

In fact, if we look deeper, we shall find that this faith in Mechanism has now struck its roots down into man's most intimate, primary sources of conviction; and is thence sending up, over his whole life and activity, innumerable stems,—fruit-bearing and poison-bearing. The truth is, men have lost their belief in the Invisible, and believe, and hope, and work only in the Visible; or, to speak it in other words: This is not a Religious age. Only the material, the immediately practical, not the divine and spiritual, is important to us. The infinite, absolute character of Virtue has passed into a finite, conditional one; it is no longer a worship of the Beautiful and Good; but a calculation of the Profitable. Worship, indeed, in any sense, is not recognized among us, or is mechanically explained into Fear of pain, or Hope of pleasure. Our true Diety is Mechanism. It has subdued external Nature for us, and we think it will do all other things. We are Giants in physical power: in a deeper than metaphorical sense, we are Titans, that strive, by heaping on mountain, to conquer Heaven also.

The strong Mechanical character, so visible in the spiritual pursuits and methods of this age, may be traced much farther into the condition and prevailing disposition of our spiritual nature itself. Consider, for example, the general fashion of Intellect in this era. Intellect, the power man has of knowing and believing, is now nearly synonymous with Logic, or the mere power of arranging and communicating. Its implement is not Meditation, but Argument. "Cause and effect" is almost the only category under which we look at, and work with, all Nature. Our first question with regard to any object is not, What is it? but, How is it? We are no longer instinctively driven to apprehend, and lay to heart, what is Good and Lovely, but rather to inquire, as onlookers, how it is produced, whence it comes, whither it goes. Our favourite Philosophers have no love and no hatred; they stand among us not to do, nor to create anything, but as a sort of Logic-mills, to grind out the true causes and effects of all that is done and created. To the eye of a Smith, a Hume or a Constant, all is well that works quietly. An Order of Ignatius Loyola, a Presbyterianism of John Knox, a Wickliffe or a Henry the Eighth, are simply so many mechanical phenomena, caused or causing.

STUDY QUESTIONS

1. What did Carlyle see as the dangers of the Industrial Revolution, just as it was "gathering steam"?
2. In what respects did Carlyle fear that a devotion to the "Mechanist" approach would subsume the individual into the group?

18.4 HENRY MAYHEW, *LONDON LABOUR AND THE LONDON POOR*, 1851

As Jacob Riis would later do for New York, Henry Mayhew (1812–1887) exposed and explored the terrible conditions of the poor in London during industrialization. Mayhew's three-volume work aimed at reforming the experiences of the day-laborers in the city, whose livelihoods were threatened by an increased value placed on mechanical and technological advances. One of seventeen

Henry Mayhew, *London Labour and the London Poor*. Edited by Robert Douglas-Fairhirst. New York: Oxford University Press, 2012.

children himself, Mayhew conducted many face-to-face interviews with working children, sweatshop laborers, prostitutes, street entertainers, hawkers, and pickpockets. Consider how his writing style creates sympathy through its detailed description of the urban bustle.

WATERCRESS GIRL

The little watercress girl who gave me the following statement although only eight years of age, had entirely lost all childish ways, and was, indeed, in thoughts and manner, a woman. There was something cruelly pathetic in hearing this infant, so young that her features had scarcely formed themselves, talking of the bitterest struggles of life, with the calm earnestness of one who had endured them all. I did not know how to talk with her. At first I treated her as a child, speaking on childish subjects; so that I might, by being familiar with her, remove all shyness, and get her to narrate her life freely. I asked her about her toys and her games with her companion; but the look of amazement that answered me soon put an end to any attempt at fun on my part. I then talked to her about the parks, and whether she ever went to them. "The parks!" she replied in wonder, "where are they?" I explained to her, telling her that they were large open places with green grass and tall trees, where beautiful carriages drove about, and people walked for pleasure, and children played. Her eyes brightened up a little as I spoke; and she asked, half doubtingly, "Would they let such as me go there—just to look?" All her knowledge seemed to begin and end with watercresses, and what they fetched. She knew no more of London than that part she has seen on her rounds, and believed that no quarter of the town was handsomer or pleasanter than it was at Farringdon-market or at Clerkenwell, where she lived. Her little face, pale and thin with privation, was wrinkled where the dimples ought to have been, and she would sigh frequently. When some hot dinner was offered to her, she would not touch it, because, if she eat too much, "it made her sick," she said; "and she wasn't used to meat, only on a Sunday."

The poor child, although the weather was severe, was dressed in a thin cotton gown, with a threadbare shawl wrapped round her shoulders. She wore no covering to her head, and the long rusty hair stood out in all directions. When she walked she shuffled along, for fear that the large carpet slippers that served her for shoes should slip off her feet.

"I go about the streets with water-creases crying. 'Four bunches a penny, water-creases.' I am just eight years old—that's all, and I've a big sister, and a brother and a sister younger than I am. On and off, I've been very near twelvemonth in the streets. Before that, I had to take care of a baby for my aunt. No, it wasn't heavy—it was only two months old; but I minded it for ever such a time—till it could walk. It was a very nice little baby, not a very pretty one; but, if I touched it under the chin, it would laugh. Before I had the baby, I used to help mother, who was in the fur trade; and, if there was any slits in the fur, I'd sew them up. My mother learned me to needle-work and to knit when I was about five. I used to go to school, too; but I wasn't there long. I've forgot all about it now, it's such a time ago; and mother took me away because the master whacked me, though the missus use'n't to never touch me. I didn't like him at all. What do you think? he hit me three times, ever so hard, across the face with his cane, and made me go dancing down the stairs; and when mother saw the marks on my cheek, she went to blow him up, but she couldn't see him—he was afraid. That's why I left school.

"The creases is so bad now, that I haven't been out with 'em for three days. They're so cold, people won't buy 'em; for when I goes up to them, they say, 'They'll freeze our bellies.' Besides, in the market, they won't see a ha'penny handful now—they're risen to a penny and tuppence. In summer there's lots, and 'most as cheap as dirt; but I have to be down at Farrington-market between four and five, or else I can't get any creases, because everyone almost—especially the Irish—is selling them, and they're picked up so quick. Some of the saleswomen—we never calls 'em ladies—is very kind to us children, and some of them altogether spiteful. The good one will give you a bunch for nothing, when they're cheap; but the others, cruel ones, if you try to bate them a farden less than they ask you, will say, 'Go along with you, you're no good.' I used to go down to market along with another girl, as must be about fourteen, 'cos she does her back hair up. When we've bought a lot, we sits down on a door-stop, and ties up the bunches. We never goes home to breakfast till we've sold out; but, if it's very late, then I buys a penn'orth of pudden, which is very nice with gravy. I don't know hardly one of the people, as goes to Farrington, to talk to; they never speaks to me, so I don't speak to them. We children never play down there, 'cos we're thinking of our living. No; people never pities me in the street—excepting one gentleman, and he says, says he, 'What do you do out so soon in the morning?' but he gave me nothink—he only walked away.

. . .

"I always give mother my money, she's so very good to me. She don't often beat me; but, when she do, she don't play with me. She's very poor, and goes out cleaning rooms sometimes, now she don't work at the fur. I ain't got no father, he's a father-in-law. No; mother ain't married again—he's a father-in-law. He grinds scissors, and he's very good to me. No; I don't mean that he says kind things to me, for he never hardly speaks. When I gets home, after selling creases, I stops at home. I put the room to rights: mother don't make me do it, I does it myself. I cleans the chairs, though there's only two to clean. I takes a tub and scrubbing-brush and flannel, and scrubs the floor—that's what I do three or four times a week.

"I don't have no dinner. Mother gives me two slices of bread-and-butter and a cup of tea for breakfast, and then I go till tea, and has the same. We has meat of a Sunday, and, of course, I should like to have it every day. Mother has just the same to eat as we has, but she takes more tea—three cups, sometimes. No; I never has no sweet-stuff; I never buy none—I don't like it. Sometimes we has a game of 'honey-pots' with the girls in the court, but not often. Me and Carry H—carries the little 'uns. We plays too, at 'kiss-in-the-ring.' I knows a good many games, but I don't play at 'em, 'cos going out with the creases tires me. On a Friday night, too, I goes to a Jew's house till eleven o'clock on Saturday night. All I has to do is to snuff the candles and poke the fire. You see they keep their Sabbath then, and they won't touch anything; so they gives me my wittals and 1 1/2*d*., I does it for 'em. I have a reg'lar good lot to eat. Supper of Friday night, and tea after that, and fried fish of a Saturday morning, and meat for dinner, and tea, and supper, and I like it very well.

. . .

"I am a capital hand at bargaining—but only at buying watercreases. They can't take me in. If the woman tries to give me a small handful of creases, I says, 'I ain't a goin' to have that for a ha'porth,' and I go to the next basket, and so on, all round. I know the quantities very well. For a penny I ought to have a full market hand, or as much as I could carry in my arms at one time, without spilling. For 3*d*. I has a lap full, enough to earn about a shilling; and for 6*d*. I gets as many as crams my basket. I can't read or write, but I knows how many pennies goes to a shilling, why, twelve, of course, but I don't know how many ha'pence there is, though there's two to a penny. When I've brought 3*d*. of creases, I ties 'em up into as many little bundles as I can. They must look biggish, or the people won't buy them, some puffs them out as much as they'll go. All my money I earns I puts in a club and draws it out to buy clothes with. It's better than spending it in sweet-stuff, for them as has no living to earn. Besides it's a like a child to care for sugar-sticks, and not like one who's got a living and vittals to earn. I ain't a child, and I shan't be a woman till I'm twenty, but I'm past eight, I am. I don't know nothing about what I earns during the year. I only know how many pennies goes to a shilling, and two ha'pence goes to a penny, and four fardens goes to a penny. I knows, too, how many fardens goes to a tuppence—eight. That's as much as I wants to know for the markets."

STUDY QUESTIONS

1. In what specific ways is this little girl's childhood being destroyed?
2. What does she envision for her future, and what might she answer to Mr. Smith's reactions to capitalism in *The Wealth of Nations*?

CHAPTER 19

THE BIRTH OF MODERN POLITICS

19.1 LAJOS KOSSUTH, SPEECH OF THE 11TH JULY, 1848

Lajos Kossuth (1802–1894) was a Hungarian political leader and lawyer. He was a key participant in the Magyar nationalist movement. As the editor of a newspaper in Pest, he gained renown for advocating for an end to Hungary's political and economic subordination to Austria, as well as widespread liberal reforms. His nationalism promoted the interests of Magyars over Slavonic Hungarians, a position that ultimately cost him his job, and contributed to the collapse of Hungary, after its 1848 revolution. During this revolution, he was appointed to the Hungarian government and became regent president of the Kingdom of Hungary. With the collapse of the Hungarian government, in 1849, Kossuth fled the country and continued his struggle for full Hungarian independence from abroad. In this speech he warns of the mounting danger of Slavic separatism to the Hungarian nationalist movement.

Gentlemen, the country is in danger. Perhaps it would suffice to say thus much; for, with the dawn of liberty, the dark veil has dropped from the nation. You know what the condition of our country is; you know that besides the troops of the line, a militia of about twelve thousand men has been organized; you know that the authorities have been empowered to place corps of the National Guard on war footing, in order to establish an effective force to defend the country, and to punish sedition, which is rife on our frontiers. This command found an echo in the nation.

Under such circumstances we took the reins of government, menaced by treachery, rebellion, reactionary movements, and by all those passions which the policy of Metternich leagued to us as a cursed inheritance. Scarcely had we assumed the government— nay, not all of us had even assembled—when we already received the most authentic information that the Panslavonic agitation had no other object than to excite the whole of the upper provinces to open rebellion, and that even the day had been fixed when the outbreak should take place. . . .

From W. H. Stiles, *Austria in 1848–49*. New York: Harper and Brothers, 1852, II, p. 384–94.

Croatia is in open rebellion! Many years have elapsed, gentlemen, when not only one or the other, but numbers, called the attention of the government to the fact, that in encouraging—the Illyric agitation, it would nourish a serpent in its bosom which would compass the ruin of the dynasty. And since the revolutionary state in which we find Europe shaking on her foundations, the gentlemen in those parts fancied they might with impunity break out in open rebellion. Had Hungary given any cause whatever for this rebellion, she would, without considering the fact that there is a revolution, ask you to be just to Croatia, and to subdue the revolt, not with the force of arms, but with the sacred name of justice.

Where is a reason to be found that, even if we take up arms to quell the disturbance, we should feel in our own hearts the conviction of having ourselves provoked the disturbance? I say, no! The rights we have acquired for ourselves, we have likewise acquired for Croatia; the liberty that was granted to the people, was likewise granted to the Croats; we extended the indemnity allowed by us to our nobility, at our own expense, to Croatia—for that country is too small and powerless to raise herself the indemnity.

With regard to nationality, Croatia entertained apprehensions—though produced by various conceptions and by erroneous ideas—for the Parliament has expressly decreed that in public life the Croats should have the fullest right to make use of their own language in accordance with their own statutes; and thus their nationality has been sanctioned by this public recognition. Their municipal rights the Parliament has not only not impaired, but extended and augmented. . . .

In one word, we have not neglected anything whatever which, within the limits of integrity, or liberty, and of the rights of the people, we could do to pacify their minds. We, gentlemen, can not, therefore, admit that on the part of the cabinet the slightest cause has been given to provoke the Croatian rebellion.

If a people think the liberty they possess too limited, and take up arms to conquer more, they certainly play a doubtful game—for a sword has two edges. Still I can understand it. But if a people say, Your liberty is too much for us, we will not have it if you give it us, but we will go and bow under the old yoke of Absolutism—that is a thing which I endeavor in vain to understand.

The case, however, stands nearly thus: in the so-called petition which was sent to his majesty by the Conventicle of Agram, they pray that they may be allowed to separate from Hungary—not to be a self-consistent, independent nation, but to submit to the Austrian ministry . . . I do not, indeed, ascribe to the sentiment of freedom so great an influence on the masses, as not to be persuaded that even this sham loyalty, in its awkward affectation, is but an empty pretext under which other purposes are concealed. On the part of the leaders it covers the reactionary tendency; but on the other hand, this idea is connected with the plan of erecting an Austro-Slavonian monarchy. They say: "Let us send deputies to Vienna; let us procure the majority for the Slavonian element, and Austria will cease to be a German empire; and what with the Bohemians, and our people down here, a new Slavonian empire will rise." This is a rather hazardous game, and Europe will probably soon decide on the question; for if we should not master these affairs, they will become a European question. This much is certain, that this combination (if of any consequence at all) will doubtless involve the ruin of the Austrian dynasty. There can be no doubt about it.

The Viennese ministers have thought proper, in the name of the Austrian emperor, to declare to the cabinet of the King of Hungary, that unless we make peace with the Croats at any price, they will act in opposition to us. This is as much as to say, that the Austrian emperor declares war to the King of Hungary, or to his own self. Whatever opinion you, gentlemen, may have formed of the cabinet, I believe you may so far rely on our patriotic feelings and on our honor, as to render it superfluous on my part to tell you that we have replied on this menace in a manner becoming the dignity of the nation.

The Austrian relations, the affairs of the countries on the Lower Danube, the Serbian disturbances, the Croation rebellion, Panslavonian agitators, and the reactionary movements—all these circumstances, taken together, cause me to say the nation is in danger, or rather, that it will be in danger unless our resolution be firm!

The danger, therefore is great, or rather, a danger threatening to become great gathers on the horizon of our country, and we ought, above all, to find ourselves the strength for its removal. That nation alone will live which in itself has sufficient vital power; that which knows not to save itself by its own strength, but only by the aid of others, has no future. I therefore demand of you, gentlemen, a great resolution. Proclaim that, in just appreciation of the extraordinary circumstances on account of which the Parliament has assembled, the nation is determined to bring the greatest sacrifices for the defense of its crown, of its liberty, and of its independence, and that, in this respect, it will at no price enter with any one into a transaction which even in the least might injure the national independence and liberty, but that it will be always ready to grant all reasonable wishes of every one. But in order to realize this important resolution, either by mediating, if possible, an honorable peace, or by fighting a victorious battle, the government is to be authorized by the nation to raise the effective strength of the army to two hundred thousand men and for this purpose to equip immediately forty thousand men, and the rest as the protection of the country and the honor of the nation may demand. . . .

Gentlemen, what I meant to say is, that this request on the part of government ought not be considered as a vote of confidence. No; we ask for your vote for the preservation of the country! And I would ask you, gentlemen, if anywhere in our country a breast sighs for liberation, or a wish waits for its fulfillment, let that breast suffer yet a while, let that wish have a little patience, until we have saved the country. (Cheers.) This is my request! You all have risen to a man, and I bow before the nation's greatness! If your energy equals your patriotism, I will make bold to say, that even the gates of hell shall not prevail against Hungary!

STUDY QUESTIONS

1. Do the goals of nationalism and liberalism contradict each other in Croatia?
2. What does the document reveal about the instabilities of the Austrian state in the period?

19.2 KARL MARX, "FIRST PREMISES OF THE MATERIALIST METHOD," *THE GERMAN IDEOLOGY*, 1846, FIRST PUBLISHED 1932

Karl Marx (1818–1883), the German socialist philosopher, worked alongside Engels to shape the Communist Party, which Marx outlined in his seminal text, *The Communist Manifesto* (1848). *The German Ideology*, also coauthored by Engels, explains Marx's theory of history as defined by relationships based on material conditions. This work responds to contemporary philosophers—such as Hegel and Feuerbach—while leading the reader step by step through Marx's materialist ideology.

From Karl Marx and Friedrich Engels, *The German Ideology*. Moscow: Progress Publishers, 1968, Vol. I. ch. 1, section A.

HISTORY: FUNDAMENTAL CONDITIONS

Since we are dealing with the Germans, who are devoid of premises, we must begin by stating the first premise of all human existence and, therefore, of all history, the premise, namely, that men must be in a position to live in order to be able to "make history." But life involves before everything else eating and drinking, a habitation, clothing and many other things. The first historical act is thus the production of the means to satisfy these needs, the production of material life itself. And indeed, this is an historical act, a fundamental condition of all history, which today, as thousands of years ago, must daily and hourly be fulfilled merely in order to sustain human life. Even when the sensuous world is reduced to a minimum, to a stick as with Saint Bruno [Bauer], it presupposes the action of producing the stick. Therefore in any interpretation of history one has first of all to observe this fundamental fact in all its significance and all its implications and to accord it its due importance. It is well known that the Germans have never done this, and they have never, therefore, had an earthly basis for history and consequently never an historian. The French and the English, even if they have conceived the relation of this fact with so-called history only in an extremely one-sided fashion, particularly as long as they remained in the toils of political ideology, have nevertheless made the first attempts to give the writing of history a materialistic basis by being the first to write histories of civil society, of commerce and industry.

The second point is that the satisfaction of the first need (the action of satisfying, and the instrument of satisfaction which has been acquired) leads to new needs; and this production of new needs is the first historical act. Here we recognise immediately the spiritual ancestry of the great historical wisdom of the Germans who, when they run out of positive material and when they can serve up neither theological nor political nor literary rubbish, assert that this is not history at all, but the "prehistoric era." They do not, however, enlighten us as to how we proceed from this nonsensical "prehistory" to history proper; although, on the other hand, in their historical speculation they seize upon this "prehistory" with especial eagerness because they imagine themselves safe there from interference on the part of "crude facts," and, at the same time, because there they can give full rein to their speculative impulse and set up and knock down hypotheses by the thousand.

The third circumstance which, from the very outset, enters into historical development, is that men, who daily remake their own life, begin to make other men, to propagate their kind: the relation between man and woman, parents and children, the family. The family, which to begin with is the only social relationship, becomes later, when increased needs create new social relations and the increased population new needs, a subordinate one (except in Germany), and must then be treated and analysed according to the existing empirical data, not according to "the concept of the family," as is the custom in Germany. These three aspects of social activity are not of course to be taken as three different stages, but just as three aspects or, to make it clear to the Germans, three "moments," which have existed simultaneously since the dawn of history and the first men, and which still assert themselves in history today.

The production of life, both of one's own in labour and of fresh life in procreation, now appears as a double relationship: on the one hand as a natural, on the other as a social relationship. By social we understand the co-operation of several individuals, no matter under what conditions, in what manner and to what end. It follows from this that a certain mode of production, or industrial stage, is always combined with a certain mode of co-operation, or social stage, and this mode of co-operation is itself a "productive force." Further, that the multitude of productive forces accessible to men determines the nature of society, hence, that the "history of humanity" must always be studied and treated in relation to the history of industry and exchange. But it is also clear how in Germany it is impossible to write this sort of history, because the Germans lack not only the necessary power of comprehension and the material but also the "evidence of their senses," for across the Rhine you cannot have any experience of these things since history has stopped happening. Thus it is quite obvious from the start that there exists a materialistic connection of men with one another, which is determined by their needs and their mode of production, and which is as old as men themselves. This connection is ever taking on new forms, and thus presents a "history" independently of the existence of any political or religious nonsense which in addition may hold men together.

Only now, after having considered four moments, four aspects of the primary historical relationships, do we find that man also possesses "consciousness," but, even so, not inherent, not "pure" consciousness. From the start the "spirit" is afflicted with the curse of being "burdened" with matter, which here makes its appearance in the form of agitated layers of air, sounds, in short, of language. Language is as old as consciousness, language is practical consciousness that exists also for other men, and for that reason alone it really exists for me personally as well; language, like consciousness, only arises from the need, the necessity, of intercourse with other men. Where there exists a relationship, it exists for me: the animal does not enter into "relations" with anything, it does not enter into any relation at all. For the animal, its relation to others does not exist as a relation. Consciousness is, therefore, from the very beginning a social product, and remains so as long as men exist at all. Consciousness is at first, of course, merely consciousness concerning the immediate sensuous environment and consciousness of the limited connection with other persons and things outside the individual who is growing self-conscious. At the same time it is consciousness of nature, which first appears to men as a completely alien, all-powerful and unassailable force, with which men's relations are purely animal and by which they are overawed like beasts; it is thus a purely animal consciousness of nature (natural religion) just because nature is as yet hardly modified historically. (We see here immediately: this natural religion or this particular relation of men to nature is determined by the form of society and vice versa. Here, as everywhere, the identity of nature and man appears in such a way that the restricted relation of men to nature determines their restricted relation to one another, and their restricted relation to one another determines men's restricted relation to nature.) On the other hand, man's consciousness of the necessity of associating with the individuals around him is the beginning of the consciousness that he is living in society at all. This beginning is as animal as social life itself at this stage. It is mere herd-consciousness, and at this point man is only distinguished from sheep by the fact that with him consciousness takes the place of instinct or that his instinct is a conscious one. This sheep-like or tribal consciousness receives its further development and extension through increased productivity, the increase of needs, and, what is fundamental to both of these, the increase of population. With these there develops the division of labour, which was originally nothing but the division of labour in the sexual act, then that division of labour which develops spontaneously or "naturally" by virtue of natural predisposition (e.g. physical strength), needs, accidents, etc. etc. Division of labour only becomes truly such from the moment when a division of material and mental labour appears. (The first form of ideologists, priests, is concurrent.) From this moment onwards consciousness can really flatter itself that it is something other than consciousness of existing practice, that it really represents something without representing something real; from now on consciousness is in a position to emancipate itself from the world and to proceed to the formation of "pure" theory, theology, philosophy, ethics, etc. But even if this theory, theology, philosophy, ethics, etc. comes into contradiction with the existing relations, this can only occur because existing social relations have come into contradiction with existing forces of production; this, moreover, can also occur in a particular national sphere of relations through the appearance of the contradiction, not within the national orbit, but between this national consciousness and the practice of other nations, i.e. between the national and the general consciousness of a nation (as we see it now in Germany).

Moreover, it is quite immaterial what consciousness starts to do on its own: out of all such muck we get only the one inference that these three moments, the forces of production, the state of society, and consciousness, can and must come into contradiction with one another, because the division of labour implies the possibility, nay the fact that intellectual and material activity—enjoyment and labour, production and consumption—evolve on different individuals, and that the only possibility of their not coming into contradiction lies in the negation in its turn of the division of labour. It is self-evident, moreover, that "spectres," "bonds," "the higher being," "concept," "scruple," are merely the idealistic, spiritual expression, the conception apparently of the isolated individual, the image of very empirical fetters and limitations, within which the mode of production of life and the form of intercourse coupled with it move.

STUDY QUESTIONS

1. How does Marx interpret human history in terms of materialistic factors?
2. What are the modes of production and the productive forces in a society?

19.3 JOHANN GEORG ECCARIUS, FROM "THE FRIEND OF THE PEOPLE," NO. 4, JANUARY 4, 1851

Johann Georg Eccarius (1818–1889) worked as a tailor until he became a dedicated Marxist in the 1840s, after which he worked in journalism and as a Communist organizer. In 1851 he moved to England to work directly with Marx and Engels; ultimately, he joined the General Council of the International Working Men's Association and became its leader. In the 1850s he helped edit "The Friend of the People," a Marxist newsletter, and contributed many articles to it; one of those articles here follows. (Eccarius's British spellings are retained.)

The social and political development of mankind is a series of phases and stages, an unavoidable process through which the human race had to pass, and is perpetually passing, to arrive at a certain end.

Nations have arisen as it were from obscurity, they have been mighty and flourishing, and then passed to decline and ruin. At some particular periods war and anarchy have been so universal that the very existence of the human species has appeared to be at stake. Powerful empires have been swept from the face of the earth. The barbarians who have conquered and ruined them have carried the ruins and trophies to distant places and founded new empires. But though nations have been extinguished, exterminating wars and revolutions have taken place, the human race has survived them all, and has incessantly tended towards improvement and perfection. Every state of society that has been overthrown has furnished the material for the establishment of a succeeding one of a more progressive character: and every newly established state of society has been the necessary result of the preceding one. Every one, according to the degree of civilisation on which it was founded, has had its social and political organization, its religion and laws, its notions of justice; and every established system has at some particular period satisfied the wants of society, and corresponded with the claims that men made upon life.

Times of great commotions, anarchy, and revolutions, have always been the periods when the existing arrangements no longer answered the wants and necessities of the population. Whenever an existing state of things has ceased to satisfy the claims of society, the ruled have commenced to question the rights and authority of the rulers; men have questioned the propriety of their religion; society has begun to revolt; strifes, struggles, and battles have ensued between the oppressors and oppressed; and the ultimate result has been the dissolution of the old, and the establishment of a new, state of society.

Every new state of society has introduced its own peculiar mode of workship, one that has always been compatible with the mode of produce, with the manner in which the different tribes or nations of the different periods obtained their means of living. Thus the ancients had their gods and goddesses to whom they sacrificed a share of their acquisitions, consisting either of the fruits of the soil, or the booties of war and plunder. The feudal system (the mission of which was to compel savage and wandering tribes to settle in fixed habitations and pursue peaceable occupations in trade and agriculture, or to protect those who were already settled against the plunderings and ravages of their barbaric neighbours) had its "right divine," and its universal catholic church commanding blind and unconditional belief and obedience. Modern society, the state of free competition in art, science, trade, and industry, has its liberty of conscience, freedom of thought, and discussion, etc., in short, free competition in religious matters, and contemplations.

One of the principal features of all the changes that have yet taken place has been a change in the relations of property, from which all the social and political organizations have originated.

At all times when society has been revolutionized, the supporters of old systems, who had privileges and advantages over others, have prophesied that the world would be ruined if new systems were adopted. On the other side, those who happened to be the champions of progress, have imagined that their peculiar systems were the only true ones, that their principles were the only principles worth fighting for, that they were inherent in human nature, and if really established and administered would be an eternal source of happiness, making all future changes and revolutions unnecessary.

The same thing has been and is still repeated, over and over again. The men of the middle age accused the ancients of idolatry, and blamed their system of slavery. They proclaimed the emancipation of the slaves, and made the slaves of the Roman empire serfs and bondmen; forgetting at the same time that the ancient world had laboured for centuries to prepare the ground on which the feudal system could be erected. The modern bourgeoisie, the discoverers of the natural rights of men, have raved and are incessantly raving against feudalism, against serfdom, and bondage. They call it the age of anarchy and oppression; yet they have commenced business with the stock which they accumulated under the wings of feudalism; they have extended that knowledge and industry which they acquired under its protection; they have abolished serfdom and bondage for their own aggrandizement, and have created a numerous proletariat—modern slaves—who have to get a scanty subsistence by working for wages.

They have been mistaken; what they considered the natural rights of man were only the rights of men living in that particular state of society.

They have in their turn become as great tyrants as were the feudal Lords and Kings; and, like their predecessors, they have for their own security been compelled to create conditions under which not only a new progressive state of society is becoming possible, but compulsory.

Thus, the bourgeoisie has fulfilled its mission in history, and no more.

It is true the accomplishments that have been made under the bourgeois regime surpass those of all former ages; but they could not have been made without having all the previous acquirements as a foundation for them. The declarations of our bourgeois politicians and economists that the essence of the present state of society is eternal, and that a deviation from it will lead to ruin and barbarism, are the more absurd, since the revolutionary volcano is continually threatening to swamp the whole system, and whatever they undertake to put a stop to, has only the effect of pouring oil on to the fire.

The events and commotions that have lately occurred are the most unmistakeable signs that the existing state of bourgeois society is in its last stage, and is verging towards ruin and dissolution. When our statesmen say that socialism and communism will lead to ruin, they are in so far right, as socialism and communism stipulate the annihilation of bourgeois society, its relations of property, its mode of appropriation, distribution, and exploitation. But mankind will not be ruined. Production and distribution will be freed from the shackles that are imposed upon them; they will not be dependent on the avidity, for gain, of some individuals, who are at present known under the denomination of "manufacturers," "merchants," "shopkeepers," etc., etc., for at present the lust of gain is the only stimulant to production, distribution, and exchange. The farmer does not cultivate the soil because society is in want of agricultural produce, but because the market price is higher than the cost of production. If society could not afford to pay that price, the farmer would abandon his land, though the majority of the people might die for the want of food. We read very often, indeed, complaints of low prices caused by overproduction or abundant harvests, while in one and the same paper we read reports of people being utterly destitute of the necessaries of life. Times of disturbance and dissolution have generally been accompanied by a comparative amount of misery and destitution, for it is misery and destitution that drive the masses to revolt and rebellion. I say comparative, because the wants and necessaries of mankind vary with the degree of civilization. What a Russian serf would consider comfort, an English proletarian might deem misery.

There has been for some years past an amount of misery in existence which is continually increasing. The "Manchester school" politicians, and economists, have told us a great deal of late about "the comparative wellbeing of the working classes." By what standard do they compare this alleged well-being? Why, by the standard of 1847—a time of universal stagnation in trade, with a famine into the bargain. A very strong argument indeed in favour of existing arrangements, that the working classes are better off in a year of unexampled prosperity than in a year of famine and commercial stagnation. Some weeks ago the Economist was highly gratified at the comparative well-being of the working classes, manifested in the increase of population and marriages during the last quarter. I very much doubt whether the increase of population and marriages, is in all cases, the result of well-being. Many a young couple join in holy matrimony, because their earnings do not enable them to live single. Their "issue," therefore, is not the result of well-being but of misery. With all the ostentatious boast of increasing trade and prosperity, our profit-mongers have not been able to reclaim more than 38,770 able-bodied paupers out of 166,828, from the 1st July 1848, till the same date 1850. On the 1st July last, society had still to keep 128,058 able-bodied paupers in the workhouses, in spite of "prosperity." Besides these there are hundreds of thousands who only get half a living, and prefer starving at home to going into workhouses.

The increase of friendly societies is also taken as a proof of increasing prosperity among the working-classes. Our Manchester politicians are greatly mistaken. The increase of friendly societies merely proves that the spare pennies of a great many are wanted to help one in case of need; and that working men are disgusted with applying for parish relief. The New Poor Law, and the cruel treatment of "in-door Paupers," do much toward increasing the number of friendly societies. They may as well tell us that our workhouses, our poor-law system, and our convict establishments, are emblems of the well-being of the working-classes. Without pauperism and crime, there would be no occasion for workhouses, poor-laws, and convict establishments. And without the wretchedness prevalent among the working-classes, there would be no occasion for societies for mutual relief and support.

Mr. Porter pretends to prove the wealth of the working-classes by the increase of the deposits in the Savings' Banks. He states that the amount of deposits in 1846 was in England, Wales, and Ireland, £ 29,669,384, —being equal to 24 s. per head,—while in 1821 the amount only averaged 12s. 8d. per head. I will not inquire how far these deposits belong to the working-classes, (the picture of pauperism just exhibited corresponds very badly), but whatever the amount belonging to working-men may be, it only shews that their earnings are not sufficient to invest them otherwise, and that their circumstances are so precarious that they are afraid to spend on luxuries and comfort that little of their income which is over and above their bare subsistence. Besides, the Savings' Banks are principally an accommodation for governments and the bourgeoisie.

Mr. Porter also attempts to disprove the position often assumed,—that the rich are becoming richer, and the poor poorer. He does so by shewing that the revenue liable to the income tax, has since 1812 increased nearly three-fold greater than the population during the same period. But Mr. Porter says nothing about the poor, whether their income has increased at the same ratio. According to his statement, the income of the bourgeoisie has increased something like five-fold. Allowing the population to be nearly double now what it was in 1812, if the income of the proletariat had increased in the same proportion, every working-man who had one pound a week, in 1812, ought to have two pounds ten shillings now. I beg Mr. Porter's pardon for maintaining that the income of the proletarian has rather shewn a tendency to decrease below the pound; and therefore Mr. Porter's figures prove nothing else but that the rich are becoming richer, and the poor poorer. The breach is becoming wider and wider; and the building must soon fall to the ground.

STUDY QUESTIONS

1. How does Eccarius describe the social and political development of humankind as a series of phases and stages?
2. Why, for Eccarius, are "the events and commotions that have lately occurred . . . the most unmistakable signs that the existing state of bourgeois society is in its last stage"? Why does Eccarius believe bourgeois society is "verging towards ruin and dissolution"?

19.4 CAROLINE NORTON, "ON THE INFANT CUSTODY BILL," 1839; "ON DIVORCE," 1855

Caroline Norton (1808–1877) was a British feminist and reformer who translated her personal experiences—of a bitter divorce and the denial of custody of her children—into activism on behalf of married women. As a direct result of her efforts, Parliament passed acts protecting women's custody, marriage rights, and property in the 1840s through 1860s. Her letter to the Lord

From Norton, Caroline Sheridan, 1808–1877. *The Separation of Mother and Child by the Law of "Custody of Infants Considered."* London: Roake and Varty, 1831; Strand, 1838, pp. 1–6.

Chancellor on the Infant Custody Bill argues eloquently but forcefully in favor of female custody. Sixteen years later, Norton aimed even higher and wrote a letter directly to the queen of England to remedy the problem that British married women had, as she phrased it, "no legal existence."

The law which regulates the Custody of Infant Children, being now under the consideration of the legislature, it is very desirable that the attention of the public and of Members of Parliament in particular, should be drawn towards a subject, upon which so much misconception and ignorance prevails.

It is a common error to suppose that every mother has a *right* to the custody of her child till it attain the age of seven years. By a curious anomaly in law, the mother of a *bastard child* HAS *this right*, while the mothers of legitimate children are excluded from it,—the law as regards to children born in wedlock being as follows.

The custody of legitimate children, is held to be the right of the Father *from the hour of their birth*: to the utter exclusion of the Mother, whose separate claim has no legal existence, and is not recognised by the Courts. No circumstance can modify or alter this admitted right of the father: though he should be living in open adultery, and his wife be legally separated from him on that account. He is responsible to no one for his motives, should he desire entirely to exclude his wife from all access to her children; nor is he accountable for the disposal of the child; that is, the law supposing the *nominal* custody to be with him, does not oblige him to make it a *bona fide* custody by a residence of the child under his roof and protection, but holds "the custody of the father" to mean, in an extended sense, the custody of whatever stranger the father may think fit to appoint in lieu of the mother; and those strangers can exert his delegated authority to exclude the mother from access to her children; without any legal remedy being possible on her part, by appeal to the Courts or otherwise; the construction of the law being, that they have *no power to interfere* with the exercise of the father's right.

Should it so happen that at the time of separation, or afterwards, the children being in the mother's possession, she should refuse to deliver them up, the father's right extends to forcibly seizing them; *even should they be infants at the breast*. Or he may obtain, on application, a writ of habeas corpus, ordering the mother to produce the child in Court, to be delivered over to him; and should this order be disobeyed, he can cause a writ of attachment to issue against her; or, in other words, cause her to be imprisoned for contempt of court. The fact of the wife being innocent and the husband guilty, or of the separation being an unwilling one on her part, does not alter his claim: the law has no power to order that a woman shall even have occasional access to her children, though she could prove that she was driven by violence from her husband's house, and that he had deserted her for a mistress. The Father's right is absolute and paramount, and can no more be affected by the mother's claim, than if she had no existence.

The result of this tacit admission by law, of an individual right so entirely despotic, (the assertion of which *can* only be called for in seasons of family disunion and bitterness of feeling), is exactly what might have been expected. Instances have arisen from time to time in which the power has been grossly and savagely abused. It has been made the means of persecution, and the instrument of vengeance: it has been exerted to compel a disposition of property in favour of the husband, where the wife has possessed an independent fortune: it has been put into force by an adulterous husband to terrify his wife from proceeding in the Ecclesiastical Courts against him: in short, there is scarcely any degree of cruelty which has not been practiced under colour of its protection.

We have given in an appendix, to which we refer our readers, a brief report of the cases quoted by Serjeant Talfourd as shewing the necessity of such measure as that which he has lately proposed; and we apprehend, that no right-minded man can read through examples there given, without admitting the necessity of some such alteration in the law, as shall afford a reasonable protection to the weak and helpless of the other sex, under circumstances of great grievance and oppression.

In one of those cases, a Frenchman marries to an Englishwoman, and wishing to compel a disposition of her property, entered by force the house where she had fled for refuge, dragged the child (which she was in the act of nursing) from the very breast; and took it away, almost naked, in an open carriage, in inclement weather. The mother appealed to the Courts: the Courts decided they had *no power to interfere.* In another case the husband being in Horsemonger jail, gave the child into the care of a woman with whom he cohabitated: his wife appealed to the Courts against the outrage: the Courts decided that they had *no power to interfere.* In a third instance the mother persuaded the schoolmistress who had charge of her child, to give it up to her, the child being sick of a disease of which two of her children had already died. The husband obtained a writ of habeas corpus, and the sick child was *taken from its mother.* In the last case decided under the present construction of "the Father's right," the wife having discovered that her husband was living with a woman of the town whom he permitted to assume his name, and passed off as his wife, withdrew from his house to that of her mother. The husband refused to part from his mistress, but claimed his infant female children; and the claim was *admitted by the Courts;* (though baffled by the mother, who fled to France taking her children with her.)

Numerous other cases exist, in which the women have attempted to establish a claim to the custody of their children, but the result has invariably been *against the mother,* except in one or two rare instances, where property was affected; for the sake of the security of which property, and not from any admission of the mother's natural claim, the decisions were made against the father.

In cases where property was not affected, no instance has occurred, in which the bad character of the father, or the cause of separation, has operated on the decisions of the Courts of Law; and though in almost all the cases reported, both counsel and judge admit the severity and injustice of the law as affecting the mother, it does not appear that any attempt has ever been made to revise or alter it.

We are told that the difficulty is, to meet every individual instance of alleged hardship, and to enter into private complaints and family disputes, as must necessarily be the case if the Court is called upon to decide the right of access of the mother, against the inclination of the father. But it is notorious that both the Court of King's Bench and the Court of Chancery do ALREADY assume to themselves the power of meeting and deciding on individual cases. They will interfere, as aforesaid, for the security of property, and on account of religious, or even political opinions; and have established a rule that *at a specified age,* namely, 14 years, a child cannot be forced back to the custody of its father, *if the child himself be unwilling to return.*

There was a direct interference in the case of Wellesley; in the case of Shelley; and others of less note. Nothing is now proposed which militates *more* against the father's right, than the power already vested in the Court of Chancery; nay, nor *so much;* for that Court *has* assumed to itself a RIGHT OF DECISION how far irreligion and immorality disqualify a man from *properly educating his children, or having the custody of them;* and though that right has been most sparingly exercised, yet its bare assumption and existence is surely a greater interference with parental power, than if the Court were to assume.

STUDY QUESTIONS

1. What might have served as the rationale for the father to have superior rights to a mother's in a property dispute?
2. Did Norton expect that she would receive an answer to her questions from either an all-male Parliament or the queen on the issue?

19.5 ISABELLA BEETON, FROM *MRS. BEETON'S BOOK OF HOUSEHOLD MANAGEMENT*, 1861

The wife of a publisher, Isabella Beeton (1836–1865) translated her cooking talent into printed how-to guides for the women of London. Her grand guide, *Mrs. Beeton's Book of Household Management*, provides nearly a thousand recipes as well as helpful tips for running a proper Victorian household. Beeton was only twenty-one years old when she began compiling the project, which sold more than fifty thousand copies in its first year. Consider the wide scope of skills Beeton thinks a proper mistress should possess.

As with the COMMANDER OF AN ARMY, or the leader of any enterprise, so is it with the mistress of a house. Her spirit will be seen through the whole establishment; and just in proportion as she performs her duties intelligently and thoroughly, so will her domestics follow in her path. Of all those acquirements, which more particularly belong to the feminine character, there are none which take a higher rank, in our estimation, than such as enter into a knowledge of household duties; for on these are perpetually dependent the happiness, comfort, and well-being of a family. In this opinion we are borne out by the author of "The Vicar of Wakefield," who says: "The modest virgins, the prudent wife, and the careful matron, are much more serviceable in life than petticoated philosophers, blustering heroines, or virago queens. She who makes her husband and her children happy, who reclaims the one from vice and trains up the other to virtue, is a much greater character than ladies described in romances, whose whole occupation is to murder mankind with shafts from their quiver, or their eyes."

. . .

In PURCHASING articles of wearing apparel, whether it be a silk dress, a bonnet, shawl, or riband, it is well for the buyer to consider three things: I. That it be not too expensive for her purse. II. That its colour harmonize with her complexion, and its size and pattern with her figure. III. That its tint allow of its being worn with the other garments she possesses. The quaint Fuller observes, that the good wife is none of our dainty dames, who love to appear in a variety of suits every day new, as if a gown, like a stratagem in war, were to be used but once. But our good wife sets up a sail according to the keel of her husband's estate; and, if of high parentage, she doth not so remember what she was by birth, that she forgets what she is by match.

To *Brunettes*, or those ladies having dark complexions, silks of a grave hue are adapted. For *Blondes*, or those having fair complexions, lighter colours are preferable, as the richer, deeper hues are too overpowering for the latter. The colours which go best together are green with violet, gold-colour with dark crimson or lilac; pale blue with scarlet; pink with black or white; and gray with scarlet or pink. A cold colour generally requires a warm tint to give life to it. Gray and pale blue, for instance, do not combine well, both being cold colours.

. . .

After luncheon, MORNING CALLS AND VISITS may be made and received. These may be divided under three heads: those of ceremony, friendship, and congratulation or condolence. Visits of ceremony, or courtesy, which occasionally merge into

From Isabella Beeton, *Mrs. Beeton's Book of Household Management*. Edited by Nicola Humble. New York: Oxford University Press, 2009, pp. 7, 11–2, 18–9, 21–4, 27, 29, 569–70.

those of friendship, are to be paid under various circumstances. Thus, they are uniformly required after dining at a friend's house, or after a ball, picnic, or any other party. These visits should be short, a stay of from fifteen to twenty minutes being quite sufficient. A lady paying a visit may remove her boa or neckerchief, but neither her shawl or bonnet.

. . .

It is not advisable, at any time, to take favourite dogs into another lady's drawing-room, for many persons have an absolute dislike to such animals; and besides this, there is always a chance of a breakage of some article occurring, through their leaping and bounding here and there, sometimes very much to the fear and annoyance of the hostess. Her children, also, unless they are particularly well-trained and orderly, and she is on exceedingly friendly terms with the hostess, should not accompany a lady in making morning calls. Where a lady, however, pays her visits in a carriage, the children can be taken in the vehicle and remain in it until the visit is over.

. . .

The HALF-HOUR BEFORE DINNER has always been considered a great ordeal through which the mistress, in giving a dinner-party, will either pass with flying colours, or, lose many of her laurels. The anxiety to receive her guests,—her hope that all will be present in due time,—her trust in the skill of her cook, and the attention of the other domestics, all tend to make these few minutes a trying time. The mistress, however, must display no kind of agitation, but show her tact in suggesting light and cheerful subjects of conversation, which will be much aided by the introduction of any particular new book, curiosity of art, or article of vertu, which may pleasantly engage the attention of the company. "Waiting for Dinner," however, is a trying time, and there are few who have not felt—

> How sad it is to sit and pine,
> The long *half-hour* before we dine!
> Upon our watches oft to look,
> Then wonder at the clock and cook
> . . .
> And strive to laugh in spite of Fate!
> But laughter forced soon quits the room,
> And leaves it in its former gloom.
> But lo! the dinner now appears,
> The object of our hopes and fears,
> The end of all our pain!

When dinner is finished, the DESSERT is placed on the table, accompanied with finger-glasses. It is the custom of some gentlemen to wet a corner of the napkin but the hostess, whose behaviour will set the tone to all the ladies present, will merely wet the tips of her fingers, which will serve all the purposes required. The French and other continentals have a habit of gargling the mouth; but it is a custom which no English gentlewoman should, in the slightest degree, imitate.

When FRUIT has been taken, and a glass or two of wine passed round, the time will have arrived when the hostess will rise, and thus give the signal for the ladies to leave the gentlemen, and retire to the drawing-room. The gentlemen of the party will rise at the same time, and he who is nearest the door, will open it for the ladies, all remaining courteously standing until the last lady had withdrawn. Dr. Johnson has a curious paragraph on the effects of a dinner on men. "Before dinner," he says, "men meet with great inequality of understanding; and those who are conscious of their inferiority have the modesty not to talk. When they have drunk wine, every man feels himself happy, and loses that modesty, and grows imprudent and vociferous; but he is not improved, he is only not sensible of his defects." This is rather severe, but there may be truth in it.

In former times, when the bottle circulated freely amongst the guests, it was necessary for the ladies to retire earlier than they do at present, for the gentlemen of the company soon became unfit to conduct themselves with that decorum which is essential in the presence of ladies. Thanks, however, to the improvements in modern society, and the high example shown to the nation by its most illustrious personages, temperance is, in these happy days, a striking feature in the character of a gentleman. Delicacy of conduct towards the female sex has increased with the esteem in which they are now universally held, and thus, the very early withdrawing of the ladies from the dining-room is to be deprecated.

A lull in the conversation will seasonably indicate the moment for the ladies' departure.

. . .

Of the manner of passing EVENINGS AT HOME, there is none pleasanter than in such recreative enjoyments as those which relax the mind from its severer duties, whilst they stimulate it with a gentle delight. Where there are young people forming a part of the evening circle, interesting and agreeable pastime should especially be promoted. It is of incalculable benefit to them that their homes should possess all the attractions of healthful amusement, comfort, and happiness; for if they do not find pleasure there, they will seek it elsewhere. It ought, therefore, to enter into the domestic policy of every parent, to make her children feel that home is the happiest place in the world; that to imbue them with this delicious home-feeling is one of the choicest gifts a parent can bestow.

. . .

Such are the onerous duties which enter into the position of the mistress of the house, and such are, happily, with a slight but continued attention, of by no means difficult performance. She ought always to remember that she is the first and the last, the Alpha and the Omega in the government of her establishment; and that is by her conduct that its whole internal policy is regulated. She is, therefore, a person of far more importance in a community than she usually thinks she is. On her pattern her daughters model themselves; by her counsels they are directed; through her virtues all are honoured;—"her children rise up and call her blessed; her husband, also, and he praiseth her." Therefore, let each mistress always remember her responsible position, never approving a mean action, nor speaking an unrefined word. Let her conduct be such that her inferiors may respect her, and such as an honourable and right-minded man may look for in his wife and the mother of his children. Let her think of the many compliments and the sincere homage that have been paid to her sex by the greatest philosophers and writers, both in ancient and modern times. Let her not forget that she has to show herself worth of Campbell's compliment when he said,—

The world was sad! the garden was a wild!
And man the hermit sigh'd, till *woman* smiled.

. . .

WILLS.—The last proof of affection which we can give to those left behind, is to leave their worldly affairs in such a state as to excite neither jealousy, nor anger, nor heartrendings of any kind, at least for the immediate future. This can only be done by a just, clear, and intelligible disposal of whatever there is to leave. Without being advocates for every man being his own lawyer, it is not to be denied that the most elaborately prepared wills have been the most fruitful sources of litigation, and it has even happened that learned judges left wills behind them which could not be carried out. Except in the cases where the property is in land or in leases of complicated tenure, very elaborate details are unnecessary; and we counsel no man to use words in making his will of which he does not perfectly understand the meaning and import.

All men over twenty-one years of age, and of sound mind, and all unmarried women of like age and sanity, may by will bequeath their property to whom they please. Infants, that is, all persons under twenty-one years of age, and married women, except where they have an estate of their "own separate use," are incapacitated, without the concurrence of the husband; the law taking the disposal of any property they die possessed of. A person born deaf and dumb cannot make a will, unless there is evidence that he could read and comprehend its contents. A person convicted of felony cannot make a will, unless subsequently pardoned; neither can persons outlawed; but the wife of a felon transported for life may make a will, and act in all respects as if she were unmarried. A suicide may bequeath real estate, but personal property is forfeited to the crown.

STUDY QUESTIONS

1. How does the wife act as an agent of the family, and how does she behave when she enters someone else's home?
2. How does Beeton compare her role to those of military generals and political leaders?

CHAPTER 20

NATIONALISM AND IDENTITY

20.1 CHARLES TREVELYAN, *THE IRISH CRISIS*, 1848

Sir Charles Trevelyan (1807–1886) spent fifteen years as a British colonial officer in India, where he pursued reform of living conditions; when he was recalled to England, he worked to combat the Irish potato famine. His account of the Great Famine (1845–1852) provides his thoughts on everything from the potato to relationships between social classes. This introductory portion of *The Irish Crisis* lays out contemporary viewpoints on the famine and frames the disaster as a failure of the "agrarian code" that drove Ireland into socioeconomic imbalance.

If, a few months ago, an enlightened man had been asked what he thought the most discouraging circumstance in the state of Ireland, we do not imagine that he would have pitched upon Absenteeism, or Protestant bigotry, or Roman Catholic bigotry, or Orangeism, or Ribbandism, or the Repeal cry, or even the system of threatening notices and midday assassinations. These things, he would have said, are evils; but some of them are curable; and others are merely symptomatic. They do not make the case desperate. But what hope is there for a nation which lives on potatoes?

. . .

The important influence which has been exercised by this root over the destinies of the human race, arises from the fact that it yields an unusually abundant produce as compared with the extent of ground cultivated, and with the labour, capital, and skill bestowed upon its cultivation. The same land, which when laid down to corn, will maintain a given number of persons, will support three times that number when used for raising potatoes. "A family in the West of Ireland, once located on from one to three or four acres of land, was provided for; a cabin could be raising in a few days without the expense of a sixpence; the potatoes, at the cost of a very little labour, supplied them with a sufficiency of food, with which, from habit, they were perfectly content; and a pig, or with some, a cow, or donkey, or pony, and occasional labour at a very low rate of wages, gave them what was necessary to pay a rent, and for such clothing and other articles as were absolutely necessary, and which, with a great proportion, were on the lowest scale of human existence.

From C. E. Trevelyan, Esq., *The Irish Crisis*. London: Longman, Brown, Green & Longmans, 1919, pp. 2, 4–9.

The foundation of the whole, however, was the possession of the bit of land; it was the one, and the only one thing absolutely necessary; the rent consequently was high, and generally well paid, being the first demand on all money received, in order to secure that essential tenure; and only what remained became applicable to other objects. Although of the lowest grade, it was an easy mode of subsistence, and led to the encouragement of early marriages, large families, and rapidly-increasing population, and at the same time afforded the proprietor very good return of profit for his land."[1]

The relations of employer and employed, which knit together the framework of society, and establish a mutual dependence and good-will, have no existence in the potato system. The Irish small holder lives in a state of isolation, the type of which is to be sought for in the islands of the South Sea, rather than in the great civilized communities of the ancient world. A fortnight for planting, a week or ten days for digging, and another fortnight for turf-cutting, suffice for his subsistence; and during the rest of the year, he is at leisure to follow his own inclinations, without even the safeguard of those intellectual tastes and legitimate objects of ambition which only imperfectly obviate the evils of leisure in the higher ranks of society.

The excessive competition for land maintained rents at a level which left the Irish peasant the bare means of subsistence; and poverty, discontent, and idleness, acting on his excitable nature, produced that state of popular feeling which furnishes the material for every description of illegal association and misdirected political agitation. That agrarian code which is at perpetual war with the laws of God and man, is more especially the offspring of this state of society, the primary object being to secure the possession of the plots of land, which, in the absence of wages, are the sole means of subsistence.

There is a gradation even in potatoes. Those generally used by the people of Ireland were of the coarsest and most prolific kind, called "Lumpers," or "Horse Potatoes," from their size, and they were, for the most part, cultivated, not in furrows, but in the slovenly mode popularly known as "lazy beds;" so that the principle of seeking the cheapest description of food at the smallest expense of labour, was maintained in all its force. To the universal dependence on the potato, and to the absence of farmers of a superior class, it was owing that agriculture of every description was carried on in a negligent, imperfect manner.[2] The domestic habits arising out of this mode of subsistence were of the lowest and most degrading kind. The pigs and poultry, which share the food of the peasant's family, became, in course, inmates of the cabin also. The habit of exclusively living on the root produced an entire ignorance of every other food and of the means of preparing it; and there is scarcely a woman of the peasant class in the West of Ireland, whose culinary art exceeds the boiling of a potato. Bread is scarcely ever seen, and an oven is unknown.

The first step to improvement was wanting to this state of things. The people had no incitement to be industrious to procure comforts which were utterly beyond their reach, and which many of them

---

[1] Sir John Burgoyne's letter to the "Times," dated October 1847.

[2] The following description of the state of agriculture in West Clare, previously to the failure in the potato crop in 1845, is taken from a narrative by Captain Mann of the Royal Navy, who had for some time previously been stationed in that district, in charge of the Coast Guard, and when the distress commenced, he took an active and very useful part in assisting in the measures of relief: "Agriculture at that period was in a very neglected state; wheat, barley, and oats, with potatoes as the food of the poor, being the produce. Of the first very little was produced, and that not good in quality; barley, a larger proportion and good; oats, much greater, but inferior for milling purposes. Various reasons were given for this inferiority in produce, the quality of the land and deteriorated seed being the cause generally assigned; but I would say that the population being content with, and relying on, the produce of the potato as food—which has with very few exceptions hitherto proved abundant—there was a general neglect and want of any attempt at improvement. Green crops were all but unknown, except here and there a little turnip or mangel wurzel in the garden or field of the better class,—the former scarcely to be purchased. Even the potatoes were tilled in the easiest way, (in beds called 'lazy beds'), not in drills, so that the hoe might in a very short time clear the weeds and lighten the soil."

perhaps had never seen. Their ordinary food being of the cheapest and commonest description, and having no value in the market, it gave them no command of butcher's meat, manufactures, colonial produce, or any other article of comfort or enjoyment. To those who subsist chiefly on corn, other articles of equal value are available, which can be substituted for it at their discretion; or if they please, they can, by the adoption of a less expensive diet, accumulate a small capital by which their future condition may be improved and secured; but the only hope for those who lived upon potatoes was in some great intervention of Providence to bring back the potato to its original use and intention as an adjunct, and not as a principal article of national food; and by compelling the people of Ireland to recur to other more nutritious means of aliment, to restore the energy and the vast industrial capabilities of that country.

STUDY QUESTIONS

1. Was the potato sufficiently resource rich to become the standard staple food for the lower classes of Ireland?
2. How did Trevelyan propose honing the skills of the immigrants, channeling their "natural capabilities" into labor?

20.2 MATTHEW ARNOLD, PREAMBLE; "ON A DEFINITION OF CULTURE," *CULTURE AND ANARCHY*, 1867

Matthew Arnold (1822–1888), the son of a famous English headmaster, grew up with a reforming mindset. He wove his Victorian concern for proper regulation and stability into poems and essays that guide the reader through his various social critiques—such as, of course, education reform. Originally a set of essays, the writings of *Culture and Anarchy* were compiled in 1869 and given an oft-quoted preface. The selection reprinted here marches through several working definitions of the idea of "culture," trying to connect it to the ennobling qualities that Arnold optimistically envisions as an English ideal.

In one of his speeches a year or two ago, that fine speaker and famous Liberal, Mr. Bright, took occasion to have a fling at the friends and preachers of culture. "People who talk about what they call culture!" said he contemptuously; "by which they mean a smattering of the two dead languages of Greek and Latin." And he went on to remark, in a strain with which modern speakers and writers have made us very

From Matthew Arnold, *Culture and Anarchy: An Essay in Political and Social*. London: Smith, Elder, and Co., 1869.

familiar, how poor a thing this culture is, how little good it can do to the world, and how absurd it is for its possessors to set much store by it. And the other day a younger Liberal than Mr. Bright, one of a school whose mission it is to bring into order and system that body of truth of which the earlier Liberals merely touched the outside, a member of the University of Oxford, and a very clever writer, Mr. Frederic Harrison, developed, in the systematic and stringent manner of his school, the thesis which Mr. Bright had propounded in only general terms. "Perhaps the very silliest cant of the day," said Mr. Frederic Harrison, "is the cant about culture. Culture is a desirable quality in a critic of new books, and sits well on a possessor of *belles lettres*; but as applied to politics, it means simply a turn for small fault-finding, love of selfish ease, and indecision in action. The man of culture is in politics one of the poorest mortals alive. For simple pedantry and want of good sense no man is his equal. No assumption is too unreal, no end is too unpractical for him. But the active exercise of politics requires common sense, sympathy, trust, resolution and enthusiasm, qualities which your man of culture has carefully rooted up, lest they damage the delicacy of his critical olfactories. Perhaps they are the only class of responsible beings in the community who cannot with safety be entrusted with power."

Now for my part I do not wish to see men of culture asking to be entrusted with power; and, indeed, I have freely said, that in my opinion the speech most proper, at present, for a man of culture to make to a body of his fellow-countrymen who get him into a committee-room, is Socrates's: Know thyself! and this is not a speech to be made by men wanting to be entrusted with power. For this very indifference to direct political action I have been taken to task by the *Daily Telegraph*, coupled, by a strange perversity of fate, with just that very one of the Hebrew prophets whose style I admire the least, and called "an elegant Jeremiah." It is because I say (to use the words which the *Daily Telegraph* puts in my mouth):—"You mustn't make a fuss because you have no vote,—that is vulgarity; you mustn't hold big meetings to agitate for reform bills and to repeal corn laws,—that is the very height of vulgarity,"—it is for this reason that I am called, sometimes an elegant Jeremiah, sometimes a spurious Jeremiah, a Jeremiah about the reality of whose mission the writer in the *Daily Telegraph* has his doubts. It is evident, therefore, that I have so taken my line as not to be exposed to the whole brunt of Mr. Frederic Harrison's censure. Still, I have often spoken in praise of culture; I have striven to make all my works and ways serve the interests of culture; I take culture to be something a great deal more than what Mr. Frederic Harrison and others call it: "a desirable quality in a critic of new books." Nay, even though to a certain extent I am disposed to agree with Mr. Frederic Harrison, that men of culture are just the class of responsible beings in this community of ours who cannot properly, at present, be entrusted with power, I am not sure that I do not think this the fault of our community rather than of the men of culture. In short, although, like Mr. Bright and Mr. Frederic Harrison, and the editor of the *Daily Telegraph*, and a large body of valued friends of mine, I am a liberal, yet I am a liberal tempered by experience, reflection, and renouncement, and I am, above all, a believer in culture. Therefore I propose now to try and enquire, in the simple unsystematic way which best suits both my taste and my powers, what culture really is, what good it can do, what is our own special need of it; and I shall seek to find some plain grounds on which a faith in culture—both my own faith in it and the faith of others,—may rest securely.

STUDY QUESTIONS

1. Can a man of culture serve a useful purpose in the real world?
2. How does Arnold incorporate allusions to both Greek and Latin literature and the Bible, and is one of these sources more important than the other?

20.3 EDWARD AUGUSTUS FREEMAN, *RACE AND LANGUAGE*, 1879

A British professor and politician, Edward Augustus Freeman (1823–1892) pursued enterprises that varied from the publishing of nearly 250 texts, to the excavation of the Palace of Knossos (Crete) with Arthur Evans, to political activism against the Ottoman Empire in the Balkans. Although his most famous work is the *History of the Norman Conquest* (1867–1879), Freeman incorporated his fascination with archeology, anthropology, and linguistics into his work *Race and Language*. This text examines the categories that humankind has developed to talk about deeply rooted values like nationalism, family development, and religious doctrine.

The plain fact is that the new lines of scientific and historical inquiry which have been opened in modern times have had a distinct and deep effect upon the politics of the age. The fact may be estimated in many ways, but its existence as a fact cannot be denied. Not in a merely scientific or literary point of view, but in one strictly practical, the world is not the same world as it was when men had not yet dreamed of the kindred between Sanscrit, Greek, and English, when it was looked on as something of a paradox to him that there was a distinction between Celtic and Teutonic tongues and nations. Ethnological and philological researches—do not forget the distinction between the two, but for the present I must group them together—have opened the way for new national sympathies, new national antipathies, such as would have been unintelligible a hundred years ago. A hundred years ago a man's political likes and dislikes seldom went beyond the range which was suggested by the place of his birth or immediate descent. Such birth or descent made him a member of this or that political community, a subject of this or that prince, a citizen— perhaps a subject—of this or that commonwealth. The political community of which he was a member had its traditional alliances and traditional enmities, and by those alliances and enmities the likes and dislikes of the members of that community were guided. But those traditional alliances and enmities were seldom determined by theories about language or race. The people of this or that place might be discontented under a foreign government; but, as a rule, they were discontented only if subjection to that foreign government brought with it personal oppression or at least political degradation. Regard or disregard of some purely local privilege or local feeling went for more than the fact of a government being native or foreign. What we now call the sentiment of nationality did not go for much; what we call the sentiment of race went for nothing at all.

There is then a distinct doctrine of race, and of sympathies founded on race, distinct from the feeling of community of religion, and distinct from the feeling of nationality in the narrower sense. It is not so simple or easy a feeling as either of those two. It does not in the same way lie on the surface; it is not in the same way grounded on obvious facts which are plain to every man's understanding. The doctrine of race is essentially an artificial doctrine, a learned doctrine. It is an inference from facts which the mass of mankind could never have found out for themselves; facts which, without a distinctly learned teaching, could never be brought home to them in any intelligible shape. Now what is the value of such a doctrine? Does it follow that, because it is confessedly artificial, because it springs, not from a spontaneous impulse, but from a learned teaching, it is therefore necessarily

From Edward Augustus Freeman, *Race and Language*, 1879.

foolish, mischievous, perhaps unnatural? It may perhaps be safer to hold that like many other doctrines, many other sentiments, it is neither universally good nor universally bad, neither inherently wise nor inherently foolish. It may be safer to hold that it may, like other doctrines and sentiments, have a range within which it may work for good, while in some other range it may work for evil. It may in short be a doctrine which is neither to be rashly accepted, nor rashly cast aside, but one which may need to be guided, regulated, modified, according to time, place, and circumstance.

The natural family is the starting-point of everything; but we must give the natural family the power of artificially enlarging itself by admitting adoptive members. A group of mankind is thus formed, in which it does not follow that all the members have any natural community of blood, but in which community of blood is the starting-point, in which those who are connected by natural community of blood form the original body within whose circle the artificial members are admitted. A group of mankind thus formed is something quite different from a fortuitous concurrence of atoms. Three or four brothers by blood, with a fourth or fifth man whom they agree to look on as filling in everything the same place as a brother by blood, form a group which is quite unlike a union of four or five men, none of whom is bound by any tie of blood to any of the others. In the latter kind of union the notion of kindred does not come in at all. In the former kind the notion of kindred is the groundwork of everything; it determines the character of every relation and every action, even though the kindred between some members of the society and others may be owing to a legal fiction and not of natural descent. All that we know of the growth of tribes, races, nations, leads us to believe that they grew in this way. Natural kindred was the groundwork, the leading and determining idea; but, by one of those legal fictions which have such an influence on all institutions adoption was in certain cases allowed to count as natural kindred.

Now it is plain, that as soon as we admit the doctrine of artificial kindred—that is, as soon as we allow the exercise of the law of adoption physical purity of race is at an end. Adoption treats a man as if he were the son of a certain father; it cannot really make him the son of that father. If a brachycephalic father adopts a dolichocephalic son, the legal act cannot change the shape of the adopted son's skull. . . . If by any chance the adopted son spoke a different language from the adopted father, the rite of adoption itself would not of itself change his language. But it would bring him under influences which would make him adopt the language of his new *gens* by a conscious act of the will, and which would make his children adopt it by the same unconscious act of the will by which each child adopts the language of his parents. The adopted son, still more the son of the adopted son, became, in speech, in feelings, in worship, in everything but physical descent, one with the gens into which he was adopted. He became one of that *gens* for all practical, political, historical purposes. . . . When the nation—the word itself keeps about it the remembrance of birth as the groundwork of everything—adopts a new citizen, that is, a new child of the State, he is said to be naturalized. That is, a legal process puts him in the same position, and gives him the same rights, as a man who is a citizen and a son by birth. It is assumed that the rights of citizenship come by nature—that is, by birth. The stranger is admitted to them only by a kind of artificial birth; he is naturalized by law; his children are in a generation or two naturalized in fact. There is now no practical distinction between the Englishman whose forefathers landed with William . . . and the Englishman whose forefathers landed with Hengest. It is for the physiologist to say whether any difference can be traced in their several skulls; for all practical purposes, historical or political, all distinction between these several classes has passed away.

STUDY QUESTIONS

1. Is it surprising to read, in a document from 1879, that the conceptualization of race is a "learned" behavior?
2. How does the idea of race result from the process of joining a community and assimilating to it, in Freeman's view?

20.4 FLORA ANNIE STEEL AND GRACE GARDINER, *COMPLETE INDIAN HOUSEKEEPER AND COOK*, 1888

Two women married to British colonial agents in India compiled their experiences in this practical guide for new "memsahibs" (Indian term of respect for married, upper-class white women) in British-controlled India. Flora Annie Steel (1847–1929) and Grace Gardiner share advice that is often humorous or outrageous as well as sophisticated. The work, called the "Mrs. Beeton of British India" (compare Document 19.5), attempts to maintain "British standards" in a country of unfamiliar food products, extreme heat, and different cultural expectations. This selection guides colonial women through what may seem like shocking changes—occasionally revealing a rather haughty tinge of colonialist superiority.

This book, it is hoped, will meet the very generally felt want for a practical guide to young housekeepers in India. A large proportion of English ladies in the country come to it newly married, to begin a new life, and take up new responsibilities under absolutely new conditions.

Few, indeed, have had any practical experience of housekeeping of any sort or kind; whilst those who have find themselves almost as much at sea as their more ignorant sisters. How can it be otherwise, when the familiar landmarks are no longer visible, and, amid the crowd of idle, unintelligible servants, there seems not one to carry on the usual routine of household work, which in England follows as a matter of course?

The kitchen is a black hole, the pantry a sink. The only servant who will condescend to tidy up is a skulking savage with a reed broom; whilst pervading all things broods the stifling, enervating atmosphere of custom, against which energy beats itself unavailingly, as against a feather bed.

. . .

It is in the hopes of supplying a little experience at second-hand that this book has been written. In it an attempt has been made to assimilate the duties of each servant to those of his or her English compeer, and thus to show the new-comer where the fault lies, if fault exists. Also, as briefly as possible, to point out bad habits which are sure to be met with, and suggest such remedies as the authors' experience has proved to be successful. And here it may be remarked, that the very possession of the book may be held to presuppose some desire on the part of the possessor to emulate the wife who does her husband good, and not evil, all the days of her life, by looking well to the ways of her household.

THE DUTIES OF THE MISTRESS

Housekeeping in India, when once the first strangeness has worn off, is a far easier task in many ways than it is in England, though it none the less requires time, and, in this present transitional period, an almost phenomenal patience; for, while one mistress enforces cleanliness according to European methods, the next may belong to the opposite faction, who, so long as the dinner is nicely served, thinks nothing of

From Flora Annie Steel and Grace Gardiner, *Complete Indian Housekeeper and Cook*. New York: Oxford University Press, 2010, pp. 6, 11–5, 55–62.

it being cooked in a kitchen which is also used as a latrine; the result being that the servants who serve one and then the other stamp of mistress, look on the desire for decency as a mere personal and distinctly disagreeable attribute of their employer, which, like a bad temper or stinginess, may be resented or evaded.

And, first, it must be distinctly understood that it is not necessary, or in the least degree desirable, that an educated woman should waste the best years of her life in scolding and petty supervision. Life holds higher duties, and it is indubitable that friction and over zeal is a sure sign of a bad housekeeper. But there is an appreciable difference between the care-worn Martha vexed in many things, and the absolute indifference displayed by many Indian mistresses, who put up with a degree of slovenliness and dirt which would disgrace a den in St. Giles, on the principle that it is no use attempting to teach the natives.

They never go into their kitchens, for the simple reason that their appetite for breakfast might be marred by seeing the *khitmutgâr* using his toes as an efficient toast-rack (*fact*); or their desire for dinner weakened by seeing the soup strained through a greasy *purgi*.

. . .

The first duty of a mistress is, of course, to be able to give intelligible orders to her servants; therefore, it is necessary she should learn to speak Hindustani. No sane Englishwoman would dream of living say, for twenty years, in Germany, Italy, or France, without making the *attempt*, at any rate, to learn the language. She would, in fact, feel that by neglecting to do so she would write herself down an ass. It would be well, therefore, if ladies in India were to ask themselves if a difference in longitude increases the latitude allowing in judging of a woman's intellect.

The next duty is obviously to insist on her orders being carried out. And here we come to the burning question, "How is this to be done?" Certainly, there is at present very little to which we can appeal in the average Indian servant, but then, until it is implanted by training, there is very little sense of duty in a child; yet in some well-regulated nurseries obedience is a foregone conclusion. The secret lies in making rules, and *keeping to them*. The Indian servant is a child in everything save age, and should be treated as a child; that is to say, kindly, but with the greatest firmness. The laws of the household should be those of the Medes and Persians, and first faults should never go unpunished. By overlooking a first offence, we lose the only opportunity we have preventing it becoming a habit.

. . .

To show what absolute children Indian servants are, the same author has for years adopted castor oil as an ultimatum in all obstinate cases, on the ground that there must be some physical cause for inability to learn or to remember. This is considered a great joke, and exposes the offender to much ridicule from his fellow-servants; so much so, that the words, "*Mem Sahib tum ko zuroor kâster ile pila dena hoga*" (*The Mem Sahib will have to give you castor oil*), is often heard in the mouths of the upper servants when new-comers give trouble.

. . .

These remarks, written ten years ago, are still applicable, though the Indian mistress has now to guard against the possibility of impertinence. It should never be overlooked for an instant.

. . .

A good mistress in India will try to set a good example to her servants in routine, method, and tidiness. Half-an-hour after breakfast should be sufficient for the whole arrangements for the day; but that half-hour should be given as punctually as possible. An untidy mistress invariably has *untidy*, a weak one, *idle* servants. It should never be forgotten that—though it is true in both hemispheres that if you want a thing done you should do it yourself—still, having to do it is a distinct confession of failure in your original intention. Anxious housewives are too apt to accept defeat in this way; the result being that the lives of educated women are wasted in doing the work of lazy servants.

The authors' advice is therefore—

"Never do work which an ordinarily good servant ought to be able to do. IF the one you have will not or cannot do it, get another who can."

In regard to engaging new servants, written certificates to character are for the most part of no use whatever, except in respect to length of service, and its implied testimony to honesty. A man who has been six or seven years in one place is not likely to be a thief, though the authors regret to say the fact is no safeguard as far as qualifications go. The best plan is to catch your servants young, promoting them to more experienced wages on the *buksheesh* theory abovementioned. They generally learn fast enough if it is made worth their while in this way. On the other hand, it is, as a rule, a mistake to keep servants *too long* in India. Officials should be especially careful on this point, as the Oriental mind connects a confidential servant with corruption.

. . .

HINTS ON BREAKFASTS, DINNER, LUNCHEONS, ETC.

Breakfasts in India are for the most part horrible meals, being hybrids between the English and the French fashions. Then the ordinary Indian cook has not an idea for breakfast beyond chops, steaks, fried fish, and quail; a *menu* rendered still less inviting by the poor quality of both fish and meat. Tea made and poured out by a *khitmugâr* at a side table, toast and butter coming in when the meal is half-finished, and the laying of the table for lunch while the breakfast-eaters are still seated, combine to make new-comers open their eyes at Indian barbarities. Of course, if breakfast is deferred till eleven or twelve o'clock, it is better to lean towards the French *dejeuner à la fourchette,* since under these circumstances lunch would be a crime; but when, as is often the case, the breakfast hour is English, there is no real reason why English fashions should not be adhered to in every way.

A breakfast table should never be crowded by flowers or fruit, but should depend for its charm on the brightness of china and silver, and on the cleanliness of the cloth. A dumb waiter is a decided convenience, if, as will be invariably the case where the mistress is wise, servants are not allowed to stay in the room at breakfast. It should never be a set meal; and even if the English plan of helping oneself cannot be fully carried out, it is at least not necessary to have a tribe of servants dancing round the table ready to snatch away your plate at the least pause. Breakfast is *par excellence* a family meal, a special opportunity to show forth mutual helpfulness, an occasion when the hostess can make her guests feel at home by admitting them to the familiar friendliness of the *vie intime.* If the servants after handing round the first dish wait outside, a touch on the handbell will bring them back when they are wanted.

. . .

When there is a large party at breakfast, it greatly conduces to the familiar comfort of all to have small sugar basins and cream or milk jugs at intervals down the table, and there should be at least two plates of butter and toast. In regard to the former, the *khitmugâr* should be generally discouraged from making it the medium for a display of his powers in plastic art; it is doubtless gratifying to observe such yearning after beauty, even in butter, but it is suggestive of too much handling to be pleasant.

Most of the recipes given under fish and eggs are suitable for breakfast while a variety of appetizing little dishes can be made by using white China scallop shells, and filling them with various mixtures . . . it should be remembered that any elaborate side-dish as too great an apparent connection with yesterday's dinner to be agreeable to the fastidious. Indeed, this lingering likeness to the immediately preceding meal is always to be striven against; and the mistress of the house where you have duck for dinner, and duck stew next morning at breakfast, may be set down as a bad manager.

In regard to tea and coffee, it may be possible to get these made satisfactorily by the servants in India; but, except in the largest establishments at home, the mistress usually does it herself.

. . .

Servants in India are particularly careless in serving up cold viands, having a contempt for them, and considering them as, in reality, the sweeper's perquisites. So it is no unusual thing to see puddings served up again as they left the table, and pies with dusty, half-dried smears of gravy clinging to the sides of the pie-dish. This should never be passed over; but both cook and *khitmugâr* taught that everything, even down to the salt in the salt-cellars, must be neat, clean, and pleasant to look at, as well as to taste.

Heavy luncheons or tiffins have much to answer for in India. It is a fact scarcely denied, that people at home invariably eat more on Sundays, because they have nothing else to do; so in the hot weather out here people seem to eat simply because it passes the time. It is no unusual thing to see a meal of four or five distinct courses placed on the table, when one light *entrée* and a dressed vegetable would be ample. Even when guests are invited to tiffin, there is no reason why they should be tempted to over-eat themselves, as they too often are, by the ludicrously heavy style of the ordinary luncheon party in India. If the object of such parties is, as it should be, to have a really pleasant time for sociable conversation between lunch and afternoon tea, stuffing the guests into a semi-torpid state certainly does not conduce to success. Yet if the *menu* be large and long, it is almost impossible for a luncheon guest to persist in refusal without making himself remarkable. He has not refuge, and, like the wedding guest, must accept his fate, although he knows that the result will be that—

> A sadder and wiser man
> He'll rise the morrow's morn.

Afternoon teas are, as it were, outclassed by tennis parties, and as these latter are a form of entertainment suitable to the limited purses of most people, a few hints may be given as to the refreshments required, &c. To begin with tea and coffee. It will be found best to have at least two teapots, and not to put more than three teaspoonfuls of tea in each. Anything more tasteless or injurious than tea which has been "stood strong" and then watered down cannot be imagined. Cream should invariably be given, and for this purpose the milk must not be boiled; even in hot weather milk will stand for twelve hours in a wide-mouthed jar placed in an earthen vessel of water, especially if a little carbonate of soda can be dissolved in the milk, while boracic acid will keep it sweet for days. Lump sugar costs very little more than grain sugar, and looks infinitely nicer. Coffee is best made double or triple strength in the morning, and diluted with boiling water when wanted. If not sufficiently hot, the bottles containing it can be placed in a saucepan of boiling water. This is the most economical plan, as this strong coffee will keep for several days; it is also the most satisfactory, as it enables the mistress to be sure of the quality of her coffee. A recipe for this coffee will be found under the chapter on the "*Khitmugâr.*" Hot milk and cold-whipped cream should be served with coffee, and brown crystallised sugar, or what is still nicer, pounded sugar candy.

. . .

In regard to eatables, plain bread and butter should invariably be a standing dish. Many people do not care for cakes, and yet find a cup of tea or coffee better for something to eat with it. . . . Cakes and bonbons suitable for tennis parties are legion, and, as a rule the one thing to be observed in selecting them is to avoid stickiness or surprises. It is not pleasant to find the first bite of a firm looking cake result in a dribble of liqueur or cream down your best dress.

. . .

Ices are best served in India in regular ice-glasses, as they do not melt so fast, being less exposed to the air.

. . .

The art of dinner-giving is a difficult subject to approach. Many people openly assert that the native plan of sending dinner on a tray to the person you desire to entertain, would remove the mountains of *ennui* and trouble for both the host and guest. But there must be something wrong in a hospitality which demands self-devotion on both sides. . . . It must not be forgotten that the dinner is not the end in itself. It is the means of making your guests enter into that contented frame of mind which conduces to good fellowship; and, to an ordinarily sympathetic guest, the sight of an anxious host or hostess is fatal to personal placidity. "*If they serve you up a barbecued puppy dog, keep a cool countenance and help the company round,*" says the young husband in "Heartsease" to his tearful wife. Never was better advice given, if we supplement it with the words, "*and have it out with the cook afterwards.*"

. . .

As it is, one is often treated to a badly-cooked dinner in the style of a third-class French restaurant, even to the *hors d'œuvres*. In regard to the latter, it is doubtful if they should ever be considered a legitimate part of the *menu* at private houses, though exceptions may be made occasionally in favour of fresh oysters. The real *raison d'etre* of the *hors d'œuvres* is *not* to stimulate the appetite. To do this it must be taken ten minutes before dinner, like bitters. It was at first nothing more or less than a restaurant dodge to while away the time (and increase the bill) whilst the dinner that had been ordered was being prepared. It therefore ceases to have any meaning in a private house, where, it is to be presumed, the guests will not have to wait for their dinners. On the other hand, it may be laid down as an axiom that no dinner, even a purely family one, is complete without a dressed vegetable of some sort of kind.

. . .

Cold sweets before the hot is a barbarism only to be equaled by serving a cheese *fondu* before jelly as a pudding.

. . .

DUTIES OF THE BEARER

The implements required by the bearer are—

6 Soft dusters.	1 Tin Putz pomade.
1 Feather broom.	2 Funnels.
1 Bottle home made furniture polish.	1 Bottle brush.
	1 Ice breaker.
1 Clothes brush.	1 Salver for cards.
1 Corkscrew.	1 Bottle benzine.
1 Pair scissors.	Hammer, tacks glue,
Chimney brush.	1 string, &c.

The bearer should be the head servant, and the greatest care should be exercised in engaging one who is honest and respectable. Being his master's valet, the other servants give weight to his opinions, and follow his lead, knowing that he has opportunities for private communication with the authorities. Ear-wigging, it must be remembered, is supposed by the Oriental to be all-powerful. The discipline and respectability of the servants' quarters depend to a great extent on the character of the bearer, who should be held responsible.

The bearer must be an early riser. He has charge of every single thing in the house, save those in the dining-room and pantry, and any loss or breakage has to be accounted for by him; therefore it is to his own advantage, one of his greatest alleviations of Indian discomfort lies in his hands; that is, keeping the house free of mosquitoes. To do this he must in the hot weather shut every window before dawn. They may be opened afterwards, but if they are not shut between four o'clock and six o'clock mosquitoes will come in.

. . .

When the sweeper has swept the outer verandahs, the upper and lower windows should be thrown open, but not till then, or the dust will come in.

One day a week the drawing-room should receive a thorough cleaning, summer and winter; and after a dust-storm a complete turning out is also necessary; but on other days the sweeper should, with a soft brush and dustpan, sweep over the whole room, shaking mats, &c., outside, as they are apt to harbour vermin. The bearer meanwhile should remove the flower-vases and place them on a table in the verandah, fold up newspapers and put them in a certain fixed receptacle, replace books in the bookshelf, restore chairs to their proper place, and sort everything up as far as possible. It is a good plan to have a separate basket for all papers, envelopes, &c., found on the floor anywhere about the house, as it is then a sure find for lost letters or memoranda. Punkahs and thermantidotes often blow scraps of paper off tables.

When this is done the whole room should be carefully dusted.

The weekly turn-out should include a polish to all articles of furniture, a smart beating of the backs of the carpets, and a cleaning of the windows. Dirty windows are the sign of a bad bearer.

. . .

After breakfast the bearer should be in attendance on his mistress at the godown, and report *openly* to her anything which has occurred in the compound during the last twenty-four hours which she ought to know. He need fear no enmity from other servants if he does this fearlessly, openly, and honestly.

. . .

The bearer should be ready to receive callers from twelve o'clock till two. Unless his mistress has told him to say *"durwâza bund"* (the Indian equivalent for not at home), he should *at once* usher the visitors into the drawing room and present their cards to his mistress, wherever she may be. He must never do this with his fingers, and a small tray for receiving the cards should always lie on the verandah or hall table.

. . .

In the evening, when the bearer lights the lamps, he should also see that each bedroom has its candle and box of matches; at the same time, he should satisfy himself that sweeper, *bheesti*, and other servants have done their work. On bringing the lamps into the drawing-room he should tidy it up, remove bits of thread, torn papers, &c., from the floor, draw the curtains, and if there is a fire, see that the wood-box is full. If the bearer is also *âbdâr*, i.e., serves the wine at the table, it is his duty to inform the *khitmutgâr* what wine-glasses will be required, and satisfy himself that they are duly placed on the table. If the *âbdâr* has to serve a large number of people, especially in the hot weather, when guests are naturally in a hurry for something cool to drink, it requires method and preparation to be successful. The ice should be broken into pieces before dinner is announced, and wrapped in a napkin. The best way of breaking up ice is to use a short sharp steel skewer; a large darning-needle fixed in a handle answers well. No hammer is required, as the lightest pressure with the sharp point will split the ice. The soda-water should be ready to hand, champagne wire removed, claret uncorked, and the wines for dessert decanted in scrupulously clean decanters. The *âbdâr* should not dodge round the table in serving guests, but go round methodically, beginning with the lady at the host's right hand.

The bearer should always be on guard against the ravages of white ants, fish insects, and other vermin; and in the rainy season he must not forget the periodical airing of all woollen clothes, blankets, rugs, &c.

Another important work of the bearer is making the beds, excepting of course, those in the *ayah*'s charge. It may generally be asserted that no native servant has the faintest idea how to make a bed, and therefore those mistresses who desire to make their guests comfortable will do well to give at least one practical lesson on this subject, insisting on the mattress being turned, the sheets evenly spread and separately tucked in, and the pillows well shaken up. An Indian bed too often consists of a hard felted surface with more than a suspicion of crumbs, and covered by frantically crooked sheets and blankets, which the slightest movement reduces to chaos, while sudden turn lets them loose in disastrous avalanche on the floor.

RECIPES FOR THE BEARER

. . .

2. Ants, to keep them from Tables, &c.—Tie a rag dipped in castor oil round the legs of the table or cupboard.

. . .

4. Brass Work, to clean.—Cut a lime in half, rub over the brass, wash the article thoroughly in soap and water, dry and polish. One teaspoon of sulphuric acid mixed in a quarter of a pint of water, and used instead of the lime, is still better. Sapolio and Brookes' soap also do well, but Putz pomade is the best.

. . .

9. Carpets, to remove Ink Stains.—Wash, if possible, while still wet, with fresh, hot boiled milk. Sponge again and again with hot water. Time and patience must be plentifully used. A weak solution of oxalic acid may be tried if the stain is very dark, but the risk of injuring the colour is very great. It is, however, possible to re-dye the injured portion, with a result certainly preferable to a black spot.

10. Chairs, to prevent the Leather from Cracking.—Rub with white of an egg beaten thin with water.

. . .

14. Glue, Strong.—Digest by gentle heat in a corked bottle 3 oz. rectified spirits of wine with 4 oz. of fine pale shellac. The Chinese use nothing else for all their wood-work. Excellent for pianos.

15. Furniture, Polish.—Mix in a bottle equal parts of linseed oil, turpentine, vinegar, and spirits of wine; or half a teacup shredded beeswax dissolved in a 1 teacup turpentine.

. . .

SIMPLE HINTS ON THE PRESERVATION OF HEALTH, AND SIMPLE REMEDIES

Much fuss is, as a rule, made about the unhealthiness of India, but, as a matter of fact, if due attention is paid to the novel conditions of life, and the same precautions which are, as a matter of course taken against the damps and chills of England be taken against the sun of India, there is no reason at all why the health should suffer. It is not only heat which the sun brings with it. That heat in its turn, combined with the intermittent and copious rain, is favourable to the development of malaria and countless bacilli of all sorts. Thus, necessarily, the risks to be run from the malarial type of disease is greater than in England. At the same time, the better class of Europeans should have immunity from a thousand dangers which have to be run at home from infection, cold, bad ventilation, and if unscientific drainage be not *perfect*, it is simply a death-trap.

. . .

In regard to the sun, it must not be forgotten that it is a *friend* as well as an enemy. Half the cases of neuraesthenia and anaemia among English ladies, and their general inability to stand the hot weather, arises from the fact that they live virtually in the dark. They feel "too languid" to go out early. "It doesn't suit them to go out before breakfast," &c. &c. Then it is too hot to leave the cool house before sunsetting. So, as the house, for the sake of what is called comfort, is kept shut up and in semi-darkness all day, it often happens that the sun is never *seen* or *felt*. The writer believes that the forced inertia caused by living without *light* is responsible for many moral and physical evils among European ladies in the Tropics. In the chapter "In the Plains" more is said on the subject of making the sun your *friend*.

Let us now think of him as an enemy, in reference, first, to clothing. On this point, also, details will be found in another chapter, that on Outfits. Flannel next to the skin day and night is, of course, the shibboleth of doctors, and doubtless they are right. The writer, however, never wore it day or night, and she never once went to the hills unless on leave with her husband, which means that two hot weathers out of every three were spent entirely in the plains. She wore *silk*, discarded stays, &c., and, as a rule, had her dresses of nuns-veiling or thick serge. And during the hot weather she used a thin white Rampore chuddar or shawl instead of a sheet. The aim and object is, however, to avoid chills and heats. To effect this, sound good sense and the energy which does not mind a little trouble are all that is necessary; unless, indeed, the claims of fashion are allowed to overbear those of comfort and health.

Food and drink should be, as in other parts of the world, simple and digestible. . . . Ice should not be taken on trust and put into drinks unless it is known to be made in a machine from pure water. . . . The writer's sole advice on this subject is to use common-sense. If you wake with a chippy mouth, and feel as if the whole world was hollow, and your doll stuffed with sawdust, you may be *sure* your liver is out of order; in which case don't blame Providence and fly to a podophyllin pill, but think over yesterday, from morn till eve, and find out whether it was that greasy side-dish at dinner, or the delay in changing to a warmer dress when you began to feel chilly, which is responsible.

. . .

Where the great heat of the sun has to be braved, a large pith hat should be worn, a real mushroom, that will protect the nape of the neck. A cork protector, made by quilting shredded cork down the middle of a sleeveless jacket, should be worn over the spine. An umbrella covered with white and dipped occasionally in water will make a hot, dangerous walk less dangerous.

. . .

The following is a list of the more common ailments and their treatment:—

Asthma.—No cure; but strong black coffee will sometimes cut short an attack. The fumes of blotting-paper which has been steeped in very strong solution of saltpeter and dried, gives relief. So, *used with caution*, will twenty grains of dried datura leaf smoked with the ordinary tobacco.

Bites of Wasps, Scorpions, &c.—A paste of ipecacuanha and water applied at once over the bite generally acts a charm. Stimulants if severe symptoms follow.

Of Mad, or even Doubtful Dogs.—Cut with a lancet or pen-knife down to the very bottom of the wound, and again across, so as to let it gape and bleed. Then cauterise remourselessly with nitrate of silver, or carbolic acid, or an actual hot iron. The object is to destroy the bitten tissue, so that you get to the *bottom*.

Of a Snake.—If in a toe, finger, or end of a limb, apply a ligature with the first thing handy. Whipcord is best, but take the first ligature that comes to hand. Twist with a stick, or any lever, as tight as you can. Apply two or more nearer the heart, at intervals of a few inches. Meanwhile, if you have help, get some one else to cut out the flesh round the fang-marks, and let it bleed freely. If the snake is known to be deadly, amputate the finger or toe at the next joint; or if you cannot do this, run the knife right round the bone, dividing the flesh completely. Let the bitten person suck the wound till you can burn it with anything at hand—carbolic, nitric acid, nitrate of silver, or actual hot iron. Give one ounce of brandy in a little water. The great object is to prevent the poison getting through the blood to the heart, so every additional pulse-beat before the ligatures are on is a danger. If symptoms of poisoning set in, give more stimulants; put mustard plasters over the heart; rub the limbs; treat, in fact, as for drowning, even to artificial respiration.

. . .

Earache.—Equal parts of opium and any sweet oil. Rub up together, soak a bit of cotton-wool in it, and insert *not too far down* the ears.

. . .

Hiccough.—Hold the right ear with the left forefinger and thumb, bringing the elbow as far across the chest as possible. An unreasonable but absolutely effective cure.

Hysteria.—Whisky and water with a little chlorodyne and a little wholesome neglect. This applies to hysterics at the time; but a nervous hysterical state generally points to functional disorders, needing active treatment.

STUDY QUESTIONS

1. How do the authors infantilize their native Indian servants, and why?
2. What concessions should an English woman make for a climate that is so hot?

20.5 THEODOR HERZL, *THE JEWISH STATE*, 1895

A Jewish Austrian writer, Theodor Herzl (1860–1904) is the father of the ideology of Zionism, which sought to create a state of Israel (achieved in 1948) that would be a center of Jewish nationalism and security for persecuted Jewish populations. Although he was disinterested in his Jewish identity as a young man, Herzl was horrified by the reality of anti-Semitic outbursts connected to the Dreyfus Affair (in which a French Jew was wrongly accused of treason). Accordingly, Herzl became convinced that only a truly Jewish state would protect Jews from pervasive anti-Semitism; his work *The Jewish State* provides reasons and methods for potential émigrés and describes the ideal of a communal Jewish identity.

From Theodor Herzl, *The Jewish State*. New York: Dover, 1968, pp. 85–96.

II. THE JEWISH QUESTION

No one can deny the gravity of the situation of the Jews. Wherever they live in perceptible numbers, they are more or less persecuted. Their equality before the law, granted by statute, has become practically a dead letter. They are debarred from filling even moderately high positions, either in the army, or in any public or private capacity. And attempts are made to thrust them out of business also: "Don't buy from Jews!"

Attacks in Parliaments, in assemblies, in the press, in the pulpit, in the street, on journeys—for example, their exclusion from certain hotels—even in places of recreation, become daily more numerous. The forms of persecutions varying according to the countries and social circles in which they occur. In Russia, imposts are levied on Jewish villages; in Rumania, a few persons are put to death; in Germany, they get a good beating occasionally; in Austria, Anti-Semites exercise terrorism over all public life; in Algeria, there are travelling agitators; in Paris, the Jews are shut out of the so-called best social circles and excluded from clubs. Shades of anti-Jewish feeling are innumerable. But this is not to be an attempt to make out a doleful category of Jewish hardships.

I do not intend to arouse sympathetic emotions on our behalf. That would be a foolish, futile, and undignified proceeding. I shall content myself with putting the following questions to the Jews: Is it not true that, in countries where we live in perceptible numbers, the position of Jewish lawyers, doctors, technicians, teachers, and employees of all descriptions becomes daily more intolerable? Is it not true, that the Jewish middle classes are seriously threatened? Is it not true, that the passions of the mob are incited against our wealthy people? Is it not true, that our poor endure greater sufferings than any other proletariat? I think that this external pressure makes itself felt everywhere. In our economically upper classes it causes discomfort, in our middle classes continual and grave anxieties, in our lower classes absolute despair.

Everything tends, in fact, to one and the same conclusion, which is clearly enunciated in that classic Berlin phrase: *"Juden Raus!"* (Out with the Jews!).

I shall now put the Question in the briefest possible form: Are we to "get out" now and where to?

Or, may we yet remain? And, how long?

Let us first settle the point of staying where we are. Can we hope for better days, can we possess our souls in patience, can we wait in pious resignation till the princes and peoples of this earth are more mercifully disposed towards us? I say that we cannot hope for a change in the current of feeling. And why not? Even if we were as near to the hearts of princes as are their other subjects, they could not protect us. They would only feel popular hatred by showing us too much favor. By "too much," I really mean less than is claimed as a right by every ordinary citizen, or by every race. The nations in whose midst Jews live are all either covertly or openly Anti-Semitic.

The common people have not, and indeed cannot have, any historic comprehension. They do not know that the sins of the Middle Ages are now being visited on the nations of Europe. We are what the Ghetto made us. We have attained pre-eminence in finance, because mediaeval conditions drove us to it. The same process is now being repeated. We are again being forced into finance, now it is the stock exchange, by being kept out of other branches of economic activity. Being on the stock exchange, we are consequently exposed afresh to contempt. At the same time we continue to produce an abundance of mediocre intellects who find no outlet, and this endangers our social position as much as does our increasing wealth. Educated Jews without means are now rapidly becoming Socialists. Hence we are certain to suffer very severely in the struggle between classes, because we stand in the most exposed position in the camps of both Socialists and capitalists.

Previous Attempts at a Solution

The artificial means heretofore employed to overcome the troubles of Jews have been either too petty—such as attempts at colonization—or attempts to convert the Jews into peasants in their present homes.

What is achieved by transporting a few thousand Jews to another country? Either they come to grief at once, or prosper, and then their prosperity creates Anti-Semitism. We have already discussed these attempts to divert poor Jews to fresh districts. This diversion is clearly inadequate and futile, if it does not actually defeat its own ends; for it merely protracts and postpones a solution, and perhaps even aggravates difficulties.

Whoever would attempt to convert the Jew into a husbandman would be making an extraordinary mistake. For a peasant is in a historical category, as proved by his costume which in some countries he has worn for centuries; and by his tools, which are identical with those used by his earliest forefathers. His plough is unchanged; he carries the seed in his apron; mows with the historical scythe, and threshes with the time-honored flail. But we know that all this can be done by machinery. The agrarian question is only a question of machinery. America must conquer Europe, in the same way as large landed possessions absorb small ones. The peasant is consequently a type which is in course of extinction. Whenever he is artificially preserved, it is done on account of the political interests which he is intended to serve. It is absurd, and indeed impossible, to make modern peasants on the old pattern. No one is wealthy or powerful enough to make civilization take a single retrograde step. The mere preservation of obsolete institutions is a task severe enough to require the enforcement of all the despotic measures of an autocratically governed State.

Are we, therefore, to credit Jews who are intelligent with a desire to become peasants of the old type? One might just as well say to them: "Here is a cross-bow: now go to war!" What? With a cross-bow, while the others have rifles and long range guns? Under these circumstances the Jews are perfectly justified in refusing to stir when people try to make peasants of them. A cross-bow is a beautiful weapon, which inspires me with mournful feelings when I have time to devote to them. But it belongs by rights to a museum.

Now, there certainly are districts to which desperate Jews go out, or at any rate, are willing to go out and till the soil. And a little observation shows that these districts—such as the enclave of Hesse in Germany, and some provinces in Russia—these very districts are the principal seats of Anti-Semitism.

For the world's reformers, who send the Jews to the plough, forget a very important person, who has a great deal to say on the matter. This person is the agriculturist, and the agriculturist is also perfectly justified. For the tax on land, the risks attached to crops, the pressure of large proprietors who cheapen labor, and American competition in particular, combine to make his life hard enough. Besides, the duties on corn cannot go on increasing indefinitely. Nor can the manufacturer be allowed to starve; his political influence is, in fact, in the ascendant, and he must therefore be treated with additional consideration.

All these difficulties are well known, therefore I refer to them only cursorily. I merely wanted to indicate clearly how futile had been past attempts—most of them well intentioned—to solve the Jewish Question. Neither a diversion of the stream, nor an artificial depression of the intellectual level of our proletariat, will overcome the difficulty. The supposed infallible expedient of assimilation has already been dealt with.

We cannot get the better of Anti-Semitism by any of these methods. It cannot die out so long as its causes are not removed. Are they removable?

Causes of Anti-Semitism

We shall not again touch on those causes which are a result of temperament, prejudice and narrow views, but shall here restrict ourselves to political and economical causes alone. Modern Anti-Semitism is not to be confounded with the religious persecution of the Jews of former times. It does occasionally take a religious bias in some countries, but the main current of the aggressive movement has now changed. In the principal countries where Anti-Semitism prevails, it does so as a result of the emancipation of the Jews. When civilized nations awoke to the inhumanity of discriminatory legislation and enfranchised us, our enfranchisement came too late. It was no longer possible to remove our disabilities in our old homes. For we had, curiously enough, developed while in the Ghetto into a bourgeois people, and we stepped out of it only to enter into fierce competition with the middle classes. Hence, our emancipation set us suddenly within this middle-class circle, where we have a double pressure to sustain, from within and from without. The Christian bourgeoisie would not be unwilling to cast us as a sacrifice to Socialism, though that would not greatly improve matters.

At the same time, the equal rights of Jews before the law cannot be withdrawn where they have once been conceded. Not only because their withdrawal would be opposed to the spirit of our age, but also because it would immediately drive all Jews, rich and poor alike, into the ranks of subversive parties. Nothing effectual can really be done to our injury. In olden days our jewels were seized. How is our movable property to be got hold of now? It consists of printed papers which are locked up somewhere or other in the world, perhaps in the coffers of Christians. It is, of course, possible to get at shares and debentures in railways, banks and industrial undertakings of all descriptions by taxation, and where the progressive income-tax is in force all our movable property can eventually be laid hold of. But all these efforts cannot be directed against Jews alone, and wherever they might nevertheless be made, severe economic crises would be their immediate consequences, which would be by no means confined to the Jews who would be the first affected. The very impossibility of getting at the Jews nourishes and embitters hatred of them. Anti-Semitism increases day by day and hour by hour among the nations; indeed, it is bound to increase, because the causes of its growth continue to exist and cannot be removed. Its remote cause is our loss of the power of assimilation during the Middle Ages; its immediate cause is our excessive production of mediocre intellects, who cannot find an outlet downwards or upwards—that is to say, no wholesome outlet in either direction. When we sink, we become a revolutionary proletariat, the subordinate officers of all revolutionary parties; and at the same time, when we rise, there rises also our terrible power of the purse.

Effects of Anti-Semitism

The oppression we endure does not improve us, for we are not a whit better than ordinary people. It is true that we do not love our enemies; but he alone who can conquer himself dare reproach us with that fault. Oppression naturally creates hostility against oppressors, and our hostility aggravates the pressure. It is impossible to escape from this eternal circle.

"No!" Some soft-hearted visionaries will say: "No, it is possible! Possible by means of the ultimate perfection of humanity."

Is it necessary to point to the sentimental folly of this view? He who would found his hope for improved conditions on the ultimate perfection of humanity would indeed be relying upon a Utopia!

I referred previously to our "assimilation." I do not for a moment wish to imply that I desire such an end. Our national character is too historically famous, and, in spite of every degradation, too fine to make its annihilation desirable. We might perhaps be able to merge ourselves entirely into surrounding races, if these were to leave us in peace for a period of two generations. But they will not leave us in peace. For a little period they manage to tolerate us, and then their hostility breaks out again and again. The world is provoked somehow by our prosperity, because it has for many centuries been accustomed to consider us as the most contemptible among the poverty-stricken. In its ignorance and narrowness of heart, it fails to observe that prosperity weakens our Judaism and extinguishes our peculiarities. It is only pressure that forces us back to the parent stem; it is only hatred encompassing us that makes us strangers once more.

Thus, whether we like it or not, we are now, and shall henceforth remain, a historic group with unmistakable characteristics common to us all.

We are one people—our enemies have made us one without our consent, as repeatedly happens in history. Distress binds us together, and, thus united, we suddenly discover our strength. Yes, we are strong enough to form a State, and, indeed, a model State. We possess all human and material resources necessary for the purpose.

This is therefore the appropriate place to give an account of what has been somewhat roughly termed our "human material." But it would not be appreciated till the broad lines of the plan, on which everything depends, have first been marked out.

The Plan

The whole plan is in its essence perfectly simple, as it must necessarily be if it is to come within the comprehension of all.

Let the sovereignty be granted us over a portion of the globe large enough to satisfy the rightful requirements of a nation; the rest we shall manage for ourselves.

The creation of a new State is neither ridiculous nor impossible. We have in our day witnessed the process in connection with nations which were not largely members of the middle class, but poorer, less educated, and consequently weaker than ourselves. The Governments of all countries scourged by Anti-Semitism will be keenly interested in assisting us to obtain the sovereignty we want.

The plan, simple in design, but complicated in execution, will be carried out by two agencies: The Society of Jews and the Jewish Company.

The Society of Jews will do the preparatory work in the domains of science and politics, which the Jewish Company will afterwards apply practically.

The Jewish Company will be the liquidating agent of the business interests of departing Jews, and will organize commerce and trade in the new country.

We must not imagine the departure of the Jews to be a sudden one. It will be gradual, continuous, and will cover many decades. The poorest will go first to cultivate the soil. In accordance with a preconceived plan, they will construct roads, bridges, railways and telegraph installations; regulate rivers; and build their own dwellings; their labor will create trade, trade will create markets and markets will attract new settlers, for every man will go voluntarily, at his own expense and his own risk. The labor expended on the land will enhance its value, and the Jews will soon perceive that a new and permanent sphere of operation is opening here for that spirit of enterprise which has heretofore met only with hatred and obloquy.

If we wish to found a State today, we shall not do it in the way which would have been the only possible one a thousand years ago. It is foolish to revert to old stages of civilization, as many Zionists would like to do. Supposing, for example, we were obliged to clear a country of wild beasts, we should not set about the task in the fashion of Europeans of the fifth century. We should not take spear and lance and go out singly in pursuit of bears; we would organize a large and active hunting party, drive the animals together, and throw a melinite bomb into their midst.

If we wish to conduct building operations, we shall not plant a mass of stakes and piles on the shore of a lake, but we shall build as men build now.

Indeed, we shall build in a bolder and more stately style than was ever adopted before, for we now possess means which men never yet possessed.

The emigrants standing lowest in the economic scale will be slowly followed by those of a higher grade. Those who at this moment are living in despair will go first. They will be led by the mediocre intellects which we produce so superabundantly and which are persecuted everywhere.

This pamphlet will open a general discussion on the Jewish Question, but that does not mean that there will be any voting on it. Such a result would ruin the cause from the outset, and dissidents must remember that allegiance or opposition is entirely voluntary. He who will not come with us should remain behind.

Let all who are willing to join us, fall in behind our banner and fight for our cause with voice and pen and deed.

Those Jews who agree with our idea of a State will attach themselves to the Society, which will thereby be authorized to confer and treat with Governments in the name of our people. The Society will thus be acknowledged in its relations with Governments as a State-creating power. This acknowledgment will practically create the State.

Should the Powers declare themselves willing to admit our sovereignty over a neutral piece of land, then the Society will enter into negotiations for the possession of this land. Here two territories come under consideration, Palestine and Argentine. In both countries important experiments in colonization have been made, though on the mistaken principle of a gradual infiltration of Jews. An infiltration is bound to end badly. It continues till the inevitable moment when the native population feels itself threatened, and forces the Government to stop a further influx of Jews. Immigration is consequently futile unless we have the sovereign right to continue such immigration.

The Society of Jews will treat with the present masters of the land, putting itself under the protectorate of the European Powers, if they prove friendly to the plan. We could offer the present possessors of the land enormous advantages, assume part of the public debt, build new roads for traffic, which our presence in the country would render necessary, and do many other things. The creation of our State would be beneficial to adjacent countries, because the cultivation of a strip of land increases the value of its surrounding districts in innumerable ways.

Palestine or Argentine?

Shall we choose Palestine or Argentine? We shall take what is given us, and what is selected by Jewish public opinion. The Society will determine both these points.

Argentine is one of the most fertile countries in the world, extends over a vast area, has a sparse population and a mild climate. The Argentine Republic would derive considerable profit from the cession of a portion of its territory to us. The present infiltration of Jews has certainly produced some discontent, and it would be necessary to enlighten the Republic on the intrinsic difference of our new movement.

Palestine is our ever-memorable historic home. The very name of Palestine would attract our people with a force of marvellous potency. If His Majesty the Sultan were to give us Palestine, we could in return undertake to regulate the whole finances of Turkey. We should there form a portion of a rampart of Europe against Asia, an outpost of civilization as opposed to barbarism. We should as a neutral State remain in contact with all Europe, which would have to guarantee our existence. The sanctuaries of Christendom would be safeguarded by assigning to them an extra-territorial status such as is well-known to the law of nations. We should form a guard of honor about these sanctuaries, answering for the fulfilment of this duty with our existence. This guard of honor would be the great symbol of the solution of the Jewish Question after eighteen centuries of Jewish suffering.

STUDY QUESTIONS

1. Are Jews constantly subjected to anti-Semitism, whether "covertly or openly," in Herzl's estimation?
2. Why does Herzl think the "rampart of Europe" should be planted in Palestine and not in Argentina?

CHAPTER 21

THE MODERN WOMAN

21.1 MARY WOLLSTONECRAFT, *A VINDICATION OF THE RIGHTS OF WOMAN*, 1792

The British activist Mary Wollstonecraft (1759–1797), mother of author Mary Shelley, wrote a letter called "A Vindication of the Rights of Men" (1790) to Edmund Burke criticizing his *Reflections on the Revolution in France* (Document 17.1) for its support of the aristocracy. Two years later, she altered the title for a feminist letter that argues for education and respect for women as valuable and contributing members of society. Now considered a founder of feminism, Wollstonecraft advocated on behalf of her fellow women in her dedication to a fellow pamphleteer, the enigmatic diplomat Talleyrand (1754–1838). Here, she outlines her main quest for education and provides a glimpse into her charm and energy.

CHAPTER 12: ON NATIONAL EDUCATION

The good effects resulting from attention to private education will ever be very confined, and the parent who really puts his own hand to the plow, will always, in some degree be disappointed, till education becomes a grand national concern. A man cannot retire into a desert with his child, and if he did, he could not bring himself back to childhood, and become the proper friend and play-fellow of an infant or youth. And when children are confined to the society of men and women, they very soon acquire that kind of premature manhood which stops the growth of every vigorous power of mind or body. In order to open their faculties they should be excited to think for themselves; and this can only be done by mixing a number of children together, and making them jointly pursue the same objects.

A child very soon contracts a benumbing indolence of mind, which he has seldom sufficient vigour to shake off, when he only asks a question instead of seeking for information, and then relies implicitly on the answer he receives. With his equals in age this could never be the case, and the subjects of inquiry, though they might be influenced, would not be entirely under the direction of men, who frequently damp, if not destroy abilities, by bringing them forward too hastily: and too hastily they will infallibly be brought forward, if the child could be

From Mary Wollstonecraft, *A Vindication of the Rights of Woman*. London: J. Johnson, 1792.

confined to the society of a man, however sagacious that man may be.

Besides, in youth the seeds of every affection should be sown, and the respectful regard, which is felt for a parent, is very different from the social affections that are to constitute the happiness of life as it advances. Of these, equality is the basis, and an intercourse of sentiments unclogged by that observant seriousness which prevents disputation, though it may not inforce submission. Let a child have ever such an affection for his parent, he will always languish to play and chat with children; and the very respect he entertains, for filial esteem always has a dash of fear mixed with it, will, if it do not teach him cunning, at least prevent him from pouring out the little secrets which first open the heart to friendship and confidence, gradually leading to more expansive benevolence. Added to this, he will never acquire that frank ingenuousness of behaviour, which young people can only attain by being frequently in society, where they dare to speak what they think; neither afraid of being reproved for their presumption, nor laughed at for their folly.

Forcibly impressed by the reflections which the sight of schools, as they are at present conducted, naturally suggested, I have formerly delivered my opinion rather warmly in favour of a private education; but further experience has led me to view the subject in a different light. I still, however, think schools, as they are now regulated, the hot-beds of vice and folly, and the knowledge of human nature, supposed to be attained there, merely cunning selfishness.

At school, boys become gluttons and slovens, and, instead of cultivating domestic affections, very early rush into the libertinism which destroys the constitution before it is formed; hardening the heart as it weakens the understanding.

I should, in fact, be averse to boarding-schools, if it were for no other reason than the unsettled state of mind which the expectation of the vacations produce. On these the children's thoughts are fixed with eager anticipating hopes, for, at least, to speak with moderation, half of the time, and when they arrive they are spent in total dissipation and beastly indulgence.

But, on the contrary, when they are brought up at home, though they may pursue a plan of study in a more orderly manner than can be adopted, when near a fourth part of the year is actually spent in idleness, and as much more in regret and anticipation; yet they there acquire too high an opinion of their own importance, from being allowed to tyrannize over servants, and from the anxiety expressed by most mothers, on the score of manners, who, eager to teach the accomplishments of a gentleman, stifle, in their birth, the virtues of a man. Thus brought into company when they ought to be seriously employed, and treated like men when they are still boys, they become vain and effeminate.

The only way to avoid two extremes equally injurious to morality, would be to contrive some way of combining a public and private education. Thus to make men citizens, two natural steps might be taken, which seem directly to lead to the desired point; for the domestic affections, that first open the heart to the various modifications of humanity would be cultivated, whilst the children were nevertheless allowed to spend great part of their time, on terms of equality, with other children.

I still recollect, with pleasure, the country day school; where a boy trudged in the morning, wet or dry, carrying his books, and his dinner, if it were at a considerable distance; a servant did not then lead master by the hand, for, when he had once put on coat and breeches, he was allowed to shift for himself, and return alone in the evening to recount the feats of the day close at the parental knee. His father's house was his home, and was ever after fondly remembered; nay, I appeal to some superior men who were educated in this manner, whether the recollection of some shady lane where they conned their lesson; or, of some stile, where they sat making a kite, or mending a bat, has not endeared their country to them?

But, what boy ever recollected with pleasure the years he spent in close confinement, at an academy near London? unless indeed he should by chance remember the poor scare-crow of an usher whom he tormented; or, the tartman, from whom he caught a cake, to devour it with the cattish appetite of selfishness. At boarding schools of every description, the relaxation of the junior boys is mischief; and of the senior, vice. Besides, in great schools what can be more prejudicial to the moral character, than the system of tyranny and abject slavery which is established amongst the boys, to say nothing of the slavery to forms, which makes religion worse than a farce? For what good can be expected from the youth who receives the sacrament of the Lord's supper, to avoid forfeiting half-a-guinea, which he probably afterwards spends in some sensual manner? Half the employment of the youths is to elude the necessity of attending public worship; and well they may, for such a constant repetition of the same thing must be a very irksome restraint on their natural vivacity. As these ceremonies have the most fatal effect on their morals, and as a ritual performed by the lips, when the heart and mind are far away, is not now stored up by our church as a bank to draw on for the fees of the poor souls in purgatory, why should they not be abolished?

But the fear of innovation, in this country, extends to every thing. This is only a covert fear, the apprehensive timidity of indolent slugs, who guard, by sliming it over, the snug place, which they consider in the light of an hereditary estate; and eat, drink, and enjoy themselves, instead of fulfilling the duties, excepting a few empty forms, for which it was endowed. These are the people who most strenuously insist on the will of the founder being observed, crying out against all reformation, as if it were a violation of justice. I am now alluding particularly to the relicks of popery retained in our colleges, where the protestant members seem to be such sticklers for the established church; but their zeal never makes them lose sight of the spoil of ignorance, which rapacious priests of superstitious memory have scraped together. No, wise in their generation, they venerate the prescriptive right of possession, as a strong hold, and still let the sluggish bell tingle to prayers, as during the days, when the elevation of the host was supposed to atone for the sins of the people, lest one reformation should lead to another, and the spirit kill the letter. These Romish customs have the most baneful effect on the morals of our clergy; for the idle vermin who two or three times a day perform, in the most slovenly manner a service which they think useless, but call their duty, soon lose a sense of duty. At college, forced to attend or evade public worship, they acquire an habitual contempt for the very service, the performance of which is to enable them to live in idleness. It is mumbled over as an affair of business, as a stupid boy repeats his task, and frequently the college cant escapes from the preacher the moment after he has left the pulpit, and even whilst he is eating the dinner which he earned in such a dishonest manner.

Nothing, indeed, can be more irreverent than the cathedral service as it is now performed in this country, neither does it contain a set of weaker men than those who are the slaves of this childish routine. A disgusting skeleton of the former state is still exhibited; but all the solemnity, that interested the imagination, if it did not purify the heart, is stripped off. The performance of high mass on the continent must impress every mind, where a spark of fancy glows, with that awful melancholy, that sublime tenderness, so near a-kin to devotion. I do not say, that these devotional feelings are of more use, in a moral sense, than any other emotion of taste; but I contend, that the theatrical pomp which gratifies our senses, is to be preferred to the cold parade that insults the understanding without reaching the heart.

Amongst remarks on national education, such observations cannot be misplaced, especially as the supporters of these establishments, degenerated into puerilities, affect to be the champions of religion. Religion, pure source of comfort in this vale of tears! how has thy clear stream been muddied by the dabblers, who have presumptuously endeavoured to confine in one narrow channel, the living waters that ever flow toward God—the sublime ocean of existence! What would life be without that peace which the love of God, when built on humanity, alone can impart? Every earthly affection turns back, at intervals, to prey upon the heart that feeds it; and the purest effusions of benevolence, often rudely damped by men, must mount as a free-will offering to Him who gave them birth, whose bright image they faintly reflect.

In public schools, however, religion, confounded with irksome ceremonies and unreasonable restraints, assumes the most ungracious aspect: not the sober austere one that commands respect whilst it inspires fear; but a ludicrous cast, that serves to point a pun. For, in fact, most of the good stories and smart things which enliven the spirits that have been concentrated at whist, are manufactured out of the incidents to which the very men labour to give a droll turn who countenance the abuse to live on the spoil.

There is not, perhaps, in the kingdom, a more dogmatical or luxurious set of men, than the pedantic tyrants who reside in colleges and preside at public schools. The vacations are equally injurious to the morals of the masters and pupils, and the intercourse, which the former keep up with the nobility, introduces the same vanity and extravagance into their families, which banish domestic duties and comforts from the lordly mansion, whose state is awkwardly aped on a smaller scale. The boys, who live at a great expence with the masters and assistants, are never domesticated, though placed there for that purpose; for, after a silent dinner, they swallow a hasty glass of wine, and retire to plan some mischievous trick, or to ridicule the person or manners of the very people they have just been cringing to, and whom they ought to consider as the representatives of their parents.

Can it then be a matter of surprise, that boys become selfish and vicious who are thus shut out from social converse? or that a mitre often graces the brow of one of these diligent pastors? The desire of living in the same style, as the rank just above them, infects each individual and every class of people, and meanness is the concomitant of this ignoble ambition; but those professions are most debasing whose ladder is patronage; yet out of one of these professions the tutors of youth are in general chosen. But, can they be expected to inspire independent sentiments, whose conduct must be regulated by the cautious prudence that is ever on the watch for preferment?

So far, however, from thinking of the morals of boys, I have heard several masters of schools argue, that they only undertook to teach Latin and Greek; and that they had fulfilled their duty, by sending some good scholars to college.

A few good scholars, I grant, may have been formed by emulation and discipline; but, to bring forward these clever boys, the health and morals of a number have been sacrificed.

The sons of our gentry and wealthy commoners are mostly educated at these seminaries, and will any one pretend to assert, that the majority, making every allowance, come under the description of tolerable scholars?

It is not for the benefit of society that a few brilliant men should be brought forward at the expence of the multitude. It is true, that great men seem to start up, as great revolutions occur, at proper intervals, to restore order, and to blow aside the clouds that thicken over the face of truth; but let more reason and virtue prevail in society, and these strong winds would not be necessary. Public education, of every denomination, should be directed to form citizens; but if you wish to make good citizens, you must first exercise the affections of a son and a brother. This is the only way to expand the heart; for public affections, as well as public virtues, must ever grow out of the private character, or they are merely meteors that shoot athwart a dark sky, and disappear as they are gazed at and admired.

Few, I believe, have had much affection for mankind, who did not first love their parents, their brothers, sisters, and even the domestic brutes, whom they first played with. The exercise of youthful sympathies forms the moral temperature; and it is the recollection of these first affections and pursuits, that gives life to those that are afterwards more under the direction of reason. In youth, the fondest friendships are formed, the genial juices mounting at the same time, kindly mix; or, rather the heart, tempered for the reception of friendship, is accustomed to seek for pleasure in something more noble than the churlish gratification of appetite.

In order then to inspire a love of home and domestic pleasures, children ought to be educated at home, for riotous holidays only make them fond of home for their own sakes. Yet, the vacations, which do not foster domestic affections, continually disturb the course of study, and render any plan of improvement abortive which includes temperance; still, were they abolished, children would be entirely separated from their parents, and I question whether they would become better citizens by sacrificing the preparatory affections, by destroying the force of relationships that render the marriage state as necessary as respectable. But, if a private education produce self-importance, or insulates a man in his family, the evil is only shifted, not remedied.

STUDY QUESTIONS

1. What errors have characteristically been made in the raising of children, in Wollstonecraft's view?
2. What are the dangers posed by "public" (i.e., private) schools, and how can they be remedied?

21.2 CAROLINE NORTON, *ENGLISH LAWS FOR WOMEN IN THE NINETEENTH CENTURY*, 1854

Before Caroline Norton (1808–1877) wrote the activist letters in Document 19.4 with the aim of improving the legal status of women in Britain, she wrote a detailed account of her own losses in her *English Laws for Women in the Nineteenth Century.* She tells her side of the mental and physical abuses she endured during her life with George Norton, a lawyer she married at the age of nineteen in 1827. Consider how revelations from her private experience may have affected a Victorian audience and fueled Norton's political quests.

I shall now give a narrative of my own case, as an example of what can be done under the English law of 1853. If the publication fail to draw any permanent attention to the law itself, at least it will remain a curious record of injustice, in a country especially boastful of its liberal and magnanimous enactments.

. . .

The treatment I received as a Wife, would be incredible if, fortunately (or unfortunately), there were not witnesses who can prove it on oath. We had been married but a few weeks when I found that a part of my lot was that which generally belongs to a lower sphere— and that, when angry, Mr. Norton resorted to personal violence.

After our honeymoon, we lived for a short time in chambers Mr. Norton had occupied as a bachelor; in Garden Court, Temple; and, on the first occasion of dispute, after some high and violent words, he flung the ink-stand, and most of the law books, which might have served a better purpose, at the head of his bride. We had no servants, only an old woman, who had taken care of these chambers for some years, and who offered me the acceptable consolation, that her master was not "sober,"—and would regret it "by-and-bye."

After this happy beginning I accompanied my husband to Scotland. We had been married about two months, when, one evening, after we had all withdrawn to our apartments, we were discussing some opinion he had expressed; I said, (very uncivilly,) that "I thought I had never heard so silly or ridiculous a conclusion." This remark was punished by a sudden and violent kick; the blow reached my side; it caused great pain for many days, and being afraid to remain with him, I sat up the whole night in another apartment.

From C. Norton, *English Laws for Women in the Nineteenth Century.* Westport, Conn.: Hyperion Press Inc., 1981, pp. 22–27, 31–3, 49–50, 54–7, 147–8, 150, 154, 158–9, 175.

Four or five months afterwards, when we were settled in London, we had returned home from a ball; I had then no personal dispute with Mr. Norton, but he indulged in bitter and coarse remarks respecting a young relative of mine, who, though married, continued to dance,—a practice, Mr. Norton said, no husband ought to permit. I defended the lady spoken of, and then stood silently looking out of the window at the quiet light of dawn, by way of contrast. Mr. Norton desired I would "cease my contemplations," and retire to rest, as he had already done; and this mandate producing no result, he suddenly sprang from the bed, seizing me by the nape of the neck, and dashed me down on the floor. The sound of my fall woke my sister and brother-in-law, who slept in a room below, and they ran up to my door. Mr. Norton locked it, and stood over me, declaring no one should enter. I could not speak,—I only moaned. My brother-in-law burst the door open, and carried me down stairs. I had a swelling on my head for many days afterwards, and the shock made my sister exceedingly ill.

On another occasion, when I was writing to my mother, Mr. Norton (who was sipping spirits and water, while he smoked his cigar) said he was sure "from the expression of my countenance," that I was "complaining." I answered, that "I seldom could do anything else." Irritated by the reply, Mr. Norton said I should not write at all, and tore the letter up. I took another sheet of paper, and recommenced. After watching and smoking for a few minutes, he rose, took one of the allumettes I had placed for his cigar, lit it, poured some of the spirits that stood by him over my writing book, and, in a moment, set the whole in a blaze. But Mr. Norton vouchsafed no other notice of my alarm, than that it would "teach me not to brave him."

On another occasion, some time before the birth of my youngest son, I being at breakfast, and my eldest child playing about the room, Mr. Norton entered; he desired me to rise and leave the place I was sitting in, as it faced the park, and it amused him to see the people pass by. I demurred, and said I was not well, and that he should have come down earlier if he had any fancy or choice about places. We had no other word of dispute. Mr. Norton then deliberately took the tea-kettle, and set it down upon my hand; I started up from the pain, and was both burnt and scalded. I ran up to the nursery, and the nurse got the surgeon who lived next door to come in and dress my hand, which remained bound up and useless for days. When this was over, I enquired where Mr. Norton was? and received for reply, that after I had been hurt, he had simply desired the servant to "brush the crumbs away," in the place he had desired me to yield; had then sat down there and breakfasted; and had since gone out—without one word of apology or enquiry.

. . .

After the trial was over, I consulted whether a divorce "by reason of cruelty" might not be pleaded for me; and I laid before my lawyers the many instances of violence, injustice, and ill-usage, of which the trial was but the crowning example. I was then told that no divorce *I* could obtain would break my marriage; that I could not plead cruelty *which I had forgiven*; that by returning to Mr. Norton I had *"condoned"* all I complained of. I learnt, too, the LAW as to my children—that the right was with the father; that neither my innocence nor his guilt could alter it; that not even his giving them into the hands of a mistress, would give me any claim to their custody. The eldest was but six years old, the second four, the youngest two and a half, when we were parted. I wrote, therefore, and *petitioned* the father and husband in whose power I was, for leave to see them—for leave to keep them, till they were a little older. Mr. Norton's answer was, that I should not have them; that if I wanted to see them, I might have an interview with them at the chambers of his attorney. I refused, and wrote as follows to my solicitor, who had conveyed his decision to me:—

> However bitter it may be to me, I must decline seeing my children in the manner proposed. I say nothing of the harshness, the inhumanity of telling me I must either see them at the chambers of his solicitor, or not at all; but I say it is not *DECENT* that the father of those children should force me, their mother, out of the very tenderness I bear them, to visit them at the chambers of the attorney who collected the evidence, examined the witnesses, and conducted the proceedings for the intended divorce.

I say it is not decent—nay, that even if I were guilty, it would not be decent to make me such a proposal. But I am innocent.—I have been pronounced innocent by a jury of my countrymen— I have been solemnly and publicly declared innocent by the nobleman against whom that ill-advised action was brought. Why, then, are my children kept from me?—from me, whom even their own witnesses proved to be a careful and devoted mother? Mr. Norton says, the Law gives him my children. I know it does, but the Law does no more; it does not compel me to endure more than separation from them; and sooner than allow them to connect my visits in their memory with secrecy and shame, I would submit never again to behold them till they were of an age to visit me without asking permission of any human being.

More than once Mr. Norton's advisers have shown more feeling for me than my husband himself; and on this occasion his solicitor wrote:—"Mr. Norton has made the appointment to see the children here—I cannot but regret it."

. . .

During the years over which my separation from these children extended, several attempts were made by Mr. Norton either to compel me to his own terms, or to bring about reconciliation. In the Spring immediately following the Trial (after my first efforts to obtain my children had been rejected) I suddenly received from him a most extraordinary note, saying, that he considered our difference *"capable of adjustment,"* and hoped I would meet him alone, in an empty house, No. 1 Berkeley street, where he would wait for me. I received this communication with doubt and distrust; increased rather than diminished by the impatience shown by Mr. Norton to obtain an answer, for which he sent twice in the course of the afternoon. He then wrote to say, that "nothing could be effected without mutual confidence," and as he could not come to my uncle's house (where I lived) he hoped I would come to his own residence. This, I consented to do. We had a long wretched interview. He besought me once more, to "forget the past" and return home. He laid the blame of all that had happened, on his friends and advisors; said the trial was against his will and judgment, and that he longed to "take me to his heart again." He complained of the coldness with which I received these proposals; but I did not refuse. He recalled my poor children from Scotland; and sent notes almost daily to my house. Those letters began, "My Carry," "My dear Carry," and were signed, "Yours affectionately." Two of them (in allusion to my fear of meeting him) bore the playful signature of "GREENACRE,"—the name of a man who had been recently hung, for enticing a woman to his house by promising marriage, and then murdering her and cutting her to pieces.

After a month of this strange correspondence, I received a note from him, to say the masculine sister had arrived to stay with him. A dispute followed, as to what I had or had not said to this lady. Mr. Norton complained that I had stated to her that I did not intend "honestly" to return to him; but "to return *for the sake of my children and my reputation;*" and that I had said "I never would live with him again." Our reconciliation was broken off: my children were sent back to Scotland; and the next notice taken of my existence, by the husband who had wooed my return; who had begged me to meet him in an empty house, assuring me nothing could be effected "without mutual confidence;"—who had signed himself GREENACRE, in familiar and caressing letters, jesting upon my fears and doubts as to trusting myself alone at that meeting;—and who had, in the first instance, desired his servant the day after my departure, to open the door of my home "with the chain across;"—the next step, I say, taken by the husband whose real story was so little known to the public, was to impose on that public by an advertisement respecting his legal liability for me, commencing,—

"Whereas on 30th March, 1836, my wife, Carolina Elizabeth Sarah, left me, her family, and home, and hath from thenceforth continued to live separate and apart from me,"&c.

Angry, and full of scorn, I consulted my solicitor whether I was compelled to bear this fresh outrage. I showed him the letters Mr. N. had written just before this pretence of being a forsaken husband:—"have I no remedy?"—"No remedy in the LAW. The LAW can do nothing for you: your case is one of singular, of incredible hardship; but there is no possible way in which the LAW could assist you." My brother did all that could be done—he desired his solicitors to publish a letter stating that "the whole of the statements contained in Mr. Norton's advertisement were false"—an imputation which remains on it to this day. After the insult of the advertisement, there was a pause of some weeks; and then Mr. Norton wrote to say he wished an arbitration in our affairs; the arbitrator he named, was Sir John Bayley; and as the history of the reference is given later, I do not here enter into it; further than to say that Mr. Norton, after solemnly pledging himself in writing, to abide whatever decision might be come to, utterly refused to be bound; quarreled with his arbitrator; and broke off the negotiation. A year and a half afterwards, he requested Sir Frederick Thesiger to act as referee; whose opinion I give in his own words:—"The accommodation proposed by Norton is one in which you are to give way upon every subject, and he is not to recede upon one; and it seems to me to be ridiculous to talk of conciliation upon such a footing." . . . "It is impossible not to be struck with the vacillating and vexatious course which Norton has pursued; exciting hopes only to disappoint them, and making promises apparently for the opportunity of breaking them." Friends mediated; men of business wasted their time in vain; Mr. Norton's promises were ropes of sand.

In 1842—two years after Mr. Norton had evaded the chance of exposure by declining to defend my petition under the Infant Custody Bill—he once more asked me to be "reconciled" to him, and to return to live with him. Though this was not arranged, yet from that time there was a degree of peace and friendliness established, which, for the sake of my sons (of whom I had already lost one), I was more than willing—I was anxious—to maintain. Mr. Norton's letters again became caressing and flattering; he visited me at the house of my uncle Mr. C. Sheridan, and after Mr. Sheridan's death, at my own. When I wrote to him from abroad, in 1848, he sent one of my letters triumphantly to my mother, to prove to her what good terms we were on. He followed me to Germany, and said he did not think I ought to "travel alone." Down to the time of my mother's death, and the dispute respecting her annuity,—whatever under-current of bitterness and distrust there might be on my part, or of caprice on his—we remained on familiar and friendly terms; and he relapsed into the old habit of entreating my interference for his interests, with such of my family or friends as had political influence; as he had done when we lived together in one home.

. . .

We will take then, first, the law as to marriage, and divorce.

The Roman Catholics have one clear unvarying rule on this subject. They make marriage a sacrament. They have laws that apply to cases of dispute,—"separation de corps et de biens,"—provision for the wife,—award as to children,—but the marriage itself is simply indissoluble; lasting, as the words of the Church ceremony imply, "till DEATH do us part."

We do not make marriage a sacrament. It is difficult to say what we hold it to be. Lord Hardwicke's Marriage Act, of 1754, declared null, all marriages not celebrated by a priest in orders: and made it indispensable that the ceremony should take place in some parish church, or public chapel, unless by special licence from the Archbiship of Canterbury. Lord John Russell's Act, of 1836, permits persons, on the contrary, to be married according to any form they choose; not sacerdotally; merely by repairing to the Registrar, and giving certain notices, and procuring certain certificates; so as to acquire a right to have the ceremony performed in places registered and appropriated for the purpose. Marriage, therefore, in England, is a religious ceremony or a mere civil contract, at the pleasure of the parties: thus meeting the requisitions of all sects of the Protestant Church. It is besides,—practically,—a sacrament for the poor, and a civil contract for the rich: as the rich break it by application to Parliament; and the poor are put frequently on trial for bigamy, from not being able to go through that expensive form. It is,—practically,—a sacrament for the wife, and a civil contract for the husband; the husband can break it almost as a matter of course, on proof of the wife's infidelity; the wife, though, nominally able to apply for a divorce, seldom or ever obtains one. I believe there are but three cases on record in the House of Lords, or marriages broken on the wife's petition.

. . .

But we have only to look back on the origin of divorce in England, to comprehend, that the protection of the woman was the last thing considered in the framing of its laws. Whether we ought to adopt the view taken by Roman Catholics, and consider marriage as a sacrament; or whether (as Milton bitterly wrote, when arguing his right to get rid of the wife who was no "help-mate" to him) persons once wedded, should be compelled, "in spight of antipathy, to fadge together and combine as they may, to their unspeakable wearisomeness;—forced to drawn in that yoke, an unmerciful day's work of sorrow, till death unharness them,"—is no longer an argument in Protestant England. Divorce, in its fullest interpretation;—divorce, which breaks the marriage utterly, and allows of a new choice; the children of which new choice shall be as legitimate and as capable of inheriting by succession, as the children of any other marriages, is the established law of our land.

. . .

Since the days of King Henry, divorce has remained an indulgence sacred to the aristocracy of England. The poorer classes have no form of divorce amongst them. The rich man makes a new marriage, having divorced his wife in the House of Lords: his new marriage is legal; his children are legitimate; his bride (if she be not the divorced partner of his sin, but simply his elected choice in his new condition of freedom), occupies, in all respects, the same social position, as if he had never previously been wedded. The poor man makes a new marriage, *not* having divorced his wife in the House of Lords; his new marriage is null; his children are bastards; and he himself is liable to be put on trial for bigamy: the allotted punishment for which crime, at one time was hanging, and is now imprisonment.

. . .

Now it is consistent with all the discretion of justice, that far greater leniency should be *practically* extended, to a sex whose passions, habits of life, and greater laxity of opinions, make their temptations greater and their resistance less, than is the case among women; and a proportionate severity may well be shewn to that other sex, whose purity is of infinitely greater importance. But to say that divorce,—if permitted at all,—should be permitted to one party only; that Lord Chancellor Thurlow's principle, (that each case should depend on its own particular circumstances for decision, and on the moral impossibility of actual reunion), should be superseded by the doctrine that only one party *can* be wronged sufficiently to deserve the extreme remedy, is surely so obvious an absurdity, that will scarce bear arguing upon: and would simply be adding one more anomaly, to laws, in which already the jealous and exclusive guarding of masculine rights, is often the foundation of most preposterous wrong.

Called upon to give assent to such a law, even Majesty might feel something of the helplessness of sex: and muse on that accident of regal birth, which has invested her with sacred and irrevocable rights, in a country where women have no rights. The one English-woman in England whom injury and injustice cannot reach: protected from it for ever: protected, not as a Woman, but as QUEEN: as England's Symbol of Royalty: and called upon in that capacity, by the law officers of the Crown and "faithful lieges in Parliament assembled," to complete and perfect by her consent, the power of men's laws. Sign manual and royal assent, necessary for perfecting and completing those laws, under a female reign,—in a country where the signatures of married women are legally worthless; where they cannot lay claim to the simplest article of personal property,—cannot make a will,—or sign a lease,—and are held to be *non-existent* in law!

. . .

If this pamphlet be an appeal to English justice, it ought not to be disregarded because it is a woman's appeal; or because it is MY appeal. On justice only, let it rest. Think if the smallest right be infringed for *men*,—if the rent of a paddock remain unpaid, or a few angry words of libel be spoken, how instantly the whole machinery of the law is set in motion, to crush out compensation; and think what it must be to spend all one's youth, as I have spent mine, in a series of vain struggles to obtain *any* legal justice! Or, do not think at all about me; forget by whose story this appeal was illustrated (I can bring you others, from your own English law books); and let *my* part in this, be only as a voice borne by the wind—as a cry coming over the waves from a shipwreck, to where you stand safe on the shore—and which you turn and listen to, not for the sake of those who call,—you do not know them,—but because it is a cry for HELP.

STUDY QUESTIONS

1. How does Norton's husband attempt to "teach her not to brave him" by means of physical violence?
2. How does the current legal system compound the abuse Norton experiences at her husband's hands?

21.3 WINNIFRED COOLEY, "THE BACHELOR MAIDEN," *THE NEW WOMANHOOD*, 1904

The American writer Winnifred Harper Cooley (1874–1967) described in depth the feminist ideal known as the "New Woman," a term popularized by the writer Henry James for characters like the protagonist in his novella *Daisy Miller*. The New Woman pushed against male dominance and sought education, independence, suffrage, and control of her own life. This chapter of *The New Womanhood* shows the shift in opinion of the unmarried woman, from poor spinster to "bachelor maiden," that occurs when a woman acts decisively to craft her own lifestyle. Consider how Cooley alerts her readers to the misstep of idealizing this figure, who may be less a woman in full control and more an inadvertent victim of her sociopolitical circumstances.

CH. XII: WOMAN AS CITIZEN (CONCERNING SUFFRAGE)

The Ballot:
"A weapon that comes down as still
As snowflakes fall upon the sod,
But executes a freeman's will,
As lightning does the Will of God!"
—John Pierpont, 1800

Could an investigating and unprejudiced stranger enter America, he would find some startling legal and industrial conditions, semi-civilized conservatisms existing within our vaunted democracy. Perhaps the most glaring inconsistency of the republic would be the fact that half the population of seventy-six millions, being in sound mind and morals, a good per cent, American born, are wholly disfranchised. From infancy, we are regaled with the foundation maxims of our national independence; "Governments derive their just power from the *consent* of the governed," "No taxation without representation," yet here are some thirty-eight million people governed without consent, and all these millions taxed without representation!

What is the cause of this singular paradox? Why did our country enter into a heartrending war to free a race of illiterate black people, making the final issue, the giving of these black men the citizen's badge of honor, the ballot; yet totally ignore the intelligent, moral white women in every home, utterly deprived of political power? Never were women so competent, so well-educated as to-day, yet the press utters not a

From Winnifred Cooley, *The New Womanhood*. New York: Broadway Publishing Co., 1904, pp. 135–45.

word against their absolute civil impotency, while it hurls stormy denunciations at a Southern State which dares disfranchise its negro men!

Let us dispassionately review for a moment the pages of history. How many of us realize that the primitive form of government was the matriarchate, or Mother Rule? Women, through their motherhood, were the arbiters of home and tribe. Paternity was uncertain, but maternity was the conservative, established fact, the unit of the family. Woman sat in the councils of war and peace; through her was the line of descent and *family name*,—at the dawn of Christianity, she was the high priestess. This state can be traced through Egyptian, Persian, German, Aryan dynasties. When men assumed sway, it was by the right of physical force. In an age of brute-strength ideals, the weaker sex naturally was relegated to an inferior position, in home, church, and state. The Roman laws retained some favorable conditions for women, until touched by the "icy fingers of canon law," which became the Saxon canon law of our fathers, which we call the English common law. Charles Kingsley says, "This will never be a good world for women until the last remnant of the canon law is swept from the face of the earth."

Of fourteen authors who have written treatises upon the modern election laws of England, only four express any doubt as to the common-law right of women to vote for members of Parliament, yet they are not permitted to vote for these.

In America, it is regarded as a huge joke, if someone says, "We may have a woman President of the United States one day!" Do we forget that Great Britain was ruled over sixty years by a woman, that Spain, the Netherlands, and many countries have had and do have girl and women sovereigns? However, we are concerned chiefly with woman's political position in our so-called democracy. In the thirteen original states, the word male was not placed in the Constitution. New York was the first to restrict some of her citizens from exercising the privilege of voting, by inserting the word "male." Massachusetts and the others quickly followed. What is, to-day, the basis of elimination? Is it a property qualification? No. Women own and manage millions of dollars' worth of property, which their negro or Swede coachmen may vote to tax. Is it educational? No. The girls of the country are flocking to the universities, in what is termed alarmingly large numbers. Is it a question of morals? No. Men in all times and climes unite in claiming that women exceed them in purity, honesty and spirituality. What then discriminates against women, preventing them from exercising the simple and undeniable right of franchise in a government of the people? Their *sex*, alone!

What can a rational, logical mind deem that sex has to do with church or state? Why should the home, the family, the personal life be dragged into the argument? Is not the home composed of *two?* If the husband can find five minutes in his great business enterprises, to steal away, and express himself upon political issues,— matters regulating schools, state institutions, local sanitation—cannot the wife leave her duties five minutes for the same purpose? The man and the woman have personal and domestic duties, but why this eternal cry of motherhood, with the tragic silence as to fatherhood? Objectors to the simple proposition that feminine as well as masculine adults should enjoy the sacred functions of citizenship, begin at once to discuss *personal functions*, as if our individual life should swallow up our civil life. They do not haggle at the admission of the illiterate foreigner, or the "immoral" negro, but woman—ah, woman's nature is a thing apart,—it is emotional, irresponsible, capricious, ungoverned!

Now, these anti-woman suffragists who insist upon woman's lack of logic, are the least logical speakers upon the platform! Instead of reading history, conning statistics, examining justice, they dash into maudlin emotionalism. With expanded chest, these orators exclaim—to an audience honestly desiring information as to woman's legal, constitutional and ethical rights—"Who will rock the cradle while the mother is at the polls?" We might reply to him, "Who rocks the cradle while mother is attending progressive euchres, or is taking in washing to support a drunken husband and eight children?" But to be convincing, we must tell him that only five per cent. of the women of the United States are taking care of young children at one time. That is, calculating the number of children born to each family, and the number of years of a woman's life, she is confined at home by the care of infants only a short period, and there are ninety-five per cent. at any one moment who may appear at the polls and assist in the purification of politics.

We assert that there is not one legal or constitutional or ethical ground upon which women should be denied full suffrage. We cannot combat sophistry. There are two grounds upon which the intellectual women of America demand the ballot: (1) justice, or their absolute right to it; and (2) their desire and ability to improve legislation. Even granting that the entrance of women into politics will not bring about speedy reforms (and we do not grant this), the justice remains the same. As we have said, the arguments against woman suffrage are of a sentimental nature. Conservatism cries: "We dare not take so radical a step." Caution declares, "Why run risks, when women do not want to vote?" What is there in it so radical? Not half a century ago, our fathers exclaimed, "What, educate our daughters, as well as our sons?—preposterous!" But an entering wedge was put through a crack in the school door, and now thousands of girls are receiving university educations. When one thinks of the enlarged opportunities of the present generation of children, reared by educated mothers as well as fathers, amid sanitary surroundings, equipped with the power to become factors in the struggle for existence, he cannot combat education.

Next, woman begged to be teacher, preacher, physician; to speak aloud if she had aught to say.—Another storm was raised, men insulted her, preachers hurled invectives at her, and quoted St. Paul! But she persisted at the expense of much that she held dear, for the weapons of ignorant conservatism are ridicule, denunciation, and slander. Now, we see thousands of women teaching our children, healing the ill and wretched, speaking at religious, literary and philanthropic conventions, preaching, doing hundreds of things well, that once were considered of a strictly masculine nature.

The next step was to plead to be placed upon school boards, boards for the management of the criminal and insane (especially unfortunate women). This has been accomplished in some twenty states, but some legislature continue to vote down such petitions, apparently preferring *such scandals, as constantly crop out, from employing men only, in institutions for women,* to placing one woman upon a board to protect her insane sisters from the barbarity still existing in men as a class!

The achievement of women, individually and as a class, during the past fifty years is marvelous, when we consider that they have been hampered by law, by conservatism, public sentiment, physical inferiority, the care of home and children. Risen they have, and their progress, when they shall be unhampered by constitutional restrictions, and popular prejudice can scarcely be predicted. *Opportunity to share in the weighty problems of government is the last favor they need ask from men.* Thereafter, co-operative labor can be carried on, hand in hand.

One of the most cruel and pathetic circumstances in history is the present demand that intelligent women, well-bred, frequently highly intellectual, the mothers of the race, should *prove* their right to the franchise; to bring all their logic and eloquence to bear to show just cause why a simple due should be granted them,—one which the most renegade young scamp inherits naturally on his twenty-first birthday, by virtue of being a male American, and one which the most illiterate and vicious emigrant gains by mere existence in the United States for one year! Those favoring woman's enfranchisement are asked if they are certain she will immediately purify the pool of politics which generations of men have made filthy!

Apart from any fore-knowledge upon this subject, or from any flattering facts of what women have accomplished where they are enfranchised, there are many weighty reasons for granting women the supreme right of citizenship. Foremost among these are: (1) Woman's need for the franchise to develop herself, and (2) the need of the community for woman. What is the most glaring lack in the average municipal management? Not brain; brilliant men abound. *The penitentiaries are full of them!* The paramount need is for conscientiousness! What class of people are super-conscientious, often morbidly so? *Women!*

In 1848, the first Convention called by women as an attempt to recover their ancient rights, was held at Seneca Falls, N. Y. Such women as Elizabeth Cady Stanton, Lucy Stone, and such men as Wendell

Phillips and Wm. Lloyd Garrison began the agitation. At this time, married women had no property rights. An heiress, finding her husband an intoxicated spendthrift, had no recourse to law. She was told that the fortune was her husband's, she a pauper. Not only money, but her very clothes belonged to the husband,—and her children were not hers in the eye of law, but her husband's, to be disposed of, as he saw fit. Divorce law was rigid. There were few grounds, not even drunkenness, upon which a woman could rid herself of an obnoxious partnership formed in youthful ignorance. A man, until ten years ago, could, in Illinois, shut up a wife for life in an insane asylum, without a physician's certificate. To-day, the common law holds good in England, that a man may beat his wife with a stick no larger around than his thumb! Slowly and painfully, law after law in each state has been attacked,—timidly, but persistently, have women gone before legislative committees, pleading for better conditions, not for themselves (often enjoying wealth and protection), but for the poor women engaged in underpaid industries, abused wives, widows struggling against injustice and poverty, young girls, who in some states were only protected against the violence of man, up to the age of *eight*.

In behalf of such, courageous women have entreated legislation, and subjected themselves to every humiliation to gain it.

In spite of being a disfranchised class, misunderstood, and working in opposition to public opinion, a few women, led by such martyr spirits as Susan B. Anthony, have altered and improved the laws of every state in the union. Yet to-day women are classed with "idiots, paupers and criminals," as the disfranchised body!

It is difficult enough to accomplish reformatory legislation with the ballot; it is almost impossible, without. In 1894, a constitutional convention held in New York, aroused much enthusiasm, and resulted in a petition bearing 625,000 names, asking that the word *male* be struck from the State Constitution. The amendment was lost by a vote of 97 to 58.

Wyoming has had equal suffrage for thirty-two years. It refused to come into the Union as a state, unless it could bring woman suffrage along with it. Colorado, nine years; Utah, seven years; Idaho, five years. Large numbers of states have school suffrage, or municipal, or both,—the logical, outcome of partial suffrage being, of course, full suffrage.

A curious thing is the universal opposition of the saloon element to the enfranchisement of women. Conversely, the suffrage in the hands of women will surely work havoc upon the saloon interests.* (Not that women as such stand for prohibition.) National legislation has been sought every year since 1869. A respectful hearing in committee is given the leading women of the country, and the bill then laid upon the table!

Women in Great Britain vote upon every issue except Parliamentary elections. Full suffrage is enjoyed in South and West Australia. In New Zealand, that Utopia where industrial conditions have approximated perfection, where there are no strikes, tramps, millionaires, or paupers, where municipal ownership of all public utilities has settled labor problems, there is universal suffrage.

Upon woman's political status, depend chiefly her civil rights. Her position in the industrial world has changed, through the introduction of machinery, which lightened her duties in the individual household,—giving her more time, and placing a monied value upon her work. She has thus been enabled to enter trades and professions, to be self-supporting,—the ethical value being that she may now remain single, or marry for love, whereas in the past, she was obliged to marry to be supported. The moral effect upon children, from marriages of inclination, rather than necessity, furnishes a vital argument in favor of woman's freedom to choose. *Industrial independence begets a desire for political independence.* Self-supporting women come into a knowledge of, and contact with, unjust discriminations against a disfranchised class. Self-support is teaching women self-respect, and inspiring in them a vital interest in governmental matters. The National Woman's Council, and the Federation of Women's Clubs (two separate organizations), the W.C.T.U., and other great bodies, are educating a race of parliamentarians. The International Council, organized in 1888, now includes the aristocracy of Europe (titled ladies, more democratic than many Americans) and the so-called working classes, laboring side by side, in the cause of woman's development, and almost universally desiring her political emancipation.

Working men are learning that it is the underpaid women in industries who are harming them by unfair competition. Equal wages and opportunities for equal work will benefit men as well as women. The industrial situation is inseparably connected with the political. *As it is the pioneers of Woman Suffrage who have gradually opened up all the avenues of wage-earning to women, so women who are engaged in industries learn that justice and equality before the law may be found only in equal suffrage.*

No man can "represent" a woman. If all humanity were divided into couples, and all couples agreed in politics, the man might be the official representative, but even then, he should cast two ballots!

Thus in cities, woman must obey the laws, pay taxes, is subject to arrest, to fines and imprisonment, but has no vote in choosing mayor, aldermen, or any of the officers upon whom depends the righteous enforcing of the laws. *Chivalry does not exempt women from taxation;* even the widow and the orphan are required to grade their streets, but are "too delicate" to vote upon questions vital to their homes and pocketbooks.

STUDY QUESTIONS

1. What threat seems to be posed by the "New Woman" to all men, and is it a serious one?
2. Is Cooley convincing in her arguments about the impact of women in professional roles and the effect of female employment on wages?

21.4 MARIA MONTESSORI, *THE MONTESSORI METHOD: SCIENTIFIC PEDAGOGY AS APPLIED TO CHILDHOOD EDUCATION*, 1912

Remembered chiefly as an education reformer, Maria Montessori (1870–1952) was also a social activist who brought the plight of Italy's urban poor to light. In this excerpt from the third chapter of her book *The Montessori Method*, she reprints an address she made at the formal opening (1907) of the first of her "Children's Houses"—this one in Rome, in the then-famous slum in the San Lorenzo district.

It may be that the life lived by the very poor is a thing which some of you here to-day have never actually looked upon in all its degradation. You may have only felt the misery of deep human poverty through the medium of some great book, or some gifted actor may have made your soul vibrate with its horror.

Let us suppose that in some such moment a voice should cry to you, "Go look upon these homes of

Translation by Clifford Backman.

misery and blackest poverty. For there have sprung up amid the terror and the suffering, oases of happiness, of cleanliness, of peace. The poor are to have an ideal house which shall be their own. In Quarters where poverty and vice ruled, a work of moral redemption is going on. The soul of the people is being set free from the torpor of vice, from the shadows of ignorance. The little children too have a 'House' of their own. The new generation goes forward to meet the new era, the time when misery shall no longer be deplored but destroyed. They go to meet the time when the dark dens of vice and wretchedness shall have become things of the past, and when no trace of them shall be found among the living." What a change of emotions we should experience! And how we should hasten here, as the wise men guided by a dream and a star hastened to Bethlehem!

I have spoken thus in order that you may understand the great significance, the real beauty, of this humble room, which seems like a bit of the house itself set apart by a mother's hand for the use and happiness of the children of the Quarter. This is the second "Children's House" which has been established within the ill-favoured Quarter of San Lorenzo.

The Quarter of San Lorenzo is celebrated, for every newspaper in the city is filled with almost daily accounts of its wretched happenings. Yet there are many who are not familiar with the origin of this portion of our city.

It was never intended to build up here a tenement district for the people. And indeed San Lorenzo is not the People's Quarter, it is the Quarter of the poor. It is the Quarter where lives the underpaid, often unemployed workingman, a common type in a city which has no factory industries. It is the home of him who undergoes the period of surveillance to which he is condemned after his prison sentence is ended. They are all here, mingled, huddled together.

The district of San Lorenzo sprang into being between 1884 and 1888 at the time of the great building fever. No standards either social or hygienic guided these new constructions. The aim in building was simply to cover with walls square foot after square foot of ground. The more space covered, the greater the gain of the interested Banks and Companies. All this with a complete disregard of the disastrous future which they were preparing. It was natural that no one should concern himself with the stability of the building he was creating, since in no case would the property remain in the possession of him who built it.

When the storm burst, in the shape of the inevitable building panic of 1888 to 1890, these unfortunate houses remained for a long time untenanted. Then, little by little, the need of dwelling-places began to make itself felt, and these great houses began to fill. Now, those speculators who had been so unfortunate as to remain possessors of these buildings could not, and did not wish to add fresh capital to that already lost, so the houses constructed in the first place in utter disregard of all laws of hygiene, and rendered still worse by having been used as temporary habitations, came to be occupied by the poorest class in the city. . . .

To this we must add the evils of crowded living, promiscuousness, immorality, crime. Every little while the newspapers uncover for us one of these intérieurs: a large family, growing boys and girls, sleep in one room; while one corner of the room is occupied by an outsider, a woman who receives the nightly visits of men.

This is seen by the girls and the boys; evil passions are kindled that lead to the crime and bloodshed which unveil for a brief instant before our eyes, in some lurid paragraph, this little detail of the mass of misery.

Whoever enters, for the first time, one of these apartments is astonished and horrified. For this spectacle of genuine misery is not at all like the garish scene he has imagined. We enter here a world of shadows, and that which strikes us first is the darkness which, even though it be midday, makes it impossible to distinguish any of the details of the room. . . .

There lies before the social crusader of the present day a problem more profound than that of the intellectual elevation of the poor; the problem, indeed, of life.

In speaking of the children born in these places, even the conventional expressions must be changed, for they do not "first see the light of day"; they come into a world of gloom. They grow among the poisonous shadows which envelope over-crowded humanity. These children cannot be other than filthy in body, since the water supply in an apartment originally intended to be occupied by three or four persons, when distributed among twenty or thirty is scarcely enough for drinking purposes!

Conditions such as I have described make it more decorous, more hygienic, for these people to take refuge in the street and to let their children live there.

But how often these streets are the scene of bloodshed, of quarrel, of sights so vile as to be almost inconceivable. The papers tell us of women pursued and killed by drunken husbands! Of young girls with the fear of worse than death, stoned by low men.

Again, we see untellable things—a wretched woman thrown, by the drunken men who have preyed upon her, forth into the gutter. There, when day has come, the children of the neighbourhood crowd about her like scavengers about their dead prey, shouting and laughing at the sight of this wreck of womanhood, kicking her bruised and filthy body as it lies in the mud of the gutter!

Such spectacles of extreme brutality are possible here at the very gate of a cosmopolitan city, the mother of civilisation and queen of the fine arts, because of a new fact which was unknown to past centuries, namely, the isolation of the masses of the poor.

In the Middle Ages, leprosy was isolated: the Catholics isolated the Hebrews in the Ghetto; but poverty was never considered a peril and an infamy so great that it must be isolated. The homes of the poor were scattered among those of the rich and the contrast between these was a commonplace in literature up to our own times. Indeed, when I was a child in school, teachers, for the purpose of moral education, frequently resorted to the illustration of the kind princess who sends help to the poor cottage next door, or of the good children from the great house who carry food to the sick woman in the neighbouring attic.

To-day all this would be as unreal and artificial as a fairy tale. The poor may no longer learn from their more fortunate neighbours lessons in courtesy and good breeding, they no longer have the hope of help from them in cases of extreme need. We have herded them together far from us, without the walls, leaving them to learn of each other, in the abandon of desperation, the cruel lessons of brutality and vice. Anyone in whom the social conscience is awake must see that we have thus created infected regions that threaten with deadly peril the city which, wishing to make all beautiful and shining according to an aesthetic and aristocratic ideal, has thrust without its walls whatever is ugly or diseased.

When I passed for the first time through these streets, it was as if I found myself in a city upon which some great disaster had fallen. It seemed to me that the shadow of some recent struggle still oppressed the unhappy people who, with something very like terror in their pale faces, passed me in these silent streets. The very silence seemed to signify the life of a community interrupted, broken. Not a carriage, not even the cheerful voice of the ever-present street vender, nor the sound of the hand-organ playing in the hope of a few pennies, not even these things, so characteristic of poor quarters, enter here to lighten this sad and heavy silence.

Observing these streets with their deep holes, the doorsteps broken and tumbling, we might almost suppose that this disaster had been in the nature of a great inundation which had carried the very earth away; but looking about us at the houses stripped of all decorations, the walls broken and scarred, we are inclined to think that it was perhaps an earthquake which has afflicted this quarter. Then, looking still more closely, we see that in all this thickly settled neighbourhood there is not a shop to be found. So poor is the community that it has not been possible to establish even one of those popular bazars where necessary articles are sold at so low a price as to put them within the reach of anyone. The only shops of any sort are the low wine shops which open their evil-smelling doors to the passer-by. As we look upon all this, it is borne upon us that the disaster which has placed its weight of suffering upon these people is not a convulsion of nature, but poverty—poverty with its inseparable companion, vice.

This unhappy and dangerous state of things, to which our attention is called at intervals by newspaper accounts of violent and immoral crime, stirs the hearts and consciences of many who come to undertake among these people some work of generous benevolence. One might almost say that every form of misery inspires a special remedy and that all have been tried here, from the attempt to introduce hygienic principles into each house, to the establishment of crêches, "Children's Houses," and dispensaries.

But what indeed is benevolence? Little more than an expression of sorrow; it is pity translated into action. The benefits of such a form of charity cannot be great, and through the absence of any continued income and the lack of organisation it is restricted to a small number of persons. The great and widespread peril of evil demands, on the other hand, a broad and comprehensive work directed toward the redemption of the entire community. Only such an organisation, as, working for the good of others, shall itself grow and prosper through the general prosperity which it has made possible, can make a place for itself in this quarter and accomplish a permanent good work.

STUDY QUESTIONS

1. How does Montessori make the connection between poverty and crime? Between poverty and immorality? What is the key factor behind the "extreme brutality" of the San Lorenzo ghetto? How does Montessori use historical examples to buttress her argument?
2. According to Montessori, what are the limitations of private charity ("benevolence")? What reasons does she put forth for the need for "broad and comprehensive work directed toward the redemption of the entire community?" Do you agree with Montessori's position?

21.5 EMMELINE PANKHURST, "FREEDOM OR DEATH," 1913

English political activist Emmeline Pankhurst (1858–1928) delivered this speech in Hartford, Connecticut, on November 13, 1913. Frequently arrested and subjected to forced feeding, Pankhurst was a tireless advocate for women's suffrage and legal rights. She founded the Women's Social and Political Union in Manchester, England, in 1903, a group dedicated to "deeds, not words." She spent several months in 1913 touring the United States and speaking on behalf of the suffrage movement.

I do not come here as an advocate, because whatever position the suffrage movement may occupy in the United States of America, in England it has passed beyond the realm of advocacy and it has entered into the sphere of practical politics. It has become the subject of revolution and civil war, and so tonight I am not here to advocate woman suffrage. American suffragists can do that very well for themselves.

Emmeline Pankhurst, "Freedom or Death," November 13, 1913.

I am here as a soldier who has temporarily left the field of battle in order to explain—it seems strange it should have to be explained—what civil war is like when civil war is waged by women. I am not only here as a soldier temporarily absent from the field at battle; I am here—and that, I think, is the strangest part of my coming—I am here as a person who, according to the law courts of my country, it has been decided, is of no value to the community at all; and I am adjudged because of my life to be a dangerous person, under sentence of penal servitude in a convict prison.

It is not at all difficult if revolutionaries come to you from Russia, if they come to you from China, or from any other part of the world, if they are men. But since I am a woman it is necessary to explain why women have adopted revolutionary methods in order to win the rights of citizenship. We women, in trying to make our case clear, always have to make as part of our argument, and urge upon men in our audience the fact—a very simple fact—that women are human beings.

Suppose the men of Hartford had a grievance, and they laid that grievance before their legislature, and the legislature obstinately refused to listen to them, or to remove their grievance, what would be the proper and the constitutional and the practical way of getting their grievance removed? Well, it is perfectly obvious at the next general election the men of Hartford would turn out that legislature and elect a new one.

But let the men of Hartford imagine that they were not in the position of being voters at all, that they were governed without their consent being obtained, that the legislature turned an absolutely deaf ear to their demands, what would the men of Hartford do then? They couldn't vote the legislature out. They would have to choose; they would have to make a choice of two evils: they would either have to submit indefinitely to an unjust state of affairs, or they would have to rise up and adopt some of the antiquated means by which men in the past got their grievances remedied.

Your forefathers decided that they must have representation for taxation, many, many years ago. When they felt they couldn't wait any longer, when they laid all the arguments before an obstinate British government that they could think of, and when their arguments were absolutely disregarded, when every other means had failed, they began by the tea party at Boston, and they went on until they had won the independence of the United States of America.

It is about eight years since the word militant was first used to describe what we were doing. It was not militant at all, except that it provoked militancy on the part of those who were opposed to it. When women asked questions in political meetings and failed to get answers, they were not doing anything militant. In Great Britain it is a custom, a time-honoured one, to ask questions of candidates for parliament and ask questions of members of the government. No man was ever put out of a public meeting for asking a question. The first people who were put out of a political meeting for asking questions, were women; they were brutally ill-used; they found themselves in jail before 24 hours had expired.

We were called militant, and we were quite willing to accept the name. We were determined to press this question of the enfranchisement of women to the point where we were no longer to be ignored by the politicians.

You have two babies very hungry and wanting to be fed. One baby is a patient baby, and waits indefinitely until its mother is ready to feed it. The other baby is an impatient baby and cries lustily, screams and kicks and makes everybody unpleasant until it is fed. Well, we know perfectly well which baby is attended to first. That is the whole history of politics. You have to make more noise than anybody else, you have to make yourself more obtrusive than anybody else, you have to fill all the papers more than anybody else, in fact you have to be there all the time and see that they do not snow you under.

When you have warfare things happen; people suffer; the noncombatants suffer as well as the combatants. And so it happens in civil war. When your forefathers threw the tea into Boston Harbour, a good many women had to go without their tea. It has always seemed to me an extraordinary thing that you did not follow it up by throwing the whiskey overboard; you sacrificed the women; and there is a good deal of warfare for which men take a great deal of glorification which has involved more practical sacrifice on women than it has on any man. It always has been so. The grievances of those who have got power, the influence of those who have got power commands a great deal of attention; but the wrongs and the grievances of those people who have no power at all are apt to be absolutely ignored. That is the history of humanity right from the beginning.

Well, in our civil war people have suffered, but you cannot make omelettes without breaking eggs; you cannot have civil war without damage to something. The great thing is to see that no more damage is done than is absolutely necessary, that you do just as much as will arouse enough feeling to bring about peace, to bring about an honourable peace for the combatants; and that is what we have been doing.

We entirely prevented stockbrokers in London from telegraphing to stockbrokers in Glasgow and vice versa: for one whole day telegraphic communication was entirely stopped. I am not going to tell you how it was done. I am not going to tell you how the women got to the mains and cut the wires; but it was done. It was done, and it was proved to the authorities that weak women, suffrage women, as we are supposed to be, had enough ingenuity to create a situation of that kind. Now, I ask you, if women can do that, is there any limit to what we can do except the limit we put upon ourselves?

If you are dealing with an industrial revolution, if you get the men and women of one class rising up against the men and women of another class, you can locate the difficulty; if there is a great industrial strike, you know exactly where the violence is and how the warfare is going to be waged; but in our war against the government you can't locate it. We wear no mark; we belong to every class; we permeate every class of the community from the highest to the lowest; and so you see in the woman's civil war the dear men of my country are discovering it is absolutely impossible to deal with it: you cannot locate it, and you cannot stop it.

"Put them in prison," they said, "that will stop it." But it didn't stop it at all: instead of the women giving it up, more women did it, and more and more and more women did it until there were 300 women at a time, who had not broken a single law, only "made a nuisance of themselves" as the politicians say.

Then they began to legislate. The British government has passed more stringent laws to deal with this agitation than it ever found necessary during all the history of political agitation in my country. They were able to deal with the revolutionaries of the Chartists' time; they were able to deal with the trades union agitation; they were able to deal with the revolutionaries later on when the Reform Acts were passed: but the ordinary law has not sufficed to curb insurgent women. They had to dip back into the middle ages to find a means of repressing the women in revolt.

They have said to us, government rests upon force, the women haven't force, so they must submit. Well, we are showing them that government does not rest upon force at all: it rests upon consent. As long as women consent to be unjustly governed, they can be, but directly women say: "We withhold our consent, we will not be governed any longer so long as that government is unjust." Not by the forces of civil war can you govern the very weakest woman. You can kill that woman, but she escapes you then; you cannot govern her. No power on earth can govern a human being, however feeble, who withholds his or her consent.

When they put us in prison at first, simply for taking petitions, we submitted; we allowed them to dress us in prison clothes; we allowed them to put us in solitary confinement; we allowed them to put us amongst the most degraded of criminals; we learned of some of the appalling evils of our so-called civilisation that we could not have learned in any other way. It was valuable experience, and we were glad to get it.

I have seen men smile when they heard the words "hunger strike," and yet I think there are very few men today who would be prepared to adopt a "hunger strike" for any cause. It is only people who feel an intolerable sense of oppression who would adopt a means of that kind. It means you refuse food until you are at death's door, and then the authorities have to choose between letting you die, and letting you go; and then they let the women go.

Now, that went on so long that the government felt that they were unable to cope. It was [then] that, to the shame of the British government, they set the example to authorities all over the world of feeding sane, resisting human beings by force. There may be doctors in this meeting: if so, they know it is one thing to feed by force an insane person; but it is quite another thing to feed a sane, resisting human being who resists with every nerve and with every fibre of her body the indignity and the outrage of forcible feeding. Now, that was done in England, and the government thought they had crushed us. But they found that it did not quell the agitation, that more and more women came in and even passed that terrible ordeal, and they were obliged to let them go.

Then came the legislation—the "Cat and Mouse Act." The home secretary said: "Give me the power to let these women go when they are at death's door, and leave them at liberty under license until they have recovered their health again and then bring them back." It was passed to repress the agitation, to make the women yield—because that is what it has really come to, ladies and gentlemen. It has come to a battle between the women and the government as to who shall yield first, whether they will yield and give us the vote, or whether we will give up our agitation.

Well, they little know what women are. Women are very slow to rouse, but once they are aroused, once they are determined, nothing on earth and nothing in heaven will make women give way; it is impossible. And so this "Cat and Mouse Act" which is being used against women today has failed. There are women lying at death's door, recovering enough strength to undergo operations who have not given in and won't give in, and who will be prepared, as soon as they get up from their sick beds, to go on as before. There are women who are being carried from their sick beds on stretchers into meetings. They are too weak to speak, but they go amongst their fellow workers just to show that their spirits are unquenched, and that their spirit is alive, and they mean to go on as long as life lasts.

Now, I want to say to you who think women cannot succeed, we have brought the government of England to this position, that it has to face this alternative: either women are to be killed or women are to have the vote. I ask American men in this meeting, what would you say if in your state you were faced with that alternative, that you must either kill them or give them their citizenship? Well, there is only one answer to that alternative, there is only one way out—you must give those women the vote.

You won your freedom in America when you had the revolution, by bloodshed, by sacrificing human life. You won the civil war by the sacrifice of human life when you decided to emancipate the negro. You have left it to women in your land, the men of all civilised countries have left it to women, to work out their own salvation. That is the way in which we women of England are doing. Human life for us is sacred, but we say if any life is to be sacrificed it shall be ours; we won't do it ourselves, but we will put the enemy in the position where they will have to choose between giving us freedom or giving us death.

So here am I. I come in the intervals of prison appearance. I come after having been four times imprisoned under the "Cat and Mouse Act," probably going back to be rearrested as soon as I set my foot on British soil. I come to ask you to help to win this fight. If we win it, this hardest of all fights, then, to be sure, in the future it is going to be made easier for women all over the world to win their fight when their time comes.

STUDY QUESTIONS

1. Why does Pankhurst contend that it is difficult for a woman to be a revolutionary? What examples does she provide to support her argument?
2. How does Pankhurst argue that governments rest on consent instead of force?
3. Why does Pankhurst believe men are unprepared to adopt hunger strikes?

21.6 REBECCA WEST, "THE STERNER SEX," 1913

Rebecca West—the pen name used by Cicily Isabel Fairfield (1892–1983)—was a prodigious British novelist, literary critic, journalist, and travel writer. Her best-known book, *Black Lamb and Grey Falcon* (1941), is an extraordinary 1,100-page account of her travels through the former Yugoslavia; the book was published soon after the Nazi invasion of the Balkans and includes the epigraph "To my friends in Yugoslavia, who are now all dead or enslaved." The selection produced here comes from the early phase of her career, when she focused principally on feminist and socialist issues. From the start of the First World War her interests turned primarily to politics and literature. The essay below appeared first in the socialist journal *The Clarion* (July 18, 1913) and was reprinted in the collection *The Young Rebecca: Writings of Rebecca West, 1911–1917* (New York, 1982), pp. 188–192.

The other day a cousin of mine was married. Though what God or myself had to do with it I do not know, but I was obliged to go to church. I object to going to church except to hear the Athanasian Creed, which stretches the power of belief and leaves one with the same pleasant, warm, tired feeling as an attack of yawning. All the same, I found myself one day last week in the porch of a somber building adorned with stained-glass windows which proved that the Apostles liked aniline dyes and everything handsome about them: I faced an usher whose eyes dropped doubtfully on the books I held in my arms. I had caught them up carelessly as I left home to read in the train, and it was an unfortunate coincidence that they happened to be the latest batch of literature issued by the Divorce Law Reform Union. With an air of resource he conducted me to a pew in the transept where any disturbance I might make would be quite ineffective. . . .

That horrid interior, distempered a deep drab picked out with a lemon-coloured dado, turned the sweetness of the music sour; and I opened "Marriage and Divorce," a pamphlet complied by the secretary of the Divorce Law Reform Union, which is largely concerned with the findings of the Royal Commission on Matrimonial Causes. That is the body which sat for three years and issued a Majority Report containing recommendations of the utmost importance to the working classes. Because it deals with sex and shocks the Archbishop of Canterbury neither the Liberals nor the Conservatives will ever have to carry it into law. Thus do men perform the task of government. My eye fell on an extraordinary conversation between Lady Frances Balfour and the Bishop of Birmingham:

"We have had evidence put before us," said Lady Frances, "that there are men who live on the prostitution of their wives. Is such a wife, being a Christian, to stick with her husband and do as he commands her?"

"Yes," replied the Bishop, probably plucking at the edge of his apron, "I am afraid so."

I felt sorry that I had come to church. It was true that Norwood is not in the diocese of Birmingham, but I did not wish to encourage the Church of England at all after this. The lack of pity for hurt flesh, the tolerance of squalid sin!

But a shadow fell across my book and I looked up into the candid gaze of two blue eyes. The bridegroom stood beside me, extending a slender hand and smiling shyly and frankly, but quite without

Rebecca West, "The Sterner Sex," *The Clarion* (18 July 1913).

coquetry. The sun lay on his fair head like a benediction, and no fretful or angry passion had ever lined that boyish brow: only the gentlest words had shaped that mouth. Personal grace of a high order was accentuated by dainty dressing; his frock-coat fitted him like the pelt of a young antelope, and his trousers had a silvery gleam like willows seen at twilight. He was a pure white rose.

How can I tell you how this flower-like radiance of untainted youth affected me, who had just come from Fleet Street? Suffice it to say that hastily I closed my book and put it from me, lest his eyes should fall on the—to his young mind—strange and disturbing title. I had an impulse to raise his gloved hands to my lips: only by some such old-fashioned courtesy could I express the million mingled feelings of love and pity, foreboding and strong hope, that rose in my heart as I saw this young creature, so grave, yet so unsuspecting of life's darker side, standing on the threshold of his new life. I did not do it. People in Norwood are so ununderstanding. He murmured a few graceful words, his delicate skin suffused with a flush, and flitted on.

An hour or so afterwards I threaded my way to my aunt through a number of people who were eating oyster patties and meringues for the same excellent reason that they had previously gone to church: because my cousin was being married. My aunt shook my hand warmly, looked out of the window into the garden, and said with deep feeling: "I shall never see geraniums and calceolarias again without remembering how I lost my little Rachel." Our conversation was at first disconnected, for it seemed that I had been dropping pamphlets on cheap divorce all round the wedding breakfast, and people were constantly retrieving them and bringing them to me. Then, casting a glance to where a trembling but composed figure stood beside my cousin's athletic form, I asked:

"What does this young man that Rachel's married do?"

"Nothing. He's in the War Office," smiled my aunt, and her attention wandered again. "I always think there's something depressing about a bridesmaid if she's over twenty. Poor things, they can't help feeling it. . . . Yes, Cyril is in the War Office. Your uncle is very pleased about that. He said to me last night, quite impressively, that a government worker is in as secure a position as any member of the royal family."

I was glad that my cousin had chosen her husband from that sheltered parterre, the Civil Service. When I go down Whitehall and meet all the cool and uncreased young men emerging from the cloister of their offices, I feel as one does when visiting an Irish convent boarding-school where girls of good family learn to paint on satin and play the harp; one feels one's voice a little loud, one's boots a little large. There is something appealing about the turning of the middle-class man to the refuge of unresponsible administrative work: The working man knows peril in his various occupations, and all women may die through motherhood; but he alone walks always in the sunlight, almost as happy as the capitalist. And so England would have her manhood. Do not the Insurance Commissioners congratulate themselves on the fact that they are spending thousands not on sick or maternity benefits, but on the employment of unskilled clerk labour? I see a day when the manhood of England will spring like a lily from an office-stool. All the same, I felt that there was a certain exuberance about the statement that a government worker is in as secure a position as any member of the royal family.

For Whitehall leads to Pimlico. And in Pimlico there are a number of government workers who seem in an extraordinarily insecure position. It is true that they are not decorative persons like Cyril, whose personal appearance is, as I have explained, such that no one could raise a hand against him save in the way of kindness: still, their humanity entitles them to a certain measure of justice. On 1 July a notice was put up in the yard which announced that the rate of pay for making soldiers' drab jackets was altered from 2*s.* 11.5*d.* to 2*s.* 6*d.*: which meant a reduction of from 1*s.* 6*d.* to 2*s.* on weekly earning which now average 17*s.* 4*d.* It was a reduction that one cannot ascribe either to the law of supply or demand or too much gold. It was simply an act of pure devilish thrift on the part of the War Office: the Army Clothing Employees' Union has just forced them to raise the rate of pay for making scarlet uniforms by 3.5 *d.*, and it is now trying to make the other workers pay for this generous rise. So six hundred women marched up

Whitehall to the War Office. Cyril, I believe, watched them from behind a blind. Cyril's superiors received them with politeness and promised that, pending the arrangement for a round-table conference, the reductions should not be carried into effect. Meantime, the authorities are hunting for some justification of the prejudice that equates in the official mind like a blind-eyed toad: that some women of exceptional skill make 25*s*. a week at this work, and it is not the will of God that a woman should earn more than a pound a week. And the need for keeping down expenses is so great. . . .

Good God enlighten us! Which of these two belongs to the sterner sex—the man who sits in Whitehall all his life on a comfortable salary, or the woman who has to keep her teeth bared lest she has her meatless bone of 17*s*. a week snatched away from her and who has to produce the next generation on her off-days? I remembered a member of the Army Clothing Employees' Union that I met a week or two ago: her brown hands were strong, every sentence she spoke bit into the truth, she had the faculty of deep and rowdy laughter. I looked at Cyril. He had sat down now and, with a solemnity that lay prettily on his Dresden-like charm, was toying with a vanilla ice. I had a vision of the world fifty years hence, when we have simply had to take over the dangerous adventures of the earth. I saw some bronzed and travel-scarred pioneer returning from the Wild West with hard-earned treasure, buying a fresh and unspoiled bridegroom who had hardly ever stirred from the office of, let us say, the Director of Public Prosecutions. I saw a world of women struggling as the American capitalist men of today struggle, to maintain a parasitic sex that is at once its tyrant and its delight. . . . We must keep men up to the mark.

STUDY QUESTIONS

1. How does West support her argument that women are the "sterner sex"? What examples does she provide?
2. What does West mean when she describes men as a "parasitic sex"?

CHAPTER 22

THE CHALLENGE OF SECULARISM

22.1 CHARLES LYELL, FROM "ON EXTINCT QUADRUPEDS," *PRINCIPLES OF GEOLOGY*, 1830–1833

Sir Charles Lyell (1797–1875), a friend of Charles Darwin, was a Scottish geologist who was so notable that to this day, in his honor, a crater on the moon and a type of armored fish both bear Lyell's name. Lyell examined the premise that the earth is governed by the same principles regardless of era and that geological evolution can be broken down into tiny changes over long spans of time—a notion that also appears in Darwin's evolutionary theory. This selection examines revolutions in climate over the eons, using evidence from, among other phenomena, mammoths preserved in ice.

Before I attempt to explain the probable causes of great vicissitudes of temperature on the earth's surface, I shall take a rapid view of some of the principal data which appear to support the popular opinions now entertained on the subject. To insist on the soundness of these inferences, is the more necessary, because some zoologists have undertaken to vindicate the uniformity of the laws of nature, not by accounting for former fluctuations in climate, but by denying the value of the evidence in their favor.

The mammoth (*E. primigenius*), already alluded to, as occurring fossil in England, was decidedly different from the two existing species of elephants, one of which is limited to Asia, south of the 31° of N. lat., the other to Africa, where it extends, as before stated, as far south as the Cape of Good Hope. The bones of the great fossil species are very widely spread over Europe and North America; but are nowhere in such profusion as in Siberia, particularly near the shores of the Frozen Ocean. Are we, then, to conclude that this animal preferred a polar climate? If so, it may well be asked, by what food was it sustained, and why does it not still survive near the arctic circle?

After more than thirty years, the entire carcass of a mammoth (or extinct species of elephant) was obtained in 1803, by Mr. Adams, much farther to the north. It fell from a mass of ice, in which it had been encased, on the banks of the Lena, in lat. 70°; and so perfectly had the soft parts of the carcass been preserved, that the flesh, as it lay, was

From Charles Lyell, "On Extinct Quadrupeds," *Principles of Geology*. London: J. Murray, 1830–1833, pp. 74–82.

devoured by wolves and bears. This skeleton is still in the museum of St. Petersburg, the head retaining its integument and many of the ligaments entire. The skin of the animal was covered, first, with black bristles, thicker than horse hair, from twelve to sixteen inches in length; secondly, with hair of a reddish brown color, about four inches long; and thirdly, with wool of the same color as the hair, about an inch in length. Of the fur, upwards of thirty pounds' weight were gathered from the wet sand-bank. The individual was nine feet high and sixteen feet long, without reckoning the large curved tusks: a size rarely surpassed by the largest living male elephants.

It is evident, then, that the mammoth, instead of being naked, like the living Indian and African elephants, was enveloped in a thick shaggy covering of fur, probably as impenetrable to rain and cold as that of the musk ox. The species may have been fitted by nature to withstand the vicissitudes of a northern climate; and it is certain that, from the moment when the carcasses, both of the rhinoceros and elephant, above described, were buried in Siberia, in latitudes 64° and 70° N., the soil must have remained frozen, and the atmosphere nearly as cold as at this day.

On considering all the facts above enumerated, it seems reasonable to imagine that a large region in central Asia, including, perhaps, the southern half of Siberia, enjoyed, at no very remote period in the earth's history, a temperate climate, sufficiently mild to afford food for numerous herds of elephants and rhinoceroses, *of species distinct from those now living.*

STUDY QUESTIONS

1. How do Lyell's detailed observations lead to his conclusion about the development of mammoths?
2. How do these observations lead him to conclusions about the distant past of the species?

22.2 ABRAHAM GEIGER, "MORAL AND LEGAL RULES," *JUDAISM AND ISLAM*, 1833

A German scholar and reforming rabbi, Abraham Geiger (1810–1874) examined the fundamental effects of Judaism on Christianity and Islam—even writing an award-winning essay entitled "What Has Muhammad Taken from Judaism?" (1833), translated as *Judaism and Islam*. The theory behind his argument was that the two later monotheisms were different methods of spreading Jewish belief to non-Jews by adapting and adopting new cultural elements to appeal to new ethnic groups. In the following passage, Geiger outlines the means and motives of the Jews who produced, revised, and translated the biblical text over the centuries. His letter to a colleague laments the misunderstanding that keeps Jewish and Christian biblical scholars at odds with one another.

Abraham Geiger and Liberal Judaism. Ed. by Max Weiner and Trans. Ernst J. Schlochauer. Hebrew Union College Press,

The Bible is now and has always been an ever-living Word, not a dead letter. It has spoken to all generations and imparted its teachings to them; it expressed the fullness of its spirit in the living, spontaneous phrase. It has ever been an immediate presence among men. It never was a sealed book of antiquity, whose meaning the student had to unlock in order to acquaint himself with the ideas of a day long past, while he himself could feel free to pursue a path of his own that might well be quite at variance with its teachings. In reading other works of antiquity, men have undertaken to interpret them in accordance with the ideas that prevailed at the times in which they had first been written, and attempted to correlate these writings with such views as they themselves held and as were prevalent in their own day. In the case of the Bible, the exact opposite has always been true. The Eternal Word was never considered part of any one era; its validity could not be dependent upon the time at which it was composed; by the same token, it could not be construed to lack any of the newer truths and insights. This is the reason why every age, every movement and every personality in history has brought its own ideas to bear upon the Bible; hence the multitude of elaborations, interpretations, and typical and symbolic attempts at explanation. All efforts notwithstanding, it seems impossible to achieve an objective interpretation of the Bible, and even the non-believer will infuse his own feelings of aversion into his attempts to explain this work. This may result in a good deal of instability in exegesis, but at the same time it points up all the more clearly the significance of the Bible as all things to all men.

In the days before the final redaction of the Bible, however, that which in later eras was accomplished by exegesis was achieved by means of textual revision. The Bible encompassed the entire spiritual life of the people and expressed it fully; every man who studied it found within it the expression of his own higher ideals. In the vigorous renaissance which characterized the first years of the Second Commonwealth . . . in the fervent endeavor to have the Bible become truth at long last, to have the contents of the Bible become fully identified with its own attitude, the national consciousness also had to find its complete expression in the Holy Book that had become its heritage. Thus the national consciousness [*of the Jewish people*] quite innocently supplied into the text that which appeared to be lacking and artlessly impressed its own stamp upon that which was already part of the original version.

No one holding an unprejudiced conception of history, no one able to transpose himself into the conditions and views that prevailed in those ancient days and to appreciate the vital force of the creative urge and the might of the spirit of revelation—though the latter was on the wane—will take exception to such textual revision. On the contrary, such a person will deem it essential and justifiable by analogy alone. He will admit that in those days entire new works were composed which then were considered equal, or almost equal, in significance to the older literature; this category, in fact, includes a major segment of the Hagiographa. He will acknowledge, too, that entire works which were composed at that time were ascribed to authors who had lived long before. The book of Ecclesiastes and the Song of Songs were not written by Solomon, nor is Daniel the author of the book bearing his name. Instead, these works were written by other authors who were fully convinced that they were speaking to their people in the spirit of these men and hence did not think it amiss to place the names of these famous personalities upon their title pages. He will also accept the fact that the latter portions of the books of Isaiah and Zachariah, a large number of psalms . . . and a major part of the book of Proverbs are of more recent origin and had only been incorporated into the older collections of biblical literature at a later date. He will understand, too, that older works and facts appear in newer writings in a completely revised form, with thorough changes in both language and conception. He will not close his eyes to the fact that, judging by a large segment of their contents, the books of Chronicles are actually revisions of the books of Samuel and Kings, and that in this case, fortunately, the older versions have also been preserved. He cannot deny the historical testimony that in those days, indeed even throughout the era of the Second Temple, and even for a century after that, there still existed complete freedom of judgment as to which of the writings should be viewed as sacred and which should not be so regarded. He will know, too, that for a long time there was considerable doubt as to whether books such as Ezekiel, Ecclesiastes, Song of Songs, and Esther should be included in the canon, until the decision was finally made in their favor. On the other hand, there were books which, though now no more a part of the biblical canon, were highly valued at one time. One such work is Ben Sirah. Particularly those Jews who lacked familiarity with Hebrew judged many books now classed with apocryphal literature as equal in sanctity with other biblical writings. Nor will a person with a broader conception of history be able to ignore the historical evidence that certain minor changes were made in all the books of the Bible, quite deliberately and from highly respectable motives, not only in olden times but long thereafter as well. . . . The religio-national consciousness [*of the Jewish people*] had fully entered into the spirit of this treasured heritage; for this reason it assimilated it also emotionally and remodeled it in accordance with its own sentiments.

. . .

In those days the Bible text in general, and thus also the copies then "circulating" in Judean Palestine, read very differently from the version we know today. It is true that, for the most part, we are now in possession of the more authentic and original text. However, at the time when one group was in the process of translating its text and the others were engaged in formulating it, that text was circulating in the altered version, and it was only at a later date that the Jews of Palestine made a careful, critical study to make their text conform more closely to the original version.

. . .

Although . . . law and legend developed independently in accordance with principles of their own, they were of necessity based on the Scriptural text. They sought to explain the simple Bible precept or Bible story in accordance with their own more advanced concepts, and so the variations in Halakhah and Agaddah naturally had a significant effect on the interpretation of Scriptures. But whereas the earlier era's later assumptions were permitted to go side by side with the actual Bible text, it is a typical phenomenon of later procedure that every effort was made to find contemporary views definitely reflected in the text of the Bible, that is, to interpret the text in such a manner as to make it appear to set forth that same more recent concept. Scholars of an earlier age did not treat the letter of the Bible with such great respect. They based their assumptions on their own views; they were not disturbed by small variations that did not alter the meaning of the whole text; indeed, they did not even shrink from making minor changes here and there in order to make the wording of the Scriptures conform more closely to their own assumptions which they regarded as firmly established. Later, however, things changed. The Bible scholars of more recent eras had to bend every effort to establish a final biblical text that would be complete and accurate. Every letter and punctuation mark offered a chance for interpretation; hence even the most minute adulteration could give rise to major variations in the construction of the biblical text. It was during that time that the correct text was established with greater care; it was then that the masoretic studies first began, and, to the extent that earlier textual changes had not become too deeply entrenched to permit the reconstruction of the original version . . . we may now assume with certainty that the text which corresponds to this more recent development is the authentic one as against the older version which had been changed by arbitrary action. This more recent text, the masoretic text, is the one which, by and large, is in our hands today.

The variations in interpretation and determination of the biblical text come to the fore most clearly in the translations dating from different periods. Even at the beginning of the Second Commonwealth, readings from the various books of the Holy Scriptures, particularly from the Pentateuch, had been introduced and it was soon deemed necessary to have some learned man provide a translation to supplement each reading. The number of those possessing an accurate knowledge of the language was not large, and even such knowledge would still not have been sufficient for the understanding of difficult passages. More than that, the actual contents, too, required interpretation—and, in fact, revision—partly in accordance with the requirements of contemporary thought, and partly out of consideration for the people as a whole. Outside of Palestine, where the vernacular had nothing in common with the language of the biblical text and thus offered no aid toward an easier understanding of that text, the translation soon became so firmly established as to supplant the original version altogether.

This happened in Egypt where a Greek translation became canonical itself, as it were, so that, eventually, its authorship was attributed to an established authoritative body of seventy (or seventy-two) elders and the work itself was surrounded by an aura of sanctity all its own. This story, however, is no more than poetic conjecture and embellishment from a later date. The same is true also of other theories concerning its origin: for example, that "five elders" had written it or that it had been composed for one of the Ptolemies, and even more so of later hypotheses which do not even have support from tradition. Briefly, the so-called Septuagint version is a translation which first was communicated orally by Greek translators, but was soon set down in writing and eventually came to be the standard text for all Greek-speaking Jews. It is therefore not the product of a deliberate literary effort; instead, it came into being in response to a definite need which it satisfied. It is an expression of the manner in which the Bible text was then understood, and, insofar as this was not prevented by translator's tendencies then prevalent . . . it faithfully reflected that contemporary interpretation. It was a faithful rendition, hewing closely to the original biblical text; yet, in many passages, it proceeded with a good deal of freedom. Now the Egyptian and other Greek-speaking Jews, who used this translation as a standard original text, were remote from the center where Scriptural interpretation, legalistic discussion and Aggadic explanation continued to flourish and develop. However the new findings that went forth from Palestine, particularly insofar as they affected practical life, penetrated to them and were probably accepted by them to a large extent. Thus the Greek speaking Jews were satisfied to accept Palestinian scholarship as authoritative. Nevertheless they still retained their own version of the Bible, namely, the standard Greek translation.

In the second century of the Christian era, however, a veritable revolution took place. The national-religious life in Palestine could no longer serve as a pattern for those living in the Diaspora. The scholars in Palestine now resolutely proceeded with the critical arrangement of the original text, and every letter in the text attained major significance because of its value in the interpretation of the whole. Besides, Christianity began to lean upon the Greek translation of the Bible and adduced from it evidence in support of Christian views. But one glance into the original Hebrew text sufficed to show that this evidence was, in fact, non-existent. Only then did it become clear how far removed the Greek text actually was from the Hebrew original. It was obvious that the old Greek translation would either have to be revised or entirely replaced by a new one. This was the cause of the work of Aquila and Theodotian. Aquila made an entirely new translation that was in accordance with the more recent point of view. Moreover, in order to preserve even in the translation the same possibilities for interpretation as were contained in the original text, Aquila proceeded with a cautious literalness that did violence to the genius of the Greek language. Theodotian, on the other hand, based his work on the Septuagint, adapting it to the newer text and to the newer viewpoint. The Jews, however, could no longer be satisfied with this one translation, and particularly not with a translation in a language of such confusing character [*as was that of Aquila*]. The Christians, for their part, looked with suspicion upon this product of the "modern" Jews. Greek Jewry as such, moreover, decreased in both numbers and importance. Hence only fragments of these later translations have been preserved, whereas the Septuagint is still with us even today.

TO PROFESSOR THEODOR NOELDECKE BERLIN, JULY 8, 1872

Our complaints at the unfair treatment of Judaism on the part of Christian scholars who are otherwise sympathetic are not based on any demand on our part that they should concern themselves more with its postbiblical literature. . . . We do not have the right to prescribe the course or direction their studies should take. But we do have the right to ask that those who are not familiar with this literature should either refrain from passing judgment on it, or at least, be circumspect in expressing their opinions. We do not have the right to denounce the ignorance of those who, despite such ignorance, and with boundless arrogance and spite, air their derogatory opinions on such matters; and we are justified in banning opinions on such matters; and we are justified in banning such persons from the company of fair and honest scholars. Of course, those Christian scholars who engage in the study of the origins of Christianity are not free to choose whether or not to study the later developments of Judaism. If they are to acquire the proper judgment they must be familiar with the conditions which prevailed within Judaism at that period, and it seems only fair that they should make use of Jewish sources for that purpose. It cannot be denied that it is difficult to get a proper understanding of these Jewish sources, but this fact does not exempt them from the duty to become familiar with them if they desire to voice opinions on subjects which can be understood only through a study of such sources. It is regrettable that we lack the aids necessary to facilitate such understanding, and that nothing is being done by the Jews who do possess this knowledge to remedy this deficiency. I am certain that this situation will be changed in the course of time. Here, too, however, the Jews are not to blame. To this very day, Jews are all but completely barred from unrestricted scholarly pursuits; much of the work is done either by rabbis who are already overburdened with official duties, or by dilettantes. How could one expect them to produce work of a nature that demands a lifetime of devoted labor?

You think that we expect you to view the dreadful discussions of Halakhah as something more than a waste of intelligence on subjects not worthy of the effort. If they are of no practical value, you need not hesitate to disregard them. But if they should prove absolutely necessary for the evaluation of a subject under study, an interested scholar can no more be exempted from studying them than a historian, desiring to present historical studies of that era in the light of their motivating forces, can afford to disregard the Church Fathers, the legendarians and the scholasticists.

I myself do not go along with the romantic predilection for modern Hebrew which many modern writers now use in their scholarly articles. However, one must consider that, by virtue of their way of life, most of these men are actually prevented from using a living language. It must therefore be deemed commendable that they communicate their observations in some idiom that can be understood. . . . I might add, though, that this undesirable state of affairs, too, is gradually disappearing.

I do not wish to enter into any further discussion on the point that complaints of the harshness of Christianity toward Judaism are unjustified because all Semitic religions have a natural bent for persecution. It is a sad thing that, on one hand, pride is taken in modern humanitarianism while at the same time one can, when it suits him, fall back on outworn Oriental attitudes. I am not telling this to you, but all the more emphatically to your colleagues.

STUDY QUESTIONS

1. Does the fact that the Bible was composed by multiple authors make its contents unreliable? Should religious people be afraid of employing the critical method with scriptural texts?
2. How was the "canon" of Jewish scripture compiled, and was it a manmade, rather than a divinely directed, process?

22.3 ERNEST RENAN, "MIRACLES," 1863

Ernest Renan (1823–1892) was one of the leaders of the "Higher Criticism" school of religious scholarship, and his *Life of Jesus* (1863) is one of the best-known works of that school. This reading presents excerpts from that book's sixteenth chapter, on the phenomenon of Jesus's supposed miracles.

In the minds of Jesus' contemporaries there were two ways in which to prove one had a supernatural mission: by performing miracles, and by fulfilling prophecies. Jesus made use of both forms of proof, and his disciples did so even more. For a long time Jesus had been convinced that the writings of the prophets [about the coming messiah] had all been written about him. Seeing himself in their sacred utterances, he thought of himself as a mirror reflecting the whole prophetic spirit of Israel, and the body of his followers strove—even within his lifetime, perhaps—to establish as proven the idea that Jesus fulfilled perfectly all that the prophets had predicted about the messiah. Many of their arguments were quite superficial and we need not trouble ourselves with them: things like simple coincidences in minor details between some event in Jesus' life and some passage or two that they remembered in the Book of Psalms or the texts of the prophets. . . .

As far as miracles are concerned, most of the people of that time regarded miracles as indisputable signs of heavenly power and proof of a prophetic vocation. The stories told about Elijah and Elisha were full of miracles, and most believers simply assumed that the messiah, when he came, would perform many miracles too. . . . Jesus was therefore confronted with the need to choose, either to become a miracle-worker or to renounce his mission as the messiah. We must bear in mind that with the exception of the great scientific school of Greece and their Roman successors, all the ancients believed in miracles. Jesus, having no notion whatsoever of a physical universe governed by fixed scientific laws, believed in them too. His understanding of these matters was no better than that of the people around him. In fact, one of his most basic assumptions was that people could control nature by means of faith and prayers—for God had so frequently granted certain people the ability to perform miracles. There was nothing unusual about it. . . .

Given the sheer number of miracle stories so tediously narrated in the Gospels, it is impossible to separate the miracles in which Jesus actually played a role from those which common rumor attributed to him. It is likewise impossible to tell whether or not the cruder elements of those miracles—the groans, the writhings, and all other actions that smack of trickery—have any factual basis, or whether they were the fruit of the imaginations of the gospel writers. Those writers were indeed suffused with the theurgy of the times, much like the "spiritualists" of our own time. Most of the miracles that Jesus believed himself to have performed—nearly all of them, in fact—appear to have been healing-miracles. Medicine in Jesus' time was what it still is in the Orient today: totally unscientific, and given over entirely to "inspired" individuals. The scientific medicine born five hundred years earlier by the Greeks was all but unknown to the Jews who lived in Palestine. . . . Jesus knew as little as his contemporaries about medicine as a rational science, and like them he believed that healing came about through religious rites. Such belief

---

Translation by Clifford Backman.

was consistent with their other beliefs. Once disease is defined as a consequence of sin or the result of a demon-spell, rather than as the product of physical factors, then the best physician was indeed a holy man with access to supernatural forces. Healing was a moral action [not a scientific one], and Jesus, keenly aware of his moral power, not surprisingly believed himself able to heal. It would have been heartless of him, if he believed that by the touch of his robe or the imposition of his hands he could ease the suffering of the sick, if he refused to do so. Healing the sick was a recognized sign of the kingdom of God, as was the liberation of the poor; both of them were signs of the great [spiritual] revolution that would end with the relief of all suffering.

The specific cure that Jesus performed most frequently was exorcism—the driving out of demons. The strange conviction that demons existed permeated Jesus' world, and indeed not just Judea but the entire world. Everyone believed that demons could, and did, seize hold of people's bodies and take control of them. A Persian demon named Aeschma-daeva in the Avesta was adopted by the Jews, who gave him the name Asmodeus, became the instigator of women's hysterical fits. Every malady imaginable for which they did not know the cause—epilepsy, nervous disorders, deafness, muteness, or anything that made someone seem like a different person—was explained as the result of demon possession. . . . The occupation of exorcist was as common as that of physician, and there is no doubt that Jesus, in his lifetime, was reputed to possess the greatest secrets of the art. There were large numbers of lunatics in Judea at that time, owing most likely to the heightened air of excitement. Mad men and women were allowed to go free, as they still are in that place, and lived in abandoned burial caves (also the common hide-outs of criminals). A thousand stories were circulated about his magical cures, stories that show in full the gullibility of the time. . . .

Numerous details suggest that Jesus became a miracle-worker late in his life, and somewhat against his own will. [In the gospels] he commonly performs his miracles only after being begged to do so, and even then he goes about it reluctantly and while criticizing the people for the coarseness of their begging. Uniquely and inexplicably, he is always careful to perform his miracles in secret, and he asks those whom he cures to tell no one. When the driven-out demons recognize him as the Son of God, he orders them to be silent. Nevertheless, they do recognize him. These elements appear especially in the gospel of Mark, who is the preeminent evangelist of miracles and exorcisms. . . .

Generally speaking, we can state with confidence that Jesus worked miracles and exorcized demons in spite of himself. It often happens that miracles are the work of the crowd rather than the performer. Jesus steadfastly avoided the performance of miracles that the crowd would have created for him. His greatest miracle would have been a refusal to perform any! That would have been a blow greater than any ever seen by the laws of history and popular psychology. Jesus' miracles were acts of violence against him, committed by the world and time he lived in. Concessions were forced from him by an immediate popular need for such.

STUDY QUESTIONS

1. What evidence does Renan provide to argue that Jesus performed miracles "in spite of himself"?
2. What historical facts does Renan offer to explain why Jesus performed so many exorcisms?

22.4 CHARLES BAUDELAIRE, "THE PAINTER OF MODERN LIFE," 1863

In his essay "The Painter of Modern Life," the French poet Charles Baudelaire (1821–1867) lays out his vision of modernism, which became perhaps the closest thing to a manifesto the movement had. In discussing the work of the painter Constantin Guys (1802–1892), Baudelaire argues that the habit of contemporary painters to look for truth or beauty in antiquity is senseless; instead, painters should, like Guys, be looking to capture the specifics of the modern age because new techniques of painting would surely uncover new perspectives on reality. Looking to the past for technique or inspiration, therefore, results in not only historically inaccurate work, but also artistic failure. But in attempting to capture the modern moment, the painter, he said, was in search of something indefinable, "something we can perhaps call modernity."

IV. MODERNITY

And so, walking or quickening his pace, he goes his way, forever in search. In search of what? We may rest assured that this man, such as I have described him, this solitary mortal endowed with an active imagination, always roaming the great desert of men, has a nobler aim than that of the pure idler, a more general aim, other than the fleeting pleasure of circumstance. He is looking for that indefinable something we may be allowed to call "modernity," for want of a better term to express the idea in question. The aim for him is to extract from fashion the poetry that resides in its historical envelope, to distil the eternal from the transitory. If we cast our eye over our exhibitions of modern pictures, we shall be struck by the general tendency of our artists to clothe all manner of subjects in the dress of the past. Almost all of them use the fashions and the furnishings of the Renaissance, as David used Roman fashions and furnishings, but there is this difference, that David, having chosen subjects peculiarly Greek or Roman, could not do otherwise than present them in the style of antiquity, whereas the painters of today, choosing, as they do, subjects of a general nature, applicable to all ages, will insist on dressing them up in the fashion of the Middle Ages, of the Renaissance, or of the East. This is evidently sheer laziness; for it is much more convenient to state roundly that everything is hopelessly ugly in the dress of a period than to apply oneself to the task of extracting the mysterious beauty that may be hidden there, however small or light it may be. Modernity is the transient, the fleeting, the contingent; it is one half of art, the other being the eternal and the immovable. There was a form of modernity for every painter of the past; the majority of the fine portraits that remain to us from former times are clothed in the dress of their own day. They are perfectly harmonious works because the dress, the hairstyle, and even the gesture, the expression and the smile (each age has its carriage, its expression and its smile) form a whole, full of vitality. You have no right to despise this transitory fleeting element, the metamorphoses of which are so frequent, nor to dispense with it. If you do, you inevitably fall into the emptiness of an abstract and indefinable beauty, like that of the One and only woman of the time before the Fall. If for the dress of the day, which is necessarily right, you substitute another, you are guilty of a piece of nonsense that only a fancy-dress ball imposed by fashion can excuse. Thus the goddesses, the nymphs, and sultanas of the eighteenth century are portraits in the spirit of their day.

No doubt it is an excellent discipline to study the old masters, in order to learn how to paint, but it can be no more than a superfluous exercise if your aim is to understand the beauty of the present day. The draperies of Rubens or Veronese will not teach you how to paint watered silk *d'antique,* or satin *à la reine,* or any other fabric produced by our mills, supported by a swaying crinoline, or petticoats of starched muslin. The texture and grain are not the same as in the fabrics of old Venice, or those worn at the court of Catherine. We may add that the cut of the skirt and bodice is absolutely different, that the pleats are arranged into a new pattern, and finally that the gesture and carriage of the woman of today give her dress a vitality and a character that are not those of the woman of former ages. In short, in order that any form of modernity may be worthy of becoming antiquity, the mysterious beauty that human life unintentionally puts into it must have been extracted from it. It is this task that M. G. particularly addresses himself to.

I have said that every age has its own carriage, its expression, its gestures. This proposition may be easily verified in a large portrait gallery (the one at Versailles, for example). But it can be yet further extended. In a unity we call a nation, the professions, the social classes, the successive centuries, introduce variety not only in gestures and manners, but also in the general outlines of faces. Such and such a nose, mouth, forehead, will be standard for a given interval of time, the length of which I shall not claim to determine here, but which may certainly be a matter of calculation. Such ideas are not familiar enough to portrait painters; and the great weakness of M. Ingres, in particular, is the desire to impose on every type that sits for him a more or less complete process of improvement, in other words a despotic perfecting process, borrowed from the store of classical ideas.

In a matter such as this, a priori reasoning would be easy and even legitimate. The perpetual correlation between what is called the soul and what is called the body is a quite satisfactory explanation of how what is material or emanates from the spiritual reflects and will always reflect the spiritual force it derives from. If a painter, patient and scrupulous but with only inferior imaginative power, were commissioned to paint a courtesan of today, and, for this purpose, were to get his inspiration (to use the hallowed term) from a courtesan by Titian or Raphael, the odds are that his work would be fraudulent, ambiguous, and difficult to understand. The study of a masterpiece of that date and of that kind will not teach him the carriage, the gaze, the come-hitherishness, or the living representation of one of these creatures that the dictionary of fashion has, in rapid succession, pigeonholed under the coarse or light-hearted rubric of unchaste, kept women, Lorettes.

The same remark applies precisely to the study of the soldier, the dandy, and even animals, dogs or horses, and of all things that go to make up the external life of an age. Woe betide the man who goes to antiquity for the study of anything other than ideal art, logic and general method! By immersing himself too deeply in it, he will no longer have the present in his mind's eye; he throws away the value and the privileges afforded by circumstance; for nearly all our originality comes from the stamp that it impresses upon our sensibility. The reader will readily understand that I could easily verify my assertions from innumerable objects other than women. What would you say, for example, of a marine painter (I take an extreme case) who, having to represent the sober and elegant beauty of a modern vessel, were to tire out his eyes in the study of the overloaded, twisted shapes, the monumental stern, of ships of bygone ages, and the complex sails and rigging of the sixteenth century? And what would you think of an artist you had commissioned to do the portrait of a thorough-bred, celebrated in the solemn annals of the turf, if he were to restrict his studies to museums, if he were to content himself with looking at equine studies of the past in the picture galleries, in Van Dyck, Bourguignon, or Van der Meulen?

M. G., guided by nature, tyrannized over by circumstance, has followed a quite different path. He began by looking at life, and only later did he contrive to learn how to express life. The result has been a striking originality, in which whatever traces of untutored simplicity may still remain take on the appearance of an additional proof of obedience to the impression, of a flattery of truth. For most of us, especially for businessmen, in whose eyes nature does not exist, unless it be in its strict utility relationship with their business interests, the fantastic reality of life becomes strangely blunted. M. G. registers it constantly; his memory and his eyes are full of it.

STUDY QUESTIONS

1. How is modernist painting seen as a rejection of previous aesthetic approaches?
2. In what ways should a modernist express "life" rather than merely copying the past?

22.5 CHARLES DARWIN, "ON SOCIABILITY," *THE DESCENT OF MAN*, AND SELECTION IN RELATION TO SEX, 1871

Charles Darwin (1809–1882), a British naturalist, propounded the theory of evolution in his famous work *On the Origin of Species* (1859). With this theory, Darwin launched a massive debate concerning the spiritual repercussions of belief in natural selection—such as the contradiction inherent in the evolution of humans from apes and the story of the Creation of Adam and Eve in the book of Genesis. This second work, *The Descent of Man*, explores the physiological connections between humans and what Darwin calls "lower animals." This selection examines the notion of sociability and how it plays out in various associations of animals; Darwin even makes a case for "lower animals" (like dogs) having characteristics that would be called "moral" in humans. Consider the impact of such "scientific discoveries" on a society that views humans as an elevated creation modeled on God.

The main conclusion here arrived at, and now held by many naturalists who are well competent to form a sound judgment, is that man is descended from some less highly organised form. The grounds upon which this conclusion rests will never be shaken, for the close similarity between man and the lower animals in embryonic development, as well as in innumerable points of structure and constitution, both of high and of the most trifling importance,—the rudiments which he retains, and the abnormal reversions to which he is occasionally liable,—are facts which cannot be disputed. They have long been known, but until recently they told us nothing with respect to the origin of man. Now when viewed by the light of knowledge of the

From Philip Appleman, ed., *Darwin: A Norton Critical Edition*, 2nd ed. New York: W. W. Norton & Company, 1980, pp. 196–203, 208.

whole organic world, their meaning is unmistakable. The great principle of evolution stands up clear and firm, when these groups or facts are considered in connection with others, such as the mutual affinities of the members of the same group, their geographical distribution in past and present times, and their geological succession. It is incredible that all these facts should speak falsely. He who is not content to look, like a savage, at the phenomena of nature as disconnected, cannot any longer believe that man is the work of a separate act of creation. He will be forced to admit that the close resemblance of the embryo of man to that, for instance, of a dog—the construction of his skull, limbs and whole frame on the same plan with that of other mammals, independently of the uses to which the parts may be put—the occasional re-appearance of various structures, for instance of several muscles, which man does not normally possess, but which are common to the Quadrumana—and a crowd of analogous facts—all point in the plainest manner to the conclusion that man is the co-descendant with other mammals of a common progenitor.

We have seen that man incessantly presents individual differences in all parts of his body and in his mental faculties. These differences or variations seem to be induced by the same general causes, and to obey the same laws as with the lower animals. In both cases similar laws of inheritance prevail. Man tends to increase at a greater rate than his means of subsistence; consequently he is occasionally subjected to a severe struggle for existence, and natural selection will have effected whatever lies within its scope. A succession of strongly marked variations of a similar nature is by no means requisite; slight fluctuating differences in the individual suffice for the work of natural selection; not that we have any reason to suppose that in the same species, all parts of the organisation tend to vary to the same degree. We may feel assured that the inherited effects of the long-continued use or disuse of parts will have done much in the same direction with natural selection. Modifications formerly of importance, though no longer of any special use, are long-inherited. When one part is modified, other parts change through the principle of correlation, of which we have instances in many curious cases of correlated monstrosities. Something may be attributed to the direct and definite action of the surrounding conditions of life, such as abundant food, heat or moisture; and lastly, many characters of slight physiological importance, some indeed of considerable importance, have been gained through sexual selection.

. . .

It must not be supposed that the divergence of each race from the other races, and of all from a common stock, can be traced back to any one pair of progenitors. On the contrary, at every stage in the process of modification, all the individuals which were in any way better fitted for their conditions of life, though in different degrees, would have survived in greater numbers than the less well-fitted. The process would have been like that followed by man, when he does not intentionally select particular individuals, but breeds from all the superior individuals, and neglects the inferior. He thus slows but surely modifies his stock, and unconsciously forms a new strain. So with respect to modifications acquired independently of selection, and due to variations arising from the nature of the organism and the action of the surrounding conditions, or from changed habits of life, no single pair will have been modified much more than the other pairs inhabiting the same country, for all will have been continually blended through free intercrossing.

. . .

The high standard of our intellectual powers and moral disposition is the greatest difficulty which presents itself, after we have been driven to this conclusion on the origin of man. But everyone who admits the principle of evolution, must see that the mental powers of the higher animals, which are the same in kind with those of man, though so different in degree, are capable of advancement. Thus the interval between the mental powers of one of the higher apes and of a fish, or between those of an ant and scale-insect, is immense; yet their development does not offer any special difficulty; for with our domesticated animals, the mental faculties are certainly variable, and the variations are inherited. No one doubts that they are of the utmost importance to animals in a state of nature. Therefore, the conditions are favourable for their development through natural selection. The same conclusion may be extended to a man; the intellect must have been all-important to him, even at a very remote period, as enabling him to invent and use language, to make weapons, tools, traps, &c., whereby with the aid of his social habits, he long ago became the most dominant of all living creatures.

A great stride in the development of the intellect will have followed, as soon as the half-art and half-instinct of language came into use; for the continued use of language will have reacted on the brain and produced an inherited effect; and this again will have reacted on the improvement of language. As Mr. Chauncey Wright has well remarked, the largeness of the brain in man relatively to his body, compared with lower animals, may be attributed in chief part to the early use of some simple form of language,—that wonderful engine which affixes signs to all sorts of objects and qualities, and excites trains of thought which would never arise from the mere impression of the sense, or if they did arise could not be followed out. The higher intellectual powers of man, such as those of ratiocination, abstraction, self-consciousness, &c., probably follow from the continued improvement and exercise of the other mental faculties.

The development of the moral qualities is a more interesting problem. The foundation lies in the social instincts, including under this term the family ties. These instincts are highly complex, and in the case of the lower animals give special tendencies towards certain definite actions; but more important elements are love, and the distinct emotion of sympathy. Animals endowed with the social instincts take pleasure in one another's company, warn one another of danger, defend and aid one another in many ways. These instincts do not extend to all the individuals of the species, but only to those of the same community. As they are highly beneficial to the species, they have in all probability been acquired through natural selection.

A moral being is one who is capable of reflecting on his past actions and their motives—of approving of some and disapproving of others; and the fact that man is the one being who certainly deserves this designation, is the greatest of all distinctions between him and the lower animals. But in the fourth chapter I have endeavoured to show that the moral sense follows, firstly, from the enduring and ever-present nature of the social instincts; secondly, from man's appreciation of the approbation and disapprobation of his fellows; and thirdly, from the high activity of his mental faculties, with past impressions extremely vivid; and in these latter respects he differs from the lower animals. Owing to this condition of mind, man cannot avoid looking both backwards and forwards, and comparing past impressions. Hence after some temporary desire or passion has mastered his social instincts; and he then feels that sense of dissatisfaction which all unsatisfied instincts leave behind them, he therefore resolves to act differently for the future,—and this is conscience. Any instinct, permanently stronger or more enduring than another, gives rise to a feeling which we express by saying that it ought to be obeyed. A pointer dog, it ought (as indeed we say of him) to have pointed at that hare and not have yielded to the passing temptation of hunting it.

Social animals are impelled partly by a wish to aid the members of their community in a general manner, but more commonly to perform certain definite actions. Man is impelled by the same general wish to aid his fellows; but has few or no special instincts. He differs also from the lower animals in the power of expressing his desires by words, which thus become a guide to the aid required and bestowed. The motive to give aid is likewise much modified in man: it no longer consists solely of a blind instinctive impulse, but is much influenced by the praise or blame of his fellows. The appreciation and bestowal of praise and blame both rest on sympathy; and this emotion, as we have seen, is one of the most important elements of the social instincts. Sympathy, though gained as an instinct, is also much strengthened by exercise or habit. As all men desire their own happiness, praise or blame is bestowed on actions and motives, according as they lead to this end; and as happiness is an essential part of the general good, the greatest-happiness principle indirectly serves as a nearly safe standard of right and wrong. As the reasoning powers advance and experience is gained, the remoter effects of certain lines of conduct on the character of the individual, and on the general good, are perceived; and then the self-regarding virtues come within the scope of public opinion, and receive praise, and their opposites blame. But with the less civilised nations reason often errs, and many bad customs and base superstitions come within the same scope, and are then esteemed as high virtues, and their breach as heavy crimes.

The moral faculties are generally and justly esteemed as of higher value than the intellectual powers. But we should bear in mind that the activity of the mind in vividly recalling past impressions is one of the fundamental though secondary bases of conscience. This affords the strongest argument for educating and stimulating in all possible ways the intellectual faculties of every human being. No doubt a man with a torpid mind, if his social affections and sympathies are well developed, will be led to good actions, and may have a fairly sensitive conscience. But whatever renders the imagination more vivid and strengthens the habit of recalling and comparing past impressions, will make the conscience more sensitive, and may even somewhat compensate for weak social affections and sympathies.

The moral nature of man has reached its present standard, partly through the advancement of his reasoning powers and consequently of a just public opinion, but especially from his sympathies having been rendered more tender and widely diffused through the effects of habit, example, instruction, and reflection. It is not improbable that after long practice virtuous tendencies may be inherited. With the more civilised races, the conviction of the existence of an all-seeing Deity has had a potent influence on the advance of morality. Ultimately man does not accept the praise or blame of his fellows as his sole guide, though few escape this influence, but his habitual convictions, controlled by reason, afford him the safest rule. His conscience then becomes the supreme judge and monitor. Nevertheless, the first foundation or origin of the moral sense lies in the social instincts, including sympathy; and these instincts no doubt were primarily gained, as in the case of the lower animals, through natural selection.

The belief in God has often been advanced as not only the greatest, but the most complete of all the distinctions between man and the lower animals. It is however impossible, as we have seen, to maintain that this belief is innate or instinctive in man. On the other hand a belief in all-pervading spiritual agencies seems to be universal; and apparently follows from a considerable advance in man's reason, and from a still greater advance in his faculties of imagination, curiosity and wonder. I am aware that the assumed instinctive belief in God has been used by many persons as an argument for His existence. But this is a rash argument, as we should thus be compelled to believe in the existence of many cruel and malignant spirits, only a little more powerful than man; for the belief in them is far more general than in a beneficent Deity. The idea of a universal and beneficent Creator does not seem to arise in the mind of man, until he has been elevated by long-continued culture.

He who believes in the advancement of man from some low organised form, will naturally ask how does this bear on the belief in the immortality of the soul. The barbarous races of man, as Sir J. Lubbock has shewn, possess no clear belief of this thing; but arguments derived from the primeval beliefs of savages are, as we have just seen, of little or no avail. Few persons feel any anxiety from the impossibility of determining at what precise period in the development of the individual, from the first trace of a minute germinal vesicle, man becomes an immortal being; and there is no greater cause for anxiety because the period cannot possibly be determined in the gradually ascending organic scale.

I am aware that the conclusions arrived at in this work will be denounced by some as highly irreligious; but he who denounces them is bound to shew why it is more irreligious to explain the origin of man as a distinct species by descent from some lower form, through the laws of variation and natural selection, than to explain the birth of the individual through the laws of ordinary reproduction. The birth both of the species and of the individual are equally parts of that grand sequence of events, which our minds refuse to accept as the result of blind chance. The understanding revolts at such a conclusion, whether or not we are able to believe that every slight variation of structure,—the union of each pair in marriage,—the dissemination of each seed,—and other such events, have all been ordained for some special purpose.

. . .

The main conclusion arrived at in this work, namely, that man is descended from some lowly organised form, will, I regret to think, be highly distasteful to many. But there can hardly be a doubt that we are descended from barbarians. The astonishment which I felt on first seeing a party of Fuegians on a wild and broken shore will never be forgotten by me, for the reflection at once rushed into my mind—such were our ancestors. These men were absolutely naked and bedaubed with paint, their long hair was tangled, their mouths, frothed with excitement, and their expression was wild, startled, and distrustful. They possessed hardly any arts, and like wild animals lived on what they could catch; they had no government and were merciless to everyone not of their own tribe. He who has seen a savage in his native land will not feel much shame, if forced to acknowledge that the blood of some more humble creature flows in his veins. For my own part I would as soon be descended from that heroic little monkey, who braved his dreaded enemy in order to save the life of his keeper, or from that old baboon, who descended from the mountains, carried away in triumph his young comrade from a crowd of astonished dogs—as from a savage who delights to torture his enemies, offers up bloody sacrifices, practises infanticide without remorse, treats his wives like slaves, knows no decency, and is haunted by the grossest superstitions.

Man may be excused for feeling some pride at having risen, though not through his own exertions, to the very summit of the organic scale; and the fact of his having thus risen, instead of having been aboriginally placed there, may give him hope for a still higher destiny in the distant future. But we are not here concerned with hopes or fears, only with the truth as far as our reason permits us to discover it; and I have given the evidence to the best of my ability. We must, however, acknowledge, as it seems to me, that man with all his noble qualities, with sympathy which feels for the most debased, with benevolence which extends not only to other men but to the humblest living creature, with his god-like intellect which has penetrated into the movements and constitution of the solar system—with all these exalted powers—Man still bears in his bodily frame the indelible stamp of his lowly origin.

STUDY QUESTIONS

1. What impact did natural selection have on the social development of early humans?
2. Does Darwin conclude that the "moral faculties" resulted from natural processes and not from direct revelation by "the Deity"?
3. How does Darwin find dignity in humans' descent from the higher mammals, even if the thought is initially "distasteful"?

22.6 JORIS-KARL HUYSMANS, *AGAINST THE GRAIN (À REBOURS)*, 1884

Joris-Karl Huysmans (1848–1907) was a French novelist and art critic and one of the early supporters of Impressionism. While he supported himself financially as a member of France's civil service, living in Paris, he was able to retire in 1898 on the back of the success of his novel

---

From Joris-Karl Huysmans, *Against Nature*. Translated by Margaret Mauldon. New York: Oxford University Press, 2010, pp. 93, 95, 96, 97, 98, 101–2.

La Cathedral. As a novelist, Huysmans had a close association with Emile Zola and the "naturalists," but later gravitated toward the "decadent" school of French literature, as illustrated by his novel *Against the Grain*, also translated as *Against Nature*. Huysmans's discontent with modern life led him to search for a spiritual solution, culminating with his conversion to Catholicism. *Against the Grain* became his best-known work, its depiction of homosexuality making it a favorite of gay literature but infamous in more conservative society. Both its style and its themes had an influence on the Irish writer Oscar Wilde, and it was used as an exhibit in that writer's trial. In this excerpt the protagonist, Des Esseintes, goes on an olfactory odyssey, mixing and experimenting with different aromas in a private perfumery.

There was one aspect of this art of perfumery which, more than any other, had always fascinated him: that of absolute accuracy in imitation.

Actually, perfumes are almost never produced from the flower whose names they bear; the artist rash enough to borrow his raw material from nature alone would produce nothing but a spurious creation, without authenticity or style, since the essence obtained by distilling the flowers can furnish only a very remote, very coarse analogy with authentic fragrance given off by the living flower growing in the ground.

Therefore, except for the inimitable jasmine, which does not admit of any counterfeit, any copy, any approximation even, all flowers are represented exactly by blends of alcohols and spirits, which usurp the very personality of the model, endowing it with that elusive something, that extra quality, that heady bouquet, that rare touch which is the stamp of a work of art.

In perfumery, in short, the artist perfects the original natural aroma by refashioning the scent and providing it with a setting, just as a jeweler improves a stone's transparency and lustre, and provides it with a mount to reveal its beauty.

. . .

Des Esseintes studied and analysed the soul of these fluids and elucidated these texts; he enjoyed and found personal satisfaction in playing the role of a psychologist, taking apart and reassembling the mechanism of a work, unscrewing the pieces that formed the structure of a composite aroma, and in so doing he had developed an almost infallibly accurate sense of smell.

. . .

He worked with amber, Tonquin musk with its terrifying potency, and patchouli, the bitterest of the vegetable perfumes whose flower, in its natural state, gives off a mouldy, mildewy odour. No matter what he did, haunting visions of the eighteenth century obsessed him; panniered and flounced skirts whirled before his eye; remembered visions of Boucher's Venuses, all plump, boneless flesh, padded with rosy cotton-wool, installed themselves on his walls; recollections of the novel *Thémidore* with the exquisite Rosette, her skirts pulled high, fiery-red with blushing despair, pursued him. Furious, he rose to his feet, and to free himself breathed in, with all his might, that pure essence of spikenard which Orientals prize so highly and Europeans find so disagreeable because of its rather too-pronounced smell of valerian. The violence of this shock left him dazed. As if pounded by a hammer, the delicate filigree of the fragrance disappeared; he took advantage of the respite to escape from vanished centuries and outdated aromas and embark, just as he had been accustomed to do in earlier days, on less limited or more novel enterprises.

. . .

With his vaporizers, he injected into the room an essence composed of ambrosia, Mitcham lavender, sweet pea, and a mixed bouquet, an essence which, when distilled by an artist, does deserve the name it has been given—"extract of meadow flowers"; next, he introduced into this meadow a precisely measured blend of tuberose, orange blossom, and almond blossom, whereupon artificial lilacs instantly appeared, while linden trees swayed in the breeze, shedding their pale efflorescence (mimicked by the London extract of tilia) on to the ground.

With this setting roughed out in a few bold strokes, and stretching, beneath his closed eyelids, far into the distance, he sprayed his room with a light mist of human, half-feline essences, redolent of skirts, heralding the appearance of powdered and rouged womankind: stephanotis, ayapana, opopanax, chypre, champaka, sarcanthus, which he overlaid with a trace of syringe, so as to add to the suggestion they exuded of a life of artifice and make-up, a natural fragrance of sweat-drenched laughter and joyful sunlit revelries.

Finally, when he had sufficiently savoured this spectacle, he quickly scattered some exotic perfumes about, used up what remained in his vaporizers, intensified his concentrated essences, and gave free reign to all his balms, so that a demented, sublimated nature exploded into the intolerably hot and stuffy room, a nature whose ever more powerful exhalations loaded the artificial breeze with frenetic alcoholates, a fraudulent, charming nature, utterly paradoxical, combining the spices of the tropics and the peppery whiffs of Chinese sandalwood and Jamaican hediosmia with the French fragrances of jasmine, hawthorn, and verbena and producing, in defiance of seasons and of climates, trees with different aromas and flowers of totally contrasting colours and fragrances, creating by the fusion and the opposition of all these tones, a collective perfume, nameless, unexpected, and strange, in which there reappeared, like a persistent refrain, the ornamental opening phrase, the scent of the great meadow fanned by the lilacs and the lime trees.

Suddenly he felt a sharp stabbing pain, as though a drill were boring into his temples.

. . .

He pushed the window wide open, glad of the cleansing gusts of fresh air; but, suddenly, it seemed to him that the breeze was wafting in a rising wave of oil of bergamot, blended with essence of jasmine, cassia, and rose-water. He gave a gasp, wondering whether he might not be in the power of one of those evil spirits which, in the Middle Ages, people had exorcised. The odour changed, transforming itself, but persisting. An indeterminate aroma of tincture of tolu, of Peruvian balsam, of saffron, bound by a few drops of amber and of musk, was rising, now, from the village which lay at the bottom of the hill, and then suddenly the metamorphosis took place, those disparate traces blended together and once again frangipani, the elements of which his sense of smell had discerned and analysed, spread from the valley of Fontenay up to the fort, assaulting his overtaxed nostrils, discomposing afresh his ruined nerves, and throwing him into such a state of prostration that he collapsed in a faint, close to death, on to the wooden sill of the window.

STUDY QUESTIONS

1. How does Huysmans link scents and sexuality?
2. How is smell related to other artistic and sensual experiences?

22.7 OSCAR WILDE, "THE SOUL OF MAN UNDER SOCIALISM," 1891

Oscar Wilde (1854–1900), Irish writer and famous wit, became one of London's most popular playwrights in the 1890s. Trained as a classicist in Dublin and then at Oxford, Wilde became a journalist in London and made a name for himself as a flamboyant proponent of the new

From Oscar Wilde, "The Soul of Man under Socialism." New York: Humboldt, 1891.

philosophy of aestheticism. After several popular stage plays, he wrote his most famous work, *The Importance of Being Ernest*, in 1895. The same year, Wilde was put on trial for homosexuality, a crime in England at that time, and imprisoned for two years. On his release, Wilde immigrated to Paris, where he died in 1900 at the age of forty-six. In *The Soul of Man*, Wilde explores the manner in which socialism, by allowing people to realize greater individualism, will provide the best context for art—Wilde's ultimate goal.

The chief advantage that would result from the establishment of Socialism is, undoubtedly, the fact that Socialism would relieve us from that sordid necessity of living for others which, in the present condition of things, presses so hardly on almost everybody. In fact, scarcely any one at all escapes.

Now and then, in the course of the century, a great man of science, like Darwin; a great poet, like Keats; a fine critical spirit, like M. Renan; a supreme artist, like Flaubert, has been able to isolate himself, to keep himself out of reach of the clamorous claims of others, to stand "under the shelter of the wall," as Plato puts it, and so to realise the perfection of what was in him, to his own incomparable gain, and to the incomparable and lasting gain of the whole world. These, however, are exceptions. The majority of people spoil their lives by an unhealthy and exaggerated altruism—are forced, indeed, so to spoil them. They find themselves surrounded by hideous poverty, by hideous ugliness, by hideous starvation. It is inevitable that they should be strongly moved by all this. The emotions of man are stirred more quickly than man's intelligence; and, as I pointed out some time ago in an article on the function of criticism, it is much more easy to have sympathy with suffering than it is to have sympathy with thought. Accordingly, with admirable, though misdirected intentions, they very seriously and very sentimentally set themselves to the task of remedying the evils that they see. But their remedies do not cure the disease: they merely prolong it. Indeed, their remedies are part of the disease.

They try to solve the problem of poverty, for instance, by keeping the poor alive; or, in the case of a very advanced school, by amusing the poor.

But this is not a solution: it is an aggravation of the difficulty. *The proper aim is to try and reconstruct society on such a basis that poverty will be impossible.* And the altruistic virtues have really prevented the carrying out of this aim. Just as the worst slave-owners were those who were kind to their slaves, and so prevented the horror of the system being realised by those who suffered from it, and understood by those who contemplated it, so, in the present state of things in England, the people who do most harm are the people who try to do most good; and at last we have had the spectacle of men who have really studied the problem and know the life—educated men who live in the East End—coming forward and imploring the community to restrain its altruistic impulses of charity, benevolence, and the like. They do so on the ground that such charity degrades and demoralises. They are perfectly right. Charity creates a multitude of sins.

There is also this to be said. It is immoral to use private property in order to alleviate the horrible evils that result from the institution of private property. It is both immoral and unfair.

Under Socialism all this will, of course, be altered. There will be no people living in fetid dens and fetid rags, and bringing up unhealthy, hunger-pinched children in the midst of impossible and absolutely repulsive surroundings. The security of society will not depend, as it does now, on the state of the weather. If a frost comes we shall not have a hundred thousand men out of work, tramping about the streets in a state of disgusting misery, or whining to their neighbours for alms, or crowded round the doors of loathsome shelters to try and secure a hunch of bread and a night's unclean lodging. Each member of the society will share in the general prosperity and happiness of the society, and if a frost comes no one will practically be anything the worse.

Upon the other hand, *Socialism itself will be* of value simply because it will lead to Individualism.

Socialism, Communism, or whatever one chooses to call it, by converting private property into public wealth, and substituting co-operation for competition, will restore society to its proper condition of a thoroughly healthy organism, and insure the material well-being of each member of the community. It will, in fact, give Life its proper basis and its proper environment. But for the full development of Life to its highest mode of perfection, something more is needed. What is needed is Individualism. If the Socialism is Authoritarian; if there are Governments armed with economic power as they are now with political power; if, in a word, we are to have Industrial Tyrannies, then the last state of man will be worse than the first. At present, in consequence of the existence of private property, a great many people are enabled to develop a certain very limited amount of Individualism. They are either under no necessity to work for the living, or are enabled to choose the sphere of activity that is really congenial to them, and gives them pleasure. These are the poets, the philosophers, the men of science, the men of culture—in a word, the real men, the men who have realised themselves, and in whom all Humanity gains a partial realisation. Upon the other hand, there are a great many people who, having no private property of their own, and being always on the brink of sheer starvation, are compelled to do the work of beasts of burden, to do work that is quite uncongenial to them, and to which they are forced by the peremptory, unreasonable, degrading Tyranny of want. These are the poor, and amongst them there is no grace of manner, or charm of speech, or civilisation, or culture, or refinement in pleasure, or joy of life. From their collective force Humanity gains much in material prosperity. But it is only the material result that it gains, and the man who is poor is in himself absolutely of no importance. He is merely the infinitesimal atom of a force that, so far from regarding him, crushes him: indeed, prefers him crushed, as in that case he is far more obedient.

. . .

Private property has crushed true Individualism, and set up an Individualism that is false. It has debarred one part of the community from being individual by starving them. It has debarred the other part of the community from being individual by putting them on the wrong road, and encumbering them. Indeed, so completely has man's personality been absorbed by his possessions that the English law has always treated offences against a man's property with far more severity than offences against his person, and property is still the test of complete citizenship. The industry necessary for the making of money is also very demoralising. In a community like ours, where property confers immense distinction, social position, honour, respect, titles, and other pleasant things of the kind, man, being naturally ambitious, makes it his aim to accumulate this property, and goes on wearily and tediously accumulating it long after he has got far more than he wants, or can use, or enjoy, or perhaps even know of. Man will kill himself by overwork in order to secure property, and really, considering the enormous advantages that property brings, one is hardly surprised. One's regret is that society should be constructed on such a basis that man has been forced into a groove in which he cannot freely develop what is wonderful, and fascinating, and delightful in him—in which, in fact, he misses the true pleasure and joy of living. He is also, under existing conditions, very insecure. An enormously wealthy merchant may be—often is—at every moment of his life at the mercy of things that are not under his control. If the wind blows an extra point or so, or the weather suddenly changes, or some trivial thing happens, his ship may go down, his speculations may go wrong, and he finds himself a poor man, with his social position quite gone. Now, nothing should be able to harm a man except himself. Nothing should be able to rob a man at all. What a man really has, is what is in him. What is outside of him should be a matter of no importance.

With the abolition of private property, then, we shall have true, beautiful, healthy Individualism.

Nobody will waste his life in accumulating things, and the symbols for things. One will live. To live is the rarest thing in the world. Most people exist, that is all.

...

Now as the State is not to govern, it may be asked what the State is to do. The State is to be a voluntary association that will organise labour, and be the manufacturer and distributor of necessary commodities. *The State is to make what is useful. The individual is to make what is beautiful.* And as I have mentioned the word labour, I cannot help saying that a great deal of nonsense is being written and talked nowadays about the dignity of manual labour. There is nothing necessarily dignified about manual labour at all, and most of it is absolutely degrading. It is mentally and morally injurious to man to do anything in which he does not find pleasure, and many forms of labour are quite pleasureless activities, and should be regarded as such. To sweep a slushy crossing for eight hours, on a day when the east wind is blowing is a disgusting occupation. To sweep it with mental, moral, or physical dignity seems to me to be impossible. To sweep it with joy would be appalling. Man is made for something better than disturbing dirt. All work of that kind should be done by a machine.

And I have no doubt that it will be so. Up to the present, man has been, to a certain extent, the slave of machinery, and there is something tragic in the fact that as soon as man had invented a machine to do his work he began to starve. This, however, is, of course, the result of our property system and our system of competition. One man owns a machine which does the work of five hundred men. Five hundred men are, in consequence, thrown out of employment, and, having no work to do, become hungry and take to thieving. The one man secures the produce of the machine and keeps it, and has five hundred times as much as he should have, and probably, which is of much more importance, a great deal more than he really wants. Were that machine the property of all, everyone would benefit by it. It would be an immense advantage to the community. All unintellectual labour, all monotonous, dull labour, all labour that deals with dreadful things, and involves unpleasant conditions, must be done by machinery. Machinery must work for us in coal mines, and do all sanitary service, and be the stoker of steamers, and clean the streets, and run messages on wet days, and do anything that is tedious or distressing. *At present machinery competes against man. Under proper conditions machinery will serve man.* There is no doubt at all that this is the future of machinery, and just as trees grow while the country gentleman is asleep, so while Humanity will be amusing itself, or enjoying cultivated leisure—which, and not labour, is the aim of man—or making beautiful things, or reading beautiful things, or simply contemplating the world with admiration and delight, machinery will be doing all the necessary and unpleasant work. The fact is, that civilisation requires slaves. The Greeks were quite right there. Unless there are slaves to do the ugly, horrible, uninteresting work, culture and contemplation become almost impossible. Human slavery is wrong, insecure, and demoralizing. On mechanical slavery, on the slavery of the machine, the future of the world depends.

...

There are three kinds of despots. There is the despot who tyrannises over the body. There is the despot who tyrannises over the soul. There is the depot who tyrannises over the soul and body alike. The first is called the Prince. The second is called the Pope. The third is called the People. The Prince may be cultivated. Many Princes have been. Yet in the Prince there is danger. One thinks of Dante at the bitter feast in Verona, of Tasso in Ferrara's madman's cell. It is better for the artist not to live with Princes. The Pope may be cultivated. Many Popes have been; the bad Popes have been. The bad Popes loved Beauty, almost as passionately, nay, with as much passion as the good Popes hated Thought. To the wickedness of the Papacy humanity owes much. The goodness of the Papacy owes a terrible debt to humanity. Yet, though the Vatican has kept the rhetoric of its thunders, and lost the rod of its lightning, it is better for the artist not to live with Popes. It was a Pope who said of Cellini to a conclave of Cardinals that common laws and common authority were not made for men such as he; but it was a Pope who thrust Cellini into prison, and kept him there till he sickened with rage, and created unreal visions for himself, and saw the gilded sun enter his room, and grew so enamoured of it he sought to escape, and crept out from tower to tower, and falling through dizzy air at dawn, maimed himself, and was by a vine-dresser covered with vine leaves, and carried in a cart to one who, loving beautiful things, had care of him. There is danger in Popes. And as for the People, what of them and their authority? Perhaps of them and their authority one has spoken enough. Their authority is a thing blind, deaf, hideous, grotesque, tragic, amusing, serious, and obscene. It is impossible for the artist to live with the People. All despots bribe. The people bribe and brutalise. Who told them to exercise authority? They were made to live, to listen, and to love. Someone has done them a great wrong. They have marred themselves by imitation of their inferiors. They have taken the scepter of the Prince. How should they use it? They have taken the triple tiara of the Pope. How should they carry its burden? They are as a clown whose heart is broken. They are as a priest whose soul is not yet born. Let all who love Beauty pity them. Though they themselves love not Beauty, yet let them pity themselves. Who taught them the trick of tyranny?

There are many other things that one might point out. One might point out how the Renaissance was great, because it sought to solve no social problem, and busied itself not about such things, but suffered the individual to develop freely, beautifully, and naturally, and so had great and individual artists, and great and individual men. One might point out how Louis XIV., by creating the modern state, destroyed the individualism of the artist, and made things monstrous in their monotony of repetition, and contemptible in their conformity to rule, and destroyed throughout all France all those fine freedoms of expression that had made tradition new in beauty, and new modes one with antique form. But the past is of no importance. The present is of no importance. It is with the future that we have to deal. For the past is what man should not have been. The present is what man ought not to be. The future is what artists are.

It will, of course, be said that such a scheme as is set forth here is quite unpractical, and goes against human nature. This is perfectly true. It is unpractical, and it goes against human nature. This is why it is worth carrying out, and that is why one proposes it. For what is a practical scheme? *A practical scheme is either a scheme that is already in existence, or a scheme that could be carried out under existing conditions.* But it is exactly the existing conditions that one objects to; and any scheme that could accept these conditions is wrong and foolish. The conditions will be done away with, and human nature will change. The only thing that one really knows about human nature is that it changes. Change is the one quality we can predicate of it. The systems that fail are those that rely on the permanency of human nature, and not on its growth and development. The error of Louis XIV. was that he thought human nature would always be the same. The result of his error was the French Revolution. It was an admirable result. All the results of the mistakes of governments are quite admirable.

STUDY QUESTIONS

1. Is Wilde deliberately writing in a serious or a sarcastic way, especially about the various "do-gooders" who espouse socialism?
2. How do aesthetics and notions of beauty shape his reactions to socialist plans?

22.8 WASSILY KANDINSKY, *ON THE SPIRITUAL ELEMENT IN ART*, 1912

Wassily Kandinsky (1866–1944) is often credited with producing the first wholly abstract works of painting. He was born in Moscow and, after attending university in Odessa, he spent most of his adult life in Germany and France. He gave up a promising career as an economist to go to art school and taught at Germany's Bauhaus School of Art from 1922 until its closure by the Nazis in 1933, whence he moved to France. Some of his paintings were exhibited by the Nazi regime, along with works by Paul Klee and Franz Marc, as examples of "degenerate art," before being destroyed. Kandinsky's writings theorized on the nature of art, exploring, among other things, the relationship of sound and color and the innate properties of geometric designs. His *Concerning the Spiritual Element in Art* is a meditation on how art can elevate the soul, especially in an era of spiritual malaise. Like Nietzsche, Kandinsky suggested that art had taken the place of religion; the only transcendence available to us, he claimed, is that experienced through aesthetic bliss.

Imagine a building, either large or small, divided into a number of rooms, each of which is filled with paintings of various sizes. Thousands of paintings, perhaps. They represent aspects of Nature, seen in full array of colors. A group of animals in sunlight or in shadow, either drinking water or standing in it, or perhaps lying on some grass. Nearby is a painting of a Crucifixion by an artist who does not believe in Christ. Then paintings of flowers, or of human beings, sitting, standing, walking, often naked. Numerous paintings, foreshortened from behind, of naked women. Apples and silverware. A formal portrait of Sir So-and-So. Sunsets. A woman in pink. A duck in flight. A portrait of Lady X. Flying geese. A woman in white. A scene of cattle in dappled sunshine, bright light and shade. A portrait of Ambassador This-and-That. A woman dressed in green. Every image is carefully reproduced in a book that lists each picture's title and the artist who painted it. People go through the rooms, from wall to wall, turning the pages of the book they hold, and reading names and title. Then they all leave, neither richer nor poorer, and resume their normal affairs, none of which have anything to do with art. Why did they come?

Every painting captures, mysteriously, the whole of a life—a life of agonies, doubts, moments of enthusiasm and inspiration. What is the direction of that life? What is the cry of the artist's soul—assuming that the soul was involved in the painting's creation? "To send light into the darkness of men's hearts is every artist's duty," wrote Schumann. "A [true] painter," wrote Tolstoy, "[is one] who draws and paints everything."

Considering the exhibition just described, we opt for the second of these judgments. Objects are recreated on canvas with varying degrees of skill, virtuosity, and energy; they are painted perhaps roughly, perhaps smoothly. To present the whole object harmoniously on the canvas is what makes a painting a work of art. Connoisseurs may admire a painter's technique (as one might admire the skills of a tightrope walker) or enjoy the quality of the painting (as one might enjoy a pastry), but those with hungry souls may still walk away [from a particular work] no less hungry.

Viewers of art must be educated to appreciate the point of view of the true artist. "Art is the product

From Wassily Kandinsky, *On the Spiritual Element in Art*. 1912. Translation by Clifford Backman.

of its time," goes the saying; but this type of art merely repeats and reproduces what is already popular among the contemporary audience. Not being germinative, it can only be the product of its time, not the fertile source of the future. It is castrated art, ephemeral, and morally dead the moment present conditions change.

There is another type of art, however, one capable of future growth even as it arises from the sensations of the moment. It echoes and reflects the present but possesses a prophetic force that has the potential for profound and pervasive change in the future.

The spiritual life to which this type of art belongs (and in which it is one of the most powerful elements) is a highly complex but distinct movement above and beyond the immediate present. At the same time, it can be simply translated. The movement is one of cognition, and while it may take a variety of forms it remains true to its essential identity and purpose.

. . .

Whenever the foundations of religion, science, and morality are shaken (the last one by the strong hand of Nietzsche), and when other foundations appear threatened, most men shift their attention away from external matters and direct their gaze inward upon themselves. Literature, music, and art are the most responsive areas in which this sort of spiritual revolution first appears, for they both reflect the darkness of the present moment and point to the significance of what was at first a mere speck of light noticed only by a few and unseen by the overwhelming majority of people. These arts may even grow dark in their turn for a while, but they turn away from the soulless-ness of the present and towards those activities and ideas that liberate the non-materialistic strivings of the soul.

One such artist, in the realm of literature, is Maeterlinck, who leads us into a world that some (justly or not) call fantastic or transcendent.[1] "La Princesse Maleine," "Les Sept Princesses," or "Les Aveugles" are not figures from the past as are, for example, the heroes in Shakespeare. Rather, they are spirits lost in a fog that threatens to choke them to death, eternally menaced by a somber force invisible to them. A spiritual darkness pervades the world through which they move, a darkness comprised of the insecurity produced by ignorance and fear. Maeterlinck may be the first of the artist-prophets, one of the first visionaries to foresee this type of cultural decadence. Spiritual gloom, the sense of a terrible hand pushing the world forward, the all-pervading fear, the feeling of being lost and without a sure guide—all these are clearly evident in his works.

. . .

In the works of another great artist, the Spaniard Pablo Picasso who now lives in Paris, there is no trace at all of conventional beauty. Constantly on the search for a new means of self-expression, he rushes from one innovation to another, often leaving so great a gulf between his different styles that his bewildered admirers are always finding him in a different place, artistically, from where they last saw him, and no sooner do they think they have him "placed" than he once more transforms himself. This is how Cubism came into being. . . . In his most recent works, Picasso has achieved nothing less than the annihilation of matter, not by dissolving it to nothingness but by a kind of parceling out of its perspectives and scattering them about the canvas. His latest work maintains an appearance of solidity, as though of a desire for it. But no innovation is too much for him. If the use of color stands in the way of his quest for pure artistic form, he simply throws it overboard and paints in brown and white. The problem of pure artistic form is the central problem of his life's work.

. . .

Each of the arts is at a different stage of development, each expressing what it can in the language that is peculiarly its own. But in spite of the differences between them—and perhaps because of them—there has never been a time when the arts come towards greater communion than they do today, as expressions of our spiritual development. Each carries the seed for a striving after the abstract and immaterial, such that, whether they realize it or not, modern

[1] Maurice Maeterlinck (1862–1949) was a Belgian-born poet and playwright, a leader in the Symbolist movement. His best-known work is the drama *Pelleas and Melisande* (1892), which tells of the doomed love affair between a princess and her brother-in-law. He won the Nobel Prize for Literature in 1911.

artists are obeying Socrates' dictum: "Know thyself." Consciously or unconsciously today's artists are examining their disciplines, testing them, weighing their spiritual value. The natural result of this, is that modern arts are drawing towards each other. Music is their best teacher. For several centuries now, with a few exceptions, music has been the art form most consistently dedicated not to reproducing the phenomena of nature but rather to express the artist's soul in sound.

Painters who no longer find satisfaction in mere representation (no matter how skilled it may be) and who yearn to express their spiritual life, can only envy the ease with which music—the most immaterial of arts—achieves this. A painter, of course, can try to apply to his art the techniques of modern music. The result of this is the search for rhythm in modern painting, for mathematical and abstract form, patterns of color, or color set in motion. But the sharing of techniques between artistic disciplines can only work when the effort is fundamental instead of superficial. The artist must first learn how a particular technique was used within the other discipline, so that a suitable sort of innovation can be imported into his own medium. Every artist must remember that he alone has the power to make a true application of each new method—but the method must be developed. . . . This is how the arts of today are approaching one another, and the proper encounter of them will result in art that is truly magnificent. Every artist who investigates the spiritual possibilities of his medium contributes vitally to the development of the spiritual triangle that will one day reach Heaven.

STUDY QUESTIONS

1. What is it the artist's duty to capture in a painting?
2. How and why did Picasso adapt his style so quickly and launch innovative changes in his art?

22.9 SIGMUND FREUD, *CIVILIZATION AND ITS DISCONTENTS*, 1929

Sigmund Freud (1856–1939), who trained as a neurologist and general psychologist, pioneered psychoanalysis, the technique of encouraging free association. From his practice he developed the theory of repression, the idea that certain thoughts were held back from both oral expression and the patient's conscious mind. His work also developed the notion of the unconscious, which he suggested was behind much of our thoughts and actions. In *Civilization and Its Discontents*, Freud argued that to be civilized is to be unhappy, because it was civilization itself that forced us to repress our natural instincts—those most notably of aggression and sexuality. In this excerpt he discusses how aggression is a primal instinct and looks at how this instinct, along with the instinct for sex, is controlled and repressed in "civilized" society, to the detriment of ultimate human happiness.

The existence of this inclination to aggression, which we can detect in ourselves and justly assume to be present in others, is the factor which disturbs our relations with our neighbor and which forces civilization into such a high expenditure [of energy]. In consequence of this primary mutual hostility of human beings, civilized society is perpetually threatened with disintegration. The interest of work in common would not hold it together; instinctual passions are stronger than reasonable interests. Civilization has to use its utmost efforts in order to set limits to man's aggressive instincts and to hold the manifestations of them in check by psychical reaction-formations. Hence, therefore, the use of methods intended to incite people into identifications and aim-inhibited relations of love, hence the restriction upon sexual life, and hence too the ideal's commandment to love one's neighbor as oneself—a commandment which is really justified by the fact that nothing else runs so strongly counter to the original nature of man. In spite of every effort, these endeavors of civilization have not so far achieved very much. It hopes to prevent the crudest excesses of brutal violence by itself assuming the right to use violence against criminals, but the law is not able to lay hold of the more cautious and refined manifestations of human aggressiveness. The time comes when each one of us has to give up as illusions the expectations which, in his youth, he pinned upon his fellow men, and when he may learn how much difficulty and pain has been added to his life by their ill-will. At the same time, it would be unfair to reproach civilization with trying to eliminate strife and competition from human activity. These things are undoubtedly indispensable. But opposition is not necessarily enmity; it is merely misused and made *occasion* for enmity.

The communists believe they have found the path to deliverance from our evils. According to them, man is wholly good and as well-disposed to his neighbor; but the institution of private property has corrupted his nature. The ownership of private wealth gives the individual power, and with it the temptation to ill-treat his neighbor; while the man who is excluded from possession is bound to rebel in hostility against his oppressor. If private property were abolished, all wealth held in common, and everyone allowed to share in the enjoyment of it, ill-will and hostility would disappear among men. Since everyone's needs would be satisfied, no one would have any reason to regard another as his enemy; all would willingly undertake the work that was necessary. I have no concern with any economic criticisms of the communist system; I cannot inquire into whether the abolition of private property is expedient or advantageous. But I am able to recognize that the psychological premises on which the system is based are an untenable illusion. In abolishing private property we deprive the human love of aggression of one of its instruments, certainly a strong one, though certainly not the strongest; but we have in no way altered the differences in power and influence which are misused by aggressiveness, nor have we altered anything in its nature. Aggressiveness was not created by property. It reigned almost before property had given up its primal, anal form; it forms the basis of every relation of affection and love among people (with the single exception, perhaps, of the mother's relation to her male child). If we do away with personal rights over material wealth, there still remains prerogative in the field of sexual relationships, which is bound to become the source of the strongest dislike and the most violent hostility among men who in other respects are on an equal footing. If we were to remove this factor, too, by allowing complete freedom of sexual life and thus abolishing the family, the germ-cell of civilization, we cannot, it is true, easily foresee what new paths the development of civilization could take; but one thing we can expect, and that is that this indestructible feature of human nature will follow it there.

It is clearly not easy for man to give up the satisfaction of this inclination to aggression. They do not feel comfortable without it. The advantage which a comparatively small cultural group offers of allowing this instinct an outlet in the form of hostility against intruders is not to be despised. It is always possible to bind together a considerable number of people in love, so long as there are other people left over to receive the manifestations of their aggressiveness. I once discussed the phenomenon that it is precisely communities with adjoining territories, and related to each other in other ways as well, who are engaged in constant feuds and in ridiculing each other—like the Spaniards and Portuguese, for instance, the North Germans and South Germans, the English and Scotch, and so on. I gave this phenomenon the name of "the narcissism of minor differences," a name which does not do much to explain it. We can now see that it is a convenient and relatively harmless satisfaction of the inclination to aggression, by means of which cohesion between the members of the community is made easier. In this respect the Jewish people, scattered everywhere, have rendered most useful services to the civilizations of the countries that have been their hosts; but unfortunately all the massacres of the Jews in the Middle Ages did not suffice to make that period more peaceful and secure for their Christian fellows. When once the Apostle Paul had posited universal love between men as the foundation of his Christian community, extreme intolerance, part of Christendom towards those who remained outside it became the inevitable consequence. To the Romans, who had not founded their communal life as a State upon love, religious intolerance was something foreign, although with them religion was a concern of the State and the State was permeated by religion. Neither was it an unaccountable chance that the dream of a Germanic world-dominion called for anti-Semitism as its complement; and it is intelligible that the attempts to establish a new, communist civilization in Russia should find its psychological support in the persecution of the bourgeois. One only wonders, with concern, what the Soviets will do after they have wiped out their bourgeois.

If Civilization imposes such great sacrifices not only on man's sexuality but on his aggressivity, we can understand better why it is hard for him to be happy in that civilization. In fact, primitive man was better off in knowing no restrictions of instinct. To counterbalance this, his prospects of enjoying this happiness for any length of time were very slender. Civilized man has exchanged a portion of his possibilities of happiness for a portion of security. We must not forget, however, that in the primal family only the head of it enjoyed this instinctual freedom; the rest lived in slavish suppression. In that primal period of civilization, the contrast between a minority who enjoyed the advantages of civilization and a majority who were robbed of those advantages was, therefore, carried to extremes. As regards the primitive peoples who exist to-day, careful researches have shown that their instinctual life is by no means to be envied for its freedom. It is subject to restrictions of a different kind but perhaps of greater severity than those attaching to modern civilized man.

When we justly find fault with the present state of our civilization for so inadequately fulfilling our demands for a plan of life that shall make us happy, and for allowing the existence of so much suffering which could probably be avoided—when, with unsparing criticism, we try to uncover the roots of its imperfection, we are undoubtedly exercising a proper right and are not showing ourselves enemies of civilization. We may expect gradually to carry through such alterations in our civilization as will better satisfy our needs and will escape our criticisms. But perhaps we may also familiarize ourselves with the idea that there are difficulties attaching to the nature of civilization which will not yield to any attempt at reform. Over and above the tasks of restricting the instincts, which we are prepared for, there forces itself on our notice the danger of a state of things which might be termed "the psychological poverty of groups." This danger is most threatening where the bonds of a society are chiefly constituted by the identification of its members with one another, while individuals of the leader type do not acquire the importance that should fall to them in the formation of a group. The present cultural state of America would give us a good opportunity for studying the damage to civilization which is thus to be feared. But I shall avoid the temptation of entering upon a critique of American civilization; I do not wish to give an impression of wanting myself to employ American methods.

STUDY QUESTIONS

1. Is aggression a natural instinct, and is it necessarily a devastating one?
2. How can aggression be channeled into positive paths, and why does this rarely happen?

22.10 POPE PIUS IX, *THE SYLLABUS OF ERRORS*, 1864

Pius IX (1792–1878) served as pope from 1846 to 1878—an exceptionally challenging time. The Industrial Revolution was changing forever the economic and social structures of the Western world; the campaign to unify the nation of Italy threatened the political freedom of the Papal State that had existed since the eighth century; and the rise of liberalism and intellectual secularism seemed to undercut not only the authority of the Church as an institution but the teachings it upheld. The following *Syllabus of Errors* was appended to a papal encyclical called *Quanta cura*, in which he lamented the rise of secularism and what he termed "religious indifferentism"—the notion that one can freely and legitimately select what one likes between religions and among religious teachings. Here he specifies eighty false ideas, grouped into ten categories, for condemnation.

I. PANTHEISM, NATURALISM AND ABSOLUTE RATIONALISM

1. There exists no Supreme, all-wise, all-provident Divine Being, distinct from the universe, and God is identical with the nature of things, and is, therefore, subject to changes. In effect, God is produced in man and in the world, and all things are God and have the very substance of God, and God is one and the same thing with the world, and, therefore, spirit with matter, necessity with liberty, good with evil, justice with injustice.
2. All action of God upon man and the world is to be denied.
3. Human reason, without any reference whatsoever to God, is the sole arbiter of truth and falsehood, and of good and evil; it is law to itself, and suffices, by its natural force, to secure the welfare of men and of nations.
4. All the truths of religion proceed from the innate strength of human reason; hence reason is the ultimate standard by which man can and ought to arrive at the knowledge of all truths of every kind.
5. Divine revelation is imperfect, and therefore subject to a continual and indefinite progress, corresponding with the advancement of human reason.
6. The faith of Christ is in opposition to human reason and divine revelation not only is not useful, but is even hurtful to the perfection of man.
7. The prophecies and miracles set forth and recorded in the Sacred Scriptures are the fiction of poets, and the mysteries of the Christian faith the result of philosophical investigations. In the books of the Old and the New Testament there are contained mythical inventions, and Jesus Christ is Himself a myth.

II. MODERATE RATIONALISM

8. As human reason is placed on a level with religion itself, so theological must be treated in the same manner as philosophical sciences.
9. All the dogmas of the Christian religion are indiscriminately the object of natural science or philosophy, and human reason, enlightened solely in an

Translated by Clifford Backman.

historical way, is able, by its own natural strength and principles, to attain to the true science of even the most abstruse dogmas; provided only that such dogmas be proposed to reason itself as its object.

10. As the philosopher is one thing, and philosophy another, so it is the right and duty of the philosopher to subject himself to the authority which he shall have proved to be true; but philosophy neither can nor ought to submit to any such authority.
11. The Church not only ought never to pass judgment on philosophy, but ought to tolerate the errors of philosophy, leaving it to correct itself.
12. The decrees of the Apostolic See and of the Roman congregations impede the true progress of science.
13. The method and principles by which the old scholastic doctors cultivated theology are no longer suitable to the demands of our times and to the progress of the sciences.
14. Philosophy is to be treated without taking any account of supernatural revelation.

III. INDIFFERENTISM, LATITUDINARIANISM

15. Every man is free to embrace and profess that religion which, guided by the light of reason, he shall consider true.
16. Man may, in the observance of any religion whatever, find the way of eternal salvation, and arrive at eternal salvation.
17. Good hope at least is to be entertained of the eternal salvation of all those who are not at all in the true Church of Christ.
18. Protestantism is nothing more than another form of the same true Christian religion, in which form it is given to please God equally as in the Catholic Church.

IV. SOCIALISM, COMMUNISM, SECRET SOCIETIES, BIBLICAL SOCIETIES, CLERICO-LIBERAL SOCIETIES

Pests of this kind are frequently reprobated in the severest terms in the Encyclical "Qui pluribus," Nov. 9, 1846, Allocution "Quibus quantisque," April 20, 1849, Encyclical "Noscitis et nobiscum," Dec. 8, 1849, Allocution "Singulari quadam," Dec. 9, 1854, Encyclical "Quanto conficiamur," Aug. 10, 1863.

V. ERRORS CONCERNING THE CHURCH AND HER RIGHTS

19. The Church is not a true and perfect society, entirely free—nor is she endowed with proper and perpetual rights of her own, conferred upon her by her Divine Founder; but it appertains to the civil power to define what are the rights of the Church, and the limits within which she may exercise those rights.
20. The ecclesiastical power ought not to exercise its authority without the permission and assent of the civil government.
21. The Church has not the power of defining dogmatically that the religion of the Catholic Church is the only true religion.
22. The obligation by which Catholic teachers and authors are strictly bound is confined to those things only which are proposed to universal belief as dogmas of faith by the infallible judgment of the Church.
23. Roman pontiffs and ecumenical councils have wandered outside the limits of their powers, have usurped the rights of princes, and have even erred in defining matters of faith and morals.
24. The Church has not the power of using force, nor has she any temporal power, direct or indirect.
25. Besides the power inherent in the episcopate, other temporal power has been attributed to it by the civil authority granted either explicitly or tacitly, which on that account is revocable by the civil authority whenever it thinks fit.
26. The Church has no innate and legitimate right of acquiring and possessing property.
27. The sacred ministers of the Church and the Roman pontiff are to be absolutely excluded from every charge and dominion over temporal affairs.
28. It is not lawful for bishops to publish even letters Apostolic without the permission of Government.
29. Favours granted by the Roman pontiff ought to be considered null, unless they have been sought for through the civil government.

30. The immunity of the Church and of ecclesiastical persons derived its origin from civil law.
31. The ecclesiastical forum or tribunal for the temporal causes, whether civil or criminal, of clerics, ought by all means to be abolished, even without consulting and against the protest of the Holy See.
32. The personal immunity by which clerics are exonerated from military conscription and service in the army may be abolished without violation either of natural right or equity. Its abolition is called for by civil progress, especially in a society framed on the model of a liberal government.
33. It does not appertain exclusively to the power of ecclesiastical jurisdiction by right, proper and innate, to direct the teaching of theological questions.
34. The teaching of those who compare the Sovereign Pontiff to a prince, free and acting in the universal Church, is a doctrine which prevailed in the Middle Ages.
35. There is nothing to prevent the decree of a general council, or the act of all peoples, from transferring the supreme pontificate from the bishop and city of Rome to another bishop and another city.
36. The definition of a national council does not admit of any subsequent discussion, and the civil authority car assume this principle as the basis of its acts.
37. National churches, withdrawn from the authority of the Roman pontiff and altogether separated, can be established.
38. The Roman pontiffs have, by their too arbitrary conduct, contributed to the division of the Church into Eastern and Western.

VI. ERRORS ABOUT CIVIL SOCIETY, CONSIDERED BOTH IN ITSELF AND IN ITS RELATION TO THE CHURCH

39. The State, as being the origin and source of all rights, is endowed with a certain right not circumscribed by any limits.
40. The teaching of the Catholic Church is hostile to the well-being and interests of society.
41. The civil government, even when in the hands of an infidel sovereign, has a right to an indirect negative power over religious affairs. It therefore possesses not only the right called that of "exsequatur," but also that of appeal, called "appellatio ab abusu."
42. In the case of conflicting laws enacted by the two powers, the civil law prevails.
43. The secular Dower has authority to rescind, declare and render null, solemn conventions, commonly called concordats, entered into with the Apostolic See, regarding the use of rights appertaining to ecclesiastical immunity, without the consent of the Apostolic See, and even in spite of its protest.
44. The civil authority may interfere in matters relating to religion, morality and spiritual government: hence, it can pass judgment on the instructions issued for the guidance of consciences, conformably with their mission, by the pastors of the Church. Further, it has the right to make enactments regarding the administration of the divine sacraments, and the dispositions necessary for receiving them.
45. The entire government of public schools in which the youth of a Christian state is educated, except (to a certain extent) in the case of episcopal seminaries, may and ought to appertain to the civil power, and belong to it so far that no other authority whatsoever shall be recognized as having any right to interfere in the discipline of the schools, the arrangement of the studies, the conferring of degrees, in the choice or approval of the teachers.
46. Moreover, even in ecclesiastical seminaries, the method of studies to be adopted is subject to the civil authority.
47. The best theory of civil society requires that popular schools open to children of every class of the people, and, generally, all public institutes intended for instruction in letters and philosophical sciences and for carrying on the education of youth, should be freed from all ecclesiastical authority, control and interference, and should be fully subjected to the civil and political power at the pleasure of the rulers, and according to the standard of the prevalent opinions of the age.
48. Catholics may approve of the system of educating youth unconnected with Catholic faith and

the power of the Church, and which regards the knowledge of merely natural things, and only, or at least primarily, the ends of earthly social life.

49. The civil power may prevent the prelates of the Church and the faithful from communicating freely and mutually with the Roman pontiff.
50. Lay authority possesses of itself the right of presenting bishops, and may require of them to undertake the administration of the diocese before they receive canonical institution, and the Letters Apostolic from the Holy See.
51. And, further, the lay government has the right of deposing bishops from their pastoral functions, and is not bound to obey the Roman pontiff in those things which relate to the institution of bishoprics and the appointment of bishops.
52. Government can, by its own right, alter the age prescribed by the Church for the religious profession of women and men; and may require of all religious orders to admit no person to take solemn vows without its permission.
53. The laws enacted for the protection of religious orders and regarding their rights and duties ought to be abolished; nay, more, civil Government may lend its assistance to all who desire to renounce the obligation which they have undertaken of a religious life, and to break their vows. Government may also suppress the said religious orders, as likewise collegiate churches and simple benefices, even those of advowson and subject their property and revenues to the administration and pleasure of the civil power.
54. Kings and princes are not only exempt from the jurisdiction of the Church, but are superior to the Church in deciding questions of jurisdiction.
55. The Church ought to be separated from the State, and the State from the Church.

VII. ERRORS CONCERNING NATURAL AND CHRISTIAN ETHICS

56. Moral laws do not stand in need of the divine sanction, and it is not at all necessary that human laws should be made conformable to the laws of nature and receive their power of binding from God.
57. The science of philosophical things and morals and also civil laws may and ought to keep aloof from divine and ecclesiastical authority.
58. No other forces are to be recognized except those which reside in matter, and all the rectitude and excellence of morality ought to be placed in the accumulation and increase of riches by every possible means, and the gratification of pleasure.
59. Right consists in the material fact. All human duties are an empty word, and all human facts have the force of right.
60. Authority is nothing else but numbers and the sum total of material forces.
61. The injustice of an act when successful inflicts no injury on the sanctity of right.
62. The principle of non-intervention, as it is called, ought to be proclaimed and observed.
63. It is lawful to refuse obedience to legitimate princes, and even to rebel against them.
64. The violation of any solemn oath, as well as any wicked and flagitious action repugnant to the eternal law, is not only not blamable but is altogether lawful and worthy of the highest praise when done through love of country.

VIII. ERRORS CONCERNING CHRISTIAN MARRIAGE

65. The doctrine that Christ has raised marriage to the dignity of a sacrament cannot be at all tolerated.
66. The Sacrament of Marriage is only a something accessory to the contract and separate from it, and the sacrament itself consists in the nuptial benediction alone.
67. By the law of nature, the marriage tie is not indissoluble, and in many cases divorce properly so called may be decreed by the civil authority.
68. The Church has not the power of establishing diriment impediments of marriage, but such a power belongs to the civil authority by which existing impediments are to be removed.
69. In the dark ages the Church began to establish diriment impediments, not by her own right, but by using a power borrowed from the State.
70. The canons of the Council of Trent, which anathematize those who dare to deny to the Church the right of establishing diriment impediments, either are not dogmatic or must be understood as referring to such borrowed power.
71. The form of solemnizing marriage prescribed by the Council of Trent, under pain of nullity, does

not bind in cases where the civil law lays down another form, and declares that when this new form is used the marriage shall be valid.

72. Boniface VIII was the first who declared that the vow of chastity taken at ordination renders marriage void.
73. In force of a merely civil contract there may exist between Christians a real marriage, and it is false to say either that the marriage contract between Christians is always a sacrament, or that there is no contract if the sacrament be excluded.
74. Matrimonial causes and espousals belong by their nature to civil tribunals.

IX. ERRORS REGARDING THE CIVIL POWER OF THE SOVEREIGN PONTIFF

75. The children of the Christian and Catholic Church are divided amongst themselves about the compatibility of the temporal with the spiritual power.
76. The abolition of the temporal power of which the Apostolic See is possessed would contribute in the greatest degree to the liberty and prosperity of the Church.

X. ERRORS HAVING REFERENCE TO MODERN LIBERALISM

77. In the present day it is no longer expedient that the Catholic religion should be held as the only religion of the State, to the exclusion of all other forms of worship.
78. Hence it has been wisely decided by law, in some Catholic countries, that persons coming to reside therein shall enjoy the public exercise of their own peculiar worship.
79. Moreover, it is false that the civil liberty of every form of worship, and the full power, given to all, of overtly and publicly manifesting any opinions whatsoever and thoughts, conduce more easily to corrupt the morals and minds of the people, and to propagate the pest of indifferentism.
80. The Roman Pontiff can, and ought to, reconcile himself, and come to terms with progress, liberalism and modern civilization.

The faith teaches us and human reason demonstrates that a double order of things exists, and that we must therefore distinguish between the two earthly powers, the one of natural origin which provides for secular affairs and the tranquillity of human society, the other of supernatural origin, which presides over the City of God, that is to say the Church of Christ, which has been divinely instituted for the sake of souls and of eternal salvation. . . . The duties of this twofold power are most wisely ordered in such a way that to God is given what is God's (Matt. 22:21), and because of God to Caesar what is Caesar's, who is great because he is smaller than heaven. Certainly the Church has never disobeyed this divine command, the Church which always and everywhere instructs the faithful to show the respect which they should inviolably have for the supreme authority and its secular rights. . . .

STUDY QUESTIONS

1. How would you describe the "false ideas" that the pope condemns? What makes these ideas pernicious?
2. How does the pope view "reason" and "rationalism"? Why does he set these in opposition to faith?

CHAPTER 23

THE GREAT LAND GRAB

23.1 WINSTON CHURCHILL, "THE BATTLE OF OMDURMAN," *THE RIVER WAR*, 1899

Twice prime minister of Britain, Sir Winston Churchill (1874–1965) led his country in uncompromising opposition to Nazi Germany during World War II. In addition to his prodigious political activity spanning a half century in government, Churchill was also a prolific writer—he won the Nobel Prize for Literature in 1953. His work *The River War* recounts his participation in the Mahdist War, an insurgency by Sudanese against Anglo-Egyptian colonial power. This selection describes the bloody Battle of Omdurman (1898), which established British control in Sudan. Whereas ten thousand Mahdists were killed, the British force under Kitchener lost fewer than fifty men. Consider how evocative imagery and selection of information reveal Churchill's point of view.

CHAPTER XV: THE BATTLE OF OMDURMAN

SEPTEMBER 2, 1898

The bugles all over the camp by the river began to sound at half-past four. The cavalry trumpets and the drums and fifes of the British division joined the chorus, and everyone awoke amid a confusion of merry or defiant notes. Then it grew gradually lighter, and the cavalry mounted their horses, the infantry stood to their arms, and the gunners went to their batteries; while the sun, rising over the Nile, revealed the wide plain, the dark rocky hills, and the waiting army. It was as if all the preliminaries were settled, the ground cleared, and nothing remained but the final act and "the rigour of the game."

Even before it became light several squadrons of British and Egyptian cavalry were pushed swiftly forward to gain contact with the enemy and learn his intentions. The first of these, under Captain Baring, occupied Surgham Hill, and waited in the gloom until the whereabouts of the Dervishes should be disclosed by the dawn. It was a perilous undertaking, for he might have found them unexpectedly near. As the sun rose, the 21st Lancers trotted out of the zeriba and

From Winston Churchill, *The River War: An Account of the Reconquest of the Sudan*. New York: Longmans, Green and Co., 1902.

threw out a spray of officers' patrols. As there had been no night attack, it was expected that the Dervish army would have retired to their original position or entered the town. It was hardly conceivable that they would advance across the open ground to attack the zeriba by daylight. Indeed, it appeared more probable that their hearts had failed them in the night, and that they had melted away into the desert. But these anticipations were immediately dispelled by the scene which was visible from the crest of the ridge.

It was a quarter to six. The light was dim, but growing stronger every minute. There in the plain lay the enemy, their numbers unaltered, their confidence and intentions apparently unshaken. Their front was now nearly five miles long, and composed of great masses of men joined together by thinner lines. Behind and near to the flanks were large reserves. From the ridge they looked dark blurs and streaks, relieved and diversified with an odd-looking shimmer of light from the spear-points. At about ten minutes to six it was evident that the masses were in motion and advancing swiftly. Their Emirs galloped about and before their ranks. Scouts and patrols scattered themselves all over the front. Then they began to cheer. They were still a mile away from the hill, and were concealed from the Sirdar's army by the folds of the ground. The noise of the shouting was heard, albeit faintly, by the troops down by the river. But to those watching on the hill a tremendous roar came up in waves of intense sound, like the tumult of the rising wind and sea before a storm.

The British and Egyptian forces were arranged in line, with their back to the river. The flanks were secured by the gunboats lying moored in the stream. Before them was the rolling sandy plain, looking from the slight elevation of the ridge smooth and flat as a table. To the right rose the rocky hills of the Kerreri position, near which the Egyptian cavalry were drawn up—a dark solid mass of men and horses. On the left the 21st Lancers, with a single squadron thrown out in advance, were halted watching their patrols, who climbed about Surgham Hill, stretched forward beyond it, or perched, as we did, on the ridge.

The ground sloped gently up from the river; so that it seemed as if the landward ends of the Surgham and Kerreri ridges curved in towards each other, enclosing what lay between. Beyond the long swell of sand which formed the western wall of this spacious amphitheatre the black shapes of the distant hills rose in misty confusion. The challengers were already in the arena; their antagonists swiftly approached.

Although the Dervishes were steadily advancing, a belief that their musketry was inferior encouraged a nearer view, and we trotted round the south-west slopes of Surgham Hill until we reached the sandhills on the enemy's side, among which the regiment had waited the day before. Thence the whole array was visible in minute detail. It seemed that every single man of all the thousands could be examined separately. The pace of their march was fast and steady, and it was evident that it would not be safe to wait long among the sandhills. Yet the wonder of the scene exercised a dangerous fascination, and for a while we tarried.

The emblems of the more famous Emirs were easily distinguishable. On the extreme left the chiefs and soldiers of the bright green flag gathered under Ali-Wad-Helu; between this and the centre the large dark green flag of Osman Sheikh-ed-Din rose above a dense mass of spearmen, preceded by long lines of warriors armed presumably with rifles; over the centre, commanded by Yakub, the sacred Black banner of the Khalifa floated high and remarkable; while on the right a great square of Dervishes was arrayed under an extraordinary number of white flags, amid which the red ensign of Sherif was almost hidden. All the pride and might of the Dervish Empire were massed on this last great day of its existence. Riflemen who had helped to destroy Hicks, spearmen who had charged at Abu Klea, Emirs who saw the sack of Gondar, Baggara fresh from raiding the Shillooks, warriors who had besieged Khartoum—all marched, inspired by the memories of former triumphs and embittered by the knowledge of late defeats, to chastise the impudent and accursed invaders.

The advance continued. The Dervish left began to stretch out across the plain towards Kerreri—as I thought, to turn our right flank. Their centre, under the Black Flag, moved directly towards Surgham. The right pursued a line of advance south of that hill. This mass of men were the most striking of all. They could not have mustered fewer than 6,000. Their array was perfect. They displayed a great number of flags—perhaps 500—which looked at the distance white, though they were really covered with texts from the Koran, and which by their admirable alignment made this division of the Khalifa's army look like the old representations of the Crusaders in the Bayeux tapestry.

The attack developed. The left, nearly 20,000 strong, toiled across the plain and approached the Egyptian squadrons. The leading masses of the centre deployed facing the zeriba and marched forthwith to the direct assault. As the whole Dervish army continued to advance, the division with the white flags, which had until now been echeloned in rear of their right, moved up into the general line and began to climb the southern slopes of Surgham Hill. Meanwhile yet another body of the enemy, comparatively insignificant in numbers, who had been drawn up behind the "White Flags," were moving slowly towards the Nile, echeloned still further behind their right, and not far from the suburbs of Omdurman. These men had evidently been posted to prevent the Dervish army being cut off from the city and to secure their line of retreat; and with them the 21st Lancers were destined to have a much closer acquaintance about two hours later.

The Dervish centre had come within range. But it was not the British and Egyptian army that began the battle. If there was one arm in which the Arabs were beyond all comparison inferior to their adversaries, it was in guns. Yet it was with this arm that they opened their attack. In the middle of the Dervish line now marching in frontal assault were two puffs of smoke. About fifty yards short of the thorn fence two red clouds of sand and dust sprang up, where the projectiles had struck. It looked like a challenge. It was immediately answered. Great clouds of smoke appeared all along the front of the British and Soudanese brigades. One after another four batteries opened on the enemy at a range of about 3,000 yards. The sound of the cannonade rolled up to us on the ridge, and was re-echoed by the hills. Above the heads of the moving masses shells began to burst, dotting the air with smoke-balls and the ground with bodies. But a nearer tragedy impended. The "White Flags" were nearly over the crest. In another minute they would become visible to the batteries. Did they realise what would come to meet them? They were in a dense mass, 2,800 yards from the 32nd Field Battery and the gunboats. The ranges were known. It was a matter of machinery. The more distant slaughter passed unnoticed, as the mind was fascinated by the approaching horror. In a few seconds swift destruction would rush on these brave men. They topped the crest and drew out into full view of the whole army. Their white banners made them conspicuous above all. As they saw the camp of their enemies, they discharged their rifles with a great roar of musketry and quickened their pace. For a moment the white flags advanced in regular order, and the whole division crossed the crest and were exposed. Forthwith the gunboats, the 32nd British Field Battery, and other guns from the zeriba opened on them. About twenty shells struck them in the first minute. Some burst high in the air, others exactly in their faces. Others, again, plunged into the sand and, exploding, dashed clouds of red dust, splinters, and bullets amid their ranks. The white banners toppled over in all directions. Yet they rose again immediately, as other men pressed forward to die for the Mahdi's sacred cause and in the defence of the successor of the True Prophet.

It was a terrible sight, for as yet they had not hurt us at all, and it seemed an unfair advantage to strike thus cruelly when they could not reply. Under the influence of the shells the mass of the "White Flags" dissolved into thin lines of spearmen and skirmishers, and came on in altered formation and diminished numbers, but with unabated enthusiasm.

And now, the whole attack being thoroughly exposed, it became the duty of the cavalry to clear the front as quickly as possible, and leave the further conduct of the debate to the infantry and the Maxim guns. All the patrols trotted or cantered back to their squadrons, and the regiment retired swiftly into the zeriba, while the shells from the gunboats screamed overhead and the whole length of the position began to burst into flame and smoke. Nor was it long before the tremendous banging of the artillery was swollen by the roar of musketry.

STUDY QUESTIONS

1. Does Churchill display any sympathy for the invaded people of the Sudan?
2. How does religion motivate the Mahdi army, and how effective were they as a result?

23.2 JOHN A. HOBSON, "CRITICISM OF IMPERIALISM," *IMPERIALISM*, 1902

John Atkinson Hobson (1858–1940) grew up during an economic depression in England that ultimately shifted his intellectual interests from literature to economics. One of his major contributions is the theory of underconsumption, which argues that low consumer demand and high supply of goods will lead to a sluggish economy. Hobson also held that imperialism could be stripped down to economic interests by the mother country: it was no more than a search for new capitalist markets. This selection explores Hobson's observed relationships among economy, international struggle, imperialism, and nationalism.

The statement, often made, that the work of imperial expansion is virtually complete is not correct. It is true that most of the "backward" races have been placed in some sort of dependence upon one or other of the "civilised" Powers as colony, protectorate, hinterland, or sphere of influence. But this in most instances marks rather the beginning of a process of imperialisation than a definite attainment of empire. The intensive growth of empire by which interference is increased and governmental control tightened over spheres of influence and protectorates is as important and as perilous an aspect of Imperialism as the extensive growth which takes shape in assertion of rule over new areas of territory and new populations.

II.IV.2

The famous saying, attributed to Napoleon, that "great empires die of indigestion" serves to remind us of the importance of the imperialist processes which still remain after formal "expansion" has been completed. During the last twenty years Great Britain, Germany, France, and Russia have bitten off huge mouthfuls of Africa and Asia which are not yet chewed, digested, or assimilated. Moreover, great areas still remain whose independence, though threatened, is yet unimpaired.

II.IV.3

Vast countries in Asia, such as Persia, Thibet, Siam, Afghanistan, are rapidly forging to the front of politics as likely subjects of armed controversy between European Powers with a view to subjugation; the Turkish dominions in Asia Minor, and perhaps in Europe, await a slow, precarious process of absorption; the paper partition of Central Africa teems with possibilities of conflict. The entrance of the United States into the imperial struggle throws virtually the whole of South America into the arena; for it is not reasonable

From John A. Hobson, *Imperialism and the Lower Races*. New York: James Pott and Co., 1902, part II, chapter IV.

to expect that European nations, with settlements and vast economic interests in the southern peninsula, will readily leave all this territory to the special protection or ultimate absorption of the United States, when the latter, abandoning her old consistent isolation, has plunged into the struggle for empire in the Pacific.

II.IV.4

Beyond and above all this looms China. It is not easy to suppose that the present lull and hesitancy of the Powers will last, or that the magnitude and manifest risks of disturbing this vast repository of incalculable forces will long deter adventurous groups of profit-seekers from driving their Governments along the slippery path of commercial treaties, leases, railway and mining concessions, which must entail a growing process of political interference.

II.IV.5

It is not my purpose to examine here the entanglement of political and economic issues which each of these cases presents, but simply to illustrate the assertion that the policy of modern Imperialism is not ended but only just begun, and that it is concerned almost wholly with the rival claims of Empires to dominate "lower races" in tropical and sub-tropical countries, or in other countries occupied by manifestly unassimilable races.

II.IV.6

In asking ourselves what are the sound principles of world policy and of national policy in this matter, we may at first ignore the important differences which should affect our conduct towards countries inhabited by what appear to be definitely low-typed unprogressive races, countries whose people manifest capacity of rapid progress from a present low condition, and countries like India and China, where an old civilisation of a high type, widely differing from that of European nations, exists.

II.IV.7

Before seeking for differences of policy which correspond to these conditions, let us try to find whether there are any general principles of guidance in dealing with countries occupied by "lower" or unprogressive peoples.

II.IV.8

It is idle to consider as a general principle the attitude of mere *laissez faire.* It is not only impracticable in view of the actual forces which move politics, but it is ethically indefensible in the last resort.

II.IV.9

To lay down as an absolute law that "the autonomy of every nation is inviolable" does not carry us very far. There can no more be absolute nationalism in the society of nations than absolute individualism in the single nation. Some measure of practical internationality, implying a "comity of nations," and some relations of "right" and "duty" between nations, are almost universally admitted. The rights of self-government, implied by the doctrine of autonomy, if binding in any sense legal or ethical on other nations, can only possess this character in virtue of some real international organisation, however rudimentary.

II.IV.10

It is difficult for the strongest advocate of national rights to assert that the people in actual occupation or political control over a given area of the earth are entitled to do what they will with "their own," entirely disregarding the direct and indirect consequences of their actions upon the rest of the world.

II.IV.11

It is not necessary to take extreme cases of a national policy which directly affects the welfare of a neighbouring State, as where a people on the upper reaches of a river like the Nile or the Niger might so damage or direct the flow as to cause plague or famine to the lower lands belonging to another nation. Few, if any, would question some right of interference from without in such a case. Or take another case which falls outside the range of directly other-regarding actions. Suppose a famine or flood or other catastrophe deprives a population of the means of living on their land, while unutilised land lies in plenty beyond their borders in another country, are the rulers of the latter entitled to refuse an entrance or a necessary settlement? As in the case of individuals, so of nations, it will be generally allowed that necessity knows no laws, which, rightly interpreted, means that the right of self-preservation transcends all other rights as the prime condition of their emergence and exercise.

II.IV.12

This carries us on an inclined plane of logic to the real issue as ably presented by Mr. Kidd, Professor Giddings, and the "Fabian" Imperialists. It is an expansion of this plea of material necessity that constitutes the first claim to a control of the tropics by "civilised" nations. The European races have grown up with a standard of material civilisation based largely upon the consumption and use of foods, raw materials of manufacture, and other goods which are natural products of tropical countries. The industries and the trade which furnish these commodities are of vital importance to the maintenance and progress of Western civilisation. The large part played in our import trade by such typically tropical products as sugar, tea, coffee, india-rubber, rice, tobacco, indicates the dependence of such countries as Great Britain upon the tropics. Partly from sheer growth of population in temperate zones, partly from the rising standard of material life, this dependence of the temperate on the tropical countries must grow. In order to satisfy these growing needs larger and larger tracts of tropical country must be cultivated, the cultivation must be better and more regular, and peaceful and effective trade relations with these countries must be maintained. Now the ease with which human life can be maintained in the tropics breeds indolence and torpor of character. The inhabitants of these countries are not "progressive people"; they neither develop the arts of industry at any satisfactory pace, nor do they evolve new wants or desires, the satisfaction of which might force them to labour. We cannot therefore rely upon the ordinary economic motives and methods of free exchange to supply the growing demand for tropical goods. The resources of the tropics will not be developed voluntarily by the natives themselves.

"If we look to the native social systems of the tropical East, the primitive savagery of Central Africa, to the West Indian Islands in the past in process of being assisted into the position of modern States by Great Britain, or the black republic of Hayti in the present, or to modern Liberia in the future, the lesson seems everywhere the same; it is that there will be no development of the resources of the tropics under native government."

II.IV.13

We cannot, it is held, leave these lands barren; it is our duty to see that they are developed for the good of the world. White men cannot "colonise" these lands and, thus settling, develop the natural resources by the labour of their own hands; they can only organise and superintend the labour of the natives. By doing this they can educate the natives in the arts of industry and stimulate in them a desire for material and more progress, implanting new "wants" which form in every society the roots of civilisation.

II.IV.14

It is quite evident that there is much force in this presentation of the case, not only on material but on moral grounds; nor can it be brushed aside because it is liable to certain obvious and gross abuses. It implies, however, two kinds of interference which require justification. To step in and utilise natural resources which are left undeveloped is one thing, to compel the inhabitants to develop them is another. The former is easily justified, involving the application on a wider scale of a principle whose equity, as well as expediency, is recognised and enforced in most civilised nations. The other interference, whereby men who prefer to live on a low standard of life with little labour shall be forced to harder or more continuous labour, is far more difficult of justification.

II.IV.15

I have set the economic compulsion in the foreground, because in point of history it is the *causa causans* of the Imperialism that accompanies or follows.

II.IV.16

In considering the ethics and politics of this interference, we must not be bluffed or blinded by critics who fasten on the palpable dishonesty of many practices of the gospel of "the dignity of labour" and "the mission of civilisation." The real issue is whether, and under what circumstances, it is justifiable for Western nations to use compulsory government for the control and education in the arts of industrial and political civilisation of the inhabitants of tropical countries and other so-called lower races. Because Rhodesian mine-owners or Cuban sugar-growers stimulate the British or American Government to Imperialism by parading motives and results which do not really concern them, it does not follow that these motives under proper guidance are unsound, or that the results are undesirable.

II.IV.17

There is nothing unworthy, quite the contrary, in the notion that nations which, through a more stimulative environment, have advanced further in certain arts of industry, politics, or morals, should communicate these to nations which from their circumstances were more backward, so as to aid them in developing alike the material resources of their land and the human resources of their people. Nor is it clear that in this work some "inducement, stimulus, or pressure" (to quote a well-known phrase), or in a single word, "compulsion," is wholly illegitimate. Force is itself no remedy, coercion is not education, but it may be a prior condition to the operation of educative forces. Those, at any rate, who assign any place to force in the education or the political government of individuals in a nation can hardly deny that the same instrument may find a place in the civilisation of backward by progressive nations.

II.IV.18

Assuming that the arts of "progress," or some of them, are communicable, a fact which is hardly disputable, there can be no inherent natural right in a nation to refuse that measure of compulsory education which shall raise it from childhood to manhood in the order of nationalities. The analogy furnished by the education of a child is *primâ facie* a sound one, and is not invalidated by the dangerous abuses to which it is exposed in practice.

II.IV.19

The real issue is one of safeguards, of motives, and of methods. What are the conditions under which a nation may help to develop the resources of another, and even apply some element of compulsion in doing so? The question, abstract as it may sound, is quite the most important of all practical questions for this generation. For, that such development will take place, and such compulsion, legitimate or illegitimate, be exercised, more and more throughout this new century in many quarters of this globe, is beyond the shadow of a doubt. It is the great practical business of the century to explore and develop, by every method which science can devise, the hidden natural and human resources of the globe.

II.IV.20

That the white Western nations will abandon a quest on which they have already gone so far is a view which does not deserve consideration. That this process of development may be so conducted as to yield a gain to world-civilisation, instead of some terrible *débâcle* in which revolted slave races may trample down their parasitic and degenerate white masters, should be the supreme aim of far-sighted scientific statecraft.

STUDY QUESTIONS

1. How does a domestic hatred of "manifestly unassimilable races" within one's own country lead to imperialism on a global scale?
2. In what ways does the "civilizing mission" of Europeans in Africa fail to match the reality of imperialism?

23.3 MARK TWAIN, *KING LEOPOLD'S SOLILOQUY*, 1905

Samuel Clemens (1835–1910), who took his pen name Mark Twain from a command shouted on riverboats, was the quintessential American writer: his major works *The Adventures of Tom Sawyer* and *The Adventures of Huckleberry Finn* are classics about the American experience. A humorist, Twain borrowed and responded to current political material in his works. This essay provides a satirical yet scathing depiction of King Leopold II of Belgium, whom Twain condemned as a heartless imperialist for his destructive policies in the Belgian Congo. Consider how Twain gets his point across while nonetheless speaking from King Leopold's point of view.

Persons will begin to ask again, as now and then in times past, how I can hope to win and keep the respect of the human race if I continue to give up my life to murder and pillage. [*Scornfully*] When have they heard me say I wanted the respect of the human race? Do they confuse me with the common herd? Do they forget that I am a king? What king has valued the respect of the human race? I mean deep down in his private heart. If they would reflect, they would know that it is impossible that a king should value the respect of the human race. He stands upon an eminence and looks out over the world and sees multitudes of meek human things worshipping the persons, and submitting to the oppressions and exactions, of a dozen human things who are in no way better or finer than themselves—made on just their own pattern, in fact, and out of the same quality of mud. When it *talks*, it is a race of whales; but a king knows it for a race of tadpoles. Its history gives it away. If men were really *men*, how could a Czar be possible? and how could I be possible? But we *are* possible; we are quite safe; and with God's help we shall continue the business at the old stand. It will be found that the race will put up with us, in its docile immemorial way. It may pull a wry face now and then, and make large talk, but it will stay on its knees all the same.

Making large talk is one of its specialties. It works itself up, and froths at the mouth, and just when you think it is going to through a brick,—it heaves a poem! Lord, what a race it is!

[*Reads*]

A CZAR—1905

A pasteboard autocrat; a despot out of date;
A fading planet in the glare of day;
A flickering candle in the bright sun's ray,
Burnt to the socket; fruit left too late,
High on a blighted bough, ripe till it's rotten.
By God forsaken and by time forgotten,
Watching the crumbling edges of his hands,
A spineless god to whom dumb millions pray,
From Finland in the West to far Cathay.
Lord of a frost-bound continent he stands,
Her seeming ruin his dim mind appalls,
And in the frozen stupor of his sleep
He hears dull thunders, pealing as she falls,
And mighty fragments dropping in the deep.

. . .

If a poet's bite were as terrible as his bark, why dear me—but it isn't. A wise king minds neither of them; but the poet doesn't know it. It's a case of little dog and lightning express. When the Czar goes thundering by, the poet skips out and rages alongside for a little distance, then returns to his kennel wagging his head with satisfaction, and thinks he has inflicted

From Mark Twain, *King Leopold's Soliloquy: A Defense of His Congo Rule*, 2nd ed. Boston: The P. R. Warren Co., 1905.

a memorable scare whereas nothing has really happened—the Czar didn't know he was around. They never bark at me; I wonder why that is. I suppose my Corruption-Department buys them. That must be it, for certainly I ought to inspire a bark or two; I'm rather choice material, I should say. Why—here *is* a yelp at me.

[*Mumbling a poem*]

. . . What gives thee holy right to murder hope
And water ignorance with human blood?

. . . .

From what high universe-dividing power
Draws't thou thy wondrous, ripe brutality?

. . . .

O horrible . . . Thou God who seest these things
Help us to blot this terror from the earth.

. . . No, I see it is "To the Czar," after all. But there are those who would say it fits me—and rather snugly, too. "Ripe brutality." They would say the Czar's isn't ripe yet, but that mine is; and not merely *ripe* but rotten. Nothing could keep them from saying that; they would think it smart.

"This terror." Let the Czar keep that name; I am supplied. This long time I have been "the monster"; that was their favorite—the monster of crime. But now I have a new one. They have found a fossil Dinosaur fifty-seven feet long and sixteen feet high, and set it up in the museum in New York and labeled it "Leopold II." But it is no matter, one does not look for manners in a republic. Um . . . that reminds me; I have never been caricatured. Could it be that the corsairs of the pencil could not find an offensive symbol that was big enough and ugly enough to do my reputation justice? [*After reflection*] There is no other way—I will buy the Dinosaur. And suppress it. [*Rests himself with some more chapter-headings . . .*]

. . .

[*Studies some photographs of mutilated negroes—throws them down. Sighs*] The kodak has been a sore calamity to us. The most powerful enemy that has confronted us, indeed.

. . .

The only witness I have encountered in my long experience that I couldn't bribe. Every Yankee missionary and every interrupted trader sent home and got one; and now—oh, well, the pictures get sneaked around everywhere, in spite of all we can do to ferret them out and suppress them. Ten thousand pulpits and ten thousand presses are saying the good word for me all the time and placidly and convincingly denying the mutilations. Then that trivial little kodak, that a child can carry in its pocket, gets up, uttering never a word, and knocks them dumb!

. . . What is this fragment? [*Reads*]

"But enough of trying to tally off his crimes! His list interminable, we should never get to the end of it. His awful shadow lies across his Congo Free State, and under it an unoffending nation of 15,000,000 is withering away and swiftly succumbing to their miseries. It is a land of graves; it is *The* Land of Graves; it is the Congo Free Graveyard. It is a majestic thought: that is, the ghastliest episode in all of human history is the work of *one man alone*; one solitary man; just a single individual—Leopold, King of the Belgians. He is personally and solely responsible for all the myriad crimes that have blackened the history of the Congo State. He is *sole* master there; he is absolute. He could have prevented the crimes by his mere command; he could stop them today with a word. He withholds the word. For his pocket's sake.

. . .

We see this awful king, this pitiless and blood-drenched kind, this money-crazy king towering toward the sky in a world-solitude of sordid crime, unfellowed and apart from the human race, sole butcher for personal gain findable in all his caste, ancient or modern, pagan or Christian, proper and legitimate target for the scorn of the lowest and the highest, and the execrations of all who hold in cold esteem the oppressor and the coward; and—well, it is a mystery, but *we do not wish to look*; for he is a king, and it hurts us, it troubles us, by ancient and inherited instinct it shames us to see a king degraded to this aspect, and we shrink from hearing the particulars of how it happened. *We shudder* and *turn away* when we come upon them in print."

Why, certainly—*that* is my protection. And you will continue to do it. I know the human race.

STUDY QUESTIONS

1. How does Twain hold King Leopold "personally and solely responsible" for the outrages against human beings in the Congo?
2. Why has there been so much reluctance to criticize this brutal figure publicly, in Twain's estimation?

23.4 MOHANDAS GANDHI, *INDIAN HOME RULE*, 1910

Mohandas Gandhi (1869–1948) wrote this book—called *Hind Swaraj* (1909) in his native language of Gujarati—on the steamer from London to South Africa, a voyage of ten days. The British banned its publication in India, but allowed Gandhi's own English translation of the book (1910) to be published, on the assumption that few in India would be able to read it. The book is written in the form of a dialogue between a Reader, who represents the colonized in India, and an Editor, who represents Gandhi's position. What follows is from Gandhi's English version.

CHAPTER 4: WHAT IS *SWARAJ*?

READER: I have now learned what the Congress has done to make India one nation, how the Partition has caused an awakening, and how discontent and unrest have spread through the land. I would now like to know your views on *swaraj*. I fear that our interpretation is not the same as yours.

EDITOR: It is quite possible that we do not attach the same meaning to the term. You and I and all Indians are impatient to obtain *swaraj*, but we are certainly not decided as to what it is. To drive the English out of India is a thought heard from many mouths, but it does not seem that many have properly considered why it should be so. I must ask you a question. Do you think that it is necessary to drive away the English, if we get all we want?

READER: I should ask of them only one thing, that is: "Please leave our country." If, after they have complied with this request, their withdrawal from India means that they are still in India, I should have no objection. Then we would understand that, in their language, the word *gone* is equivalent to *remained*.

EDITOR: Well then, let us suppose that the English have retired. What will you do then?

READER: That question cannot be answered at this stage. The state after withdrawal will depend largely upon the manner of it. If, as you assume, they retire, it seems to me we shall still keep their constitution and shall carry on the Government. If they simply retire for the asking, we should have an army, etc. ready at hand. We should, therefore, have no difficulty in carrying on the Government.

EDITOR: You may think so; I do not. But I will not discuss the matter just now. I have to answer your question, and that I can do well by asking you several questions. Why do you want to drive away the English?

READER: Because India has become impoverished by their Government. They take away our money from year to year. The most important posts are reserved for themselves. We are kept in a state of slavery. They behave insolently towards us and disregard our feelings.

EDITOR: If they do not take our money away, become gentle, and give us responsible posts, would you still consider their presence to be harmful?

READER: That question is useless. It is similar to the question whether there is any harm in associating with a tiger if he changes his nature. Such a question is sheer waste of time. When a tiger changes his nature, Englishmen will change theirs. This is not possible, and to believe it to be possible is contrary to human experience.

EDITOR: Supposing we get Self-Government similar to what the Canadians and the South Africans have, will it be good enough?

READER: That question also is useless. We may get it when we have the same powers; we shall then hoist our own flag. As is Japan, so must India be. We must own our navy, our army, and we must have our own splendor, and then will India's voice ring through the world.

EDITOR: You have drawn the picture well. In effect it means this: that we want English rule without the Englishman. You want the tiger's nature, but not the tiger; that is to say, you would make India English. And when it becomes English, it will be called not *Hindustan* but *Englistan*. This is not the *swaraj* that I want.

READER: I have placed before you my idea of *swaraj* as I think it should be. If the education we have received be of any use, if the works of Spencer, Mill, and others be of any importance, and if the English Parliament be the Mother of Parliaments, I certainly think that we should copy the English people, and this to such an extent that, just as they do not allow others to obtain a footing in their country, so we should not allow others to obtain it in ours. What they have done in their own country has not been done in any other country. It is, therefore, proper for us to import their institutions. But now I want to know your views.

EDITOR: There is need for patience. My views will develop of themselves in the course of this discourse. It is as difficult for me to understand the true nature of *swaraj* as it seems to you to be easy. I shall therefore, for the time being, content myself with endeavoring to show that what you call *swaraj* is not truly *swaraj*.

CHAPTER 5: THE CONDITION OF ENGLAND

READER: Then from your statement I deduce that the Government of England is not desirable and not worth copying by us.

EDITOR: Your deduction is justified. The condition of England at present is pitiable. I pray to God that India may never be in that plight. That which you consider to be the Mother of Parliaments is like a sterile woman and a prostitute. Both of these are harsh terms, but exactly fit the case. That Parliament has not yet, of its own accord, done a single good thing. Hence I have compared it to a sterile woman. The natural condition of that Parliament is such that, without outside pressure, it can do nothing. It is like a prostitute because it is under the control of ministers who change from time to time. Today it is under Mr. Asquith, tomorrow it may be under Mr. Balfour.

READER: You have said this sarcastically. The term "sterile woman" is not applicable. The Parliament, being elected by the people, must work under public pressure. This is its quality.

EDITOR: You are mistaken. Let us examine it a little more closely. The best men are supposed to be elected by the people. The members serve without pay and therefore, it must be assumed, only for the public weal. The electors are considered to be educated and therefore we should assume that they would not generally make mistakes in their choice. Such a Parliament should not need the spur of petitions or any other pressure. Its work should be so smooth that its effects would be more apparent day by day. But, as a matter of fact, it is generally acknowledged that the members are hypocritical and selfish. Each thinks of his own little interest. It is fear that is the guiding motive. What is done today may be undone tomorrow. *It is not possible to recall a single instance in which finality can be predicted for its work.* When the greatest questions are debated, its members have been seen to stretch themselves and to doze. Sometimes the members talk away until the listeners are disgusted. Carlyle has called it the "talking shop of the world." Members vote for their party without a thought. Their so-called discipline binds them to it. If any member, by way of exception, gives an independent vote, he is considered a renegade. If the money and the time wasted by Parliament were entrusted to a few good men, the English nation would be occupying a much higher platform. These views are by no means peculiar to me. Some great English thinkers have expressed them. One of the members of that Parliament recently said that a true Christian could not become a member of it. Another said that it was a baby. And if it has remained a baby after an existence of seven hundred years, when will it outgrow its babyhood?

READER: You have set me thinking; you do not expect me to accept at once all you say. You give me entirely novel views. I shall have to digest them. Will you now explain the epithet "prostitute"?

EDITOR: That you cannot accept my views at once is only right. If you will read the literature on this subject, you will have some idea of it. Parliament is without a real master. Under the Prime Minister, its movement is not steady but it is buffeted about like a prostitute. The Prime Minister is more concerned about his power than about the welfare of Parliament. His energy is concentrated upon securing the success of his party. His care is not always that Parliament shall do right. Prime Ministers are known to have made Parliament do things merely for party advantage. All this is worth thinking over.

READER: Then you are really attacking the very men whom we have hitherto considered to be so patriotic and honest?

EDITOR: Yes, that is true; I can have nothing against Prime Ministers, but what I have seen leads me to think that they cannot be considered really patriotic. If they are to be considered honest because they do not take what are generally known as bribes, let them be so considered, but they are open to subtler influences. In order to gain their ends, they certainly bribe people with honors. I do not hesitate to say that they have neither real honesty nor a living conscience.

READER: As you express these views about Parliament, I would like to hear you on the English people, so that I may have your view of their Government.

EDITOR: To the English voters their newspaper is their Bible. They take their cue from their newspapers which are often dishonest. The same fact is differently interpreted by different newspapers, according to the party in whose interests they are edited. One newspaper would consider a great Englishman to be a paragon of honesty, another would consider him dishonest. What must be the condition of the people whose newspapers are of this type?

READER: You shall describe it.

EDITOR: These people change their views frequently. It is said that they change them every seven years. These views swing like the pendulum of a clock and are never steadfast. The people would follow a powerful orator or a man who gives them parties, receptions, etc. As are the people, so is their Parliament. They have certainly one quality very strongly developed. They will never allow their country to be lost. If any person were to cast an evil eye on it, they would pluck out his eyes. But that does not mean that the nation possesses every other virtue or that it should be imitated. If India copies England, it is my firm conviction that she will be ruined.

READER: To what do you ascribe this state of England?

EDITOR: It is not due to any peculiar fault of the English people, but the condition is due to modern civilization. It is a civilization only in name. Under it the nations of Europe are becoming degraded and ruined day by day.

CHAPTER 7: WHY WAS INDIA LOST?

READER: You have said much about civilization—enough to make me ponder over it. I do not know what I should adopt and what I should avoid from the nations of Europe, but one question comes to my lips immediately. If civilization is a disease and if it has attacked England, why has she been able to take India, and why is she able to retain it?

EDITOR: Your question is not very difficult to answer, and we shall presently be able to examine the true nature of *swaraj*; for I am aware that I have still to answer that question. I will, however, take up your previous question. The English have not taken India; we have given it to them. They are not in India because of their strength, but because we keep them. Let us now see whether these propositions can be sustained. They came to our country originally for purposes of trade. . . . Who was tempted at the sight of their silver? Who bought their goods? History testifies that we did all this. In order to become rich all at once we welcomed [the East India] Company's officers with open arms. We assisted them. . . . A true servant of India will have to go to the root of the matter. If an excess of food has caused me indigestion, I shall certainly not avoid it by blaming water. He is a true physician who probes the cause of disease, and if you pose as a physician for the disease of India, you will have to find its true cause. . . . [England was] unhampered by questions of morality. Its object was to increase its commerce and to make money. It accepted our assistance, and increased the number of its warehouses. To protect the latter it employed an army which was utilized by us also. Is it not then useless to blame the English for what we did at that time? The Hindus and the Mahomedans were at daggers drawn. This too gave [England] its opportunity and thus we created the circumstances that gave [them] control over India. . . .

CHAPTER 14: HOW CAN INDIA BECOME FREE?

READER: I appreciate your views about civilization. I will have to think over them. I cannot take them in all at once. What, then, holding the views you do, would you suggest for freeing India?

EDITOR: I do not expect my views to be accepted all of a sudden. My duty is to place them before readers like yourself. Time can be trusted to do the rest. We have already examined the conditions for Freeing India, but we have done so indirectly; we will now do so directly. It is a world-known maxim that the removal of the cause of a disease results in the removal of the disease itself. Similarly if the cause of India's slavery be removed, India can become free.

READER: If Indian civilization is, as you say, the best of all, how do you account for India's slavery?

EDITOR: This civilization is unquestionably the best, but it is to be observed that all civilizations have been on their trial. That civilization which is permanent outlives it. Because the sons of India were found wanting, its civilization has been placed in jeopardy. But its strength is to be seen in its ability to survive the shock. Moreover, the whole of India is not touched. Those alone who have been affected by Western civilization have become enslaved. We measure the universe by our own miserable foot-rule. When we are slaves, we think that the whole universe is enslaved. Because we are in an abject condition, we think that the whole of India is in that condition. As a matter of fact, it is not so, yet it is as well to impute our slavery to the whole of India. But if we bear in mind the above fact, we can see that if we become free, India is free. And in this thought you have a definition of *swaraj*.

It is *swaraj* when we learn to rule ourselves. It is therefore in the palm of our hands.

STUDY QUESTIONS

1. How does the Reader's interpretation of *swaraj* differ from the Editor's? Why does the Editor argue that the Reader's vision of *swaraj* will merely turn India into an "Englistan"?
2. What does the Editor see as the main defects of British "civilization"? How does he reconcile these weaknesses with the fact that India is ruled by the British? What does the Editor mean when he says that "the civilization which is permanent outlives it"?

23.5 FREDERICK TAYLOR, *THE PRINCIPLES OF SCIENTIFIC MANAGEMENT*, 1911

Frederick Winslow Taylor (1856–1915) was a mechanical engineer (and champion tennis player) who aimed to increase industrial efficiency by training laborers to work with minimal movement and maximum speed to make their efforts in tune with the mechanical efficiency of the machines they operated. Only a scientific study of labor—the number of physical movements required, for example, to bolt an automobile tire onto its mount, or the ideal pace at which workers should shovel coal into a blast furnace to maintain steady heat—could bring about the efficiency made possible by machinery. Taylor's *Principles of Scientific Management* (1911) was for many years the foundational text used at the Harvard Business School, established in 1908. The following excerpt comes from the book's opening chapter.

The principal object of management should be to secure the maximum prosperity for the employer, coupled with the maximum prosperity for each employee. The words "maximum prosperity" are used, in their broad sense, to mean not only large dividends for the company or owner, but the development of every branch of the business to its highest state of excellence, so that the prosperity may be permanent. In the same way maximum prosperity for each employ[ee] means not only higher wages than are usually received by men of his class, but, of more importance still, it also means the development of each man to his state of maximum efficiency, so that he may be able to do, generally speaking, the highest grade of work for which his natural abilities fit him, and it further means giving him, when possible, this class of work to do. . . . Scientific management . . . has for its very foundation the firm conviction that the true interests of the two are one and the same; that prosperity for the employer cannot exist through a long term of years unless it is accompanied by prosperity for the employee and vice versa; and that it is possible to give the workman what he most wants—high wages—and the employer what he wants—a low labor cost—for his manufactures. . . .

The greatest prosperity can exist only as the result of the greatest possible productivity of the men and machines of the establishment—that is, when each man and each machine are turning out the largest possible output; because unless your men and your machines are daily turning out more work than others around you, it is clear that competition will prevent your paying higher wages to your workmen than are paid to those of your competitor. And what is true as to the possibility of paying high wages in the case of two companies competing close beside one another is also true as to whole districts of the country and even as to nations which are in competition. In a word, that maximum prosperity can exist only as the result of maximum productivity. . . . These principles appear to be so self-evident that many men may think it almost childish to state them. Let us, however, turn to the facts, as they actually exist in this country and in England. The English and American peoples are the greatest sportsmen in the world. Whenever an American workman plays baseball, or an English workman plays cricket, it is safe to say that he strains every nerve to secure victory for his side. He does his very best to make the largest possible number of runs. The universal sentiment is so strong that any man who fails to give out all there is in him in sport is branded as a "quitter," and treated with contempt by those who are around him. When the same workman returns to work on the following day, instead of using every effort to turn out the largest possible amount of work, in a majority of the cases this man deliberately plans to do as little as he safely can—to turn out far less work than he is well able to do—in many instances to do not more than one-third to one-half of a proper day's work. And in fact if he were to do his best to turn out his largest possible day's work, he would be abused by his fellow-workers for so doing, even more than if he had proved himself a "quitter" in sport. Underworking, that is, deliberately working slowly so as to avoid doing a full day's work—"soldiering," as it is called in this country, "hanging it out," as it is called in England—is almost universal in industrial establishments, and prevails also to a large extent in the building trades; and the writer asserts without fear of contradiction that this constitutes the greatest evil with which the working-people of both England and America are now afflicted. . . . America and England have been recently agitated over such subjects as the tariff, the control of the large corporations on the one hand, and of hereditary power on the other hand, and over various more or less socialistic proposals for taxation, etc. On these subjects both peoples have been profoundly stirred, and yet hardly a voice has been raised to call attention to this vastly greater and more important subject of "soldiering," which directly and powerfully affects the wages, the prosperity, and the life of almost every working-man, and also quite as much the prosperity of every industrial establishment in the nation. The elimination of "soldiering" and of the several causes of slow working would so lower the cost of production that both our home and foreign markets would be greatly enlarged, and we could compete on more than even terms with our rivals. . . . It would insure higher wages and make shorter working hours and better working and home conditions possible. Why is it, then, in the face of the self-evident fact that maximum prosperity can exist only as the result of the determined effort of each workman to turn out each day his largest possible day's work, that the great majority of our men are deliberately doing just the opposite, and that even when the men have the best of intentions their work is in most cases far from efficient? There are three causes for this condition, which may be briefly summarized as: First. The fallacy, which has from time immemorial been almost universal among workmen, that a material increase in the output of each man or each machine in the trade would result in the end in throwing a large number of men out of work. Second. The defective systems of management which are in common use, and which make it necessary for each workman to soldier, or work slowly, in order that he may protect his own best interests. Third. The inefficient rule-of-thumb methods, which are still almost universal in all trades, and in practicing which our workmen waste a large part of their effort. . . .

First. The great majority of workmen still believe that if they were to work at their best speed they would be doing a great injustice to the whole trade by throwing a lot of men out of work, and yet the history of the development of each trade shows that each improvement, whether it be the invention of a new machine or the introduction of a better method, which results in increasing the productive capacity of the men in the trade and cheapening the costs, instead of throwing men out of work make in the end work for more men. The cheapening of any article in common use almost immediately results in a largely increased demand for that article. Take the case of shoes, for instance. The introduction of machinery for doing every element of the work which was formerly done by hand has resulted in making shoes at a fraction of their former labor cost, and in selling them so cheap that now almost every man, woman, and child in the working-classes buys one or two pairs of shoes per year, and wears shoes all the time, whereas formerly each workman bought perhaps one pair of shoes every five years, and went barefoot most of the time, wearing shoes only as a luxury or as a matter of the sternest necessity. In spite of the enormously increased output of shoes per workman, which has come with shoe machinery, the demand for shoes has so increased that there are relatively more men working in the shoe industry now than ever before. The workmen in almost every trade have before them an object lesson of this kind, and yet, because they are ignorant of the history of their own trade even, they still firmly believe, as their fathers did before them, that it is against their best interests for each man to turn out each day as much work as possible.

Under this fallacious idea a large proportion of the workmen of both countries each day deliberately work slowly so as to curtail the output. Almost every labor union has made, or is contemplating making, rules which have for their object curtailing the output of their members, and those men who have the greatest influence with the working-people, the labor leaders as well as many people with philanthropic feelings who are helping them, are daily spreading this fallacy and at the same time telling them that they are overworked. A great deal has been and is being constantly said about "sweat-shop" work and conditions. The writer has great sympathy with those who are overworked, but on the whole a greater sympathy for those who are under paid. For every individual, however, who is overworked, there are a hundred who intentionally underwork—greatly underwork—every day of their lives, and who for this reason deliberately aid in establishing those conditions which in the end inevitably result in low wages. And yet hardly a single voice is being raised in an endeavor to correct this evil.

Second. As to the second cause for soldiering—the relations which exist between employers and employees under almost all of the systems of management which are in common use—it is impossible in a few words to make it clear to one not familiar with this problem why it is that the ignorance of employers as to the proper time in which work of various kinds should be done makes it for the interest of the workman to "soldier." The writer therefore quotes herewith from a paper read before The American Society of Mechanical Engineers, in June, 1903, entitled "Shop Management," which it is hoped will explain fully this cause for soldiering: "This loafing or soldiering proceeds from two causes. First, from the natural instinct and tendency of men to take it easy, which may be called natural soldiering. Second, from more intricate second thought and reasoning caused by their relations with other men, which may be called systematic soldiering." . . . This common tendency to "take it easy" is greatly increased by bringing a number of men together on similar work and at a uniform standard rate of pay by the day. . . . The younger and less experienced men are taught this by their elders, and all possible persuasion and social pressure is brought to bear upon the greedy and selfish men to keep them from making new records which result in temporarily increasing their wages, while all those who come after them are made to work harder for the same old pay. . . . Unfortunately for the character of the workman, soldiering involves a deliberate attempt to mislead and deceive his employer, and thus upright and straightforward workmen are compelled to become more or less hypocritical. The employer is soon looked upon as an antagonist, if not an enemy, and the mutual confidence which should exist between a leader and his men, the enthusiasm, the feeling that they are all working for the same end and will share in the results is entirely lacking. . . .

Third. As to the third cause for slow work, considerable space will later in this paper be devoted to illustrating the great gain, both to employers and employs, which results from the substitution of scientific for rule-of-thumb methods in even the smallest details of the work of every trade. The enormous saving of time and therefore increase in the output which it is possible to effect through eliminating unnecessary motions and substituting fast for slow and inefficient motions for the men working in any of our trades can be fully realized only after one has personally seen the improvement which results from a thorough motion and time study, made by a competent man. To explain briefly: owing to the fact that the workmen in all of our trades have been taught the details of their work by observation of those immediately around them, there are many different ways in common use for doing the same thing, perhaps forty, fifty, or a hundred ways of doing each act in each trade, and for the same reason there is a great variety in the implements used for each class of work. Now, among the various methods and implements used in each element of each trade there is always one method and one implement which is quicker and better than any of the rest. And this one best method and best implement can only be discovered or developed through a scientific study and analysis of all of the methods and implements in use, together with accurate, minute, motion and time study. This involves the gradual substitution of science for rule of thumb throughout the mechanic arts.

This paper will show that the underlying philosophy of all of the old systems of management in common use makes it imperative that each workman shall be left with the final responsibility for doing his job practically as he thinks best, with comparatively little help and advice from the management. And it will also show that because of this isolation of workmen, it is in most cases impossible for the men working under these systems to do their work in accordance with the rules and laws of a science or art, even where one exists. The writer asserts as a general principle (and he proposes to give illustrations tending to prove the fact later in this paper) that in almost all of the mechanic arts the science which underlies each act of each workman is so great and amounts to so much that the workman who is best suited to actually doing the work is incapable of fully understanding this science, without the guidance and help of those who are working with him or over him, either through lack of education or through insufficient mental capacity.

In order that the work may be done in accordance with scientific laws, it is necessary that there shall be a far more equal division of the responsibility between the management and the workmen than exists under any of the ordinary types of management. Those in the management whose duty it is to develop this science should also guide and help the workman in working under it, and should assume a much larger share of the responsibility for results than under usual conditions is assumed by the management. The body of this paper will make it clear that, to work according to scientific laws, the management must take over and perform much of the work which is now left to the men; almost every act of the workman should be preceded by one or more preparatory acts of the management which enable him to do his work better and quicker than he otherwise could. And each man should daily be taught by and receive the most friendly help from those who are over him, instead of being, at the one extreme, driven or coerced by his bosses, and at the other left to his own unaided devices. This close, intimate, personal cooperation between the management and the men is of the essence of modern scientific or task management. It will be shown by a series of practical illustrations that, through this friendly cooperation, namely, through sharing equally in every day's burden, all of the great obstacles (above described) to obtaining the maximum output for each man and each machine in the establishment are swept away. The 30 percent to 100 percent increase in wages which the workmen are able to earn beyond what they receive under the old type of management, coupled with the daily intimate shoulder to shoulder contact with the management, entirely removes all cause for soldiering. And in a few years, under this system, the workmen have before them the object lesson of seeing that a great increase in the output per man results in giving employment to more men, instead of throwing men out of work, thus completely eradicating the fallacy that a larger output for each man will throw other men out of work.

It is the writer's judgment, then, that while much can be done and should be done by writing and talking toward educating not only workmen, but all classes in the community, as to the importance of obtaining the maximum output of each man and each machine, it is only through the adoption of modern scientific management that this great problem can be finally solved. Probably most of the readers of this paper will say that all of this is mere theory. On the contrary, the theory, or philosophy, of scientific management is just beginning to be understood, whereas the management itself has been a gradual evolution, extending over a period of nearly thirty years. And during this time the employees of one company after another, including a large range and diversity of industries, have gradually changed from the ordinary to the scientific type of management. At least 50,000 workmen in the United States are now employed under this system; and they are receiving from 30 percent to 100 percent higher wages daily than are paid to men of similar caliber with whom they are surrounded, while the companies employing them are more prosperous than ever before. In these companies the output, per man and per machine, has on an average been doubled. During all these years there has never been a single strike among the men working under this system. In place of the suspicious watchfulness and the more or less open warfare which characterizes the ordinary types of management, there is universally friendly cooperation between the management and the men. . . .

Scientific management fundamentally consists of certain broad general principles, a certain philosophy, which can be applied in many ways, and a description of what any one man or men may believe to be the best mechanism for applying these general principles should in no way be confused with the principles themselves. It is not here claimed that any single panacea exists for all of the troubles of the working-people or of employers. As long as some people are born lazy or inefficient, and others are born greedy and brutal, as long as vice and crime are with us, just so long will a certain amount of poverty, misery, and unhappiness be with us also. No system of management, no single expedient within the control of any man or any set of men can insure continuous prosperity to either workmen or employers. Prosperity depends upon so many factors entirely beyond the control of any one set of men, any state, or even any one country, that certain periods will inevitably come when both sides must suffer, more or less. It is claimed, however, that under scientific management the intermediate periods will be far more prosperous, far happier, and more free from discord and dissension. And also, that the periods will be fewer, shorter and the suffering less. And this will be particularly true in any one town, any one section of the country, or any one state which first substitutes the principles of scientific management for the rule of thumb. That these principles are certain to come into general use practically throughout the civilized world, sooner or later, the writer is profoundly convinced, and the sooner they come the better for all the people.

STUDY QUESTIONS

1. What is "scientific" about Taylor's principles of management?
2. What benefits does Taylor put forward for scientific management? How will scientific management ease discord between workers and owners and increase prosperity?

23.6 PRESIDENTIAL ADDRESS OF CHITTA RANJAN DAS, INDIAN NATIONAL CONGRESS AT GAYA, DECEMBER 1922

Chitta Ranjan Das (1870–1925) was an Indian nationalist politician, as well as leader of the Swaraj (Independence) Party in Bengal, during British rule in India. Although educated in England, he returned to India to play a major role in the independence movement, including such episodes as the "Non-Cooperation" movement of 1919–1920. Like the better-known Gandhi, Das was a believer in nonviolence and was trained as a lawyer, perhaps influencing his constitutionalist approach to independence. Along with pacifism he also saw Muslim–Hindu cooperation as an essential element of Indian independence and national success. It was at the Gaya meeting in

From Presidential Address of Chitta Ranjan Das, Indian National Congress at Gaya, December 1922. An appendix to P. C. Ray, *Life and Times of C. R. Das*. Oxford: Oxford University Press, 1927, pp. 261–74.

1922 that he formed the Swaraj Party, having lost a motion to Gandhi's faction. In this excerpt from his speech, Das discusses how Indian nationalism must not copy the aggressive, competitive nationalism of Europe, but must find its place in a greater Humanity of which it is a part.

The conclusion is irresistible that is not by acquiescence in the doctrine of law and order that the English people have obtained the recognition of their fundamental rights. It follows from the survey that I have made, firstly, that no regulation is law unless it is based on the consent of the people; secondly, where such consent is wanting the people are under no obligation to obey; thirdly, where such laws are not only based on the consent of the people but profess to attack their fundamental rights, the subjects are entitled to compel their withdrawal by force or insurrections; fourthly, that law and order is, and has always been, a plea for absolutism; and lastly, there can be neither law nor order before the real reign of law begins. . . .

What is the ideal which we must set before us? The first and foremost is the ideal of nationalism. Now what is nationalism? It is, I conceive, a process through which a nation expresses itself and finds itself, not in isolation from other nations, not in opposition to other nations, but as part of a great scheme by which, in seeking its own expression and therefore its own identity, it materially assists the self-expression and self-realization of other nations as well: Diversity is as real as unity. And in order that the unity of the world may be established it is essential that each nationality should proceed on its own line and find fulfillment in self-expression and self-realization. The nationality of which I am speaking must not be confused with the conception of nationality as it exists in Europe today. Nationalism in Europe is an aggressive nationalism, a selfish nationalism, a commercial nationalism of gain and loss. The gain of France is the loss of Germany, and the gain of Germany is the loss of France. Therefore French nationalism is nurtured on the hatred of Germany, and German nationalism is nurtured on the hatred of France. It is not yet realized that you cannot hurt Germany without hurting Humanity, and in consequence hurting France; and that you cannot hurt France without hurting Humanity, and in consequence hurting Germany. That is European nationalism; that is not the nationalism of which I am speaking to you today. I contend that each nationality constitutes a particular stream of the great unity, but no nation can fulfil itself unless and until it becomes itself and at the same time realizes its identity with Humanity. The whole problem of nationalism is therefore to find that stream and to face that destiny. If you find the current and establish a continuity with the past, then the process of self-expression has begun, and nothing can stop the growth of nationality.

Throughout the pages of Indian history, I find a great purpose unfolding itself. Movement after movement has swept over this vast country, apparently creating hostile forces, but in reality stimulating the vitality and moulding the life of the people into one great nationality. If the Aryans and the non-Aryans met, it was for the purpose of making one people out of them, Brahmanism with its great culture succeeded in binding the whole of India and was indeed a mighty unifying force. Buddhism with its protests against Brahmanism served the same great historical purpose; and from Magadba to Taxila was one great Buddhistic empire which succeeded not only in broadening the basis of Indian unit, but in creating, what is perhaps not less important, the greater India beyond the Himalayas and beyond the seas, so much so that the sacred city where we have met may be regarded as a place of pilgrimage of millions and millions of people of Asiatic races. Then came the Mahomedans of diverse races, but with one culture which was their common heritage. For a time it looked as if here was disintegrating force, an enemy to the growth of Indian nationalism, but the Mahomedans made their home in India, and, while they brought a new outlook and a wonderful vitality to the Indian life, with infinite wisdom, they did as little as possible to disturb the growth of life in the villages where India really lives. This new outlook was necessary for India; and if the two sister streams met, it was only to fulfil themselves and face the destiny of Indian history. Then came the English with their alien culture, their foreign methods, delivering a rude shock of this growing nationality; but the shock has only completed the unifying process so that the purpose of history is practically fulfilled. The great Indian nationality is in sight. It already stretches its hands across the Himalayas not only to Asia but to the whole of the world, not aggressively, but to demand its recognition, and to offer its contribution. . . .

We have, therefore, to foster the spirit of Nationality. True development of the Indian nation must necessarily lie in the path of Swaraj. A question has often been asked as to what is Swaraj. Swaraj is indefinable and is not to be confused with any particular system of Government. . . . Swaraj is the natural expression of the national mind. The full outward expression of that mind covers, and must necessarily cover, the whole life history of a nation. Yes it is true that Swaraj begins when the true development of a nation begins, because, as I have said, Swaraj is the expression of the national mind. The question of nationalism, therefore, looked at from another point of view, is the same question as that of Swaraj. The question of all questions in India today is the attainment of Swaraj.

I now come to the question of method. I have to repeat that it has been proved beyond any doubt that the method of non-violent non-co-operation is the only method which we must follow to secure a system of Government which may in reality be the foundation of Swaraj. It is hardly necessary to discuss the philosophy of non-co-operation. I shall simply state the different viewpoints from which this question may be discussed. From the national point of view the method of non-co-operation means the attempt of the nation to concentrate upon its own energy and to stand on its own strength. From the ethical point of view, non-co-operation means the method of self-purification, the withdrawal from that which is injurious to the development of the nation, and therefore to the good of humanity. From the spiritual point of view, Swaraj means that isolation which in the language of Sadhana is called *protyahar*—that withdrawal from the forces which are foreign to our nature—and isolation and withdrawal which is necessary in order to bring out from our hidden depths the soul of the nation in all her glory. I do not desire to labour the point, but from every conceivable point of view, the method of non-violent non-co-operation must be regarded as the true method of "following in the path of Swaraj." . . .

I believe in revolutions, but I repeat, violence defeats freedom. . . .

Non-violence is not an idle dream. It was not in vain that Mahatma declared "put up thy sword into the sheath." Let those who are "of the truth" hear his voice as those others heard a mightier voice two thousand years ago. . . .

I shall place before you one by one the items of work, which, in my opinion, the Indian National Congress should prescribe for the nation.

It should commence its work for the year by a clearer declaration of the rights of the different communities in India under the Swaraj Government. So far as the Hindus and the Mahomedans are concerned there should be a clearer and emphatic confirmation of what is known as the Lucknow Compact, and along with that there should be an emphatic recognition of each other's rights, and each should be prepared to undergo some kind of sacrifice in favour of the other. Let me give an instance to make my meaning clear. Every devout Musalman objects to any music in front of a mosque, and every devout and orthodox Hindu objects to cows being slaughtered. May not the Hindus and the Musalmans of India enter into a solemn compact so that there may not be any music before any mosque and that no cows may be slaughtered? Other instances may be quoted. There should be a scheme of a series of sacrifices to be suffered by each community so that they may advance shoulder to shoulder in the path of Swaraj. As regards the other communities such as Sikhs, Christians and Parsees, the Hindus and the Mahomedans who constitute the bulk of the people should be prepared to give them even more than the proportional share in the Swaraj administration. I suggest that the Congress should bring about real agreement between all these communities by which the rights of every minority should be clearly recognized in order to remove all doubts which may arise and all apprehensions which probably exist. I need hardly add that I include among Christians not only pure Indians, but also Anglo-Indians and other people who have chosen to make India their home. Such an agreement as I have indicated was always necessary, but such an agreement is specially necessary in view of the work which faces us today.

I further think that the policy of exclusiveness which we have been following during the last two years should not be abandoned. There is in every country a number of people who are selfless followers of liberty and who desire to see every country free. We can no longer afford to lose their sympathy and co-operation. In my opinion, there should be established Congress Agencies in America and in every European country. We must keep ourselves in touch with world movements and be in constant communication with the lovers of freedom all over the world.

Even more important than this participation of India is the great Asiatic Federation, which I see in the course of formation. I have hardly any doubt that the Pan-Islamic movement, which was started on a somewhat narrow basis, has given way or is about to give way to the great Federation of all Asiatic people. It is the union of the oppressed nationalities of Asia. Is India to remain outside this union? I admit that our freedom must be won by ourselves but such a bond of friendship and love, or sympathy and co-operation, between India and the rest of Asia, nay, between India and all the liberty-loving people of the world, is destined to bring about world peace. World peace to my mind means the freedom of every nationality, and I go further and say that no nation on the face of the earth can be really free when other nations are in bondage. The policy which we have hitherto pursued was absolutely necessary for the concentration of the work which we took upon ourselves to perform, and I agreed to that policy whole-heartedly. The hope of the attainment of Swaraj or a substantial basis of Swaraj in the course of the year made such concentration absolutely necessary. Today that very work demands broader sympathy and a wider outlook.

STUDY QUESTIONS

1. How does Das look to history to justify his current course?
2. Of what specific terms does the principle of nonviolence consist?

23.7 FRANCIS GALTON, "AFRICA FOR THE CHINESE," 1873

Sir Francis Galton (1822–1911) was a British sociologist and psychologist, and a leader of the British Association for the Advancement of Science. Although he worked in many fields, the central theme of his research was the understanding of both the biologically determined and culturally acquired differences in human beings—what came to be known as the "nature vs. nurture" debate. He was a distant cousin of Charles Darwin, whose works influenced him profoundly, although their personal contact was not great. He pioneered the use of questionnaires in sociological research, and as a statistician he established the notions of standard deviation and regression toward the mean. He also helped to establish the analysis of fingerprints as a means

Francis Galton, "Africa for the Chinese: To the Editor of The Times." *The Times*, June 5, 1873.

of identification. Galton coined the term *eugenics* and was an ardent supporter of its practice. (He once wrote, somewhat laconically, "There exists a sentiment, for the most part quite unreasonable, against the gradual extinction of an inferior race.") In 1873 he wrote the following letter to the editor of the *London Times*.

Sir,—In a few days Sir Bartle Frere[1] will return to England, and public attention will be directed to the East Coast of Africa. I am desirous of availing myself of the opportunity to ventilate some speculations of my own, which you may, perhaps, consider of sufficient interest to deserve publication in the Times. My proposal is to make the encouragement of the Chinese settlements at one or more suitable places on the East Coast of Africa a part of our national policy, in the belief that the Chinese immigrants would not only maintain their position, but that they would multiply and their descendants supplant the inferior Negro race. I should expect the large part of the African seaboard, now sparsely occupied by lazy, palavering savages living under the nominal sovereignty of the Zanzibar, or Portugal, might in a few years be tenanted by industrious, order loving Chinese, living either as a semi-detached dependency of China, or else in perfect freedom under their own law. In the latter case their [position] would be similar to that of the inhabitants of Liberia, in West Africa, the territory which was purchased 50 years ago and set apart as an independent State for the reception of freed negroes from America.

The opinion of the public on the real worth of the Negro race has halted between the extreme views which have been long and loudly proclaimed. It refuses to follow those of the early abolitionists, that all the barbarities in Africa are to be traced to the effects of a foreign slave trade, because travelers continually speak of similar barbarities existing in regions to which the slave trade has not penetrated. Captain Colomb[2] has written a well-argued chapter on this matter, in his recent volume. On the other hand, the opinion of the present day repudiates the belief that the negro is an extremely inferior being, because there are notorious instances of negroes possessing high intelligence and culture, some of whom acquire large fortunes in commerce, and others become considerable men in other walks of life. The truth appears to be that individuals of the mental caliber I have just described are much more exceptional in the negro than in the Anglo-Saxon race, and that average negroes possess too little intellect, self-reliance, and self-control to make it possible for them to sustain the burden of any respectable form of civilization without a large measure of external guidance and support. The Chinaman is a being of another kind, who is endowed with a remarkable aptitude for a high material civilization. He is seen to the least advantage in his own country, where a temporary dark age still prevails, which has not sapped the genius of the race, though it has stunted the developed the of each member of it, by the rigid enforcement of an effete system of classical education which treats originality as a social crime. All the bad parts of his character, as his lying and servility, spring from timidity due to an education that has cowed him, and no treatment is better calculated to remedy that evil than location in a free settlement. The natural capacity of the Chinaman shows itself by the success with which, notwithstanding his timidity, he competes with strangers, wherever he may reside. The Chinese emigrants possess an extraordinary instinct for political and social organization; they contrive to establish for themselves a police and internal government, and they give no trouble to their rulers so long as they are left to manage those matters by themselves. They are good-tempered, frugal, industrious, saving, commercially inclined, and extraordinarily prolific. They thrive in all countries, the natives of the Southern provinces being perfectly able to labor and multiply in the hottest climates. Of all known varieties of mankind there is none so appropriate as the Chinaman to

---

[1] The governor of India from 1862 to 1867.

[2] Philip Howard Colomb (1831–1899) was a British naval officer and historian.

become the future occupant of the enormous regions which lie between the tropics, whose extent is far more vast than it appears, from the cramped manner in which those latitudes are pictured in the ordinary maps of the world. But take a globe and examine it, and consider the huge but poorly-peopled bulk of Africa, by whose side the areas of India and of China look insignificant, and think what a field lies there for the development of a suitable race. The Hindoo cannot fulfil the required conditions nearly as well as the Chinaman, for he is inferior to him in strength, industry, aptitude for saving, business habits, and prolific power. The Arab is little more than an eater up of other men's produce; he is a destroyer rather than a creator, and he is unprolific.

The history of the world tells a tale of the continual displacement of populations, each by a worthier successor, and humanity gains thereby. We ourselves are no descendants of the aborigines of Britain, and our colonists were invaders of the regions they now occupy as their lawful home. But the countries into which the Anglo-Saxon race can be transfused are restricted to those where the climate is temperate. The Tropics are not for us, to inhabit permanently; the greater part of Africa is the heritage of people differently constituted to ourselves. On that continent, as elsewhere, one population continually drives out another. Consider its history as it extends over successive centuries. We note how Arab, Tuarick, Fellatah, Negroes of uncounted varieties, Cadre, Hottentot surge and reel to and fro in the struggle for existence. It is into this free flight among all present that I wish to see a new competitor introduced—namely, the Chinaman. The gain would be immense to the whole civilized world if we were to out-breed and finally displace the negro, as completely as the latter has displaced the aborigines of the West Indies. The magnitude of the gain may be partly estimated by making the converse supposition, namely, the loss that would ensue if China were somehow to be depopulated and restocked by Negroes.

The pressure of population in China is enormous, and its outflow is great and increasing. There is no lack of material for a suitable immigration into Africa. I do not say that it would be possible at any moment to persuade communities of men and women from Southern China to establish themselves in Africa; but I am assured, by excellent authorities, that occasions of political disturbances frequently arise when it would be practicable to do so by the promise of a free, or nearly free, grant of land. The Chinese have a land hunger, as well as a love for petty traffic, and they would find a field in which to gratify both of these tastes on the East African Coast. There are many Chinese capitalists resident in foreign parts who might speculate in such a system and warmly encourage it. If once successfully started, it ought to maintain itself. The colonist could not starve; and when they began to succeed they would send money to their relatives to enable them to follow, just as they now do from the many other parts of the world where they are located. For these reasons it is probable that the streams of emigration from China have sufficient "head" to enable them to reach and overflow the coasts of Eastern Africa if they were watched and judiciously diverted in that direction.

I have finally to speak of the political effort necessary to secure a free right of occupancy and of settlement at suitable points on the coast. No very serious obstacle seems to stand in the way; certainly none was met with when Liberia was founded. It is probable that as the success of such an enterprise would be of equally great value to all nations commercially interested in those parts, no national jealousy would be excited by its promotion, and the necessary territory could be obtained with little difficulty and at a small cost, to be advanced in the first instance as a charge on the land and hereafter to be redeemed.

STUDY QUESTIONS

1. Why does Galton feel that the Chinese are superior to the Africans? What evidence does he offer to support his argument?
2. Why does Galton feel that the Chinese should colonize Africa?

CHAPTER 24

THE WORLD AT WAR (PART I)

24.1 RUDYARD KIPLING, *FRANCE AT WAR*, 1915

Rudyard Kipling (1865–1936) was an India-born British writer best known for his many volumes of short stories and of poetry, as well as his novel *Kim* (1901). He was awarded the Nobel Prize for Literature in 1907. A champion of British imperialism, he ardently supported the entry in World War I—although his enthusiasm received a severe blow when news arrived of his son's death in battle in September 1915. His book *France at War*, which was published in that year, was part of a series of stories commissioned by the British government to entertain the nation and promote support for the war effort by depicting the atrocities of the Germans, the heroism of the British men, and the steadfast courage of French and British women. Portions of the first chapter ("On the Frontier of Civilisation") appear below.

"It's a pretty park," said the French artillery officer. "We've done a lot for it since the owner left. I hope he'll appreciate it when he comes back."

The car traversed a winding drive through woods, between banks embellished with little chalets of a rustic nature. At first, the chalets stood their full height above ground, suggesting tea-gardens in England. Further on they sank into the earth till, at the top of the ascent, only their solid brown roofs showed. Torn branches drooping across the driveway, with here and there a scorched patch of undergrowth, explained the reason of their modesty.

The chateau that commanded these glories of forest and park sat boldly on a terrace. There was nothing wrong with it except, if one looked closely, a few scratches or dints on its white stone walls, or a neatly drilled hole under a flight of steps. One such hole ended in an unexploded shell. "Yes," said the officer. "They arrive here occasionally."

Something bellowed across the folds of the wooded hills; something grunted in reply. Something passed overhead, querulously but not without dignity. Two clear fresh barks joined the chorus, and a man moved lazily in the direction of the guns.

"Well. Suppose we come and look at things a little," said the commanding officer.

AN OBSERVATION POST

There was a specimen tree—a tree worthy of such a park—the sort of tree visitors are always taken to admire. A ladder ran up it to a platform. What little wind there was swayed the tall top, and the ladder creaked like a ship's gangway. A telephone bell tinkled 50 foot overhead. Two invisible guns spoke fervently for half a minute, and broke off like terriers choked on a leash. We climbed till the topmost platform swayed sicklily beneath us. Here one found a rustic shelter, always of the tea-garden pattern, a table, a map, and a little window wreathed with living branches that gave one the first view of the Devil and all his works. It was a stretch of open country, with a few sticks like old tooth-brushes which had once been trees round a farm. The rest was yellow grass, barren to all appearance as the veldt.

"The grass is yellow because they have used gas here," said an officer. "Their trenches are—. You can see for yourself."

The guns in the woods began again. They seemed to have no relation to the regularly spaced bursts of smoke along a little smear in the desert earth two thousand yards away—no connection at all with the strong voices overhead coming and going. It was as impersonal as the drive of the sea along a breakwater.

Thus it went: a pause—a gathering of sound like the race of an incoming wave; then the high-flung heads of breakers spouting white up the face of a groyne. Suddenly, a seventh wave broke and spread the shape of its foam like a plume overtopping all the others.

"That's one of our torpilleurs—what you call trench-sweepers," said the observer among the whispering leaves.

Some one crossed the platform to consult the map with its ranges. A blistering outbreak of white smoke rose a little beyond the large plume. It was as though the tide had struck a reef out yonder.

Then a new voice of tremendous volume lifted itself out of a lull that followed. Somebody laughed. Evidently the voice was known.

"That is not for us," a gunner said. "They are being waked up from—" he named a distant French position. "So and so is attending to them there. We go on with our usual work. Look! Another torpilleur."

"THE BARBARIAN"

Again a big plume rose; and again the lighter shells broke at their appointed distance beyond it. The smoke died away on that stretch of trench, as the foam of a swell dies in the angle of a harbour wall, and broke out afresh half a mile lower down. In its apparent laziness, in its awful deliberation, and its quick spasms of wrath, it was more like the work of waves than of men; and our high platform's gentle sway and glide was exactly the motion of a ship drifting with us toward that shore.

"The usual work. Only the usual work," the officer explained. "Sometimes it is here. Sometimes above or below us. I have been here since May."

A little sunshine flooded the stricken landscape and made its chemical yellow look more foul. A detachment of men moved out on a road which ran toward the French trenches, and then vanished at the foot of a little rise. Other men appeared moving toward us with that concentration of purpose and bearing shown in both Armies when—dinner is at hand. They looked like people who had been digging hard.

"The same work. Always the same work!" the officer said. "And you could walk from here to the sea or to Switzerland in that ditch—and you'll find the same work going on everywhere. It isn't war."

"It's better than that," said another. "It's the eating-up of a people. They come and they fill the trenches and they die, and they die; and they send more and those die. We do the same, of course, but—look!"

He pointed to the large deliberate smoke-heads renewing themselves along that yellowed beach. "That is the frontier of civilization. They have all civilization against them—those brutes yonder. It's not the local victories of the old wars that we're after. It's the barbarian—all the barbarian. Now, you've seen the whole thing in little. Come and look at our children."

SOLDIERS IN CAVES

We left that tall tree whose fruits are death ripened and distributed at the tingle of small bells. The observer returned to his maps and calculations; the telephone-boy stiffened up beside his exchange as the amateurs went out of his life. Some one called down through the branches to ask who was attending to—Belial, let us say, for I could not catch the gun's name. It seemed to belong to that terrific new voice which had lifted itself for the second or third time. It appeared from the reply that if Belial talked too long he would be dealt with from another point miles away.

The troops we came down to see were at rest in a chain of caves which had begun life as quarries and had been fitted up by the army for its own uses. There were underground corridors, ante-chambers, rotundas, and ventilating shafts with a bewildering play of cross lights, so that wherever you looked you saw Goya's pictures of men-at-arms.

Every soldier has some of the old maid in him, and rejoices in all the gadgets and devices of his own invention. Death and wounding come by nature, but to lie dry, sleep soft, and keep yourself clean by forethought and contrivance is art, and in all things the Frenchman is gloriously an artist.

Moreover, the French officers seem as mother-keen on their men as their men are brother-fond of them. Maybe the possessive form of address: "Mon general," "mon capitaine," helps the idea, which our men cloke in other and curter phrases. And those soldiers, like ours, had been welded for months in one furnace. As an officer said: "Half our orders now need not be given. Experience makes us think together." I believe, too, that if a French private has an idea—and they are full of ideas—it reaches his C.O. quicker than it does with us.

THE SENTINEL HOUNDS

The overwhelming impression was the brilliant health and vitality of these men and the quality of their breeding. They bore themselves with swing and rampant delight in life, while their voices as they talked in the side-caverns among the stands of arms were the controlled voices of civilization. Yet, as the lights pierced the gloom they looked like bandits dividing the spoil. One picture, though far from war, stays with me. A perfectly built, dark-skinned young giant had peeled himself out of his blue coat and had brought it down with a swish upon the shoulder of a half-stripped comrade who was kneeling at his feet with some footgear. They stood against a background of semi-luminous blue haze, through which glimmered a pile of coppery straw half covered by a red blanket. By divine accident of light and pose it reminded one of St. Martin giving his cloak to the beggar. There were scores of pictures in these galleries—notably a rock-hewn chapel where the red of the cross on the rough canvas altar-cloth glowed like a ruby. Further inside the caves we found a row of little rock-cut kennels, each inhabited by one wise, silent dog. Their duties begin in at night with the sentinels and listening-posts. "And believe me," a proud instructor, "my fellow here knows the difference between the noise of our shells and the Boche shells."

When we came out into the open again there were good opportunities for this study. Voices and wings met and passed in the air, and, perhaps, one strong young tree had not been bending quite so far across the picturesque park-drive when we first went that way.

"Oh, yes," said an officer, "shells have to fall somewhere, and," he added with fine toleration, "it is, after all, against us that the Boche directs them. But come you and look at my dug-out. It's the most superior of all possible dug-outs."

"No. Come and look at our mess. It's the Ritz of these parts." And they joyously told how they had got, or procured, the various fittings and elegancies, while hands stretched out of the gloom to shake, and men nodded welcome and greeting all through that cheery brotherhood in the woods.

WORK IN THE FIELDS

The voices and the wings were still busy after lunch, when the car slipped past the tea-houses in the drive, and came into a country where women and children worked among the crops. There were large raw shell holes by the wayside or in the midst of fields, and often a cottage or a villa had been smashed as a bonnet-box is smashed by an umbrella. That must be part of Belial's work when he bellows so truculently among the hills to the north.

We were looking for a town that lives under shellfire. The regular road to it was reported unhealthy—not that the women and children seemed to care. We took byways of which certain exposed heights and corners were lightly blinded by wind-brakes of dried tree-tops. Here the shell holes were rather thick on the ground. But the women and the children and the old men went on with their work with the cattle and the crops; and where a house had been broken by shells the rubbish was collected in a neat pile, and where a room or two still remained usable, it was inhabited, and the tattered window-curtains fluttered as proudly as any flag. And time was when I used to denounce young France because it tried to kill itself beneath my car wheels; and the fat old women who crossed roads without warning; and the specially deaf old men who slept in carts on the wrong side of the road! Now, I could take off my hat to every single soul of them, but that one cannot traverse a whole land bareheaded. The nearer we came to our town the fewer were the people, till at last we halted in a well-built suburb of paved streets where there was no life at all. . . .

A WRECKED TOWN

The stillness was as terrible as the spread of the quick busy weeds between the paving-stones; the air smelt of pounded mortar and crushed stone; the sound of a footfall echoed like the drop of a pebble in a well. At first the horror of wrecked apartment-houses and big shops laid open makes one waste energy in anger. It is not seemly that rooms should be torn out of the sides of buildings as one tears the soft heart out of English bread; that villa roofs should lie across iron gates of private garages, or that drawing-room doors should flap alone and disconnected between two emptinesses of twisted girders. The eye wearies of the repeated pattern that burst shells make on stone walls, as the mouth sickens of the taste of mortar and charred timber. One quarter of the place had been shelled nearly level; the facades of the houses stood doorless, roofless, and windowless like stage scenery. This was near the cathedral, which is always a favourite mark for the heathen. They had gashed and ripped the sides of the cathedral itself, so that the birds flew in and out at will; they had smashed holes in the roof; knocked huge cantles out of the buttresses, and pitted and starred the paved square outside. They were at work, too, that very afternoon, though I do not think the cathedral was their objective for the moment. We walked to and fro in the silence of the streets and beneath the whirring wings overhead. Presently, a young woman, keeping to the wall, crossed a corner. An old woman opened a shutter (how it jarred!), and spoke to her. The silence closed again, but it seemed to me that I heard a sound of singing—the sort of chant one hears in nightmare-cities of voices crying from underground.

IN THE CATHEDRAL

"Nonsense," said an officer. "Who should be singing here?" We circled the cathedral again, and saw what pavement-stones can do against their own city, when the shell jerks them upward. But there was singing after all—on the other side of a little door in the flank of the cathedral. We looked in, doubting, and saw at least a hundred folk, mostly women, who knelt before the altar of an unwrecked chapel. We withdrew quietly from that holy ground, and it was not only the eyes of the French officers that filled with tears. Then there came an old, old thing with a prayer-book in her hand, pattering across the square, evidently late for service.

"And who are those women?" I asked.

"Some are caretakers; people who have still little shops here. (There is one quarter where you can buy things.) There are many old people, too, who will not go away. They are of the place, you see."

"And this bombardment happens often?" I said.

"It happens always. Would you like to look at the railway station? Of course, it has not been so bombarded as the cathedral."

We went through the gross nakedness of streets without people, till we reached the railway station, which was very fairly knocked about, but, as my friends said, nothing like as much as the cathedral. Then we had to cross the end of a long street down which the Boche could see clearly. As one glanced up it, one perceived how the weeds, to whom men's war is the truce of God, had come back and were well established the whole length of it, watched by the long perspective of open, empty windows.

STUDY QUESTIONS

1. Why does Kipling portray the British and French trenches as the "frontiers of civilization"? What does this say about the German forces that are positioned on the other side of the trenches?
2. In his depiction of the soldiers, of women and children working in the fields, of the voices filling the cathedral with song, how does Kipling portray the French?

24.2 EXTRACTS FROM THE TREATY OF VERSAILLES, 1919

The Treaty of Versailles concluded World War I. Signed between the Axis powers and the victorious Allies, it was drafted primarily by the "Big Three," Britain, France, and the United States, represented by their leaders, David Lloyd George, Georges Clemenceau, and Woodrow Wilson, respectively. Signed at the Palace of Versailles, outside Paris, the treaty reflected the different positions of the victors. France looked to permanently end any future threat from Germany and exact vengeance for wartime losses, whereas President Wilson's "Fourteen Points" offered a somewhat softer landing for Germany. The British government walked a fine line between its public's demands for vengeance and its own concerns that Germany should remain a solid wall against Russia's Communism. The final treaty imposed heavy reparation costs and territorial losses on Germany, however, and its severity played a role in the rise of Hitler and World War II.

PART III. POLITICAL CLAUSES FOR EUROPE

SECTION III.LEFT BANK OF THE RHINE

Article 42

Germany is forbidden to maintain or construct any fortifications either on the left bank of the Rhine or on the right bank to the west of a line drawn 50 kilometres to the East of the Rhine.

SECTION IV.SAAR BASIN

Article 45

As compensation for the destruction of the coal mines in the north of France and as partial payment towards the total reparation due from Germany for the damage resulting from the war, Germany cedes to France in full and absolute possession, with exclusive rights of exploitation,

From Jonathan F. Scott and Alexander Baltzly, *Readings in European History since 1814*. New York: F. S. Crofts & Co., 1930, pp. 546–50.

unencumbered and free from all debts and charges of any kind, the coal mines situated in the Saar Basin as defined in Article 48. [Article 48 outlines boundaries. Editor's note.]

Article 49

Germany renounces in favour of the League of Nations, in the capacity of trustee, the government of the territory defined above.

At the end of fifteen years from the coming into force of the present Treaty the inhabitants of the said territory shall be called upon to indicate the sovereignty under which they desire to be placed.

Article 50, Annex, Chapter II

16

The Government of the territory of the Saar Basin shall be entrusted to a Commission representing the League of Nations. The Commission shall sit in the territory of the Saar Basin.

17

The Governing Commission provided for by paragraph 16 shall consist of five members chosen by the Council of the League of Nations, and will include one citizen of France, one native inhabitant of the Saar Basin, not a citizen of France, and three members belonging to three countries other than France or Germany.

The members of the Governing Commission shall be appointed for one year and may be re-appointed. They can be removed by the Council of the League of Nations, which will provide for their replacement.

The members of the Governing Commission will be entitled to a salary which will be fixed by the Council of the League of Nations, and charged on the local revenues.

18

The Chairman of the Governing Commission shall be appointed for one year from among the members of the Commission by the Council of the League of Nations and may be re-appointed.

The Chairman will act as the executive of the Commission. . . .

SECTION V. ALSACE-LORRAINE

The High Contracting Parties, recognising the moral obligation to redress the wrong done by Germany in 1871 both to the rights of France and to the wishes of the population of Alsace and Lorraine, which were separated from their country in spite of the solemn protest of their representatives at the Assembly of Bordeaux,

Agree upon the following Articles:

Article 51

The territories which were ceded to Germany in accordance with the Preliminaries of Peace signed at Versailles on February 26, 1871, and the Treaty of Frankfort of May 10, 1871, are restored to French sovereignty as from the date of the Armistice of November 11, 1918.

The provisions of the Treaties establishing the delimitation of the frontiers before 1871 shall be restored.

SECTION VI. AUSTRIA

Article 80

Germany acknowledges and will respect strictly the independence of Austria, within the frontiers which may be fixed in a Treaty between that State and the Principal Allied and Associated Powers; she agrees that this independence shall be inalienable, except with the consent of the Council of the League of Nations.

SECTION VII. CZECHO-SLOVAK STATE

Article 81

Germany, in conformity with the action already taken by the Allied and Associated Powers, recognises the complete independence of the Czecho-Slovak State which will include the autonomous territory of the Ruthenians to the south of the Carpathians. Germany hereby recognises the frontiers of this State as determined by the Principal Allied and Associated Powers and the other interested States.

SECTION VIII. POLAND

Article 87

Germany, in conformity with the action already taken by the Allied and Associated Powers, recognises the complete independence of Poland. . . .

Article 89

Poland undertakes to accord freedom of transit to persons, goods, vessels, carriages, wagons and mails in transit between East Prussia and the rest of Germany over Polish territory, including territorial waters, and to treat them at least as favourably as the persons, goods, vessels, carriages, wagons and mails respectively of Polish or of any other more favoured nationality, origin, importation, starting-point, or ownership as regards facilities, restrictions and all other matters. . . .

SECTION VIII.FREE CITY OF DANZIG

Article 102

The Principal Allied and Associated Powers undertake to establish the town of Danzig, together with the rest of the territory described in Article 100, as a Free City. It will be placed under the protection of the League of Nations.

SECTION XIV.RUSSIA AND RUSSIAN STATES

Article 116

Germany acknowledges and agrees to respect as permanent and inalienable the independence of all the territories which were part of the former Russian Empire on August 1, 1914.

In accordance with the provisions of Article 259 of Part IX (Financial Clauses) and Article 292 of Part X (Economic Clauses) Germany accepts definitely the abrogation of the Brest–Litovsk Treaties and of all other treaties, conventions and agreements entered into by her with the Maximalist Government in Russia.

The Allied and Associated Powers formally reserve the rights of Russia to obtain from Germany restitution and reparation based on the principles of the present Treaty.

PART IV. GERMAN RIGHTS AND INTERESTS OUTSIDE GERMANY

SECTION I.GERMAN COLONIES

Article 119

Germany renounces in favour of the Principal Allied and Associated Powers all her rights and titles over her oversea possessions.

PART V. MILITARY, NAVAL AND AIR CLAUSES

SECTION I.MILITARY CLAUSES

Article 159

The German military forces shall be demobilised and reduced as prescribed hereinafter.

Article 160

(1) By a date which must not be later than March 31, 1920, the German Army must not comprise more than seven divisions of infantry and three divisions of cavalry.

After that date the total number of effectives in the Army of the States constituting Germany must not exceed one hundred thousand men, including officers and establishments of depots. The Army shall be devoted exclusively to the maintenance of order within the territory and to the control of the frontiers.

The total effective strength of officers, including the personnel of staffs, whatever their composition, must not exceed four thousand. . . .

SECTION II.NAVAL CLAUSES

Article 181

After the expiration of a period of two months from the coming into force of the present Treaty the German naval forces in commission must not exceed:

6 battleships of the *Deutschland* or *Lotharingen* type,
6 light cruisers,

12 destroyers,
12 torpedo boats,
or an equal number of ships constructed to replace them as provided in Article 190.

No submarines are to be included.

All other warships, except where there is provision to the contrary in the present Treaty, must be placed in reserve or devoted to commercial purposes.

SECTION III. AIR CLAUSES

Article 198

The armed forces of Germany must not include any military or naval air forces. . . .

PART VIII. REPARATION

SECTION I. GENERAL PROVISIONS

Article 231

The Allied and Associated Governments affirm and Germany accepts the responsibility of Germany and her allies for causing all the loss and damage to which the Allied and Associated Governments and their nationals have been subjected as a consequence of the war imposed upon them by the aggression of Germany and her allies.

Article 232

The Allied and Associated Governments recognise that the resources of Germany are not adequate, after taking into account permanent diminutions of such resources which will result from other provisions of the present Treaty, to make complete reparation for all such loss and damage.

The Allied and Associated Governments, however, require, and Germany undertakes, that she will make compensation for all damage done to the civilian population of the Allied and Associated Powers and to their property during the period of the belligerency of each as an Allied or Associated Power against Germany by such aggression by land, by sea and from the air, and in general all damage as defined in Annex *I* hereto. . . .

Article 233

The amount of the above damage for which compensation is to be made by Germany shall be determined by an Inter-Allied Commission, to be called the *Reparation Commission* and constituted in the form and with the powers set forth hereunder and in Annexes II to VII inclusive hereto.

This Commission shall consider the claims and give to the German Government a just opportunity to be heard.

The findings of the Commission as to the amount of damage defined as above shall be concluded and notified to the German Government on or before May 1, 1921, as representing the extent of that Government's obligations. . . .

Article 234

The Reparation Commission shall after May 1, 1921, from time to time, consider the resources and capacity of Germany, and, after giving her representatives a just opportunity to be heard, shall have discretion to extend the date, and to modify the form of payments, such as are to be provided for in accordance with Article 233; but not to cancel any part, except with the specific authority of the several Governments represented upon the Commission.

STUDY QUESTIONS

1. In what respects does Article 231 form the basis for the rest of the treaty terms?
2. How did the treaty aim to humiliate the German economy permanently?
3. Are the treaty terms consistent with President Wilson's goals of national self-determination?

24.3 ERNST JÜNGER, *STORM OF STEEL*, 1920

German officer Ernst Jünger (1895–1998) was wounded a total of fourteen times during World War I, including five times by bullets, one of which went through his chest. He survived, however, to be awarded the Iron Cross, 1st Class, and publish his memoir, *Storm of Steel*, an account of fighting on the Western Front. This was one of the first accounts of trench warfare. Largely unexpurgated on publication, it contained graphic passages, which shocked much of its audience, detailing the utter destruction this new kind of warfare wrought on the people and the landscape.

21.11—I took an entrenching party from the Altenburg Redoubt to C sector. One of them, Landsturmsman Diener, climbed on to a ledge in the side of the trench to shovel earth over the top. He was scarce up when a shot fired from the sap got him in the skull and laid him dead on the floor of the trench. He was married and had four children. His comrades lay in wait a long while behind the parapet to take vengeance. They sobbed with rage. It is remarkable how little they grasp the war as an objective thing. They seem to regard the Englishman who fired the fatal shot as a personal enemy. I can understand it.

. . .

One morning, when, thoroughly wet through, I went up out of the dugout into the trench, I could scarcely believe my eyes. The field of battle that hitherto had been marked by the desolation of death itself had taken on the appearance of a fair. The occupants of the trenches on both sides had been driven to take to the top, and now there was a lively traffic and exchange going on in schnaps, cigarettes, uniform buttons, etc., in front of the wire. The crowds of khaki-coloured figures that streamed from the hitherto so deserted English trenches had a most bewildering effect.

Suddenly there was a shot that dropped one of our fellows dead in the mud. . . . Whereupon both sides disappeared like moles into their trenches.

. . .

It has always been my ideal in war to eliminate all feelings of hatred and to treat my enemy as an enemy only in battle and to honour him as a man according to his courage. It is exactly in this that I have found many kindred souls among British officers. It depends, of course, on not letting oneself be blinded by an excessive national feeling, as the case generally is between the French and the Germans. The consciousness of the importance of one's own nation ought to reside as a matter of course and unobtrusively in everybody, just as an unconditional sense of honour does in the gentleman. Without this it is impossible to give others their due.

. . .

We spent Christmas Eve in the line. The men stood in the mud and sang Christmas carols that were drowned by the enemy machine-guns. On Christmas Day we lost a man in No. 3 platoon by a flanking shot through the head. Immediately after, the English attempted a friendly overture and put up a Christmas tree on their parapet. But our fellows were so embittered that they fired and knocked it over. And this in turn was answered with rifle grenades. In this miserable fashion we celebrated Christmas Day.

. . .

At night when I lay down on my plank bed I always had the pleasant consciousness of having in

From Ernst Jünger, *Der Kampf als inneres Erlebnis*. Berlin: E.G. Mittler & Sohn, 1929, pp. xi–xv, 1–5, as quoted in Roger Griffin, *Fascism*, Oxford: Oxford University Press, 1995, pp. 108–9.

my sphere fulfilled the expectations those at home had of me. I had given all my energies to the defence of my two hundred metres of the front line, and cared for the well-being of my sixty men.

It was only now when there was time for it that I was able to experience this feeling to the full. In the winter months we had not a thought in the trenches but of digging and "Will this damned business never end?" It is not danger, however extreme it may be, that depresses the spirit of the men so much as over-fatigue and wretched conditions. People who have leisure can afford themselves every luxury, even that of heroic feelings. This is true for the people as a whole. Its moral worth can only reach its full height when the pressure of work is not crushing upon any section of it.

. . .

The villages we passed through as we marched to the front line had the appearance of lunatic asylums let loose. Whole companies were pushing walls down or sitting on the roofs of the houses throwing down the slates. Trees were felled, window-frames broken, and smoke and clouds of dust rose from heap after heap of rubbish. In short, an orgy of destruction was going on. The men were chasing round with incredible zeal, arrayed in the abandoned wardrobes of the population, in women's dresses and with top hats on their heads. With positive genius they singled out the main beams of the houses and, tying ropes round them, tugged with all their might, shouting out in time with their pulls, till the whole house collapsed. Others swung hammers and smashed whatever came in their way, from flowerpots on the window ledges to the glass-work of conservatories.

Every village up to the Siegfried line was a rubbish heap. Every tree felled, every road mined, every well fouled, every water-course dammed, every cellar blown up or made into a death-trap with concealed bombs, all supplies or metal sent back, all rails ripped up, all telephone wire rolled up, everything burnable burned. In short, the country over which the enemy were to advance had been turned into an utter desolation.

The moral justification of this has been much discussed. However, it seems to me that the gratified approval of arm-chair warriors and journalists is incomprehensible. When thousands of peaceful persons are robbed of their homes, the self-satisfaction of power may at least keep silence.

As for the necessity, I have of course, as a Prussian officer, no doubt whatever. War means the destruction of the enemy without scruple and by any means. War is the harshest of all trades, and the masters of it can only entertain humane feelings so long as they do no harm. It makes no difference that these operations which the situation demanded were not very pretty.

. . .

Even modern battle has its great moments. One hears it said very often and very mistakenly that the infantry battle has degenerated to an uninteresting butchery. On the contrary, to-day more than ever it is the individual that counts. Every one knows that who has seen them in their own realm, these princes of the trenches, with their hard, set faces, brave to madness, tough and agile to leap forward or back, with keen bloodthirsty nerves, whom no despatch ever mentions. Trench warfare is the bloodiest, wildest, and most brutal of all warfare, yet it too has had its men, men whom the call of the hour has raised up, unknown foolhardy fighters. Of all the nerve-racking moments of war none is so formidable as the meeting of two storm-troop leaders between the narrow walls of the trench. There is no retreat and no mercy then. Blood sounds in the shrill cry that is wrung like a nightmare from the breast.

. . .

After fourteen days I was lying on the feather mattress of a hospital train. Once again a German landscape flitted by me, tinged this time with the first dyes of autumn, and once again, as on that time at Heidelberg I was gripped by the sad and proud feeling of being more closely bound to my country because of the blood shed for her greatness. Why should I conceal that tears smarted in my eyes when I thought of the end of the enterprise in which I had borne my share? I had set out to the war gaily enough, thinking we were to hold a festival on which all the pride of youth was lavished, and I had thought little, once I was in the thick of it, about the ideal that I had to stand for. Now I looked back: four years of development in the midst of a generation predestined to death, spent in caves, smoke-filled trenches, and shell-illumined wastes; years enlivened only by the pleasures of a mercenary, and nights of guard after guard in an endless perspective; in short, a monotonous calendar full of hardships and privation, divided by the red-letter days of battles. And almost without any thought of mine, the idea of the Fatherland had been distilled from all these afflictions in a clearer and brighter essence. That was the final winnings in a game on which so often all had been staked: the nation was no longer for me an empty thought veiled in symbols; and how could it have been otherwise when I had seen so many die for its sake, and been schooled myself to stake my life for its credit every minute, day and night, without a thought? And so, strange as it may sound, I learned from this very four years' schooling in force and in all the fantastic extravagance of material warfare that life has no depth of meaning except when it is pledged for an ideal, and that there are ideals in comparison with which the life of an individual and even of a people has no weight. And though the aim for which I fought as an individual, as an atom in the whole body of the army, was not to be achieved, though material force cast us, apparently, to the earth, yet we learned once and for all to stand for a cause and if necessary to fall as befitted men.

Hardened as scarcely another generation ever was in fire and flame, we could go into life as though from the anvil; into friendship, love, politics, professions, into all that destiny had in store. It is not every generation that is so favoured.

STUDY QUESTIONS

1. How does Jünger reveal a sympathy with an understanding of the enemy?
2. What is the point Jünger makes about the famous "Christmas Truce" of 1914?
3. How does he underscore the poorly understood and unusually horrific nature of this conflict?

24.4 ROBERT GRAVES, *GOODBYE TO ALL THAT*, 1929

Robert Graves (1895–1985) was a British writer whose talents spanned a wide range of genres, from novels and poetry to biography, history, mythology, and translation. He was born in 1895 in the London suburb of Wimbledon and lived most of his adult life on the Balearic island of Mallorca. *Goodbye to All That*, which he wrote when he was thirty-four, deals with his early life and his reasons for leaving England, never to make it his home again. But a large part of it also discusses his experiences in World War I, and the title may be a reference to the passing of the old order that the war represented. Along with the trauma and destruction of war, Graves comments on the social disruptions—and innovations—which accompanied the period, including the rise of feminism, pacifism, socialism, and atheism and the changes in literary and artistic expression that were to be so large a part of the early twentieth century.

From Robert Graves, *Goodbye to All That*. New York: Penguin Books, 2001, pp. 96, 97–8, 100–1, 103, 105–6, 190–2, 197–8, 199. By permission of Carcanet Press Limited and the estate of Robert Graves.

They began singing. Instead of the usual music-hall songs they sang Welsh hymns, each man taking a part. The Welsh always sang when pretending not to be scared; it kept them steady. And they never sang out of tune.

We marched towards the flashes, and could soon see the flare-lights curving across the distant trenches. The noise of the guns grew louder and louder. Presently we were among the batteries. From about two hundred yards behind us, on the left of the road, a salvo of four shells whizzed suddenly over our heads. This broke up *Aberystwyth* in the middle of a verse, and sent us off our balance for a few seconds; the column of fours tangled up. The shells went hissing away eastward; we saw the red flash and heard the hollow bang where they landed in German territory. The men picked up their step again and began chaffing. A lance-corporal dictated a letter home: "Dear auntie, this leaves me in the pink. We are at present wading in blood up to our necks. Send me fags and a life-belt. This war is a booger. Love and kisses."

. . .

Those were early days of trench warfare, the days of the jam-tin bomb and the gas-pipe trench-mortar: still innocent of Lewis or Stokes guns, steel helmets, telescopic rifle-sights, gas-shells, pill-boxes, tanks, well-organized trench-raids, or any of the later refinements of trench warfare.

After a meal of bread, bacon, rum, and bitter stewed tea sickly with sugar, we went through the broken trees to the east of the village and up a long trench to battalion headquarters. The wet and slippery trench ran through dull red clay. I had a torch with me, and saw that hundreds of field mice and frogs had fallen into the trench but found no way out. The light dazzled them, and because I could not help treading on them, I put the torch back in my pocket. We had no mental picture of what the trenches would be like, and were almost as ignorant as a young soldier who joined us a week or two later.

I reported to the company commander.

. . .

I had expected a grizzled veteran with a breastful of medals; but Dunn was actually two months younger than myself—one of the fellowship of "only survivors." Captain Miller of the Black Watch in the same division was another. Miller had escaped from the Rue du Bois massacre by swimming down a flooded trench. Only survivors had great reputations. Miller used to be pointed at in the streets when the battalion was back in reserve billets. "See that fellow? That's Jock Miller. Out from the start and hasn't got it yet." Dunn did not let the war affect his morale at all. He greeted me very easily with: "Well, what's the news from England? Oh, sorry, first I must introduce you. This is Walker—clever chap from Cambridge, fancies himself as an athlete. This is Jenkins, one of those elder patriots who chucked up their jobs to come here. This is Price—joined us yesterday, but we liked him at once: he brought some damn good whisky with him. Well, how long is the war going to last, and who's winning? We don't know a thing out here. And what's all this talk about war-babies? Price pretends ignorance on the subject." I told them about the war, and asked them about the trenches.

"About trenches," said Dunn. "Well, we don't know as much about trenches as the French do, and not near as much as Fritz does. We can't expect Fritz to help, but the French might do something. They are too greedy to let us have the benefit of their inventions. What wouldn't we give for their parachute-lights and aerial torpedoes! But there's never any connexion between the two armies, unless a battle is on, and then we generally let each other down."

. . .

"Time we all got to work. Look here, Graves, you lie down and have a doss on that bunk. I want you to take the watch before 'stand-to.' I'll wake you up and show you around. Where the hell's my revolver? I don't like to go out without it. Hello, Walker, what was wrong?"

Walker laughed. "A chap from the new draft. He had never fired his musketry course at Cardiff, and tonight he fired ball for the first time. It went to his head. He'd had a brother killed up at Ypres, and sworn to avenge him. So he blazed off all his own ammunition at nothing, and two bandoliers out of the ammunition-box besides. They call him the 'Human Maxim' now. His foresight's misty with heat. Corporal Parry should have stopped him; but he just leant up against the traverse and shrieked with laughter. I gave them both a good cursing. Some other new chaps started blazing away too. Fritz retaliated with machine-guns and whizz-bangs. No casualties. I don't know why. It's all quiet now. Everybody ready?"

. . .

I spent the rest of my watch in acquainting myself with the geography of the trench-section, finding how easy it was to get lost among culs-de-sac and disused alleys. Twice I overshot the company frontage and wandered among the Munster Fusiliers on the left. Once I tripped and fell with a splash into deep mud. My watch ended when the first signs of dawn showed. I passed the word along the line for the company to stand-to-arms. The N.C.O.s whispered hoarsely into the dugouts: "Stand-to, stand-to," and out the men tumbled with their rifles in their hands. Going towards company headquarters to wake the officers I saw a man lying on his face in a machine-gun shelter. I stopped and said: "Stand-to, there!" I flashed my torch on him and saw that one of his feet was bare.

The machine-gunner beside him said: "No good talking to him, sir."

I asked: "What's wrong? Why has he taken his boot and sock off?"

"Look for yourself, sir!"

I shook the sleeper by the arm and noticed suddenly the hole in the back of his head. He had taken off the boot and sock to pull the trigger of his rifle with one toe; the muzzle was in his mouth.

"Why did he do it?" I asked.

"He went through the last push, sir, and that sent him a bit queer; on top of that he got bad news from Limerick about his girl and another chap."

He belonged to the Munsters—their machine-guns overlapped the left of our company—and his suicide had already been reported. Two Irish officers came up. "We've had several of these lately," one of them told me. Then he said to the other: "While I remember, Callaghan, don't forget to write to his next-of-kin. Usual sort of letter; tell them he died a soldier's death, anything you like. I'm not going to report it as suicide."

. . .

Propaganda reports of atrocities were, it was agreed, ridiculous. We remembered that while the Germans *could* commit atrocities against enemy civilians, Germany itself, except for an early Russian cavalry raid, had never had the enemy on her soil. We no longer believed the highly-coloured accounts of German atrocities in Belgium; knowing the Belgians now at first-hand. By atrocities we meant, specifically, rape, mutilation, and torture—not summary shootings of suspected spies, harbourers of spies, *francs-tireurs*, or disobedient local officials. If the atrocity-list had to include the accidental-on-purpose bombing or machine-gunning of civilians from the air, the Allies were now committing as many atrocities as the Germans. French and Belgian civilians had often tried to win our sympathy by exhibiting mutilations of children—stumps of hands and feet, for instance—representing them as deliberate, fiendish atrocities when, as likely as not, they were merely the result of shell-fire. We did not believe rape to be any more common on the German side of the line than on the Allied side. And since a bully-beef diet, fear of death, and absence of wives made ample provision of women necessary in the occupied areas, no doubt the German army authorities provided brothels in the principal French towns behind the line, as the French did on the Allied side. We did not believe stories of women's forcible enlistment in these establishments. "What's wrong with the voluntary system?" we asked cynically.

As for atrocities against soldiers—where should one draw the line? The British soldier, at first, regarded as atrocious the use of bowie-knives by German patrols. After a time, he learned to use them himself; they were cleaner killing weapons than revolvers or bombs. The Germans regarded as equally atrocious the British Mark VII rifle bullet, which was more apt to turn on striking than the German bullet. For true atrocities, meaning personal rather than military violations of the code of war, few opportunities occurred—except in the interval between the surrender of prisoners and their arrival (or non-arrival) at headquarters. Advantage was only too often taken of this opportunity. Nearly every instructor in the mess could quote specific instances of prisoners having been murdered on the way back. The commonest motives were, it seems, revenge for the death of friends or relatives, jealousy of the prisoner's trip to a comfortable prison camp in England, military enthusiasm, fear of being suddenly overpowered by the prisoners, or, more simply, impatience with the escorting job. In any of these cases the conductors would report on arrival at headquarters that a German shell had killed the prisoners; and no questions would be asked. We had every reason to believe that the same thing happened on the German side, where prisoners, as useless mouths to feed in a country already short of rations, would be even less welcome. None of us had heard of German prisoners being more than threatened at headquarters to get military information from them. The sort that they could give was not of sufficient importance to make torture worthwhile; and anyhow, it had been found that, when treated kindly, prisoners were anxious in gratitude to tell as much as they knew. German intelligence officers had probably discovered that too.

. . .

The troops, while ready to believe in the Kaiser as a comic personal devil, knew the German soldier to be, on the whole, more devout than himself. In the instructors' mess we spoke freely of God and Gott as opposed tribal deities. For Anglican regimental chaplains we had little respect. If they had shown one-tenth the courage, endurance, and other human qualities that the regimental doctors showed, we agreed, the British Expeditionary Force might well have started a religious revival. But they had not, being under orders to avoid getting mixed up with the fighting and to stay behind with the transport. Soldiers could hardly respect a chaplain who obeyed these orders, and yet not one in fifty seemed sorry to obey them. Occasionally, on a quiet day in a quiet sector, the chaplain would make a daring afternoon visit to the support line and distribute a few cigarettes, before hurrying back. But he was always much to the fore in rest-billets. Sometimes the colonel would summon him to come up with the rations and bury the day's dead; he would arrive, speak his lines, and shoot off again. The position was complicated by the respect that most commanding officers had for the cloth—though not all. The colonel in one battalion I served with got rid of four new Anglican chaplains in four months; finally, he applied for a Roman Catholic, alleging a change of faith in the men under his command. For the Roman Catholic chaplains were not only permitted to visit posts of danger, but definitely enjoyed to be wherever fighting was, so that they could give extreme unction to the dying. And we had never heard of one who failed to do all that was expected of him and more. Jovial Father Gleeson of the Munsters, when all the officers were killed or wounded at the first battle of Ypres, had stripped off his black badges and, taking command of the survivors, held the line.

. . .

I felt better after a few weeks at Harfleur, though the knowledge that this was merely a temporary relief haunted me all the time. One day I left the mess to begin the afternoon's work on the drill-ground, and passed the place at which bombing instruction went on. A group of men stood around a table where the various types of bombs were set out for demonstration. I heard a sudden crash. A sergeant of the Royal Irish Rifles had been giving a little unofficial instruction before the proper instructor arrived. He picked up a No. 1 percussion-grenade and said: "Now lads, you've got to be careful here! Remember that if you touch anything while you're swinging this chap, it'll go off." To illustrate the point, he rapped the grenade against the table edge. It killed him and the man next to him and wounded twelve others more or less severely.

STUDY QUESTIONS

1. What divisions have opened up *among* the Allied armies, in Graves's description?
2. Why was the suicide not reported, and what caused it?

24.5 NORMAN ANGELL, *THE GREAT ILLUSION*, 1933

Norman Angell (1872–1967), after spending several years in the United States working variously as cowboy, farm laborer, and reporter, became the Paris-based editor of the English *Daily Mail* newspaper. He was an executive for the Committee against War and Fascism and a member of the executive committee of the League of Nations Union. During his tenure at the *Daily Mail* he produced his most memorable written work, *The Great Illusion*, which was an expanded version of a pamphlet he had written entitled "Europe's Optical Illusion." In this piece he made the case that a European war would be disastrous because the economies of Europe were so interdependent. Any disruption to a single commercial sector would affect every sector. Angell took a decidedly business-oriented approach in this book, seeing an appeal to economic interests as the only way to counter society's romanticism over bloody conflict. After a decade in politics back in Britain, Angell was awarded the Nobel Peace Prize.

The fact that Germany has of late come to the front as an industrial nation, making giant strides in general prosperity and well-being, is deemed also to be the result of her military successes and the increasing political power which she is coming to exercise in Continental Europe. These things, alike in Great Britain and in Germany, are accepted as the axioms of the problem. . . .

We know that in the world as it exists today, in spheres other than those of international rivalry, the race is to the strong, and the weak get scant consideration. Industrialism and commercialism are as full of cruelties as war itself—cruelties, indeed, that are longer drawn out, more refined, if less apparent, and, it may be, appealing less to the ordinary imagination than those of war. With whatever reticence we may put the philosophy into words, we all feel that conflict of interests in this world is inevitable, and that what is an incident of our daily lives should not be shirked as a condition of those occasional titanic conflicts which mold history.

The virile man doubts whether he ought to be moved by the plea of the "inhumanity" of war. The masculine mind accepts suffering, death itself, as a risk which we are all prepared to run even in the most unheroic forms of money-making. None of us refuses to use the railway train because of the occasional smash, to travel because of the occasional shipwreck. Indeed, peaceful industry demands in the long run a heavier toll even in life and blood than does war. It suffices to note the physique of the thousands—women as well as men—who pour through the factory gates of the north; the health of the children left at home, the kind of life that industry involves for millions, to say nothing of the casualty statistics in railroading, fishing, mining, and seamanship, to be persuaded of that fact. Even in the "conscious" brutality which we usually deem special to war, such peaceful industries as fishing and shipping reveal a dreadful plenty.[1] Our peaceful administration of the

From Norman Angell, *The Great Illusion*. New York: G. P. Putnam's Sons, 1933, pp. 65, 67–9, 71, 72.

[1] The *Matin* newspaper recently made a series of revelations, in which it was shown that the master of a French cod-fishing vessel had, for some trivial insubordinations, nearly disemboweled his cabin-boy, put salt into the intestines, and then thrown the quivering body into the hold with the cod-fish. So inured were the crew to brutality that they did not effectively protest, and the incident was only brought to light months later by wine-shop chatter. The *Matin* quotes this as the sort of brutality that marks the Newfoundland cod-fishing industry in French ships.

tropics not only takes its heavy toll in the health and lives of good men, but much of it involves a moral deterioration of human character as great—as does so much of our "peaceful" industry and trade.

Besides these peace sacrifices the "price of war" does not seem unduly high, and many may well feel that the trustees of a nation's interests ought not to shrink from paying that price should the efficient protection of those interests demand it. If the ordinary man is prepared, as we know he is, to risk his life in a dozen dangerous trades and professions for no object higher than that of improving his position or increasing his income, why should the statesman shrink from such sacrifices as the average war demands, if thereby the great interests which have been confided to him can be advanced? If it be true, as even the pacifist admits that it may be true, that the vital interests of a nation can be advanced by warfare; if, in other words, warfare can play some large part in the protection of the nation's heritage, the promotion of its welfare, then the rulers of a courageous people are justified in disregarding the suffering and the sacrifice that it may involve. And he will continue to receive the support of "the common man" so long as the latter feels that military predominance gives his nation the efficient protection of rights, its due share in the world's wealth and economic opportunity, enlarged commercial opportunities, wider markets, protection against the aggression of commercial rivals, all translatable into welfare and prosperity, not at all necessarily for himself personally, but for his people—those who should come first, by whom he feels he should stick as a matter of plain and simple loyalty. He faces the risk of war in the same spirit as that in which a sailor or a fisherman faces the risk of drowning, or a miner that of the choke-damp, or a doctor that of a fatal disease, because he would rather take the supreme risk than accept for himself and his dependents a lower situation, a narrower and meaner existence, with complete safety. He also asks whether the lower path is altogether free from risks. If he knows much of life, he knows that in so very many circumstances the bolder way is the safer way.

. . .

Not long since, an English Divine said that the root cause of all war was the selfishness and avarice of man. One thought of the spectacle which almost any war affords us, of tens of thousands of youngsters going to their deaths as to a feast, of the mothers who bid them good-by with smiling faces and breaking hearts; of the fathers who are so proud of them; of the millions who starve and skimp and suffer through the years without murmur. Selfishness? Avarice?

War does not arise because consciously wicked men take a course which they know to be wrong, but because good men on both sides pursue a course which they believe to be right, stand, as Lincoln stood when he made war, for the right as they see it. It is a case not of conscious and admitted wrong challenging unquestioned and admitted right; but of misunderstanding of right.

. . .

This, of course, does not imply that the economic motive should dominate life, but rather that it will unless the economic problem is solved: a hungry people is a people thinking first and last of bread. To turn their minds to other things, they must be fed.

. . .

1. Until economic difficulties are so far solved as to give the mass of the people the means of secure and tolerable physical existence, economic considerations and motives will tend to exclude all others. The way to give the spiritual a fair chance with ordinary men and women is not to be magnificently superior to their economic difficulties, but to find a solution for them. Until the economic dilemma is solved, no solution of moral difficulties will be adequate. If you want to get rid of the economic preoccupation, you must solve the worst of the economic problem.

STUDY QUESTIONS

1. Was the Great War in any sense an "average war," and who benefited and lost from it?
2. Why did "good men" on both sides of the conflict believe they were right, and what lessons can we learn from that factor?

CHAPTER 25

RADICAL REALIGNMENTS

25.1 JOHN MAYNARD KEYNES, *THE ECONOMIC CONSEQUENCES OF THE PEACE*, 1919

John Maynard Keynes (1883–1946) was born in Cambridge, England, and attended King's College, Cambridge, where he studied mathematics. While working in the British civil service he wrote his first book on economics, *Indian Currency and Finance*, an exploration of the Indian monetary system. After briefly lecturing at Cambridge, he returned to government service and worked his way up the bureaucracy at the Treasury. He was the British Treasury's principal representative at the Versailles negotiations, but he resigned his position because he felt that the treaty imposed such a financial burden on Germany as to make her politically unstable in the future. *The Economic Consequences of the Peace* laid out his case, and its publication in 1919 made Keynes a celebrity. In addition to his cogent and prophetic economic analysis, the book also provided a perceptive account of the motivations of the main negotiators, Britain's David Lloyd George, France's Clemenceau, and president Woodrow Wilson, all three of whom had their own specific agendas at Versailles.

EUROPE AFTER THE TREATY

This chapter must be one of pessimism. . . .

. . .

What then is our picture of Europe? A country population able to support life on the fruits of its own agricultural production but without the accustomed surplus for the towns, and also (as a result of the lack of imported materials and so of variety and amount in the saleable manufactures of the towns) without the usual incentives to market food in return for other wares; an industrial population unable to keep its strength for lack of food, unable to earn a livelihood for lack of materials, and so unable to make good by imports from abroad the failure of productivity at home. Yet, according to Mr. Hoover, "a rough estimate would indicate that the population of Europe is at least 100,000,000 greater than can be supported without imports, and must live by the production and distribution of exports."

John Maynard Keynes, *The Economic Consequences of the Peace*. New York: Harcourt, Brace and Howe, 1920, pp. 226, 234–5, 237–8, 250–1.

. . .

We are thus faced in Europe with the spectacle of an extraordinary weakness on the part of the great capitalist class, which has emerged from the industrial triumphs of the nineteenth century, and seemed a very few years ago our all-powerful master. The terror and personal timidity of the individuals of this class is now so great, their confidence in their place in society and in their necessity to the social organism so diminished, that they are the easy victims of intimidation. This was not so in England twenty-five years ago, any more than it is now in the United States. Then the capitalists believed in themselves, in their value to society, in the propriety of their continued existence in the full enjoyment of their riches and the unlimited exercise of their power. Now they tremble before every insult;—call them pro-Germans, international financiers, or profiteers, and they will give you any ransom you choose to ask not to speak of them so harshly. They allow themselves to be ruined and altogether undone by their own instruments, governments of their own making, and a press of which they are the proprietors. Perhaps it is historically true that no order of society ever perishes save by its own hand. In the complexer world of Western Europe the Immanent Will may achieve its ends more subtly and bring in the revolution no less inevitably through a Klotz or a George than by the intellectualisms, too ruthless and self-conscious for us, of the bloodthirsty philosophers of Russia.

. . .

. . . Economic privation proceeds by easy stages, and so long as men suffer it patiently the outside world cares little. Physical efficiency and resistance to disease slowly diminish, but life proceeds somehow, until the limit of human endurance is reached at last and counsels of despair and madness stir the sufferers from the lethargy which precedes the crisis. Then man shakes himself, and the bonds of custom are loosed. The power of ideas is sovereign, and he listens to whatever instruction of hope, illusion, or revenge is carried to him on the air. As I write, the flames of Russian Bolshevism seem, for the moment at least, to have burnt themselves out, and the peoples of Central and Eastern Europe are held in a dreadful torpor. The lately gathered harvest keeps off the worst privations, and Peace has been declared at Paris. But winter approaches. Men will have nothing to look forward to or to nourish hopes on. There will be little fuel to moderate the rigors of the season or to comfort the starved bodies of the town-dwellers.

But who can say how much is endurable, or in what direction men will seek at last to escape from their misfortunes?

STUDY QUESTIONS

1. In what specific respects does Keynes expect the worst, as a result of the Versailles settlement?
2. What long-term economic plans does he believe are necessary?

25.2 PAUL VALÉRY, *A CRISIS OF THE MIND*, 1919

Paul Valéry (1871–1945) was a French writer whose interests were so broad that he was known as a polymath (someone whose interests and abilities span many different areas). He produced plays, essays, novels, and other works of nonfiction, including symbolist poetry (symbolism being a

---

From Paul Valéry, *A Crisis of the Mind*, 1919.

late nineteenth-century art movement). He was born and raised in the south of France, where he received a Roman Catholic education before moving to Paris, where he lived for most of his life. By 1919, when he wrote *A Crisis of the Mind*, Valéry was a literary giant in France. In it he suggested that Europe was in decline. Looking back at the great civilizations of antiquity, he memorialized them and went on to point out that Europe, although once great, was not immune to the forces that had undermined Babylon, or Nineveh, or the Ancient Persian Empire, among other ancient civilizations.

We later civilizations . . . we too know that we are mortal.

We had long heard tell of whole worlds that had vanished, of empires sunk without a trace, gone down with all their men and all their machines into the unexplorable depths of the centuries, with their gods and their laws, their academies and their sciences pure and applied, their grammars and their dictionaries, their Classics, their Romantics, and their Symbolists, their critics and the critics of their critics. . . . We were aware that the visible earth is made of ashes, and that ashes signify something. Through the obscure depths of history we could make out the phantoms of great ships laden with riches and intellect; we could not count them. But the disasters that had sent them down were, after all, none of our affair.

Elam, Ninevah, Babylon were but beautiful vague names, and the total ruin of those worlds had as little significance for us as their very existence. But France, England, Russia . . . these too would be beautiful names. Lusitania too, is a beautiful name. And we see now that the abyss of history is deep enough to hold us all. We are aware that a civilization has the same fragility as a life. The circumstances that could send the works of Keats and Baudelaire to join the works of Menander are no longer inconceivable; they are in the newspapers. That is not all. The searing lesson is more complete still. It was not enough for our generation to learn from its own experience how the most beautiful things and the most ancient, the most formidable and the best ordered, can perish by accident; in the realm of thought, feeling, and common sense, we witnessed extraordinary phenomena: paradox suddenly become fact, and obvious fact brutally believed.

I shall cite but one example: the great virtues of the German peoples have begotten more evils, than idleness ever bred vices. With our own eyes, we have seen conscientious labor, the most solid learning, the most serious discipline and application adapted to appalling ends.

. . .

An extraordinary shudder ran through the marrow of Europe. She felt in every nucleus of her mind that she was no longer the same, that she was no longer herself, that she was about to lose consciousness, a consciousness acquired through centuries of bearable calamities, by thousands of men of the first rank, from innumerable geographical, ethnic, and historical coincidences.

So—as though in desperate defense of her own physiological being and resources—all her memory confusedly returned. Her great men and her great books came back pell-mell. Never has so much been read, nor with such passion, as during the war: ask the booksellers. . . . Never have people prayed so much and so deeply: ask the priests. All the saviors, founders, protectors, martyrs, heroes, all the fathers of their country, the sacred heroines, the national poets invoked. . . .

And in the same disorder of mind, at the summons of the same anguish, all cultivated Europe underwent the rapid revival of her innumerable ways of thought: dogmas, philosophies, heterogeneous ideals; the three hundred ways of explaining the World, the thousand and one versions of Christianity, the two dozen kinds of positivism; the whole spectrum of intellectual light spread out its incompatible colors, illuminating with a strange contradictory glow the death agony of the European soul. While inventors were feverishly searching their imaginations and the annals of former wars for the means of doing away with barbed wire, of outwitting submarines or paralyzing the flight of airplanes, her soul was intoning at the same time all the incantations it ever knew, and giving serious consideration to the most bizarre prophecies; she sought refuge, guidance, consolation throughout the whole register of her memories, past acts, and ancestral attitudes. Such are the known effects of anxiety, the disordered behavior of mind fleeing from reality to nightmare and from nightmare back to reality, terrified, like a rat caught in a trap.

. . .

But hope is only man's mistrust of the clear foresight of his mind. Hope suggests that any conclusion unfavorable to us must be an error of the mind. And yet the facts are clear and pitiless; thousands of young writers and artists have died; the illusion of a European culture has been lost, and knowledge has been proved impotent to save anything whatsoever; science is mortally wounded in its moral ambitions and, as it were, put to shame by the cruelty of its applications; idealism is barely surviving, deeply stricken, and called to account for its dreams; realism is hopeless, beaten, routed by its own crimes and errors; greed and abstinence are equally flouted; faiths are confused in their aim—cross against cross, crescent against crescent; and even the skeptics, confounded by the sudden, violent, and moving events that play with our minds as a cat with a mouse . . . even the skeptics lose their doubts, recover, and lose them again, no longer master of the motions of their thought.

. . .

Standing, now, on an immense sort of terrace of Elsinore that stretches from Basel to Cologne, bordered by the sands of Nieuport, the marshes of the Somme, the limestone of Champagne, the granites of Alsace . . . our Hamlet of Europe is watching millions of ghosts.

But he is an intellectual Hamlet, meditating on the life and death of truths; for ghosts, he has all the subjects of our controversies; for remorse, all the title of our frame. He is bowed under the weight of all the discoveries and varieties of knowledge, incapable of resuming the endless activity; he broods on the tedium of rehearsing the past and the folly of always trying to innovate. He staggers between two abysses—for two dangers never cease threatening the world: order and disorder.

Every skull he picks up is an illustrious skull. This one was *Leonardo*. He invented the flying man, but the flying man has not exactly served his inventor's purposes. We know that, mounted on his great swan (*il grande uccello sopra del dosso del suo magnio cicero*) he has other tasks in our day than fetching snow from the mountain peaks during the hot season to scatter it on the streets of towns. And that other skull was *Leibnitz*, who dreamed of universal peace. And this one was *Kant . . . and Kant begat Hegel, and Hegel begat Marx, and Marx begat. . . .*

Hamlet hardly knows what to make of so many skulls. But suppose he forgets them! Will he still be himself? His terribly lucid mind contemplates the passage from war to peace: darker, more dangerous than the passage from peace to war; all peoples are troubled by it. . . . "What about Me," he says, "what is to become of Me, the European intellect? . . . And what is peace? *Peace is perhaps that state of things in which the natural hostility between men is manifested in creation, rather than destruction as in war.* Peace is a time of creative rivalry and the battle of production; but am I not tired of producing? Have I not exhausted my desire for radical experiment, indulged too much in cunning compounds? . . . Should I not perhaps lay aside my hard duties and transcendent ambitions? Perhaps follow the trend and do like Polonius who is now director of a great newspaper; like Laertes, who is something in aviation; like Rosencrantz, who is doing God knows what under a Russian name?

"Farewell, ghosts! The world no longer needs you—or me. By giving the names of progress to its own tendency to a fatal precision, the world is seeking to add to the benefits of life the advantages of death. A certain confusion still reigns; but in a little while all will be made clear, and we shall witness at last the miracle of an animal society, the perfect and ultimate anthill."

STUDY QUESTIONS

1. Is the "rats caught in a trap" image, applied to European society generally, an appropriate one?
2. How is discarding the ghosts of the past essential to progress and in what fields especially?

25.3 HENRY FORD, *THE INTERNATIONAL JEW*, 1920

Henry Ford (1863–1947) was the founder of the Ford Motor Company, which produced the world's first affordable cars. Although he was known as a pacifist in World War I, in World War II he made his anti-Semitic views widely known in publications such as *The International Jew*, which was printed as a four-volume series of booklets published by the Dearborn Publishing Company, which he owned. His *Dearborn Independent* newspaper also published a series of his anti-Semitic articles. In *The International Jew*, Ford recirculates many of the traditional anti-Semitic arguments—for instance, those concerning a Jewish conspiracy for global dominance via behind-the-scenes methods. In this excerpt he discusses the Jews in Germany and reiterates many widespread arguments concerning the extent of Jewish involvement in contemporary Germany's financial and political woes.

GERMANY'S REACTION AGAINST THE JEW

Humanity has become wise enough to discuss those forms of physical sickness over which it formerly drew the veil of shame and secrecy, but political hygiene is not so far advanced. The main source of the sickness of the German national body is charged to be the influence of the Jews, and although this was apparent to acute minds years ago, it is now said to have gone so far as to be apparent to the least observing. The eruption has broken out on the surface of the body politic, and no further concealment of this fact is possible. It is the belief of all classes of the German people that the collapse which has come since the armistice, and the revolution from which they are being prevented a recovery, are the result of Jewish intrigue and purpose. They declare it with assurance; they offer a mass of facts to confirm it; they believe that history will provide the fullest proof.

The Jew in Germany is regarded as only a guest of the people; he has offended by trying to turn himself into the host. There are no stronger contrasts in the world than the pure Germanic and pure Semitic races; therefore, there has been no harmony between the two in Germany; the German has regarded the Jew strictly as a guest, while the Jew, indignant at not being given the privileges of the nation-family, has cherished animosity against his host. In other countries the Jew is permitted to mix more readily with the people, he can amass his control unchallenged; but in Germany the case was different. Therefore, the Jew hated the German people; therefore, the countries of the world which were most dominated by the Jews

From Henry Ford, *The International Jew: The World's Foremost Problem*, 1920.

showed the greatest hatred of Germany during the recent regrettable war. Jewish hands were in almost exclusive control of the engines of publicity by which public opinion concerning the German people was molded. The sole winners of the war were Jews.

But assertion is not enough; proof is wanted; therefore, consider the evidence. What occurred immediately upon the change from the old regime to the new? The cabinet composed of six men, which substituted the Minister of State, was dominated by the Jews Haase and Landsberg. Haase had control of foreign affairs; his assistant was the Jew Kautsky, a Czech, who in 1918 was not even a German citizen. Also associated with Haase were the Jews Cohn and Herzfeld. The Jew Schiffer was Financial Minister of State, assisted by the Jew Bernstein. The Secretary of the Interior was the Jew Preuss, with the Jew Dr. Freund for his assistant. The Jew Fritz Max Cohen, who was correspondent of the *Frankfurter Zeitung* in Copenhagen, was made government publicity agent.

The kingdom of Prussia duplicated this condition of affairs. The Jews Hirsch and Rosenfeld dominated the cabinet, with Rosenfeld controlling the Department of Justice and Hirsch in the Department of the Interior. The Jew Simon was in charge of the Treasury Department. The Prussian Department of Justice was wholly manned and operated by Jews. The Director of Education was the Jew Furtran with the assistance of the Jew Arndt. The Director of the Colonial Office was the Jew Meyer-Gerhard. The Jew Kastenberg was the director of the Department of Art. The War Food Supply Department was directed by the Jew Wurm, while in the State Food Department were the Jews Prof. Dr. Hirsch and the Geheimrat Dr. Stadthagen. The Soldiers' and Workmen's Committee was directed by the Jew Cohen, with the Jews Stern, Herz, Lowenberg, Frankel, Israelowicz, Laubenheim, Seligsohn, Katzenstein, Laufenberg, Heimann, Schlesinger, Merz and Weyl having control of various activities of that committee.

The Jew Ernst is chief of police at Berlin; in the same office at Frankfurt is the Jew Sinzheimer; in Munich the Jew Steiner; in Essen the Jew Levy. It will be remembered that the Jew Eisner was President of Bavaria, his financial minister being the Jew Jaffe. Bavaria's trade, commerce and industry were in control of the half-Jew Brentano. The Jews Lipsinsky and Schwarz were active in the government of Saxony; the Jews Thalheimer and Heiman in Wurtemberg; the Jew Fulda in Hessen.

Two delegates sent to the Peace Conference were Jews and a third was notoriously the tool of Jewish purposes. In addition Jews swarmed through the German delegation as experts and advisor—Max Warburg, Dr. Von Strauss, Merton, Oskar Oppenheimer, Dr. Jaffe, Deutsch, Brentano, Bernstein, Struck, Rathenau, Wassermann, and Mendelsohn-Bartholdi.

As to the part which Jews from other countries had in the Peace Conference, German observers declare that any candid student may discover by reading the accounts of impartial non-Jewish recorders of that event. Only the non-Jewish historians seem to have been struck by the fact; the multitude of Jewish writers apparently judged it wise to conceal it.

Jewish influence in German affairs came strongly to the front during the war. It came with all the directness and attack of a flying wedge, as if previously prepared. The Jews of Germany were not German patriots during the war, and although this will not appear a crime in the eyes of the nations who were opposed to Germany, it may throw some light on the Jew's assertion of patriotic loyalty to the land where he lives. Thoughtful Germans hold that it is impossible for a Jew to be a patriot, for reasons which will presently be given.

The point to be considered is the general claim that the persons already named would not have obtained the positions in which they were found had it not been for the Revolution, and the Revolution would not have come had not they brought it. It is true that there were unsatisfactory conditions in Germany, but they could and would have been adjusted by the people themselves; the conditions which destroyed the people's morale and were made impossible of reform were in control of the Jews.

The principal Jewish influences which are charged with bringing about the downfall of German order may be named under three heads: (a) the spirit of Bolshevism which masqueraded under the name of German Socialism; (b) Jewish ownership and control of the Press; (c) Jewish control of the food supply and the industrial machinery of the country. There was a fourth, "higher up," but these worked upon the German people directly.

As it is possible that German conclusions upon this matter may be received doubtfully by people whose public opinion has been shaped by Jewish influence, it may help to quote George Fitter-Wilson, of the *London Globe,* who wrote early in April, 1919, "Bolshevism is the dispossession of the Christian nations of the world to such an extent that no capital will remain in the hands of the Christians, that all Jews may jointly hold the world in their hands and reign wherever they choose." As early as the second year of the war, German Jews were preaching that Germany's defeat was necessary to the rise of the proletariat, at which time Strobel declared, "I openly admit that a full victory of the country would not be in the interest of the Social Democrats." Everywhere it was preached that "the exaltation of the proletariat after a won victory is an impossibility." These instances, out of many, are cited not to reopen the military question but to show how the so-called German Jew forgot loyalty to the country in which he lived and joined the outside Jews in accomplishing the collapse of Germany, and not merely, as we shall see, to rid Germany of militarism, which every thoughtful German desired, but to throw the country into such confusion as to permit them to seize control.

The press of Germany echoed this plan of the Jewish spokesmen, at first faintly, then boldly. The *Berliner Tageblatt* and the *Munchner Neuester Nachrichten* were during the whole war official and semi-official organs of the government. They were owned and controlled by Jews, as was also the *Frankfurter Zeitung* and a host of smaller papers that were their spiritual dependents. These papers, it is charged, were really German editions of the Jew-controlled press of the Allied countries, and their purpose was the same. One of the great pieces of research that ought to be undertaken for the purpose of showing the world how its thought is manufactured for it every day, and for what ulterior purposes, is this union of the Jewish press, which passes for the Public Press, throughout the world.

The food and supplies of the people quickly passed into Jewish hands as soon as the war emergency came, and then began a period of dishonesty which destroyed the confidence of the bravest. Like all other patriotic people, the German people knew that war meant sacrifice and suffering, and like other people they were willing to share the common lot. But they found themselves preyed upon by a class of Jews who had prepared everything to make profit out of the common distress. Immediately Jews appeared in banks, war companies, distribution societies, and the ministries of supplies—wherever the life of the people could be speculated in or taxed. Articles that were plentiful disappeared, only to reappear again at high prices. The war companies were exclusively Jewish, and although the government attempted to regulate the outgo of food in the interests of all the people, it became notorious that those with money could get all of anything they wanted, regardless of the food cards. The Jews simply trebled the price of the goods they let go without the cards, and so kept a stream of the nation's gold flowing into their private treasuries. None of the government's estimates of the food stocks could be depended on, because of the hidden hoards on which these speculators drew. This began to disturb the morale of the people, and complaints were made and prosecutions started; but as soon as the cases came up it was discovered that the prosecutor appointed to charge and the commissioner appointed to judge were also Jews, and so the cases usually wore themselves out without results. When, however, a German merchant was caught, great noise was made about it, and the penalty placed upon him was equal to what all the others should have had. Go the length and breadth of Germany today, say the reports, study the temper of the people, and you will discover that the abuse of power by the Jews has burned across Germany's memory like a hot iron.

STUDY QUESTIONS

1. How does Ford incorporate the "stab in the back theory" into his treatment of the background of Germany's ambassadors to Versailles?
2. How does he conflate Jews and Bolsheviks, and why?

25.4 ADOLF HITLER, EXCERPTS FROM A SPEECH DELIVERED TO OPEN THE CONGRESS OF THE NATIONAL SOCIALIST PARTY, 1933

Adolf Hitler (1889–1945) was appointed to the chancellorship in January 1933. One month later a young Dutch Communist, Marinus van der Lubbe (1909–1934), set fire to the Reichstag building; by his own admission, he committed arson as a desperate attempt to rally the German working class against the Nazis. (He was tried, found guilty, and guillotined.) Using the fire as an excuse, Hitler dissolved the parliament and assumed emergency powers—which led directly to his ultimate declaration of dictatorial authority as Führer. Several months later, Hitler addressed the annual Congress of the Nazi Party.

In the year 1919, when the National Socialist Movement sprang to life in order to create a new Reich in place of the Marxist-Democratic Republic, it seemed a hopelessly foolish enterprise. Above all, the flighty intellectuals with their superficial knowledge of history had no more than a pitying smile for such an undertaking. Most of them knew perfectly well that Germany was about to fall on evil times. Most of the so-called intelligentsia understood very well that the rulers of the November Republic were either too evil or too incompetent to lead our people. But they did not recognize that this new regime would succumb to those forces which for fifty years have steadily retreated before the attacks of Marxism, and would finally, in the hour of greatest emergency, capitulate utterly. Perhaps part of the reason for this was that the political leaders of the nation were aged, out-dated. They could not or would not recognize that the time had come for the restoration of the nation's strength. What separated us National Socialists from the urbane world of the "intellectuals" was the fact that we made it clear, and then acted on the conviction, that the necessary first step in our nation's recovery was the defeat of Marxism. . . .

Lacking all understanding of organic development, the rootless intellectual tries to get around the law of growth by quick experiments. National Socialism, on the other hand, was ready from the very first day to undertake the long and painful task of building anew the tools that would later destroy Marxism. But because this was not understood by the shallow intelligence of our politicized bourgeoisie, the new Movement could at first develop only among those groups closest to nature. What the intellect of the intellectual could not see was understood immediately by the soul, the heart, and the instinct of this simple, primitive, sturdy man. One of our tasks for the future will be to re-establish the connection between feeling and intellect; that is, to teach a thus-far unspoiled generation to understand with absolute clarity the eternal law of organic development and at the same time to remain true to the primitive instinct.

National Socialism directed its appeal for the formation of a new Movement to the broad masses of the people, and hence its first task was to inspire by suggestion those few whom it had first won over with the belief that they would in fact one day be the saviors of their Fatherland. This problem of getting men to believe in themselves, and to have confidence in themselves, was as necessary as it was difficult. Men who socially and economically had lowly origins and were

Translation by Clifford Backman.

frequently oppressed had to be given, as the first rung on the ladder, the political conviction that some day they would represent the leadership of the nation. . . .

The former leaders of the bourgeois world talked endlessly about making "quiet progress" and proclaimed supposedly profound theories at tea parties, but National Socialism marched directly into the hearts of the people. We held hundreds and thousands of demonstrations. . . . They blathered on and on about democracy, but kept away from the people. National Socialism talked about authority, but it engaged with the people, wrestled with the people, as no movement in German history had ever done. . . . The National Socialist Revolution has now overthrown a republic based on treason and lies, and in its place has created once more a Reich of honor, loyalty, and decency. . . .

And now, as the sole possessor of state power, our Party understands, as it must, that it is responsible for the entire course of German history. The work of education which the Movement must carry on is tremendous, for it is not enough to organize the state in accordance with sound principles: it is necessary to educate the inner souls of the people. Only if the people have an intimate sympathy with the principles and methods which inspire and move the organization of their state, will there grow up a living organism instead of a dead, because purely formal and mechanical, bureaucracy. . . .

The rise and astonishing victory of the National Socialist Movement would never have occurred if our Party had ever accepted the principle that in our ranks every one can do as he likes. That particular watchword of democratic freedom led only to insecurity, indiscipline, and at length to the downfall and destruction of all authority. Our opponents may object that we too once made use of democratic rights [by coming to power through elections]—but their objections will not hold water, for what we did was to make use of an unreasonable right, which was part and parcel of an unreasonable system, in order to overthrow the unreason of that system. . . . When Old Germany fell, it betrayed its inner weaknesses, just as the November Republic's weaknesses have now been revealed. . . .

While we may reject the principles of democracy and parliamentary government, and deny the parliamentary-democratic principle, we passionately believe in the people's right to govern themselves. But parliaments, we insist, do not express the real will of the masses but actually pervert and violate that will. The will of the people finds its only true and effective expression in its most gifted leaders. . . .

The greater the tasks with which we are faced, the greater must be the authority of those who accomplish these tasks. It is important that the self-assurance of the leaders of the whole organization in their decisions should arouse in the members and followers of the Party an untroubled confidence. . . . The Party must be convinced that it will be able to cope with all problems, that because it has chosen its human material in living struggle, its leaders are politically the most competent men in Germany. . . . Power and its ruthless application can accomplish much. . . . And to save a nation one must think heroically. But the heroic thinker must always be willing to renounce the approval of his contemporaries where truth is at stake. . . .

May the very manner of this demonstration renew our understanding that the government of the nation must never harden into a purely bureaucratic machine; it must forever remain a living leadership. . . . Forms and institutions can pass, but what does and must remain is the living substance of flesh and blood. All of us desire that the German people shall forever remain upon this earth, and we believe that by our struggle we are but carrying out the will of the Creator, who imbued all creatures with the instinct of self-preservation. Long live our nation! Long live the National Socialist Party!

STUDY QUESTIONS

1. How does Hitler describe intellectuals? Marxists? The bourgeoisie? How does he contrast democracy with the National Socialist Movement?
2. What are the goals and the work that Hitler sets out for the National Socialist Movement? How will it achieve its aims?

25.5 BENITO MUSSOLINI, "FORCE AND CONSENT," 1923

Benito Mussolini (1883–1945) ruled Italy from 1922 to 1943. As the leader of the Fascist Party, he governed the nation as prime minister, according to the constitution, until January 1925, when he dropped all pretense and began to rule as dictator. He liked to think of himself as combining the traits of a scholar with those of a man of action—and his collected works fill twelve volumes. In the following essay, published in 1923 in a monthly journal (*Gerarchia*) for which he himself served as editor in chief, he contrasts the virtues of Fascism ("Force") with the vices of Liberalism ("Consent").

Italian Liberalism, which likes to think of itself as the sole upholder of true, eternal principles, actually bears a remarkable resemblance to half-dead Socialism, since, like Socialism, it is based on indisputable, scientific truths that apply to all times, places, and situations. But clearly, this is absurd. Liberalism is not the final, definitive word on anything, including the subject of government. In politics—an extraordinarily difficult and delicate art that requires one to work with refractory materials in a constant state of flux (that is, with living people rather than lifeless matter)—one does not find the Aristotelian unities of time, place, and action. Men have been and can be effectively governed in a myriad of ways. Liberalism is a product of the 19th century, a technique of governance. It is not a stupid technique, as Daudet would have it. Stupidity and intelligence can be found, waxing and waning alike, now increasing, now declining, in every century. But there is no reason to assume that Liberalism—a technique of governance suited to the 19th century (dominated as it was by the two phenomena of capitalist expansion and the increase in nationalist sentiment)—should suit the 20th century, an era that even now is already characterized by features that strongly distinguish it from the earlier period. Facts mean more than theories, and experience trumps doctrines. And the experience of the post-war period makes it unmistakably clear that Liberalism's awkward demise has begun—history acting out before our very eyes. Both Russia and Italy right now are proving that governments can succeed entirely outside, above, and in opposition to Liberal ideology. Both Communism and Fascism thrive outside the parameters of Liberalism.

Really, though, what is this Liberalism that today's enemies of Fascism are so showily enthusiastic about? Does Liberalism entail universal suffrage and all that goes with it? Does Liberalism mean keeping parliaments in perpetual meeting—an indecent display that everyone loathes? Does it mean destroying everyone's freedom in order to preserve the liberty of a few—and to do so, supposedly, "in the name of Freedom"? Is it Liberalism to permit the free action of those who declare themselves enemies of the State and who actually work to destroy it? If this is Liberalism, then it is nothing more than the theory and practice of despair and failure! Liberty is a means, not an end; and as a means it must be controlled and dominated.

But now we must speak of Force. I challenge all Liberals, everywhere: Tell me of any instance in history of a government based solely on popular consent that renounced the use of force under any circumstance. There never has been such a government, and there never will be. Consent is like the sand on

---

Translation by Clifford Backman.

a seashore—always shifting, always changing, never permanent, never complete. Nor has there ever been a government that has made all of its people happy. The solution to any problem—any problem—creates unhappiness somewhere for someone, even if that solution was inspired by the Celestial Wisdom itself. Throughout all these centuries, geometry has never managed to square a circle and politics has failed even more. If one accepts the proposition that every system of government creates discontented people, how does one prevent their discontent from building up and up until they present a menace to the stability of the State? The answer: by force. By marshaling the greatest force one can, and by applying this force whenever it is necessary. Take away from any government its force (and I mean physical, armed force), leaving it with only its high-minded principles, and I tell you that that government will fall victim to the first organized group determined to overthrow it.

Fascism throws those principles out to rot. When a group or party is in power, it has an obligation to strengthen itself and defend itself against all rivals, for it is a simple truth—clear to everyone whose brain has not been warped by high-minded principles—that people today have grown tired of freedom. They have made an orgy of it. Freedom today is not the chaste and strict maiden fought for and died for by the people of the first half of the nineteenth century. No, for the brave, restless, angry, youthful people of today, they are inspired by other values: order, hierarchy, discipline. Italian Liberalism sighs pathetically while continuing its futile struggle for more freedom. It is behind the times, beyond comprehension, and no longer remotely possible. Such ridiculous ideas! They are like seeds that die under the cover of winter. Fascism, though, which never feared to call itself reactionary when most of today's Liberals lay flat on their faces before its triumphal march, is not ashamed to call itself illiberal and even anti-Liberal. Fascism will never resort to trickery.

Have no doubt about it: Fascism knows no idols and worships no fetishes. And it has already trampled the generally putrid corpse of the goddess called "Liberty"—and it won't hesitate to do so again, if need be.

STUDY QUESTIONS

1. Why has liberalism failed, according to Mussolini? Is there any chance it could be reformed or saved? Why or why not?
2. What makes Mussolini's Fascism different from the absolutism of Thomas Hobbes?

25.6 OSWALD SPENGLER, *THE DECLINE OF THE WEST*, 1918

Oswald Spengler (1880–1936) may not have been the obvious candidate to produce the most talked-about book of his age. A somewhat sickly loner, he nonetheless touched something in the collective European consciousness, a melancholic postwar mood that enabled *The Decline of the West* to become a bestseller. Civilizations, being "organic," have life cycles, he argued, just

From Oswald Spengler, *The Decline of the West*, 1918.

like biological entities. He went on to argue that Western civilization has evolved through three major stages—the Magian, the Apollonian, and the Faustian. These correspond, respectively, to the belief in magic (including the major religions), the striving for order (classical Greece and Rome), and the pursuit of power and knowledge (the modern West). The West had achieved its high point; from here, things would take a downhill turn. In this excerpt he discusses what he calls the "world-city," a cosmopolitan mélange of people and cultures composed of rootless individuals without traditions, territorial identity, or religion—what Spengler contemptuously refers to as "a mob."

Civilizations are the most external and artificial states of which a species of developed humanity is capable. They are a conclusion, the thing-become succeeding the thing-becoming, death following life, rigidity following expansion, intellectual age and the stone-built, petrifying world-city following mother-earth and the spiritual childhood of Doric and Gothic. They are an end, irrevocable, yet by inward necessity reached again and again.

. . .

The transition from Culture to Civilization was accomplished for the Classical world in the fourth, for the Western in the nineteenth century. From these periods onward the great intellectual decisions take place, no longer all over the world where not a hamlet is too small to be unimportant, but in three or four world-cities that have absorbed into themselves the whole content of History, while the old wide landscape of the Culture, become merely provincial, serves only to feed the cities with what remains of its higher mankind. *World-city and province*—the two basic ideas of every civilization—bring up a wholly new form-problem of History, the very problem that we are living through today with hardly the remotest conception of its immensity. In place of a world, there is a *city, a point*, in which the whole life of broad regions is collecting while the rest dries up. In place of a type-true people, born of and grown on the soil, there is a new sort of nomad, cohering unstably in fluid masses, the parasitical city dweller, traditionless, utterly matter-of-fact, religionless, clever, unfruitful, deeply contemptuous of the country gentlemen. This is a very great stride towards the inorganic, towards the end—what does it signify?

The world-city means cosmopolitanism in place of "home." . . . The world-city belongs not to a folk but a mob. Its uncomprehending hostility to all the traditions representative of the Culture (nobility, church, privileges, dynasties, convention in art and limits of knowledge in science), the deep and cold intelligence that confounds the wisdom of the peasant, the new fashioned naturalism that in relation to all matters of sex and society goes back far to quite primitive instincts and conditions, the reappearance of the *panem et circenses* in the form of wage-disputes and sports stadia—all these things betoken the definite closing down of the Culture and the opening of a quite new phase of human existence—anti-provincial, late, futureless, but quite inevitable.

. . .

. . . There are no eternal truths. Every philosophy is the expression of its own and only its own time . . . no two ages possess the same philosophic intentions. The difference is not between perishable and imperishable doctrines but between doctrines which live their day and doctrines which never live at all. The immortality of thoughts-become is an illusion—the essential is, what kind of man comes to expression in them. The greater the man, the truer the philosophy, with the inward truth that in a great work of art transcends all proof of its several elements or even of the compatibility with one another. At highest, the philosophy may absorb the entire content of an epoch, realize it within itself and then, embodying it in some grand form or personality, pass it on to be developed further and further. Only its necessity to life decides the eminence of a doctrine.

For me, therefore, the test of value to be applied to a thinker is his eye for the great facts of his own time. Only this can settle whether he is merely a clever architect of systems and principles versed in definitions and analyses, or whether it is the very soul of his time that speaks in his works and his intuitions. . . .

. . .

And herein, I think, all the philosophers of the newest age are open to a serious criticism. What they do not possess is real standing in actual life. Not one of them has intervened effectively, either in higher politics, in the development of modern technics, in matters of communication, in economics or in any other big actuality, with a single act or a single compelling idea. Not one of them counts in mathematics, in physics, in the science of government, even to the extent that Kant counted. Let us glance at other times. Confucius was several times a minister. Pythagoras was the organizer of an important political movement akin to the Cromwellian, the significance of which is even now far underestimated by Classical researchers. Goethe, besides being a model executive minister—though lacking, alas, the operative sphere of a great state—was interested in the Suez and Panama canals (the dates of which he foresaw with accuracy) and their effects on the economy of the world, . . .

. . .

Whenever I take up a work by a modern thinker, I find myself asking: Has he any idea whatever of the actualities of world-politics, world-city problems, capitalism, the future of the state, the relation of technics to the course of civilization, Russia, Science? Goethe would have understood all this and reveled in it, but there is not one living philosopher capable of taking it in. . . .

. . .

With that, the claim of higher thought to possess general and eternal truths falls on the ground. Truths are truths only in relation to a particular mankind. Thus, my own philosophy is able to express and reflect only the Western (as distinct from the Classical, Indian or other) soul, and that soul only in its present civilized phase by which its conception of the world, its practical range and its sphere of effect are specified.

STUDY QUESTIONS

1. Can a philosopher be useful in the real world, especially in political leadership?
2. What trajectory does Spengler see laid out before philosophers in his immediate future?

25.7 FRIEDRICH HAYEK, "ECONOMIC CONTROL AND TOTALITARIANISM," 1944

Friedrich Hayek (1899–1992) was born in Vienna, when it was still the vibrant capital of the Austrian–Hungarian empire. After the war, he studied economics and law at the University of Vienna. He published his first book, on monetary theory, in 1929, on the strength of which he was appointed to the post of professor at the London School of Economics. Here he stayed until

From Friedrich A. Hayek, *The Road to Serfdom*. Chicago: University of Chicago Press, 2008, pp. 93–4, 96–8, 100.

1950. He also taught at the universities of Chicago and Freiburg. Throughout the 1930s and 1940s he challenged the other prominent British economist, John Maynard Keynes, book for book and article for article. Hayek endorsed the pre-1848 vision of classical economic liberalism, emphasizing the importance of private property, individual liberty, personal responsibility, and the free market. In *The Road to Serfdom* (1944) he argues that government intrusion into a free economy is the first step toward totalitarianism.

Our freedom of choice in a competitive society rests on the fact that, if one person refuses to satisfy our wishes, we can turn to another. But if we face a monopolist we are at his mercy. And an authority directing the whole economic system would be the most powerful monopolist conceivable. While we need probably not be afraid that such an authority would exploit this power in the manner in which a private monopolist would do so, while its purpose would presumably not be the extortion of maximum financial gain, it would have complete power to decide what we are to be given and on what terms. It would not only decide what commodities and services were to be available and in what quantities; it would be able to direct their distribution between districts and groups and could, if it wished, discriminate between persons to any degree it liked. If we remember why planning is advocated by most people, can there be much doubt that this power would be used for the ends of which the authority approves and to prevent the pursuits of ends which it disapproves?

The power conferred by the control of production and prices is almost unlimited. In a competitive society the prices we have to pay for a thing, the rate at which we can get one thing for another, depend on the quantities of other things of which by taking one, we deprive the other members of society. This price is not determined by the conscious will of anybody. And if one way of achieving our ends proves too expensive for us, we are free to try other ways. The obstacles in our path are not due to someone's disapproving of our ends but to the fact that the same means are also wanted elsewhere. In a directed economy, where the authority watches over the ends pursued, it is certain that it would use its powers to assist some ends and to prevent the realization of others. Not our own view, but somebody else's, of what we ought to like or dislike would determine what we should get. And since the authority would have the power to thwart any efforts to elude its guidance, it would control what we consume almost as effectively as if it directly told us how to spend our income.

Not only in our capacity as consumers, however, and not even mainly in that capacity, would the will of the authority shape and "guide" our daily lives. It would do so even more in our position as producers. These two aspects of our lives cannot be separated; and as for most of us the time we spend at our work is a large part of our whole lives, and as our job usually also determines the place where and the people among whom we live, some freedom in choosing our work is, probably, even more important for our happiness than freedom to spend our income during the hours of leisure.

. . .

That in a competitive society most things can be had at a price—though it is often a cruelly high price we have to pay—is a fact the importance of which can hardly be overrated.

. . .

To take only one example: We could, of course, reduce casualties by automobile accidents to zero if we were willing to bear the cost—if in no other way—by abolishing automobiles. And the same is true of thousands of other instances in which we are constantly risking life and health and all the fine values of the spirit, of ourselves and of our fellowmen, to further what we at the same time contemptuously describe as our material comfort. Nor can it be otherwise, since all our ends compete for the same means; and we could not strive for anything but these absolute values if they were on no account to be endangered.

That people should wish to be relieved of the bitter choice which hard facts often impose upon them is not surprising. But few want to be relieved through having the choice made for them by others. People just wish that the choice should not be necessary at all. And they are only too ready to believe that the choice is not really necessary, that it is imposed upon them merely by the particular economic system under which we live.

. . .

During the liberal era the progressive division of labor has created a situation where almost every one of our activities is part of a social process. This is a development which we cannot reverse, since it is only because of it that we can maintain the vastly increased population at anything like present standards. But, in consequence, the substitution of central planning for competition would require central direction of a much greater part of our lives than was ever attempted before. It could not stop at what we regard as our economic activities, because we are now for almost every part of our lives dependent on somebody else's economic activities.[1] The passion for the "collective satisfaction of our needs," with which our socialists have so well prepared the way for totalitarianism, and which wants us to take our pleasures as well as our necessities at the appointed time and in the prescribed form, is, of course, partly intended as a means of political education. But it is also the result of the exigencies of planning, which consists essentially in depriving us of choice, in order to give us whatever fits best into the plan and that at a time determined by the plan.

It is often said that political freedom is meaningless without economic freedom. This is true enough, but in a sense almost opposite from that in which the phrase is used by our planners. The economic freedom which is the prerequisite of any other freedom cannot be the freedom from economic care which the socialists promise us and which can be obtained only by relieving the individual at the same time of the necessity and of the power of choice; it must be the freedom of our economic activity which, with the right of choice, inevitably also carries the risk and the responsibility of that right.

[1] It is no accident that in the totalitarian countries, be it Russia or Germany or Italy, the question of how to organize the people's leisure has become a problem of planning. The Germans have even invented for this problem the horrible and self-contradictory name of *Freizeitgestaltung* (literally: the shaping of the use made of the people's free time), as if it were still "free time" when it has to be spent in the way ordained by authority.

STUDY QUESTIONS

1. In what sense was Hayek at odds with the overall economic and political developments of the early twentieth century?
2. How does he connect the concept of "freedom" (including even the "freedom to fail") to economic and political life?

CHAPTER 26

THE WORLD AT WAR (PART II)

26.1 ALDOUS HUXLEY, *AN ENCYCLOPAEDIA OF PACIFISM*, 1937

The British novelist and critic Aldous Huxley (1894–1963) was also known as a writer on history, travel, and many other subjects, as well as a sometime poet. He attended the University of Oxford, where he received a degree in literature. Unable to pursue his two first choices of profession—scientist or Air Force pilot—because of poor eyesight, he turned instead to writing. He spent most of the 1920s and 1930s living in Italy and France, where he wrote his best-known novel *Brave New World* (1932) before moving to America in 1937. Huxley was a lifelong pacifist, but in the 1930s he was particularly active. His book *Ends and Means* (1937) explored the causes of war, its consequences, and how although humanity agrees on what it wants, it has failed to agree on how to get there. His *Encyclopaedia of Pacifism* extended his interest in the subject, looking critically at all historical, social, biological, and psychological aspects of conflict.

BIOLOGY AND WAR

War is often described as a Law of Nature. This is not true. Among the lower animals war is unknown. True, there are carnivores which prey upon other animals; but their activities are no more war-like than are the activities of fishermen or butchers. Moreover, the existence of carnivores should not blind us to the fact that there is at least as much co-operation in nature as strife.

Individuals of the same species often fight together; but these fights are seldom pushed to a finish; the conquered is rarely killed or even permanently hurt. Such duels waged in the heat of passion, under the stress of hunger or sexual impulse, are quite unlike war, which is mass murder, scientifically prepared in cold blood.

In nature, it is only among the social insects, such as the ants and termites, that we meet with anything

From Aldous Huxley, ed., *An Encyclopaedia of Pacifism*. London: Chatto & Windus, 1937, pp. 7–9, 7–8, 72–5, 104–6, 122.

resembling war. And even here the resemblance is only superficial. Insect wars are conducted by members of one species against members of another species. Man is the only creature to organize mass murder of his own species.

It is often argued that war is inevitable, since man is descended from pugnacious ancestors, akin to the gorilla. This is probably not the case. Most zoologists are now of the opinion that man's ancestor was not a gorilla-like ape, but a gentle, sensitive creature, something like a tarsier. In any case, the gifts which brought man his extraordinary biological success were not ruthlessness and brute strength (plenty of animals are much stronger and fiercer than he is), but co-operation, intelligence, wondering curiosity and sensitiveness. In the words of Charles Darwin, "The small strength and speed of man and his want to natural weapons are more than counterbalanced, firstly, by his intellectual faculties (chiefly or exclusively gained for the benefit of the community), and secondly, by those social qualities which led him to give and receive aid from his fellowmen."

Another biological argument often invoked in defence of war is the following: War is civilization's equivalent of natural selection; it acts as nature's pruning-hook, ensuring the survival of the fittest. This is obviously untrue. War tends to kill off the young and healthy and children. In the second place, there is no reason to suppose that warlike peoples are superior to unwarlike peoples. Even if the violent were to survive (and war is just as likely to kill them off as to ensure the persistence of their stock), this would not necessarily mean the survival of the most satisfactory type of human being. The most violent are not the best human beings; nor, conversely, are the most valuable necessarily the strongest. In so far as war is an agent of selection it selects dysgenically, ensuring the survival, not of the more desirable, but of the less desirable human strains. In the past, war's capacity to do harm was limited by the fact that the instruments of destruction at men's disposal were crude and inadequate. Today, thanks to technological progress, they are enormously efficient. War, therefore, has not become as dangerous to human societies, and even to the whole human species, as cancer is to the human body. War is "natural" to exactly the same extent as cancer is "natural."

. . .

COMMUNISM AND FASCISM

The way in which violence begets violence is very clearly illustrated by the history of the rise of Communism and Fascism. The Communist revolution in Russia was the fruit of violence. Tsarist tyranny had prepared the ground, sowing hatred and resentment among the oppressed masses. In 1917 the fabric of Russian society had been reduced to chaos by the impact of war. Military violence gave the revolutionaries their opportunity; violently, they seized it. More military violence, in the shape of the White Russian and allied attacks upon the Bolsheviks, confirmed the new régime in its essentially anti-pacifist principles. Marxian theory had from the first insisted upon the necessity of violence; but even if they had not desired to do so, circumstances would have compelled the Bolsheviks to put the Marxian theory of violence into practice. Communism became a militant, even a militaristic creed.

Communist violence in Italy, itself produced in large measure by the disruptive violence of war, evoked violent reaction. Fascism was born and, after a period of civil strife, came to power.

In the case of Germany, the allies were given ample opportunity to behave with justice and generosity; but, during the fifteen years which preceded the accession of Hitler, Germany was treated with consistent injustice. Such concessions as were made were always made reluctantly and so late that they never did anything to allay the bitterness of German public opinion. In Nazism, Frenchmen and Englishmen are reaping the fruits of their governments' stupid inhumanity and injustice. Hitler's violence is the answer to the arrogance of France and England and, to a less extent, to the militant propaganda of Russian Communism—itself, as we have seen, a product of earlier violence.

Anti-Communists call upon us to suppress Communism by violence; anti-Fascists exhort us to answer the threats of Nazism with counter-threats. Both parties would have us reply to violence with violence. In other words both would have us do precisely those things which, as the history of the last twenty years makes so abundantly clear, are certain to produce the greatest possible amount of tyranny, war and civil strife. Pacifists are people who profit by the lessons of history; militarists, whether of the right or the left, are people who are determined not to learn by experience. . . .

MORALITY OF PACIFISM

It is often objected that pacifism is morally unjustifiable. "Your position in society," the critic of pacifism argues, "is that of a parasite. You are profiting by what the armed forces of your country are doing to preserve you and your family from danger but you refuse to undertake defence work yourself and you try to persuade others to follow your example. You have no right to take from the society in which you live without giving anything in return."

Several answers to these criticisms present themselves:

(1) In the contemporary world, the armed forces of a country do not provide its inhabitants with protection. On the contrary, their existence is one of the principal sources of national danger. There is no more effective way of provoking people to attack than to threaten them. At the present time Great Britain combines extreme vulnerability with formidable aggressive armament. Our policy of rearmament with weapons of aggression is one which positively invites attack. The pacifist is criticized as a shirker who seeks security behind a line of soldiers, sailors and airmen, whom he refuses to help. In reality, his dearest wish is to get rid of the soldiers, sailors and airmen, and all their machinery of destruction; for he knows that so long as they are there, security will be unattainable. Tanks, bombers and battleships do not give security; on the contrary, they are a constant source of danger.

(2) Those who accuse pacifists of being parasites upon the society in which they live should pause for a moment to consider a few facts and figures. Since the last war this country has spent sixteen hundred millions of pounds upon its armaments, and the rate of expenditure is now to be increased. The world as a whole spends nearly two thousand millions a year on its "defence forces." These "defence forces" live at the expense of the working community, performing no constructive work, absorbing an increasing amount of the world's energy and not only failing to provide the individual citizens of the various nations with adequate protection, but actually inviting attack from abroad. To the inhabitant of a bombarded London it will be no satisfaction to learn that the planes for which he has been paying so heavily in taxation are bombarding some foreign capital.

(3) Refusal to obey the government of the society of which one is a member is a very serious matter. Still, most moralists and political philosophers have been of opinion that individuals are fully justified in disobeying the State if the State commands them to do something which they are convinced to be wrong. Social solidarity is not always desirable. There is such a thing as solidarity with evil as well as solidarity with good. A man who finds himself on a pirate ship is morally justified in refusing to co-operate with his shipmates in their nefarious activities. All reformers have been men who refused to co-operate, on some important issue, with the societies of which they were members. That is why so many of them have been persecuted by their contemporaries. The Christian religion takes its name from a persecuted reformer.

Criticisms and answers:

(1) The State provided free schools, libraries, pensions, etc. In return the individual should do what the State demands of him.

Answer: (*a*) The individual pays for State services in taxation.

(*b*) The State is not God and its demands are not categorical imperatives. The State was made for man, not man for the State. The State is a convenience, like drains or the telephone; its demand that it should be treated as an all-wise divinity is inadmissible and leads, as the history of tyrannies and dictatorships shows, to every kind of crime and disaster.

(*c*) If the State may justifiably demand of an individual that he should commit murder for the sake of his country, then it is equally justified in demanding that he should commit lesser crimes. But we can imagine the outcry that would be raising by pious militarists if, for example, in an effort to raise the birth-rate and improve the quality of the race, the State were to conscribe all women and compel them to have sexual intercourse with eugenically selected men.

(2) "The pacifist method of dealing with war is too slow and there will be another war before there are enough pacifists to stop it."

The pacifist method is certainly slow; but the militarist's method is far slower. Indeed, the militarist's method is foredoomed to make no advance whatever towards the goal of peace. War produces more war. Only non-violence can produce non-violence. Pacifism is admittedly slow and hard to practice; but the fact remains that it is the only method of getting universal peace which promises to be in the least effective.

(3) "There is something worse than war, and that is injustice." But war inevitably commits injustices far greater and more widespread than those it was called upon to redress.

(4) "Pacifism tends to increase the arrogance and power of dictators."

(*a*) None of the modern dictators has been faced with large-scale pacifism. Where non-violence has been used on a large scale even violent and ruthless rulers have been nonplussed.

(*b*) What increases the arrogance of dictators is not so much pacifism as the half-hearted use of their own violent methods. The violence of dictators must be opposed either by violence greater than theirs (with the certainty of prolonging the war habit and the possibility of doing irreparable damage to civilization) or else by complete pacifism (which, however slow and difficult, will ultimately lead to the establishment of peace).

PROPAGANDA

On the outbreak of war it is as necessary to inflame public opinion into a state of indignation and hatred of her enemy as it is to supply the fighting forces with munitions. The case against the enemy must be stated with complete bias and a suitable amount of exaggeration. Any arguments in support of the enemy's case must be suppressed. As early as possible atrocities perpetrated by the enemy must be circulated and the enemy's cruel treatment of prisoners described in order to prevent desertions. In the official circular issued during the Great War, when an endeavor was made to collect the necessary material, it was written: "Essential not literal truth and correctness are necessary. Inherent probability being respected, the thing imagined may be as serviceable as the thing seen." Lies, therefore, are circulated by each government to stir up resentment in their people. In a country which has not conscription they have to be more lurid and more frequent than in conscripted nations. Faked photographs are useful and studios for the photography of hideous mutilations can be set up. A good catch-phrase is of special value. In the Great War the Kaiser's supposed reference to the British expeditionary force as "the contemptible little army" helped recruiting more than any other effort that was made. It was only discovered after the war was over that he never said anything of the kind and was not even at the place where he was supposed to have made this statement. No invention about the enemy published independently by the press is ever checked. But any attempt to plead for peace or to say a good word for the enemy may be ruthlessly punished.

It will thus be seen that there was unlimited use, not only of physical violence, but also of fraud. Lies are as necessary in war as shells or planes. Meanwhile militarists assure us that war is the school of virtue. (Consult *Falsehood in Wartime*, by Lord Ponsonby.)

Where the intervals of peace are used for the preparation of fresh wars, propaganda also plays an important part. It is a significant fact that it is precisely in those countries where military preparations are carried on most intensively that truth is most carefully distorted and suppressed. In the liberal countries there is no official peace-time censorship, such as exists in the totalitarian states. But this does not mean, unhappily, that there is no suppression or distortion of truth in the press of these countries. Newspapers are now run almost exclusively for profit. The result is that nothing must be printed that may dry up the sources of profit. Anything which might frighten away advertisers is kept out of the papers. Nor must we forget the power of the socially irresponsible rich men who own newspapers. These men dictate policy to their editors according to the whim of the moment of their own pecuniary interests. Private, plutocratic censorship takes the place in liberal countries of the official state censorship of totalitarian countries. Luckily, the whims and the financial interests of the plutocrats are not identical. What one suppresses, another allows to appear. More truth gets through in the liberal than in the totalitarian countries. Still, the system in both is thoroughly vicious. (Consult Hamilton Fyfe's *Press Parade.*)

. . .

WOMEN IN MODERN WAR, POSITION OF

Between 1914 and 1918 the part played by women in carrying on the war was considerable. In France, for example, towards the end of the war, 1,500,000 women were employed in the war industries alone. In England the number of women employed in industry at large was about three millions. Of these, a considerable proportion worked in munition factories. Most of the rest took the place of men who were thus released for military service.

In the last war, women gave their services voluntarily. In the next, they will almost certainly be subject to conscription. In the words of a French military writer, Colonel Émile Mayer, "It is the function of the military authority to exploit its human materials [*sic*] as best it can, in the interests of national defence, without regard to the age of the individuals." Again, in time of national crisis, every citizen "is at the disposal of the State, whatever his or her sex." In any future war there will be, not merely military conscription, but also industrial, intellectual and moral conscription: and the whole population, women, children and the aged, as well as men, will be subjected to this State-imposed slavery. War is no longer an affair conducted by a small body of professionals; it has become totalitarian. Women are as intimately concerned in it as men.

STUDY QUESTIONS

1. In what terms does Huxley dismiss the argument that warfare is a "natural" state for humans?
2. In what way does he see pacifism as both a just and a practical policy?

26.2 VIRGINIA WOOLF, *THREE GUINEAS*, 1938

Virginia Woolf (1882–1941) was one of the foremost British modernist writers. A member of the influential set of writers, artists, and philosophers known as the Bloomsbury Group, her best-known works include the novels *Mrs. Dalloway, To the Lighthouse*, and *Orlando*, as well as the nonfiction essay "A Room of One's Own." Woolf was at the height of fame as a novelist when she wrote *Three Guineas*. Divided into three distinct essays, it takes the form of letters in response to requests for financial support for various admirable causes. The third essay acts both as a statement of radical pacifism and as an attempt to decode the root of all wars, which she sees as a distinctly male desire for aggression. To resist Fascism directly, therefore, is to extend the male need for dominance and not to control or terminate that desire. In this excerpt, she asks her correspondent why he thinks she should be of any use in coming up with a solution to the war.

From Virginia Woolf, *Three Guineas*. London: Hogarth Press, 1938, Part 3.

Women, after all, have been shut out of education and public office throughout history, so in what ways can they be expected to solve the muddles made of public life by men? While she recognizes the acute global crisis underway, she explores the even deeper cultural malaise of patriarchy that underlies it.

Here then is your own letter. In that, as we have seen, after asking for an opinion as to how to prevent war, you go on to suggest certain practical measures by which we can help you to prevent it. These are it appears that we should sign a manifesto, pledging ourselves "to protect culture and intellectual liberty"; that we should join a certain society, devoted to certain measures whose aim is to preserve peace; and, finally, that we should subscribe to that society which like the others is in need of funds.

First, then, let us consider how we can help you to prevent war by protecting culture and intellectual liberty, since you assure us that there is a connection between those rather abstract words and these very positive photographs—the photographs of dead bodies and ruined houses.

But if it was surprising to be asked for an opinion how to prevent war, it is still more surprising to be asked to help you in the rather abstract terms of your manifesto to protect culture and intellectual liberty. Consider, Sir, in the light of the facts given above, what this request of yours means. It means that in the year 1938 the sons of educated men are asking the daughters to help them to protect culture and intellectual liberty. And why, you may ask, is that so surprising? Suppose that the Duke of Devonshire, in his star and garter, stepped down into the kitchen and said to the maid who was peeling potatoes with a smudge on her cheek: "Stop your potato peeling, Mary, and help me to construe this rather difficult passage in Pindar," would not Mary be surprised and run screaming to Louisa the cook, "Lawks, Louie, Master must be mad!" That, or something like it, is the cry that rises to our lips when the sons of educated men ask us, their sisters, to protect intellectual liberty and culture. But let us try to translate the kitchen-maid's cry into the language of educated people.

Once more we must beg you, Sir, to look from our angle, from our point of view, at Arthur's Education Fund. Try once more, difficult though it is to twist your head in that direction, to understand what it has meant to us to keep that receptacle filled all these centuries so that some 10,000 of our brothers may be educated every year at Oxford and Cambridge. It has meant that we have already contributed to the cause of culture and intellectual liberty more than any other class in the community. For have not the daughters of educated men paid into Arthur's Education Fund from the year 1262 to the year 1870 all the money that was needed to educate themselves, bating such miserable sums as went to pay the governess, the German teacher, and the dancing master? Have they not paid with their own education for Eton and Harrow, Oxford and Cambridge, and all the great schools and universities on the continent—the Sorbonne and Heidelberg, Salamanca and Padua and Rome? Have they not paid so generously and lavishly if so indirectly, that when at last, in the nineteenth century, they won the right to some paid-for education for themselves, there was not a single woman who had received enough paid-for education to be able to teach them? And now, out of the blue, just as they were hoping that they might filch not only a little of that same university education for themselves but some of the trimmings—travel, pleasure, liberty—for themselves, here is your letter informing them that the whole of that vast, that fabulous sum—for whether counted directly in cash, or indirectly in things done without, the sum that filled Arthur's Education Fund is vast—has been wasted or wrongly applied. With what other purpose were the universities of Oxford and Cambridge founded, save to protect culture and intellectual liberty? For what other object did your sisters go without teaching or travel or luxuries themselves except that with the money so saved their brothers should go to schools and universities and there learn to protect culture and intellectual liberty? But now since you proclaim them in danger and ask us to add our voice to yours, and our sixpence to your guinea, we must assume that the money so spent was wasted and that those societies have failed. Yet, the reflection must intrude, if the public schools and universities with their elaborate machinery for mind-training and body-training have failed, what reason is there to think that your society, sponsored though it is by distinguished names, is going to succeed, or that your manifesto, signed though it is by still more distinguished names, is going to convert? Ought you not, before you lease an office, hire a secretary, elect a committee and appeal for funds, to consider why those schools and universities have failed?

That, however, is a question for you to answer. The question which concerns us is what possible help we can give you in protecting culture and intellectual liberty—we, who have been shut out from the universities so repeatedly, and are only now admitted so restrictedly; we who have received no paid-for education whatsoever, or so little that we can only read our own tongue and write our own language, we who are, in fact, members not of the intelligentsia but of the ignorantsia? To confirm us in our modest estimate of our own culture and to prove that you in fact share it there is Whitaker with his facts. Not a single educated man's daughter, Whitaker says, is thought capable of teaching the literature of her own language at either university. Nor is her opinion worth asking, Whitaker informs us, when it comes to buying a picture for the National Gallery, a portrait for the Portrait Gallery, or a mummy for the British Museum. How then can it be worth your while to ask us to protect culture and intellectual liberty when, as Whitaker proves with his cold facts, you have no belief that our advice is worth having when it comes to spending the money, to which we have contributed, in buying culture and intellectual liberty for the State? Do you wonder that the unexpected compliment takes us by surprise? Still, there is your letter. There are facts in that letter, too. In it you say that war is imminent; and you go on to say, in more languages than one—here is the French version: *Seule la culture désintéressée peut garder le monde de sa ruine*—you go on to say that by protecting intellectual liberty and our inheritance of culture we can help you to prevent war. And since the first statement at least is indisputable and any kitchen-maid even if her French is defective can read and understand the meaning of "Air Raid Precautions" when written in large letters upon a blank wall, we cannot ignore your request on the plea of ignorance or remain silent on the plea of modesty. Just as any kitchen-maid would attempt to construe a passage in Pindar if told that her life depended on it, so the daughters of educated men, however little their training qualifies them, must consider what they can do to protect culture and intellectual liberty if by so doing they can help you to prevent war. So let us by all means in our power examine this further method of helping you, and see, before we consider your request that we should join your society, whether we can sign this manifesto in favour of culture and intellectual liberty with some intention of keeping our word.

What, then, is the meaning of those rather abstract words? If we are to help you to protect them it would be well to define them in the first place. But like all honorary treasurers you are pressed for time, and to ramble through English literature in search of a definition, though a delightful pastime in its way, might well lead us far. Let us agree, then, for the present, that we know what they are, and concentrate upon the practical question how we can help you to protect them. Now the daily paper with its provision of facts lies on the table; and a single quotation from it may save time and limit our inquiry. "It was decided yesterday at a conference of head masters that women were not fit teachers for boys over the age of fourteen." That fact is of instant help to us here, for it proves that certain kinds of help are beyond our reach. For us to attempt to reform the education of our brothers at public schools and universities would be to invite a shower of dead cats, rotten eggs and broken gates from which only street scavengers and locksmiths would benefit, while the gentlemen in authority, history assures us, would survey the tumult from their study windows without taking the cigars from their lips or ceasing to sip, slowly as its bouquet deserves, their admirable claret. The teaching of history, then, reinforced by the teaching of the daily paper, drives us to a more restricted position. We can only help you to defend culture and intellectual liberty by defending our own culture and our own intellectual liberty. That is to say, we can hint, if the treasurer of one of the women's colleges asks us for a subscription, that some change might be made in that satellite body when it ceases to be satellite; or again, if the treasurer of some society for obtaining professional employment for women asks us for a subscription, suggest that some change might be desirable, in the interests of culture and intellectual liberty, in the practice of the professions. But as paid-for education is still raw and young, and as the number of those allowed to enjoy it at Oxford and Cambridge is still strictly limited, culture for the great majority of educated men's daughters must still be that which is acquired outside the sacred gates, in public libraries or in private libraries, whose doors by some unaccountable oversight have been left unlocked. It must still, in the year 1938, largely consist in reading and writing our own tongue. The question thus becomes more manageable. Shorn of its glory it is easier to deal with. What we have to do now, then, Sir, is to lay your request before the daughters of educated men and to ask them to help you to prevent war, not by advising their brothers how they shall protect culture and intellectual liberty, but simply by reading and writing their own tongue in such a way as to protect those rather abstract goddesses themselves.

This would seem, on the face of it, a simple matter, and one that needs neither argument nor rhetoric. But we are met at the outset by a new difficulty. We have already noted the fact that the profession of literature, to give it a simple name, is the only profession which did not fight a series of battles in the nineteenth century. There has been no battle of Grub Street. That profession has never been shut to the daughters of educated men. This was due of course to the extreme cheapness of its professional requirements. Books, pens and paper are so cheap, reading and writing have been, since the eighteenth century at least, so universally taught in our class, that it was impossible for any body of men to corner the necessary knowledge or to refuse admittance, except on their own terms, to those who wished to read books or to write them. But it follows, since the profession of literature is open to the daughters of educated men, that there is no honorary treasurer of the profession in such need of a guinea with which to prosecute her battle that she will listen to our terms, and promise to do what she can to observe them. This places us, you will agree, in an awkward predicament. For how then can we bring pressure upon them—what can we do to persuade them to help us? The profession of literature differs, it would seem, from all the other professions. There is no head of the profession; no Lord Chancellor as in your own case: no official body with the power to lay down rules and enforce them. We cannot debar women from the use of libraries; or forbid them to buy ink and paper; or rule that metaphors shall only be used by one sex, as the male only in art schools was allowed to study from the nude; or rule that rhyme shall be used by one sex only as the male only in Academies of music was allowed to play in orchestras. Such is the inconceivable licence of the profession of letters that any daughter of an educated man may use a man's name—say George Eliot or George Sand—with the result that an editor or a publisher, unlike the authorities in Whitehall, can detect no difference in the scent or savour of a manuscript, or even know for certain whether the writer is married or not.

STUDY QUESTIONS

1. How costly does Woolf consider the financial barriers that have traditionally kept women from literary careers?
2. What does she see as the irrational aspects of keeping women firmly within the "ignorantsia"?

26.3 ADOLF HITLER, SPEECH FROM SEPTEMBER 19, 1939

Adolf Hitler's (1889–1945) promises of desire for *Lebensraum* ("living space") and a renewal of the former glory of the empire appealed to German nationalism. In 1938, Hitler set his sights on Poland, claiming that the large German ethnic population in the port city of Danzig needed protection and should be under German control. After Germany invaded Poland on September 1, 1939, Hitler traveled to Danzig on September 19 and delivered this speech.

My District Leader, My Dear Danzigers:

Not only you experience this moment with deepest emotion; nay, the entire German nation experiences it with you, and I, too, am aware of the greatness of the hour when I, for the first time, tread on the soil which German settlers occupied five centuries ago and which for five centuries was German, and which—thereof you may rest assured—will remain German. . . .

The fact that a province was torn from the German Reich and that other German territories were given to the Polish State was explained on the grounds of national necessity. Later, plebiscites everywhere showed that no one wished to become a part of the Polish State—that Polish State which arose out of the blood of countless German regiments. It then expanded at the expense of old settlement areas and above all at the expense of intelligence and economic possibility.

One thing has been clearly proved in the last twenty years; the Poles who had not founded that culture also were not able to maintain it. It has been shown again that only he who is himself culturally creative can permanently maintain real cultural performance.

Thirty years would have been sufficient to reduce again to barbarism those territories which the Germans, painstakingly and with industry and thrift, had saved from barbarism. Everywhere traces of this retrogression and decay were visible.

Poland itself was a "nationalities State." That very thing had been created here which had been held against the old Austrian State. At the same time Poland was never a democracy. One very thin anemic upper class here ruled not only foreign nationalities but also its so-called own people.

It was a State built on force and governed by the truncheons of the police and the military. The fate of Germans in this State was horrible. There is a difference whether people of lower cultural value has the misfortune to be governed by a culturally significant people or whether a people of high cultural significance has forced upon it the tragic fate of being oppressed by an inferior.

In this inferior people all its inferiority complexes will be compensated upon a higher culture-bearing people. This people will be horribly and barbarically mistreated and Germans have been evidence of this fate for twenty years.

It was, as already emphasized, tragic and painful. Nevertheless, as everywhere else, I tried to find a solution here which might have led to a fair adjustment. I have tried in the West and then later in the South to maintain final frontier delineations in order thus to deliver region upon region from uncertainty and assure peace and justice for the future. I made the greatest efforts to attain the same thing here also. . . .

The world, which immediately sheds tears when Germany expels a Polish Jew who only a few decades

Translation by Clifford Backman.

ago came to Germany, remained dumb and deaf toward the misery of those who, numbering not thousands but millions, were forced to leave their home country on account of Versailles—that is, if these unfortunates were Germans. What was for us and also for me most depressing was the fact that we had to suffer all this from a State which was far inferior to us; for, after all, Germany is a Great Power, even though madmen believed the vital rights of a great nation could be wiped out by a crazy treaty or by dictation.

Germany was a big power and had to look on while a far inferior people of a far inferior State maltreated these Germans. There were two especially unbearable conditions: First, this city whose German character nobody could deny was not only prevented from returning to the Reich but in addition an attempt was made to Polonize it by all kinds of devices; second, the province [East Prussia] severed from the German Reich had no direct contact with the Reich, but traffic with this province was dependent upon all kinds of chicanery or upon the good will of this Polish State.

No power on earth would have borne this condition as long as Germany. I do not know what England would have said about a similar peace solution at its expense or how America or France would have accepted it. I attempted to find a solution—a tolerable solution—even for this problem. I submitted this attempt to the Polish rulers in the form of verbal proposals. You know these proposals. They were more than moderate. . . .

I do not know what mental condition the Polish Government was in when it refused these proposals. I know, however, that millions of Germans sighed with relief, since they felt I had gone too far. As an answer, Poland gave the order for the first mobilization. Thereupon wild terror was initiated, and my request to the Polish Foreign Minister to visit me in Berlin once more to discuss these questions was refused. Instead of going to Berlin, he went to London. For the next weeks and months there were heightened threats, threats which were hardly bearable for a small State but which were impossible for a Great Power to bear for any length of time.

We could read in Polish publications that the issue at stake was not Danzig but the problem of East Prussia, which Poland was to incorporate in a short time. That increased. Other Polish newspapers stated that East Prussia would not solve the problem, but that Pomerania must, under all circumstances, come to Poland.

Finally, it became questionable in Poland whether the Oder would be enough as a boundary or whether Poland's natural boundary was not the Oder but the Elbe. It was debated whether our armies would be smashed before or behind Berlin.

The Polish Marshal, who miserably deserted his armies, said that he would hack the German Army to pieces. And martyrdom began for our German nationals. Tens of thousands were dragged off, mistreated, and murdered in the vilest fashion. Sadistic beasts gave vent to their perverse instincts, and this pious democratic world watched without blinking an eye.

I have often asked myself: Who can have so blinded Poland? Does anyone really believe that the German nation will permanently stand that from such a ridiculous State? Does anyone seriously believe that? It must have been believed because certain quarters described it as possible to the Poles, certain quarters which general warmongers have occupied decades long, yes, hundreds of years long and which they occupy even today.

These quarters declared that Germany was not even to be considered as a Power. The Poles were told that they would easily be able to resist Germany, and, going a step further, assurance was given that if their own resistance was not enough they could depend on the resistance and assistance of others. The guarantee was given which put it into the hands of a small State to begin a war, or again perhaps not to do so.

For these men Poland, too, was only a means to an end. Because today it is being declared quite calmly that Poland was not the primary thing, but that the German regime is. I always warned against these men. You will recall my Saarbrücken and Wilhelmshaven speeches. In both these speeches I pointed out the danger that in a certain country such men could rise and unmolested preach the necessity of war—Herren Churchill, Eden, Duff-Cooper, etc.

I pointed out how dangerous this is, especially in a country where one does not know whether these men may not be the Government in a short time. I was then told that that would never happen. In my opinion they are now the Government. It happened exactly as I then foresaw. I then decided for the first time to warn the German nation against them. But I also have left no doubt that Germany, under no circumstances, will capitulate to the threats or coercion of these people.

On account of this answer I have been strongly attacked: because certain practices have gradually been developed in democracies: namely, in democracies war may be advocated. There foreign regimes and statesmen may be attacked, calumniated, insulted, sullied because there reign freedom of speech and the press. In authoritarian States, on the other hand, one may not defend one's self because there reigns discipline.

You know, of course, of those August days. I believe it would have been possible in those last August days, without the British guarantee and without agitation by these warmongers, to have reached an understanding. At a certain moment England herself offered to bring us into direct discussion with Poland. I was ready. Of course, it was the Poles who did not come.

I came to Berlin with my Government and for two days waited and waited. Meanwhile, I had worked out a new proposal. You know it. I had the British Ambassador informed of it on the evening of the first day. It was read to him sentence by sentence and the Reich Foreign Minister gave him a supplementary explanation. Then came the next day and nothing occurred except for Polish general mobilization, renewed acts of terror, and finally attacks against Reich territory.

Now in the life of nations, patience must not always be interpreted as weakness. For years I patiently looked on these continuous provocations. What keen suffering I underwent in these years only few can imagine, because there was hardly a month or week in which deputations from these districts did not come to me depicting unbearable conditions and imploring me to interfere.

I have always begged them to try again. This continued for years, but I have recently also warned that this could not go on forever. After again waiting and even receiving new proposals I finally decided, as I declared in the Reichstag, to talk with Poland in the same language as they talked to us, or believed they could talk to us—the language which alone they seem to understand.

Also, at this moment peace could have been saved. Friendly Italy and Il Duce came in and made a suggestion for mediation. France agreed. I also expressed my agreement. Then England rejected also that suggestion and replied that, instead, Germany might be served with a two-hour ultimatum with impossible demands. England erred in one thing. There once was a government in Germany in November, 1918, that was kept by England, and they confound the present German regime with one they kept and confound the present German nation with the misled and blinded nation of that time.

One does not send ultimatums to the Germany of today.—May London make note!

In the last six years I had to stand intolerable things from States like Poland—nevertheless I sent no ultimatum. The German Reich is not inclined and will not be addressed in such a tone. I knew if Poland chose war she chose it because others drove her into war, those others who believed they might make their biggest political and financial killing in this war. But it will not be their biggest killing, but their biggest disappointment.

Poland chose to fight and she received a fight. She chose this fight light-heartedly because certain statesmen assured her they had detailed proof of the worthlessness of Germany and her armed forces, of the inferiority of our armament, of the poor morale of our troops, of defeatism within the Reich, of a discrepancy between the German people and its leadership.

The Poles were persuaded that it would be easy not only to resist but also to throw our army back. Poland constructed her campaign on these assurances of the Western general staffs. Since then eighteen days have passed, and hardly elsewhere in history can the following be said with more truth: The Lord has struck them down with horse, with man and with wagon.

As I speak to you our troops stand along a great line from Brest-Litovsk to Lwow, and at this moment endless columns of the smashed Polish Army have been marching as prisoners from that sector since yesterday afternoon. Yesterday morning there were

20,000; yesterday afternoon 50,000; this morning 70,000. I do not know how great the number is now, but I know one thing: what remains of the Polish Army west of that line will capitulate within a few days, they will lay down their arms or be crushed. At this moment, our thankful hearts fly to our men. The German Army gave those genius-statesmen, who were so well-informed as to conditions within the Reich, a necessary lesson. . . .

At this moment we want to give the Polish soldier absolute justice. At many points the Pole fought bravely. His lower leadership made desperate efforts, his middle-grade leadership was too unintelligent, his highest leadership was bad, judged by any standard. His organization was—Polish. . . .

I ordered the German Air Force to conduct humanitarian warfare—that is, to attack only fighting troops. The Polish Government and army leadership ordered the civilian population to carry on the war as *francs-tireurs* [civilian auxiliary troops] from ambush. It is very difficult under these circumstances to hold one's self back. I want to stress that the democratic States should not imagine it must be that way. If they want it otherwise, they can have it otherwise. My patience can have limits here also. . . .

So, we have beaten Poland within eighteen days and thus created a situation which perhaps makes it possible one day to speak to representatives of the Polish people calmly and reasonably.

Meantime, Russia felt moved, on its part, to march in for the protection of the interests of the White Russian and Ukrainian people in Poland. We realize now that in England and France this German and Russian co-operation is considered a terrible crime. An Englishman even wrote that it is perfidious—well, the English ought to know. I believe England thinks this co-operation perfidious because the co-operation of democratic England with bolshevist Russia failed, while National Socialist Germany's attempt with Soviet Russia succeeded.

I want to give here an explanation: Russia remains what she is; Germany also remains what she is. About only one thing are both regimes clear: neither the German nor the Russian regime wants to sacrifice a single man for the interest of the Western democracies. A lesson of four years was sufficient for both peoples. We know only too well that alternately, now one then the other, would be granted the honor to fill the breach for the ideals of the Western democracies.

We therefore thank both peoples and both States for this task. We intend henceforth to look after our interests ourselves, and we have found that we best have been able to look after them when two of the largest peoples and States reconcile each other. And this is made simpler by the fact that the British assertion as to the unlimited character of German foreign policy is a lie. I am happy now to be able to refute this lie for British statesmen. British statesmen, who continually maintain that Germany intends to dominate Europe to the Urals now will be pleased to learn the limits of German political intentions. I believe this will deprive them of a reason for war because they profess to have to fight against the present regime because it today pursues unlimited political goals.

Now, gentlemen of the great British Empire, the aims of Germany are closely limited. We discussed the matter with Russia—they, after all, are the most immediately interested neighbor—and if you are of the opinion that we might come to a conflict on the subject—we will not.

Britain ought to welcome the fact that Germany and Soviet Russia have come to an understanding, for this understanding means the elimination of that nightmare which kept British statesmen from sleeping because they were so concerned over the ambitions of the present [German] regime to conquer the world. It will calm you to learn that Germany does not, and did not, want to conquer the Ukraine. We have very limited interests, but we are determined to maintain those interests despite all dangers, despite anyone.

And that we did not permit ourselves to be trifled with in those past eighteen days may have been proved sufficiently. How a definite settlement of State conditions in this conflict will look depends first and foremost upon the two countries which there have their most important vital interests.

Germany has there limited but unalterable claims, and she will realize those claims one way or another. Germany and Russia will put in place the hotbed of conflict in the European situation which later will be valued only as a relaxation of tension.

If the Western Powers now declare that this must not be, under any circumstances, and if especially England declares that she is determined to oppose this in a three- or five- or eight-year war, then I want to say something in reply:

Firstly, Germany, by extensive yielding and renunciation in the west and south of the Reich, has accepted definite boundaries. Germany tried by these renunciations to attain lasting pacification. And we believe we would have succeeded were it not that certain warmongers could be interested in disturbing the European peace.

I have neither toward England nor France any war claims, nor has the German nation since I assumed power. I tried gradually to establish confidence between Germany and especially its former war enemies. I attempted to eliminate all tensions which once existed between Germany and Italy, and I may state with satisfaction that I fully succeeded.

That ever closer and more cordial relations were established was due also to personal and human relations between Il Duce and myself. I went still further, I tried to achieve the same between Germany and France. Immediately after the settlement of the Saar question I solemnly renounced all further frontier revisions, not only in theory but in practice. I harnessed all German propaganda to this end in order to eliminate everything which might lead to doubt or anxiety in Paris.

You know of my offers to England. I had only in mind the great goal of attaining the sincere friendship of the British people. Since this now has been repulsed, and since England today thinks it must wage war against Germany, I would like to answer thus:

Poland will never rise again in the form of the Versailles Treaty. That is guaranteed not only by Germany but also guaranteed by Russia.

It is said in England that this war, of course, is not for Poland. That is only secondary. More important is the war against the regime in Germany. And I receive the honor of special mention as a representative of this regime. If that is now set up as a war aim, I will answer the gentlemen in London thus:

It is for me the greatest honor to be thus classed. On principle I educated the German people so that any regime which is lauded by our enemies is poison for Germany and will therefore be rejected by us. If, therefore, a German regime would get the consent of Churchill, Duff-Cooper and Eden it would be paid and kept by these gentlemen and hence would be unbearable for Germany. That, certainly, is not true with us. It is, therefore, only honorable for us to be rejected by these gentlemen. I can assure these gentlemen only this: If they should praise, this would be a reason for me to be most crestfallen. I am proud to be attacked by them.

But if they believe they can thereby alienate the German people from me, then they either think the German people are as lacking in character as themselves or as stupid as themselves. They err in both. National Socialism did not educate the German people in vain during the past twenty years. We are all men who, in their long struggle, have been nothing but attacked. That only tended to increase the love of our followers and created an inseparable union. And as the National Socialist party took upon itself this years-long struggle, finally to win it, thus the National Socialist Reich and the German people take up the fight and those gentlemen may be convinced: By their ridiculous propaganda the German people will not be undermined. Those bunglers will have become our apprentices for many years before they can even attempt propaganda.

If peoples go to pieces it will not be the German people, who are fighting for justice, who have no war aims and who were attacked.

Rather, those peoples will break when they gradually find out what their misleaders plan, and gradually grasp for what little reason they are fighting, and that the only reasons for war are the profits or political interests of a very small clique. A part of it declared in Britain that this war will last three years. Then I can only say: My sympathies are with the French poilu. What he is fighting for he does not know. He knows only that he has the honor to fight at least three years. But if it should last three years, then the word capitulation will not stand at the end of the third, and at the end of the fourth year the word capitulation also will not be, and not in the fifth either, and also not in the sixth or seventh year.

These gentlemen should take note of the following: Today you have the Germany of Frederick the Great before you. These gentlemen can believe this. The German people will not split up in this fight but become more unified. If anything splits up it will be those States that are not so homogeneous, those empires built on the oppression of peoples. We are fighting only for our naked beings. We are not able ourselves to be misled by propaganda.

Just imagine! There are people who say there are those ruling in another land who do not please us, so now we have war with them. Naturally they do not carry on the war themselves, but look about for someone to conduct it for them. They provide cannon and grenades while others provide grenadiers and soldiers. Such an utter lack of conscience!

What would be said if one of us should say that the present regime in France or Britain does not suit us and consequently we are conducting a war? What immeasurable lack of conscience. For that, millions of persons are whipped into death. These gentlemen can say that calmly, for they themselves never have been on the battlefield for even an hour.

But we will see how long they keep nations at war. There can be no doubt of one thing. however. We will take up the gauntlet and we will fight as the enemy fights. England, with lies and hypocrisy, already has begun to fight against women and children. They found a weapon which they think is invincible: namely, sea power. And because they cannot be attacked with this weapon they think they are justified in making war with it against women and children—not only of enemies but also of neutrals if necessary.

Let them make no mistake here, however. The moment could come very suddenly in which we could use a weapon with which we cannot be attacked. I hope then they do not suddenly begin to think of humaneness and of the impossibility of waging war against women and children. We Germans do not like that. It is not in our nature. In this campaign I gave an order to spare human beings. When columns cross a market-place it can occur that someone else becomes the victim of attack.

In those places where insane or crazy people did not offer resistance not one windowpane was broken. In Cracow, except for the air field, railroads and the railroad station, which were military objectives, not one bomb fell. On the other hand, in Warsaw the war is carried on by civilian shootings in all streets and houses. There, of course, the war will take in the whole city. We followed these rules and would like to follow them in the future. It is entirely up to England to carry out her blockade in a form compatible with international law or incompatible with international law. We will adapt ourselves thereto.

But there should be no doubt about one thing:

England's goal is not "a fight against the regime" but a fight against the German people, women and children. Our reaction will be compatible, and one thing will be certain: This Germany does not capitulate. We know too well what fate would be in store for Germany. Mr. King-Hall [Commander Stephen King-Hall, retired naval officer who writes a privately-circulated newsletter] told us in the name of his masters: A second Versailles, only worse.

What can be worse? The first Versailles Treaty was intended to exterminate 20,000,000 Germans. Thus the second can only realize this intention. We received more detailed illustrations of what has been intended, what Poland shall have, what crowns will be placed on what heads in France, etc. The German people take notice of this and shall fight accordingly. . . .

We are determined to carry on and stand this war one way or another. We have only this one wish, that the Almighty, who now has blessed our arms, will now perhaps make other peoples understand and give them comprehension of how useless this war, this debacle of peoples, will be intrinsically, and that He may perhaps cause reflection on the blessings of peace which they are sacrificing because a handful of fanatic warmongers, persons who stand to gain by war, want to involve peoples in war.

STUDY QUESTIONS

1. How does Hitler present the Treaty of Versailles as the cause for Germany's invasion of Poland?
2. How does Hitler present the condition of Germans living in Poland? What is the rationale he gives for invasion? Why does he express contempt for Britain and France?

26.4 GUSTAVE GILBERT, *NUREMBURG DIARY*, 1947

Gustave Gilbert (1911–1977) was an American military officer and prison psychologist during the Nuremburg trials. On October 20, 1945, the International Military Tribunal received indictments of twenty-three Nazi war criminals, among them Hermann Goering, senior Nazi leader and head of the Luftwaffe, and other high-ranking Nazis. It was Gilbert's role to maintain close contact with the prisoners for the duration of the trial, monitoring their state of morale, and to provide mental examinations with the prison psychologist. His *Nuremburg Diary* is a verbatim account of his conversations with the prisoners and a compilation of some of the essays he asked them to write. In doing so, Gilbert began to expose what had motivated these men to create the nightmarish Aryan dystopia that was the Third Reich.

MARCH 20

GOERING'S CROSS-EXAMINATION

Morning Session: A nip-and-tuck word duel between Goering and Prosecutor Jackson. In spite of Goering's evasive tactics, it was established that Goering was responsible for supporting anti-Semitic decrees. In spite of his claim to being a moderating force in the Jewish question, he had to admit participating in the taking over of Jewish-owned business and property as director of the Four-Year Plan, proclaiming the Nuremburg Laws as President of the Reichstag, levying a fine of a billion marks on the Jewish population, ordering Himmler and Heydrich to settle the elimination of the Jews from German economic life. After the riots of November 9–10, 1938 he declared to Heydrich, "I wish you had killed 200 Jews and not destroyed such valuable property." He had then turned the destruction of Jewish property to the profit of the insurance companies and the government.

*****

Lunch Hour: At lunch Fritzsche said he was now surprised that Goering had interceded on Goebbels' behalf, when Goebbels was in the dog house with Hitler over his philandering, and was about to be ousted. The incident of Goering's quarrel and apparent opposition to Goebbels occurred only 8 weeks before Goering interceded for Goebbels. With typical naïveté, Fritzsche drew the conclusion that Goering must have done it out of chivalry toward an opponent. The more plausible explanation that Goering really did not want to get rid of a strong anti-Semite who suited the Nazi program of looting Jewish property, apparently did not occur to him.

Funk tried to explain the necessity for putting the aryanization of Jewish property on a legal basis, after the reckless excesses of hoodlums who smashed thousands of Jewish store windows in the "spontaneous" uprising at Goebbels' instigation.

"That is almost more disgraceful," I commented, "—putting robbery on a legal basis and giving it official sanction."

"Oh, I don't justify it in the slightest—the whole policy was wrong—I do not mean that—it was entirely unjustifiable."

*****

Afternoon Session: Funk's concern over the legality of organizing Jewish property became understandable as

From G. M. Gilbert, *Nuremburg Diary*. New York: Farrar, Straus and Company, 1947, pp. 205–11.

Prosecutor Jackson continued to present documentary proof that Funk as well as Heydrich were involved in Goering's plan for the elimination of Jews from economic and public life and their segregation in ghettos. Then came Goering's looting of art treasures from occupied countries, by the trainload. Goering insisted he was only building an art collection for the future cultural interest of the State. He had similar rationalizations for his use of PW and slave labor, confiscation of food and property in occupied territories.

*****

During the intermission there was general agreement that it was not a very proud spectacle to have one of their statesmen trying to explain how he came by 50 million marks worth of art property while Germans were being exhorted to undergo sacrifices for their "ideals."

*****

However, at the end of the day, Goering was apparently quite proud of his performance, and told the others, "If you all handle yourselves half as well as I did, you will do all right.—You have to be careful—every other word can be twisted around."

After he went down, Speer remarked scornfully to Seyss-Inquart, "Well, even Hermann made some bad slips; he needn't be so pleased with himself."

"All that talking isn't going to do him any good," Seyss-Inquart replied coolly. "They have it all in black and white."

MARCH 21

Morning Session: Sir David Maxwell-Fyfe made Goering sweat over the murdering of British RAF officers who had escaped from the Sagon PW camp and handing Russian PW's over to the Gestapo. Goering quibbled and denied responsibility. [Fritzsche pointed out during the intermission that the really damaging part of the testimony was that Goering turned the administration of PW camps over to someone else, after the Sagon incident, rather than insisting on changing the system.] Goering had to be asked several times by the court to stop evading direct answers to questions.

Sir David continued to make Goering squirm over the hypocritical intrigue in connection with his attempt to "prevent war" by his negotiation behind Hitler's back, while acquiescing in Hitler's aggressive plans.

*****

Afternoon Session: At the beginning of the afternoon session, Sir David asked Goering whether he still maintained his loyalty to the Führer in the face of all these murders. Goering replied that he did not approve of the murders, but maintained his loyalty in difficult times as well as in good times. Pressed further about atrocities, he weakly maintained that he did not think the Führer knew the extent of them, and he himself certainly did not. He had merely known about a few instances of extermination and "certain preparations."

MARCH 22

EGOTISM, LOYALTY, AND BIGOTRY

Morning Session: Goering's defense ended on a note of anticlimax as General Rudenko terminated his brief cross-examination and the French prosecutor said he had nothing further to add. On re-examination, the court ruled that they were not interested in any further speeches, and the defense counsel brought his examination to an abrupt end.

EVENING IN JAIL

Goering's Cell: When I visited Goering in his cell, to see what he had to say after the completion of his defense, he made an outright bid for applause for his performance.

"Well, I didn't cut a petty figure, did I?" he asked for the third time.

"No, I cannot say you did."

"Don't forget I had the best legal brains of England, America, Russia, and France arrayed against me with their whole legal machinery—and there I was, alone!" He couldn't help admiring himself, and paused for a moment to do so. He then expressed satisfaction with the court's ruling that the others did not have to go over the history and program of the Nazi Party again, since he had been given free rein to do so once and for all. Yes, he was quite satisfied with his figure in history. "Why, I bet even the prosecution had to admit that I did well, didn't they? Did you hear anything?" The test of his medieval heroism was admiration by the enemy. I shrugged my shoulders.

He then began to go over the two days' defense in detail. Being cut off from making more speeches at the end was slightly frustrating. He said he had wanted to tell the court that he accepted the formal responsibility for the anti-Semitic measures, even though he did not know it would lead to such horrible excesses. I told him that he could say that in his final speech anyway, but what was more important was whether he considered that policy correct.

"*Nein, um Gotteswillen!*—After what I know now?—For heaven's sake, do you think I would ever have supported it if I had had the slightest idea that it would lead to mass murder? I assure you we never for a moment had such things in mind. I only thought we would eliminate Jews from positions in big business and government, and that was that.—But don't forget they carried on a terrific campaign against us too, all over the world."

"Do you blame them? It is understood that they would not accept this persecution lying down."

"That is the trouble. That is the mistake we made," he admitted.

He agreed that it would have been better not to have started the persecution altogether. He had just never considered it important one way or the other.

He returned to the more pleasant topic of his duel with the prosecutors. "That guy Rudenko was more nervous than I was, that's a sure thing. Hoho! but he pulled a boner when I slipped in that one about the Russians transporting 1,680,000 Poles and Ukrainians to Russia. Instead of saying, 'We are not interested in your accusations,' he said, 'You do not have to bring up Soviet *actions*.'—'*Actions*,' he said. Hoho! I bet he gets a hot wire from old Joe on that one! He sure fell into it!—I also gave him a good dig when he asked me why I didn't refuse to obey Hitler's orders. I answered 'Then I certainly would not have had to worry about my health.' That's the technical terminology for liquidation in a dictatorship. He understood me, all right."

I then broached the subject of loyalty again, to get more of a revelation on this point in his system of values. "By the way, I noticed that you gave Sir David the same answer you gave me on your loyalty to the Führer. Of course, you didn't answer his question directly."

"I know, that was a very dangerous question. Somebody else might have been trapped by it. He asked me, 'Do you still seek to justify and glorify Hitler after you know he was a murderer?' That was a tough one—a very dangerous one. I told him that I did not justify him, but kept my oath, in hard times as well as in good times."

"Yes, and then I remembered what you had said about being impressed by figures in history who kept their loyalty even in difficult times. Do you remember any examples?"

"Oh, yes, that impressed me even as a little boy.—You know the story about the *Nibelungen*—and how Hagen killed Siegfried because Günther wished it. And then Krimhilde demanded revenge from her three brothers. But they said to Hagen, 'Nay, though thou art our enemy, we must bow to thy loyalty to thy king.'—I can see it now—how they held their shields before him and said they would protect him against any attack for what he did in loyalty to his king." I didn't get the analogy to this loyalty to the Führer, unless he was trying to convey that even Goering's enemies should respect his loyalty, even if it condoned murder.

He then launched into a tirade on the homosexuality of the Catholic clergy, to show that his anti-Catholicism also had some basis. "Did you ever see one of their seminaries? There are 14, 15, 16, and 17-year-olds from all over the world, and you can see at 10 paces that they are selected pederasts. It stands to reason. You cannot go against human nature. When we arrested their priests because of homosexuality, they hollered that we were persecuting the Church.—Some persecution!—We had to pay them close to a billion marks a year in taxes anyway.—But that Catholic clergy—don't you think I know what goes on behind drawn curtains in those confessions, or between the priests and the nuns.—The nuns are 'brides of Christ' you know.—What a setup!" There was an obvious streak of Streicher-like lewd bigotry in all this, that had not been revealed before. It was interesting only in view of his pretended sympathetic interest in the Catholic Church when the Catholic chaplain came around to see him at lunch yesterday.

He mentioned off-handedly that he did not think America would get away with its Negro problem so easily. This was apparently recently borrowed from Rosenberg, indicating the Nazi fear lest they die without leaving behind some heritage of racial hatred somewhere, to prove in a macabre sort of way that they were right after all.

*****

Speer's Cell: (Went to test out the effect on the opposition.) Speer felt that all in all the prosecution had succeeded in penetrating Goering's heroic armor. "It is all well and good for him to claim loyalty to the Führer in grandiloquent terms, but when they pin him right down to take the blame for specific crimes, what does he do? He says he made intrigues behind Hitler's back, he didn't know about this, he disagreed with that. I had to laugh.—He was claiming opposition to Hitler almost as much as I was, after bawling me out for it. Yet he maintains the pose of the loyal servant to the very end. It is just a lot of words.—He knows perfectly well they can't hang him for *saying* he is loyal, but he dodges responsibility wherever he can, when they pin him right down to facts. And when he can't dodge it, he comes out bravely and says, 'Yes, I take full responsibility!'

"You know, when Jackson cross-examines Goering, you can see that they just represent two entirely opposite worlds—they don't even understand each other. Jackson asks him if he didn't help plan the invasion of Holland and Belgium and Norway, expecting Goering to defend himself against a criminal accusation, but instead Goering says, Why yes, of course, it took place thus and so, as if it is the most natural thing in the world to invade a neutral country if it suits your strategy.

"Anyway, it is remarkable how he held up under the strain. Your prison discipline has certainly had a sobering effect on him. You should have seen him in the old days.—A lazy, selfish, corrupt, irresponsible dope addict. Now he cuts a dashing figure, and the people admire his nerve. I hear from my attorney that they are saying, 'That Goering is quite a guy [*Mordskerl*]'—But you should have seen him before. They were all corrupt cowards in the country's hour of crisis. Why do you suppose Goering wasn't in Berlin, to stand by his beloved Führer? Because it was too hot in Berlin when the Russians closed in. The same with Himmler. But not one of them gave any thought to sparing the people any more of this madness, You know, I get furious again every time I think of it.—No, none of them must go down in history as the least bit worthy of respect. Let the whole damn Nazi system and all who participated in it, including myself, go down with the ignominy and disgrace it deserves!—And let the people forget and start to build a new life on some sensible democratic basis."

STUDY QUESTIONS

1. What caused Goering to "sweat" and "squirm" the most, according to this record of his interrogation?
2. How did Goering differentiate between "loyalty" and "condoning murder," and why does he draw on a Wagnerian allusion?

26.5 ARTHUR KOESTLER, *THE GOD THAT FAILED*, 1949

Born in Budapest and educated in Austria, Arthur Koestler (1905–1983) was a member of the Communist Party from 1931 to 1938, when he resigned his membership. He wrote many novels, essays, and other works of nonfiction, and in 1968 he was awarded the Sonning prize for "outstanding contribution to European culture." *The God That Failed*, published in 1949, was made up of six essays on the shared theme of disillusionment with Communism. Billed as "a confession," the six contributing writers tell the stories of their ultimately disappointing relationship with Communism.

I became converted because I was ripe for it and lived in a disintegrating society thirsting for faith. But the day when I was given my Party card was merely the climax of a development which had started long before I had read about the drowned pigs or heard the names of Marx and Lenin. Its roots reach back into childhood; and though each of us, comrades of the Pink Decade, had individual roots with different twists in them, we are products of, by and large, the same generation and cultural climate. It is this unity underlying diversity which makes me hope that my story is worth telling.

. . .

Even by a process of pure elimination, the Communists, with the mighty Soviet Union behind them, seemed the only force capable of resisting the onrush of the primitive horde with its swastika totem. But it was not by a process of elimination that I became a Communist. Tired of electrons and wave-mechanics, I began for the first time to read Marx, Engels, and Lenin in earnest. By the time I had finished with *Feuerbach* and *State and Revolution*, something had clicked in my brain which shook me like a mental explosion. To say that one had "seen the light" is a poor description of the mental rapture which only the convert knows (regardless of what faith he has been converted to). The new light seems to pour from all directions across the skull; the whole universe falls into pattern like the stray pieces of a jigsaw puzzle assembled by magic at one stroke. There is now an answer to every question, doubts and conflicts are a matter of the tortured past—a past already remote, when one had lived in dismal ignorance in the tasteless, colorless world of those who *don't know*. Nothing henceforth can disturb the convert's inner peace and serenity—except the occasional fear of losing faith again, losing thereby what alone makes life worth living, and falling back into the outer darkness, where there is wailing and gnashing of teeth. This may explain how Communists, with eyes to see and brains to think with, can still act in subjective *bona fides*, anno Domini 1949. At all times and in all creeds only a minority has been capable of courting excommunication and committing emotional hara-kiri in the name of an abstract truth.

. . .

It was not usual to apply for membership by writing to the Central Committee; I did it on the advice of friends in close touch with the Party. The normal

From Arthur Koestler, *The God That Failed*. New York: Harper's, 1949, pp. 17, 23, 24, 29–31, 48–9, 71–2, 74–5. Edited by Richard H.S. Crossman.

procedure was to join one of the Party-cells, the basic units of the Party's organizational network. There were two types of cells: "workshop-cells" (*Betriebs-Zellen*), which comprised the Party members of a given factory, workshop, office or any other enterprise; and "street-cells" (*Strassen-Zellen*), organized according to residential blocks. Most wage-earners belonged both to the workshop-cells of the place where they were employed, and to the street-cell of their homes. This system was universal in all countries where the Party led a legal existence. It was an iron rule that each Party member, however high up in the hierarchy, must belong to a cell. There was, so we were told, a "workshop-cell" even in the Kremlin, in which members of the Politbureau, sentries and charwomen discussed the policy of the Party in fraternal democracy at the usual weekly meeting, and where Stalin was told off if he forgot to pay his membership fee.

. . .

The new recruit to the Party found himself plunged into a strange world, as if he were entering a deep-sea aquarium with its phosphorescent light and fleeting, elusive shapes. It was a world populated by people with Christian names only—Edgars and Paulas and Ivans—without surname or address. This was true not only of the people of the various Apparat nets—and the majority of the Party members had some indirect contact with one Apparat or the other—but even of the rank and file in the cells. It was a paradoxical atmosphere—a blend of fraternal comradeship and mutual distrust. Its motto might have been: Love your comrade, but don't trust him an inch—both in your own interest, for he may betray you; and in his, because the less he is tempted to betray, the better for him.

. . .

Before we parted, Schneller said with his embarrassed smile: "Now that you are a member of the Party, you must say 'thou' to me and Paula, not 'you.'" I felt like a knight who had just received his accolade.

. . .

During the next few weeks my only Party activities consisted in dictating, once or twice a week, reports to Paula. Sometimes Edgar dropped in too and listened with his smooth, slightly ironical smile, while pacing up and down the room. As I am also in the habit of treading the carpet while dictating, we sometimes both marched at right angles across my sitting-room, which created an atmosphere of fraternal collaboration. That is about as much warmth as I got out of the Party at that stage.

. . .

A special feature of Party life at that period was the cult of the proletarian and abuse of the intelligentsia. It was the obsession, the smarting complex of all Communist intellectuals of middle-class origin. We were in the Movement on sufferance, not by right; this was rubbed into our consciousness night and day. We had to be tolerated because Lenin had said so, and because Russia could not do without the doctors, engineers and scientists of the pre-revolutionary intelligentsia, and without the hated foreign specialists. But we were no more trusted or respected than the category of "Useful Jews" in the Third Reich who were allowed to survive and were given distinctive armlets so that they should not by mistake be pushed into a gas-chamber before their span of usefulness expired. The "Aryans" in the Party were the Proletarians, and the social origin of parents and grandparents was as weighty a factor both when applying for membership and during the biannual routine purges as Aryan descent was with the Nazis. The ideal Proletarians were the Russian factory workers, and the élite among the latter were those of the Putilov Works in Leningrad and of the oil fields in Baku. In all books which we read or wrote, the ideal proletarian was always broad-shouldered, with an open face and simple features; he was fully class-conscious, his sexual urge was kept well under control; he was strong and silent, warm-hearted but ruthless when necessary, had big feet, horny hands and a deep baritone voice to sing revolutionary songs with. Proletarians who were not Communists were not real proletarians—they belonged either to the Lumpen-Proletariat or to the Workers' Aristocracy. No movement can exist without a heroic archetype; Comrade Ivan Ivanovich of the Putilov Works was our Buffalo Bill.

. . .

At no time and in no country have more revolutionaries been killed and reduced to slavery than in Soviet Russia. To one who himself for seven years found excuses for every stupidity and crime committed under the Marxist banner, the spectacle of these dialectical tight-rope acts of self-deception, performed by men of good will and intelligence, is more disheartened than the barbarities committed by the simple in spirit. Having experienced the almost unlimited possibilities of mental acrobatism on that tight-rope stretched across one's conscience, I know how much stretching it takes to make that elastic rope snap.

. . .

I served the Communist Part for seven years—the same length of time as Jacob tended Laban's sheep to win Rachel his daughter. When the time was up, the bride was led into his dark tent; only the next morning did he discover that his ardors had been spent not on the lovely Rachel but on the ugly Leah.

I wonder whether he ever recovered from the shock of having slept with an illusion. I wonder whether afterwards he believed that he had ever believed in it. I wonder whether the happy end of the legend will be repeated; for at the price of another seven years of labor, Jacob was given Rachel too, and the illusion became flesh.

And the seven years seemed unto him but a few days, for the love he had for her.

STUDY QUESTIONS

1. How does Koestler cast his "conversion" to Communism, and did he have reason to exaggerate some aspects of this conversion later?
2. What caused him to see his faith as an illusion, and what role did the Soviet Union play in this discovery?

26.6 VICTIMS OF THE SHOAH

Nearly six million Jews were killed in the Shoah. The great majority were killed in a spasm of unthinkable violence between 1942 and the middle of 1944. Millions of Russians, Poles, Roma, and other persecuted groups were also victims of the Nazis' industrialized murder.

The Principal Targets: The Jewish Victims of the Concentration Camps

Country of Origin	Prewar Jewish Population	Estimated Number of Jews Murdered	Percentage Killed
Poland	3,300,000	3,000,000	90
Baltic nations	253,000	228,000	90
Germany/Austria	240,000	210,000	90
Bohemia/Moravia	90,000	80,000	89
Slovakia	90,000	75,000	83

Country of Origin	Prewar Jewish Population	Estimated Number of Jews Murdered	Percentage Killed
Greece	70,000	54,000	77
The Netherlands	140,000	105,000	75
Hungary	650,000	450,000	70
Belorussia	375,000	245,000	65
Ukraine	1,500,000	900,000	60
Belgium	65,000	40,000	60
Yugoslavia	43,000	26,000	60
Romania	600,000	300,000	50
Norway	1,800	900	50
France	350,000	90,000	26
Bulgaria	64,000	14,000	22
Italy	40,000	8,000	20
Luxembourg	5,000	1,000	20
Russia	975,000	107,000	11
Denmark	8,000	?	?
Finland	2,000	?	?

The Non-Jewish Victims of the Concentration Camps

Soviet POWs	2,000,000–3,000,000
Poles	2,000,000
Roma (Gypsies)	350,000
The Disabled	250,000
Freemasons	120,000
Homosexuals	15,000
Jehovah's Witnesses	4,000

CHAPTER 27

THEATER OF THE ABSURD: THE POSTWAR WORLD

27.1 SIMONE WEIL, "THE LOVE OF RELIGIOUS PRACTICES," 1950

Simone Weil (1900–1943) was among the most committed of philosophers. Apart from her intellectual work, in her brief life she volunteered as a farmhand, a teacher, a factory worker, a trade union organizer, and a member of the French Resistance. In every aspect of her life, she insisted that the only way to find meaning and value in existence was in paying attention to others. Her essay on Homer, "The Iliad, or the Poem of Force," while a work of literary criticism, provides an excellent introduction to one of the central themes of her thought and life: a call for awareness of and resistance to all the elements in life—military, social, cultural, economic, and religious—that dehumanize us by urging us to live for our own pleasure, pride, and reputation. Raised in a non-practicing, intellectual Jewish family, she converted to Catholicism although she never formally joined the Church. The excerpts from the following essay, which was written by Weil in 1942 but not published until after her death as *Attente de Dieu* (*Waiting for God*), illustrates her attitude towards all institutions, even spiritual ones.

The love of institutional religion, in which the name of God is inevitably evoked, is not an explicit but an implicit love of God since it does not involve direct, unmediated contact with Him. Certainly God is present in such practices, whenever they are pure, in the same way and to the same extent that He is present in our neighbor or in the beauty of the world. Love of a religion can take many forms in the soul, and it differs tremendously depending on the circumstances of our lives; indeed, some circumstances prevent the birth of this love, while others kill it before it even has a chance to develop. Suffering causes many people, even without their realizing it, to develop a hateful contempt for religion on account of the cruelty, pride, and corrupt

Excerpt from Simone Weil, "Formes de l'amour implicite de Dieu." In *Attente de Dieu*. Paris: Fayard, 1950. Translation by Clifford Backman.

behavior that some of its ministers have made them suffer. Some have been raised since childhood in an atmosphere of this sort, and we must take hope that by God's mercy their love for their neighbors or for the world's beauty, if these are sufficiently strong and pure in intent, will suffice to enlighten their spirits. The love of institutional religion in most cases is directed at whatever is the prevailing religion of the nation or society in which one is raised, and it is simply out of habit that whenever one thinks about organized religious services, this is what one thinks of. . . .

Generally speaking, the relative value of different religions is extremely difficult to discern—indeed, almost impossible since any religion can only be truly known from the inside. Catholics say this of Catholicism but it is true of all religions. Religion, after all, is a form of nourishment, and one cannot appreciate the flavor and nutritional value of something one has never tasted. Comparing different religions, if it is possible at all, can only be achieved through a miraculous gift for sympathy. To have any kind of true knowledge of another person requires that while we perceive him or her from the outside we also manage by sympathy to join our soul with theirs, at least for a time, and in the same way our study of different religions cannot result in a true knowledge of them unless we give our soul over to them for a while and share in the faith that is at the very center of whichever ones we are studying. In saying "share in the faith" I mean it in the deepest sense. This hardly ever happens, of course, for many people either have no faith to begin with or have it only in their one religion; in such cases, they look at the other religion with only the same kind of attention they use to study strangely shaped seashells. Some people think they can view religions with impartiality precisely because they themselves have no real faith and thus can turn their minds in any direction, but just the opposite is true. One must give all of one's attention, commitment, and love to one religion before one can think of another with the same attention, commitment, and love it deserves—just as only those who are capable of true friendship can take a true interest in a total stranger. Love is not real unless it is directed at a specific person or thing, in any aspect of life. . . .

The virtue of any religious practice results from the contact it makes with what is pure and has the result of destroying what is evil. Nothing here on earth is perfectly pure except the beauty of the universe in its entirety, a beauty we cannot truly perceive until we have made great progress towards spiritual perfection. This beauty cannot be contained in anything tangible, although it itself is a kind of tangible thing. Religious practices are a unique type of tangible thing since they both exist here on earth and are perfectly pure; but this purity derives from no particular quality of their own. A church building may be ugly, the singing within it out of tune, the priest corrupt, and the congregants inattentive, but none of these things matter. If a geometrician draws a figure in order to illustrate a proof, if does not matter if the lines are not straight and the circles are not round. Religious actions are pure by right, theoretically, hypothetically, and by tradition, and thus their purity untrammeled and without stain. . . .

The perfect purity of religious actions, in fact, is shown in the form of their beauty whenever faith and love do not fail. The words of the liturgy, for example, are supremely beautiful; so are the words of the prayer taught us by Christ. Romanesque architecture and Gregorian chant are beautiful too. Even in the midst of all these, though, if there is no clear evidence of purity of spirit, and if actions are performed out of mere habit, everything is shorn of all beauty. It cannot be otherwise. Architecture, singing, language—even if the words spoken are those of Christ Himself—all fall short of genuine purity of spirit. Anything presented to our senses as a pure thing, if it is the result of mere habit, is just that—a habitual thing, nothing more. . . .

Once we have learned to recognize perfect purity, the shortness of human life is the only thing that prevents us from believing that we can attain perfection here on earth if only we stop pretending, for since we are finite beings the evil that is within us is finite too. The pure beauty available to our eyes is infinite. . . . One of the central truths of Christianity, although it is hardly even recognized today, is that *seeing what is* is what saves us. . . . At those times when we are "in a bad mood," as the saying goes, when we feel most incapable of the spiritual elevation that befits holy things, that is precisely when we most need to turn our eyes to the universe's perfect purity, since that is the time when evil—which is really banality—comes to the soul's surface and is most vulnerable to being quenched by divine fire. . . . The work that brings a soul to salvation is the work of looking and listening; it is like the spirit with which a fiancée accepts her lover. It is simple attention and consent, not an exertion of will. . . . Our obedience to God is therefore passive, requiring no exertion of will. No matter what difficulties we may face or however great our efforts may seem to be, no part of it is analogous to muscular effort. There is only patience, attentiveness, silence, stillness, and remaining steadfast through both suffering and joy. The crucifixion of Christ is the perfect model of obedience. This passive activity is the highest form of activity, perfectly described in the Bhagavad Gita and by Lao Tsu, a spiritual union of opposites in the Pythagorean sense. . . . Aeschylus wrote, "There is no effort required in what is divine." Indeed, there is an easiness to salvation that is harder for us than all our strenuous efforts. One of Grimm's folktales tells of a contest between a giant and a little tailor, to see who is the stronger. The giant takes a stone and throws it so high into the sky that it takes a long, long time for it to come down again, but the tailor lets a bird fly and it does not come down at all.

Anything without wings will always come down again. It is because human will-power has no power to bring about salvation that the idea of secular morality is absurd. What most people think of as morality boils down, essentially, to a willingness to perform actions that require some sort of physical effort, whereas true religion corresponds to desire—the desire is what saves us. The Romans made a caricature of Greek Stoicism by associating it with physical action, whereas true Stoicism, the philosophy from which St. John and perhaps Jesus Himself borrowed the terms *Logos* [Word] and *Pneuma* [Spirit], is simply to be filled with desire, piety, love, and humility. On this point and many others the Christianity of today has let itself be corrupted by its critics. The metaphor of *searching for God* implies an effort of the will . . . but in the Gospels, those great symbols of mythology and folklore, it is always God Who seeks man. *Quaerens me sedisti lassus.*[1] Nowhere in the Gospels does it ever speak of a search [for God] undertaken by a person. . . . To long for God and renounce everything else, that alone can save us. . . .

Attentiveness animated by loving desire is the foundation of all religious practices, which is why no system of secular morality can take their place. . . . It should be proclaimed aloud that religion is nothing else but attentiveness, and insofar as it claims to be anything else it deserves to be locked up inside churches lest it ruin everything it touches everywhere. The role of religion in society is nothing other than what pertains to the divine love in our souls. People who give charity too large a visible and conscious place in their soul cheapen it. Our Father lives only in secret, and love should always go hand-in-hand with humility. True faith needs to be discreet. It is a secret between God and us, one in which we play hardly any part at all. . . . Love for our neighbor, love for the beauty of the world, and the love of religion are in this way unselfish loves.

---

[1] From the Gospel of John, ch. 5. "Searching for me, you sat down, tired."

STUDY QUESTIONS

1. How does Weil distinguish between the love of institutional religion and the love of religious practice? What, for Weil, are the main differences, and why are these differences important?
2. Weil writes that "one of the central truths of Christianity, although it is hardly ever recognized today, is that *seeing what is* is what saves us." What do you think Weil means by this? How is Weil's assertion connected to her later statement that "it is always God Who seeks man"?

27.2 ALBERT CAMUS, *THE MYTH OF SISYPHUS*, 1942

Albert Camus (1913–1960) was a French author, journalist, and philosopher. He is one of the founders of absurdism, a philosophy that developed in Europe immediately after World War II that views the tendency of humans to seek inherent value and meaning in life as impossible goals. He was awarded the Nobel Prize in Literature in 1957.

There is only one truly serious philosophical problem: suicide. To decide whether or not life is worth living is to answer philosophy's most fundamental question. Everything else—like wondering whether the universe exists in three dimensions, or whether the mind has nine categories or twelve—is secondary, mere games. One must answer the first question first. If Nietzsche was right when he said that no philosopher deserves respect who does not preach by example, then you understand the importance of that first answer. It comes before everything else. These are simple facts that one knows in one's heart, but one must examine them closely before they become clear to the mind.

If I ask myself, "How do you know that this question is more urgent than the rest?" I can only answer that one judges such things by their consequences. I have never seen anyone die of the Ontological Argument. Galileo knew a scientific truth of the first order, and yet he foreswore it easily as soon as it put his life in danger. He was right to do so, in one sense, for the truth at stake wasn't worth the risk. It does not matter a bit whether the earth revolves around the sun, or vice-versa. It is a pointless question, really. By contrast, I have seen many people die because they deemed life not worth living. There are others, paradoxically, who get themselves killed for the ideas or beliefs that give their existence meaning; yet what some call a reason to live may be also a perfectly good reason to die. This is why I conclude that the meaning of life is the most important of philosophical questions. But how can one answer it? There are probably only two ways to approach the truly crucial problems in life (by which I mean those that either risk death or those that intensify the desire to live): those of La Palice and of Don Quixote. Only by balancing empiricism and lyricism can one achieve genuine feeling and clear thought at the same time. . . .[1]

Suicide has many causes, of which the most obvious are not necessarily the most potent. It is rarely the result of deep reflection, although we must admit that that is sometimes the case. Rather, what triggers the crisis is almost always something unverifiable. Newspaper reports often cite personal problems or incurable illness as the cause of a suicide, and these are indeed plausible explanations, but one really must know, in any particular case, whether a friend of a man-in-crisis happened to brush him off on that particular day. If so, he is the guilty one, for his action

[1] *Lapalissade* is a French term meaning an empty platitude or a bromide.

Albert Camus, *Le mythe de Sisyphe*. Paris: Gallimard, 1942. Translation by Clifford Backman from Parts 1 and 4 of the original.

was enough to ignite all the bitterness and boredom still held in check by the man in question.

As hard as it is, though, to know the precise instant of the unspoken decision to prefer death to life, it is relatively easy to determine from the act itself the rush of consequences it sets off. In a sense, as we can see it happen in a melodrama, to kill oneself is to confess something—to confess that life is simply too unbearable and incomprehensible. . . . it is, in other words, not worth the trouble. Obviously, living is never easy. One keeps going through the motions required by existence for a host of reasons, the primary one being sheer habit. To choose to die implies that one recognizes instinctively the absurdity of that habit, the absence of any real reason to go on living, the senselessness of daily troubles, the uselessness of suffering. . . .

The subject of this essay is exactly the relationship between that absurdity and suicide, and the precise degree to which suicide is simply the solution to the absurdity of life. A basic premise: unless one is discussing someone who is fundamentally dishonest, whatever a man or woman believes to be true determines his or her actions. To believe in the absurdity of life, if one does so, determines one's conduct. . . . But this is too simplistic and allowance must be made for those who keep questioning the value of life without ever reaching a decision about it—that is, the majority of people. . . . On the other hand, it often happens that those who do kill themselves actually believe in life's meaning. Such contradictions are everywhere. . . . In the face of them, however, must we conclude that there is no relationship between what one believes about life and the decision to abandon it? Let us not exaggerate here. There is something stronger than the sum of the world's miseries in the desire to continue living. The body itself has an opinion, one as legitimate as the mind's, and the body recoils from the idea of annihilation. We acquire the habit of living long before we acquire the habit of thinking, and in the race of life, which day by day brings us closer to death, the body has a commanding lead over the mind. . . .

Deep feelings, like great deeds, always mean more than they are aware of. . . . and all of them have ridiculous origins. Great deeds are born on street corners or in a restaurant's revolving door. So it is with life's absurdity. The absurd world, more than any other, derives its nobility from its low birth. To answer "Nothing" when asked what one is thinking of may or may not be a pretense, depending on the situation (as anyone who has been in love will know). But if that "Nothing" is spoken sincerely, that is, if it expresses that curious state of mind in which Nothingness acquires voice and in which the chain of everyday gestures is broken, or in which the heart searches in vain for something to connect to again, then that "Nothing" is the first sign of the Absurd.

The stage sets collapse. One rises from bed, rides a streetcar, spends four hours in the office or the factory, eats a meal, rides another streetcar, another four hours of work, then another meal, and then sleep. Monday, Tuesday, Wednesday, Thursday, Friday, and Saturday, all according to the exact same rhythm. It is easy to live this way most of the time. But one day the question "Why?" arises and everything henceforth begins with a sense of amazed weariness. "Begins," that's important. Weariness of this sort is the result of a mechanical life, and yet it also marks the start of consciousness. It wakes the mind and inspires everything that follows—which is either the choice to return to one's chains or to awaken absolutely. If the latter, the result can only be recovery or suicide. There is something sickening to this sort of weariness, which forces me to conclude that it is good, for everything real begins with consciousness and nothing real is possible without it. There is nothing original in my saying this, but it is nonetheless obvious and that is enough for now, in this quick sketch of the origins of the Absurd. As Heidegger noted, anxiety is the source of everything.

Likewise with Time, which carries us forward through every day of our unremarkable lives. But a moment always comes when we must carry it. We live for the future. "Tomorrow." "A bit later on." "Once you have gained success." "You'll understand when you're older." Such phrases are ridiculous, since life is all a matter of dying. A day comes when one notices or tells another that one is thirty, thereby asserting one's youth. But this very act situates one permanently in time; you enter it and acknowledge that you stand at a specific point in its trajectory and must follow it to the end. You now belong to time, and in the horror of that fact you finally recognize your worst enemy. Tomorrow—you always looked forward to tomorrow, whereas everything in you ought to run from it. The revolt of your flesh is the Absurd. . . .

I come now to Death and our attitude toward it. Everything that can be said about it has already been said; here it is necessary only to avoid pathos. It surprises one, but never sufficiently so, that everyone lives as though they don't know about Death. Because they have not experienced it. We can only know what we have ourselves experienced and consciously lived. Therefore, it is only possible (and even this, barely so) to speak of having experienced other people's deaths. It is a mirage, an illusion that can never quite persuade us, a sad, unconvincing happenstance. In reality, the true horror results from the mathematical aspect of the event. Time frightens us because it works out the problem and the solution comes later. All the pretty speeches one has heard about "the soul" come undone in an instant; the soul cannot be perceived in a motionless body on which a slap leaves no mark. This elementary and definitive quality of the experience constitutes the Absurd. In the fatal light of that destiny, life's uselessness becomes evident, and no code of ethics or action are justifiable *a priori* in the face of the cruel mathematics that henceforth monopolizes our attention. . . .

To feel the Absurd, however, is not the same thing as knowing it. It lays the foundations for it, but that is all; neither is it limited to knowing it, except for that brief instant when the Absurd passes judgment on the universe. As a result it has a chance to go a bit farther. It is alive. In other words, the sense of the Absurd must either die or reverberate. . . . [For example,] if I were to accuse an innocent man of a monstrous crime, or if I were to criticize a virtuous man of lusting after his own sister, each would reply that my accusation was Absurd. Each fellow's indignation would be comical in a way but would also be perfectly based in reason. The virtuous man's response would indicate the absolute contradistinction between the act I have accused him of and the ethical principles he has observed all his life. "That's Absurd!" in this case would mean "That's impossible!" or "That makes no sense!" If I were to witness another man, one armed only with a sword, attack a battery of machine guns, I would consider his action an Absurd one—but it would be Absurd only because of the disproportion between his goal and the reality he would be soon confronting. I would be aware of the contradiction between his aim and the reality of his ability. We consider the verdict handed down in a courtroom trial to be Absurd when we perceive that verdict to contradict the facts presented in the case. Similarly, the Absurd is made manifest when we juxtapose the consequences of poor reasoning with the logical reality that we hope to achieve. In all of these cases, from the simple to the more complex, the degree of Absurdity is in direct proportion to the distance between the two things I am contrasting. There are Absurd marriages, Absurd wagers, Absurd animosities, Absurd silences, Absurd wars. Even Absurd peace treaties. In each and every case the Absurdity springs from a contrast. Therefore, I have some justification in stating that the sense of Absurdity does not result from the mere observation of a fact or impression, but from the contrast between that fact and a certain hard reality—in other words, between an action and the world that transcends it. The Absurd is essentially a divorce: it consists of neither of the two things being contrasted, only their confrontation.

In this way, and in regard to the understanding, I can therefore conclude that the Absurd is not a quality of mankind, nor is it a quality of the world. . . . it consists of their existence together. It is the only bond uniting them, in time. Let me limit myself to simple facts: I know what a man wants and I know what the world offers him, and now I can state that I also know what links the two. There is no need to dig any deeper; this simple certainty is enough. One has only to consider the consequences that derive from it.

The first consequence is a rule of method. The curious trinity [—mankind, the world, their Absurd relation—] that we see is hardly a startling discovery; it resembles the data of everyday experience, insofar as it is both incredibly simple and incredibly complex. The first distinguishing feature of this trinity is that it cannot be sundered. To destroy one of its elements is to destroy the whole. The Absurd does not exist outside the human mind, and along with everything else the Absurd ends with death. But the Absurd does not exist outside the world either. By this simple reasoning I am convinced that the notion of the Absurd is essential and can stand as the first of my truths. By the rule of rule described above, if I regard a thing as true then I must preserve it. If I try to solve a problem, then I must solve it in a way that does not magically erase one of the terms of that problem. The single hard fact [of life], in my opinion, is the Absurd. . . .

If I carry out this logic of the Absurd to its end I am forced to admit that the struggle of life implies a complete absence of hope (which is not the same thing as despair), a continual rejection (which is not the same thing as renunciation), and a conscious discontent (which is not the same thing as moody unrest). Anything that destroys, does away with, or dispels these necessities . . . ruins the Absurd and devalues the attitude that must be proposed to confront it. In the end, the Absurd has meaning only to the degree that it is not agreed to.

The [ancient Greek] gods had condemned Sisyphus to an eternal fate of rolling a boulder to the top of a mountain, from which it would then roll back down, by force of its weight. Endlessly. For some reason, they believed there could be no more dreadful punishment than an eternity of pointless, hopeless labor.

According to Homer, this Sisyphus was one of the wisest and most sensible of men. A different tradition held that he was more in the way of thug. I see no contradiction in this. But as for the reason he was condemned to pointless labor in the underworld, numerous opinions exist. First of all, he was accused of disrespect for the gods, some of whose secrets he supposedly stole. . . . Another claim is that when Sisyphus was near death he decided to test his wife's love by ordering her not to bury his corpse but have it thrown into the town square. When he awoke in the underworld [which could only have happened because his wife gave him a proper burial] he was angry that his wife had placed obedience to the gods over her love for him. With Pluto's permission, he returned to the world in order to chastise his wife. But once he had again beheld the world, its waters and sunlight, its warm stones and the sea, he refused to return to the shadows of the underworld despite the gods' commands, warnings, and threats. Sisyphus spent many years enjoying the sight of beaches, the sparkling sea, and the delights of the warmth, until finally the gods ordered Hermes to seize him and drag him back to the underworld—where his boulder was waiting for him.

It is evident that Sisyphus is a hero of the Absurd and that he is such as much through his passions and through the torture he endures. His scorn for the gods, his rejection of death and passion for life are what earned him the dreadful punishment of having his entire being dedicated to accomplishing nothing throughout eternity. Such is the price to pay, for love of life. We are told nothing else about Sisyphus in the afterlife. It is the nature of myths that they need our imagination to breathe life into them. In this case, one sees only the strain of a body against a huge stone, pushing it, rolling it up a slope, a hundred times over. One sees his face grimacing, his cheek and shoulder braced against the stone, his foot wedging it underneath. Or starting anew with arms outstretched, the human strength of his two dirt-caked hands. And at the end of every long effort carried out in skyless space and time without measure, he achieves his purpose—only then to see the boulder crash back down toward the lower depths from which he will have to push it up again, to the same place. Sisyphus thus treads slowly back down the hill.

It is at that precise point, the moment of his return to the depths, that Sisyphus is of greatest interest. A face that strains so close to rock is already rock itself. I see him going back downhill with a heavy but regular step toward the punishment he will never know the end of. That window of time offers a breathing space, one that recurs as regularly as his torment; it is the hour of consciousness, and during each of these hours when he leaves the summit and climbs back down to the abode of the gods he is superior to his fate. He is stronger than the rock itself.

If the myth of Sisyphus is a tragedy, it is because Sisyphus possesses consciousness. What "torture" would it be if he had with him at all times a hope of success? . . . Happiness and the Absurd are the offspring of the same earth, and they are inseparable. It makes no sense to say that happiness results from the discovery of the Absurd, for it is equally true that the sense of the Absurd results from happiness.

"I conclude that all is well," says Oedipus—a remark that is sacred and echoes in the chaotic, finite universe of mankind. It teaches us that not everything has been exhausted. It expels from this world a god who had come into it already dissatisfied and with a penchant for useless suffering. It makes our fate a purely human matter, one that we must resolve ourselves.

All of Sisyphus' private joy consists of this knowledge: his fate belongs to him. His rock is his purpose. . . . Without darkness, there can be no light; and it is necessary to know the dark. The Absurd man acknowledges this, and once he does so his labors will never end. . . . So let us leave Sisyphus at the foot of his mountain. One's torments are never far off. But Sisyphus teaches us a higher duty, one that lifts rocks and negates the gods. Like Oedipus, he too concludes that "all is well" and that this unmastered universe seems to be neither pointless or meaningless. Every atom of his stone, every molecule of that dark mountain, forms a world unto itself. The struggle to attain the heights is enough to fill the human heart. One can only imagine Sisyphus to be happy.

STUDY QUESTIONS

1. How does Camus argue that suicide is simply the solution to the absurdity of life?
2. Why is Sisyphus a hero of the Absurd?

27.3 NIKOLAI NOVIKOV, *ON POSTWAR AMERICAN POLICY*, 1946

Just as the United States distrusted the Soviet Union, so the Soviet Union distrusted the United States, believing it to be inherently imperialist and bent on Soviet destruction. Intended as a retort to George Kennan's "Long Telegram," in which the American diplomat described Soviet postwar intentions, here Soviet ambassador to the United States Nikolai Novikov (1900–1976) described how he saw American foreign policy, suggesting in particular that what drove the United States were the imperialist tendencies of "monopolistic capitalism." His view both informed and expressed the core of Soviet foreign policy in the postwar years.

The foreign policy of the United States, which reflects the imperialist tendencies of American monopolistic capital, is characterized in the post-war period by a striving for world supremacy. This is the real meaning of the many statements by President Truman and other representatives of American ruling circles; that the United States has the right to lead the world. All the forces of American diplomacy—the army, the air force, the navy, industry, and science—are enlisted in the service of their foreign policy.

"The Novikov Telegram Washington, September 27, 1946." *Diplomatic History* 15, no. 4 (1991): 527–38.

For this purpose, broad plans for expansion have been developed and are being implemented through diplomacy and the establishment of a system of naval and air bases stretching far beyond the boundaries of the United States, through the arms race, and through the creation of ever newer types of weapons.

. . .

3. Obvious indications of the U.S. effort to establish world dominance are also to be found in the increase in military potential in peacetime and in the establishment of a large number of naval and air bases both in the United States and beyond its borders.

In the summer of 1946, for the first time in the history of the country, Congress passed a law on the establishment of a peacetime army, not on a volunteer basis but on the basis of universal military service. . . . Expenditures on the army and navy have risen colossally, amounting to $13 billion according to the budget for 1946–47 (about 40 percent of the total budget of $36 billion). This is more than 10 times greater than corresponding expenditures in the budget for 1938, which did not amount to even $1 billion.

Along with maintaining a large army, navy, and air force, the budget provides that these enormous amounts also will be spent on establishing a very extensive system of naval and air bases in the Atlantic and Pacific oceans. According to existing official plans, in the course of the next few years 228 bases, points of support, and radio stations are to be constructed in the Atlantic Ocean and 258 in the Pacific. A large number of these bases and points of support are located outside the boundaries of the United States. . . . The establishment of American bases on the islands that are often 10,000 to 12,000 kilometers from the territory of the United States and are on the other side of the Atlantic and Pacific oceans clearly indicates the offensive nature of the strategic concepts of the commands of the U.S. army and navy. . . . All of these facts show clearly that a decisive role in the realization of plans for world dominance by the United States is played by its armed forces.

. . . It must be kept in mind . . . that incidents such as the visit by the American battleship *Missouri* to the Black Sea straits, the visit of the American fleet to Greece, and the great interest that U.S. diplomacy displays in the problem of the straits have a double meaning. On the one hand, they indicate that the United States has decided to consolidate its position in the Mediterranean basin to support its interests in the countries of the Near East and that it has selected the navy as the tool for this policy. On the other hand, these incidents constitute a political and military demonstration against the Soviet Union. The strengthening of U.S. positions in the Near East and the establishment of conditions for basing the American navy at one or more points on the Mediterranean Sea (Trieste, Palestine, Greece, Turkey) will therefore signify the emergence of a new threat to the security of the southern regions of the Soviet Union.

. . .

The present policy of the American government with regard to the USSR is also directed at limiting or dislodging the influence of the Soviet Union from neighboring countries. In implementing this policy in former enemy or Allied countries adjacent to the USSR, the United States attempts, at various international conferences or directly in these countries themselves, to support reactionary forces with the purpose of creating obstacles to the process of democratization of these countries. In so doing, it also attempts to secure positions for the penetration of American capital into their economics.

STUDY QUESTIONS

1. What does Novikov consider proof of U.S. plans for global domination?
2. How are American ambitions in the world tied to their economic goals, particularly in the Middle East?

27.4 WINSTON CHURCHILL, "IRON CURTAIN" SPEECH, MARCH 5, 1947

Winston Churchill's (1874–1965) speech at Westminster College in Fulton, Missouri, delivered when Churchill was no longer prime minister of the United Kingdom, introduced the phrase "Iron Curtain" to describe the division of Europe between the Soviet Bloc and the West. This division is often taken to mark the beginning of the Cold War because it defined the deepening rift between the former allies and the widening gap between the ideologies of Communism and capitalist democracy. In his speech, Churchill outlines the emerging geopolitics of the era, in particular the dangers of nuclear confrontation, the need for increasing global cooperation, and the role of a strong United Nations.

I have a strong admiration and regard for the valiant Russian people and for my wartime comrade, Marshal Stalin. There is deep sympathy and goodwill in Britain—and I doubt not here also—towards the peoples of all the Russias and a resolve to persevere through many differences and rebuffs in establishing lasting friendships. . . . It is my duty however, for I am sure you would wish me to state the facts as I see them to you, to place before you certain facts about the present position in Europe. From Stettin in the Baltic to Trieste in the Adriatic, an iron curtain has descended across the Continent. Behind that line lie all the capitals of the ancient states of Central and Eastern Europe. Warsaw, Berlin, Prague, Vienna, Budapest, Belgrade, Bucharest and Sofia, all these famous cities and the populations around them lie in what I must call the Soviet sphere, and all are subject in one form or another, not only to Soviet influence but to a very high and, in many cases, increasing measure of control from Moscow. . . . The Communist parties, which were very small in all these Eastern States of Europe, have been raised to preeminence and power far beyond their numbers and are seeking everywhere to obtain totalitarian control. Police governments are prevailing in nearly every case, and so far, except in Czechoslovakia, there is no true democracy. . . . Whatever conclusions may be drawn from these facts—and facts they are—this is certainly not the Liberated Europe we fought to build up. Nor is it one which contains the essentials of permanent peace.

. . . I do not believe that Soviet Russia desires war. What they desire is the fruits of war and the indefinite expansion of their power and doctrines. But what we have to consider here today, while time remains, is the permanent prevention of war and the establishment of conditions of freedom and democracy as rapidly as possible in all countries. Our difficulties and dangers will not be removed by closing our eyes to them. They will not be removed by mere waiting to see what happens; nor will they be removed by a policy of appeasement. What is needed is a settlement, and the longer this is delayed, the more difficult it will be and the greater our dangers will become.

From what I have seen of our Russian friends and Allies during the war, I am convinced that there is nothing they admire so much as strength, and there is nothing for which they have less respect than for weakness, especially military weakness. For that reason the old doctrine of a balance of power is

From Jussi Hanhimäki and Odd Arne Westad, *The Cold War: A History in Documents and Eyewitness Accounts*. New York: Oxford University Press, © 2004.

unsound. We cannot afford, if we can help it, to work on narrow margins, offering temptations to a trial of strength. If the Western Democracies stand together in strict adherence to the principles of the United Nations Charter, their influence for furthering those principles will be immense and no one is likely to molest them. If however they become divided or falter in their duty and if these all-important years are allowed to slip away, then indeed catastrophe may overwhelm us all.

STUDY QUESTIONS

1. Why and in what terms does Churchill allude to "appeasement" in this context?
2. If he can succeed in having his audience recognize the existence of the Iron Curtain, what does he then recommend that the democracies do?

27.5 THE UNIVERSAL DECLARATION OF HUMAN RIGHTS, 1948

The *Universal Declaration of Human Rights*, adopted by the United Nations General Assembly on December 10, 1948, was one of the most significant and lasting results of World War II. The League of Nations, created after World War I, had failed to prevent the beginning of another even more catastrophic and costly conflict. The United Nations was planned throughout the war as a substitute mechanism for global peace and security, but world leaders also believed that a document was necessary to affirm the rights of individuals throughout the entire world. A formal drafting committee, consisting of members from eight countries, was charged with the task. The committee chair was Eleanor Roosevelt, the widow of President Roosevelt and a strong advocate for human rights in her own right. By its Resolution 217 A (III), the General Assembly, meeting in Paris, adopted the *Universal Declaration of Human Rights*. Eight nations abstained from the vote, but none dissented.

PREAMBLE

Whereas recognition of the inherent dignity and of the equal and inalienable rights of all members of the human family is the foundation of freedom, justice and peace in the world,

Whereas disregard and contempt for human rights have resulted in barbarous acts which have outraged the conscience of mankind, and the advent of a world in which human beings shall enjoy freedom of speech and belief and freedom from fear and want has been proclaimed as the highest aspiration of the common people,

Whereas it is essential, if man is not to be compelled to have recourse, as a last resort, to rebellion against tyranny and oppression, that human rights should be protected by the rule of law,

Whereas it is essential to promote the development of friendly relations between nations,

Whereas the peoples of the United Nations have in the Charter reaffirmed their faith in fundamental human rights, in the dignity and worth of the human person and in the equal rights of men and women and have determined to promote social progress and better standards of life in larger freedom,

Whereas Member States have pledged themselves to achieve, in co-operation with the United Nations, the promotion of universal respect for and observance of human rights and fundamental freedoms,

Whereas a common understanding of these rights and freedoms is of the greatest importance for the full realization of this pledge,

Now, Therefore THE GENERAL ASSEMBLY proclaims THIS UNIVERSAL DECLARATION OF HUMAN RIGHTS as a common standard of achievement for all peoples and all nations, to the end that every individual and every organ of society, keeping this Declaration constantly in mind, shall strive by teaching and education to promote respect for these rights and freedoms and by progressive measures, national and international, to secure their universal and effective recognition and observance, both among the peoples of Member States themselves and among the peoples of territories under their jurisdiction.

ARTICLE 1

All human beings are born free and equal in dignity and rights. They are endowed with reason and conscience and should act towards one another in a spirit of brotherhood.

ARTICLE 2

Everyone is entitled to all the rights and freedoms set forth in this Declaration, without distinction of any kind, such as race, colour, sex, language, religion, political or other opinion, national or social origin, property, birth or other status. Furthermore, no distinction shall be made on the basis of the political, jurisdictional or international status of the country or territory to which a person belongs, whether it be independent, trust, non-self-governing or under any other limitation of sovereignty.

ARTICLE 3

Everyone has the right to life, liberty and security of person.

ARTICLE 4

No one shall be held in slavery or servitude; slavery and the slave trade shall be prohibited in all their forms.

ARTICLE 5

No one shall be subjected to torture or to cruel, inhuman or degrading treatment or punishment.

ARTICLE 6

Everyone has the right to recognition everywhere as a person before the law.

. . .

ARTICLE 15

1. Everyone has the right to a nationality.
2. No one shall be arbitrarily deprived of his nationality nor denied the right to change his nationality.

ARTICLE 16

1. Men and women of full age, without any limitation due to race, nationality or religion, have the right to marry and to found a family. They are entitled to equal rights as to marriage, during marriage, and at its dissolution.
2. Marriage shall be entered into only with the free and full consent of the intending spouses.
3. The family is the natural and fundamental group unit of society and is entitled to protection by society and the State.

ARTICLE 17

1. Everyone has the right to own property alone as well as in association with others.
2. No one shall be arbitrarily deprived of his property.

ARTICLE 18

Everyone has the right to freedom of thought, conscience and religion; this right includes freedom to change his religion or belief, and freedom, either alone or in community with others and in public or private, to manifest his religion or belief in teaching, practice, worship and observance.

ARTICLE 19

Everyone has the right to freedom of opinion and expression; this right includes freedom to hold opinions without interference and to seek, receive and impart information and ideas through any media and regardless of frontiers.

ARTICLE 23

1. Everyone has the right to work, to free choice of employment, to just and favorable conditions of work and to protection against unemployment.
2. Everyone, without any discrimination, has the right to equal pay for equal work.
3. Everyone who works has the right to just and favorable remuneration ensuring for himself and his family an existence worthy of human dignity, and supplemented, if necessary, by other means of social protection.
4. Everyone has the right to form and to join trade unions for the protection of his interests.

ARTICLE 24

Everyone has the right to rest and leisure, including reasonable limitation of working hours and periodic holidays with pay.

ARTICLE 25

1. Everyone has the right to a standard of living adequate for the health and well-being of himself and of his family, including food, clothing, housing and medical care and necessary social services, and the right to security in the event of unemployment, sickness, disability, widowhood, old age or other lack of livelihood in circumstances beyond his control.
2. Motherhood and childhood are entitled to special care and assistance. All children, whether born in or out of wedlock, shall enjoy the same social protection.

ARTICLE 26

1. Everyone has the right to education. Education shall be free, at least in the elementary and fundamental stages. Elementary education shall be compulsory. Technical and professional education shall be made generally available and higher education shall be equally accessible to all on the basis of merit.
2. Education shall be directed to the full development of the human personality and to the strengthening of respect for human rights and fundamental freedoms. It shall promote understanding, tolerance and friendship among all nations, racial or religious groups, and shall further the activities of the United Nations for the maintenance of peace.
3. Parents have a prior right to choose the kind of education that shall be given to their children.

STUDY QUESTIONS

1. What, according to the *Universal Declaration of Human Rights*, would be the practical benefits of guaranteeing human rights for the entire human family?
2. How likely were these goals to be applied globally in 1948? Which articles remained to be fulfilled at that point—and perhaps even today?

27.6 SIMONE DE BEAUVOIR, INTRODUCTION TO *THE SECOND SEX*, 1949

Encouraged by the successful strategy and tactics of the civil rights and antiwar movements, a new assertiveness also marked the drive for women's rights after the conclusion of World War II. A leading voice in the movement for women's freedoms was that of a leading French philosopher and intellectual, Simone de Beauvoir (1908–1986). Her lengthy, detailed, and compelling study *The Second Sex*, published in 1949, challenged women to take action on their own behalf to gain full equality with their male counterparts. Her analysis traced the origins of sexism and a sense of women's inferiority to the unique circumstances of girlhood and to society's instilling of "feminine" characteristics within young women. Only by breaking the barriers of societal expectations for "well-bred young girls," she argued, could women achieve the goal of true and complete equality with men.

I have long hesitated to write a book on woman. The topic is irritating, especially for women; neither is it new. Feminist quarrels have provoked much debate, and these have now been settled: let's not discuss it further. And, yet, there is still talk about it. Is there a "problem" after all? And what might this problem be? Do women even exist? Admittedly, many still believe in the "eternal feminine." Some whisper that, "Even in Russia, at least, women are still womanly." But others who claim to be well-informed—and they are sometimes the same people—bemoan that, "womanliness is being lost, woman will be lost." One no longer truly knows whether women still exist, whether they will exist in the future, whether one should wish for their survival, what place they occupy in the world, and what place they should occupy. "Where are women?" a magazine's recent headline asked. But, first, what is a woman? One remarks: "Tota mulier in utero: it is a womb." Nonetheless, others who proclaim themselves experts decree upon commenting on some women, that, "these ones are not women" although they possess, like others, a uterus. Everyone seems to agree that the human species contains females: they make up today, as they have yesterday, more-or-less half of humankind; and yet, we are told that, "femininity is endangered;" we are urged to "Be women, stay women, become women." Does this mean that every female human being is not necessarily a woman? She must participate in this mysterious and imperiled fact of femininity. Is femininity a product of one's ovaries? Or frozen within a Platonic sky? Would one merely need a rustled skirt to make it come down to earth? Although many women strive to embody [this femininity], it has never been copyrighted. Instead, it is described in vague and shimmering terms almost borrowed from a fortune-teller's vocabulary. [. . .] Social and biological sciences no longer subscribe to the belief in immutable and fixed concepts that determine the characteristics of beings like Woman, the Jew, the Black; they deem one's character to be the secondary reaction to a situation. If there isn't any femininity nowadays, that is because it has never existed. Does this mean that there is any substance to the word "woman?" [. . .] Surely, woman is, like man, a human being: but such a claim remains abstract; the fact of the matter is that every real human being is always individually situated.

To reject the notion of an eternal feminine, a black soul, a jewish character does not mean denying that jews, blacks, and women exist; this denial only means for those concerned an inauthentic flight, rather than emancipation. It is obvious that no woman can pretend to be beyond her sex, unless she is of bad faith. [. . .]

The category of the Other is as old as consciousness itself. One can find a duality of the Same and the Other in the most primitive societies and in the most ancient mythologies; Originally, this division was not placed under the sign of sexual difference and did not depend upon empirical facts: this is what the works of Granet on Chinese thought, Dumézil on India and Rome have shown. No feminine element is identified in the couples Varuna-Mitra, Ouranos-Zeus, Sun-Moon, Day-Night; neither does it appear in the opposition between Good and Evil, auspicious and harmful principles, left and right, God and Lucifer. Otherness is an essential category in human thought. No collectivity will define itself as One without first expressing that there is an Other it faces. One only needs to put three travelers together in a same traincar for the rest of the train's travelers to be considered vaguely hostile "others." Villagers consider all those who do not belong to the village as suspicious "others"; a country's native resident will look at other countries' inhabitants as "foreigners"; the anti-Semite believes Jews are "others", American racists do the same with Blacks, as do colonizers with indigenous people, and the owning classes with the working-classes. [. . .]

There have been cases when, for a while, a category of people was able to dominate another completely. This privilege has often been the result of numerical inequality: the majority imposes its law upon a minority, and even persecutes it. But women are not a minority like American Blacks or like Jews: there are as many women as men on earth. Often, at first, these two groups existed independently: they sometimes ignored one another, or each recognized the other's autonomy; and one was subordinated to the other through a historical event: the Jewish diaspora, the introduction of slavery in America, colonial conquests—these are historical facts. In these cases, those oppressed can point to a before: [as a group,] they have a common past, tradition, sometimes a religion, or culture. Maybe it is the comparison between woman and the working-classes that Bebel first made that might be the most appropriate: proletarians are not numerically inferior, nor are they a separate group. It was not so much one event, but rather a historical development that explains their existence as a class and that sheds light on the subjection of these individuals within this particular class. There have not always been proletarians: there have always been women; they are women because of their physiological structure; and, as long as one goes back in history, women have subordinated to men: [. . .] it is in part because this [subordination] does not seem to have come about as the accidental result of historical events that otherness here appears like an absolute. After all, a situation created over time can be undone over time: Haitian Blacks have clearly proved it; whereas, it seems, on the contrary that a natural condition cannot change. However, in truth, like history, nature is not an unchanging fact. [. . .]

STUDY QUESTIONS

1. Why does Beauvoir focus on the question of otherness? What point is she trying to make? Why does she compare women to "Jews," "Blacks," and workers?
2. How does Beauvoir conceive of power relations in society? For her, what is the role of history in shaping societies?

27.7 ABBA EBAN, "THE ARAB REFUGEE PROBLEM," 1958

Abba Eban (1915–2002) was an Israeli diplomat who served as minister of education and culture (1960–1963), deputy prime minister (1963–1966), and minister of foreign affairs (1966–1974). From 1949 to 1959 he served as the first ambassador to the United Nations for the newly established state of Israel. The speech from which this selection is excerpted provided the Israeli view of the question of the Palestinian refugees.

The Arab refugee problem was caused by a war of aggression, launched by the Arab States against Israel in 1947 and 1948. Let there be no mistake. If there had been no war against Israel, with its consequent harvest of bloodshed, misery, panic, and flight, there would be no problem of Arab refugees today. Once you determine the responsibility for that war, you have determined the responsibility for the refugee problem. Nothing in the history of our generation is clearer or less controversial than the initiative of Arab governments for the conflict out of which the refugee tragedy emerged. The historic origins of that conflict are clearly defined by the confessions of the Arab governments themselves: "This will be a war of extermination," declared the Secretary General of the Arab League, speaking for the governments of six Arab States; "It will be a momentous massacre to be spoken of like the Mongolian massacre and the Crusades." . . .

On the day of Israel's Declaration of Independence, on May 14, 1948, the armed forces of Egypt, Jordan, Syria, Lebanon, and Iraq, supported by contingents from Saudi Arabia and the Yemen, crossed their frontiers and marched against Israel. . . . Caught up in the havoc and tension of war, demoralized by the flight of their leaders, urged on by irresponsible promises that they would return to inherit the spoils of Israel's destruction, hundreds of thousands of [Palestinian] Arabs sought the shelter of Arab lands. A survey by an international body in 1957 described these violent events in the following terms: "As early as the first months of 1948 the Arab League issued orders exhorting the [Palestinian] people to seek a temporary refuge in neighboring countries, later to return to their abodes in the wake of the victorious Arab armies and obtain their share of abandoned Jewish property." . . . On September 15, 1948, Mr. Emile Ghoury, who had been the Secretary of the Arab Higher Committee at the time of the Arab invasions if Israel, declared: "I do not want to impugn anyone but only to help the refugees. The fact that there are these refugees is the direct consequence of the action of the Arab States in opposing partition and the Jewish State. The Arab States agreed upon this policy unanimously, and they must share in the solution of the problem." . . .

Apart from the question of its origin, the perpetuation of this refugee problem is an unnatural event, running against the whole course of experience and precedent. Since the end of the Second World War, problems affecting forty million refugees have confronted Governments in various parts of the world. In no case, except that of the Arab refugees, amounting to less than two percent of the whole, has the international community shown constant responsibility and provided lavish aid. In every other case a solution has been found by the integration of refugees

Ministry of Foreign Affairs of Israel. "Statement to the Special Political Committee of the United Nations General Assembly by Ambassador Eban." November 17, 1958. https://www.gov.il/en/Departments/General/11-statement-to-the-special-political-committee-of-unga-by-ambassador-eban-17-november-1958.

into their host countries. Nine million Koreans; 900,000 refugees from the conflict in Viet Nam; 8 1/2 million Hindus and Sikhs leaving Pakistan for India; 6 1/2 million Muslims fleeing India to Pakistan; 700,000 Chinese refugees in Hong Kong; 13 million Germans from the Sudetenland, Poland, and other East European States reaching West and East Germany; thousands of Turkish refugees from Bulgaria; 440,000 Finns separated from their homeland by a change of frontier; 450,000 refugees from Arab lands arrived destitute in Israel; and an equal number converging on Israel from the remnants of the Jewish holocaust in Europe—these form the tragic procession of the world's refugee population in the past two decades. *In every case but that of the Arab refugees now in Arab lands, the countries in which the refugees sought shelter have facilitated their integration.* In this case alone has integration been obstructed.

The paradox is the more astonishing when we reflect that the kinship of language, religion, social background, and national sentiment existing between the Arab refugees and their Arab host countries has been at least as intimate as those existing between any other host countries and any other refugee groups. It is impossible to escape the conclusion that the integration of Arab refugees into the life of the Arab world is an objectively feasible process which has been resisted for political reasons. . . .

Any settlement of this problem revolves around the two themes of resettlement, and what is called "repatriation." There is a growing skepticism about the feasibility of repatriation. These hundreds of thousands of Arab refugees are now in Arab lands on the soil of their kinsmen. They have been nourished for ten years on a single theme—hatred of Israel; refusal to recognize Israel's sovereignty; resentment against Israel's existence; the dream of securing Israel's extinction. . . .

Repatriation would mean that hundreds of thousands of people would be introduced into a State whose existence they oppose, whose flag they despise, and whose destruction they are resolved to seek. The refugees are all Arabs, and the countries in which they find themselves are Arab countries. Yet the advocates of repatriation contend that these Arab refugees should be settled in a non-Arab country, in the only social and cultural environment which is alien to their background and tradition. The Arab refugees are to be uprooted from the soil of nations to which they are akin and loyal—and placed in a State to which they are alien and hostile. Israel, whose sovereignty and safety are already assailed by the States surrounding her, is invited to add to its perils by the influx from hostile territories of masses of people steeped in the hatred of her existence. All of this is to happen in a region where the Arab nations possess unlimited opportunities for resettling their kinsmen, and in which Israel has already contributed to the solution of the refugee problems of Asia and Africa by receiving 450,000 refugees from Arab lands among its immigrants. . . .

I do not believe it necessary to speak at any length on the point that resettlement in Arab countries is free from all the disadvantages which adhere to repatriation. Every condition which has ever contributed to a solution of refugee problems by integration is present in this case. With its expanse of territory, its great rivers, its resources of mineral wealth, in accessibility to international aid, the Arab world is easily capable of absorbing an additional population, not only without danger to itself, but with actual reinforcement of its security and welfare. . . .

STUDY QUESTIONS

1. According to Abba Eban, why are Arab states to blame for the Arab refugee problem?
2. Why does Abba Eban propose repatriation as the solution to the refugee problem? How do you think most Palestinians responded to his proposal?

27.8 DECOLONIZATION AROUND THE WORLD

The dismantling of the European empires began as soon as World War II ended. Decolonization came via a variety of methods—few of them completely peaceful—and set the stage for the Cold War as each newly liberated country became a site of the ideological tug-of-war between the democratic West and Communist Russia. As shown in the following table, territories that had been colonized by the Ottomans were the first to gain independence, before World War II. Next came those of the Japanese Empire, followed by European-held colonies in South Asia, Southeast Asia, and Africa. By 1970 the process was nearly complete.

Decolonized Territories

Year of Independence	Country [Colonial Name]	Colonized by	Year Colonized
1932	Iraq	Ottoman Empire	1638
1932	Saudi Arabia [Arabia]	Ottoman Empire	1517
1941	Ethiopia [Abyssinia]	Italy	1936
1943	Lebanon	Ottoman Empire	1516
1945	Korea	Japan	1910
1946	Philippines	United States	1898
1946	Syria	Ottoman Empire	1517
1947	India	United Kingdom	1850
1947	Pakistan [India]	United Kingdom	1850
1947	Israel [Palestine]	Ottoman Empire	1517
1948	Jordan	Ottoman Empire	1518
1948	Myanmar [Burma]	United Kingdom	1886
1948	Sri Lanka [Ceylon]	United Kingdom	1796
1949	Indonesia [Dutch East Indies]	Netherlands	1602
1951	Libya	Italy	1912
1953	Cambodia	France	1863
1954	Egypt	Ottoman Empire	1517
1954	Laos [French Indochina]	France	1893
1954	Vietnam [French Indochina]	France	1862
1956	Morocco	France	1912
1956	Tunisia	France	1883
1957	Ghana [Gold Coast]	United Kingdom	1850
1960	Burkina Faso [French West Africa]	France	1896
1960	Chad [French Equatorial Africa]	France	1910

Year of Independence	Country [Colonial Name]	Colonized by	Year Colonized
1960	Central African Republic	France	1894
1960	Congo	France	1888
1960	Gabon	France	1886
1960	Democratic Republic of Congo	Belgium	1885
1960	Ivory Coast [French West Africa]	France	1893
1960	Madagascar	France	1896
1960	Mali [French West Africa]	France	1904
1960	Niger [French West Africa]	France	1921
1960	Nigeria	United Kingdom	1861
1960	Somalia	Italy	1885
1960	Togo	Germany	1884
1961	Cameroon	Germany	1884
1961	Sierra Leone	United Kingdom	1808
1961	Tanzania [East Africa]	Germany	1885
1962	Algeria	France	1830
1962	Jamaica	United Kingdom	1655
1962	Trinidad-Tobago	United Kingdom	1797
1962	Uganda	United Kingdom	1896
1963	Kenya	United Kingdom	1895
1963	Malaysia [Malaya]	United Kingdom	1867
1964	Malawi [Nyasaland]	United Kingdom	1891
1964	Malta	United Kingdom	1814
1964	Zambia [Northern Rhodesia]	United Kingdom	1899
1965	Gambia	United Kingdom	1843
1965	Singapore	United Kingdom	1867
1966	Botswana [Bechuanaland]	United Kingdom	1885
1966	Guyana [Guiana]	United Kingdom	1796
1966	Lesotho [Basutoland]	United Kingdom	1868
1967	Yemen	Ottoman Empire	1517
1971	Bangladesh	East Pakistan	1850
1975	Angola	Portugal	1491
1975	Mozambique	Portugal	1508
1975	Papua New Guinea	Germany	1884
1975	Surinam	Netherlands	1667
1980	Zimbabwe [Southern Rhodesia]	United Kingdom	1891
1981	Belize [British Honduras]	United Kingdom	1782
1990	Namibia [Southwest Africa]	Germany	1884
1997	Hong Kong	United Kingdom	1843
1999	Macao	Portugal	1557

TERRITORIES STILL COLONIZED TODAY

The United Nations identifies the following seventeen territories that are still in effect colonies of Western nations. The specific term used by the UN is "Non-Self-Governing Territories." Seven of them are in the Caribbean, six in the South Pacific, two in the South Atlantic, one in Africa, and one in Europe. In 2023 they have a combined population of two million people.

American Samoa	United States
Anguilla	United Kingdom
Bermuda	United Kingdom
British Virgin Islands	United Kingdom
Cayman Islands	United Kingdom
Falkland Islands	United Kingdom
French Polynesia	France
Gibraltar	United Kingdom
Guam	United States
Montserrat	United Kingdom
New Caledonia	France
Pitcairn Island	United Kingdom
Saint Helena	United Kingdom
Tokelau	New Zealand
Turks and Caicos Islands	United Kingdom
United States Virgin Islands	United States
Western Sahara	[disputed]

CHAPTER 28

SOMETHING TO BELIEVE IN

28.1 DIETRICH BONHOEFFER, SERMON OF JANUARY 21, 1934

Dietrich Bonhoeffer (1906–1945) was a Lutheran pastor, theologian, writer, and staunch resister of the Nazi Party. His political resistance largely took the form of trying to prevent the Nazis from controlling German Protestant churches; to this effect he was a founding member of the Confessing Church, a branch of the German Protestant Church created especially to resist the Nazi efforts at religious control. He was arrested in 1943, on Hitler's express orders, and sent to a concentration camp, where he was executed in 1945. His legacy as a theologian is somewhat contested, however. While opposing the Nazi Party, he raised questions that he was unable to resolve before his early death; he took traditionally Christian views toward the Jews, which meant viewing them as a people who would eventually accept Jesus as a Messiah.

SERMON ON JEREMIAH 20:7.

LONDON, THIRD SUNDAY AFTER EPIPHANY, JANUARY 21, 1934

Jer. 20:7:

O Lord, you have enticed me,
and I was enticed;
you have overpowered me,
and you have prevailed.

Jeremiah was not eager to become a prophet of God. When the call came to him all of a sudden, he shrank back, he resisted, he tried to get away. No, he did not want to be a prophet and a witness for this God. But as he was running away, he was seized by the word, by the call. Now he cannot get away anymore, it's all up with him, or as one passage says, the arrow of the Almighty has struck down the hunted game. Jeremiah is his prophet.

It comes over a person from the outside, not from the longings of one's own heart; it does not rise up out of one's most unseen wishes and hopes. The word that confronts us, seizes us, takes us captive, binds us fast, does not come from the depths of our souls. It is the foreign, the unfamiliar, unexpected, forceful, overpowering word of the Lord that calls into

From "Sermon on Jeremiah 20:7." London, Third Sunday after Epiphany, January 21, 1934.

his service whomsoever and whenever God chooses. Then it is no good trying to resist, for God's answer is: Before I formed you in the womb I knew you. You are mine. Fear not! I am your God, I will uphold you.

And then all at once this foreign, this faraway, unfamiliar, overwhelming word becomes the incredibly familiar, incredibly near, persuading, captivating, enticing word of the Lord's love, yearning for his creature. It has thrown a lasso over the person's head, and there is no getting away anymore. Any attempt to struggle only shows even more how impossible it is, for the lasso will only pull tighter, a painful reminder of one's captivity. So the person is now captive and must simply follow the path ordained for him or her. It is the path of someone from God who will not let go anymore, who will never again be without God: this means the path of someone who will never again, come good or evil, be God-less.

This path will lead right down into the deepest situation of human powerlessness. The follower becomes a laughingstock, scorned and taken for a fool, but a fool who is extremely dangerous to people's peace and comfort, so that he or she must be beaten, locked up, tortured, if not put to death right away. That is exactly what became of this man Jeremiah, because he could not get away from God. He was accused of fantasizing, being stubborn, disturbing the peace, and being an enemy of the people, as have those in every age even up to the present day who were seized and possessed by God—for whom God had become too strong.

Imagine how Jeremiah would have preferred to talk differently—how gladly he would have joined with others in shouting "Peace" and "Well-being!" where there was in fact strife and disaster. How happy he would have been to have kept quiet and agreed that they were right to say so. But he simply couldn't; he was compelled and under pressure, as if someone were breathing down his neck and driving him on from one prophecy of truth to the next and from agony to agony. He was no longer his own master, no longer in control of himself. Someone else had power over him and possessed him; he was possessed by another. And Jeremiah was just as much flesh and blood as we are, a human being like ourselves. He felt the pain of being continually humiliated and mocked, of the violence and brutality others used against him. After one episode of agonizing torture that had lasted a whole night, he burst out in prayer: "O Lord, you have enticed me, and I was enticed; you have overpowered me, and you have prevailed."

God, it was you who started this with me. It was you who pursued me and would not let me go, and who always appeared in front of me wherever I went, who enticed and captivated me. It was you who made my heart submissive and willing, who talked to me about your yearning and eternal love, about your faithfulness and might. When I looked for strength you strengthened me; when I looked for something to hold onto, you held me; when I sought forgiveness, you forgave my guilt. I would not have wanted it thus, but you overcame my will, my resistance, my heart. God, you enticed me so irresistibly that I gave myself up to you. O Lord, you have enticed me, and I was enticed. I had no idea what was coming when you seized me—and now I cannot get away from you anymore; you have carried me off as your booty. You tie us to your victory chariot and pull us along behind you, so that we have to march, chastened and enslaved, in your victory procession. How could we know that your love hurts so much, that your grace is so stern?

You have overpowered me, and you have prevailed. When the thought of you grew strong in me, I became weak. When you won me over, I lost; my will was broken; I had too little power; I had to follow the way of suffering. I could no longer resist, I could no longer turn back; the decision about my life had been made. It was not I who decided, but you who decided for me. You have bound me to you for better or worse. God, why are you so terrifyingly near to us?

Today in our home church, thousands of parishioners and pastors are facing the hander of oppression and persecution because of their witness for the truth. They have not chosen this path out of arbitrary defiance, but because they were led to it; they simply had to follow it—often against their own wills and against their own flesh and blood. They followed it because God had become too strong for them, because they could not withstand God any longer, because a door had closed behind them, and they could no longer go back beyond the point where they received the word, the call, the command of God. How often they must have wished that peace and calm and quietness would finally return; how often they must have wished that they did not have to keep on threatening, warning, protesting, and bearing witness to the truth! But necessity is laid upon them. "Woe to me if I do not proclaim the gospel! God, why are you so close to us?"

Not to be able to get away from God is the constant disquieting thing in the life of every Christian. If you once let God into your life, if you once allow yourself to be enticed by God, you will never get away again—as a child never gets away from its mother, as a man never gets away from the woman whom he loves. The person to whom God has once spoken can never forget him entirely but will always know that God is near, in good times and in bad, that God pursues him, as close as one's shadow. And this constant nearness of God becomes too much, too big for the person, who will sometimes think, Oh if only I had never started walking with God! It is too heavy for me. It destroys my soul's peace and my happiness. But these thoughts are of no use; one cannot get away, one must simply keep going forward, with God, come what may. And if someone thinks he can no longer bear it and must make an end of things—then he realizes that even this is not a way to escape from the presence of God, whom he has allowed into his life, by whom he has been enticed. We remain at God's mercy; we remain in God's hands.

Yet at this very point, when someone feels unable to go any further on the path with God, because it is too hard—and such times come to each one of us—when God has become too strong for us, when a Christian breaks down under God's presence, and despairs, then God's nearness, God's faithfulness, God's strength become our comfort and our help. Then we finally, truly recognize God and the meaning of our lives as Christians. Not being able to get away from God means that we will experience plenty of fear and in bad times we can no longer be Godless. It means God is with us everywhere we go, in times of faith and times of sin, in facing persecution, mockery, and death.

So why be concerned about ourselves, our life, our happiness, our peace, our weakness, our sins? If only the word and the will and the power of God can be glorified in our weak, mortal, sinful lives, if only our powerlessness can be a dwelling place for divine power. Prisoners do not wear fancy clothes; they wear chains. Yet with those chains we glorify the victorious one who is advancing through the world, through all humankind. With our chains and ragged clothes and the scars we must bear, we praise the one whose truth and love and grace are glorified in us. . . . The triumphal procession of truth and justice, of God and the gospel, continues through this world, pulling its captives after it in the wake of the victory chariot.

Oh, that God would bind us at the last to his victory chariot, so that we, although enslaved and in chains, might share in the holy victory! God has persuaded us, become too strong for us, and will never let us go. What do our chains matter, or our burdens, our sins, sorrows, and death?? It is God who holds us fast and never lets us go. Lord, entice us every day anew and become ever stronger in our lives, that we may believe in you alone, live and die to you alone, that we may taste your victory.

STUDY QUESTIONS

1. Why does Bonhoeffer think it is unwise to resist when God pursues?
2. Why does he see it as an advantage to be bound to God's victory chariot, and what does this mean in practical terms?

28.2 PAUL TILLICH, *COLLECTIVE GUILT*, 1943

Paul Tillich (1886–1965) was a German American theologian and a Christian existentialist philosopher. Born and raised in Germany, Tillich attended several universities there before becoming a Lutheran minister in the province of Brandenburg. It was while he was teaching in Frankfurt am Main between 1929 and 1933 that he came into conflict with the Nazi Party because of his lectures and speeches throughout Germany, and he was fired after Hitler came to power in 1933. Soon thereafter, Tillich moved to the United States, where he became a citizen in 1940. Tillich's work as a philosopher was tied to questions of ontology (the study of being). Whereas his philosophy concentrated on generating questions about what it means to be human, his interest in theology sought to generate answers. Tillich saw the idea of "correlation" as the concept that linked his interest in philosophical questions and theological answers. In *Collective Guilt*, he takes a somewhat mystical approach to the idea that the Germans as a whole were guilty in the "destiny" of Germany, that the crimes perpetuated by individuals were representative of the destiny of the wider German community.

MY GERMAN FRIENDS!

One of the proudest German cities is a heap of ruins. Ten thousand are buried in the ruins. A hundred thousand are without a home, dependent on the hospitality of strangers or the help of the state, in grief over the loss of everything that made life dear to them: people, property, work, the city of their fathers or their choice, in whose brilliance they shared. The ancient story of the rain of fire that fell on Sodom and Gomorrah has become truth in one city, which was famous throughout the entire world and which was proud of its spiritual and moral culture. Many people of Hamburg will ask: why has this struck so dreadfully, directly at us, when we were surely the least ready to open our doors to the destroyers of Germany? What is our particular guilt; why are we, of all people, chosen among the seventy million Germans? And perhaps the refugees from the other destroyed cities will follow and ask: why us of all people? And perhaps, then, those will join in whose husbands or sons or fathers have died on the battlefields and will ask: why me, why me of all people? And perhaps the masses of the German nation will hear this question and will likewise ask: why our nation? Why have we become the victims and tools of the National Socialists, in order to become the victims, now, of the rain of fire and of want and of death on the battlefields and of inevitable defeat?

. . .

And many have answered: I am conscious of no guilt. Why, then, is it hitting me in particular? And others have answered: I am as guilty as all others, not more and not less. Why am I punished more than the others? And yet others have answered: yes, I am especially guilty, because I could have better understood and was blinded and led into destruction. Countless people in the German nation will swing to and fro among these three answers. The superficial ones will exonerate themselves of any complicity in the evil. The deeper ones will grasp that there is a collective guilt, and the finest and best in the nation will lay the greatest blame on themselves. They will

---

Ronald H. Stone and Matthew Lon Weaver, eds., Paul Tillich's Wartime Addresses to Nazi Germany. Trans. Matthew Lon Weaver. (Louisville, Ky.: Westminster John Knox Press) © 1999.

say to themselves and to others among: if we had been stronger and braver and wiser, we could have prevented the destroyers of the German nation from having won power over it.

. . .

There is a collective guilt of humanity in every disaster that strikes humanity, in wartime as in peacetime. Only fools and hypocrites exclude themselves from this collective guilt, which is acknowledged by all sages and saints and prophets. The misery that a wicked social order brings to the masses of people is a collective sin in the same way as the misery that war brings to two nations. And the misfortune that the world wars of the twentieth century have brought to all of humanity is a collective sin in the same way as the indigence and desperation of the unemployed in all the world, which was one of the most important causes for the emergence of dictatorships. No one in the whole world should be brought by political propaganda and nationalist blindness to where he acquits himself of this collective guilt and lays all the blame on others. Whoever does this only creates the conditions for the next disaster that will come upon the nations.

But least of all should you, my German friends, acquit yourselves of the collective guilt, and I believe—indeed, I know—that you are not doing so. Because on this basis humanity's collective guilt, the particular guilt of the individual nation rises up.

. . .

A nation can be reborn only if it perceives its guilt and has parted with it. The guilt of the German nation is that it has permitted the National Socialists to become masters over it. Surely, it is due to the collective guilt of humanity that it could come to this, and the honest and decent people in other countries acknowledge that. But it still took place not in the other countries but in Germany, and for this reason, in the midst of the collective guilt of the nations, there is still a particular German guilt. Hitler was long seen coming, and many who inwardly despised National Socialism supported it because they all believed they could do business with it and then get rid of it. And thus, they became guilty. All Germans have heard of the horrible crimes that have taken place in the concentration camps. But they hardened their hearts and did nothing and, as a result, made themselves culpable. Every German knew of the extermination campaign against Jewish people. Everyone knew Jewish people about whom he felt sorry, but no protest arose. Not once did the churches take their place with the persecuted of the nation from which Christ came; and thus, they all became culpable. The entire army saw, and keeps seeing, what is occurring in the occupied regions through the Gestapo's henchmen. Generals and soldiers know about it and turn their eyes away, often in shame, but never with an action that could save Germany from this disgrace. And so they have become culpable.

. . .

Why is this happening to us; why our generation? So ask the people in all nations. And the answer is: because they all share in collective guilt. Why is this happening to us, to those of us from Germany, to those of us from Hamburg, to our families, to me? So ask the people in Germany. And the answer is: because all Germans share in a particular guilt, namely, to have given power to those who have brought doom on Germany and the world.

STUDY QUESTIONS

1. How does Tillich demonstrate that the Germans are collectively responsible for the guilt of the Holocaust?
2. In what sense does he see this culpability as a long-term opportunity?

28.3 REINHOLD NIEBUHR, SERMON ON HUMOR AND FAITH, 1946

Reinhold Niebuhr (1892–1971) was one of the most prominent public intellectuals in the United States in the twentieth century. The son of German immigrants, Niebuhr was ordained a pastor in the German Evangelical Church (a forerunner of today's United Church of Christ), a denomination composed of elements drawn equally from the Lutheran and Calvinist traditions. Niebuhr's early pastoral work and writings focused on the needs of working-class blue-collar families, and he espoused ideas that were tinged with Socialism. The spread of Fascism in the 1920s and 1930s affected his thinking, and he became more explicitly political. He described his approach to religion and politics as "Christian realism"—that is, a way of looking at the world that retains the idealism of Christian values as guiding principles of action but recognizes as well the need to deal with the hard and messy realities of the real world that may require us to compromise on those ideals. The essence of his thought is evident in the titles he gave to two of his best-known books: *Moral Man and Immoral Society* (1932) and *The Children of Light and the Children of Darkness* (1944). Below is a sermon he delivered at Union Theological Seminary in New York.

He that sitteth in the heavens shall laugh: the Lord shall have them in derision.

—Psalm 2, verse 4

This word of the second Psalm is the only instance in the Bible in which laughter is attributed to God. God is not frequently thought of as possessing a sense of humor, though that quality would have to be attributed to any perfect personality. There are critics of religion who regard it as deficient in the sense of humor, and they can point to the fact that there is little laughter in the Bible. Why is it that Scriptural literature, though filled with rejoicings and songs of praise, is not particularly distinguished for the expression of laughter? There are many sayings of Jesus which betray a touch of ironic humor, but on the whole one must agree with the critics who do not find much humor or laughter in the Bible.

This supposed defect will, however, appear less remarkable if the relation of humor to faith is understood. Humor is, in fact, a prelude to faith; and laughter is the beginning of prayer. Laughter must be heard in the outer courts of religion; and the echoes of it should resound in the sanctuary; but there is no laughter in the holy of holies. There laughter is swallowed up in prayer and humor is fulfilled by faith.

[. . .]

Laughter is a sane and healthful response to the innocent foibles of men; and even to some which are not innocent. All men betray moods and affectations, conceits and idiosyncrasies, which could become the source of great annoyance to us if we took them too seriously. It is better to laugh at them. A sense of humor is indispensable to men of affairs who have the duty of organizing their fellowmen in common endeavors. It reduces the frictions of life and makes the foibles of men tolerable. There is, in the laughter with which we observe and greet the foibles of others, a nice mixture of mercy and judgment, of censure and forbearance. We would not laugh if

From Reinhold Niebuhr, *Discerning the Times: Sermons for Today and Tomorrow*. New York: Charles Scribner's Sons, 1946, pp. 111–31.

we regarded these foibles as altogether fitting and proper. There is judgment, therefore, in our laughter. But we also prove by the laughter that we do not take the annoyance too seriously. However, if our fellows commit a serious offense against the common good, laughter no longer avails. If we continue to indulge in it, the element of forbearance is completely eliminated from it. Laughter against real evil is bitter. Such bitter laughter of derision has its uses as an instrument of condemnation. But there is no power in it to deter the evil against which it is directed.

There were those who thought that we could laugh Mussolini and Hitler out of court. Laughter has sometimes contributed to the loss of prestige of dying oligarchies and social systems. Thus Cervantes' *Don Quixote* contributed to the decline of feudalism, and Boccaccio's *Decameron* helped to signal the decay of medieval asceticism. But laughter alone never destroys a great seat of power and authority in history. Its efficacy is limited to preserving the self-respect of the slave against the master. It does not extend to the destruction of slavery. Thus, all the victims of tyranny availed themselves of the weapon of wit to preserve their sense of personal self-respect. Laughter provided them with a little private world in which they could transvalue the values of the tyrant, and reduce his pompous power to the level of the ridiculous. Yet there is evidence that the most insufferable forms of tyranny (as in the concentration camps, for instance) could not be ameliorated by laughter.

Laughter may turn to bitterness when it faces serious evil, partly because it senses its impotence. But, in any case, serious evil must be seriously dealt with. The bitterness of derision is serious enough; but where is the resource of forgiveness to come from? It was present in the original forbearance of laughter, but it cannot be brought back from the bitterness of derision. The contradiction between judgment and mercy cannot be resolved by humor but only by vicarious pain [. . .] Not humor but the Cross is the meeting point of justice and mercy, once both judgment and mercy have become explicit. Laughter can express both together, when neither is fully defined. But when it becomes necessary to define each explicitly, laughter can no longer contain them both. Mercy is expelled and only bitterness remains.

What is true of our judgments of each other is true of the judgment of God. In the word of our text, God is pictured laughing at man and having him in derision because of the vanity of man's imagination and pretensions. There is no suggestion of a provisional geniality in this divine laughter. Derisiveness is pure judgment. It is not possible to resolve the contradiction between mercy and judgment, on the level of the divine, through humor because the divine judgment is ultimate judgment [. . .]

The sense of humor is even more important provisionally in dealing with our own sins than in dealing with the sins of others. Humor is a proof of the capacity of the self to gain a vantage point from which it is able to look at itself. The sense of humor is thus a by-product of self-transcendence. People with a sense of humor do not take themselves too seriously. They are able to "stand off" from themselves, see themselves in perspective, and recognize the ludicrous and absurd aspects of their pretensions. All of us ought to be ready to laugh at ourselves because all of us are a little funny in our foibles, conceits, and pretensions. What is funny about us is precisely that we take ourselves too seriously. We are rather insignificant little bundles of energy and vitality in a vast organization of life. But we pretend that we are the very center of this organization. This pretension is ludicrous, and its absurdity increases without lack of awareness of it. The less we are able to laugh at ourselves the more it becomes necessary and inevitable that others laugh at us [. . .] This means that the ability to laugh at oneself is the prelude to the sense of contrition. Laughter is a vestibule to the temple of confession [. . .] If we recognize the real evil of sin, laughter cannot deal with the problem. If we continue to laugh after having recognized the depth of evil, our laughter becomes the instrument of irresponsibility. Laughter is thus not only the vestibule of the temple of confession but the no-man's land between cynicism and contrition [. . .]

The incongruity of man's greatness and weakness, of his mortality and immortality, is the source of his temptation to evil. Some men seek to escape from their greatness to their weakness; they try to deny the freedom of their spirit in order to achieve the serenity of nature. Some men seek to escape from their weakness to their greatness. But these simple methods of escape are unavailing. The effort to escape into the weakness of nature leads not to the desired serenity but to sensuality. The effort to escape from weakness to greatness leads not to the security but to the evils of greed and lust for power, or to the opposite evils of a spirituality which denies the creaturely limitations of human existence.

The philosophies of the ages have sought to bridge the chasm between the inner and the outer world, between the world of thought in which man is so great and the world of physical extension in which man is so small and impotent. But philosophy cannot bridge the chasm. It can only pretend to do so by reducing one world to the dimensions of the other. Thus naturalists, materialists, mechanists, and all philosophers who view the world as primarily a system of physical relationships construct a universe of meaning from which man as the full dimension of spirit can find no home. The idealistic philosophers, on the other hand, construct a world of rational coherence in which mind is the very stuff of order, the very foundation of existence. But their systems do not do justice to the large areas of chaos in the world; and they fail to give an adequate account of man himself, who is something less, as well as something more, than mind [. . .]

The Christian faith declares that the ultimate order and meaning of the world lies in the powers and wisdom of God who is both Lord of the whole world of creation and the father of human spirits. It believes that incongruities of human existence are finally overcome by the power and the love of God [. . .] This faith is not some vestigial remnant of a credulous and prescientific age with which "scientific" generations may dispense. There is no power in any science or philosophy, whether in a pre- or post-scientific age, to leap the chasm of incongruity by pure thought. Thought which begins on one side of the chasm can do no more than deny the reality on the other side. It seeks either to prove that death is no reality because spirit is eternal, or that spirit is not eternal because death is a reality. But the real situation is that man, as a part of the natural world, brings his years to an end like a tale that is told; and that man as a free spirit finds the brevity of his years incongruous and death an irrationality; and that man as a unity of body and spirit can neither by taking thought reduce the dimension of his life to the limit of nature, nor yet raise it to the dimension of pure spirit. Either his incomplete and frustrated life is completed by a power greater than his own, or it is not completed.

Faith is therefore the final triumph over incongruity, the final assertion of the meaningfulness of existence. There is no other triumph and will be none, no matter how much human knowledge is enlarged. Faith is the final assertion of the freedom of the human spirit, but also the final acceptance of the weakness of man and the final solution for the problem of life through the disavowal of any final solutions in the power of man.

Insofar as the sense of humor is a recognition of incongruity, it is more profound than any philosophy which seeks to devour incongruity in reason. But the sense of humor remains healthy only when it deals with immediate issues and faces the obvious and surface irrationalities. It must move toward faith or sink into despair when the ultimate issues are raised.

That is why there is laughter in the vestibule of the temple, the echo of laughter in the temple itself, but only faith and prayer, and no laughter, in the holy of holies.

STUDY QUESTIONS

1. Niebuhr described his approach to religion and politics as "Christian realism." What features of his sermon exemplify Christian realism?
2. What hard realities of the real world does Niebuhr describe in his sermon that may require believers to compromise their Christian values?

28.4 JEAN-PAUL SARTRE, "THE HUMANISM OF EXISTENTIALISM," 1947

Jean-Paul Sartre (1905–1980) was perhaps the most famous European philosopher of the twentieth century, but more people have read his novels and plays than his philosophical works. He is sometimes described erroneously as the founder of existentialism, but while existentialist ideas emerged a generation before Sartre, he is the one who weaved the ideas into a systematic whole with his masterpiece *Being and Nothingness*, which was published in French in 1943, with the first English translation appearing five years later. The following essay, which appeared in an anthology published in 1947, discusses the link between existentialism and atheism. The nonexistence of God, according to Sartre, requires that we create our own identities and values and that we do so through the actions we take. "Existence precedes essence," he claims—meaning, in rough terms, that what we do makes us what we are, rather than the other way around.

I represent *atheistic Existentialism* . . . which asserts that, whereas God does not exist, there is still one being whose existence precedes his essence, a being, in other words, whose existence is real before it can be defined by any pre-existing concept—and that this being is Man. . . . But what does it mean, to say that "existence precedes essence"? In the first place, it means simply that Man exists, is present, appears on the scene, first, and that he defines himself afterward. If the Existentialist conception is correct that Man is indefinable, it is because he is at first nothing, and will be something only after he will himself have made himself into something. There is no such thing as *human nature*, since there is no God to create it. Man is only what he conceives himself to be, and what he wills himself to be once he has come into existence.

Man is nothing other than what he makes of himself—this is the first principle of Existentialism; it is also what is meant by the term *subjectivity*. . . . What do we mean by this? Only that Man possesses greater dignity than a rock or a table? No. We mean that Man first exists—that is, that he is the being who propels himself toward a future and who consciously imagines himself as having a future. From the start of his existence, man (unlike, say, a patch of moss, a piece of rubbish, or a cauliflower) perceives his awareness of himself. Nothing at all exists prior to this self-perception—nothing in any heaven. Man will be whatever he plans to be. *Plans*, not *wills*, for the word *will* usually implies a conscious decision, which is something that we realize *after* we have made of ourselves whatever we make of ourselves. For example, I may desire to join a political party, to write a book, or to get married; but these things are only manifestations of an earlier, spontaneous choice that is called *will*. Thus, since existence really does precede essence, every Man is responsible for what he is and what he becomes, and for this reason the first task of Existentialism is to make everyone aware of what he or she is and to teach them to take responsibility for their own existence. Moreover, when we say that Man is responsible for himself we mean not only that he is responsible for his own individual existence but for that of all Men.

There are two meanings to the word *subjectivism*, and our detractors play on both of them. On the one

Translation by Clifford Backman.

hand, subjectivism means that an individual makes choices and in so doing makes himself; on the other hand, it means the impossibility for any man to transcend human subjectivity. The second definition is the very essence of Existentialism. When we say that Man chooses his own self, we mean that every one of us does the very same; but we also mean that in making his choice, Man chooses for all mankind. Simply put, in creating the man we want to be, every single one of our acts creates an image of mankind that we think ought to exist. To choose to be one thing, as opposed to another, is to affirm, at the same time, the value of the thing we choose. We can never choose evil, and hence we always choose what is good—and nothing can be good for us that is not, at the same time, good for everyone. . . .

If I am a simple laborer, for example, and if I choose to join a Christian trade-union rather than the Communist party, and if by joining the trade-union I hope to show that the best thing for Man is to resign himself to the fact that the true Kingdom is not of this world—then I am saying that I want everyone to be so resigned. My action has implicated all of humanity. Or to use a more personal example: say that I want to get married and have children. Even if this marriage results solely from my own circumstances, desires, or wishes, I am in essence involving all of mankind (and not merely myself) in the choice of monogamy. This is why I say that in being responsible for myself I am responsible for everyone. . . . For every person, everything happens as if all mankind was watching him or her and was taking its lead from whatever he or she does, and this is why we ought always to ask ourselves, "Am I the kind of person whose actions ought by right to serve as the model of all mankind?" . . .

Existentialists find it deeply distressing that God does not exist because without Him there is no possibility of finding a set of absolute values in some heaven of ideas; there can be no such thing as an *a priori* Good, since there is no Infinite and Perfect Being to think it. Nowhere is it written that Goodness exists, or that we must be honest and must not lie—because we exist in a space where there are only human beings. Dostoevsky once said, "If God didn't exist, everything would be permissible"—and this statement is the absolute starting point of Existentialism, for in fact everything *is* permissible if God does not exist. This truth results in mankind's misery, for we have nothing internal or external to ourselves to cling to, and there are no excuses for what we make of our lives. . . .

This is what I mean when I say that Man is condemned to be free—*condemned*, because he did not create himself; *free*, because, once launched into the world, he alone is responsible for everything he does. . . . Existentialism maintains that cowards make themselves cowardly, and heroes make themselves heroic. After all, a coward can always choose not to be cowardly, and a hero can always choose to stop behaving heroically. What matters is the totality of one's actions, not any one particular action or set of circumstances. . . .

[Thus] Existentialism is not a philosophy of quietism, since it defines Man in terms of actions. Nor is it a pessimistic view of Man; indeed, it is the most optimistic of doctrines, since Man's destiny is entirely up to him. It does not discourage action; rather, it insists that hope exists solely in his acting. Taking action is the only thing that makes it possible to live. . . .

But some might object: *You are basically just moving things from one pocket to another. Your values aren't true, since you are merely choosing the ones you want.* To which I reply: I am sorry, but that is the way things are! Without a God, someone else has to invent values. You have to take things as they are. Besides, to say that we invent our own values really is to say nothing more than that human life has no *a priori* meaning. Before you are born, your life is nothing; once you are born, it is up to you to give it meaning. Values are nothing but the meaning that you choose. . . .

Consequently, no one can pass judgment on Mankind. Existentialism vitiates any such judgment, and never considers Mankind as an end because he is always in the making. . . . [To an Existentialist,] *humanism* has a different meaning [from what others mean by the word]. It means that Man is constantly outside of himself. In pressing forward from himself—that is, in losing himself outside of himself—he creates his existence. The pursuit of transcendent goals is what makes existence bearable. . . . There is no universe other than the human universe, the universe of human subjectivity.

STUDY QUESTION

1. How does Sartre show the link between existentialism and atheism? Do you agree with Sartre's argument?
2. Why does Sartre believe that people need to create their own identities and values? What importance does he place on action?

28.5 POPE JOHN XXIII, *PACEM IN TERRIS*, 1963

Pope John XXIII (1881–1963) died from cancer shortly after issuing this papal encyclical (letter formally sent out to all bishops). In it he addressed not only Catholics, but also all mankind, which is perhaps understandable if you view this work in its Cold War context. Issued two years after the erection of the Berlin Wall and two months after the Cuban missile crisis, the world was focused on the rising tensions between the Soviet Union and the United States and as such was poised for disaster. The full title of the encyclical, *On Establishing Universal Peace in Truth, Justice, Charity, and Liberty,* covers the scope of the document, which is divided into four sections. The first discusses the relations between the individual and humanity in general; the second deals with the relationship between the individual and the state; the third talks about how the state entails rights and duties for citizens, as well as the need for equality among states; and the fourth tackles the need for collective assistance among states.

To Our Venerable Brethren the Patriarchs, Primates, Archbishops, Bishops, and all other Local Ordinaries who are at Peace and in Communion with the Apostolic See, and to the Clergy and Faithful of the entire Catholic World, and to all Men of Good Will. Venerable Brethren and Dearest Sons, Health and Apostolic Benediction.

Peace on Earth—which man throughout the ages has so longed for and sought after—can never be established, never guaranteed, except by the diligent observance of the divinely established order.

ORDER IN THE UNIVERSE

2. That a marvelous order predominates in the world of living beings and in the forces of nature, is the plain lesson which the progress of modern research and the discoveries of technology teach us. And it is part of the greatness of man that he can appreciate that order, and devise the means for harnessing those forces for his own benefit.
3. But what emerges first and foremost from the progress of scientific knowledge and the inventions of technology is the infinite greatness of God Himself, who created both man and the universe. Yes; out of nothing He made all things, and filled them with the fullness of His own wisdom and goodness. Hence, these are the words the holy psalmist used in praise of God: "O Lord, our Lord: how admirable is thy name in the whole earth!" (1) And elsewhere he says: "How great are thy works, O Lord! Thou hast

From *Pacem in Terris. Encyclical of Pope John XXIII, On Establishing Universal Peace in Truth, Justice, Charity, and Liberty.* April 11, 1963.

made all things in wisdom." (2) Moreover, (2a) God created man "in His own image and likeness," (3) endowed him with intelligence and freedom, and made him lord of creation. All this the psalmist proclaims when he says: "Thou hast made him a little less than the angels: thou hast crowned him with glory and honor, and hast set him over the works of thy hands. Thou hast subjected all things under his feet." (4)

ORDER IN HUMAN BEINGS

4. And yet there is a disunity among individuals and among nations which is in striking contrast to this perfect order in the universe. One would think that the relationships that bind men together could only be governed by force.
5. But the world's Creator has stamped man's inmost being with an order revealed to man by his conscience; and his conscience insists on his preserving it. Men "show the work of the law written in their hearts. Their conscience bears witness to them." (5) And how could it be otherwise? All created being reflects the infinite wisdom of God. It reflects it all the more clearly, the higher it stands in the scale of perfection. (6)
6. But the mischief is often caused by erroneous opinions. Many people think that the laws which govern man's relations with the State are the same as those which regulate the blind, elemental forces of the universe. But it is not so; the laws which govern men are quite different. The Father of the universe has inscribed them in man's nature, and that is where we must look for them; there and nowhere else.
7. These laws clearly indicate how a man must behave toward his fellows in society, and how the mutual relationships between the members of a State and its officials are to be conducted. They show too what principles must govern the relations between States; and finally, what should be the relations between individuals or States on the one hand, and the world-wide community of nations on the other. Men's common interests make it imperative that at long last a world-wide community of nations be established.

I. ORDER BETWEEN MEN

8. We must devote our attention first of all to that order which should prevail among men.
9. Any well-regulated and productive association of men in society demands the acceptance of one fundamental principle: that each individual man is truly a person. His is a nature, that is, endowed with intelligence and free will. As such he has rights and duties, which together flow as a direct consequence from his nature. These rights and duties are universal and inviolable, and therefore altogether inalienable. (7)
10. When, furthermore, we consider man's personal dignity from the standpoint of divine revelation, inevitably our estimate of it is incomparably increased. Men have been ransomed by the blood of Jesus Christ. Grace has made them sons and friends of God, and heirs to eternal glory.

Rights

11. But first We must speak of man's rights. Man has the right to live. He has the right to bodily integrity and to the means necessary for the proper development of life, particularly food, clothing, shelter, medical care, rest, and, finally, the necessary social services. In consequence, he has the right to be looked after in the event of ill health; disability stemming from his work; widowhood; old age; enforced unemployment; or whenever through no fault of his own he is deprived of the means of livelihood. (8)

Rights Pertaining to Moral and Cultural Values

12. Moreover, man has a natural right to be respected. He has a right to his good name. He has a right to freedom in investigating the truth, and—within the limits of the moral order and the common good—to freedom of speech and publication, and to freedom to pursue whatever profession he may choose. He has the right, also, to be accurately informed about public events.
13. He has the natural right to share in the benefits of culture, and hence to receive a good general education, and a technical or professional training consistent with the degree of educational

development in his own country. Furthermore, a system must be devised for affording gifted members of society the opportunity of engaging in more advanced studies, with a view to their occupying, as far as possible, positions of responsibility in society in keeping with their natural talent and acquired skill. (9)

The Right to Worship God According to One's Conscience

14. Also among man's rights is that of being able to worship God in accordance with the right dictates of his own conscience, and to profess his religion both in private and in public. According to the clear teaching of Lactantius, "this is the very condition of our birth, that we render to the God who made us that just homage which is His due; that we acknowledge Him alone as God, and follow Him. It is from this ligature of piety, which binds us and joins us to God, that religion derives its name." (10)

    Hence, too, Pope Leo XIII declared that "true freedom, freedom worthy of the sons of God, is that freedom which most truly safeguards the dignity of the human person. It is stronger than any violence or injustice. Such is the freedom which has always been desired by the Church, and which she holds most dear. It is the sort of freedom which the Apostles resolutely claimed for themselves. The apologists defended it in their writings; thousands of martyrs consecrated it with their blood." (11)

The Right to Choose Freely One's State in Life

15. Human beings have also the right to choose for themselves the kind of life which appeals to them: whether it is to found a family—in the founding of which both the man and the woman enjoy equal rights and duties—or to embrace the priesthood or the religious life. (12)
16. The family, founded upon marriage freely contracted, one and indissoluble, must be regarded as the natural, primary cell of human society. The interests of the family, therefore, must be taken very specially into consideration in social and economic affairs, as well as in the spheres of faith and morals. For all of these have to do with strengthening the family and assisting it in the fulfilment of its mission.
17. Of course, the support and education of children is a right which belongs primarily to the parents. (13)

Economic Rights

18. In the economic sphere, it is evident that a man has the inherent right not only to be given the opportunity to work, but also to be allowed the exercise of personal initiative in the work he does. (14)
19. The conditions in which a man works form a necessary corollary to these rights. They must not be such as to weaken his physical or moral fibre, or militate against the proper development of adolescents to manhood. Women must be accorded such conditions of work as are consistent with their needs and responsibilities as wives and mothers. (15)
20. A further consequence of man's personal dignity is his right to engage in economic activities suited to his degree of responsibility. (16) The worker is likewise entitled to a wage that is determined in accordance with the precepts of justice. This needs stressing. The amount a worker receives must be sufficient, in proportion to available funds, to allow him and his family a standard of living consistent with human dignity. Pope Pius XII expressed it in these terms: "Nature imposes work upon man as a duty, and man has the corresponding natural right to demand that the work he does shall provide him with the means of livelihood for himself and his children. Such is nature's categorical imperative for the preservation of man." (17)
21. As a further consequence of man's nature, he has the right to the private ownership of property, including that of productive goods. This, as We have said elsewhere, is "a right which constitutes so efficacious a means of asserting one's personality and exercising responsibility in every field, and an element of solidity and security for family life, and of greater peace and prosperity in the State." (18)
22. Finally, it is opportune to point out that the right to own private property entails a social obligation as well. (19)

The Right of Meeting and Association

23. Men are by nature social, and consequently they have the right to meet together and to form associations with their fellows. They have the right to confer on such associations the type of organization which they consider best calculated to achieve their objectives. They have also the right to exercise their own initiative and act on their own responsibility within these associations for the attainment of the desired results. (20)
24. As We insisted in Our encyclical *Mater et Magistra*, the founding of a great many such intermediate groups or societies for the pursuit of aims which it is not within the competence of the individual to achieve efficiently, is a matter of great urgency. Such groups and societies must be considered absolutely essential for the safeguarding of man's personal freedom and dignity, while leaving intact a sense of responsibility. (21)

The Right to Emigrate and Immigrate

25. Again, every human being has the right to freedom of movement and of residence within the confines of his own State. When there are just reasons in favor of it, he must be permitted to emigrate to other countries and take up residence there. (22) The fact that he is a citizen of a particular State does not deprive him of membership in the human family, nor of citizenship in that universal society, the common, world-wide fellowship of men.

Political Rights

26. Finally, man's personal dignity involves his right to take an active part in public life, and to make his own contribution to the common welfare of his fellow citizens. As Pope Pius XII said, "man as such, far from being an object or, as it were, an inert element in society, is rather its subject, its basis and its purpose; and so must he be esteemed." (23)
27. As a human person he is entitled to the legal protection of his rights, and such protection must be effective, unbiased, and strictly just. To quote again Pope Pius XII: "In consequence of that juridical order willed by God, man has his own inalienable right to juridical security. To him is assigned a certain, well-defined sphere of law, immune from arbitrary attack." (24)

Duties

28. The natural rights of which We have so far been speaking are inextricably bound up with as many duties, all applying to one and the same person. These rights and duties derive their origin, their sustenance, and their indestructibility from the natural law, which in conferring the one imposes the other.
29. Thus, for example, the right to live involves the duty to preserve one's life; the right to a decent standard of living, the duty to live in a becoming fashion; the right to be free to seek out the truth, the duty to devote oneself to an ever deeper and wider search for it.

Reciprocity of Rights and Duties Between Persons

30. Once this is admitted, it follows that in human society one man's natural right gives rise to a corresponding duty in other men; the duty, that is, of recognizing and respecting that right. Every basic human right draws its authoritative force from the natural law, which confers it and attaches to it its respective duty. Hence, to claim one's rights and ignore one's duties, or only half fulfill them, is like building a house with one hand and tearing it down with the other.

. . .

STUDY QUESTIONS

1. In what terms, and in appealing to what sources, does the pope establish the rights of individuals?
2. The pope declares the duty to respect the rights of others, but does he call into service an enforcement mechanism for these rights?

28.6 NSC (NATIONAL SECURITY COUNCIL) MEMORANDUM 68: APRIL 14, 1950

This report from the National Security Council to president Harry S. Truman (1884–1972) laid out the framework for the policy of "containment" that guided US actions throughout the Cold War. Its main author was Paul H. Nitze, then the director of policy planning for the Department of State. The passage below discusses the conflict of ideas and values between the United States and the Soviet Union.

IV. THE UNDERLYING CONFLICT IN THE REALM OF IDEAS AND VALUES BETWEEN THE U.S. PURPOSE AND THE KREMLIN DESIGN

A. NATURE OF CONFLICT

The Kremlin regards the United States as the only major threat to the conflict between the idea of slavery under the grim oligarchy of the Kremlin, which has come to a crisis with the polarization of power described in Section I, and the exclusive possession of atomic weapons by the two protagonists. The idea of freedom, moreover, is peculiarly and intolerably subversive of the idea of slavery. But the converse is not true. The implacable purpose of the slave state to eliminate the challenge of freedom has placed the two great powers at opposite poles. It is this fact which gives the present polarization of power the quality of crisis.

The free society values the individual as an end in himself, requiring of him only that measure of self-discipline and self-restraint which make the rights of each individual compatible with the rights of every other individual. The freedom of the individual has as its counterpart, therefore, the negative responsibility of the individual not to exercise his freedom in ways inconsistent with the freedom of other individuals and the positive responsibility to make constructive use of his freedom in the building of a just society.

From this idea of freedom with responsibility derives the marvelous diversity, the deep tolerance, the lawfulness of the free society. This is the explanation of the strength of free men. It constitutes the integrity and the vitality of a free and democratic system. The free society attempts to create and maintain an environment in which every individual has the opportunity to realize his creative powers. It also explains why the free society tolerates those within it who would use their freedom to destroy it. By the same token, in relations between nations, the prime reliance of the free society is on the strength and appeal of its idea, and it feels no compulsion sooner or later to bring all societies into conformity with it.

For the free society does not fear, it welcomes, diversity. It derives its strength from its hospitality even to antipathetic ideas. It is a market for free trade in ideas, secure in its faith that free men will take the best wares, and grow to a fuller and better realization of their powers in exercising their choice.

The idea of freedom is the most contagious idea in history, more contagious than the idea of submission to authority. For the breadth of freedom cannot be tolerated in a society which has come under the domination of an individual or group of individuals with a will to absolute power. Where the despot holds

National Archives.

absolute power—the absolute power of the absolutely powerful will—all other wills must be subjugated in an act of willing submission, a degradation willed by the individual upon himself under the compulsion of a perverted faith. It is the first article of this faith that he finds and can only find the meaning of his existence in serving the ends of the system. The system becomes God, and submission to the will of God becomes submission to the will of the system. It is not enough to yield outwardly to the system—even Gandhian non-violence is not acceptable—for the spirit of resistance and the devotion to a higher authority might then remain, and the individual would not be wholly submissive.

The same compulsion which demands total power over all men within the Soviet state without a single exception, demands total power over all Communist Parties and all states under Soviet domination. Thus Stalin has said that the theory and tactics of Leninism as expounded by the Bolshevik party are mandatory for the proletarian parties of all countries. A true internationalist is defined as one who unhesitatingly upholds the position of the Soviet Union and in the satellite states true patriotism is love of the Soviet Union. By the same token the "peace policy" of the Soviet Union, described at a Party Congress as "a more advantageous form of fighting capitalism," is a device to divide and immobilize the non-Communist world, and the peace the Soviet Union seeks is the peace of total conformity to Soviet policy.

The antipathy of slavery to freedom explains the iron curtain, the isolation, the autarchy of the society whose end is absolute power. The existence and persistence of the idea of freedom is a permanent and continuous threat to the foundation of the slave society; and it therefore regards as intolerable the long-continued existence of freedom in the world. What is new, what makes the continuing crisis, is the polarization of power which now inescapably confronts the slave society with the free.

The assault on free institutions is world-wide now, and in the context of the present polarization of power a defeat of free institutions anywhere is a defeat everywhere. The shock we sustained in the destruction of Czechoslovakia was not in the measure of Czechoslovakia's material importance to us. In a material sense, her capabilities were already at Soviet disposal. But when the integrity of Czechoslovak institutions was destroyed, it was in the intangible scale of values that we registered a loss more damaging than the material loss we had already suffered.

Thus, unwillingly our free society finds itself mortally challenged by the Soviet system. No other value system is so wholly irreconcilable with ours, so implacable in its purpose to destroy ours, so capable of turning to its own uses the most dangerous and divisive trends in our own society, no other so skillfully and powerfully evokes the elements of irrationality in human nature everywhere, and no other has the support of a great and growing center of military power.

B. OBJECTIVES

The objectives of a free society are determined by its fundamental values and by the necessity for maintaining the material environment in which they flourish. Logically and in fact, therefore, the Kremlin's challenge to the United States is directed not only to our values but to our physical capacity to protect their environment. It is a challenge which encompasses both peace and war and our objectives in peace and war must take account of it.

Thus, we must make ourselves strong, both in the way in which we affirm our values in the conduct of our national life, and in the development of our military and economic strength. We must lead in building a successfully functioning political and economic system in the free world. It is only by practical affirmation, abroad as well as at home, of our essential values, that we can preserve our own integrity, in which lies the real frustration of the Kremlin design. But beyond thus affirming our values our policy and actions must be such as to foster a fundamental change in the nature of the Soviet system, a change toward which the frustration of the design is the first and perhaps the most important step. Clearly it will not only be less costly but more effective if this change occurs to a maximum extent as a result of internal forces in Soviet society. In a shrinking world, which now faces the threat of atomic warfare, it is not an adequate objective merely to seek to check the Kremlin design, for the absence of order among nations is becoming less and less tolerable. This fact imposes on us, in our own interests, the responsibility of world leadership. It demands that we make the attempt, and accept the risks inherent in it, to bring about order and justice by means consistent with the principles of freedom and democracy. We should limit our requirement of the Soviet Union to its participation with other nations on the basis of equality and respect for the rights of others. Subject to this requirement, we must with our allies and the former subject peoples seek to create a world society based on the principle of consent. Its framework cannot be inflexible. It will consist of many national communities of great and varying abilities and resources, and hence of war potential. The seeds of conflicts will inevitably exist or will come into being. To acknowledge this is only to acknowledge the impossibility of a final solution. Not to acknowledge it can be fatally dangerous in a world in which there are no final solutions.

All these objectives of a free society are equally valid and necessary in peace and war. But every consideration of devotion to our fundamental values and to our national security demands that we seek to achieve them by the strategy of the cold war. It is only by developing the moral and material strength of the free world that the Soviet regime will become convinced of the falsity of its assumptions and that the pre-conditions for workable agreements can be created. By practically demonstrating the integrity and vitality of our system the free world widens the area of possible agreement and thus can hope gradually to bring about a Soviet acknowledgement of realities which in sum will eventually constitute a frustration of the Soviet design. Short of this, however, it might be possible to create a situation which will induce the Soviet Union to accommodate itself, with or without the conscious abandonment of its design, to coexistence on tolerable terms with the non-Soviet world. Such a development would be a triumph for the idea of freedom and democracy. It must be an immediate objective of United States policy.

There is no reason, in the event of war, for us to alter our overall objectives. They do not include unconditional surrender, the subjugation of the Russian peoples or a Russia shorn of its economic potential. Such a course would irrevocably unite the Russian people behind the regime which enslaves them. Rather these objectives contemplate Soviet acceptance of the specific and limited conditions requisite to an international environment in which free institutions can flourish, and in which the Russian peoples will have a new chance to work out their own destiny. If we can make the Russian people our allies in the enterprise we will obviously have made our task easier and victory more certain.

The objectives outlined in NSC 20/4 (November 23, 1948) . . . are fully consistent with the objectives stated in this paper, and they remain valid. The growing intensity of the conflict which has been imposed upon us, however, requires the changes of emphasis and the additions that are apparent. Coupled with the probable fission bomb capability and possible thermonuclear bomb capability of the Soviet Union, the intensifying struggle requires us to face the fact that we can expect no lasting abatement of the crisis unless and until a change occurs in the nature of the Soviet system.

C. MEANS

The free society is limited in its choice of means to achieve its ends.

Compulsion is the negation of freedom, except when it is used to enforce the rights common to all. The resort to force, internally or externally, is therefore a last resort for a free society. The act is permissible only when one individual or groups of individuals within it threaten the basic rights of other individuals or when another society seeks to impose its will upon it. The free society cherishes and protects as fundamental the rights of the minority against the will of a majority, because these rights are the inalienable rights of each and every individual.

The resort to force, to compulsion, to the imposition of its will is therefore a difficult and dangerous act for a free society, which is warranted only in the face of even greater dangers. The necessity of the act must be clear and compelling; the act must commend itself to the overwhelming majority as an inescapable exception to the basic idea of freedom; or the regenerative capacity of free men after the act has been performed will be endangered.

The Kremlin is able to select whatever means are expedient in seeking to carry out its fundamental design. Thus, it can make the best of several possible worlds, conducting the struggle on those levels where it considers it profitable and enjoying the benefits of a pseudo-peace on those levels where it is not ready for a contest. At the ideological or psychological level, in the struggle for men's minds, the conflict is worldwide. At the political and economic level, within states and in the relations between states, the struggle for power is being intensified. And at the military level, the Kremlin has thus far been careful not to commit a technical breach of the peace, although using its vast forces to intimidate its neighbors, and to support an aggressive foreign policy, and not hesitating through its agents to resort to arms in favorable circumstances. The attempt to carry out its fundamental design is being pressed, therefore, with all means which are believed expedient in the present situation, and the Kremlin has inextricably engaged us in the conflict between its design and our purpose.

We have no such freedom of choice, and least of all in the use of force. Resort to war is not only a last resort for a free society, but it is also an act which cannot definitively end the fundamental conflict in the realm of ideas. The idea of slavery can only be overcome by the timely and persistent demonstration of the superiority of the idea of freedom. Military victory alone would only partially and perhaps only temporarily affect the fundamental conflict, for although the ability of the Kremlin to threaten our security might be for a time destroyed, the resurgence of totalitarian forces and the re-establishment of the Soviet system or its equivalent would not be long delayed unless great progress were made in the fundamental conflict.

Practical and ideological considerations therefore both impel us to the conclusion that we have no choice but to demonstrate the superiority of the idea of freedom by its constructive application, and to attempt to change the world situation by means short of war in such a way as to frustrate the Kremlin design and hasten the decay of the Soviet system.

For us the role of military power is to serve the national purpose by deterring an attack upon us while we seek by other means to create an environment in which our free society can flourish, and by fighting, if necessary, to defend the integrity and vitality of our free society and to defeat any aggressor. The Kremlin uses Soviet military power to back up and serve the Kremlin design. It does not hesitate to use military force aggressively if that course is expedient in the achievement of its design. The differences between our fundamental purpose and the Kremlin design, therefore, are reflected in our respective attitudes toward and use of military force.

Our free society, confronted by a threat to its basic values, naturally will take such action, including the use of military force, as may be required to protect those values. The integrity of our system will not be jeopardized by any measures, covert or overt, violent or non-violent, which serve the purposes of frustrating the Kremlin design, nor does the necessity for conducting ourselves so as to affirm our values in actions as well as words forbid such measures, provided only they are appropriately calculated to that end and are not so excessive or misdirected as to make us enemies of the people instead of the evil men who have enslaved them.

But if war comes, what is the role of force? Unless we so use it that the Russian people can perceive that our effort is directed against the regime and its power for aggression, and not against their own interests, we will unite the regime and the people in the kind of last-ditch fight in which no underlying problems are solved, new ones are created, and where our basic principles are obscured and compromised. If we do not in the application of force demonstrate the nature of our objectives we will, in fact, have compromised from the outset our fundamental purpose. In the words of the Federalist (No. 28) "The means to be employed must be proportioned to the extent of the mischief." The mischief may be a global war or it may be a Soviet campaign for limited objectives. In either case we should take no avoidable initiative which would cause it to become a war of annihilation, and if we have the forces to defeat a Soviet drive for limited objectives it may well be to our interest not to let it become a global war. Our aim in applying force must be to compel the acceptance of terms consistent with our objectives, and our capabilities for the application of force should, therefore, within the limits of what we can sustain over the long pull, be congruent to the range of tasks which we may encounter.

STUDY QUESTIONS

1. What are the different values and ideas between the United States and the USSR that Nitze outlines in his memorandum?
2. What positions does Nitze put forward to argue in favor of military force to counter the perceived threat from the Soviets?

28.7 POPE PAUL VI, *HUMANAE VITAE*, 1968

Pope Paul VI (1897–1978) took office at a time of reform in the Catholic Church. In the wake of Vatican II (1962–1965), he extended the reforming spirit of John XXIII. Nonetheless, in the 1960s, attendance at Catholic Mass continued to decline. Conservatives argued that the reforms were to blame. Liberals argued that the church's ban on contraception and its refusal to allow women priests were the real culprits. The availability of "the pill" in 1961 put contraception front and center in the church. "*Humanae Vitae*" ("Of Human Life"), Paul VI's historic encyclical, was the result of several years of research on his part. Sex, he argued, produces offspring but also expresses human love. As such, all forms of artificial contraception were to be rejected, leaving every sexual union open to the possibility of new life. This line of reasoning did not bring new converts to the church, and indeed it is often cited as a principal reason why many have abandoned it. The encyclical's footnotes are omitted here.

To the venerable Patriarchs, Archbishops and other local ordinaries in peace and communion with the Apostolic See, to priests, the faithful and to all men of good will.

Venerable brothers and beloved sons:

THE TRANSMISSION OF LIFE

1. The most serious duty of transmitting human life, for which married persons are the free and responsible collaborators of God the Creator, has always been a source of great joys to them, even if sometimes accompanied by not a few difficulties and by distress.

At all times the fulfillment of this duty has posed grave problems to the conscience of married persons, but, with the recent evolution of society, changes have taken place that give rise to new questions which the Church could not ignore, having to do with a matter which so closely touches upon the life and happiness of men.

I. NEW ASPECTS OF THE PROBLEM AND COMPETENCY OF THE MAGISTERIUM

NEW FORMULATION OF THE PROBLEM

2. The changes which have taken place are in fact noteworthy and of varied kinds. In the first

From Pope Paul VI, *Humanae Vitae. American Ecclesiastical Review* 159: 290–300 (1968).

place, there is the rapid demographic development. Fear is shown by many that world population is growing more rapidly than the available resources, with growing distress to many families and developing countries, so that the temptation for authorities to counter this danger with radical measures is great. Moreover, working and housing conditions, as well as increased exigencies both in the economic field and in that of education, often make the proper education of a large number of children difficult today. A change is also seen both in the manner of considering the person of woman and her place in society, and in the value to be attributed to conjugal love in marriage, and also in the appreciation to be made of the meaning of conjugal acts in relation to that love.

Finally, and above all, man has made stupendous progress in the domination and rational organization of the forces of nature, such that he tends to extend this domination to his own total being: to the body, to psychical life, to social life and even to the laws which regulate the transmission of life.

3. This new state of things gives rise to new questions. Granted the conditions of life today, and granted the meaning which conjugal relations have with respect to the harmony between husband and wife and to their mutual fidelity would not a revision of the ethical norms, in force up to now, seem to be advisable, especially when it is considered that they cannot be observed without sacrifices, sometimes heroic sacrifices?

And again: by extending to this field the application of the so-called "principle of totality," could it not be admitted that the intention of a less abundant but more rationalized fecundity might transform a materially sterilizing intervention into a licit and wise control of birth? Could it not be admitted, that is, that the finality of procreation pertains to the ensemble of conjugal life, rather than to its single acts? It is also asked whether, in view of the increased sense of responsibility of modern man, the moment has not come for him to entrust to his reason and his will, rather than to the biological rhythms of this organism, the task of regulating birth.

COMPETENCY OF THE *MAGISTERIUM*

4. Such questions required from the teaching authority of the Church a new and deeper reflection upon the principles of the moral teaching on marriage: a teaching founded on the natural law, illuminated and enriched by divine revelation.

No believer will wish to deny that the teaching authority of the Church is competent to interpret even the natural moral law. It is, in fact, indisputable, as our predecessors have many times declared, that Jesus Christ, when communicating to Peter and to the Apostles His divine authority and sending them to teach all nations His commandments, constituted them as guardians and authentic interpreters of all the moral law, not only, that is, of the law of the Gospel, but also of the natural law, which is also an expression of the will of God, the faithful fulfillment of which is equally necessary for salvation.

Conformable to this mission of hers, the Church has always provided—and even more amply in recent times—a coherent teaching concerning both the nature of marriage and the correct use of conjugal rights and the duties of husband and wife.

SPECIAL STUDIES

5. The consciousness of that same mission induced us to confirm and enlarge the study commission which our predecessor Pope John XXIII of happy memory had instituted in March, 1963. That commission which included, besides several experts in the various pertinent disciplines, also married couples, had as its scope the gathering of opinions on the new questions regarding conjugal life, and in particular on the regulation of births, and of furnishing suitable elements of information so that the *magisterium* could give an adequate reply to the expectation not only of the faithful, but also of world opinion.

The work of these experts, as well as the successive judgments and counsels spontaneously forwarded by or expressly requested from a good number of our brothers in the episcopate, have permitted us to measure exactly all the aspects of this complex matter. Hence with all our heart we express to each of them our lively gratitude.

REPLY OF THE *MAGISTERIUM*

6. The conclusions at which the commission arrived could not, nevertheless, be considered by us as definitive, nor dispense us from a personal examination of this serious question; and this also because, within the commission itself, no full concordance of judgments concerning the moral norms to be proposed had been reached, and above all because certain criteria of solutions had emerged which departed from the moral teaching of marriage proposed with constant firmness by the teaching authority of the Church.

Therefore, having attentively sifted the documentation laid before us, after mature reflection and assiduous prayers, we now intend, by virtue of the mandate entrusted to us by Christ, to give our reply to these, grave questions.

II. DOCTRINAL PRINCIPLES

A TOTAL VISION OF MAN

7. The problem of birth, like every other problem regarding human life, is to be considered, beyond partial perspectives—whether of the biological or psychological, demographic or sociological orders—in the light of an integral vision of man and of his vocation, not only his natural and earthly, but also his supernatural and eternal vocation. And since, in the attempt to justify artificial methods of birth control, many have appealed to the demands both of conjugal love and of "responsible parenthood," it is good to state very precisely the true concept of these two great realities of married life, referring principally to what was recently set forth in this regard, and in a highly authoritative form, by the Second Vatican Council in its pastoral constitution *Gaudium et Spes.*

CONJUGAL LOVE

8. Conjugal love reveals its true nature and nobility when it is considered in its supreme origin, God, who is love, "the Father, from whom every family in heaven and on earth is named."

Marriage is not, then, the effect of chance or the product of evolution of unconscious natural forces; it is the wise institution of the Creator to realize in mankind His design of love. By means of the reciprocal personal gift of self, proper and exclusive to them, husband and wife tend towards the communion of their beings in view of mutual personal perfection, to collaborate with God in the generation and education of new lives.

For baptized persons, moreover, marriage invests the dignity of a sacramental sign of grace inasmuch as it represents the union of Christ and of the Church.

ITS CHARACTERISTICS

9. Under this light, there clearly appear the characteristic marks and demands of conjugal love, and it is of supreme importance to have an exact idea of these.

This love is first of all fully human, that is to say, of the senses and of the spirit at the same time. It is not, then, a simple transport of instinct and sentiment, but also, and principally, an act of the free will, intended to endure and to grow by means of the joys and sorrows of daily life, in such a way that husband and wife become only one heart and only one soul, and together attain their human perfection.

Then, this love is total, that is to say, it is a very special form of personal friendship, in which husband and wife generously share everything, without undue reservations or selfish calculations. Whoever truly loves his marriage partner loves not only for what he receives, but for the partner's self, rejoicing that he can enrich his partner with the gift of himself.

Again, this love is faithful and exclusive until death. Thus, in fact, do bride and groom conceive it to be on the day when they freely and in full awareness assume the duty of the marriage bond. A fidelity, this, which can sometimes be difficult, but is always possible, always noble and meritorious, as no one can deny. The example of so many married persons down through the centuries shows, not only that fidelity is according to the nature of marriage, but also that it is a source of profound and lasting happiness and finally, this love is fecund for it is not exhausted by the communion between husband and wife, but is destined to continue, raising up new lives. "Marriage and conjugal love are by their nature ordained toward the begetting and educating of children. Children are really the supreme gift of marriage and contribute very substantially to the welfare of their parents."

RESPONSIBLE PARENTHOOD

10. Hence conjugal love requires in husband and wife an awareness of their mission of "responsible parenthood," which today is rightly much insisted upon, and which also must be exactly understood. Consequently, it is to be considered under different aspects which are legitimate and connected with one another.

In relation to the biological processes, responsible parenthood means the knowledge and respect of their functions; human intellect discovers in the power of giving life biological laws which are part of the human person.

In relation to the tendencies of instinct or passion, responsible parenthood means that necessary dominion which reason and will must exercise over them.

In relation to physical, economic, psychological and social conditions, responsible parenthood is exercised, either by the deliberate and generous decision to raise a large family, or by the decision, made for grave motives and with due respect for the moral law, to avoid for the time being, or even for an indeterminate period, a new birth.

Responsible parenthood also and above all implies a more profound relationship to the objective moral order established by God, of which a right conscience is the faithful interpreter. The responsible exercise of parenthood implies, therefore, that husband and wife recognize fully their own duties towards God, towards themselves, towards the family and towards society, in a correct hierarchy of values.

In the task of transmitting life, therefore, they are not free to proceed completely at will, as if they could determine in a wholly autonomous way the honest path to follow; but they must conform their activity to the creative intention of God, expressed in the very nature of marriage and of its acts, and manifested by the constant teaching of the Church.

RESPECT FOR THE NATURE AND PURPOSE OF THE MARRIAGE ACT

11. These acts, by which husband and wife are united in chaste intimacy, and by means of which human life is transmitted, are, as the council recalled, "noble and worthy," and they do not cease to be lawful if, for causes independent of the will of husband and wife, they are foreseen to be infecund, since they always remain ordained towards expressing and consolidating their union. In fact, as experience bears witness, not every conjugal act is followed by a new life. God has wisely disposed natural laws and rhythms of fecundity which, of themselves, cause a separation in the succession of births. Nonetheless the Church, calling men back to the observance of the norms of the natural law, as interpreted by their constant doctrine, teaches that each and every marriage act *(quilibet matrimonii usus)* must remain open to the transmission of life.

TWO INSEPARABLE ASPECTS: UNION AND PROCREATION

12. That teaching, often set forth by the *magisterium*, is founded upon the inseparable connection, willed by God and unable to be broken by man on his own initiative, between the two meanings of the conjugal act: the unitive meaning and the procreative meaning. Indeed, by its intimate structure, the conjugal act, while most closely uniting husband and wife, empowers them to generate new lives, according to laws inscribed in the very being of man and of woman. By safeguarding both these essential aspects, unitive and the procreative, the conjugal act preserves in its fullness the sense of true mutual love and its ordination towards man's most high calling to

parenthood. We believe that the men of our day are particularly capable of seizing the deeply reasonable and human character of this fundamental principle.

FAITHFULNESS TO GOD'S DESIGN

13. It is in fact justly observed that a conjugal act imposed upon one's partner without regard for his or her condition and lawful desires is not a true act of love, and therefore denies an exigency of right moral order in the relationships between husband and wife. Hence, one who reflects well must also recognize that a reciprocal act of love, which jeopardizes the disponsibility to transmit life which God the Creator, according to particular laws, inserted therein is in contradiction with the design constitutive of marriage, and with the will of the Author of life. To use this divine gift destroying, even if only partially, its meaning and its purpose is to contradict the nature both of man and of woman and of their most intimate relationship and therefore, it is to contradict also the plan of God and His will. On the other hand, to make use of the gift of conjugal love while respecting the laws of the generative process means to acknowledge oneself not to be the arbiter of the sources of human life, but rather the minister of the design established by the Creator. In fact, just as man does not have unlimited dominion over his body in general, so also, with particular reason, he has no such dominion over his generative faculties as such, because of their intrinsic ordination towards raising up life, of which God is the principle. "Human life is sacred," Pope John XXIII recalled; "from its very inception it reveals the creating hand of God."

ILLICIT WAYS OF REGULATING BIRTH

14. In conformity with these landmarks in the human and Christian vision of marriage, we must once again declare that the direct interruption of the generative process already begun, and, above all, directly willed and procured abortion, even if for therapeutic reasons, are to be absolutely excluded as licit means of regulating birth.

Equally to be excluded, as the teaching authority of the Church has frequently declared, is direct sterilization, whether perpetual or temporary whether of the man or of the woman. Similarly excluded is every action which, either in anticipation of the conjugal act, or in its accomplishment, or in the development of its natural consequences, proposes, whether as an end or as a means to render procreation impossible.

To justify conjugal acts made intentionally infecund, one cannot invoke as valid reasons the lesser evil, or the fact that such acts would constitute a whole together with the fecund acts already performed or to follow later, and hence would share in one and the same moral goodness. In truth, if it is sometimes licit to tolerate a lesser evil in order to avoid a greater evil or to promote a greater good it is not licit, even for the gravest reasons, to do evil so that good may follow therefrom, that is, to make into the object of a positive act of the will something which is intrinsically disordered, and hence unworthy of the human person, even when the intention is to safeguard or promote individual, family, or social well-being. Consequently, it is an error to think that a conjugal act which is deliberately made infecund and so is intrinsically dishonest could be made honest and right by the ensemble of a fecund conjugal life.

LICITNESS OF THERAPEUTIC MEANS

15. The Church, on the contrary, does not at all consider illicit the use of those therapeutic means truly necessary to cure diseases of the organism, even if an impediment to procreation, which may be foreseen, should result therefrom, provided such impediment is not, for whatever motive, directly willed.

LICITNESS OF RECOURSE TO INFECUND PERIODS

16. To this teaching of the Church on conjugal morals, the objection is made today, as we observed earlier (no. 3), that it is the prerogative of the human intellect to dominate the energies offered by irrational nature and to orientate them towards an end conformable to the good of man. Now, some may ask: in the present case, is it not

reasonable in many circumstances to have recourse to artificial birth control if, thereby, we secure the harmony and peace of the family, and better conditions for the education of the children already born? To this question it is necessary to reply with clarity: the Church is the first to praise and recommend the intervention of intelligence in a function which so closely associates the rational creature with his Creator; but she affirms that this must be done with respect for the order established by God.

If, then, there are serious motives to space out births, which derive from the physical or psychological condition of husband and wife, or from external conditions, the Church teaches that it is then licit to take into account the natural rhythms immanent in the generative functions, for the use of marriage in the infecund periods only, and in this way to regulate birth without offending the moral principles which have been recalled earlier.

The Church is consistent with herself when she considers recourse to the infecund periods to be licit, while at the same time condemning, as being always illicit, the use of means directly contrary to fecundation, even if such use is inspired by reasons which may appear honest and serious. In reality, there are essential differences between the two cases; in the former, the married couple make legitimate use of a natural disposition; in the latter, they impede the development of natural processes. It is true that, in the one and the other case, the married couple are in agreement in the positive will of avoiding children for plausible reasons, seeking the certainty that offspring will not arrive; but it is also true that only in the former case are they able to renounce the use of marriage in the fecund periods when, for just motives, procreation is not desirable, while making use of it during infecund periods to manifest their affection and to safeguard their mutual fidelity. By so doing, they give proof of a truly and integrally honest love.

GRAVE CONSEQUENCES OF METHODS OF ARTIFICIAL BIRTH CONTROL

17. Upright men can even better convince themselves of the solid grounds on which the teaching of the Church in this field is based, if they care to reflect upon the consequences of methods of artificial birth control. Let them consider, first of all, how wide and easy a road would thus be opened up towards conjugal infidelity and the general lowering of morality. Not much experience is needed in order to know human weakness, and to understand that men—especially the young, who are so vulnerable on this point—have need of encouragement to be faithful to the moral law, so that they must not be offered some easy means of eluding its observance. It is also to be feared that the man, growing used to the employment of anti-conceptive practices, may finally lose respect for the woman and, no longer caring for her physical and psychological equilibrium, may come to the point of considering her as a mere instrument of selfish enjoyment, and no longer as his respected and beloved companion.

Let it be considered also that a dangerous weapon would thus be placed in the hands of those public authorities who take no heed of moral exigencies. Who could blame a government for applying to the solution of the problems of the community those means acknowledged to be licit for married couples in the solution of a family problem? Who will stop rulers from favoring, from even imposing upon their peoples, if they were to consider it necessary, the method of contraception which they judge to be most efficacious? In such a way men, wishing to avoid individual, family, or social difficulties encountered in the observance of the divine law, would reach the point of placing at the mercy of the intervention of public authorities the most personal and most reserved sector of conjugal intimacy.

Consequently, if the mission of generating life is not to be exposed to the arbitrary will of men, one must necessarily recognize unsurmountable limits to the possibility of man's domination over his own body and its functions; limits which no man, whether a private individual or one invested with authority, may licitly surpass. And such limits cannot be determined otherwise than by the respect due to the integrity of the human's organism and its functions, according to the principles recalled earlier, and also according to the correct understanding of the "principle of totality" illustrated by our predecessor Pope Pius XII.

THE CHURCH GUARANTOR OF TRUE HUMAN VALUES

18. It can be foreseen that this teaching will perhaps not be easily received by all: Too numerous are those voices—amplified by the modern means of propaganda—which are contrary to the voice of the Church. To tell the truth, the Church is not surprised to be made, like her divine founder, a "sign of contradiction," yet she does not because of this cease to proclaim with humble firmness the entire moral law, both natural and evangelical. Of such laws the Church was not the author, nor consequently can she be their arbiter; she is only their depository and their interpreter, without ever being able to declare to be licit that which is not so by reason of its intimate and unchangeable opposition to the true good of man.

In defending conjugal morals in their integral wholeness, the Church knows that she contributes towards the establishment of a truly human civilization; she engages man not to abdicate from his own responsibility in order to rely on technical means; by that very fact she defends the dignity of man and wife. Faithful to both the teaching and the example of the Saviour, she shows herself to be the sincere and disinterested friend of men, whom she wishes to help, even during their earthly sojourn, "to share as sons in the life of the living God, the Father of all men."

III. PASTORAL DIRECTIVES

THE CHURCH MATER ET MAGISTRA

19. Our words would not be an adequate expression of the thought and solicitude of the Church, mother and teacher of all peoples, if, after having recalled men to the observance and respect of the divine law regarding matrimony, we did not strengthen them in the path of honest regulation of birth, even amid the difficult conditions which today afflict families and peoples. The Church, in fact, cannot have a different conduct towards men than that of the Redeemer: She knows their weaknesses, has compassion on the crowd, receives sinners; but she cannot renounce the teaching of the law which is, in reality, that law proper to a human life restored to its original truth and conducted by the spirit of God.

POSSIBILITY OF OBSERVING THE DIVINE LAW

20. The teaching of the Church on the regulation of birth, which promulgates the divine law, will easily appear to many to be difficult or even impossible of actuation. And indeed, like all great beneficent realities, it demands serious engagement and much effort, individual, family, and social effort. More than that, it would not be practicable without the help of God, who upholds and strengthens the good will of men. Yet, to anyone who reflects well, it cannot but be clear that such efforts ennoble man and are beneficial to the human community.

MASTERY OF SELF

21. The honest practice of regulation of birth demands first of all that husband and wife acquire and possess solid convictions concerning the true values of life and of the family, and that they tend towards securing perfect self-mastery. To dominate instinct by means of one's reason and free will undoubtedly requires ascetical practices, so that the affective manifestations of conjugal life may observe the correct order, in particular with regard to the observance of periodic continence. Yet this discipline which is proper to the purity of married couples, far from harming conjugal love, rather confers on it a higher human value. It demands continual effort yet, thanks to its beneficent influence, husband and wife fully develop their personalities, being enriched with spiritual values. Such discipline bestows upon family life fruits of serenity and peace, and facilitates the solution of other problems; it favors attention for one's partner, helps both parties to drive out selfishness, the enemy of true love; and deepens their sense of responsibility. By its means, parents acquire the capacity of having a deeper and

more efficacious influence in the education of their offspring; little children and youths grow up with a just appraisal of human values, and in the serene and harmonious development of their spiritual and sensitive faculties.

CREATING AN ATMOSPHERE FAVORABLE TO CHASTITY

22. On this occasion, we wish to draw the attention of educators, and of all who perform duties of responsibility in regard to the common good of human society, to the need of creating an atmosphere favorable to education in chastity, that is, to the triumph of healthy liberty over license by means of respect for the moral order.

Everything in the modern media of social communications which leads to sense excitation and unbridled habits, as well as every form of pornography and licentious performances, must arouse the frank and unanimous reaction of all those who are solicitous for the progress of civilization and the defense of the common good of the human spirit. Vainly would one seek to justify such depravation with the pretext of artistic or scientific exigencies, or to deduce an argument from the freedom allowed in this sector by the public authorities.

APPEAL TO PUBLIC AUTHORITIES

23. To Rulers, who are those principally responsible for the common good, and who can do so much to safeguard moral customs, we say: Do not allow the morality of your peoples to be degraded; do not permit that by legal means practices contrary to the natural and divine law be introduced into that fundamental cell, the family. Quite other is the way in which public authorities can and must contribute to the solution of the demographic problem: namely, the way of a provident policy for the family, of a wise education of peoples in respect of moral law and the liberty of citizens.

We are well aware of the serious difficulties experienced by public authorities in this regard, especially in the developing countries. To their legitimate preoccupations we devoted our encyclical letter *Populorum Progressio*. But with our predecessor Pope John XXIII, we repeat: no solution to these difficulties is acceptable "which does violence to man's essential dignity" and is based only on an utterly materialistic conception of man himself and of his life. The only possible solution to this question is one which envisages the social and economic progress both of individuals and of the whole of human society, and which respects and promotes of true human values. Neither can one, without grave injustice, consider divine providence to be responsible for what depends, instead, on a lack of wisdom in government, on an insufficient sense of social justice, on selfish monopolization, or again on blameworthy indolence in confronting the efforts and the sacrifices necessary to ensure the raising of living standards of a people and of all its sons.

May all responsible public authorities—as some are already doing so laudably—generously revive their efforts. And may mutual aid between all the members of the great human family never cease to grow. This is an almost limitless field which thus opens up to the activity of the great international organizations.

TO MEN OF SCIENCE

24. We wish now to express our encouragement to men of science, who "can considerably advance the welfare of marriage and the family, along with peace of conscience, if by pooling their efforts they labor to explain more thoroughly the various conditions favoring a proper regulation of births." It is particularly desirable that, according to the wish already expressed by Pope Pius XII, medical science succeed in providing a sufficiently secure basis for a regulation of birth, founded on the observance of natural rhythms. In this way, scientists and especially Catholic scientists will contribute to demonstrate in actual fact that, as the Church teaches, "a true contradiction cannot exist between the divine laws pertaining to the transmission of life and those pertaining to the fostering of authentic conjugal love."

TO CHRISTIAN HUSBANDS AND WIVES

25. And now our words more directly address our own children, particularly those whom God calls

to serve Him in marriage. The Church, while teaching imprescriptible demands of the divine law, announces the tidings of salvation, and by means of the sacraments opens up the paths of grace, which makes man a new creature, capable of corresponding with love and true freedom to the design of his Creator and Saviour, and of finding the yoke of Christ to be sweet.

Christian married couples, then, docile to her voice, must remember that their Christian vocation, which began at baptism, is further specified and reinforced by the sacrament of matrimony. By it husband and wife are strengthened and as it were consecrated for the faithful accomplishment of their proper duties, for the carrying out of their proper vocation even to perfection, and the Christian witness which is proper to them before the whole world. To them the Lord entrusts the task of making visible to men the holiness and sweetness of the law which unites the mutual love of husband and wife with their co-operation with the love of God, the author of human life.

We do not at all intend to hide the sometimes serious difficulties inherent in the life of Christian married persons; for them as for everyone else, "the gate is narrow and the way is hard, that leads to life." But the hope of that life must illuminate their way, as with courage they strive to live with wisdom, justice and piety in this present time, knowing that the figure of this world passes away.

Let married couples, then, face up to the efforts needed, supported by the faith and hope which "do not disappoint . . . because God's love has been poured into our hearts through the Holy Spirit, who has been given to us." Let them implore divine assistance by persevering prayer; above all, let them draw from the source of grace and charity in the Eucharist. And if sin should still keep its hold over them, let them not be discouraged, but rather have recourse with humble perseverance to the mercy of God, which is poured forth in the sacrament of Penance. In this way they will be enabled to achieve the fullness of conjugal life described by the Apostle: "husbands, love your wives, as Christ loved the Church . . . husbands should love their wives as their own bodies. He who loves his wife loves himself. For no man ever hates his own flesh, but nourishes and cherishes it, as Christ does the Church . . . this is a great mystery, and I mean in reference to Christ and the Church. However, let each one of you love his wife as himself, and let the wife see that she respects her husband."

APOSTOLATE IN HOMES

26. Among the fruits which ripen forth from a generous effort of fidelity to the divine law, one of the most precious is that married couples themselves not infrequently feel the desire to communicate their experience to others. Thus, there comes to be included in the vast pattern of the vocation of the laity a new and most noteworthy form of the apostolate of like to like; it is married couples themselves who become apostles and guides to other married couples. This is assuredly, among so many forms of apostolate, one of those which seem most opportune today.

TO DOCTORS AND MEDICAL PERSONNEL

27. We hold those physicians and medical personnel in the highest esteem who, in the exercise of their profession, value above every human interest the superior demands of their Christian vocation. Let them persevere, therefore, in promoting on every occasion the discovery of solutions inspired by faith and right reason, let them strive to arouse this conviction and this respect in their associates. Let them also consider as their proper professional duty the task of acquiring all the knowledge needed in this delicate sector, so as to be able to give to those married persons who consult them wise counsel and healthy direction, such as they have a right to expect.

TO PRIESTS

28. Beloved priest sons, by vocation you are the counselors and spiritual guides of individual persons and of families. We now turn to you with confidence. Your first task—especially in the case of those who teach moral theology—is to expound the Church's teaching on marriage without ambiguity. Be the first to give, in the exercise of your ministry, the example of loyal internal and external obedience to the teaching authority of the Church.

That obedience, as you know well, obliges not only because of the reasons adduced, but rather because of the light of the Holy Spirit, which is given in a particular way to the pastors of the Church in order that they may illustrate the truth. You know, too, that it is of the utmost importance, for peace of consciences and for the unity of the Christian people, that in the field of morals as well as in that of dogma, all should attend to the *magisterium* of the Church, and all should speak the same language. Hence, with all our heart we renew to you the heartfelt plea of the great Apostle Paul: "I appeal to you, brethren, by the name of Our Lord Jesus Christ, that all of you agree and that there be no dissensions among you, but that you be united in the same mind and the same judgment."

29. To diminish in no way the saving teaching of Christ constitutes an eminent form of charity for souls. But this must ever be accompanied by patience and goodness, such as the Lord himself gave example of in dealing with men. Having come not to condemn but to save, he was indeed intransigent with evil, but merciful towards individuals.

In their difficulties, many married couples always find, in the words and in the heart of a priest, the echo of the voice and the love of the Redeemer.

Speak out confidently, beloved sons, with the conviction that the Spirit of God, while assisting the *Magisterium* in propounding doctrine, enlightens internally the hearts of the faithful, and invites them to give their assent. Teach married couples the necessary way of prayer, and prepare them to have recourse frequently and with faith to the sacraments of the Eucharist and Penance, without ever allowing themselves to be disheartened by their weakness.

TO BISHOPS

Beloved and venerable brothers in the episcopate, with whom we most intimately share the solicitude of the spiritual good of the people of God, at the conclusion of this encyclical our reverent and affectionate thoughts turn to you. To all of you we extend an urgent invitation. At the head of the priests, your collaborators, and of your faithful, work ardently and incessantly for the safeguarding and the holiness of marriage, so that it may always be lived in its entire human and Christian fullness. Consider this mission as one of your most urgent responsibilities at the present time. As you know, it implies concerted pastoral action in all the fields of human activity, economic, cultural and social; for, in fact, only a simultaneous improvement in these various sectors will make it possible to render the life of parents and of children within their families not only tolerable, but easier and more joyous, to render the living together in human society more fraternal and peaceful, in faithfulness to God's design for the world.

FINAL APPEAL

31. Venerable brothers, most beloved sons, and all men of good will, great indeed is the work of education, of progress and of love to which we call you, upon the foundation of the Church's teaching, of which the successor of Peter is, together with his brothers in the episcopate, the depositary and interpreter. Truly a great work, as we are deeply convinced, both for the world and for the Church, since man cannot find true happiness—towards which he aspires with all his being—other than in respect of the laws written by God in his very nature, laws which he must observe with intelligence and love. Upon this work, and upon all of you, and especially upon married couples, we invoke the abundant graces of the God of holiness and mercy, and in pledge thereof we impart to you all our apostolic blessing.

Given at Rome, from St. Peter's, this 25th day of July, feast of St. James the Apostle, in the year 1968, the sixth of our pontificate.

STUDY QUESTIONS

1. Whose rights should take priority if the rights of a pregnant woman and those of a developing fetus come into conflict?
2. On what basis are certain forms of birth control declared "illicit" here?

28.8 GAMAL ABDEL NASSER, RESIGNATION SPEECH, 1967

On June 9, 1967, president Gamal Abdel Nasser (1918–1970) of Egypt resigned his office, after the failure of the Egyptian-led Six-Day War against Israel. Nasser had held the presidency since 1956. He was out of office only briefly, however, because a series of nationwide demonstrations by the people called for his reinstatement. He remained in power until his death in 1970. In this speech, he blames the Arab defeat in the war on a secret alliance among Israel, Britain, and the United States and ends with a renewed call for Arab nationalism and unity.

Brothers, at times of triumph and tribulation, in the sweet hours and bitter hours, we have become accustomed to sit together and discuss things, to speak frankly of facts, believing that only in this way can we always find the right path however difficult circumstances may be.

We cannot hide from ourselves the fact that we have met with a grave setback in the last few days, but I am confident that we all can, and in a short time will, overcome our difficult situation—although this calls for much patience and wisdom, as well as moral courage and ability to work, on our part. Before that, brothers, we need to cast a glance back over past events, so that we shall be able to follow developments and the line of our march leading to the present conditions.

All of us know how the crisis started in the Middle East. At the beginning of last May there was an enemy plan for the invasion of Syria, and the statements by his politicians and all his military leaders openly said so. There was plenty of evidence concerning the plan. Sources of our Syrian brothers were categorical on this, and our own reliable information confirmed it. Add to this the fact that our friends in the Soviet Union warned the parliamentary delegation, which was on a visit to Moscow, at the beginning of last month, that there was a premeditated plot against Syria. We considered it our duty not to accept this silently. This was the duty of Arab brotherhood; it was also the duty of national security. Whoever starts with Syria will finish with Egypt. . . .

Accurate calculations were made of the enemy's strength and showed us that our armed forces, at the level of equipment and training which they had reached, were capable of repelling the enemy and deterring him. We realized that the possibility of an armed clash existed and [we] accepted the risk. . . .

In the morning of last Monday, 5th June, the enemy struck. If we say now it was a stronger blow than we had expected, we must say at the same time, and with complete certainty, that it was bigger than the potential at his disposal. It became very clear from the first moment that there were other powers behind the enemy—they came to settle their accounts with the Arab national movement. Indeed, there were surprises worthy of note:

1. The enemy, whom we were expecting from the east and north, came from the west—a fact which clearly showed that facilities exceeding his own capacity and his calculated strength had been made available to him.
2. The enemy covered at one go all military and civilian airfields in the [United Arab Republic].

Walter Laqueur and Barry Rubin, *The Arab–Israeli Reader: A Documentary History of the Middle East Conflict*, 7th ed. New York: Penguin, 2008, pp. 103–5.

This means that he was relying on some force other than his own normal strength to protect his skies against any retaliatory action from our side. The enemy was also leaving other Arab fronts to be tackled with outside assistance, which he had been able to attain.

3. There is clear evidence of imperialist collusion with the enemy—an imperialist collusion trying to benefit from the lesson of the open collusion of 1956 by resorting this time to abject and wicked concealment. Nevertheless, what is now established is that American and British aircraft carriers were off the shores of the enemy, helping his war effort. Also, British aircraft raided, in broad daylight, positions on the Syrian and Egyptian fronts, in addition to operations by a number of American aircraft reconnoitering some of our positions. The inevitable result of this was that our land forces, fighting most violent and brave battles in the open desert, found themselves at the difficult time without adequate air cover in the face of the decisive superiority of the enemy air forces. Indeed, it can be said without emotion or exaggeration that the enemy was operating with an air force three times stronger than his normal force. . . .

We now have several urgent tasks before us. The first is to remove the traces of this aggression against us, and to stand by the Arab nation resolutely and firmly; despite the setback, the Arab nation, with all its potential and resources, is in a position to insist on the removal of the traces of the aggression.

The second task is to learn the lesson of the setback. In this connection there are three vital facts. First, the elimination of imperialism in the Arab world will leave Israel with its own intrinsic power; yet, whatever the circumstances, and however long it may take, the Arab intrinsic power is greater and more effective. Second, redirecting Arab interests in the service of Arab rights is an essential safeguard; the American Sixth Fleet moved with Arab oil, and there are Arab bases, placed forcibly and against the will of the peoples, in the service of aggression. Third, the situation now demands a united word from the entire Arab nation; this, in the present circumstances, is an irreplaceable guarantee.

Now we arrive at an important point in this heart-searching, by asking ourselves: does this mean that we do not bear responsibility for the consequences of the setback? I tell you truthfully, and despite any factors on which I might have based my attitude during the crisis, that I am ready to bear the whole responsibility. I have taken a decision in which I want you all to help me. I have decided to give up, completely and finally, every official post and every political role, and return to the ranks of the masses and do my duty with them like every other citizen. . . .

In doing this I am not liquidating the revolution—indeed, the revolution is not the monopoly of any one generation of revolutionaries. I take pride in the brothers of this generation of revolutionaries. It has brought to pass the evacuation of British imperialism, has won the independence of Egypt and defined its Arab personality, and has combated the policy of "spheres of influence" in the Arab world. It has led the social revolution and created a deep transformation in the Egyptian reality by establishing the people's control over the sources of their wealth and the result of Arab action. It recovered the Suez Canal and laid down the foundation of industrial upsurge in Egypt. It built the High Dam to bring fertile greenness to barren desert. It laid down a power network over the whole of the north of the Nile Valley. It made oil resources gush out after a long wait. More important still, it gave the leadership of political action to the alliance of the people's working forces, the constant source of renewed leaderships carrying the banners of Egyptian and Arab struggle through its successive stages, building socialism, succeeding and triumphing.

I have unlimited faith in this alliance as the leader of national action: the peasants, the workers, the soldiers, the intellectuals, and [our] national capital. Its unity and cohesion and creative response within the framework of this unity are capable of creating—through work, serious work, difficult work, as I have said more than once—colossal miracles for this country in order to be a strength for itself, for its Arab nation, for the movement of national revolution, and for world peace based on justice.

The sacrifices made by our people and their burning spirit during the crisis, and the glorious pages of heroism written by the officers and soldiers of our armed forces with their blood, will remain an unquenchable torch in our history and a great inspiration for the future and its great hopes. The people were splendid as usual. The members of our armed forces were an honorable example of Arab man in every age and every place. They defended the grains of sand in the desert to the last drop of their blood. In the air, they were, despite enemy supremacy, legends of dedication and sacrifice, of courage and willingness to perform their duty in the best way.

This is an hour for action, not sorrow. It is a situation calling for ideals, not for selfishness and personal feelings. All my heart is with you, and I want all your hearts to be with me. May God be with us, a hope in our hearts, a light and guidance. Peace and the blessing of God be with you.

STUDY QUESTIONS

1. How does Nasser describe Egypt's defeat in the Six-Day War as the result of "an imperialist collusion"?
2. For Nasser, why will the socialist revolution continue despite this recent defeat? What are the achievements of the revolution?

28.9 ENOCH POWELL, "RIVERS OF BLOOD" SPEECH, 1968

Enoch Powell (1912–1998) was a member of Parliament in Britain's Conservative Party in the 1960s. He gave his "Rivers of Blood" speech in the spring of 1968 at the general meeting of the West Midlands Area Conservative Political Centre. The speech is so named because, although the phrase "rivers of blood" is not actually used, he refers to a line in the Roman poet Virgil's *Aeneid*, which talks about the river Tiber foaming with blood. Allegedly reporting the concerns of his constituents in Wolverhampton southwest, Powell laments the influx of immigrants into Britain from the nation's former colonies and notes the dismay of native residents of some towns and cities who find themselves in a beleaguered white minority. He suggests that integration is not on the minds of immigrants and predicts coming racial tensions. He then goes on to suggest re-emigration of large numbers of immigrants. The reaction to Powell's speech was strong and swift; he was fired from his government position as shadow defense secretary, his speech being seen as inflammatory and damaging to race relations.

From Enoch Powell, "Rivers of Blood," 1968.

The supreme function of statesmanship is to provide against preventable evils. In seeking to do so, it encounters obstacles which are deeply rooted in human nature. One is that by the very order of things such evils are not demonstrable until they have occurred: At each stage in their onset there is room for doubt and for dispute whether they be real or imaginary. By the same token, they attract little attention in comparison with current troubles, which are both indisputable and pressing: whence the besetting temptation of all politics to concern itself with the immediate present at the expense of the future.

Above all, people are disposed to mistake predicting troubles for causing troubles and even for desiring troubles: "if only," they love to think, "if only people wouldn't talk about it, it probably wouldn't happen." Perhaps this habit goes back to the primitive belief that the word and the thing, the name and the object, are identical. At all events, the discussion of future grave but, with effort now, avoidable evils is the most unpopular and at the same time the most necessary occupation for the politician. Those who knowingly shirk it, deserve, and not infrequently receive, the curses of those who come after.

A week or two ago I fell into conversation with a constituent, a middle-aged, quite ordinary working man employed in one of our nationalized industries. After a sentence or two about the weather, he suddenly said: "If I had the money to go, I wouldn't stay in this country." I made some deprecatory reply, to the effect that even this Government wouldn't last for ever; but he took no notice, and continued: "I have three children, all of them have been through grammar school and two of them married now, with family. I shan't be satisfied till I have seen them settled overseas. In this country in fifteen or twenty years' time the black man will have the whip hand over the white man."

I can already hear the chorus of execration. How dare I say such a horrible thing? How dare I stir up trouble and inflame feelings by repeating such a conversation? The answer is that I do not have the right not to do so. Here is a decent, ordinary fellow Englishman, who in broad daylight in my own town says to me, his Member of Parliament, that this country will not be worth living in for his children. I simply do not have the right to shrug my shoulders and think about something else. What he is saying, thousands and hundreds of thousands are saying and thinking—not throughout Great Britain, perhaps, but in the areas that are already undergoing the total transformation to which there is no parallel in a thousand years of English history.

In fifteen or twenty years, on present trends, there will be in this country 3 1/2 million Commonwealth immigrants and their descendants. That is not my figure. That is the official figure given to Parliament by the spokesman of the Registrar General's office. There is no comparable official figure for the year 2000, but it must be in the region of 5–7 million, approximately one-tenth of the whole population, and approaching that of Greater London. Of course, it will not be evenly distributed from Margate to Aberystwyth and from Penzance to Aberdeen. Whole areas, towns and parts of towns across England will be occupied by different sections of the immigrant and immigrant-descended population.

As time goes on, the proportion of this total who are immigrant descendants, those born in England, who arrived here by exactly the same route as the rest of us, will rapidly increase. Already by 1985 the native-born would constitute the majority. It is this fact above all which creates the extreme urgency of action now, of just that kind of action which is hardest for politicians to take, action where the difficulties lie in the present but the evils to be prevented or minimized lie several parliaments ahead.

The natural and rational first question with a nation confronted by such a prospect is to ask: "How can its dimensions be reduced?" Granted it be not wholly preventable, can it be limited, bearing in mind that numbers are of the essence: the significance and consequences of an alien element introduced into a country or population are profoundly different according to whether that element is 1 per cent or 10 per cent. The answers to the simple and rational question are equally simple and rational: by stopping or virtually stopping, further inflow, and by promoting the maximum outflow. Both answers are part of the official policy of the Conservative Party.

It almost passes belief that at this moment twenty or thirty additional immigrant children are arriving from overseas in Wolverhampton alone every week—and that means fifteen or twenty additional families of a decade or two hence. Those whom the gods wish to destroy, they first make mad. We must be mad, literally mad, as a nation to be permitting the annual inflow of some 50,000 dependants, who are for the most part the material of the future growth of the immigrant-descended population. It is like watching a nation busily engaged in heaping up its own funeral pyre. So insane are we that we actually permit unmarried persons to immigrate for the purpose of founding a family with spouses and fiancées whom they have never seen.

Let no one suppose that the flow of dependents will automatically tail off. On the contrary, even at the present admission rate of only 5,000 a year by voucher, there is sufficient for a further 325,000 dependents per annum ad infinitum, without taking into account the huge reservoir of existing relations in this country—and I am making no allowance at all for fraudulent entry. In these circumstances nothing will suffice but that the total inflow for settlement should be reduced at once to negligible proportions, and that the necessary legislative and administrative measures be taken without delay. I stress the words "for settlement."

This has nothing to do with the entry of Commonwealth citizens, any more than of aliens, into this country, for the purposes of study or of improving their qualifications, like (for instance) the Commonwealth doctors who, to the advantage of their own countries, have enabled our hospital service to be expanded faster than would otherwise have been possible. These are not, and never have been, immigrants.

I turn to re-emigration. If all immigration ended tomorrow, the rate of growth of the immigrant and immigrant-descended population would be substantially reduced, but the prospective size of this element in the population would still leave the basic character of the national danger unaffected. This can only be tackled while a considerable proportion of the total still comprises persons who entered this country during the last ten years or so. Hence the urgency of implementing now the second element of the Conservative Party's policy: the encouragement of re-emigration.

Nobody can make an estimate of the numbers which, with generous grants and assistance, would choose either to return to their countries of origin or to go to other countries anxious to receive the manpower and the skills they represent. Nobody knows, because no such policy has yet been attempted. I can only say that, even at present, immigrants in my own constituency from time to time come to me, asking if I can find them assistance to return home. If such a policy were adopted and pursued with the determination which the gravity of the alternative justifies, the resultant outflow could appreciably alter the prospects for the future.

It can be no part of any policy that existing family should be kept divided; but there are two directions in which families can be reunited, and if our former and present immigration laws have brought about the division of families, albeit voluntary or semi-voluntarily, we ought to be prepared to arrange for them to be reunited in their countries of origin. In short, suspension of immigration and encouragement of re-emigration hang together, logically and humanly, as two aspects of the same approach.

The third element of the Conservative Party's policy is that all who are in this country as citizens should be equal before the law and that there shall be no discrimination or difference made between them by public authority. As Mr. Heath has put it, we will have no "first-class citizens" and "second-class citizens." This does not mean that the immigrant and his descendants should be elevated into a privileged or special class or that the citizen should be denied his right to discriminate in the management of his own affairs between one fellow citizen and another or that he should be subjected to inquisition as to his reasons and motives for behaving in one lawful manner rather than another.

There could be no grosser misconception of the realities than is entertained by those who vociferously demand legislation as they call it "against discrimination," whether they be leader-writers of the same kidney and sometimes on the same newspapers which year after year in the 1930s tried to blind this country to the rising peril which confronted it, or archbishops who live in palaces, faring delicately with the bedclothes pulled right over their heads.

They have got it exactly and diametrically wrong. The discrimination and the deprivation, the sense of alarm and resentment, lies not with the immigrant population but with those among whom they have come and are still coming. This is why to enact legislation of the kind before Parliament at this moment is to risk throwing a match on to the gunpowder. The kindest thing that can be said about those who propose and support it is they know not what they do.

Nothing is more misleading than comparison between the Commonwealth immigrant in Britain and the American Negro. The Negro population of the United States, which was already in existence before the United States became a nation, started literally as slaves and were later given the franchise and other rights of citizenship, to the exercise of which they have only gradually and still incompletely come. The Commonwealth immigrant came to Britain as a full citizen, to a country which knows no discrimination between one citizen and another, and he entered instantly into the possession of the rights of every citizen, from the vote to free treatment under the National Health Service. Whatever drawbacks attended the immigrants—and they were drawbacks which did not, and do not, make admission into Britain by hook or by crook appear less than desirable—arose not from the law or from public policy or from administration but from those personal circumstances and accidents which cause, and always will cause, the fortunes and experience of one man to be different from another's.

But while to the immigrant entry to this country was admission to privileges and opportunities eagerly sought, the impact upon the existing population was very different. For reasons which they could not comprehend, and in pursuance of a decision by default, on which they were never consulted, they found themselves made strangers in their own country. They found their wives unable to obtain hospital beds in childbirth, their children unable to obtain school places, their homes and neighbourhoods changed beyond recognition, their plans and prospects for the future defeated; at work they found that employers hesitated to apply to the immigrant worker the standards of discipline and competence required of the native-born worker; they began to hear, as time went by, more and more voices which told them that they were now the unwanted. On top of this, they now learn that a one-way privilege is to be established by Act of Parliament: a law, which cannot, and is not intended, to operate to protect them or redress their grievances, is to be enacted to give the stranger, the disgruntled and the agent provocateur the power to pillory them for their private actions.

In the hundreds upon hundreds of letters I received when I last spoke on this subject two or three months ago, there was one striking feature which was largely new and which I find ominous. All Members of Parliament are used to the typical anonymous correspondent; but what surprised and alarmed me was the high proportion of ordinary, decent, sensible people, writing a rational and often well-educated letter, who believed that they had to omit their address because it was dangerous to have committed themselves to paper to a Member of Parliament agreeing with the views I had expressed, and that they would risk either penalties or reprisals if they were known to have done so. The sense of being a persecuted minority which is growing among ordinary English people in the areas of the country which are affected is something that those without direct experience can hardly imagine. I am going to allow just one of those hundreds of people to speak for me. She did give her name and address, which I have detached from the letter which I am about to read. She was writing from Northumberland about something which is happening at this moment in my own constituency:

Eight years ago in a respectable street in Wolverhampton a house was sold to a Negro. Now only one white (a woman old-age pensioner) lives there. This is her story. She lost her husband and both her sons in the war. So she turned her seven-roomed house, her only asset, into a boarding house. She worked hard and did well, paid off her mortgage and began to put something by for her old age. Then the immigrants moved in. With growing fear, she saw one house after another taken over. The quiet streets became a place of noise and confusion.

Regretfully, her white tenants moved out.

The day after the last one left, she was awakened at 7 a.m. by two Negroes who wanted to use her phone to contact their employer. When she refused, as she would have refused any stranger at such an hour, she was abused and feared she would have been attacked but for the chain on her door. Immigrant families have tried to rent rooms in her house, but she always refused. Her little store of money went, and after paying her rates, she had less than £2 per week. She went to apply for a rate reduction and was seen by a young girl, who on hearing she had a seven-roomed house, suggested she should let part of it. When she said the only people she could get were Negroes, the girl said "racial prejudice won't get you anywhere in this country." So she went home.

The telephone is her lifeline. Her family pay the bill, and help her out as best they can. Immigrants have offered to buy her house—at a price which the prospective landlord would be able to recover from his tenants in weeks, or at most in a few months. She is becoming afraid to go out.

Windows are broken. She finds excreta pushed through her letterbox. When she goes to the shops, she is followed by children, charming, wide-grinning piccaninnies. They cannot speak English, but one word they know. "Racialist," they chant. When the new Race Relations Bill is passed, this woman is convinced she will go to prison. And is she so wrong? I begin to wonder.

The other dangerous delusion from which those who are willfully or otherwise blind to realities suffer, is summed up in the word "integration." To be integrated into a population means to become for all practical purposes indistinguishable from its other members. Now, at all times, where there are marked physical differences, especially of colour, integration is difficult though, over a period, not impossible. There are among the Commonwealth immigrants who have come to live here in the last fifteen years or so, many thousands whose wish and purpose is to be integrated and whose every thought and endeavour is bent in that direction. But to imagine that such a thing enters the heads of a great and growing majority of immigrants and their descendants is a ludicrous misconception, and a dangerous one to boot.

We are on the verge here of a change. Hitherto it has been force of circumstance and of background which has rendered the very idea of integration inaccessible to the greater part of the immigrant population—that they never conceived or intended such a thing, and that their numbers and physical concentration meant the pressures towards integration which normally bear upon any small minority did not operate. Now we are seeing the growth of positive forces acting against integration, of vested interests in the preservation and sharpening of racial and religious differences, with a view to the exercise of action domination, first over fellow immigrants and then over the rest of the population. The cloud no bigger than a man's hand, that can so rapidly overcast the sky, has been visible recently in Wolverhampton and has shown signs of spreading quickly. The words I am about to use, verbatim as they appeared in the local press on 17 February, are not mine, but those of a Labour Member of Parliament who is a Minister in the present Government.

> The Sikh communities' campaign to maintain customs inappropriate in Britain is much to be regretted. Working in Britain, particularly in the public services, they should be prepared to accept the terms and conditions of their employment. To claim special communal rights (or should one say rites?) leads to a dangerous fragmentation within society. This communalism is a canker: whether practised by one colour or another it is to be strongly condemned.

All credit to John Stonehouse for having had the insight to perceive that, and the courage to say it.

For these dangerous and divisive elements the legislation proposed in the Race Relations Bill is the very pabulum they need to flourish. Here is the means of showing that the immigrant communities can organize to consolidate their members, to agitate and campaign against their fellow citizens, and to overawe and dominate the rest with the legal weapons which the ignorant and the ill-informed have provided. As I look ahead, I am filled with foreboding.

Like the Roman, I seem to see "the River Tiber foaming with much blood." That tragic and intractable phenomenon which we watch with horror on the other side of the Atlantic but which there is interwoven with the history and existence of the States itself, is coming upon us here by our own volition and our own neglect. Indeed, it has all but come. In numerical terms, it will be of American proportions long before the end of the century.

Only resolute and urgent action will avert it even now. Whether there will be the public will to demand and obtain that action, I do not know. All I know is that to see, and not to speak, would be the great betrayal.

STUDY QUESTIONS

1. What is the nightmare vision Powell constructs for the future of Britain?
2. What images does he incorporate into his vision of the consequences of unrestricted immigration, and is the language inherently racist?

28.10 VACLAV HAVEL, "THE POWER OF THE POWERLESS," 1978

Vaclav Havel (1936–2011) was a playwright and political dissident in Communist Czechoslovakia who became the nation's first president of the post-Communist era (1989–1993) and then was elected the first president of the independent Czech Republic (1993–2003). His essay "The Power of the Powerless" was suppressed by the Communist government but circulated widely in the Czech underground network; in it, Havel discusses methods of resistance in a "post-totalitarian" society—that is, a society that no longer conforms to the models of totalitarianism from earlier in the twentieth century. A post-totalitarian society is one in which people are not oppressed from an authority above them but are instead enmeshed in a complex web of power struggles, interdependencies, mutual distrust, and self-censorship.

A specter is haunting Eastern Europe: the specter of what in the West is called "dissent." This specter has not appeared out of thin air. It is a natural and inevitable consequence of the present historical phase of the system it is haunting. It was born at a time when this system, for a thousand reasons, can no longer base itself on the unadulterated, brutal, and arbitrary application of power, eliminating all expressions of non-conformity. What is more, the system has become so ossified politically that there is practically no way for such nonconformity to be implemented within its official structures. . . .

Translation by Paul Wilson, in *The Power of the Powerless: Citizens against the State in Central Eastern Europe*, edited by John Keane (1985).

Our system is most frequently characterized as a dictatorship or, more precisely, as the dictatorship of a political bureaucracy over a society which has undergone economic and social leveling. I am afraid that the term "dictatorship," regardless of how intelligible it may otherwise be, tends to obscure rather than clarify the real nature of power in this system. . . . Even though our dictatorship has long since alienated itself completely from the social movements that give birth to it, the authenticity of these movements (and I am thinking of the proletarian and socialist movements of the nineteenth century) gives it undeniable historicity. These origins provided a solid foundation of sorts on which it could build until it became the utterly new social and political reality it is today, which has become so inextricably a part of the structure of the modern world. . . . It commands an incomparably more precise, logically structured, generally comprehensible and, in essence, extremely flexible ideology that, in its elaborateness and completeness, is almost a secularized religion. It offers a ready answer to any question whatsoever; it can scarcely be accepted only in part, and accepting it has profound implications for human life. In an era when metaphysical and existential certainties are in a state of crisis, when people are being uprooted and alienated and are losing their sense of what this world means, this ideology inevitably has a certain hypnotic charm. . . .

The profound difference between our system—in terms of the nature of power—and what we traditionally understand by dictatorship, a difference I hope is clear even from this quite superficial comparison, has caused me to search for some term appropriate for our system, purely for the purposes of this essay. If I refer to it henceforth as a "post-totalitarian" system, I am fully aware that this is perhaps not the most precise term, but I am unable to think of a better one. I do not wish to imply by the prefix "post" that the system is no longer totalitarian; on the contrary, I mean that it is totalitarian in a way fundamentally different from classical dictatorships, different from totalitarianism as we usually understand it. . . .

The manager of a fruit-and-vegetable shop places in his window, among the onions and carrots, the slogan: "Workers of the world, unite!" Why does he do it? What is he trying to communicate to the world? Is he genuinely enthusiastic about the idea of unity among the workers of the world? Is his enthusiasm so great that he feels an irrepressible impulse to acquaint the public with his ideals? Has he really given more than a moment's thought to how such a unification might occur and what it would mean?

I think it can safely be assumed that the overwhelming majority of shopkeepers never think about the slogans they put in their windows, nor do they use them to express their real opinions. That poster was delivered to our greengrocer from the enterprise headquarters along with the onions and carrots. He put them all into the window simply because it has been done that way for years, because everyone does it, and because that is the way it has to be. If he were to refuse, there could be trouble. He could be reproached for not having the proper decoration in his window; someone might even accuse him of disloyalty. He does it because these things must be done if one is to get along in life. It is one of the thousands of details that guarantee him a relatively tranquil life "in harmony with society," as they say.

Obviously the greengrocer . . . does not put the slogan in his window from any personal desire to acquaint the public with the ideal it expresses. This, of course, does not mean that his action has no motive or significance at all, or that the slogan communicates nothing to anyone. The slogan is really a sign, and as such it contains a subliminal but very definite message. Verbally, it might be expressed this way: "I, the greengrocer XY, live here and I know what I must do. I behave in the manner expected of me. I can be depended upon and am beyond reproach. I am obedient and therefore I have the right to be left in peace." This message, of course, has an addressee: it is directed above, to the greengrocer's superior, and at the same time it is a shield that protects the greengrocer from potential informers. The slogan's real meaning, therefore, is rooted firmly in the greengrocer's existence. It reflects his vital interests. But what are those vital interests?

Let us take note: if the greengrocer had been instructed to display the slogan "I am afraid and therefore unquestioningly obedient;" he would not be nearly as indifferent to its semantics, even though the statement would reflect the truth. The greengrocer would be embarrassed and ashamed to put such an unequivocal statement of his own degradation in the shop window, and quite naturally so, for he is a human being and thus has a sense of his own dignity. To overcome this complication, his expression of loyalty must take the form of a sign which, at least on its textual surface, indicates a level of disinterested conviction. It must allow the greengrocer to say, "What's wrong with the workers of the world uniting?" Thus the sign helps the greengrocer to conceal from himself the low foundations of his obedience, at the same time concealing the low foundations of power. It hides them behind the facade of something high. And that something is ideology.

Ideology is a specious way of relating to the world. It offers human beings the illusion of an identity, of dignity, and of morality while making it easier for them to part with them. As the repository of something suprapersonal and objective, it enables people to deceive their conscience and conceal their true position and their inglorious modus vivendi, both from the world and from themselves. It is a very pragmatic but, at the same time, an apparently dignified way of legitimizing what is above, below, and on either side. It is directed toward people and toward God. It is a veil behind which human beings can hide their own fallen existence, their trivialization, and their adaptation to the status quo. It is an excuse that everyone can use, from the greengrocer, who conceals his fear of losing his job behind an alleged interest in the unification of the workers of the world, to the highest functionary, whose interest in staying in power can be cloaked in phrases about service to the working class. The primary excusatory function of ideology, therefore, is to provide people, both as victims and pillars of the post-totalitarian system, with the illusion that the system is in harmony with the human order and the order of the universe. . . .

The post-totalitarian system touches people at every step, but it does so with its ideological gloves on. This is why life in the system is so thoroughly permeated with hypocrisy and lies: government by bureaucracy is called popular government; the working class is enslaved in the name of the working class; the complete degradation of the individual is presented as his ultimate liberation; depriving people of information is called making it available; the use of power to manipulate is called the public control of power, and the arbitrary abuse of power is called observing the legal code; the repression of culture is called its development; the expansion of imperial influence is presented as support for the oppressed; the lack of free expression becomes the highest form of freedom; farcical elections become the highest form of democracy; banning independent thought becomes the most scientific of world views; military occupation becomes fraternal assistance. Because the regime is captive to its own lies, it must falsify everything. It falsifies the past. It falsifies the present, and it falsifies the future. It falsifies statistics. It pretends not to possess an omnipotent and unprincipled police apparatus. It pretends to respect human rights. It pretends to persecute no one. It pretends to fear nothing. It pretends to pretend nothing.

Individuals need not believe all these mystifications, but they must behave as though they did, or they must at least tolerate them in silence, or get along well with those who work with them. For this reason, however, they must live within a lie. They need not accept the lie. It is enough for them to have accepted their life with it and in it. For by this very fact, individuals confirm the system, fulfill the system, make the system, are the system. . . .

Why in fact did our greengrocer have to put his loyalty on display in the shop window? Had he not already displayed it sufficiently in various internal or semipublic ways? At trade union meetings, after all, he had always voted as he should. He had always taken part in various competitions. He voted in elections like a good citizen. He had even signed the "anti-Charter." Why, on top of all that, should he have to declare his loyalty publicly? After all, the people who walk past his window will certainly not stop to read that, in the greengrocer's opinion, the workers of the world ought to unite. The fact of the matter is, they don't read the slogan at all, and it can be fairly assumed they don't even see it. If you were to ask a woman who had stopped in front of his shop what she saw in the window, she could certainly tell whether or not they had tomatoes today, but it is highly unlikely that she noticed the slogan at all, let alone what it said.

It seems senseless to require the greengrocer to declare his loyalty publicly. But it makes sense nevertheless. People ignore his slogan, but they do so because such slogans are also found in other shop windows, on lampposts, bulletin boards, in apartment windows, and on buildings; they are everywhere, in fact. They form part of the panorama of everyday life. Of course, while they ignore the details, people are very aware of that panorama as a whole. And what else is the greengrocer's slogan but a small component in that huge backdrop to daily life?

The greengrocer had to put the slogan in his window, therefore, not in the hope that someone might read it or be persuaded by it, but to contribute, along with thousands of other slogans, to the panorama that everyone is very much aware of. This panorama, of course, has a subliminal meaning as well: it reminds people where they are living and what is expected of them. It tells them what everyone else is doing, and indicates to them what they must do as well, if they don't want to be excluded, to fall into isolation, alienate themselves from society, break the rules of the game, and risk the loss of their peace and tranquility and security. . . .

Let us now imagine that one day something in our greengrocer snaps and he stops putting up the slogans merely to ingratiate himself. He stops voting in elections he knows are a farce. He begins to say what he really thinks at political meetings. And he even finds the strength in himself to express solidarity with those whom his conscience commands him to support. In this revolt the greengrocer steps out of living within the lie. He rejects the ritual and breaks the rules of the game. He discovers once more his suppressed identity and dignity. He gives his freedom a concrete significance. His revolt is an attempt to live within the truth. . . .

The bill is not long in coming. He will be relieved of his post as manager of the shop and transferred to the warehouse. His pay will be reduced. His hopes for a holiday in Bulgaria will evaporate. His children's access to higher education will be threatened. His superiors will harass him and his fellow workers will wonder about him. Most of those who apply these sanctions, however, will not do so from any authentic inner conviction but simply under pressure from conditions, the same conditions that once pressured the greengrocer to display the official slogans. They will persecute the greengrocer either because it is expected of them, or to demonstrate their loyalty, or simply as part of the general panorama, to which belongs an awareness that this is how situations of this sort are dealt with, that this, in fact, is how things are always done, particularly if one is not to become suspect oneself. The executors, therefore, behave essentially like everyone else, to a greater or lesser degree: as components of the post-totalitarian system, as agents of its automatism, as petty instruments of the social auto-totality.

Thus, the power structure, through the agency of those who carry out the sanctions, those anonymous components of the system, will spew the greengrocer from its mouth. The system, through its alienating presence in people, will punish him for his rebellion. It must do so because the logic of its automatism and self-defense dictate it. The greengrocer has not committed a simple, individual offense, isolated in its own uniqueness, but something incomparably more serious. By breaking the rules of the game, he has disrupted the game as such. He has exposed it as a mere game. He has shattered the world of appearances, the fundamental pillar of the system. He has upset the power structure by tearing apart what holds it together. He has demonstrated that living a lie is living a lie. He has broken through the exalted facade of the system and exposed the real, base foundations of power. He has said that the emperor is naked. And because the emperor is in fact naked, something extremely dangerous has happened: by his action, the greengrocer has addressed the world. He has enabled everyone to peer behind the curtain. He has shown everyone that it is possible to live within the truth. Living within the lie can constitute the system only if it is universal. The principle must embrace and permeate everything. There are no terms whatsoever on which it can co-exist with living within the truth, and therefore everyone who steps out of line denies it in principle and threatens it in its entirety. . . .

The original and most important sphere of activity, one that predetermines all the others, is simply an attempt to create and support the independent life of society as an articulated expression of living within the truth. In other words, serving truth consistently, purposefully, and articulately, and organizing this service. This is only natural, after all: if living within the truth is an elementary starting point for every attempt made by people to oppose the alienating pressure of the system, if it is the only meaningful basis of any independent act of political import, and if, ultimately, it is also the most intrinsic existential source of the "dissident" attitude, then it is difficult to imagine that even manifest "dissent" could have any other basis than the service of truth, the truthful life, and the attempt to make room for the genuine aims of life.

STUDY QUESTIONS

1. What types of resistance does Havel describe in a "post-totalitarian" society?
2. According to Havel, what are the features of a post-totalitarian society?

28.11 AYATOLLAH KHOMEINI, *MESSAGE*, 1980

Sayyed Ruhollah Mostafavi Mosavi Khomeini, or Ayatollah Khomeini (1902–1989), was the leader of the Iranian revolution of 1979. After the downfall of the ruling shah (king), Khomeini, who had been living in exile in Paris, returned to Iran and became the supreme leader, the highest political and spiritual office in the country. He held this position until his death. Under his rule, the principle of *Velayet-e-faqih*—a Shi'a political concept that gave religious clerics political power—was enshrined in the postrevolutionary constitution. This excerpt from his *Message* puts the struggles in Iran in a global context, as many nations around the world were caught up in proxy wars between the superpowers of the Cold War, the Soviet Union and the United States. Trumpeting a new Muslim unity (*tawhid*), Khomeini depicts Muslim leaders who make deals with the "infidel" Americans as traitors, prefiguring the coming fundamentalist Islamic opposition to both superpowers, especially the Soviets in Afghanistan, but notably the resistance to American power in the Middle East.

Greetings to the visitors to God's Sacred House who have gathered at the local point of revelation, the place where God's angels alight. Greetings to the believers who have migrated from their own houses to the House of God. . . . Greetings to those who have grasped the sense of God Almighty's summons and set out, in response, to His House.

. . .

At a time when all the Muslims in the world are about to join together and achieve mutual

---

From Jussi Hanhimäki and Odd Arne Westad, *The Cold War: A History in Documents and Eyewitness Accounts*. New York: Oxford University Press, 2004, pp. 563–4. *The Cold War: A History in Documents and Eyewitness Accounts*. New York: Oxford University Press, © 2004.

understanding between the different schools of thought in Islam, in order to deliver their nations from the foul grasp of the superpowers; at a time when the arms of the Eastern and Western oppressors are about to be fore-shortened in Iran, by means of unity of purpose and reliance on God Almighty—precisely at this time, the Great Satan has summoned its agents and instructed them to sow dissension among the Muslims by every imaginable means, giving rise to hostility and dispute among brothers in faith who share the belief in *tauhid*, so that nothing will stand in the way of complete domination and plunder. . . . Thus, it is that precisely at the time Iran is waging a determined struggle to ensure the unity of all Muslims in the world on the basis of *tauhid* and true Islam, the Great Satan gives its orders to one of the pawns in the region, one of the dead Shah's friends, to obtain decrees from Sunni *fuqaha* and *muftis* to the effect that the Iranians are unbelievers. These pawns of America say that the Islam of Iran is different from the Islam of those who support the pawns of America, like Sadat and Begin, who extend the hand of friendship to the enemies of Islam and flaunt the commands of God Almighty, and who leave no like and calumny unuttered in their efforts to create disunity among the Muslims. The Muslims of the world must be aware of these people who are attempting to spread dissension, and must frustrate their foul conspiracy.

At a time when the superpowers are attacking Muslim countries like Afghanistan, inflicting pitiless and savage massacres on the Afghan Muslims who wish the destiny of their country to be free from foreign interference, at a time when America has a hand in every form of corruption; at a time when criminal Israel is unleashing a comprehensive onslaught against the Muslims in its beloved Lebanon and Palestine, and is preparing to transfer its capital to Jerusalem and intensity and extend its crimes against the Muslim it has driven from their homelands; in short, at a time when the Muslims stand in greater need than ever of unity, Sadat, the traitor and servant of America, the friend and brother of Begin and the dead, deposed Shah, and Saddam, another humble servant of America, are trying to sow dissension among the Muslims and will not hesitate to commit any crime their masters enjoin upon them in order to achieve their goal.

. . .

Muslims the world over who believe in the truth of Islam, arise and gather beneath the banner of *tauhid* and the teachings of Islam. Repel the treacherous superpowers from your countries and your abundant resources. Restore the glory of Islam, and abandon your selfish disputes and differences, for you possess everything! Rely on the culture of Islam, resist Western imitation, and stand on your own feet. Attack those intellectuals who are infatuated with the West and the East, and recover your true identity. Realize that intellectuals in the pay of foreigners have inflicted disaster upon their people and countries.

STUDY QUESTIONS

1. Why does the ayatollah see the "Great Satan" as being engaged in a war against Islam itself?
2. How does he sketch out the need for Muslim unity as the key to dislodging the power of Islam's enemies?

28.12 FOUNDING CHARTER OF THE ISLAMIC RESISTANCE MOVEMENT (HAMAS), 1987

The Islamic Resistance Movement, commonly known as Hamas, is an affiliate of the Muslim Brotherhood. Founded in 1987, Hamas is a *waqf*—an Islamic charitable trust—that does indeed do significant social work among the Palestinians; but it also has a military wing that engages in terrorism against Israel. Since 2007 it has been the de facto government of the Gaza Strip, while the Palestinian Liberation Organization has been the titular power in the West Bank. As its founding charter makes clear, the political aim of Hamas is the destruction of the state of Israel. It sees no opportunity for compromise on the issue and sees jihadi militancy as an absolute religious obligation. What follows is the group's founding charter, in its official English version. I have edited out the charter's frequent quotations from the Qur'an and hadith and have stabilized its English usage.

This Covenant of the IRM (HAMAS), clarifies its picture, reveals its identity, outlines its stand, explains its aims, speaks about its hopes, and calls for its support, adoption and joining its ranks. Our struggle against the Jews is very great and very serious. It needs all sincere efforts. It is a step that inevitably should be followed by other steps. The Movement is but one squadron that should be supported by more and more squadrons from this vast Arab and Islamic world, until the enemy is vanquished and Allah's victory is realized. . . .

ARTICLE ONE—IDEOLOGICAL STARTING POINTS

The IRM's program is Islam. From it, it draws its ideas, ways of thinking and understanding of the universe, life and man. It resorts to it for judgement in all its conduct, and it is inspired by it for guidance of its steps.

ARTICLE TWO—THE IRM'S RELATION WITH THE MOSLEM BROTHERHOOD GROUP

The IRM is one of the wings of Moslem Brotherhood in Palestine. Moslem Brotherhood Movement is a universal organization which constitutes the largest Islamic movement in modern times. It is characterized by its deep understanding, accurate comprehension and its complete embrace of all Islamic concepts of all aspects of life, culture, creed, politics, economics, education, society, justice and judgement, the spreading of Islam, education, art, information, science of the occult and conversion to Islam.

ARTICLE SIX—CHARACTERISTICS AND INDEPENDENCE

The IRM is a distinguished Palestinian movement, whose allegiance is to Allah, and whose way of life is Islam. It strives to raise the banner of Allah over every inch of Palestine, for under the wing of Islam followers of all religions can coexist in security and safety where their lives, possessions and rights are concerned. In the absence of Islam, strife will be rife, oppression spreads, evil prevails and schisms and wars will break out. . . .

ARTICLE SEVEN—THE UNIVERSALITY OF THE IRM

. . . The IRM is one of the links in the chain of the struggle against the Zionist invaders. It goes back to 1939, to the emergence of the martyr Izz al-Din al

Hamas Covenant 1988. http://avalon.law.yale.edu/20th_century/hamas.asp.

Kissam and his brethren the fighters, members of Moslem Brotherhood. It goes on to reach out and become one with another chain that includes the struggle of the Palestinians and Moslem Brotherhood in the 1948 war and the Jihad operations of the Moslem Brotherhood in 1968 and after.

Moreover, if the links have been distant from each other and if obstacles, placed by those who are the lackeys of Zionism in the way of the fighters obstructed the continuation of the struggle, the IRM aspires to the realization of Allah's promise, no matter how long that should take. The Prophet, Allah bless him and grant him salvation, has said:

> The Day of Judgement will not come about until Moslems fight the Jews (killing the Jews), when the Jew will hide behind stones and trees. The stones and trees will say O Moslems, O Abdulla, there is a Jew behind me, come and kill him. Only the Gharkad tree, (evidently a certain kind of tree) would not do that because it is one of the trees of the Jews. (related by al-Bukhari and Moslem).

ARTICLE EIGHT—THE SLOGAN OF THE IRM

Allah is its target, the Prophet is its model, the Koran its constitution: Jihad is its path and death for the sake of Allah is the loftiest of its wishes.

ARTICLE ELEVEN—STRATEGIES OF THE IRM: PALESTINE IS AN ISLAMIC WAQF

The IRM believes that the land of Palestine is an Islamic *waqf* consecrated for future Moslem generations until Judgement Day. It, or any part of it, should not be squandered: it, or any part of it, should not be given up. Neither a single Arab country nor all Arab countries, neither any king or president, nor all the kings and presidents, neither any organization nor all of them, be they Palestinian or Arab, possess the right to do that. Palestine is an Islamic Waqf land consecrated for Moslem generations until Judgement Day. This being so, who could claim to have the right to represent Moslem generations till Judgement Day?

This is the law governing the land of Palestine in the Islamic Sharia (law) and the same goes for any land the Moslems have conquered by force, because during the times of (Islamic) conquests, the Moslems consecrated these lands to Moslem generations till the Day of Judgement. . . .

ARTICLE THIRTEEN—PEACEFUL SOLUTIONS, INITIATIVES, AND INTERNATIONAL CONFERENCES

Initiatives, and so-called peaceful solutions and international conferences, are in contradiction to the principles of the Islamic Resistance Movement. Abusing any part of Palestine is abuse directed against part of religion. Nationalism of the IRM is part of its religion. Its members have been fed on that. For the sake of hoisting the banner of Allah over their homeland they fight. "Allah will be prominent, but most people do not know."

Now and then the call goes out for the convening of an international conference to look for ways of solving the (Palestinian) question. Some accept, others reject the idea, for this or other reason, with one stipulation or more for consent to convening the conference and participating in it. Knowing the parties constituting the conference, their past and present attitudes towards Moslem problems, the IRM does not consider these conferences capable of realising the demands, restoring the rights or doing justice to the oppressed. These conferences are only ways of setting the infidels in the land of the Moslems as arbitrators. When did the infidels do justice to the believers?

There is no solution for the Palestinian question except through Jihad. Initiatives, proposals and international conferences are all a waste of time and vain endeavors. The Palestinian people know better than to consent to having their future, rights and fate toyed with. . . .

ARTICLE FIFTEEN—THE JIHAD FOR THE LIBERATION OF PALESTINE IS AN INDIVIDUAL DUTY

The day that enemies usurp part of Moslem land, Jihad becomes the individual duty of every Moslem. In face of the Jews' usurpation of Palestine, it is compulsory that the banner of Jihad be raised. To do this requires the diffusion of Islamic consciousness among the masses, both on the regional, Arab and Islamic levels. It is necessary to instill the spirit of Jihad in the heart of the nation so that they would confront the enemies and join the ranks of the fighters.

It is necessary that scientists, educators and teachers, information and media people, as well as the educated masses, especially the youth and sheikhs of the Islamic movements, should take part in the operation of awakening (the masses). It is important that basic changes be made in the school curriculum, to cleanse it of the traces of ideological invasion that affected it as a result of the orientalists and missionaries who infiltrated the region following the defeat of the Crusaders at the hands of Salah el-Din (Saladin). The Crusaders realized that it was impossible to defeat the Moslems without first having ideological invasion pave the way by upsetting their thoughts, disfiguring their heritage and violating their ideals. Only then could they invade with soldiers. This, in its turn, paved the way for the imperialistic invasion that made Allenby declare on entering Jerusalem: "Only now have the Crusades ended." General Guru stood at Salah el-Din's grave and said: "We have returned, O Salah el-Din." Imperialism has helped towards the strengthening of ideological invasion, deepening, and still does, its roots. All this has paved the way towards the loss of Palestine.

It is necessary to instill in the minds of the Moslem generations that the Palestinian problem is a religious problem, and should be dealt with on this basis. Palestine contains Islamic holy sites. In it there is al-Aqsa Mosque which is bound to the great Mosque in Mecca in an inseparable bond as long as heaven and earth speak of Isra' (Mohammed's midnight journey to the seven heavens) and Mi'raj (Mohammed's ascension to the seven heavens from Jerusalem). . . .

ARTICLE SEVENTEEN—THE ROLE OF THE MOSLEM WOMAN

The Moslem woman has a role no less important than that of the Moslem man in the battle of liberation. She is the maker of men. Her role in guiding and educating the new generations is great. The enemies have realised the importance of her role. They consider that if they are able to direct and bring her up the way they wish, far from Islam, they would have won the battle. That is why you find them giving these attempts constant attention through information campaigns, films, and the school curriculum, using for that purpose their lackeys who are infiltrated through Zionist organizations under various names and shapes, such as Freemasons, Rotary Clubs, espionage groups and others, which are all nothing more than cells of subversion and saboteurs. These organizations have ample resources that enable them to play their role in societies for the purpose of achieving the Zionist targets and to deepen the concepts that would serve the enemy. These organizations operate in the absence of Islam and its estrangement among its people. The Islamic peoples should perform their role in confronting the conspiracies of these saboteurs. The day Islam is in control of guiding the affairs of life, these organizations, hostile to humanity and Islam, will be obliterated.

ARTICLE EIGHTEEN

Woman in the home of the fighting family, whether she is a mother or a sister, plays the most important role in looking after the family, rearing the children and imbuing them with moral values and thoughts derived from Islam. She has to teach them to perform the religious duties in preparation for the role of fighting awaiting them. That is why it is necessary to pay great attention to schools and the curriculum followed in educating Moslem girls, so that they would grow up to be good mothers, aware of their role in the battle of liberation.

She has to be of sufficient knowledge and understanding where the performance of housekeeping matters are concerned, because economy and avoidance of waste of the family budget, is one of the requirements for the ability to continue moving forward in the difficult conditions surrounding us. She should put before her eyes the fact that the money available to her is just like blood which should never flow except through the veins so that both children and grownups could continue to live.

ARTICLE TWENTY—SOCIAL MUTUAL RESPONSIBILITY

Moslem society is a mutually responsible society. The Prophet, prayers and greetings be unto him, said: "Blessed are the generous, whether they were in town or on a journey, who have collected all that they had and shared it equally among themselves."

The Islamic spirit is what should prevail in every Moslem society. The society that confronts a vicious enemy which acts in a way similar to Nazism, making no differentiation between man and woman, between children and old people—such a society is entitled to this Islamic spirit. Our enemy relies on the methods of collective punishment. He has deprived people of their homeland and properties, pursued them in their places of exile and gathering, breaking bones, shooting at women, children and old people, with or without a reason. The enemy has opened detention camps where thousands and thousands of people are thrown and kept under sub-human conditions. Added to this, are the demolition of houses, rendering children orphans, meting cruel sentences against thousands of young people, and causing them to spend the best years of their lives in the dungeons of prisons.

In their Nazi treatment, the Jews made no exception for women or children. Their policy of striking fear in the heart is meant for all. They attack people where their breadwinning is concerned, extorting their money and threatening their honor. They deal with people as if they were the worst war criminals. Deportation from the homeland is a kind of murder.

To counter these deeds, it is necessary that social mutual responsibility should prevail among the people. The enemy should be faced by the people as a single body which if one member of it should complain, the rest of the body would respond by feeling the same pains.

ARTICLE TWENTY-ONE

Mutual social responsibility means extending assistance, financial or moral, to all those who are in need and joining in the execution of some of the work. Members of the IRM should consider the interests of the masses as their own personal interests. They must spare no effort in achieving and preserving them. They must prevent any foul play with the future of the upcoming generations and anything that could cause loss to society. The masses are part of them and they are part of the masses. Their strength is theirs, and their future is theirs. Members of the Islamic Resistance Movement should share the people's joy and grief, adopt the demands of the public and whatever means by which they could be realized. The day that such a spirit prevails, brotherliness would deepen, cooperation, sympathy and unity will be enhanced and the ranks will be solidified to confront the enemies.

ARTICLE TWENTY-TWO—SUPPORTIVE FORCES BEHIND THE ENEMY

For a long time, the enemies have been planning, skillfully and with precision, for the achievement of what they have attained. They took into consideration the causes affecting the current of events. They strived to amass great and substantive material wealth which they devoted to the realization of their dream. With their money, they took control of the world media, news agencies, the press, publishing houses, broadcasting stations, and others. With their money they stirred revolutions in various parts of the world with the purpose of achieving their interests and reaping the fruit therein. They were behind the French Revolution, the Communist revolution and most of the revolutions we heard and hear about, here and there. With their money they formed secret societies, such as Freemasons, Rotary Clubs, the Lions and others in different parts of the world for the purpose of sabotaging societies and achieving Zionist interests. With their money they were able to control imperialistic countries and instigate them to colonize many countries in order to enable them to exploit their resources and spread corruption there.

You may speak as much as you want about regional and world wars. They were behind World War I, when they were able to destroy the Islamic Caliphate, making financial gains and controlling resources. They obtained the Balfour Declaration, formed the League of Nations through which they could rule the world. They were behind World War II, through which they made huge financial gains by trading in armaments, and paved the way for the establishment of their state. It was they who instigated the replacement of the League of Nations with the United Nations and the Security Council to enable them to rule the world through them. There is no war going on anywhere, without having their finger in it.

The imperialistic forces in the Capitalist West and Communist East, support the enemy with all their might, in money and in men. These forces take turns in doing that. The day Islam appears, the forces of infidelity would unite to challenge it, for the infidels are of one nation.

ARTICLE TWENTY-THREE—OUR ATTITUDES TOWARDS ISLAMIC MOVEMENTS

The IRM views other Islamic movements with respect and appreciation. If it were at variance with them on one point or opinion, it is in agreement with them on other points and understandings. It considers these movements, if they reveal good intentions and dedication to Allah, that they fall into the category of those who are trying hard since they act within the Islamic circle. Each active person has his share.

The IRM considers all these movements as a fund for itself. It prays to Allah for guidance and directions for all and it spares no effort to keep the banner of unity raised, ever striving for its realization in accordance with the Koran and the Prophet's directives.

ARTICLE TWENTY-FIVE—OUR ATTITUDES TOWARDS NATIONALIST MOVEMENTS IN THE PALESTINE ARENA

The IRM respects these movements and appreciates their circumstances and the conditions surrounding and affecting them. It encourages them as long as they do not give their allegiance to the Communist East or the Crusading West. It confirms to all those who are integrated in it, or sympathetic towards it, that the Islamic Resistance Movement is a fighting movement that has a moral and enlightened look of life and the way it should cooperate with the other (movements). It detests opportunism and desires only the good of people, individuals and groups alike. It does not seek material gains, personal fame, nor does it look for a reward from others. It works with its own resources and whatever is at its disposal "and prepare for them whatever force you can," for the fulfilment of the duty, and the earning of Allah's favor. It has no other desire than that.

The Movement assures all the nationalist trends operating in the Palestinian arena for the liberation of Palestine, that it is there for their support and assistance. It will never be more than that, both in words and deeds, now and in the future. It is there to bring together and not to divide, to preserve and not to squander, to unify and not to throw asunder. It evaluates every good word, sincere effort and good offices. It closes the door in the face of side disagreements and does not lend an ear to rumors and slanders, while at the same time fully realizing the right for self-defense.

Anything contrary or contradictory to these trends, is a lie disseminated by enemies or their lackeys for the purpose of sowing confusion, disrupting the ranks and occupy them with side issues.

ARTICLE TWENTY-SEVEN—OUR ATTITUDES TOWARDS THE PLO

The PLO is the closest to the heart of the *Islamic Resistance Movement*. It contains the father and the brother, the next of kin and the friend. The Moslem does not estrange himself from his father, brother, next of kin or friend. Our homeland is one, our situation is one, our fate is one and the enemy is a joint enemy to all of us.

Because of the situations surrounding the formation of the Organization, of the ideological confusion prevailing in the Arab world as a result of the ideological invasion under whose influence the Arab world has fallen since the defeat of the Crusaders and which was, and still is, intensified through orientalists, missionaries and imperialists, the Organization adopted the idea of the secular state. And that is how we view it.

Secularism completely contradicts religious ideology. Attitudes, conduct and decisions stem from ideologies.

That is why, with all our appreciation for the PLO—and what it can develop into—and without belittling its role in the Arab–Israeli conflict, we are unable to exchange the present or future Islamic Palestine with the secular idea. The Islamic nature of Palestine is part of our religion and whoever takes his religion lightly is a loser. . . .

The day the PLO adopts Islam as its way of life, we will become its soldiers, and fuel for its fire that will burn the enemies. . . .

ARTICLE TWENTY-EIGHT—OUR ATTITUDES TOWARDS ARAB AND ISLAMIC COUNTRIES, INSTITUTIONS, AND INTELLECTUALS

The Zionist invasion is a vicious invasion. It does not refrain from resorting to all methods, using all evil and contemptible ways to achieve its end. It relies greatly in its infiltration and espionage operations on the secret organizations it gave rise to, such as the Freemasons, the Rotary and Lions clubs, and other sabotage groups. All these organizations, whether secret or open, work in the interest of Zionism and according to its instructions. They aim at undermining societies, destroying values, corrupting consciences, deteriorating character and annihilating Islam. It is behind the drug trade and alcoholism in all its kinds so as to facilitate its control and expansion.

Arab countries surrounding Israel are asked to open their borders before the fighters from among the Arab and Islamic nations so that they could consolidate their efforts with those of their Moslem brethren in Palestine.

As for the other Arab and Islamic countries, they are asked to facilitate the movement of the fighters from and to it, and this is the least thing they could do.

We should not forget to remind every Moslem that when the Jews conquered the Holy City in 1967, they stood on the threshold of the Aqsa Mosque and proclaimed that "Mohammed is dead, and his descendants are all women."

Israel, Judaism and Jews challenge Islam and the Moslem people. "May the cowards never sleep."

The IRM hopes that all these groupings will side with it in all spheres, would support it, adopt its stand and solidify its activities and moves, work towards rallying support for it so that the Islamic people will be a base and a stay for it, supplying it with strategic depth an all human material and informative spheres, in time and in place. This should be done through the convening of solidarity conferences, the issuing of explanatory bulletins, favorable articles and booklets, enlightening the masses regarding the Palestinian issue, clarifying what confronts it and the conspiracies woven around it. They should mobilize the Islamic nations, ideologically, educationally and culturally, so that these peoples would be equipped to perform their role in the decisive battle of liberation, just as they did when they vanquished the Crusaders and the Tatars and saved human civilization. Indeed, that is not difficult for Allah.

ARTICLE THIRTY

Writers, intellectuals, media people, orators, educators and teachers, and all the various sectors in the Arab and Islamic world—all of them are called upon to perform their role, and to fulfill their duty, because of the ferocity of the Zionist offensive and the Zionist influence in many countries exercised through financial and media control, as well as the consequences that all this led to in the greater part of the world.

Jihad is not confined to the carrying of arms and the confrontation of the enemy. The effective word, the good article, the useful book, support and solidarity—together with the presence of sincere purpose for the hoisting of Allah's banner higher and higher—all these are elements of the Jihad for Allah's sake. . . .

ARTICLE THIRTY-ONE—OUR ATTITUDES TOWARDS FOLLOWERS OF OTHER RELIGIONS

The IRM is a humanistic movement. It takes care of human rights and is guided by Islamic tolerance when dealing with the followers of other religions. It does not antagonize anyone of them except if it is antagonized by it or stands in its way to hamper its moves and waste its efforts.

Under the wing of Islam, it is possible for the followers of the three religions—Islam, Christianity and Judaism—to coexist in peace and quiet with each other. Peace and quiet would not be possible except under the wing of Islam. Past and present history are the best witness to that.

It is the duty of the followers of other religions to stop disputing the sovereignty of Islam in this region, because the day these followers should take over there will be nothing but carnage, displacement and terror. Every one of them is at variance with his fellow-religionists, not to speak about followers of other religionists. Past and present history are full of examples to prove this fact.

Islam confers upon everyone his legitimate rights. Islam prevents the incursion on other people's rights. The Zionist Nazi activities against our people will not last for long. "For the state of injustice lasts but one day, while the state of justice lasts till Doomsday."

ARTICLE THIRTY-TWO—THE ATTEMPT TO ISOLATE THE PALESTINIAN PEOPLE

World Zionism, together with imperialistic powers, try through a studied plan and an intelligent strategy to remove one Arab state after another from the circle of struggle against Zionism, in order to have it finally face the Palestinian people only. Egypt was, to a great extent, removed from the circle of the struggle, through the treacherous Camp David Agreement. They are trying to draw other Arab countries into similar agreements and to bring them outside the circle of struggle.

The IRM calls on Arab and Islamic nations to take up the line of serious and persevering action to prevent the success of this horrendous plan, to warn the people of the danger emanating from leaving the circle of struggle against Zionism. Today it is Palestine, tomorrow it will be one country or another. The Zionist plan is limitless. After Palestine, the Zionists aspire to expand from the Nile to the Euphrates. When they will have digested the region they overtook, they will aspire to further expansion, and so on. Their plan is embodied in the "Protocols of the Elders of Zion," and their present conduct is the best proof of what we are saying.

Leaving the circle of struggle with Zionism is high treason, and cursed be he who does that, "for whoso shall turn his back unto them on that day, unless he turneth aside to fight, or retreateth to another party of the faithful, shall draw on himself the indignation of Allah, and his abode shall be hell; an ill journey shall it be thither." (*The Spoils*—verse 16). There is no way out except by concentrating all powers and energies to face this Nazi, vicious Tatar invasion. The alternative is loss of one's country, the dispersion of citizens, the spread of vice on earth and the destruction of religious values. Let every person know that he is responsible before Allah, for "the doer of the slightest good deed is rewarded in like, and the doers of the slightest evil deed is also rewarded in like."

The IRM consider itself to be the spearhead of the circle of struggle with world Zionism and a step on the road. The Movement adds its efforts to the efforts of all those who are active in the Palestinian arena. Arab and Islamic Peoples should augment by further steps on their part; Islamic groupings all over the Arab world should also do the same, since all of these are the best-equipped for the future role in the fight with the warmongering Jews.

ARTICLE THIRTY-FIVE

The IRM views seriously the defeat of the Crusaders at the hands of Salah ed-Din al-Ayyubi and the rescuing of Palestine from their hands, as well as the defeat of the Tatars at Ein Galot, breaking their power at the hands of Qataz and Al-Dhaher Bivers and saving the Arab world from the Tatar onslaught which aimed at the destruction of every meaning of human civilization. The Movement draws lessons and examples from all this. The present Zionist onslaught has also been preceded by Crusading raids from the West and other Tatar raids from the East. Just as the Moslems faced those raids and planned fighting and defeating them, they should be able to confront the Zionist invasion and defeat it. This is indeed no problem for the Almighty Allah, provided that the intentions are pure, the determination is true and that Moslems have benefited from past experiences, rid themselves of the effects of ideological invasion and followed the customs of their ancestors.

ARTICLE THIRTY-SIX—THE IRM IS COMPOSED OF SOLDIERS

While paving its way, the IRM, emphasizes time and again to all the sons of our people, to the Arab and Islamic nations, that it does not seek personal fame, material gain, or social prominence. It does not aim to compete against any one from among our people, or take his place. Nothing of the sort at all. It will not act against any of the sons of Moslems or those who are peaceful towards it from among non-Moslems, be they here or anywhere else. It will only serve as a support for all groupings and organizations operating against the Zionist enemy and its lackeys.

The IRM adopts Islam as its way of life. Islam is its creed and religion. Whoever takes Islam as his way of life, be it an organization, a grouping, a country or any other body, the Islamic Resistance Movement considers itself as their soldiers and nothing more.

The last of our prayers will be praise to Allah, the Master of the Universe.

STUDY QUESTIONS

1. Why does Hamas see jihadi militancy as an absolute religious obligation? Why is the destruction of Israel its central political aim?
2. According to the charter, what role do women play in fulfilling Hamas's mission?

28.13 HÉLÈNE CIXOUS, "THE LAUGH OF THE MEDUSA," 1975

Hélène Cixous (b. 1937) began her academic career as a scholar of English literature (her first book was a study of James Joyce) but soon branched out into feminist theory, philosophy, and social and literary criticism, as well as writing numerous novels, plays, and poetry-volumes. She is one of the three central figures in establishing the French "third wave" of poststructuralist feminist theory (the other two being Luce Irigaray and Julia Kristeva), and her most famous, influential work is the essay "The Laugh of the Medusa." This essay both asserts the need for and exemplifies the use of *écriture feminine* (as a neologism, "womanwriting"). Cixous's point is that Western culture and intellectual life are based on a fundamentally masculine form of domination and explanation, a goal-oriented rationalism that she contrasts with a feminine form of expression that is based on sensation, intuition, stream-of-consciousness, and acceptance of ambiguity. As a consequence, she abjures traditional styles of argument and norms of language, even of grammar and syntax. Her essay's title is an expression of the amusement women feel at the fear men have for the way women think, speak, feel, and exist.

Excerpt from Hélène Cixous. "The Laugh of the Medusa," translated by Keith Cohen and Paula Cohen. *Signs* 1, no. 4 (Summer 1974), pp. 875–93. Published by the University of Chicago Press.

I shall speak about women's writing: about *what it will do*. Woman must write herself: must write about women and bring women to writing, from which they have been driven away as violently as from their bodies—for the same reasons, by the same law, with the same fatal goal. Woman must put herself into the text—as into the world and into history—by her own movement.

The future must no longer be determined by the past. I do not deny that the effects of the past are still with us. But I refuse to strengthen them by repeating them, to confer upon them an irremovability the equivalent of destiny, to confuse the biological and the cultural. Anticipation is imperative.

Since these reflections are taking shape in an area just on the point of being discovered, they necessarily bear the mark of our time—a time during which the new breaks away from the old, and, more precisely, the "feminine" new from the old. Thus, as there are no grounds for establishing a discourse, but rather an arid millennial ground to break, what I say has at least two sides and two aims: to break up, to destroy; and to foresee the unforeseeable, to project.

I write this as a woman, toward women. When I say "woman," I'm speaking of woman in her inevitable struggle against conventional man, and of a universal woman subject who must bring women to their senses and to their meaning in history. But first it must be said that in spite of the enormity of the repression that has kept them in the "dark"—that dark which people have been trying to make them accept as their attribute—there is, at this time, no general woman, no one typical woman. What they have *in common* I will say. But what strikes me is the infinite richness of their individual constitutions: you can't talk about *a* female sexuality, uniform, homogenous, classifiable into codes—any more than you can talk about one unconscious resembling another. Women's imaginary is inexhaustible, like music, painting, writing: their stream of phantasms is incredible. . . .

It is time to liberate the New Woman from the Old by coming to know her—by loving her for getting by, for getting beyond the Old without delay, by going out ahead of what the New Woman will be, as an arrow quits the bow with a movement that gathers and separates the vibrations musically, in order to be more than her self.

I say that we must, for, with a few rare exceptions, there has not yet been any writing that inscribes femininity; exceptions so rare, in fact, that, after plowing through literature across languages, cultures, and ages, one can only be startled at this vain scouting mission. It is well known that the number of women writers (while having increased very slightly from the nineteenth century on) has always been ridiculously small. This is a useless and deceptive fact unless from their species of female writers we do not first deduct the immense majority whose workmanship is in no way different from male writing, and which either obscures women or reproduces the classic representations of women (as sensitive—intuitive—dreamy, etc.).

Let me insert here a parenthetical remark. I mean it when I speak of male writing. I maintain unequivocally that there is such a thing as *marked* writing; that, until now, far more extensively and repressively than is ever suspected or admitted, writing has been run by a libidinal and cultural—hence political, typically masculine—economy; that this is a locus where the repression of women has been perpetuated, over and over, more or less consciously, and in a manner that's frightening since it's often hidden or adorned with the mystifying charms of fiction; that this locus has grossly exaggerated all the signs of sexual opposition (and not sexual difference), where woman has never *her* turn to speak—this being all the more serious and unpardonable in that writing is precisely *the very possibility of change*, the space that can serve as a springboard for subversive thought, the precursory movement of a transformation of social and cultural structures.

Nearly the entire history of writing is confounded with the history of reason, of which it is at once the effect, the support, and one of the privileged alibis. It has been one with the phallocentric tradition. It is indeed the same self-admiring, self-stimulating, self-congratulatory phallocentrism.

With some exceptions, for there have been failures—and if it weren't for them, I wouldn't be writing (I-woman, escapee)—in that enormous machine that has been operating and turning out its "truth" for centuries. There have been poets who would go to any lengths to slip something by at odds with tradition—men capable of loving love and hence capable of loving others and of wanting them, of imagining the woman who would hold out against oppression and constitute herself as a superb, equal, hence "impossible" subject, untenable in a real social framework. Such a woman the poet could desire only by breaking the codes that negate her. Her appearance would necessarily bring on, if not revolution—for the bastion was supposed to be immutable—at least harrowing explosions.

But only the poets—not the novelists, allies of representationalism. Because poetry involves gaining strength through the unconscious and because the unconscious, that other limitless country, is the place where the repressed manage to survive: women, or as Hoffmann would say, fairies.

She must write her self, because this is the invention of a *new insurgent* writing which, when the moment of her liberation has come, will allow her to carry out the indispensable ruptures and transformations in her history, first at two levels that cannot be separated.

a) Individually. By writing her self, woman will return to the body which has been more than confiscated from her, which has been turned into the uncanny stranger on display—the ailing or dead figure, which so often turns out to be the nasty companion, the cause and location of inhibitions. Censor the body and you censor breath and speech at the same time. . . .
b) An act that will also be marked by woman's *seizing* the occasion to *speak*, hence her shattering entry into history, which has always been based *on her suppression*. To write and thus to forge for herself the antilogos weapon. To become *at will* the taker and initiator, for her own right, in every symbolic system, in every political process.

It is time for women to start scoring their feats in written and oral language.

Every woman has known the torment of getting up to speak. Her heart racing, at times entirely lost for words, ground and language slipping away—that's how daring a feat, how great a transgression it is for a woman to speak—even just open her mouth—in public. A double distress, for even if she transgresses, her words fall almost always upon the deaf male ear, which hears in language only that which speaks in the masculine.

It is by writing, from and toward women, and by taking up the challenge of speech which has been governed by the phallus, that women will confirm women in a place other than that which is reserved in and by the symbolic, that is, in a place other than silence. Women should break out of the snare of silence. They shouldn't be conned into accepting a domain which is the margin or the harem. . . .

The new history is coming; it's not a dream, though it does extend beyond men's imagination, and for good reason. It's going to deprive them of their conceptual orthopedics, beginning with the destruction of their enticement machine.

It is impossible to *define* a feminine practice of writing, and this is an impossibility that will remain, for this practice can never be theorized, enclosed, coded—which doesn't mean that it doesn't exist. But it will always surpass the discourse that regulates the phallocentric system; it does and will take place in areas other than those subordinated to philosophico-theoretical domination. It will be conceived of only by subjects who are breakers of automatisms, by peripheral figures that no authority can ever subjugate.

Hence the necessity to affirm the flourishes of this writing, to give form to its movement, its near and distant byways. Bear in mind to begin with (1) that sexual opposition, which has always worked for man's profit to the point of reducing writing, too, to his laws, is only a historico-cultural limit. There is, there will be more and more rapidly pervasive now, a fiction that produces irreducible effects of femininity. (2) That it is through ignorance that most readers, critics, and writers of both sexes hesitate to admit or deny outright the possibility or the pertinence of a distinction between feminine and masculine writing. . . .

The Dark Continent is neither dark nor unexplorable.—It is still unexplored only because we've been made to believe that it was too dark to be explorable. And because they want to make us believe that what interests us is the white continent, with its monuments to Lack. And we believed. They riveted us between two horrifying myths: between the Medusa and the abyss. That would be enough to set half the world laughing, except that it's still going on. For the phallocentric sublation is with us, and it's militant, regenerating the old patterns, anchored in the dogma of castration. They haven't changed a thing: they've theorized their desire for reality! Let the priests tremble, we're going to show them our sexts!

Too bad for them if they fall apart upon discovering that women aren't men, or that the mother doesn't have one. But isn't this fear convenient for them? Wouldn't the worst be, isn't the worst, in truth, that women aren't castrated, that they have only to stop listening to the Sirens (for the Sirens were men) for history to change its meaning? You have only to look at the Medusa straight on to see her. And she's not deadly. She's beautiful and she's laughing.

Men say that there are two unrepresentable things: death and the feminine sex. That's because they need femininity to be associated with death; it's the jitters that gives them a hard-on! For themselves! They need to be afraid of us. Look at the trembling Perseuses moving backward toward us, clad in apotropes [warning signs]. What lovely backs! Not another minute to lose. Let's get out of here.

Let's hurry: the continent is not impenetrably dark. I have been there often. . . .

Almost everything is yet to be written by women about femininity: about their sexuality, that is, its infinite and mobile complexity, about their eroticization, sudden turn-ons of a certain miniscule-immense area of their bodies; not about destiny, but about the adventure of such and such a drive, about trips, crossings, trudges, abrupt and gradual awakenings, discoveries of a zone at one time timorous and soon to be forthright. A woman's body, with its thousand and one thresholds of ardor—once, by smashing yokes and censors, she lets it articulate the profusion of meanings that run through it in every direction—will make the old single-grooved mother tongue reverberate with more than one language.

We've been turned away from our bodies, shamefully taught to ignore them, to strike them with that stupid sexual modesty; we've been made victims of the old fool's game: each one will love the other sex. I'll give you your body and you'll give me mine. But who are the men who give women the body that women blindly yield to them? Why so few texts? Because so few women have as yet won back their body. Women must write through their bodies, they must invent the impregnable language that will wreck partitions, classes, and rhetorics, regulations and codes, they must submerge, cut through, get beyond the ultimate reserve-discourse, including the one that laughs at the very idea of pronouncing the word "silence," the one that, aiming for the impossible, stops short before the word "impossible" and writes it as "the end." . . .

More so than men who are coaxed toward social success, toward sublimation, women are body. More body, hence more writing. For a long time it has been in body that women have responded to persecution, to the familial-conjugal enterprise of domestication, to the repeated attempts at castrating them. Those who have turned their tongues 10,000 times seven times before not speaking are either dead from it or more familiar with their tongues and their mouths than anyone else. Now, I-woman am going to blow up the Law: an explosion henceforth possible and ineluctable; let it be done, right now, in language.

Let us not be trapped by an analysis still encumbered with the old automatisms. It's not to be feared that language conceals an invincible adversary, because it's the language of men and their grammar. We mustn't leave them a single place that's any more theirs alone than we are.

If woman has always functioned "within" the discourse of man, a signifier that has always referred back to the opposite signifier which annihilates its specific energy and diminishes or stifles its very different sounds, it is time for her to dislocate this "within," to explode it, turn it around, and seize it; to make it hers, containing it, taking it in her own mouth, biting that tongue with her very own teeth to invent for herself a language to get inside of. And you'll see what ease will spring forth from that "within"—the "within" where once she so drowsily crouched—to overflow at the lips she will cover the foam.

Nor is it the point to appropriate their instruments, their concepts, their places, or to begrudge them their position of mastery. Just because there's a risk of identification doesn't mean that we'll succumb. Let's leave it to the worriers, to masculine anxiety and its obsession with how to dominate the way things work—knowing "how it works" in order to "make it work." For us the point is not to take possession in order to internalize or manipulate, but rather to dash through and to "fly."

Flying is woman's gesture—flying in language and making it fly. We have all learned the art of flying and its numerous techniques; for centuries we've been able to process anything only by flying; we've lived in flight, stealing away, finding, when desired, narrow passageways, hidden crossovers. It's no accident that *voler* has a double meaning, that it plays on each of them and thus throws off the agents of sense. It's no accident: women take after birds and robbers just as robbers take after women and birds. They go by, fly the coop, take pleasure in jumbling the order of space, in disorienting it, in changing around the furniture, dislocating things and values, breaking them all up, emptying structures, and turning propriety upside down.

What woman hasn't flown/stolen? Who hasn't felt, dreamt, performed the gesture that jams sociality? Who hasn't crumbled, held up to ridicule, the bar of separation? Who hasn't inscribed with her body the differential, punctured the system of couples and opposition? Who, by some act of transgression, hasn't overthrown successiveness, connection, the wall of circumfusion?

A feminine text cannot fail to be more than subversive. It is volcanic; as it is written it brings about an upheaval of the old property crust, carrier of masculine investments; there's no other way. There's no room for her if she's not a he. If she's a her-she, it's in order to smash everything, to shatter the framework of institutions, to blow up the law, to break up the "truth" with laughter. . . .

STUDY QUESTIONS

1. What reasons does Cixous provide for asserting the need for *écriture feminine*?
2. How does Cixous contrast Western culture with a feminine form of expression?

28.14 ANDREI DMITRIEVICH SAKHAROV, "HOW I CAME TO DISSENT," 1974

Andrei Dmitrievich Sakharov (1921–1989) was one of the Soviet Union's leading nuclear physicists and in the 1960s became an ardent pro-reform and antiwar activist. He was awarded the Nobel Peace Prize in 1975, but Soviet authorities did not allow him to travel to Stockholm to collect the award. He spent most of the 1970s and 1980s in internal exile in the city of Gorky (now Nizhny Novgorod), under constant government surveillance and effectively under house arrest. In 1986, Mikhail Gorbachev gave Sakharov and his wife, Yelena Bonner (likewise a human rights activist), permission to return to Moscow. Sakharov died there three years later.

From *The New York Review of Books*, March 21, 1974. Translation by Guy Daniels.

I was born in 1921 in Moscow, into a cultured and close family. My father was a teacher of physics and the author of several widely-known textbooks and popular-science books. From childhood I lived in an atmosphere of decency, mutual help and tact, a liking for work, and respect for the mastery of one's chosen profession. In 1938 I completed high school and entered Moscow State University, from which I was graduated in 1942. Between 1942 and 1945 I worked as an engineer at a war plant, where I developed several inventions having to do with methods of quality control.

Between 1945 and 1947 I did graduate work under the guidance of a well-known Soviet scientist, the theoretical physicist Igor Evgenevich Tamm. A few months after defending my dissertation in the spring of 1948, I was included in a research group working on the problem of a thermonuclear weapon. I had no doubts about the vital importance of creating a Soviet superweapon—for our country and for the balance of power throughout the world. Carried away by the immensity of the task, I worked very strenuously and became the author or co-author of several key ideas. In the Western press I have often been called "the father of the hydrogen bomb." This description reflects very inaccurately the real (and complex) situation of collective invention—something I shall not discuss in detail.

In the summer of 1950, almost simultaneously with the beginning of work on the thermonuclear weapon, I. E. Tamm and I began work on the problem of controlled thermonuclear reaction: i.e. on the use of the nuclear energy of light elements for purposes of industrial energetics. In 1950 we formulated the idea of the magnetic thermos-isolation of high-temperature plasma, and completed estimates on the parameters for thermonuclear synthesis installations. . . . I mention these things here by way of explaining that my contributions were not limited to military problems. . . . Our research group became part of a special institute. For the next eighteen years I found myself caught up in the rotation of a special world of military designers and inventors, special institutes, committees and learned councils, pilot plants and proving grounds. Every day I saw the huge material, intellectual, and nervous resources of thousands of people being poured into creating the means of total destruction, a force potentially capable of annihilating all human civilization. I noticed that the control levers were in the hands of people who, although talented in their own way, were cynical. Until the summer of 1953 the top boss of the atomic project was [Lavrentiy] Beria, who ruled over millions of slave-prisoners. Almost all the construction was done with their labor. Beginning in the late Fifties, one got an increasingly clearer picture of the collective might of the military-industrial complex and of its vigorous, unprincipled leaders, blind to everything except their "job." . . .

Beginning in 1957 (not without the influence of statements on this subject made throughout the world by such people as Albert Schweizer, Linus Pauling, and others) I felt myself responsible for the problem of radioactive contamination from nuclear explosions. As is known, the absorption of the radioactive products of nuclear explosions by the billions of people inhabiting the earth leads to an increase in the incidence of several diseases and birth defects because of so-called sub-threshold biological effects; for example, because of damage to DNA molecules—the bearers of heredity. When the radioactive products of an explosion get into the atmosphere, each megaton of the power of a nuclear explosion means thousands of victims. And each series of tests of a nuclear weapon (whether they be conducted by the US, the USSR, Great Britain, China, or France) involves tens of megatons; i.e. tens of thousands of victims.

In my attempts to explain this problem, I encountered great difficulties—and a reluctance to understand. I wrote memorandums . . . and I spoke at conferences. I remember that in the summer of 1961 there was a meeting between atomic scientists and the chairman of the Council of Ministers, [Nikita] Khrushchev. It turned out that we were to prepare for a series of tests which would bolster up the new policy of the USSR on the German question (the Berlin Wall). I wrote a note to Khrushchev, saying: "To resume tests after a three-year moratorium would undermine the talks on banning tests and on disarmament, and would lead to a new round in the armaments race—especially in the sphere of intercontinental missiles and anti-missile defense."

I passed it up the line. Khrushchev put the note in his breast pocket and invited all present to dine.

At the dinner table he made an off-the-cuff speech which I remember for its frankness, and which did not merely reflect his personal position. He said more or less the following: *Sakharov is a good scientist. But leave it to us, who are specialists in this tricky business, to make foreign policy.* . . .

Early in 1968 I began work on a book which I called *Thoughts on Progress, Peaceful Coexistence, and Intellectual Freedom*. I wanted that book to reflect my thoughts on the most important problems facing mankind: thoughts on war and peace, on dictatorship, on the prohibited subject of Stalinist terror and freedom of thought, on demographic problems and the pollution of the environment, on the role that can be played by science and technological progress. The general tenor of the book was affected by the time of its writing—the height of the "Prague Spring." . . . Today I regard this work as eclectic, pretentious in places, and imperfect ("raw") in terms of form. Nonetheless its basic ideas are dear to me. In it I formulated the thesis (which strikes me as very important) that the rapprochement of the socialist and capitalist systems, accompanied by democratization, demilitarization, and social and technological progress, is the only alternative to the ruin of mankind.

Beginning in May and June of 1968, *Thoughts* was widely distributed in the USSR. This was the first work of mine which was taken up by samizdat. In July and August came the first foreign reports of my book. Subsequently *Thoughts* was repeatedly published abroad in large printings and provoked a great flow of responses in the press of many countries. . . . The publication of *Thoughts* abroad immediately resulted in my being taken off secret projects (in August of 1968). . . .

Events in society and an inner need to oppose injustice continued to urge me toward new actions. Early in 1970 another open letter to the leaders of the state was published . . . on the inter-dependence of the problems of democratization and techno-economic progress. In June I took an active part in the campaign to free the biologist Zhores Medvedev from illegal confinement in a psychiatric hospital. About the same time I joined in a collective supervisory protest to the Procurator's Office USSR on the case of General P. G. Grigorenko, who by decision of a Tashkent court had been sent for compulsory treatment to a special prison-type hospital. . . . The reason for this was the fact that Grigorenko had repeatedly made public appeals in defense of political prisoners and in defense of the rights of the Crimean Tatars, who in 1944 had been resettled from the Crimea with great cruelties under the Stalinist tyranny, and who today cannot return to their homeland. . . . I was thus brought into contact with what was perhaps one of the most shameful aspects of present-day Soviet reality: illegality and the cynical persecution of persons coming out in defense of basic human rights. . . .

Before proceeding further, I should like to say a few words about why I attach so much importance to the matter of defending political prisoners—defending the freedom of one's convictions. In the course of fifty-six years our country has undergone great shocks, sufferings, and humiliations, the physical annihilation of millions of the best people (best both morally and intellectually), decades of official hypocrisy and demagoguery, or internal and external time-serving. The era of terror, when tortures and special conferences threatened everyone, when they seized the most devoted servants of the regime simply for the general count and to create an atmosphere of fright and submission—that era is now behind us.

But we are still living in the spiritual atmosphere created by that era. Against those few who do not go along with the prevalent practice of compromise, the government uses repression as before. Together with judicial repressions, the most important and decisive role in maintaining this atmosphere of internal and external submission is played by the power of the state, which manipulates all the levers of economic and social control. This, more than anything else, keeps the body and soul of the majority of people in a state of dependence.

Another major influence on the psychological situation in the country is the fact that people are weary of endless promises of economic flowering in the very near future, and have ceased altogether to believe in fine words. The standard of living (food, clothing, housing, possibilities for leisure), social conditions (children's facilities, medical and educational institutions, pensions, labor protections, etc.)—all this lags far behind the level in advanced countries. An indifference to social problems—an attitude of consumerism and selfishness—is developing among the broad strata of the population. And among the majority, protest against the deadening official ideology has an unconscious, latent character. The religious and national movements are the broadest and most conscious. Among those who fill the camps or are subjected to other persecutions are many believers and representatives of national minorities.

One of the mass forms of protest is the desire to leave the country. Unfortunately, it must be noted that sometimes the striving toward a national revival takes on chauvinistic traits, and borders on the traditional "everyday" hostility toward "aliens." Russian anti-Semitism is an example of this. Thus a part of the Russian opposition intelligentsia is beginning to manifest a paradoxical closeness to the secret Party-State doctrine of nationalism, which in fact is increasingly replacing the antinational and antireligious myth of Bolshevism. Among some people the same feeling of dissatisfaction and internal protest takes on other asocial forms (drunkenness, crime).

It is very important that the façade of prosperity and enthusiasm not conceal from the world this real picture of things. Our experience must not come to nothing. And it is equally important that our society gradually emerge from the dead end of unspirituality, which closes off the possibilities not only for the development of spiritual culture but for progress in the material sphere. . . .

I should like to talk about that part of the Western liberal intelligentsia (still a small part) which extends its activities to the socialist countries as well. These people look to the Soviet dissenters for a reciprocal, analogous international position with respect to other countries. But there are several important circumstances they do not take into account: the lack of information; the fact that a Soviet dissenter is not only unable to go to other countries but is deprived, within his own country, of the majority of sources of information; that the historical experience of our country has weaned us away from excessive "leftism," so that we evaluate many facts differently from the "leftist" intelligentsia of the West; that we must avoid political pronouncements in the international arena, where we are so ignorant (after all, we do not engage in political activity in our own country); that we must avoid getting into the channel of Soviet propaganda, which so often deceives us.

We know that in the Western countries there are vigilant and influential forces which protest (better and more effectively than we do) against injustice and violence there. We do not justify injustice or violence, wherever they appear. We do not feel that there is necessarily more of both in our country than in other countries. But at the moment our strength cannot suffice for the whole world. We ask that all this be taken into account, and that we be forgiven the errors we sometimes make in the dust kicked up by polemics.

STUDY QUESTIONS

1. How does Sakharov describe the spiritual and psychological atmosphere of the Soviet Union in 1974?
2. What are the reasons Sakharov gives for defending the rights of political prisoners?
3. How does Sakharov view Western "liberal intelligentsia"?

28.15 RONALD REAGAN AND MIKHAIL GORBACHEV, *ON NUCLEAR DEFENSE*, 1985–1987

The 1980s were the final decade of the Cold War. Whereas the period between 1942 and 1962 marked the most hostile stage and 1962 to 1979 was the era of détente, the final stage saw the Soviet invasion of Afghanistan and the rise of Mikhail Gorbachev (1931–2022). The invasion cost the Soviets dearly and taxed their military heavily. Gorbachev exerted efforts (successfully, it turned out) to democratize his country's political system and decentralize the Soviet economy. His support of reformist Communist leaders in Soviet bloc countries in Eastern Europe led to their eventual secession from the USSR, and his reforms over several years between 1985 and 1991 led to the fall of the Berlin Wall. Gorbachev's counterpart in the United States, Ronald Reagan (1911–2004), was a former actor who became president in 1981 and presided over American foreign policy during this period, becoming one of the most popular modern presidents. In these excerpts, tension over weapons of mass destruction is still front and center in relations between the two countries, notwithstanding the imminent collapse of the Soviet system.

REAGAN ON SDI

My fellow Americans:

In a television address to the nation on March 23, 1983, I challenged the scientific community to change the course of history by embarking on a research effort to counter Soviet threats with measures purely defensive—measures to reassure people their security no longer depends alone on threats of mutual nuclear annihilation to deter a Soviet attack, but measures enabling us to interpret and destroy ballistic missiles before they reach our soil or that of our allies. A nonnuclear strategic defense makes good sense. It's better to protect lives than to avenge them. But another reason, equally simple and compelling, persuades us to its merit. As the Book of Luke says: "If a strong man shall keep his court well guarded, he shall live in peace." Well, SDI, our Strategic Defense Initiative, could prove crucial to guarding security and peace for America and her allies.

The strategic challenges we face are far different from those in 1972, when the United States and the Soviet Union signed the SALT I and antiballistic missile treaties. When those treaties were signed, certain assumptions about the Soviets were made that—well, to put it charitably—have not proven justified. For example, it was assumed that the treaties would lead to a stable balance and, ultimately, to real reductions in strategic arms. But the Soviet Union has never accepted any meaningful and verifiable reduction in offensive nuclear arms—none. It was assumed the treaties were based on acceptance of parity in offensive weapon systems, but the Soviets have continued to race for superiority. As former Secretary of Defense Harold Brown put it, "When we build, they build." It was assumed that the Soviets would accept the innocent notion that being mutually vulnerable to attack was in our common interest. They haven't.

From Jussi Hanhimäki and Odd Arne Westad, *The Cold War: A History in Documents and Eyewitness Accounts*. New York: Oxford University Press, 2004, pp. 307–10. *The Cold War: A History in Documents and Eyewitness Accounts*. New York: Oxford University Press, © 2004.

The Soviets have repeatedly condemned as provocative our research on defense against their first-strike missiles, while blanketing their own country with the most sophisticated air defense system ever seen to protect against our second-strike bombers. And while we dismantled our long ABM system 10 years ago, the Soviets have consistently improved the world's only missile defense system deployed around Moscow. They've also developed and deployed the world's only operational killer satellite system and then proceeded to condemn the United States for daring even to test such a weapon.

It was assumed that an effective defense would not be feasible until 1972. But in that very year, Soviet Marshal Grechko testified to the Supreme Soviet: "The treaty on limiting ABM systems imposes no limitations on the performance of research and experimental work aimed at resolving the problem of defending the country against nuclear missile attack." Thus, the Soviets have devoted a huge share of the military budget to a sophisticated strategic defense program which, in resources already allocated, far exceeds what the United States anticipates spending in the current decade.

Finally, it was assumed that the agreements signed would be complied with, but the Soviets are seriously violating them in both offensive and defensive areas. It is the Soviet Union that has violated the 1972 ABM treaty with its construction of a massive radar facility at Krasnoyarsk. Further, the Soviet Union has tested and deployed sophisticated air defense systems which we judge may have capabilities against ballistic missiles.

Given these facts, is it not preposterous for the Soviets, already researching defense technologies for two decades, to now condemn our embryonic SDI program? As Paul Nitze, one of my chief arms control advisors, pointed out, Soviet hypocrisy is even more glaring when we realize who's taking advantage of our open society to propagandise against our SDI program. A letter to the *New York Times* denouncing SDI was signed by the very Soviet scientists who've been developing the Soviet strategic defense program; other Soviet scientists who signed have spent their entire careers developing offensive weapons. I intend to mention this when I meet with Mr. Gorbachev in Geneva this November. I will tell him that the United States not only has the right to go forward with research for a strategic missile defense, but in the light of the scale of their program we'd be the greatest fools on Earth not to do so.

We're going to put our best scientists to work. We're going to cooperate with our allies. We're going to push forward compliance with the ABM treated on a broad-based research program, whose results to date are immensely encouraging. And, yes, I hope we will one day develop a security shield that destroys weapons, not people.

Until next week, thanks for listening. God bless you.

MIKHAIL GORBACHEV ON THE ARMS RACE, 1987

Pondering the question of what stands in the way of good Soviet–American relations, one arrives at the conclusion that, for the most part, it is the arms race. I am not going to describe its history. Let me just note once again that at almost all its stages the Soviet Union has been the party catching up. By the beginning of the seventies we had reached approximate military–strategic parity, but on a level that is really frightening. Both the Soviet Union and the United States now have the capacity to destroy each other many times over.

It would seem logical, in the face of strategic stalemate, to halt the arms race and get down to disarmament. But the reality is different. Armouries already overflowing continue to be filled with sophisticated new types of weapons, and new areas of military technology are being developed. The U.S. sets the tone in this dangerous, if not fatal pursuit.

It shall not disclose any secret if I tell you that the Soviet Union is doing all that is necessary to maintain up-to-date and reliable defenses. This is our duty to our own people and our allies. At the same time I wish to say quite definitely that this is not our choice. It has been imposed on us.

All kinds of doubts are being spread among Americans about Soviet intentions in the field of disarmament. But history shows that we can keep the word we have and that we honor the obligations assumed. Unfortunately, this cannot be said of the United States. The administration is conditioning public opinion, intimidating it with a Soviet threat, and does so with particular stubbornness when a new military budget has to be passed through Congress. We have to ask ourselves why all this is being done and what aim the U.S. pursues.

. . .

We sincerely advise Americans: try to get rid of such an approach to our country. Hopes of using any advantages in technology or advanced equipment so as to gain superiority over our country are futile. To act on the assumption that the Soviet Union is in a "hopeless position" and that it is necessary just to press it harder to squeeze out everything the U.S. wants is to err profoundly. Nothing will come of these plans. In real politics there can be no wishful thinking. If the Soviet Union, when it was much weaker than now, was in a position to meet all the challenges that it faced, then indeed only a blind person would be unable to see that our capacity to maintain strong defences and simultaneously resolve social and other tasks has enormously increased.

I shall repeat that as far as the United States foreign policy is concerned, it is based on at least two delusions. The first is the belief that the economic system of the Soviet Union is about to crumble and that the USSR will not succeed in restructuring. The second is calculated on Western superiority in equipment and technology and, eventually, in the military field. These illusions nourish a policy geared toward exhausting socialism through the arms race, so as to dictate terms later. Such is the scheme; it is naïve.

STUDY QUESTIONS

1. In what terms and with what degree of success does Reagan advocate the desirability of his Strategic Defense Initiative (SDI)?
2. Why was the prospect of SDI so frightening to the Soviets?

CHAPTER 29

GLOBAL WARMINGS

29.1 HALIDÉ EDIB ADIVAR, *MEMOIRS*, 1926 AND 1928

Halidé Edib Adivar (1884–1964) was a Turkish feminist and writer, best known for novels focusing on the status of Turkish women. Born in Constantinople (Istanbul), she was connected by family to the court of the Ottoman sultan Abdul Hamid II and educated in a multilingual environment, where she learned Arabic, English, and French. One of a new generation of women, her experiences spanned the old world of harems as well as the new world of professional women. Her early career involved writing articles on education for newspapers and work for the ministry of education. Her memoir is not particularly personal, focusing as it largely does on Turkey's struggle for nationhood after the fall of the Ottoman Empire in World War I and the nationalist politics of its first "modern" leader, Kemal Ataturk.

One night about this time I begged granny to allow me to learn to read. "Thy father does not want thee to learn before thou art seven," she said. "It is stupid of him. *I* started at three, and in my days children of seven knew the Quran by heart." In spite of this I kept bothering her and even speaking to father about it, so that he at last consented, although I was not fully six yet. Thereupon the house began to get ready to celebrate my *bashlanmak*, my entrance into learning.

Little children in Turkey started to school in those days with a pretty ceremony. A little girl was dressed in silk covered with jewels, and a gold-embroidered bag, with an alphabet inside, was hung round her neck with a gold-tasselled cord. She sat in an open carriage, with a damask silk cushion at her feet. All the pupils of the school walked in procession after the carriage, forming two long tails on either side. The older ones were the hymn-singers, usually singing the very popular hymn, "The rivers of paradise, as they flow, murmur, 'Allah, Allah.' The angels in paradise, as they walk, sing, 'Allah. Allah.'" At the end of each stanza hundreds of little throats shouted, *"Amin, amin!"*

From H. Edib, *The Memoirs of Halidé Edib*. London: John Murray, 1926, pp. 11–4, 85–8, 142–8. Halidé Edib, *The Turkish Ordeal: Further Memoirs*. London: John Murray, 1928, pp. 25–34 (excerpts). Internet Archive via Public Library of India.

They went through several streets in this way, drawing into the procession the children and waifs from the quarters they passed through until they reached school. In the school the new pupil knelt on her damask cushion before a square table, facing the teacher. Kissing the hand of the instructor, she repeated the alphabet after her. Some sweet dish would then be served to the children, and each child received a bright new coin given by the parents of the pupil to be. After this sort of consecration, the little one went every day to school, fetched by the *kalfa*, an attendant who went from one house to another collecting the children from the different houses.

The ceremony was as important as a wedding, and fond parents spent large sums in the effort to have a grander ceremony than their neighbours. Each family who could afford a costly *bashlanmak* would arrange for a few poor children of the quarter to share the ceremony and would thenceforward pay their schooling, as well as that of their own child. The old systematic philanthropy of the Ottomans, although fast disappearing, was not entirely dead yet.

The sight of a children's procession with the grand carriage had always caused me a certain excitement, mixed, however, with a longing to be the little girl in the carriage and fear of being the centre of attraction in public.

Father had arranged that I was not to begin by going to school, but a hodja was to come and give me lessons at home. The *bashlanmak* too in my case was not to be the usual one. There was to be a big dinner at home for the men, and the ceremony was to take place at home after the night prayers.

Granny had her own way about my dress for once. She could not bear to have me begin my reading of the holy Quran in a blue serge dress. I remember well the champagne-coloured silk frock with lovely patterns on it, and the soft silk veil of the same colour, that she got for me instead.

A large number of guests arrived, both from our own neighbourhood and also from the palace.

Some one held a mirror in front of me after I was dressed, and I looked strange with the veil over my hair and bedecked with the really beautiful jewels of the palace lady. Fikriyar was moved to tears. "Thou shalt wear a bride's dress and I will hold thy train one day," she said. She was wishing me the one possible felicity for a Turkish woman.

. . . All ceremonies in Turkey, even marriages and Bairams, tend to take on a sad and solemn tone; always the women with wet eyes and the men in softened silent mood. What makes other people rejoice makes the Turk sad.

. . .

I believe indeed that there are as many degrees and forms of jealousy as there are degrees and forms of human affection. But even supposing that time and education are able to tone down this very elemental feeling, the family problem will still not be solved; for the family is the primary unit of human society, and it is the integrity of this smallest division which is, as a matter of fact, in question. The nature and consequences of the suffering of a wife, who in the same house shares a husband lawfully with a second and equal partner, differs both in kind and in degree from that of the woman who shares him with a temporary mistress. In the former case, it must also be borne in mind, the suffering extends to two very often considerable groups of people—children, servants, and relations—two whole groups whose interests are from the very nature of the case more or less antagonistic, and who are living in a destructive atmosphere of mutual distrust and a struggle for supremacy.

In my own childhood, polygamy and its results produced a very ugly and distressing impression. The constant tension in our home made every simple family ceremony seem like a physical pain, and the consciousness of it hardly ever left me.

The rooms of the wives were opposite each other, and my father visited them by turns. When it was Teizé's turn everyone in the house showed a tender sympathy to Abla, while when it was her turn no one heeded the obvious grief of Teizé. It was she indeed who could conceal her suffering least. She would leave the table with eyes full of tears, and one could be sure of finding her in her room either crying or fainting. Very soon I noticed that father left her alone with her grief.

. . .

The wives never quarreled, and they were always externally polite, but one felt a deep mutual hatred accumulating in their hearts, to which they gave vent only when each was alone with father. He wore the look of a man who was getting more than his just punishment now. Finally, he took to having a separate room, where he usually sat alone. But he could not escape the gathering storm in his new life. Hava Hanum not inaptly likened his marriage to that of Nassireddin Hodja. She told it to us as if she was glad to see father unhappy. The hodja also wanted to taste the blessed state of polygamy, and took to himself a young second wife. Before many months were out his friends found the hodja completely bald, and asked him the reason. "My old wife pulls out all my black hairs so that I may look as old as she; my young wife pulls out my white hairs so that I may look as young as she. Between them I am bald."

. . .

THE OCCUPATION OF SMYRNA

I had another telephone call the next morning. It was from the Ojak.

"Come at once," said the voice. "We are going to have a meeting to protest against the massacres in Smyrna; all the student associations have joined."

. . .

"Going to the mountain" is a Turkish term which means the raising of the standards of revolt. I had a profound sympathy with any "going to the mountain" feeling at the moment. I was feeling most bitter not only against the Allies, who had inaugurated their policy of spoliation in Turkey with such ugly bloodshed, but also against all the Turkish leaders, past and present, who had driven the poor Turks into the adventure of the great war, or who were now at each other's throats from more or less personal motives, complicating and endangering the people's chances of ever standing on their feet. Somehow neither the presence of the Allied armies nor the sorry state of Turkish politics prevented a great number of Turkish youths from going to the Smyrna mountains before many months had passed after the events I am recording.

. . .

The people had gathered in big groups before the square in front of the municipality building. They were to be addressed from the balcony. As I looked up and realized how far my voice would have to carry, over a mass of people estimated at fifty thousand, I quailed; but at that instant, by a dramatic coincidence, something happened which engulfed me in a great storm of sorrow, to the exclusion of every other feeling. There, over the red flags and their white crescents, which were hanging down and waving in the gentle breeze, an enormous black drapery was being lowered. This sight, so sudden and so dramatic, roused such emotion—coming as it did on top of my small material fear for my voice—that I immediately had the poignant feeling of a woman who sees her most beloved covered with a shroud. As the soft black draperies swayed, patches or bits of brilliant red slits appeared and disappeared like streaks of flowing blood. Some one evidently with an unconscious feeling for the psychology of the masses had conceived the idea. But I was caught by its symbolic tragedy as much as any simple man in the street; the palpitation and its pain were so strong that I had actually to lean against the railings of the garden and wait before I could proceed. . . .

Leaning over the black draperies on the railings of the balcony I fell under the spell of a sea of faces.

The centre of the mass was formed by a compact group of soldiers and officers. In the front and around the soldiers was a thick circular human wall composed of women dressed in black, mostly young, and their faces, the drapery of their black veils shading them from the shimmering sun, were strangely quivering with emotion and ecstasy. The rest seemed all white turbans, red fezzes, and a few hats. But one had a very dim impression of the coloured tops—the necks seemed to be screwed backward, all the faces seemed to be screwed upward and kept in that position with absolute immobility. And there were eyes, thousands of them, glistening, shooting their message and their desire. This feeling of what they wanted me to say was so clear that I had the sense of repeating what they were thinking. I realized that their supreme demand was identical with mine. We all longed for hope, for absolute belief in our rights and in our own strength, and I gave them what they wanted: "Brothers, sisters, countrymen, Moslems: When the night is darkest and seems eternal, the light of dawn is nearest." I began thus, and my voice as I spoke struck against the broken column opposite, a memorial for the airmen killed in the war, and came back to me in a distant echo. It was a strange coincidence that this column should be the agent which kept my voice in the square and made it audible to each one in the crowd. Somehow, between my voice and the faces screwed round on the necks below, there was a wonderfully intimate communication. I hardly thought it was my voice speaking. I listened to what it said as a creature aloof, believing in and feeling comforted by its message as much as any one of the crowd down below. The voice was telling them to trust in their own rights and to lean on their own strength, the strength which is not of machines but of brave hearts and unconquerable ideals. We were hardly conscious of two aeroplanes which policed the crowd and flew so low sometimes that in ordinary circumstances we would have been terrified.

. . .

As I set foot on the tribune I knew that one of the rare, one of the very rare, moments of my life had come to me. I was galvanized in every atom of my being by a force which at any other time would have killed me, but which at that crisis gave me the power to experience—to know—the quintessence of the suffering and desire of those two hundred thousand souls.

I believe that the Halidé of Sultan Ahmed is not the ordinary, everyday Halidé. The humblest sometimes can be the incarnation of some great ideal of some great nation. That particular Halidé was very much alive, palpitating with the message of Turkish hearts, a message which prophesied the great tragedy of the coming years.

STUDY QUESTIONS

1. How did women's roles in this society contrast with those of men at every stage of their lives?
2. What did young women and men share in Turkey in the aftermath of World War I?

29.2 FATIMA MERNISSI, "THE STORY OF A FEMALE PSYCHIC," 1989

Fatima Mernissi (1940–2015) was a Moroccan feminist and sociologist. After studying at the Sorbonne in Paris, she received her PhD from Brandeis University before returning to Morocco. Mernissi's work largely focused on the role of women within Islam, and she examined the ways in which traditional Islamic cultures have treated women versus how the Qur'an (the source of much of Islamic "orthodoxy") treats them. Her first book, *Beyond the Veil* (1975), became a classic in the fields of anthropology and sociology. *Doing Daily Battle: Interviews with Moroccan Women* (1989) was prompted in part by the suggestion that feminism was a Western concern. For the book, Mernissi interviewed a hundred women, mostly from the lower classes, and collected a great deal of material on diverse subjects such as culinary culture, spirituality, sex, and family.

As for my present condition, that began when I was a small child. My brothers and sisters would begin to tickle me and I would black out. I wouldn't regain consciousness until they put my hand in water or had me inhale something that had been burned in fire. If someone tickled me, I would run away from there like mad. My father, may Allah rest his soul, would yell at the children, ordering them to stop: "Leave your sister alone, don't tickle her any more," he told them over and over.

Q: *How old were you when it began?*

A: I was ten or eleven. You see, I was very young. . . . There was an animal that had a terrible effect on me, worse even than the tickling: I mean frogs. I was terrified of frogs. It was enough for someone to say the word in front of me for me to go crazy. If I had something in my hand, I threw it; I became aggressive, chased other people. Yes, I became crazy. I began to scream like a mad person, screaming until I lost consciousness. My poor father tried to prevent this from happening, to protect me. He forbade my brothers and sisters to torment me. And because of all that, this thing that I have began to get worse. I remember one day when I was invited to visit my brother. My son Muhammad was still a baby. Someone said the word "*jrana*" [frog] in front of me. I fell upon my baby and I nearly killed him. I lost consciousness. My brother was so upset that he swore that from then on he would take to court anybody who tried to excite me: "You know perfectly well that my sister has an attack when she hears that word, so avoid saying it in front of her!"

Q: *Was your first husband aware of the situation?*

A: Yes, I used to have attacks when I was living with him after our marriage, if someone upset me. But, you see, he didn't believe in it; he used to say to me, "You are crazy." He didn't have faith, he didn't believe at all in that. So when he saw me having a seizure, he would cry out, "I think this woman is crazy." In fact, he was rather inflexible; he didn't believe at all in the power of the djinns. He was a very ordinary man; I never understood him. He had an odd manner about him. I stayed with him for five or six years.

Q: *He didn't believe in those things?*

A: He didn't believe in them at all. But when I had an attack, you see I have to admit that he did take care of me. But he had a sort of pride, it was as if he was ashamed in front of others when this happened to me. We lived on a farm in the country, and he didn't want people to see me in that state or to know about it. When there were strangers in the house, he would lock me up and ask neighbouring women to take care of me.

Q: *And your second husband? What is his attitude about the djinns? Did you tell him about it before you got married?*

A: Yes, he knew all about it when he married me. You see, although he doesn't have any legs, he helps me when I have an attack. If the seizure comes upon me when I am near a puddle of water, he throws himself on top of me, tries to pull me away, and calls people to my aid. He gets them to carry me to a clean place; then he washes off my clothes, rubs me with benzoin, puts my head on his shoulder, and calms me. Life went on like this until I got pregnant. I got pregnant two or three times with him, but it always came to nothing. You see, he had been married before meeting me. The parents of his first wife came and threatened me in order to make me leave him and thus force him to return to their daughter. They threatened me with a knife, and that incident made my seizures worse.

. . .

A: . . . I began to see things after having made the "blood sacrifice." I bought a cow for 800 dirhams without giving a thought to the price. I invited the *muqaddam*, who came accompanied by fourteen people, not counting the women.

. . .

A: . . . You know, there are several kinds of spirits. We leave people free; we try to be flexible with them; but in fact, each person is possessed by their own *malik*, their own master spirit. Each one of us, the possessed, dances their own dance: one handles fire, another pours water on the head to feel well, and still another must tear their clothes to find relief. Another, seeing a person they don't like, runs after him and hits him. That's the way it is in our world. When I had carried out the celebration and danced and cured some people, I began to receive others. For the next Prophet's birthday, I paid the expenses of a Ganawi celebration. The tray that I offered to Lalla

Malika cost me 200 dirhams; I had to put on it a variety of things, such as *siwak*, watermelon, seeds, figs. The piles of things must be placed on this tray so that there will be *hajba*.

Q: *What does hajba mean?*

A: Hajba means the tray must be isolated in a room which no one goes into, especially children. You cover the tray, which has been very carefully arranged. If someone enters the room and takes something without permission, they put their life in danger. One of my nieces, who was seventeen years old, was touched that night. She didn't know what was going on, the poor thing. Now she is touched, she too.

Q: *She went into the room where the tray was?*

A: No, it happened when we put the scarf on the horns of the cow.

Q: *When the cow was being sacrificed? At that moment?*

A: Yes, just then. When she saw the cow with the scarves, she let out a crazy laugh. Then "they" struck her. Now she dances more than I do. I stopped after a certain time; she, the poor thing, continues. I have really tried to intervene with "them" to free her, but in vain. One time a participant at the Hamdushi ceremony that I had organised got up to dance. In twelve years Lalla Aisha had never made an appearance to her. That night Lalla Aisha came. I begged her to free my niece: "Why has my niece been chosen? She is only a child. It is right for you to choose me, who is beginning to age, who has lived a long time and has accepted life's hard knocks. But she is a girl; she still knows nothing of life." She replied to me: "We want our family to grow. You don't want to be our only kin, do you? That's why we are going to keep her among us." So, my niece was obliged to pay all the expenses necessary for the ceremonies; she had to finance all the activities for healing, and today she is possessed. She "sees" everything. She sees everything just as I see everything.

Q: *Does she practice as a psychic, like you?*

A: No, she doesn't "see" for others. She sees imaginary beings. Sometimes she sees Lalla Aisha beside her; she sees herself travelling with Lalla Aisha, accompanying her everywhere. As soon as she sees her, she laughs in her face. She has never recovered, the poor thing.

. . .

Q: *How long have you been practicing as a psychic?*

A: Three years.

The visit of a young black man . . .

Q: *You began by charging two dirhams for a séance?*

A: Yes, exactly. The day that Allah willed that my resources be augmented, I saw a young black man, black as that young man there across from you. He was like him, very similar in appearance, except that his hair stood on end.

Q: *Did you see that young man in a dream or in reality?*

A: I saw him in a dream. Latifa, a "teacher" like me, was here. She had just come to tell me that someone was at the door and wanted to see me. I opened the door and found myself face to face with this young black man. We greeted each other, and then he said at once: "Are you the woman who uses the *ladun*?" "Yes," I answered. Then he put me to a test: "What do you do for someone who comes to you sick?" "If you want to see what I do, then come in. I will show you. If you are a believer, you are welcome." I was very afraid of him. "Why are you afraid?" he asked me. "Master, people are afraid of me, and I am afraid of you. In the name of God, who are you?" "I am the Master of the *Ladun*." I grabbed him by his clothes and pulled him with all my strength to the sofa where I pushed him down. "How do you use the *ladun*?" he asked. "I give it to my visitor to hold in the hand; then I throw it in the fire, and then in cold water. Afterwards I look into it, and I see." "Next time do the same thing, but on the head of your visitor, like this," he said, acting out his words. Then he ordered me to "do" the *ladun* on him. I began by passing the *ladun* over his head with my right hand. He grabbed my hand in his, saying, "Very good, seventy rials [three and a half dirhams], and you really deserve it." You know, I remember every detail of that dream. It was five months ago that I met that man in my dream, but the dream remains engraved in my memory in its smallest details . . . and its consequences.

The next day I didn't dare announce the new fee to my visitors. At the beginning I used to accept any donation at all, even just a bit of benzoin. I was embarrassed to announce this rise in my fee to my visitors. I could already hear what they would say: "You know our Morocco." Once their tongues were loosened, if they decided to attack me, they would not try to look for the reason that had impelled me to act. So the day after that dream, I was unwilling to announce the rise to my clientele. That same evening a black woman appeared to me in a dream. She wore three rings, one in her nose, another in her ear, and a third was hanging from her lower lip. She made them clang against each other and lashed out at me: "You refused to obey orders. You refused to announce to people that your fee would be seventy rials from now on. You will see what is going to happen to you now. You will suffer the consequences of your act. We are going to burn you. You were more afraid of people than of us. We are going to burn your mouth. Your wound will linger for a year." I was terrified. I had already been suffering for a year from a wound in the foot that wouldn't heal. And now I was supposed to have committed an offence against "them"! I had already lost a finger in this business. So, with these threats, I was terrified and had to announce the new fee to my clientele.

One day, at eleven o'clock in the morning, there was a knock at the door. There was no one there, just thirty rials on the ground. I called to my daughter, "You are irresponsible, dropping coins in the face of His Majesty Hassan II on the ground." But it was not she who had put the money there. I realised then that it had to be the spirits, because the thirty rials was the amount of the rise in my fee. So I announced my new fee to everyone. To those who protested, I said that I was going to put my life in danger and there was nothing I could do for them. I showed them the marks of the three burns on my leg, three scars as big as a rial, which appeared after the dream. I still have those marks. Here, look. [Habiba then showed me her leg, where the traces could actually be seen.]

. . .

AN ILLITERATE WOMAN WRITES CHARMS

Q: *And writing charms, how does that go?*

A: It depends on the age of the client. If it's for a sick child, I write it for 200 rials. If it's for a grownup, I charge double, 400 rials. Sometimes people simply have to burn a selection of things in a brazier at home; the smoke is supposed to be purifying and dissipates the *thiqaf*. They give me money—it is not a fixed sum—and it is I who then buy them the necessary items. The other day two men came to see me.

. . .

Q: *How is it done? Do you write while awake or asleep?*

A: I write while awake, but in fact it is not I who writes. My hand moves by itself, as if it were connected to a machine, in the space of a few minutes. I can write forty or fifty charms very easily. But it is not I who writes. All I do is carry out the orders of my *faqih*, whom I obey and in whom I have total confidence. It is he who writes for me. I write charms for different problems: to help a young girl get married, to solve work problems, etc. I write charms in the evening. It is my *faqih*, who instructs me; he reveals things to me, shows me things I don't know about.

STUDY QUESTIONS

1. Was belief in djinns inconsistent with Islamic belief and practice in this society?
2. What role does the interviewer play in eliciting the subject's comments?

29.3 FRANCIS FUKUYAMA, "OUR PESSIMISM," 1992

Francis Fukuyama (b. 1952) is an American political scientist and author best known, perhaps, for his 1992 book *The End of History and the Last Man*. Fukuyama received a doctorate in political science from Harvard University and worked at the Rand Corporation and the US Department of State, specializing in Middle East and then European affairs. He has also taught at Johns Hopkins University and at Stanford. In *The End of History,* Fukuyama made the case that the ideological struggles that had beset Europe in the twentieth century had largely been resolved with the end of the Cold War in favor of the West, or at least of the Western idea of liberal democracy. This had triumphed over Communism, bringing the "end point of mankind's ideological evolution and the universalization of Western liberal democracy as the final form of human government."

The twentieth century, it is safe to say, has made all of us into deep historical pessimists.

As individuals, we can of course be optimistic concerning our personal prospects for health and happiness. By long-standing tradition, Americans as a people are said to be continually hopeful about the future. But when we come to larger questions, such as whether there has been or will be progress in history, the verdict is decidedly different. The soberest and most thoughtful minds of this century have seen no reason to think that the world is moving toward what we in the West consider decent and humane political institutions—that is, liberal democracy. Our deepest thinkers have concluded that there is no such thing as History—that is, a meaningful order to the broad sweep of human events. Our own experience has taught us, seemingly, that the future is more likely than not to contain new and unimagined evils, from fanatical dictatorships and bloody genocides to the banalization of life through modern consumerism, and that unprecedented disasters await us from nuclear winter to global warming.

The pessimism of the twentieth century stands in sharp contrast to the optimism of the previous one. Though Europe began the nineteenth century convulsed by war and revolution, it was by and large a century of peace and unprecedented increases in material well-being. There were two broad grounds for optimism. The first was the belief that modern science would improve human life by conquering disease and poverty. Nature, long man's adversary, would be mastered by modern technology and made to serve the end of human happiness. Second, free democratic governments would continue to spread to more and more countries around the world. The "Spirit of 1776," or the ideals of the French Revolution, would vanquish the world's tyrants, autocrats, and superstitious priests. Blind obedience to authority would be replaced by rational self-government, in which all men, free and equal, would have to obey no masters but themselves. In light of the broad

From Francis Fukuyama, *The End of History and the Last Man*. New York: Free Press, 2006, pp. 3–8; Reprinted with the permission of The Free Press, a Division of Simon & Schuster, Inc.

movement of civilization, even bloody wars like those of Napoleon could be interpreted by philosophers as socially progressive in their results, because they fostered the spread of republican government.

. . .

The extreme pessimism of our own country is due at least in part to the cruelty with which these earlier expectations were shattered.

. . .

Nineteenth-century theories of progress associated human evil with a backward state of social development. While Stalinism did arise in a backward, semi-European country known for its despotic government, the Holocaust emerged in a country with the most advanced industrial economy and one of the most cultured and well-educated populations in Europe. If such events could happen in Germany, why then could they not happen in any other advanced country? And if economic development, education, and culture were not a guarantee against a phenomenon like Nazism, what was the point of historical progress?

. . .

The traumatic events of the twentieth century formed the backdrop to a profound intellectual crisis as well. It is possible to speak of historical progress only if one knows where mankind is going. Most nineteenth-century Europeans thought that progress meant progress toward democracy. But for most of this century, there has been no consensus on this question. Liberal democracy was challenged by two major rival ideologies—fascism and communism—which offered radically different visions of a good society. People in the West themselves came to question whether liberal democracy was in fact a general aspiration of all mankind, and whether their earlier confidence that it was did not reflect a narrow ethnocentrism on their part. As Europeans were forced to confront the non-European world, first as colonial masters, then as patrons during the Cold War and theoretical equals in a world of sovereign nation states, they came to question the universality of their own ideals. The suicidal self-destructiveness of the European state system in two world wars gave the lie to the notion of superior Western rationality, while the distinction between civilized and barbarian that was instinctive to Europeans in the nineteenth century was much harder to make after the Nazi death camps. Instead of human history leading in a single direction, there seemed to be as many goals as there were peoples or civilizations, with liberal democracy having no particular privilege among them.

In our own time, one of the clearest manifestations of our pessimism was the almost universal belief in the permanence of a vigorous, communist-totalitarianism alternative to Western liberal democracy.

. . .

As recently as 1983, Jean-François Revel declared that "democracy may, after all, turn out to have been a historical accident, a brief parenthesis that is closing before our eyes."

STUDY QUESTIONS

1. What does Fukuyama see as the prospects for liberal democracy after its "challengers" had been defeated in the twentieth century?
2. Does democracy need a rival to continue being relevant?

29.4 LUCE IRIGARAY, FROM *AN ETHICS OF SEXUAL DIFFERENCE*, 1993

Born in Belgium in 1930, feminist, philosopher, and psychoanalyst Luce Irigaray earned PhDs in philosophy and linguistics and studied psychology at the University of Paris. She trained as a psychoanalyst under the well-known theorist and analyst Jacques Lacan. In the 1960s she began to work at the Centre Nationale de Recherche Scientifiques, where she became director. Irigaray played a significant role in the women's movement (MLF: Mouvement de libération des femmes) in the 1970s, being a leading figure in third wave feminism. The central theme of her work is the struggle to create an authentic understanding of femaleness. Ideas of gender, she says, are socially constructed around a system of binary relations, and these revolve around a male "norm" that is based in "gendered" language. *An Ethics of Sexual Difference* puts forward the idea that all thought and language is gendered, there being no purely neutral thought.

LOVE OF THE OTHER

If we are to have a sense of the other that is not projective or selfish, we have to attain an intuition of the infinite:

- either the intuition of a god or divine principle aiding in the birth of the other without pressuring it with our own desire,
- or the intuition of a subject that, at each point in the present, remains unfinished and open to a becoming of the other that is neither simply passive nor simply active.

If we fail to turn toward the other in this way, hatred becomes the *apeiron*, the dimension of the unfinished or of the Infinite [*de l'in-fini ou Infini*]. With this dimension being transmuted by and into a theory or a set of concepts which are not worked out on the basis of love of the other. As is virtually the norm in our tradition.

Consequently, the *Other* often stands in our tradition for *product of a hatred* for the *other.* Not intended to be open to interpretation. The Other constitutes a love of sameness that has no recognition of itself as such and is raised to the dimension of a transcendent that ensures and guards the whole world entity. In this way God functions as the keystone of language, of sign and symbol systems.

God is beyond this world, but supposedly he already ensures its coherence here and now. Fluid, an interstitial flux, that cements the unity of everything and allows us to believe that the love of sameness has been overcome, whereas in fact that love has been raised to an incalculable power and swallows up the love of the other—the maternal-feminine other—which has been assimilated to sameness. Equally annihilated by sameness is the nonthetic love of self, which still finds no representation.

This Other, placed as keystone to the whole order of language, of semantic architecture, has for centuries been scrupulously protected by the word of men, sometimes only by that of the clerics, in a kind of inescapable circularity or tautology: in order to protect that which or He Who offered them protection.

Nietzsche used to say that we would continue to believe in God as long as we believed in grammar. Yet even, or perhaps particularly after the fall of a certain God, discourse still defends its untouchable status. To say that discourse has a *sex*, especially in its syntax, is to question the last bastion of semantic order. It amounts to taking issue with the God of men in his most traditional form. Even if language is emptied of meaning?—respect for its technical architecture must remain intact. Discourse would be the erection of the *totem* and the *taboo* of the world of man.

And the more man strives to analyze the world, the universe, himself, the more he seems to resist *upsetting the foundations of discourse.* His analysis would serve only to confirm and double discourse's immutability. From the start, discourse would be for man that other of nature, that mother, that nature-womb, within which he lived, survived, and risked being lost. The discourse that had been intended as his tool for breaking ground and cultivating the world changed into an intangible, sacred horizon for him. That which is most his own and yet most alien to him? His home within the universe. And, inside that tentacular technical machine that man has made, a machine that threatens him today, not only stark reality but also by assimilation to his fantasies and the nightmares he has of a devouring mother, man seems to cling ever tighter to that semblance of familiarity he finds in both his everyday and his scientific discourse. As if that technical universe and that language were not his creation, which, because of its failure to preserve the other, fails to preserve him too. The work of his hand, in which he cannot even recognize himself, in which he has drowned the other, now threatens to drown him in turn. He has all the animist fears of a child in the face of nature. He is afraid to touch his machine in case it is activated by his approach, as if it were a mechanism owed respect because of its transcendence. Language, in all its shapes and sizes, would dimly represent for man the all-powerful and ever-unknown mother as well as the transcendent God. *Both.* Man cannot or will not recognize or reinterpret in his symbols this duality in his technical productions.

The most obvious symbol, that closest to hand and also most easily forgotten, is the *living symbol* of sexual difference. But theory would claim that this symbolizes only itself. And women would serve only as a potential symbol to be exchanged by men, by peoples, and would never achieve symbolism or be able to use symbols. Does the symbol constituted by sexual difference implacably split into two? The female would fall into the category of fallow land, matter to be made into a product, or currency symbol, mother or virgin without any identity as a woman. The masculine would no longer enter into the body or the flesh of the symbol but fashion it or pass it from hand to hand from the outside.

The bond between or the function shared by the pieces would be achieved secretly thanks to the female; the exchange of symbols would be assured by the masculine. By serving in this way as mediation from within the symbol, the feminine would have no access to sharing, exchanging, or coining symbols. In particular, the mother–daughter relationship, the attraction between mother and daughter, would be hidden in the symbol. Daughters, wives, and indeed mothers would not have, or would no longer have, signs available for their own relationships, or the means of designating a reality transcendent to themselves—their Other, their God or divine being. No articulated language would help women escape from the sameness of man or from an uninhabitable sameness of their own, lacking a passage from the inside to the outside of themselves, among themselves. Because they are used in mediation, as mediators, women can have within themselves and among themselves a *same*, an *Other* only if they move out of the existing systems of exchange. Their only recourse is flight, explosion, implosion, into an immediate relationship to nature or to God.

The cultural functions that women might have performed have been judged asocial and hence have been barred to them. They were accused of being *witches*, or *mystics*, because of the potency of the relations they maintained with the cosmos and the divine, even though they lacked any extrinsic or intrinsic way to express them, or express themselves. Useful in the elaboration of the Other of the masculine world, women could have only a forbidden Other of their own. Which was often called demonic possession whereas in fact it involves an ability to perceive the divine (*daimon*) to which man in his shell, his various shells, remains a stranger. In so far as he is alien to a sensible transcendental—the dimension of the divine par excellence—and of its grace, man would remain a little outside the religious world, unless he is initiated into it by women. And this happens in certain traditions. Even in our own, if one knows how to read certain texts: from the New Testament, from the Song of Songs, from the mystics, and so on. Given that our "tradition" is in fact a sedimentation laid down in its time by earlier traditions.

The sameness of women, among women, would always occur from and within *openness*, expansion. Generation. Threshold. Their Other without capital letters. Which is not to say that it has no reality or dimension that goes beyond the capital letters. Perhaps going beyond certain graphics or discourses already written down and consecrated? A cosmic, creative fermentation that is always and forever free. Though this is not it say it has no signs, no rhythms, no symbols, no god(s).

STUDY QUESTIONS

1. What are the consequences of females being gendered as "Other" in both language and society?
2. What results from the gendering of "God" as male?

29.5 MARTHA NUSSBAUM, "THE IDEA OF WORLD CITIZENSHIP," FROM *CULTIVATING HUMANITY: A CLASSICAL DEFENSE OF REFORM IN LIBERAL EDUCATION*, 1998

Martha Nussbaum (b. 1947) teaches philosophy and law at the University of Chicago and has written two dozen books and hundreds of articles. Her range is wide: from Stoic philosophy to modern feminism, from literary criticism to analyses of developing-world economies and systems of justice. Her 1997 book *Cultivating Humanity: A Classical Defense of Reform in Liberal Education* argues for the importance of humanistic studies in higher education advocates the study of non-Western cultures and the study of domestic minorities, including African American Studies and Women's Studies, and makes a nuanced and heavily qualified argument for universal political principles. While recognizing that we should celebrate what is unique and worthy in each culture, she upholds the idea of ethical universals that all peoples share.

From *Cultivating Humanity: A Classical Defense of Reform in Liberal Education* by Martha C. Nussbaum, Cambridge, Mass.: Harvard University Press,

Asked where he came from, the ancient Greek Cynic philosopher Diogenes replied, "I am a citizen of the world." He meant by this that he refused to be defined simply by his local origins and group memberships, associations central to the self-image of a conventional Greek male; he insisted on defining himself in terms of more universal aspirations and concerns. The Stoics who followed his lead developed his image of the *kosmopolitês*, or world citizen, more fully, arguing that each of us dwells, in effect, in two communities—the local community of our birth, and the community of human argument and aspiration that "is truly great and truly common." It is the latter community that is, most fundamentally, the source of our moral and social obligations. With respect to fundamental moral values such as justice, "we should regard all human beings as our fellow citizens and local residents." This attitude deeply influenced the subsequent philosophical and political tradition, especially as mediated through the writings of Cicero, who reworked it so as to allow a special degree of loyalty to one's own local region or group. Stoic ideas influenced the American republic through the writings of Thomas Paine, and also through Adam Smith and Immanuel Kant, who themselves influenced the Founders. Later on, Stoic thought was a major formative influence on both Emerson and Thoreau.

This form of cosmopolitanism is not peculiar to Western traditions. It is, for example, the view that animates the work of the influential Indian philosopher, poet, and educational leader Rabindranath Tagore. Tagore drew his own cosmopolitan views from older Bengali traditions although he self-consciously melded them with Western cosmopolitanism. It is also the view recommended by Ghanaian philosopher Kwame Anthony Appiah, when he writes, concerning African identity: "We will only solve our problems if we see them as human problems arising out of a special situation, and we shall not solve them if we see them as African problems generated by our being somehow unlike others." But for people who have grown up in the Western tradition it is useful to understand the roots of this cosmopolitanism in ancient Greek and Roman thought. These ideas are an essential resource for democratic citizenship. Like Socrates' ideal of critical inquiry, they should be at the core of today's higher education.

. . .

Contemporary debates about the curriculum frequently imply that the idea of a "multicultural" education is a new fad, with no antecedents in long-standing educational traditions. In fact, Socrates grew up in an Athens already influenced by such ideas in the fifth century BC. Ethnographic writers such as the historian Herodotus examined the customs of distant countries, both in order to understand their ways of life and in order to attain a critical perspective on their own society. Herodotus took seriously the possibility that Egypt and Persia might have something to teach Athens about social values. A cross-cultural inquiry, he realized, may reveal that what we take to be natural and normal is merely parochial and habitual. One cultural group thinks that corpses must be buried; another, that they must be burnt; another, that they must be left in the air to be plucked clean by the birds. Each is shocked by the practices of the other, and each, in the process, starts to realize that its habitual ways may not be the way designed by nature for all times and persons.

Awareness of cultural difference gave rise to a rich and complex debate about whether our central moral and political values exist in the nature of things (by *phusis*), or merely by convention (*nomos*). That Greek debate illustrates most of the positions now familiar in debates about cultural relativism and the source of social norms. It also contains a crucial insight: if we should conclude that our norms are human and historical rather than immutable and eternal, it does not follow that the search for a rational justification of moral norms is futile.

In the conventional culture of fifth-century BC Athens, recognition that Athenian customs were not universal became a crucial precondition of Socratic teaching. So long as young men were educated in the manner of Aristophanes' Old Education, an education stressing uncritical assimilation of traditional values, so long as they marched to school in rows and sang the old songs without discussion of alternatives, ethical questioning could not get going. Ethical inquiry requires a climate in which the young are encouraged to be critical of their habits and conventions, and such critical inquiry, in turn, requires awareness that life contains other possibilities.

Pursuing these comparisons, fifth-century Athenians were especially fascinated by the example of Sparta, Athens' primary rival, a hierarchical and nondemocratic culture that understood the goal of civic education in a very un-Athenian way. As the historian Thucydides depicts them, Spartan educators carried to an extreme the preference for uniformity and rule-following that characterized the Old Education of Athens in Aristophanes' nostalgic portrait. Conceiving the good citizen as an obedient follower of tradition, they preferred uncritical subservience to Athenian public argument and debate. Denying the importance of free speech and thought, they preferred authoritarian to democratic politics. . . .

Plato, writing in the early to mid-fourth century BC, alludes frequently to the study of other cultures, especially those of Sparta, Crete, and Egypt. In his *Republic,* which alludes often to Spartan practices, the plan for an ideal city is plainly influenced by reflection about customs elsewhere. One particularly fascinating example of the way in which reflection about history and other cultures awakens critical reflection occurs in the fifth book of that work, where Plato's character Socrates produces the first serious argument known to us in the Western tradition for an equal education for women. Here Socrates begins by acknowledging that the idea of women's receiving both physical and intellectual education equal to that of men will strike most Athenians as very weird and laughable. . . . But he then reminds Glaucon that many good things once seemed weird in just this way. For example, the unclothed public exercise that Athenians now prize as a norm of manliness once seemed foreign, and the heavy clothing that they think barbaric once seemed natural. However, he continues, when the practice of stripping for athletic contests had been in effect for some time, its advantages were clearly seen—and then "the appearance of absurdity ebbed away under the influence of reason's judgment about the best." So it is with women's education, Socrates argues. Right now it seems absurd, but once we realize that our conventions don't by themselves supply reasons for what we ought to do, we will be forced to ask ourselves whether we really do have good reasons for denying women the chance to develop their intellectual and physical capacities. . . .

Cross-cultural inquiry up until this time had been relatively unsystematic, using examples that the philosopher or historian in question happened to know through personal travel or local familiarity. Later in the fourth century, however, the practice was rendered systematic and made a staple of the curriculum, as Aristotle apparently instructed his students to gather information about 153 forms of political organization, encompassing the entire known world, and to write up historical and constitutional descriptions of these regimes. The Athenian Constitution, which was written either by Aristotle or by one of his students, is our only surviving example of the project; it shows an intention to record everything relevant to critical reflection about that constitution and its suitability. . . . But it was neither Plato nor Aristotle who coined the term "citizen of the world." It was Diogenes the Cynic. Diogenes (404–323 BC) led a life stripped of the usual protections that habit and status supply. Choosing exile from his own native city, he defiantly refused protection from the rich and powerful for fear of losing his freedom, and lived in poverty, famously choosing a tub set up in the market-place as his "home" in order to indicate his disdain for convention and comfort. He connected poverty with independence of mind and speech, calling freedom of speech "the finest thing in human life." Once, they say, Plato saw him washing some lettuce and said, "If you had paid court to Dionysius, you would not be washing lettuce." Diogenes replied, "If you had washed lettuce, you would not have paid court to Dionysius."

Diogenes left no written work behind, and it is difficult to know how to classify him. "A Socrates gone mad" was allegedly Plato's description—and a good one, it seems. For Diogenes clearly followed the lead of Socrates in disdaining external markers of status and focusing on the inner life of virtue and thought. His search for a genuinely honest and virtuous person, and his use of philosophical arguments to promote that search, are recognizably Socratic. What was "mad" about him was the public assault on convention that accompanied his quest. Socrates provoked people only by his questions. He lived a conventional life. But Diogenes provoked people by his behavior as well, spitting in a rich man's face, even masturbating in public. What was the meaning of this shocking behavior?

It appears likely that the point of his unseemly behavior was itself Socratic—to get people to question their prejudices by making them consider how difficult it is to give good reasons for many of our deeply held feelings. Feelings about the respect due to status and rank and feelings of shame associated with sexual practices are assailed by this behavior—as Herodotus' feelings about burial were assailed by his contact with Persian and Egyptian customs. The question is whether one can then go on to find a good argument for one's own conventions and against the behavior of the Cynic. . . .

Set in this context, the invitation to consider ourselves citizens of the world is the invitation to become, to a certain extent, philosophical exiles from our own ways of life, seeing them from the vantage point of the outsider and asking the questions an outsider is likely to ask about their meaning and function. Only this critical distance, Diogenes argued, makes one a philosopher. In other words, a stance of detachment from uncritical loyalty to one's own ways promotes the kind of evaluation that is truly reason based. When we see in how many different ways people can organize their lives we will recognize, he seems to think, what is deep and what is shallow in our own ways, and will consider that "the only real community is one that embraces the entire world." In other words, the true basis for human association is not the arbitrary or the merely habitual; it is that which we can defend as good for human beings—and Diogenes believes that these evaluations know no national boundaries.

The Stoic philosophers, over the next few centuries, made Diogenes' insight respectable and culturally fruitful. They developed the idea of cross-cultural study and world citizenship much further in their own morally and philosophically rigorous way. . . . The meaning of the idea of political life is made especially clear in Cicero's work *On Duties* (*De officiis*), written in 44 BC. . . . Cicero argues that the duty to treat humanity with respect requires us to treat aliens on our soil with honor and hospitality. It requires us never to engage in wars of aggression, and to view wars based on group hatred and wars of extermination as especially pernicious. It requires us to behave honorably in the conduct of war, shunning treachery even toward the enemy. In general, it requires us to place justice above political expediency, and to understand that we form part of a universal community of humanity whose ends are the moral ends of justice and human well-being. Cicero's book has been among the most influential in the entire Western philosophical tradition. . . . Stoics hold, then, that the good citizen is a "citizen of the world." They hold that thinking about humanity as it is realized in the whole world is valuable for self-knowledge: we see ourselves and our customs more clearly when we see our own ways in relation to those of other reasonable people. They insist, furthermore, that we really will be better able to solve our problems if we face them in this broader context, our imaginations unconstrained by narrow partisanship. No theme is deeper in Stoicism than the damage done by faction and local allegiances to the political life of a group. Stoic texts show repeatedly how easy it is for local or national identities and their associated hatreds to be manipulated by self-seeking individuals for their own gain—whereas reason is hard to fake, and its language is open to the critical scrutiny of all. . . .

To be a citizen of the world, one does not, the Stoics stress, need to give up local affiliations, which can frequently be a source of great richness in life. They suggest instead that we think of ourselves as surrounded by a series of concentric circles. The first one is drawn around the self; the next takes in own's immediate family; then follows the extended family; then, in order, one's neighbors or local group, one's fellow city-dwellers, one's fellow countrymen—and we can easily add to this list groups formed on the basis of ethnic, religious, linguistic, historical, professional, and gender identities. Beyond all these circles is the largest one, that of humanity as a whole. Our task as citizens of the world, and as educators who prepare people to be citizens of the world, will be to "draw the circles somehow toward the center," making all human beings like our fellow city-dwellers. In other words, we need not give up our special affections and identifications, whether national or ethnic or religious; but we should work to make all human beings part of our community of dialogue and concern, showing respect for the human wherever it occurs, and allowing that respect to constrain our national or local politics.

STUDY QUESTIONS

1. What argument does Nussbaum make for the importance of humanistic studies in higher education?
2. Why, for Nussbaum, is multiculturalism such an important part of education?

29.6 RICHARD RORTY, "FAILED PROPHECIES, GLORIOUS HOPES," 1998

Richard Rorty (1931–2007) was an American philosopher who taught at Stanford, Princeton, and the University of Virginia. Rorty became associated with a form of American philosophy known as pragmatism, which followed the writing of the philosopher John Dewey. He came to believe, following Wittgenstein's philosophy of language, that meaning was a sociolinguistic product and did not exist in and of itself. In *Failed Prophecies, Glorious Hopes*, Rorty, an avowed atheist, argues that we should not ignore the inspirational qualities of great works such as the gospels or the *Communist Manifesto*, simply because their predictions fell short of reality. Christianity and Communism, he wrote, need not be judged for their predictive qualities but for their appeals to what Abraham Lincoln referred to as the "Better Angels of our Nature." They stirred men and women to good deeds, which arguably benefitted society in general.

Failed prophecies often make invaluable inspirational reading. Consider two examples: the New Testament and the *Communist Manifesto*. Both were intended by their authors as predictions of what was going to happen—predictions based on superior knowledge of the forces which determine human history. Both sets of predictions have, so far, been ludicrous flops. Both claims to knowledge have become objects of ridicule.

Christ did not return. Those who claim that He is about to do so, and that it would be prudent to become a member of a particular sect or denomination in order to prepare for this event, are rightly viewed with suspicion. To be sure, nobody can prove that the Second Coming will not occur, thus producing empirical evidence for the Incarnation. But we have been waiting for a long time.

Analogously, nobody can prove that Marx and Engels were wrong when they proclaimed that "the bourgeoisie has forged the weapons that bring death to itself." It may be that the globalization of the labour market in the next century will reverse the progressive bourgeoisization of the European and North American proletariat, and that it will become true that "the bourgeoisie is incapable of continuing to rule, since it is unable even to assure an existence to the slaves within their slavery." Maybe the breakdown of capitalism, and the assumption of the

From Richard Rorty, "Failed Prophecies, Glorious Hopes." *Constellations* 6, no. 2 (June 1999), 216–21. Reprinted with permission of John Wiley & Sons, Inc.; permission conveyed through Copyright Clearance Center, Inc.

political power by a virtuous and enlightened proletariat, will then come to pass. Maybe, in short, Marx and Engels just got the timing a century or two wrong. Still, capitalism has overcome many crises in the past, and we have been waiting a long time for the emergence of this proletariat.

. . .

Just as the New Testament is still read by millions of people who spend little time wondering whether Christ will someday return in glory, so the *Communist Manifesto* is still read even by those of us who hope and believe that full social justice can be attained without a revolution of the sort Marx predicted: that a classless society, a world in which "the free development of each is the condition of the free development of all" can come about as a result of what Marx despised as "bourgeois reformism." Parents and teachers should encourage young people to read both books. The young will be morally better for having done so.

We should raise our children to find it intolerable that we who sit behind desks and punch keyboards are paid ten times as much as people who get their hands dirty cleaning our toilets, and a hundred times as much as those who fabricate our keyboards in the Third World. We should ensure that they worry about the fact that the countries which industrialized first have a hundred times the wealth of those which have not yet industrialized. Our children need to learn, early on, to see the inequalities between their own fortunes and those of other children as neither the Will of God nor the necessary price for economic efficiency, but as an evitable tragedy. They should start thinking, as early as possible, about how to the world might be changed so as to ensure that no one goes hungry while others have a surfeit.

The children need to read Christ's message of human fraternity alongside Marx and Engel's account of how industrial capitalism and free markets—indispensable as they have turned out to be—make it very difficult to institute that fraternity. They need to see their lives as given meaning by efforts towards the realization of the moral potential inherent in our ability to communicate our needs and our hopes to one another. They should learn stories both about Christian congregations meeting in the catacombs and about workers' rallies in city squares. For both have played equally important roles in the long process of actualizing their potentiality.

The inspirational value of the New Testament and the *Communist Manifesto* is not diminished by the fact that many millions of people were enslaved, tortured or starved to death by sincere, morally earnest people who recited passages from one or the other text in order to justify their deeds. Memories of the dungeons of the Inquisition and the interrogation rooms of the KGB, of the ruthless greed and arrogance of the Christian clergy and of the Communist nomenklatura, should indeed make us reluctant to hand over power to people who claim to know what God, or History, wants. But there is a difference between knowledge and hope. Hope often takes the form of false prediction, as it did in both documents. But hope for social justice is nevertheless the only basis for a worthwhile human life.

. . .

Insofar as history presents a *moral* spectacle, it is the struggle to break such monopolies. The use of Christian doctrine to argue for the abolition of slavery (and to argue against the American equivalent of the Nuremberg Laws—the racial segregation statutes) shows Christianity at its best. The use of Marxist doctrine to raise the consciousness of workers—to make it clear to them how they are being cheated—shows Marxism at its best. When the two have coalesced, as they did in the "Social Gospel" movement, in the theologies of Paul Tillich and Walter Rauschenbusch, and in the most socialistic of the papal encyclicals, they have enabled the struggle for social justice to transcend the controversies between theists and atheists. Those controversies *should* be transcended: we should read the New Testament as saying that how we treat each other on earth matters a great deal more than the outcome of debate concerning the existence or nature of another world.

. . .

The *Manifesto* inspired the founders of most of the great unions of modern times. By quoting its words, the founders of the unions were able to bring millions of people out on strike against degrading conditions and starvation wages. Those words buttressed the faith of the strikers that their sacrifice—their willingness to see their children without sufficient food rather than to yield to the owners' demand for a higher return on investment—would not be in vain. A document which has accomplished that much will always remain among the treasures of our intellectual and spiritual heritage. For the *Manifesto* spelled out what the workers were gradually coming to realize: that "instead of rising with the progress of industry," the worker was in danger of "sinking deeper and deeper below the conditions of existence of his own class." This danger was avoided, at least temporarily, in Europe and North America thanks to the courage of workers who had read the *Manifesto* and who, as a result, were emboldened to demand their share of political power. Had they waited for the Christian kindness and charity of their superiors, their children would still be illiterate and badly fed.

. . .

It would be best, of course, if we could find a new document to provide our children with inspiration and hope—one which was as free of the defects of the New Testament as of those of the *Manifesto*. It would be good to have a reformist text, one which lacked the apocalyptic character of both books—which did not say that all things must be made new, or that justice "can be attained only by the forcible overthrow of all existing social conditions." It would be well to have a document which spelled out the details of a this-worldly utopia without assuring us that this utopia will emerge full-blown, and quickly, as soon as some single decisive change has occurred—as soon as private property is abolished, or as soon as we have all taken Jesus into our hearts.

It would be best, in short, if we could get along without prophecy and claims to knowledge of the forces which determine history—if generous hope could sustain itself without such reassurances. Someday perhaps we shall have a new text to give to our children—one which abstains from prediction yet still expresses the same yearning for fraternity as does the New Testament, and is as filled with sharp-eyed descriptions of our most recent forms of inhumanity to each other as the *Manifesto*. But in the meantime we should be grateful for two texts which have helped make us better—have helped us overcome, to some degree, our brutish selfishness and our cultivated sadism.

STUDY QUESTIONS

1. Can stories be a source of inspiration and values even if their religious content is not endorsed?
2. Is Rorty assuming that hope for a better future is necessary, especially for young people?

29.7 GEORGE W. BUSH, SPEECH TO CONGRESS, SEPTEMBER 20, 2001

Less than two weeks after the terrorist attacks of September 11, 2001, president George W. Bush (b. 1946) addressed Congress. In his speech, he attempted to walk a fine line between pointing the finger at the Muslim terrorists who attacked the World Trade Center and the Pentagon and

From George W. Bush, "Address to the Nation." Washington, DC, September 20, 2001.

reassuring Muslims that America was not an enemy of Islam. He argued that the Muslims who carried out the attacks "blasphemed the name of Allah," that they were "traitors to their own faith." In the speech, he defined what was to become his "War on Terror," vowing not only to bring the terrorists to justice, but also to take on any government that harbored them (such as Afghanistan and its Taliban). He also claimed that the terrorists acted because they "hate our freedoms," pitting Islamic militancy staunchly against democracy.

Mr. Speaker, Mr. President Pro Tempore, members of Congress, and fellow Americans:

In the normal course of events, Presidents come to this chamber to report on the state of the Union. Tonight, no such report is needed. It has already been delivered by the American people.

We have seen it in the courage of passengers, who rushed terrorists to save others on the ground—passengers like an exceptional man named Todd Beamer. And would you please help me to welcome his wife, Lisa Beamer, here tonight. (Applause.)

We have seen the state of our Union in the endurance of rescuers, working past exhaustion. We have seen the unfurling of flags, the lighting of candles, the giving of blood, the saying of prayers—in English, Hebrew, and Arabic. We have seen the decency of a loving and giving people who have made the grief of strangers their own.

My fellow citizens, for the last nine days, the entire world has seen for itself the state of our Union—and it is strong. (Applause.)

Tonight we are a country awakened to danger and called to defend freedom. Our grief has turned to anger, and anger to resolution. Whether we bring our enemies to justice, or bring justice to our enemies, justice will be done. (Applause.)

I thank the Congress for its leadership at such an important time. All of America was touched on the evening of the tragedy to see Republicans and Democrats joined together on the steps of this Capitol, singing "God Bless America." And you did more than sing; you acted, by delivering $40 billion to rebuild our communities and meet the needs of our military.

Speaker Hastert, Minority Leader Gephardt, Majority Leader Daschle and Senator Lott, I thank you for your friendship, for your leadership and for your service to our country. (Applause.)

And on behalf of the American people, I thank the world for its outpouring of support. America will never forget the sounds of our National Anthem playing at Buckingham Palace, on the streets of Paris, and at Berlin's Brandenburg Gate.

We will not forget South Korean children gathering to pray outside our embassy in Seoul, or the prayers of sympathy offered at a mosque in Cairo. We will not forget moments of silence and days of mourning in Australia and Africa and Latin America.

Nor will we forget the citizens of 80 other nations who died with our own: dozens of Pakistanis; more than 130 Israelis; more than 250 citizens of India; men and women from El Salvador, Iran, Mexico and Japan; and hundreds of British citizens. America has no truer friend than Great Britain. (Applause.) Once again, we are joined together in a great cause—so honored the British Prime Minister has crossed an ocean to show his unity of purpose with America. Thank you for coming, friend. (Applause.)

On September the 11th, enemies of freedom committed an act of war against our country. Americans have known wars—but for the past 136 years, they have been wars on foreign soil, except for one Sunday in 1941. Americans have known the casualties of war—but not at the center of a great city on a peaceful morning. Americans have known surprise attacks—but never before on thousands of civilians. All of this was brought upon us in a single day—and night fell on a different world, a world where freedom itself is under attack.

Americans have many questions tonight. Americans are asking: Who attacked our country? The evidence we have gathered all points to a collection of loosely affiliated terrorist organizations known as al Qaeda. They are the same murderers indicted for bombing American embassies in Tanzania and Kenya, and responsible for bombing the USS *Cole*.

Al Qaeda is to terror what the mafia is to crime. But its goal is not making money; its goal is remaking the world—and imposing its radical beliefs on people everywhere.

The terrorists practice a fringe form of Islamic extremism that has been rejected by Muslim scholars and the vast majority of Muslim clerics—a fringe movement that perverts the peaceful teachings of Islam. The terrorists' directive commands them to kill Christians and Jews, to kill all Americans, and make no distinction among military and civilians, including women and children.

This group and its leader—a person named Osama bin Laden—are linked to many other organizations in different countries, including the Egyptian Islamic Jihad and the Islamic Movement of Uzbekistan. There are thousands of these terrorists in more than 60 countries. They are recruited from their own nations and neighborhoods and brought to camps in places like Afghanistan, where they are trained in the tactics of terror. They are sent back to their homes or sent to hide in countries around the world to plot evil and destruction.

The leadership of al Qaeda has great influence in Afghanistan and supports the Taliban regime in controlling most of that country. In Afghanistan, we see al Qaeda's vision for the world.

Afghanistan's people have been brutalized—many are starving and many have fled. Women are not allowed to attend school. You can be jailed for owning a television. Religion can be practiced only as their leaders dictate. A man can be jailed in Afghanistan if his beard is not long enough.

The United States respects the people of Afghanistan—after all, we are currently its largest source of humanitarian aid—but we condemn the Taliban regime. (Applause.) It is not only repressing its own people, it is threatening people everywhere by sponsoring and sheltering and supplying terrorists. By aiding and abetting murder, the Taliban regime is committing murder.

And tonight, the United States of America makes the following demands on the Taliban: Deliver to United States authorities all the leaders of al Qaeda who hide in your land. (Applause.) Release all foreign nationals, including American citizens, you have unjustly imprisoned. Protect foreign journalists, diplomats and aid workers in your country. Close immediately and permanently every terrorist training camp in Afghanistan, and hand over every terrorist, and every person in their support structure, to appropriate authorities. (Applause.) Give the United States full access to terrorist training camps, so we can make sure they are no longer operating.

These demands are not open to negotiation or discussion. (Applause.) The Taliban must act, and act immediately. They will hand over the terrorists, or they will share in their fate.

I also want to speak tonight directly to Muslims throughout the world. We respect your faith. It's practiced freely by many millions of Americans, and by millions more in countries that America counts as friends. Its teachings are good and peaceful, and those who commit evil in the name of Allah blaspheme the name of Allah. (Applause.) The terrorists are traitors to their own faith, trying, in effect, to hijack Islam itself. The enemy of America is not our many Muslim friends; it is not our many Arab friends. Our enemy is a radical network of terrorists, and every government that supports them. (Applause.)

Our war on terror begins with al Qaeda, but it does not end there. It will not end until every terrorist group of global reach has been found, stopped and defeated. (Applause.)

Americans are asking, why do they hate us? They hate what we see right here in this chamber—a democratically elected government. Their leaders are self-appointed. They hate our freedoms—our freedom of religion, our freedom of speech, our freedom to vote and assemble and disagree with each other.

They want to overthrow existing governments in many Muslim countries, such as Egypt, Saudi Arabia, and Jordan. They want to drive Israel out of the Middle East. They want to drive Christians and Jews out of vast regions of Asia and Africa.

These terrorists kill not merely to end lives, but to disrupt and end a way of life. With every atrocity, they hope that America grows fearful, retreating from the world and forsaking our friends. They stand against us, because we stand in their way.

We are not deceived by their pretenses to piety. We have seen their kind before. They are the heirs of all the murderous ideologies of the 20th century. By sacrificing human life to serve their radical visions—by abandoning every value except the will to power—they follow in the path of fascism, and Nazism, and totalitarianism. And they will follow that path all the way, to where it ends: in history's unmarked grave of discarded lies. (Applause.)

Americans are asking: How will we fight and win this war? We will direct every resource at our command—every means of diplomacy, every tool of intelligence, every instrument of law enforcement, every financial influence, and every necessary weapon of war—to the disruption and to the defeat of the global terror network.

This war will not be like the war against Iraq a decade ago, with a decisive liberation of territory and a swift conclusion. It will not look like the air war above Kosovo two years ago, where no ground troops were used and not a single American was lost in combat.

Our response involves far more than instant retaliation and isolated strikes. Americans should not expect one battle, but a lengthy campaign, unlike any other we have ever seen. It may include dramatic strikes, visible on TV, and covert operations, secret even in success. We will starve terrorists of funding, turn them one against another, drive them from place to place, until there is no refuge or no rest. And we will pursue nations that provide aid or safe haven to terrorism. Every nation, in every region, now has a decision to make. Either you are with us, or you are with the terrorists. (Applause.) From this day forward, any nation that continues to harbor or support terrorism will be regarded by the United States as a hostile regime.

Our nation has been put on notice: We are not immune from attack. We will take defensive measures against terrorism to protect Americans. Today, dozens of federal departments and agencies, as well as state and local governments, have responsibilities affecting homeland security. These efforts must be coordinated at the highest level. So tonight I announce the creation of a Cabinet-level position reporting directly to me—the Office of Homeland Security.

And tonight I also announce a distinguished American to lead this effort, to strengthen American security: a military veteran, an effective governor, a true patriot, a trusted friend—Pennsylvania's Tom Ridge. (Applause.) He will lead, oversee and coordinate a comprehensive national strategy to safeguard our country against terrorism, and respond to any attacks that may come.

These measures are essential. But the only way to defeat terrorism as a threat to our way of life is to stop it, eliminate it, and destroy it where it grows. (Applause.)

Many will be involved in this effort, from FBI agents to intelligence operatives to the reservists we have called to active duty. All deserve our thanks, and all have our prayers. And tonight, a few miles from the damaged Pentagon, I have a message for our military: Be ready. I've called the Armed Forces to alert, and there is a reason. The hour is coming when America will act, and you will make us proud. (Applause.)

This is not, however, just America's fight. And what is at stake is not just America's freedom. This is the world's fight. This is civilization's fight. This is the fight of all who believe in progress and pluralism, tolerance and freedom.

We ask every nation to join us. We will ask, and we will need, the help of police forces, intelligence services, and banking systems around the world. The United States is grateful that many nations and many international organizations have already responded—with sympathy and with support. Nations from Latin America, to Asia, to Africa, to Europe, to the Islamic world. Perhaps the NATO Charter reflects best the attitude of the world: An attack on one is an attack on all.

The civilized world is rallying to America's side. They understand that if this terror goes unpunished, their own cities, their own citizens may be next.

Terror, unanswered, can not only bring down buildings, it can threaten the stability of legitimate governments. And you know what—we're not going to allow it. (Applause.)

Americans are asking: What is expected of us? I ask you to live your lives, and hug your children. I know many citizens have fears tonight, and I ask you to be calm and resolute, even in the face of a continuing threat.

I ask you to uphold the values of America, and remember why so many have come here. We are in a fight for our principles, and our first responsibility is to live by them. No one should be singled out for unfair treatment or unkind words because of their ethnic background or religious faith. (Applause.)

I ask you to continue to support the victims of this tragedy with your contributions. Those who want to give can go to a central source of information, libertyunites.org, to find the names of groups providing direct help in New York, Pennsylvania, and Virginia.

The thousands of FBI agents who are now at work in this investigation may need your cooperation, and I ask you to give it.

I ask for your patience, with the delays and inconveniences that may accompany tighter security; and for your patience in what will be a long struggle.

I ask your continued participation and confidence in the American economy. Terrorists attacked a symbol of American prosperity. They did not touch its source. America is successful because of the hard work, and creativity, and enterprise of our people. These were the true strengths of our economy before September 11th, and they are our strengths today. (Applause.)

And, finally, please continue praying for the victims of terror and their families, for those in uniform, and for our great country. Prayer has comforted us in sorrow, and will help strengthen us for the journey ahead.

Tonight I thank my fellow Americans for what you have already done and for what you will do. And ladies and gentlemen of the Congress, I thank you, their representatives, for what you have already done and for what we will do together.

Tonight, we face new and sudden national challenges. We will come together to improve air safety, to dramatically expand the number of air marshals on domestic flights, and take new measures to prevent hijacking. We will come together to promote stability and keep our airlines flying, with direct assistance during this emergency. (Applause.)

We will come together to give law enforcement the additional tools it needs to track down terror here at home. (Applause.) We will come together to strengthen our intelligence capabilities to know the plans of terrorists before they act, and find them before they strike. (Applause.)

We will come together to take active steps that strengthen America's economy, and put our people back to work.

Tonight we welcome two leaders who embody the extraordinary spirit of all New Yorkers: Governor George Pataki, and Mayor Rudolph Giuliani. (Applause.) As a symbol of America's resolve, my administration will work with Congress, and these two leaders, to show the world that we will rebuild New York City. (Applause.)

After all that has just passed—all the lives taken, and all the possibilities and hopes that died with them—it is natural to wonder if America's future is one of fear. Some speak of an age of terror. I know there are struggles ahead, and dangers to face. But this country will define our times, not be defined by them. As long as the United States of America is determined and strong, this will not be an age of terror; this will be an age of liberty, here and across the world. (Applause.)

Great harm has been done to us. We have suffered great loss. And in our grief and anger we have found our mission and our moment. Freedom and fear are at war. The advance of human freedom—the great achievement of our time, and the great hope of every time—now depends on us. Our nation—this generation—will lift a dark threat of violence from our people and our future. We will rally the world to this cause by our efforts, by our courage. We will not tire, we will not falter, and we will not fail. (Applause.)

It is my hope that in the months and years ahead, life will return almost to normal. We'll go back to our lives and routines, and that is good. Even grief recedes with time and grace. But our resolve must not pass. Each of us will remember what happened that day, and to whom it happened. We'll remember the moment the news came—where we were and what we were doing. Some will remember an image of a fire, or a story of rescue. Some will carry memories of a face and a voice gone forever.

And I will carry this: It is the police shield of a man named George Howard, who died at the World Trade Center trying to save others. It was given to me by his mom, Arlene, as a proud memorial to her son. This is my reminder of lives that ended, and a task that does not end. (Applause.)

I will not forget this wound to our country or those who inflicted it. I will not yield; I will not rest; I will not relent in waging this struggle for freedom and security for the American people.

The course of this conflict is not known, yet its outcome is certain. Freedom and fear, justice and cruelty, have always been at war, and we know that God is not neutral between them. (Applause.)

Fellow citizens, we'll meet violence with patient justice—assured of the rightness of our cause, and confident of the victories to come. In all that lies before us, may God grant us wisdom, and may He watch over the United States of America.

Thank you. (Applause.)

STUDY QUESTIONS

1. What further steps, beyond the punishment of al-Qaeda, did Bush advocate in this speech?
2. Was he advancing an overly simplistic view that "they hate our freedoms"?

29.8 EUROPEAN COUNCIL ON FATWA AND RESEARCH, DECREES REGARDING MUSLIM WOMEN IN EUROPE, 2001

The European Council on Fatwa and Research (ECFR) is a private organization of Islamic scholars and clergy dedicated to resolving conflicts between Islamic law and tradition, on the one hand, and the secular laws and traditions of the European Community, on the other. It aims to preserve Islamic identity and integrity within a European context. In other words, how can European Muslims be both European and Muslim? The ECFR meets annually, publishes scholarly analyses of problems, issues authoritative resolutions, and enacts binding *fatwas* (religious judgments) over individual cases. It should be noted that despite its European focus, roughly one third of the ECFR's membership consists of Muslim leaders who do not live in the West and may not be fully aware of European values and expectations. The ECFR has had a close relationship with the Muslim Brotherhood from its start and, like its affiliate, has been accused of anti-Semitism. Here is a sampler of resolutions and *fatwas* enacted since 1995 regarding Muslim women in Europe.

8TH SESSION, JULY 18–22, 2001.

RESOLUTION 3/8: A WOMAN EMBRACES ISLAM AND HER HUSBAND DOES NOT.

On this issue, the Council issued the following:

Having considered the numerous papers and studies submitted for its attention over three consecutive sessions, and which carried a variety of perspectives and opinions all dealing with this problem in detail and length, observing the objectives of *Sharia* [Islamic law] and relating those to principles of *Fiqh* [Islamic jurisprudence]. The Council also recognises and acknowledges the conditions in which the new Muslim sisters in the West find themselves when their husbands choose to remain on their religion.

The Council affirms and repeats that it is forbidden for a Muslim female to establish marriage to a non-Muslim male. This has been an issue of consensus throughout the history of this nation. However, in the case of marriage being established prior to the female entering Islam, the Council has decided the following:

First: If both husband and wife revert to Islam and there is no *Sharia* objection to their marriage in the first place, such as particular blood relations or relations established as a result of breast-feeding, which deems the very establishment of marriage unlawful, the marriage shall be deemed valid and correct.

Second: If the husband reverts to Islam alone, and no object to the establishment of marriage exists and the woman is a Jew or a Christian, then the marriage shall be deemed valid and correct.

Third: If the wife reverts to Islam and her husband remains on his religion, the Council sees the following:

- If her reversion to Islam occurred and the marriage is yet to be consummated, then they must immediately separate.
- If her reversion to Islam occurred after the consummation of marriage, and the husband also embraced Islam before the expiry of her period of waiting, then the marriage is deemed valid and correct.
- If her reversion to Islam occurred after the consummation of marriage, and the period of waiting expired, she is allowed to wait for him to embrace Islam even if that period was a lengthy one. Once he does so and reverts to Islam, then their marriage is deemed valid and correct.
- If the wife chose to marry another man after the expiration of the period of waiting, she must first request a dissolution of marriage through legal channels.

Fourth: According to the four main schools of jurisprudence, it is forbidden for the wife to remain with her husband, or indeed to allow him conjugal rights, once her period of waiting has expired. However, some scholars see that it is for her to remain with him, allowing him and enjoying full conjugal rights, if he does not prevent her from exercising her religion and she has hope in him reverting in Islam. The reason for this is for women not to reject entering into Islam if they realise that they are to separate from their husbands and desert their families by doing so.

10TH SESSION, JANUARY 22–26, 2003.

FATWA 10/1: SURROGACY (A WOMAN HIRING HER WOMB TO CARRY AN EMBRYO)

In terms of *Shari'ah* it is impermissible for a woman to hire her womb to carry an embryo in it. It is impermissible even if it were done *gratis*, for this involves introducing the sperm of a man that is not her husband, and it would lead to mixing up and confusing ancestry or genealogy because by giving birth to the child she would be its mother, as Allah Almighty says: "Their mothers are none but those who have given them birth," although the embryo does not belong to her own ovum that has been fertilized by her husband. This, of course, does not apply by analogy, to a woman's breastfeeding somebody else's child, for this provides the child with external nutrients and does not involve holding it inside her body. Moreover, taking a wet nurse is legalized by texts from the *Quran* and the *Sunnah*.

The prohibition of this case, which is termed "the nursing womb" or surrogacy, has been confirmed by a decision passed by the International Islamic *Fiqh* Academy. Poverty is not an excuse for a woman to hire her womb; she had better seek her sustenance through other permissible means and remember the Saying of Allah: "And if you fear poverty, soon will Allah enrich you, if He wills, out of His Bounty" (IX: 28). Nobody refrains from something unlawful but Allah will compensate him for that with something lawful and good.

FATWA 10/2: A MARRIAGE THAT WAS CONTRACTED IN THE CHURCH

Contracting marriage in a church is not recommended by *Shari'ah*, and it is *haram* (unlawful) if it involves participation in the rituals related to their religion, or if the marriage in the church leads to something that is prohibited by *Shari'ah*, such as the pledge of the husband to educate the children on non-Islamic principles.

Yet, the marriage contract will be valid if all its legal (Islamic) requisites and conditions are observed, and the marriage will be correct and all its consequences should be observed. But just as a precaution, the person who had to do so should repeat the contract outside the church to publicize the marriage among the Muslims. The Council is keen to advise the Muslim youths against doing this impermissible deed that implies the husband's complying with the wishes of the wife in matters displeasing Allah (swt), and will expose him to the risk of accepting the conditions concerning the education of the children according to non-Islamic principles.

FATWA 10/3: CERTAIN METHODS OF CONTRACEPTION

There is no objection in the light of *Shari'ah* to using what prevents reproduction temporarily, regardless of the age of the woman. Therefore, the use of the coil is not objectionable, but tying the ovary, for example, is not permissible because it prevents reproduction forever and is therefore only permissible when there is a medical necessity.

FATWA 10/4: ABORTING A FETUS THAT SUFFERS FROM SERIOUS DEFECTS

It is impermissible to abort a fetus after the age of four months even if its deformation is confirmed, or even if its survival after its birth depends on using resuscitating apparatus. It is permissible however, to remove the apparatus if it has not been placed for a therapeutic purpose, but just for keeping it alive. Many decisions have been passed by one of the forums of the Islamic Organization for Medical Sciences and adopted by the Islamic *Fiqh* Academy concerning the two issues (the prohibition of aborting a fetus of more than four months of age because of deformations—and the permissibility of removing the resuscitating apparatus from any person for whom it has not been set up to continue useful therapy).

11TH CONFERENCE, JULY 1–7, 2003.

FATWA 11/1

QUESTION: A husband married for five years complains that his wife does not observe the prayers and that as a result, his children do not perform the prayers except when he is present with them. His wife also treats the children cruelly (She for example, beat her child and broke his arm, slapped her daughter leaving the impression of her fingers marked on her cheek for several weeks.) When her husband discussed with her a certain matter, she would say: "O Allah! Kill me," for example, or "relieve me of this world!" What is the ruling of Shari'ah on this woman? Should her husband divorce her?

ANSWER: Whoever does not perform the prayers out of laziness but does not believe that it is not obligatory is a *fasiq*, disobedient to Allah Almighty in the opinion of the majority of scholars. From your question one understands that your wife does not observe the prayers out of laziness; therefore, you should advise and admonish her and remind her and be patient with her and treat her gently and help her with all that you can so that she may fulfill her obligations towards Allah Almighty and her children. As to what you mention of her indifference and violence against her children, it may be caused by casual circumstances she is experiencing, so you have to try hard to deal with the matter, seeking aid through supplication and then through strengthening your relationship with other Muslim families in your community. Divorce is not the correct solution, nor is it obligatory as you inferred in your question, for that would entail the disintegration of the family and the loss of the children. Never despair of reforming her, for the believer does not despair of Allah's soothing Mercy. Allah Almighty says: "Truly, no one despairs of Allah's Soothing Mercy except those who have no faith" (XII: 87). Some of the prophets, such as Noah and Lot, kept patient with their wives and did not despair of preaching them benevolently although they were infidels.

13TH SESSION, JULY 7–10, 2004.

FATWA 13/6

I have been married to my wife for fourteen years. I heard that in the past she had wanted to marry an indecent person. My wife swore that she did not but he claimed she had endeavored to marry him. I do not trust my wife any more. I do not know which one is a liar. What can I do?

ANSWER: The questioner has heard a bad rumor about his wife. When he asked her she denied and swore that it was a lie. The entire story might be false and vexatious. If the husband does not have proof, then holding a good opinion of Muslims is an obligation and is essential between husband and wife. Originally everyone is innocent and certainty is not removed with suspicion. The husband is not supposed to listen any more to the person he described as indecent. In this case we need to recall the rule regarding the accusation of the chaste women as stated in Surah An-Nur. It states the necessity of witnesses or confession. Moreover, we advise the wife to find another job away from that man to eliminate the problem and restore the trust between the husband and the wife.

14TH SESSION, 23–27 FEBRUARY, 2005.

RESOLUTION 7/14: DOMESTIC VIOLENCE AND THE SOLUTION

Upon deliberating on the issue of Domestic Violence and the Solution and the researches submitted in this regard, the ECFR reached the following resolution:

Definition of Domestic Violence:

First: Violence is the application of material or abstract force in an illegal way to cause harm to others.

Second: Domestic Violence encompasses husband's abuse of his wife, wife's abuse of her husband, parents' abuse of their children and visa versa. It includes physical abuse, sexual abuse, verbal abuse and threatening, social abuse and ideological abuse. The worst type of violence is killing for honour.

Third: The reasons of violence can be summed up as follows:

1. Misunderstanding and weak religious conscience
2. Wrong upbringing and rearing in a rough location
3. Non-existence of dialogue and consultation among family members
4. Wrong choice and discrepancies between the bride and the bridegroom in all aspects including the ideological ones
5. Difficult circumstances e.g. poverty and unemployment

Fourth: Domestic violence has critical repercussions on the bride and the bridegroom, children and society. Consequently the ECFR resolved that all types of Domestic Violence are prohibited in Islam. A Muslim is supposed to refrain therefrom since all sorts of oppression and harm are prohibited and that has been crystallized in many parts of the Islamic literature, let alone the Domestic Violence. The relationship among family members is established on mercy, love and tranquility.

The ECFR stressed the Islamic means to prevent the Domestic Violence. The most important of which are:

1. Raising the religious conscience, applying the right methods in children's upbringing and observing dialogue and consultation among the family members.
2. Choosing one's spouse in the right way.
3. Raising awareness of the repercussions of oppression, hitting, cursing and insult via preaching and guidance.
4. Arbitration.
5. Upon exhausting every possible means, divorce as a final solution can be reached through judicial authorities or the two arbitrators.

The ECFR recommends Muslim minorities to shun hitting wives within the family following the example of the prophet—Peace be upon him—who never tapped. The prophet—Peace be upon him—said: "The best amongst ye wilt not tap." Moreover, it will incur repercussions and it violates the law.

15TH SESSION, 29 JUNE–3 JULY, 2005.

FATWA 5/15

I got married to a man who is more than twenty years older than I. Nevertheless, I would have never seen the difference in age as a barrier that separates me from him or turn me away from him, had he shown me a cheerful face and a good tongue and love. Alas, he has deprived me of the cheerful face, sweet word and the active emotion that makes woman feel her femininity and her place in the heart of her husband. He is not mean when it comes to my clothing and expenditure, nor does he hurt me. But this is not everything a woman needs from her husband. I do not think I mean anything to him other than as a chef or a unit of pleasure whenever he wills. This makes me feel bored and hate my life especially when I see my friends and peeresses whose husbands are filling their lives with love and euphoria.

Once I complained to him against this treatment and he said: Do you think I do not fulfill my duties towards you? Am I mean regarding your expenditure and clothing?

For husbands and wives to know I raise the following question: Are the financial needs in terms of food, clothing and accommodation the only Islamic duties that the husband owes his wife? Is the psychological aspect valueless in the Islamic view? According to my limited knowledge and by nature I do not think so. Please elaborate on this issue since it dramatically affects the continuity and happiness of the Muslim family.

ANSWER: This sister with her sound nature and limited knowledge realized the correct opinion that Islam states.

According to the Islamic *Shari'a*, the husband is obliged to provide his wife with her financial needs e.g. expenditure, clothing, accommodation, medication etc. in a way suitable to his circumstances and hers or as the *Qur'an* states "In a reasonable way."

The *Shari'a* does not neglect the psychological aspects that man cannot do without. Moreover the Qur'an describes marriage as one of Allah's signs and one of His graces on people. Allah said: "And among His signs is this, that He has created for you mates from among yourselves, that you may dwell in tranquility with them and He has put love and mercy between your hearts. Verily, in that are signs for those who reflect"(Trans. 30:21). This verse specifies the aims of marital life or its components as tranquility, love and mercy between the wife and the husband and these are psychological, and not material, components. Hence, marital life is meaningless in the case of the absence of these meanings when it turns into bodily closure and emotional separation.

On this basis, many good husbands are wrong when they think that the duties they owe their wives are naught but expenditure, clothing and accommodation neglecting that as the woman needs food, clothing and other material needs, she needs, and needs more, the good word, the wide smile, the tender touch, the entertaining kiss, loving treatment and dalliance that remove life burdens and achieve happiness.

Prophet Muhammad—peace be upon him—set the highest example in this regard. In spite of his huge burdens of *Da'wah* [preaching], establishing the rules of Islam, educating the Muslims, establishing the Muslim state intrinsically and protecting it against the extrinsic enemy, in addition to his love to his Lord and eagerness to perform continuous worship e.g. fasting, reciting the *Qur'an*, night prayer until his feet swelled and cry until his beard was wet. He—peace be upon him—never neglected his wives' rights. His spiritual aspects never drove him to the negligence of their human aspects in terms of quenching the thirst of their feelings that could not be satisfied with food and clothing.

Imam Ibn Al-Qayim described his attitude towards his wives saying: "Prophet Muhammad's life with his wives was founded on good company and good ethics. He—peace be upon him—used to send girls from Ansar to play with his wife 'Aish. Whenever she asked for something permissible he agreed. When she drank from a cup he would take it and put his lips on the same place she put her lips and drink and when she ate meat he would take the bones and put his mouth on the place of hers and eat. He—peace be upon him—used to put his head on her lap and recite Qur'an when she might be in her monthly period. When she was in her monthly period he used tell her to wear *Izar* [a wrap garment] so that intimacy can be practiced indirectly, and then he would have intercourse with her. He—peace be upon him—used to kiss her while he was fasting. Out of his morals he would enable her to play and carry her over his shoulder to show her the Abyssinians when playing in his mosque. He—peace be upon him—raced her twice. He used to say: 'The best among you is the best to his wife and I'm the best to my wife.' When he prayed *'Asr* [afternoon prayers] he used to pass by his wives and get informed of their affairs and when night came he would go to the one according to the turn. 'Aisha said: 'He never stayed with any of us more than the others and it rarely happened that he did not visit all of us and come closer to each of us without touching until he reached the one who had the turn so he would overnight with her.'"

When we consider this piece of the prophet's biography regarding the way he treated his wives, we can see clearly that he looked after them all, visited them all and drew nigh to them all. But he used to pay more attention to 'Aisha and that was not for nothing or bias but rather due to her young age and virginity. He—peace be upon him—married her when she was a virgin and he was her first and last husband. Such a girl would need more from her husband than an old woman. Her need is not the mere need for expenditure and clothing or even sexual intercourse, but rather the psychological aspects of the feelings which are deeper and of greater importance. It is not strange to see prophet Muhammad—peace be upon him—having great interest in the psychological aspects even though he was overwhelmed with a wide range of burdens in terms of *Da'wah* and establishing the Muslim nation and state. Allah said: "Indeed, in the messenger of Allah you have a good example to follow" (Trans. 33:21).

18TH SESSION, 1–5 JULY, 2008.

1/18 A MUSLIM LADY MARRYING A NON-MUSLIM

QUESTION: I am a girl and I am twenty years old. A Christian man, who is ready to respect Islamic obligations and does not mind our children to be Muslims, propose to me. Is it permissible to marry him?

ANSWER: It is not permissible for a Muslim woman to marry a non-Muslim man, even though he is from the people of the Book or promises to respect her religion after marriage. With regard to mixed marriage, Allah only permits a Muslim man to marry a chaste woman from the people of the Book. Allah said: "This day are (all) things good and pure made lawful unto you. The food of the People of the Book is lawful unto you and yours is lawful unto them. (Lawful unto you in marriage) are (not only) chaste women who are Believers, but chaste women among the People of the Book, revealed before your time" (5:5). The rule that forbids a Muslim woman from marrying a non-Muslim man is to enable her to preserve her religion, leaving no room for any, intentional or accidental, repercussions caused by this marriage on her or her offspring. Since the man is responsible for his family and should care for them, the husband is in a better position than his wife to affect her and his children. According to Islam, it is permissible for a Muslim man to marry a chaste woman from the people of the Book since if he affects her; she will embrace the true religion. In addition, according to Islam, it is not permissible for him to disrespect her religion or impose Islam on her.

In support of the above-mentioned rule, most scholars quote: Allah said: "Do not marry unbelieving women until they believe" "Nor marry (your girls) to Unbelievers until they believe." Then Allah made exception "(Lawful unto you in marriage) are (not only) chaste women who are Believers, but chaste women among the People of the Book, revealed before your time." Hence, it is permissible for a Muslim man to marry a chaste woman from the people of the Book, but it is not permissible for a Muslim woman to marry a non-Muslim man.

24TH SESSION, 16–19 AUGUST, 2014.

RESOLUTION 2/24: WOMAN'S POLITICAL RIGHTS

The ECFR resolves the following:

- Islam, prior to all the other systems, has stated woman's rights in general and her right of equality in all fields of viceregency on the earth, the concept of sincerity, fidelity and support between believing men and believing women, freedom of belief, social and civil rights, eligibility, financial rights and rewards.
- Islam states that there are differences between men and women but these differences are due to their being males and females and they are meant to create a comprehensive equilibrium in the universe and *Shari'ah*.
- Woman has the right to head organizations and states provided that her post does not cause repercussions on her family and suitable ethical atmosphere is available. Muslim scholars expressed a number of opinions regarding woman's right to be a Caliph. It is worth mentioning here that in today's time there is no Caliphate. Based on the afore-mentioned argument woman has the right, for instance, to vote in political elections, run political elections and take part in political parties, ministries and others.

In this context the ECFR exhorts Muslim woman in Europe, in order to serve her society and promote her community in light of succession of priorities taking into consideration Islamic rules, to participate in political activities, while being equipped with knowledge, faith, awareness and morality.

RESOLUTION 3/24: TREATING *NUSHUZ* [A REBELLIOUS WIFE]

The ECFR resolves the following: There are a number of essential principles that should be implemented in order to reach the authentic rule pertinent to the issue of treating a rebellious wife:

- Caring for one's family, deemed to be the corner stone in every good society, and its protection are included among the fundamental objectives of *Shari'ah*.
- Since marital relations should be founded on tranquility, mercy and love, husband and wife should cooperate and support one another, respect and forgive one another. The believers are brethren, sincere to each other and support one another.
- In the case of family disagreement, it might be that a husband does not like a characteristic of his wife's but surely he likes another. Even if he does not like her, it might be that Allah makes her a source of abundant good for him. Hence, he should not make his complaint against his wife his duty overlooking his shortcomings. Only the prophets were perfect.
- In the case when family problems become magnificently serious and husband hates his wife and the wife ill-treats her husband such as dealing with him arrogantly, despising him or neglecting her duties specified by Allah and clarified by His Prophet, peace be upon him, an attitude named in the Qur'an *NUSHUZ*, verse No. 34 in Surah No. 4 instructs the husband to adopt a wise approach and reason issues of concern with his wife to reach a fair solution. If this does not result in satisfactory solutions, he has the right to refrain peacefully from intimacy as an expression of disapproval hoping that his wife may stop causing him harm in action or word and may not upset him and recognize the responsibility Allah assigned to husbands i.e. *Qiwamah* and leadership of family on the basis of justice, consultation and understanding between husbands and their wives.
- In the case when the above-mentioned procedures fail there is no religious harm in divorce. Although it is permissible, Islam does not encourage divorce if there is a solution of lesser harm than divorce to protect family unit and

avert many repercussions caused by family disintegration.

- As for the third step referred to in the above-named verse "Hit them lightly," it should be understood in light of the way in which Allah honours woman as He honours man and that He prohibits despising and insulting woman. Moreover, the *Sunnah* in clear words forbids it and this is what can be understood from the context of "Hit them lightly." The best interpretation for this verse can be in the life of the Prophet Muhammad, peace be upon him, since to him Allah assigned the duty of interpreting the *Qur'an*. The Prophet Muhammad, peace be upon him, never hit a wife of his and condemned those who did it.

In our opinion, pondering over Islamic texts while taking into consideration inclusive as well as partial objectives of *Shari'ah*, the preponderant approach is to exclude light hitting in conformity with contemporary norms and effective laws harmonious with the Prophet Muhammad's guidance.

Based on the afore-mentioned the ECFR recommends Muslims in Europe and elsewhere to:

- Abide by the *Qur'an* and the *Sunnah* regarding mutual and integrated rights and duties of husbands and wives including taking early preventative procedures against complicated family problems and not to resort to hitting whether it is light or not following the example of the Prophet Muhammad, peace be upon him.
- Raise awareness of Islamic teaching to enlighten Muslim men and women about their religion especially in relation to family affairs and avert misinterpreting the above-mentioned verse.

STUDY QUESTIONS

1. How do the *fatwas* attempt to preserve Islamic identity and integrity within a European context?
2. Taking into account that nearly one third of the Councils members do not live in Europe, do the *fatwas* show full awareness of European values and expectations?

29.9 MOHAMMED ARKOUN, "IN PRAISE OF SUBVERSIVE REASON: BEYOND DIALOGUE AND THE QUEST FOR IDENTITY," 2005

Mohammed Arkoun (1918–2010), an Algerian Berber by birth, was a professor of Islamic Studies at the New Sorbonne University in Paris. The author of many books, his work focused on the relationship between Islam and modern European society. The text below is an excerpt from his contribution to the celebration of the fiftieth anniversary of the European Cultural Convention (a program under the direction of the Council of Europe), held in Strasbourg, September 8–9, 2005. This paper synthesizes Arkoun's position that the Greater West experienced a rift in ways of thinking, at some point in its past, with the Judeo-Christian European world adopting a form of Enlightenment rationalism and scientific reasoning and the Islamic world adopting a reliance of revealed tradition. Arkoun argues that we are today, post 9/11, confronted not with a simple choice between one or the other, but with the larger challenge of adopting "subversive reason"—a mode of inquiry and value formation that embraces and challenges both ways of thinking.

On 20–21 September 2001, the Council of Europe organised a colloquy on the challenge of religious, spiritual and cultural identities. It was my privilege to be there, and to present a paper on inter-religious dialogue and interculturalism. That meeting was one of the first responses to the terrorist attacks of 11 September 2001; several participants voiced their personal reactions, and various experts went confidently over the ins and outs of the tragedy which had jarred the world's consciousness. And now here we are again, brought together by the same Council of Europe to discuss the same obsessive question—a question still asked, but rarely illuminated, let alone rendered obsolete, in terms not just of analysis, but also of practical solutions, particularly in the fields of research on, and teaching of, the various cultures and religions which now co-exist in the European political and cultural area. . . .

My long experience of colloquies on Euro-Arab, Islamo-Christian and Judeo-Islamo-Christian dialogue, the clash of civilisations, interculturalism, and so on have led me to adopt a more radical stance. . . . [regarding] the failures, the omissions, the backings-off, the tiresome redundancies, the forgettings, the systematic elimination and the arrogance of Euro-Western attitudes to everything which has been relegated to the rest of the world since the "end of history" and the "clash of civilisations" were proclaimed in the US. . . .

The aftermath of [9/11] revealed the full extent of the crisis which now affects modern reason and the "values" trumpeted by the West as it calls for a "just war"—using terms which have much the same ring as those used by the popes who backed the crusaders against an Islam whose intellectual and cultural influence was powerfully felt throughout the Mediterranean. I employ this historical parallel, although I have repeatedly denounced its ritual use as ideological justification by many Arab Muslim intellectuals. What I am thinking of here is the persistence of a certain scholastic strain in Euro-Western thought, which briefly told us in the 1970s that the grand narratives were finished, and that post-modernity had come. What our bold talk of post-modernity actually implies is that modernity itself still thinks and acts in terms of the grand narrative which it constructed as a basis for the joint sovereignty of intellect and politics, which it substituted for the earlier sovereignty of theology and politics reimagined by Spinoza. Strengthened by the great scientific discoveries and the colonial empires, that grand narrative fed our vision of salvation through scientific progress. As happened with the grand founding narratives of the world's religions, modern reason has—like scholastic reason—profoundly refashioned the conditions in which human existence unfolds in historical terms. The mytho-historical narratives associated with these two stages in the history of reason spoke, first, of values eternal because they were "divine" and, later, of values both secular and universal. But all the time, the really universal aspects of the human condition were (and still are) ignored and suppressed in many countries, even in those which invented modernity—and particularly when women, children and "foreigners" are the issue.

In America as in Europe, the "intellectuals" who attracted most media attention after [9/11] are fervent supporters of the "just war" which has been waged in the Middle East and the rest of the world since 1945. We have to go back to that date to form a clearer picture (at least in the medium term) of the successive abdications of that reason which we still call modern, although intellectual modernity is still waiting for historians of thought capable of applying to it an anthropological approach which is equally critical of the systems of thought and social constructions of reality generated by all the world's cultures. High-profile philosophers and essayists may focus attention on "the defeat of thought," "disposable" culture and thought, the performance society, compulsive consumption, and commodification of the body and soul, but the market still tyrannises those very countries most radically stripped of their assets, liberties and basic human dignity. In those countries, isolated elites forge ties of solidarity with their western counterparts in a social, economic and cultural environment given over to the implacable forces of structural violence. To avert global collapse of the market, the pace of consumption must be sustained at all costs. This law is simply stated, but it stultifies all the efforts of even the most inventive thinkers to restore primacy of the human person. . . .

This is where the instrumental, managerial and pragmatic reasoning employed by those human resource engineers and experts, who are becoming ever more indispensable, reveals its limitations and its hold on what I would call the rights and duties of subversive reason. I use that term because the term "modern reason" has lost all its conceptual validity, all its links with the intellectual euphoria of Enlightenment reasoning, and all its ability to resist the rise of "disposable thought" and the pleasure/leisure culture—the only things capable of pushing up the TV ratings and generating the profits needed to create jobs. In this connection, I have noticed in the last ten years the growing popularity of French-language women's magazines in the countries of North Africa. In every detail, these are exact clones of their Parisian models. They give advertisers privileged access to the vital women's market, which is why they have succeeded so fast and so durably—although the information and ideas circulated in these societies, where women are still so disregarded, is as superficial, hasty, fragmentary and conformist as in all other parts of the world. Nonetheless, the isolated elite targeted by these publications are proud to have a national magazine as glossily produced as any of its western models. And this lavish outlay—money which could be used to publish theses and scientific works of far more use to far more people—is part and parcel of "disposable culture" in countries where development is otherwise the main priority.

Thus, the things "special" to Europe and the West are both taken for granted and still invoked as a source of identity. Historically, the political and legal revolutions ushered in by new epistemic and epistemological departures in the exercise of reason are, undeniably, one of the main things special to Europe. The industrial and urban revolution, and the later turmoil of our computer age, are also part of that distinctive historical process which has no parallels in other parts of the world. . . . We have got used to the idea that modernity—the intellectual, scientific, cultural, legal and economic adjunct of European history since the 16th century—works by regularly plunging set ways of thinking into crisis, allowing us to transcend our assumptions, principles and procedures as soon as they become inadequate, prove ideologically flawed or lose their practical utility. As the processes of history have accelerated and become more complex, so crises have become more frequent and the simultaneous existence of disparate thought systems has increasingly sparked political and social violence. Owing to lack of time, the old rule that the validity of all scientific truths and heuristic theories must be constantly questioned and tested cannot produce all its fruitful effects, particularly in the human and social sciences. This is another constraint specific to our history, which is dominated by omnipresent and omnipotent technology. . . .

In the case of Catholicism and Protestantism, dominant ideology has been freed—not by its own choice—of the obligations and concerns of the state. In the case of Islam, however, the state directly controls the management of religious affairs. Judaism, for its part, remains in a state of lively tension with its orthodox elements. . . .

The three great revolutions, English, American and French, took the eschatological hope of eternal salvation and replaced it with a vision of here-and-now happiness and peace through scientific progress and democracy. How much of that new hope remains after the European wars which soon became world wars, the Cold War, the so-called wars of liberation, and the civil wars which have been raging since the post-colonial party-states emerged? The question is a huge one, and is regularly dodged, suppressed, circumvented and transformed by the managers of globalisation into a mirage-version of the right of people and peoples to self-determination. A secular alliance of philosophy, politics and democratic systems has replaced the alliance of theology and politics which typifies monotheistic religions, and the monarchies and theocracies which some countries still have. . . .

All the types and levels of dialogue practised so far have been constrained . . . by rules accepted as categorical imperatives—rules on listening to others, and on tolerance, self-control, self-protection and silence on anything which might offend, violate a taboo, or prevent the meeting from proceeding smoothly. Meaningless platitudes are the norm as soon as sensitive religious or political issues come up. There are even scientists who feel obliged, in the name of "tolerance," to conceal the implications of any research which seems likely to shake the faith of people who follow other religions. In other words, as scholars, they apply all the rules of critical enquiry to their own religion, and leave other believers to do the same for theirs. Is this intellectual good practice, or simply a case of reason's shirking its primary task of universalising scientific knowledge, which must clearly be subject to debate? What this amounts to in practice is leaving a rubble-strewn wasteland to believers who lack the intellectual and material resources needed for all basic scientific research. This is what many Western experts on Islam have done to Islam itself and to Islamic societies.

It is true that good relations and personal contacts are precious and enriching, and that dialogue promotes them—but their benefits increase if we encourage what I call subversive thought to contribute. So far, I have said nothing of the attitudes of states, civil societies, political parties, and professional groups in Islamic contexts, to the events of [9/11] and to the later terrorist acts triggered by the punitive war waged by the new US-led alliance. Although the US and Europe have made intercultural dialogue a necessary concomitant of a tragically unequal and unjustified war, Muslims have persisted in proclaiming their innocence, their eternal victimhood—and thus the need to "defend" themselves by any means available. But there are also many who have chased the mirage of formal dialogue, saying all the right things, swamping the media with "sensible" comment, and roundly condemning all acts of terrorism. They denounce the "false" Muslims who have gone astray and are holding the "real" Islam hostage. Real Islam and modern Muslims have become useful talking partners for Westerners who are deeply convinced that Islam has been nurturing violence ever since it was instrumentalised by lawful (but not legitimate) states, and by inflamed masses left a prey to the blind workings of a global liberalism which extends to even the poorest societies. To call for dialogue between cultures and religions in a situation like this, where radical inequality exists on all levels, is to go on giving Machtpolitik and Réalpolitik the alibi they need to realise their true designs while posing as friends of humanity. This marks a systemic break with that concern for the human spirit which is still cultivated by various ahistorical abstract spiritualities, and that practical humanism which increasingly isolated European voices are still evoking.

Many facts and examples taken from our history since 1945 could be used to illustrate these hastily made points. However, we would soon lose our way in unmapped jungles of data and practices, if we applied the same critical, searching scrutiny to the immense diversity of the Islamic world, and also of "the West," which is hugely creative—but less and less able to curb the excesses of its own drive for power. Above all, the ideological polarisation of "Islam" and "the West" has hardened to such an extent since [9/11] that dispassionate, impartial analysis, which aims to be exhaustive, as well as scientifically and philosophically rigorous, has given way to lumbering erudition, which is itself obstructed by the current heavy emphasis on "disposable" thought and information. Am I going too far if I say that many of the things said and written on the various forms of dialogue are themselves in this "disposable" category?

Historical solidarity is one fruitful theme which is scarcely mentioned by the many commentators on the Islam/West antithesis. In sermon-like tones, people call for tolerance, peace, understanding, a readiness to listen to others, and respect for their values and achievements. But they rarely suggest ways of making the transition from the instinctive, "natural" forms of solidarity which exist in patriarchal families, clans, tribes, corporations, political parties, trade unions, sects, and religious and/or national communities in a given state, empire or kingdom, to broader forms of solidarity, progressively widening from one's native area to the whole of humanity. This has nothing to do with the universal "values" which are ritually celebrated in interreligious dialogue necessarily haunted by the eternal teaching of the divine word. . . . We know how the champions of sovereignty resist this move towards solidarity. Also against it are the people who cling loyally to "values" more imagined than lived—values which have never been subjected to that critical scrutiny which all inherited values demand. These are the "sociological" obstacles which delay beneficial changes, or even block them completely if creative imagination and a critical spirit are both lacking. The success of the EU gives us new reason to hope that humanity may yet be emancipated, and that hope rests on sounder historical and cultural foundations than those offered by the history of the US. In Europe, our memory of the past embodies several collective memories, and this plurality enriches our vision and gives us a basis for innovative approaches to global solidarity. It offers us a real possibility of shaking off outworn codes and practices, which fall far short of the challenges the EU has faced, and the things it has ringingly achieved, after the tragic lessons of the intra-European wars, and particularly the 1940–45 war.

All of this ties in with the subversive campaign to violate and transcend the binary opposites: church/state, spiritual/temporal, faith/reason, culture of belief/culture of unbelief, tradition/modernity, conservatism/progress, under-development/development, fundamentalism/tolerance, etc. These opposites still weigh heavily on inter-religious and intercultural dialogue, since European thought—which generated modernity and has managed it so far—is itself far from free of the psycholinguistic and ideological constraints inherent in binary thinking (although it was widely studied and criticised during the brief post-modernist phase). The subversive writings of Michel Houellebecq dissolve our era's disposable values, and discredit deceptive reversions to false distinctions and "murderous identities"—but without offering us alternative paths to creative imagination and to plural thinking, which is obstinately innovative and systematically subversive. In the field of philosophical enquiry, one notes the same discrepancy between the noisy pronouncements of popular authors with high media profiles and thinkers who are less accessible to the general public, more traditional and, above all, confined within the European and American logosphere and systems. This would apply to J. Habermas, P. Ricoeur and E. Lévinas. I single them out because they have worked and thought on the arbitrarily drawn chronological line which leads from the Greco-Latin and biblical heritage up to our own day, without paying the slightest attention to the mediating role played by Arab thought from the 7th to the 13th centuries. Modish or traditional, many thinkers confirm, by their silence and indifference, the persistence of the ideological boundary traced by the Belgian historian Henri Pirenne in his 1936 book, *Mahomet et Charlemagne*, which has again become topical since the western imagination seized on the Islam/West antithesis.

The massive influx of immigrants, who first came to meet industrial Europe's manpower needs in the 1960s–70s, and later as refugees from authoritarian regimes, is now starting to nurture the new forms of historical solidarity of which I spoke just now. Hardly anything is said about these immigrants, who are refuting the old paradigms by integrating—not along the lines more imagined than thought out by the integration councils, but within the historical dynamic which has gone into building the EU. Even the most immigrant-friendly political parties have failed to notice, and above all support, these new patterns of personal development, which some writers, artists, researchers and intellectuals have looked at boldly. The many essays and books already published encourage me to say a few words about my own career which, as will be seen, stands for numerous others.

I am one of those new citizens who—with the same convictions, the same commitment and the same critical requirements—simultaneously cultivate several interlocking forms of historical solidarity. My starting point was the little village of Taouririt-Mimoun, 1100 metres up a hill in the Djurdjura. Solidarity there means solidarity with one's physical surroundings, with the collective memory of a community which has shrunk to a minority, and so is united by a powerful sense of identity. Successive enlargements later extended that solidarity to the whole of Algeria, to the Maghreb, the Arab–Islamic logosphere and simultaneously, from my sixth year on, the Francophone and, later, Anglophone logosphere as well. These successive or simultaneous enlargements are so many linguistic, cultural and intellectual paths through the dialectic of forces constituted by the state, writing, academic culture, religious and political orthodoxies, and the residues left by those forces in societies which have no central state, no written tradition, no academic culture and no centralising orthodoxy (oral culture or literature, and animistic or polytheistic beliefs, termed heresies by the orthodox authorities). For me, it was at this point that the transition from the instinctive, unconditional forms of solidarity to historical forms which were thought out, freely accepted, and deliberately reinforced as a basis for new ways of coming to grips with the human condition, took on attractive meanings and fed definite hopes.

Along the way, I had to weigh the humanist implications of each successive level of solidarity. That was why I set out, in addition to my French schooling, to master the intellectual and scientific heritage of what I have called the Arab–Islamic logosphere. . . . That was also why the humanist question remained central to my process of thought and enquiry: I wanted to be able to connect my broadening solidarities with that vision, which was capable of becoming universal, but never prematurely proclaimed as such. This same desire to push back the boundaries of solidarity in a critical spirit is the guiding principle behind the things I am fighting and working for in the European area—on paths marked to a greater or lesser degree by Islam and the history of Arab thought. . . .

This brief autobiographical excursion seems essential to forestall any misunderstanding concerning the thing I practise under the deliberately provocative name, subversive thought. Why subversive? What am I subverting? And for whom or for what am I subverting it? . . . First of all, subversive thought is a determination to rethink and rewrite the history of all the systems of thought and culture which have marked the Mediterranean area, trying all the time to reconceptualise them. I am not, a priori, privileging the Mediterranean area over the other great centres of thought and culture. The fact is, that historically, the intellectual, spiritual, legal and cultural roots of the Europe which became the West lie in that area. . . . Islam and the West have become portmanteau words filled with bombs, violence, mutual ignorance, and mutual rejections—all of which have been piling up since the days of Pax Romana in the Mare Nostrum, all the way up to that severance on which I refuse to set a date until the professional historians have done so. At present, public opinion feeds on summary official reports, themselves outrageously simplified by magazines and dailies which supposedly deal in "information." But one cannot speak of some great original divide, of the kind wanted by monotheistic religions, each anxious to keep for itself the eternal privilege of divine election, or, from the 19th century on, by the colonialists, who set out to bring the lands conquered by Islam back to the one true faith, and the new hopes offered by modernity.

How can we refocus the attention of the various Euro-Western and Muslim communities on a history spanning a very long period, at a time when disposable thought and the culture of leisure, pleasure and desire so powerfully promoted by the media have more or less wiped their own countries' histories from their memories? We are urged to speak of intercultural and inter-religious dialogue even though forgetfulness of the past, as national historians have recorded it since the 19th century, is either semi-irreversible, or likely to remain, for many years to come, an endemic part of the Euro-Western vision of the things now regarded as constituting Europe's identity. Who shapes this vision of an identity distinct from all the others which compete for "universal" recognition? The "new history" proclaimed and practised in the 1970s–80s set out to admit other collective memories, and incorporate them into a critical historical consciousness, focused on achieving a shared knowledge of our various pasts. Since we were told that history had ended and the clash of civilisations had begun, political failures, murderous and devastating violence, the aberrations of economic thought, the arbitrary operations of the great monopolies, and the growing effects of unchecked liberalism have been compromising the first tentative steps towards more effective and more durable forms of liberation.

STUDY QUESTIONS

1. According to Arkoun, what is "subversive thought"? What is it attempting to change?
2. According to Arkoun, what is the crisis in the Greater West that the aftermath of 9/11 has exposed?

29.10 WORLD ECONOMIC FORUM, GLOBAL GENDER GAP REPORT, 2010

The Global Gender Gap Report was introduced by the World Economic Forum in 2006 to analyze disparities between genders in a worldwide context. It assesses national gender gaps in political, economic, health, and education-related areas and ranks countries according to data, allowing comparisons across regions, time, and income groups. According to the report's introduction, these rankings "are designed to create greater awareness among a global audience of the challenges posed by gender gaps and the opportunities created by reducing them." This excerpt looks at women's impact on economic growth through increased education, participation in the labor force, and women's role as consumers, or the "power of the purse."

There are several interconnected areas that may serve as conduits for the demonstrated link between gender equality and productivity, growth and development.

- *Girls' education*: Research demonstrates that investment in girls' education has significant multiplier effects: it reduces high fertility rates, lowers infant and child mortality rates, lowers maternal mortality rates, increases women's labour force participation rates and earnings and fosters educational investment in children. These outcomes not only improve the quality of life, they also foster faster economic growth and development. A substantial body of literature has shown investing in girls' education to be one of the highest-return investments that a developing economy can make. Out of the world's 130 million out-of-school youth, 70 percent are girls; even where there is parity in enrolment, there are discrepancies between the quality of boys' and girls' education. Education remains the key for many of the low-ranking countries covered in this *Report*.
- *Women's labour force participation*: According to recent research, a reduction in the male–female employment gap has been an important driver of European economic growth in the last decade. Closing this gap would have huge economic implications for developed economies, boosting US GDP by as much as 9%, Euro zone GDP by as

From "The Global Gender Gap," World Economic Forum, Switzerland, 2010. https://www3.weforum.org/docs/WEF_GenderGap_Report_2010.pdf.

much as 13% and Japanese GDP by as much as 16%. Greater economic opportunity for women in these countries could also play a key role in addressing the future problems posed by ageing populations and mounting pension burdens. Moreover, in countries in which it is relatively easy for women to combine work with having children, female employment and female fertility both tend to be higher. A report by the United Nations Economic and Social Commission for Asia and the Pacific Countries found that restricting job opportunities for women is costing the region between US$42 and US$46 billion a year. Research by the World Bank demonstrates that similar restrictions have also imposed massive costs throughout the Middle East, where decades of substantial investment have dramatically reduced the gender gap in education but the gender gap in economic opportunity remains the widest in the world.

- *Women as consumers:* There is new research on the growing "power of the purse" and how this will be among the drivers of growth in the post-crisis economy. The combined impact of growing gender equality, the emerging middle class and women's spending priorities will lead to rising household savings rates and shifting spending patterns that are likely to benefit sectors such as food, healthcare, education, childcare, apparel, consumer durables and financial services, particularly in emerging markets. The study predicts that over the next five years, these effects will be seen most clearly in China and Russia, and to a lesser extent in Vietnam, Mexico, Brazil and Indonesia. In the subsequent decade (2015–25), these dynamics are likely to remain strong in Mexico and Russia, and to continue to strengthen in China, Indonesia, Vietnam, India and the Philippines. India's middle class will see rapid growth off a very low base, but the shifts in spending that we outline are likely to remain constrained by women's relatively low status, at least for the next 10 to 15 years.
- *Women and spending decisions:* Research has shown that women are likely to invest a larger proportion of their household income than men would in the education and health of their children. There is some evidence from India to suggest that women in local government roles also make decisions with better outcomes for communities when charged with budget decisions; they also appear to be more competent representatives than men, obtaining more resources for their constituencies despite having significantly lower education and relevant labor market experience.
- *Women and leadership:* Innovation requires new, unique ideas—and the best ideas flourish in a diverse environment. This implies that companies benefit by successfully integrating the female half of the available talent pool across their internal leadership structures. This is particularly relevant in many developed countries, where women now account for more than half of the college and university graduates. As they begin to take up half of entry-level positions in several industries, it is a loss for companies if these high-skilled women are forced into a choice between work and family at later stages of their career as evident in the data from several OECD countries. Studies exploring the link between women in leadership positions and business performance have shown a positive correlation between gender diversity on top leadership teams and a company's financial results. Over the last two years, in the midst of the global economic downturn, several new themes have emerged about gender equality in the workplace and its impact. Biologists, behavioural economists and psychologists have contributed to discussions on some of the decisions and excesses that led to the financial crisis and have suggested that more diverse teams make better informed decisions, leading to less risk-taking and more successful outcomes for companies.

Over time, therefore, a nation's competitiveness depends significantly on whether and how it educates and utilizes its female talent. To maximize its competitiveness and development potential, each country should strive for gender equality—that is, to give women the same rights, responsibilities and opportunities as men. It has been shown through our own research as well as that of others that the current economic participation of women, even in countries where they are as healthy and as educated as men, is far from optimal. Business leaders and policy-makers must ensure that barriers to women's entry to the workforce are removed and put in place practices and policies that will provide equal opportunities for rising to positions of leadership within companies. Such practices will ensure that all existing resources are used in the most efficient manner and that the right signals are sent regarding the future flow of talent.

TRACKING THE GENDER GAP OVER TIME

The Global Gender Gap Index was first published in 2006 with a view to creating a comprehensive gender parity index that is able to track gaps over time relative to an equality benchmark, thus providing information on a country's progress relative to itself as well as other countries.

Based on the five years of data available for the 114 countries that have been part of the *Report* since its inception, we find that, on the whole, much of the world has made progress on closing gender gaps. . . . In 2006, 14% of the global political empowerment gap had been closed; in 2010, almost 18% of this gap has been closed. In 2006, 56% of the economic participation gap had been closed; in 2010, more than 59% of this gap has been closed. In 2006, almost 92% of the educational attainment gap had been closed; in 2010, over 93% of this gap has been closed. On health and survival, however, there has been a small deterioration between 2006 and 2010. The Asia and the Pacific, Latin America and North America regional categories have displayed improvement over the last five years on the Index score; the Middle East and North Africa, sub-Saharan Africa and Europe and Central Asia have deteriorated.

STUDY QUESTIONS

1. What does the report suggest are the long-term economic consequences for all people in a society once women and men are made more equal?
2. What were the causes of the deterioration for the status of women in certain regions over the course of this evaluation?

29.11 VLADIMIR PUTIN, "ON THE HISTORICAL UNITY OF RUSSIANS AND UKRAINIANS," 2021

Since coming to power in Moscow, Vladimir Putin (b. 1952) has consistently opposed the spread of the European Union and of NATO into Eastern Europe and has argued that such expansions represent existential threats to Russia's national security. When the people of Ukraine overthrew

Excerpt from "Article by Vladimir Putin 'On the Historical Unity of Russians and Ukrainians.'" July 12, 2021. Translation published by the Kremlin: http://en.kremlin.ru/events/president/news/66181. "Vladimir Putin, President of Russia (CC BY 4.0)."

their corrupt government in 2014 and elected a new president, Petro Poroshenko, who initiated moves to join the EU and NATO, Putin attacked. His forces moved into the Crimea and his government declared a formal annexation of the region, and in early 2022, after a long buildup, his forces invaded the rest of the country. His propaganda office provided a justification for Russia's actions with an essay that appeared on the Kremlin's website. Excerpts from that essay follow, highlighting the extent to which nineteenth-century ethnic nationalism still influences political thinking in today's world.

. . . [M]odern Ukraine is entirely the product of the Soviet era. We know and remember well that it was shaped—for a significant part—on the lands of historical Russia. To make sure of that, it is enough to look at the boundaries of the lands reunited with the Russian state in the 17th century and the territory of the Ukrainian SSR [i.e., Soviet Socialist Republic] when it left the Soviet Union.

The Bolsheviks treated the Russian people as inexhaustible material for their social experiments. They dreamt of a world revolution that would wipe out national states. That is why they were so generous in drawing borders and bestowing territorial gifts. It is no longer important what exactly the idea of the Bolshevik leaders who were chopping the country into pieces was. We can disagree about minor details, background and logics [*sic*] behind certain decisions. One fact is crystal clear: Russia was robbed, indeed.

When working on this article, I relied on open-source documents that contain well-known facts rather than on some secret records. The leaders of modern Ukraine and their external "patrons" prefer to overlook these facts. They do not miss a chance, however, both inside the country and abroad, to condemn "the crimes of the Soviet regime," listing among them events with which neither the CPSU [Communist Party of the Soviet Union], not the USSR, let alone modern Russia, have anything to do. At the same time, the Bolsheviks' efforts to detach from Russia its historical territories are not considered a crime. And we know why: if they brought about the weakening of Russia, our ill-wishe[r]s are happy with that.

Of course, inside the USSR, borders between republics were never seen as state borders; they were nominal within a single country, which, while featuring all the attributes of a federation, was highly centralized—this, again, was secured by the CPSU's leading role. But in 1991, all those territories, and, which is more important, people, found themselves abroad overnight, taken away, this time indeed, from their historical motherland.

What can be said to this? Things change: countries and communities are no exception. Of course, some part of a people in the process of its development, influenced by a number of reasons and historical circumstances, can become aware of itself as a separate nation at a certain moment. How should we treat that? There is only one answer: with respect! . . .

Ukraine and Russia have developed as a single economic system over decades, and centuries. The profound cooperation we had 30 years ago is an example for the European Union to look up to. We are natural complementary economic partners. Such a close relationship can strengthen competitive advantages, increasing the potential of both countries.

Ukraine used to possess great potential, which included powerful infrastructure, gas transportation system, advanced shipbuilding, aviation, rocket and instrument engineering industries, as well as world-class scientific design and engineering schools. Taking over this legacy and declaring independence, Ukrainian leaders promised that the Ukrainian economy would be one of the leading ones and the standard of living would be among the best in Europe.

Today, high-tech giants that once were the pride of Ukraine and the entire Union, are sinking. Engineering output has dropped by 42 percent over ten years. The scale of deindustrialization and overall economic degradation is visible in Ukraine's electricity production, which has seen a nearly two-time[s] decrease in 30 years. Finally, according to

IMF reports, in 2019, before the coronavirus pandemic broke out, Ukraine's GDP per capita had been below USD 4 thousand. This is less than in the Republic of Albania, the Republic of Moldova, or unrecognized Kosovo. Nowadays, Ukraine is Europe's poorest country.

Who is to blame for this? Is it the people of Ukraine's fault? Certainly not. It was the Ukrainian authorities who waisted [*sic*] and frittered away the achievements of many generations. We know how hardworking and talented the people of Ukraine are. They can achieve success and outstanding results with perseverance and determination. And these qualities, as well as their openness, innate optimism and hospitality have not gone. The feelings of millions of people who treat Russia not just well but with great affection, just as we feel about Ukraine, remain the same.

Until 2014, hundreds of agreements and joint projects were aimed at developing our economies, business and cultural ties, strengthening security, and solving common social and environmental problems. They brought tangible benefits to people—both in Russia and Ukraine. This is what we believed to be most important. And that is why we had a fruitful interaction with all, I emphasize, with all the leaders of Ukraine.

Even after the events in Kiev of 2014, I charged the Russian government to elaborate options for preserving and maintaining our economic ties within relevant ministries and agencies. However, there was and is still no mutual will to do the same. Nevertheless, Russia is still one of Ukraine's top three trading partners, and hundreds of thousands of Ukrainians are coming to us to work, and they find a welcome reception and support. So that [is] what the "aggressor state" is.

When the USSR collapsed, many people in Russia and Ukraine sincerely believed and assumed that our close cultural, spiritual and economic ties would certainly last, as would the commonality of our people, who had always had a sense of unity at their core. However, events—at first gradually, and then more rapidly—started to move in a different direction.

In essence, Ukraine's ruling circles decided to justify their country's independence through a denial of its past, however, except for border issues. They began to mythologize and rewrite history, edit out everything that united us, and refer to the period when Ukraine was part of the Russian Empire and the Soviet Union as an occupation. The common tragedy of collectivization and famine of the early 1930s was portrayed as the genocide of the Ukrainian people.

Radicals and neo-Nazis were open and more and more insolent about their ambitions. They were indulged by both the official authorities and local oligarchs, who robbed the people of Ukraine and kept their stolen money in Western banks, ready to sell their motherland for the sake of preserving their capital. To this should be added the persistent weakness of state institutions and the position of a willing hostage to someone else's geopolitical will.

I recall that long ago, well before 2014, the US and EU countries systematically and consistently pushed Ukraine to curtail and limit economic cooperation with Russia. We, as the largest trade and economic partner of Ukraine, suggested discussing the emerging problems in the Ukraine-Russia-EU format. But every time we were told that Russia had nothing to do with it and that the issue concerned only the EU and Ukraine. De facto Western countries rejected Russia's repeated calls for dialogue.

Step by step, Ukraine was dragged into a dangerous geopolitical game aimed at turning Ukraine into a barrier between Europe and Russia, a springboard against Russia. Inevitably, there came a time when the concept of "Ukraine is not Russia" was no longer an option. There was a need for the "anti-Russia" concept which we will never accept.

. . .

Nor were the interests of the Ukrainian people thought of in February 2014. The legitimate public discontent, caused by acute socio-economic problems, mistakes, and inconsistent actions of the time, was simply cynically exploited. Western countries directly interfered in Ukraine's internal affairs and supported the coup. Radical nationalist groups served as its battering ram. Their slogans, ideology, and blatant aggressive Russophobia have to a large extent become defining elements of state policy in Ukraine.

All the things that united us and bring us together so far came under attack. First and foremost, the Russian language. Let me remind you that the new "Maidan" authorities first tried to repeal the law on state language policy. Then there was the law on the "purification of power," the law on education that virtually cut the Russian language out of the educational process.

Lastly, as early as May of this year, the current president introduced a bill on "indigenous peoples" to the Rada [i.e., Ukrainian parliament]. Only those who constitute an ethnic minority and do not have their own state entity outside Ukraine are recognized as indigenous. The law has been passed. New seeds of discord have been sown. And this is happening in a country, as I have already noted, that is very complex in terms of its territorial, national and linguistic composition, and its history of formation.

There may be an argument: if you are talking about a single large nation, a triune nation, then what difference does it make who people consider themselves to be—Russians, Ukrainians, or Belarusians. I completely agree with this. Especially since the determination of nationality, particularly in mixed families, is the right of every individual, free to make his or her own choice.

But the fact is that the situation in Ukraine today is completely different because it involves a forced change of identity. And the most despicable thing is that the Russians in Ukraine are being forced not only to deny their roots, generations of their ancestors but also to believe that Russia is their enemy. It would not be an exaggeration to say that the path of forced assimilation, the formation of an ethnically pure Ukrainian state, aggressive towards Russia, is comparable to the use of weapons of mass destruction against us. As a result of such a harsh and artificial division of Russians and Ukrainians, the Russian people in all may decrease by hundreds of thousands or even millions.

Our spiritual unity has also been attacked. As in the days of the Grand Duchy of Lithuania, a new ecclesiastical [policy?] has been initiated. The secular authorities, making no secret of their political aims, have blatantly interfered in church life and brought things to a split, to the seizure of churches, the beating of priests and monks. Even extensive autonomy of the Ukrainian Orthodox Church while maintaining spiritual unity with the Moscow Patriarchate strongly displeases them. They have to destroy this prominent and centuries-old symbol of our kinship at all costs.

. . .

This is what is actually happening. First of all, we are facing the creation of a climate of fear in Ukrainian society, aggressive rhetoric, indulging neo-Nazis and militarizing the country. Along with that we are witnessing not just complete dependence but direct external control, including the supervision of the Ukrainian authorities, security service and armed forces by foreign advisers, military "development" of the territory of Ukraine and deployment of NATO infrastructure. It is no coincidence that the aforementioned flagrant law on "indigenous peoples" was adopted under the cover of large-scale NATO exercises in Ukraine.

This is also a disguise for the takeover of the rest of the Ukrainian economy and the exploitation of its natural resources. The sale of agricultural land is not far off, and it is obvious who will buy it up. From time to time, Ukraine is indeed given financial resources and loans, but under their own conditions and pursuing their own interests, with preferences and benefits for Western companies. By the way, who will pay these debts back? Apparently, it is assumed that this will have to be done not only by today's generation of Ukrainians but also by their children, grandchildren and probably great-grandchildren.

The Western authors of the anti-Russia project set up the Ukrainian political system in such a way that presidents, members of parliament and ministers would change but the attitude of separation from and enmity with Russia would remain. Reaching peace was the main election slogan of the incumbent president. He came to power with this. The promises turned out to be lies. Nothing has changed. And in some ways the situation in Ukraine and around Donbas has even degenerated.

In the anti-Russia project, there is no place either for a sovereign Ukraine or for the political forces that are trying to defend its real independence. Those who talk about reconciliation in Ukrainian society, about dialogue, about finding a way out of the current impasse are labelled as "pro-Russian" agents.

Again, for many people in Ukraine, the anti-Russia project is simply unacceptable. And there are millions of such people. But they are not allowed to raise their heads. They have had their legal opportunity to defend their point of view in fact taken away from them. They are intimidated, driven underground. Not only are they persecuted for their convictions, for the spoken word, for the open expression of their position, but they are also killed. Murderers, as a rule, go unpunished.

Today, the "right" patriot of Ukraine is only the one who hates Russia. Moreover, the entire Ukrainian statehood, as we understand it, is proposed to be further built exclusively on this idea. Hate and anger, as world history has repeatedly proved this, are a very shaky foundation for sovereignty, fraught with many serious risks and dire consequences.

All the subterfuges associated with the anti-Russia project are clear to us. And we will never allow our historical territories and people close to us living there to be used against Russia. And to those who will undertake such an attempt, I would like to say that this way they will destroy their own country.

The incumbent authorities in Ukraine like to refer to Western experience, seeing it as a model to follow. Just have a look at how Austria and Germany, the USA and Canada live next to each other. Close in ethnic composition, culture, in fact sharing one language, they remain sovereign states with their own interests, with their own foreign policy. But this does not prevent them from the closest integration or allied relations. They have very conditional, transparent borders. And when crossing them the citizens feel at home. They create families, study, work, do business. Incidentally, so do millions of those born in Ukraine who now live in Russia. We see them as our own close people.

Russia is open to dialogue with Ukraine and ready to discuss the most complex issues. But it is important for us to understand that our partner is defending its national interests but not serving someone else's, and is not a tool in someone else's hands to fight against us.

We respect the Ukrainian language and traditions. We respect Ukrainians' desire to see their country free, safe and prosperous.

I am confident that true sovereignty of Ukraine is possible only in partnership with Russia. Our spiritual, human and civilizational ties formed for centuries and have their origins in the same sources, they have been hardened by common trials, achievements and victories. Our kinship has been transmitted from generation to generation. It is in the hearts and the memory of people living in modern Russia and Ukraine, in the blood ties that unite millions of our families. Together we have always been and will be many times stronger and more successful. For we are one people.

Today, these words may be perceived by some people with hostility. They can be interpreted in many possible ways. Yet, many people will hear me. And I will say one thing—Russia has never been and will never be "anti-Ukraine." And what Ukraine will be—it is up to its citizens to decide.

STUDY QUESTIONS

1. What arguments does Putin make to support his assertion that Ukraine and Russia enjoy a historical unity?
2. According to Putin, how does the West undermine the spiritual unity of Ukraine and Russia?

Printed in the USA/Agawam, MA
January 4, 2024

858732.020